Karl Marx

Karl Marx

The Burden of Reason (Why Marx Rejected Politics and the Market)

Allan Megill

ROWMAN & LITTLEFIELD PUBLISHERS, INC.
Lanham • Boulder • New York • Oxford

ROWMAN & LITTLEFIELD PUBLISHERS, INC.

Published in the United States of America
by Rowman & Littlefield Publishers, Inc.
4720 Boston Way, Lanham, Maryland 20706
www.rowmanlittlefield.com

12 Hid's Copse Road
Cumnor Hill, Oxford OX2 9JJ, England

British Library Cataloguing in Publication Information Available

Library of Congress Cataloging-in-Publication Data

Megill, Allan.
Karl Marx : the burden of reason (why Marx rejected politics and the market) / Allan Megill.
p. cm.
Includes bibliographical references and index.
ISBN 0-7425-1165-0 (alk. paper) — ISBN 0-7425-1166-9 (pbk. : alk. paper)
1. Marx, Karl, 1818–1883—Philosophy. 2. Marx, Karl, 1818–1883—Political and social views. 3. Historical materialism. 4. Dialectical materialism. I. Title.

HX39.5 .M414 2002
335.4'01—dc21 2001048266

Printed in the United States of America

∞™ The paper used in this publication meets the minimum requirements of American National Standard for Information Sciences—Permanence of Paper for Printed Library Materials, ANSI/NISO Z.39.48-1992.

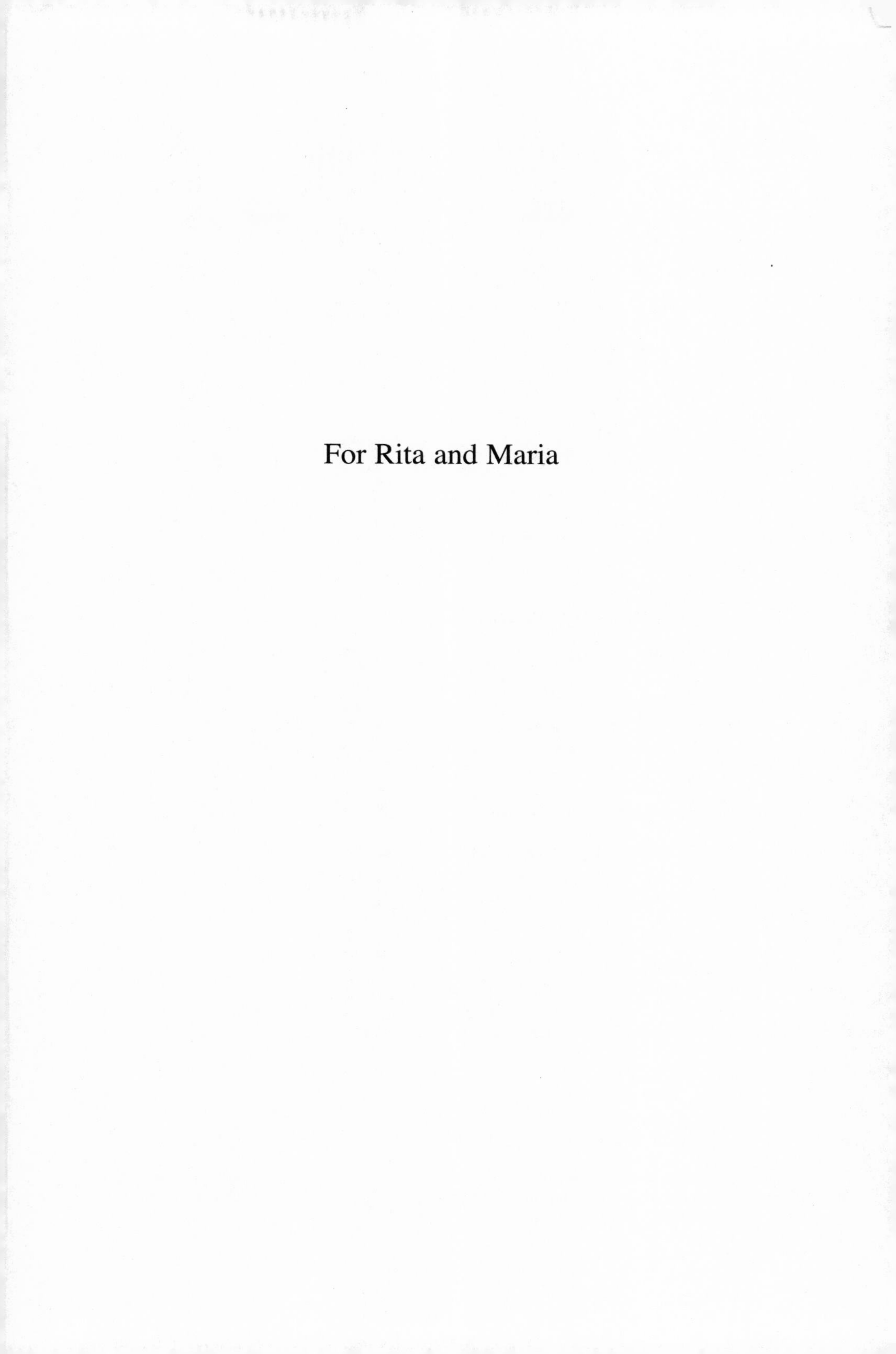

For Rita and Maria

Philosophy comes into the world amid the loud cries of its enemies, who betray their inner infection by wild shouts for help against the fiery ardor of ideas.

—Karl Marx, "The Leading Article in No. 179 of the *Kölnische Zeitung*," *Rheinische Zeitung* No. 191, July 10, 1842 (*MEGA2* 1.1: 183/*MECW* 1: 196).

Ancient metaphysics had . . . a higher conception of thinking than is current today. For it based itself on the fact that the knowledge of things obtained through thinking is alone what is really true in them. . . . Thus this metaphysics believed that thinking (and its determinations) is not anything alien to the object, but rather is its essential nature. . . .

—G. W. F. Hegel, *Science of Logic* trans. A. V. Miller, foreword by J. N. Findlay (London: George Allen & Unwin, 1969; orig. published 1812–16), introduction, 45.

Given for one instant an intellect that could comprehend all the forces by which nature is moved and the respective situations of the beings that compose it, and if, besides, it was sufficiently vast to submit these data to analysis, it would embrace in the same formula the movements of the greatest bodies of the universe and those of the lightest atom: nothing would be uncertain for it, and the future, like the past, would be present before its eyes.

—Pierre Laplace, *Théorie analytique des probabilités*, 3. éd., rev. et augm. (Paris, 1820), ii–iii.

The mortal danger for every being lies in losing itself. Hence lack of freedom is the real mortal danger for mankind.

—Karl Marx, "Proceedings of the Sixth Rhine Province Assembly. First Article. Debates on Freedom of the Press and Publication of the Proceedings of the Assembly of the Estates," *Rheinische Zeitung* No. 135, May 15, 1842 (*MEGA2* 1.1: 152/*MECW* 1:164).

Contents

Abbreviations

Here I indicate the meanings of the abbreviated references that I use in this book. Most of my references to Marx's and Engels's writings include citations to the text in its original language (almost always German) and in an English translation. Wherever possible I cite the original-language text in the authoritative "New *MEGA*" edition of Marx and Engels (*MEGA2*: see below). Where the appropriate volume of the New *MEGA* is not yet available, I cite the less authoritative *Werke* (*MEW*: again, see below). I cite the English translation that appears in *Collected Works* (*MECW*: likewise see below). In addition, I often cite an English translation appearing in an accessible paperback edition. The paperbacks that win the prize for frequency of citation are the Pelican Marx Library's *Early Writings* (*EW*) and, to a lesser extent, that convenient standby *The Marx-Engels Reader*, 2d ed. (*MER*), which is published by Norton. Few English readers will be able to run out and buy the fifty volumes of *MECW*, but *EW* and *MER* will be within reach of many. I have sometimes amended the English translations that I quote. I separate the different citations (which are, of course, all to the same text) by means of the slash sign, as in the following example: (*MEGA2* 1.2: 463/*MECW* 3: 206/*EW* 420). Note that in citing the German original of *Capital* volume 1, I have preferred to cite the 1873 edition (in *MEGA2* 2.6) rather than the original 1867 edition (in *MEGA2* 2.5), because of its improved division into chapters and sections (which is closer to, although still not the same as, the chapter divisions in the English editions [as Draper notes, DRAP 2: 28]).

The "New *MEGA*" is divided into four *Abteilungen* (divisions), each containing individual *Bände* (volumes). Accordingly, the reference *MEGA2* 1.2: 463 refers the reader to division 1, volume 2, page 463. Individual *MEGA2 Bände* are themselves divided into separately bound *Text* and *Apparat* volumes, but I have ignored this distinction in my references because the pagination of each *Text* volume carries over into the corresponding *Apparat* volume. References to

MECW are uncomplicated: *MECW* 1: 11 refers to Marx and Engels, *Collected Works*, volume 1, page 11.

I sometimes cite works parenthetically in the text, after an initial full citation in an endnote. Where there is no chance of ambiguity or hesitation I include a page reference alone; otherwise, I also include the author's name. Normally, when any of my parenthetical references is *followed* by a period, the reference refers only to material in the immediately preceding sentence. When a reference refers to material in two or more sentences, it is *not* followed by a period. However, since there is no chance of ambiguity in extracted text, the period always precedes the parenthetical reference.

CAP Karl Marx, *Capital: A Critique of Political Economy*, introduced by Ernest Mandel, trans. Ben Fowkes (vol. 1) and David Fernbach (vols. 2 and 3) (3 vols.; Harmondsworth, Middlesex: Penguin, 1976, 1978, 1981 [Pelican Marx Library]). In the United States these books have also appeared under the Random House Vintage Books imprint.

DRAP Hal Draper, *The Marx-Engels Cyclopedia* (3 vols.; New York: Schocken, 1985). Vol. 1: *The Marx-Engels Chronicle: A Day-by-Day Chronology of Marx and Engels's Life and Activity*. Vol. 2: *The Marx-Engels Register: A Complete Bibliography of Marx and Engels' Individual Writings*. Vol. 3: *The Marx-Engels Glossary: Glossary to the Chronicle and Register, and Index to the Glossary*.

EPM "Economic and Philosophical Manuscripts," in *EW*.

EW Karl Marx, *Early Writings*, introduced by Lucio Colletti, trans. Rodney Livingstone and Gregor Benton (Harmondsworth, Middlesex: Penguin, 1975 [Pelican Marx Library]). In the United States this book has also appeared under the Random House Vintage Books imprint.

GRUND Karl Marx, *Grundrisse: Foundations of the Critique of Political Economy*, trans. Martin Nicolaus, foreword by Martin Nicolaus (Harmondsworth, Middlesex: Penguin, 1973 [Pelican Marx Library]). In the United States this book has also appeared under the Random House Vintage Books imprint.

LHP G. W. F. Hegel, *Lectures on the History of Philosophy*, trans. E. S. Haldane and Frances H. Simson (3 vols.; London: Routledge and Kegan Paul, 1955 [translation, originally published in 1896, of the 2d, altered German edition of the *Vorlesungen über die Geschichte der Philosophie*, published as vols. 13–15 of Hegel's *Werke* in 1840, 1842, and 1844, respectively; the first German edition of the *Vorlesungen* was originally published in 1833 and 1836 and constituted a different vols. 13–15 of Hegel's *Werke*]).

LPW Karl Marx, *Later Political Writings*, trans. and ed. Terrell Carver (Cambridge: Cambridge University Press, 1996).

MECW Institute of Marxism-Leninism, Moscow, Karl Marx and Frederick Engels, *Collected Works* (50 vols.; New York: International Publishers, 1975–2003[?]). As of September 2001, volumes 48–50 are not available, but are promised soon.

MEGA2 Institut für Marxismus-Leninismus beim Zentralkomitee der Kommunistischen Partei der Sowjetunion and Institut für Marxismus-Leninismus beim Zentralkomitee der Sozialistischen Einheitspartei Deutschlands, *Karl Marx Friedrich Engels Gesamtausgabe* (*MEGA*) (eventually 114 conceptual volumes [and many more physical volumes]; Berlin: Dietz, 1972–). From 1990, the body responsible for this edition has been the Internationale Marx-Engels-Stiftung.

MER Karl Marx and Friedrich Engels, *The Marx-Engels Reader*, ed. Robert C. Tucker, 2d ed. (New York: Norton, 1978).

MEW Institut für Marxismus-Leninismus beim Zentralkomitee der Sozialistischen Einheitspartei Deutschlands, *Karl Marx Friedrich Engels Werke* (43 vols.; Berlin: Dietz, 1956–83).

Preface

The Fish in the Water

Marxism exists in nineteenth-century thought like a fish in water.

—Michel Foucault, *The Order of Things*, trans. anon. (New York: Random House, 1970), 262.

This book aims to explain why Marx adhered to certain positions that many intelligent observers now find unwarranted. In writing it, I have focused especially on Marx's conviction that politics and the market will ultimately disappear from the human social order. Paradoxically, a man who thought that science will come to replace politics engaged in unceasing political activity throughout his adult life. It is perhaps slightly less paradoxical that a man who rejected the market in his scientific work was able to do that work only because his friend and collaborator, Friedrich Engels, bankrolled him with profits from the flourishing textile enterprise in which he, Engels, was a partner. Nietzsche once wrote: "One is fruitful only at the price of being rich in contradictions."[1] Marx's contradictions were perhaps the price that he, and we, have to pay for the immense richness of his thinking.

In explaining why Marx came to his theoretical rejection of politics and the market, I also seek to change the image of Marx by which we are possessed. As I write these words Marx is widely considered to be utterly passé, a dead dog. In certain circles it is well known that riches lie hidden in Marx's work. But those circles are small. More common are two other views: the view that everything worth knowing about Marx is already known and can be conveyed in a few simple statements, and the view that there is no need to know anything at all about Marx. Both views are mistaken. As a theorist, Marx went deeply wrong in some ways, but in other ways he was on the right track. By uncovering the source of some of the error, I make easier the task of winnowing out what is valuable from what is not valuable in his work. In part, this book is a postmortem on Marx. But it is more than a postmortem: it is also an invitation, if not to a resurrection, then at least to a very serious reconsideration. I concentrate on what I find to be dead or defective in Marxist theory, for only if we understand the source of the deadness (which I locate in a too-rigid conception of science) do we have the possibility of thinking our way beyond Marx, yet with Marx. I tell a historical story, but I do so in the interests of theoretical advance.

Most professors teach, and their teaching has an impact on what they write. Since 1976 I have regularly taught a course on Marx. I was doing so at the University of Iowa in fall 1989, when the Berlin Wall came down and the "German Democratic Republic" disappeared. I was teaching Marx again at another university in fall 1991, when the Soviet Union trembled and then collapsed. The conjunction of a rereading of Marx with the events of 1989, and especially with those of 1991, led me to think differently about the reading. Not that I had ever considered myself a Marxist: I came from a place that made such a thing unlikely. Since there had never been a conversion to Marx, there was never a deconversion. Nonetheless, the events of 1989–91 led me to think differently about Marx. They did so by inviting me to see Marx as an object of *historical* reflection. Before 1989 I would analyze Marx's major works in front of a class every few semesters—because I found it interesting to explore and reexplore Marx's vivid and bracing mind, and because students were interested in the subject. But I had not thought to write about him: for a decade and a half it had been sufficient to read a little more of his work each time I taught the class, to read a little more about him, to talk about him, and to reflect on the responses, mine and the students', to what we had read.

In 1966, in his quirky and brilliant *The Order of Things*, Michel Foucault insisted that Marxism was a characteristically nineteenth-century product—that it was a fish in the water of nineteenth-century thought.[2] To be sure, there also exists a rich body of twentieth-century Marxist thought: "Marxism" is not solely a nineteenth-century product, as the work of such twentieth-century intellectuals as Georg Lukács, Walter Benjamin, Herbert Marcuse, and the later Jean-Paul Sartre showed.[3] But Marxism in its original form was unequivocally both in and of the nineteenth century: it drew its resources overwhelmingly from things that were characteristic of that century. One can quibble in minor ways with Foucault's "fish in the water" statement but one cannot deny it. In part (but only in part), the present book tries to show the fish in the water: it tries to show how a particular assumption (or family of assumptions) deeply rooted in nineteenth-century theory permeates Marx's theorizing and by extension permeates Marxism. In deference to Foucault we might call the assumption an "epistemic" view, since it tends to ground an entire way of thinking (an *episteme*, to use Foucault's term). The view that I have in mind originated well before the nineteenth century, but it was most pervasive in that century and it had a distinctively nineteenth-century form. The approach in the present book is to locate this view in Marx's thought, to say something about its particular shape therein, and to show how it affected both Marx's general way of thinking and the positions that he adopted on particular issues.

This book is not intended as a comprehensive study of Marx. Deliberately, it does not offer a narrative account of Marx's life and work. A number of such accounts have been written: why duplicate what has been done already?[4] Accordingly, this book is not at all an intellectual biography. Nor does it offer a comprehensive analytical account of Marx's thought—an account that would survey Marx's thought in general and would attempt to address all its major themes.[5] Rather, I focus on what I take to be *essential* and *distinctive* about Marx's mode of theorizing. I concentrate on a few strategic topics in Marx's work, with an emphasis on the earliest phases of his intellectual career but with a constant awareness of its entire course. (Engels's work is also discussed whenever it casts light on Marx's.) From early in his career Marx himself favored the search for essences. (He was confident, also, that everything could ultimately be reduced to a single essence—a position that I call "unitarism." I do not share this confidence.) In one of the "Notebooks on Epicurean Philosophy" that he filled up while preparing to write his doctoral dissertation, he stated that the historian of philosophy should seek to reveal, in each philosophical system, "the determinations themselves, the thoroughgoing actual crystallizations . . . the silent, continuously working mole of actual philosophical knowledge. . . . Anyone who writes the history of philosophy separates essential from inessential. . ." (*MEGA 2* 4.1: 137/*MECW* 1: 506). I try to follow this advice.

In examining Marx's theory I do not aim to solve what Alvin Gouldner called the "nuclear contradiction" of Marxism, namely, the contradiction between science and activism (or, more fully, between Marx's claim that human society is determined by certain structural laws, and his claim that we ought to stand up and try to radically change society).[6] In fact, I do not believe that the tension between science and activism, between understanding and remaking, *can* be resolved. Nor do I believe that the tension *ought* to be resolved, even assuming it could be, for understanding the world well requires maintaining a certain distance from what is. Marx would have agreed with me—but only insofar as his own, unredeemed time was concerned. My claim is rather that the tension can never be resolved; or, to put the matter differently, that all times are unredeemed, all are contradictory and generative of contradiction. I shall time and again insist on the contradictoriness of Marx's theoretical positions and of his project generally. I intend no condemnation of

Marx here, for I am persuaded that, almost always, his contradictions do not result from banal error. Rather, they come from his own rigor and consistency, which runs up against the complexities of the world. Marx's insistence on developing his positions in a manner that was as uncompromising as possible is what most often generates the contradictions, which tend to have the character of unavoidable *aporoi*, of blocked pathways that are blocked in reality as well. In short, Marx's contradictoriness is no reason to dismiss his project.

Nor do I examine Marx with a view to addressing the problem of what strategy "left intellectuals"—whatever that term might mean—ought to adopt now. I examine Marx in order to understand his project and to learn from both its merits and its limitations, not in order to offer prescriptions for policy or action. With unrivaled passion and deep persistence Marx tried to understand the human world. To grasp the core of what he did, and in particular to see where he fired rightly and where he misfired, is not a negligible thing. Moreover, in the twenty-first century we are far enough from Marx, and well enough situated historically, to see with clarity things that, until recently, were difficult if not impossible to see. My thought is that Marx is to be both emulated and left behind. The questions, then, are: In what ways emulated? In what ways left behind? I must also say that, although this investigation of Marx's work does not offer policy prescriptions, it does have policy implications. I do not claim that the implications need to be derived from a critical examination of Marx's project, for it is clear that they can be discovered from other starting points as well. But a critical examination of the basis of Marx's thinking makes these implications more vivid than would otherwise be the case.

Historical study, rightly pursued, needs to be both connected to and disconnected from the present. Consider one of the discarded working titles of this book: "Marx Disentangled from the Nineteenth Century." It was a cumbrous title, but it well conveys the approach that is taken. I have aimed to look at Marx's theorizing as an object in its own right. I have thus wished to avoid the contextualist error of turning Marx into a reflection of his circumstances. But to disentangle honestly and well, one must first of all entangle. To separate Marx's theory from the contexts out of which it emerged, one must have some sense of how it was related to those contexts. The contexts in question were multiple, perhaps even infinite. One cannot deal with all of them. The focus of the present study, in its contextualist moment, is on situating Marx *intellectually* in his time. I want to contribute to the wider, collective project of showing how Marx comes out of a particular set of intellectual traditions. The traditions in question were connected primarily to philosophy and to a lesser extent to natural science, or at least to the *idea* of natural science. Marx's everyday life experiences also fed into his theorizing, but those experiences were mediated through the grid of his philosophical presuppositions; they had to be, to have any effect on the theory.

To the degree that I situate Marx within a set of intellectual traditions I am engaging in a variant of contextual intellectual history.[7] But I am far more interested in Marx than I am in the contexts out of which he came. I zero in on Marx; everything else I sketch. How do I justify highlighting text to a greater degree than context? An initial and obvious point is that any thinker worthy of the name breaks away from the constraints of the tradition or traditions that gave rise to his (her) work. Someone completely entangled in the ways of thinking of his (her) own time would be of no philosophical interest. Such a person might be worthy of study as an exemplar of a past mode of thought that deserves historical reconstruction. With Marx, however, we are not dealing with someone who was in that sense an exemplary thinker. Rather, he is of interest because he burst out beyond the constraints of nineteenth-century theory (in part because he intensified certain of its characteristic features). Marx was a synthesizer of ideas that were already extant, but an original synthesizer, whose own situation and studies led him along paths different from what one would have expected from a mere ventriloquizer of the *Zeitgeist*. In other words, Marx in part disentangled himself from the nineteenth century, and the method of this study follows therefrom.

With the benefit of hindsight we can disentangle Marx still further, thus engaging in a theoretical and not only in a historiographical act. As Michel de Certeau and others have shown, perhaps the most important contribution that history-writing makes to knowledge and to life is to explore and develop a breach or break between the present and the past—highlighting the otherness or strangeness of the past, its difference from us.[8] Only on the assumption of a break or crisis dividing past from present can one hope to arrive in any degree at a *critical* history-writing. A critical history-writing keeps alive alternative possibilities for the present. It shows us how people have lived their lives or have thought about their worlds in other ways than "we" do now. It makes us aware of ways that are not our ways and perhaps cannot be our ways, but whose difference helps us see ourselves and our limits more fully. By juxtaposing to the present something that is not the present, history of this kind helps to keep the present from becoming everything that is. It stops the present from becoming a stifling prison house marked by a closed horizon whose closedness is invisible.

The point that I make about history-writing's relation to the present is also, *mutatis mutandis*, applicable to its relation to the past. History properly pursued ought to highlight the contingency of both the present and the past. History carries with it the danger of a retrospective illusion: we look back and see a past that followed a particular path, and (perhaps unconsciously) we come to think that this was history's rational trajectory, the way things had to be. This is a Marxian view (and a Hegelian view before it was Marxian). While much of the present study is concerned with showing what led Marx to the particular theoretical positions and historical interpretations that he came to, in articulating these explanations I do not want the reader to lose sight of the paths that Marx did not take. I "contextualize" Marx (seeing him as part of a necessitarian tradition in philosophy and science) in part so that I can make visible those points where we might make choices different from the ones he made.

Marx rejected politics and the market because he found it impossible to understand politics and the market in a way that conformed to his idea of science. I want to indicate another road than the road Marx took. This other road involves an acceptance of markets (because of their superiority, in general, over all alternatives for the production of material goods in a complex society). It also involves an acceptance of the necessity and legitimacy of a political order in which people would subordinate market mechanisms to the vision of a free, egalitarian, and humane society. This is social democracy, and it requires an application of state power in its pursuit of freedom for all. As for Marx's theory, in spite of Marx's humanistic focus on freedom it ended up unintendedly hostile to freedom. It is unfortunate that this was so; indeed, it was one of the great tragedies of the twentieth century. I imagine a rescuing of Marx from himself, by thinking out a position more accepting of contingency and of the uncertainty resulting from contingency. But there is still much in Marx that ought to be preserved—above all, the vigor and thoroughness of his critical-theoretical project. This is why I see this book not as the last word on Marx but as part of a new beginning.

* * *

The literature on Marx is immense. Much of it is of low quality or is simply outdated, but it also includes a great many insightful works. In the 1950s and 1960s a sense of intellectual excitement surrounded the investigation of Marx's thought. Those years saw a coming to terms with manuscripts from the Marx-Engels *Nachlass* that had appeared in print only in the years 1927–41 in the "old" *Marx-Engels Gesamtausgabe* (*MEGA2*) (published 1927–35) and in the "raw draft" of *Capital*, the so-called *Grundrisse* (published 1939–41). Political repression in Germany and in Russia, where the *MEGA* volumes were published, and the disruptions of economic depression and war, meant that these writings remained largely unavailable in practical terms until well after 1945. The *Grundrisse*, which was published in Moscow under unfortunate circumstances, remained almost totally inaccessible until the East Germans republished it in 1953. Only in the mid- to late 1950s did scholars begin to come to grips with the most important of Marx's manuscripts and with the implications they had for understanding Marx's project generally.9 Only in the 1960s did some of the manuscripts come to be widely known: in particular, the "Economic and Philosophical Manuscripts" (1844) became the focus of much attention.[10]

More recently, in 1972, the so-called New *MEGA* (*MEGA2*), the first edition of Marx's and Engels's writings to be edited according to adequate standards of textual scholarship, began to appear, edited by expert scholars mainly located in East Germany. By that time the earlier great interest in Marx's manuscripts, and in Marx generally, had dissipated. The spate of original Marx scholarship from the late 1950s and 1960s had slackened off, while for many people in the wider world Marxism came to seem less and less the bearer of hope for the future and more and more a sclerotic apologetics for the (as we now know) dying Soviet system. And so an edition that is beautifully done, offering access to complex and often all but illegible manuscripts, was underused. The present study has been much stimulated by the New *MEGA* (which an international team of scholars coordinated by the Internationale Marx-Engels-Stiftung, headquartered in Amsterdam, continues to carry forward after the collapse of the German Democratic Republic). Although I arrived at the idea of writing this book before engaging with the New *MEGA*, several of the ideas that I advance here could not have come to me without that edition's clear laying out of some crucial Marx manuscripts. The New *MEGA*'s treasures are immense: the danger of such a rich edition is that one will drown in the all too fascinating material, and never publish one's own work.

* * *

This is an original and quite heavily documented study, not a mere popularization, and so the style is sometimes heavy (although I hope that a certain verve and energy also show through). Readers do not need to read the endnotes to get the basic argument. They can be read glancingly, perhaps by turning to them only after the reading of an entire chapter. They are copious for a reason. Even though this is not a comprehensive study of Marx (indeed, in part *because* it is not a comprehensive study), I want readers to be able to find their way to the sources and to the secondary literature, in case they wish to have fuller documentation for the claims that I make or if they wish to explore some particular topic in more detail.[11] But most readers can do without the copiousness.

The book can be thought of as a set of linked essays that, taken together, highlight the early Marx's particular way of thinking and show how that way of thinking influenced his theorizing about politics, economics, and history generally. Chapter 1 is essential for understanding the book, whereas the other chapters are somewhat optional and can be tackled according to the reader's own set of interests. In chapter 1 I introduce something that until now has not been clearly seen: Marx's "rationalism." I define this rationalism and explicate the four criteria that Marx saw as involved in it. In chapter 2 I examine Marx's attempt to come to grips with politics. I turn in chapter 3 to his attempt to come to grips with economics, and most especially with the market. In chapter 4 I examine "the materialist conception of history" (also known as "historical materialism"), which, I contend, reactivated in a different register the philosophically oriented rationalism sketched out in chapter 1. Historical materialism is a theory or interpretation of the human world in general; it gives us Marx's scientific project in its widest possible extension; it is the putative theoretical underpinning for all specific assertions that Marx and Engels would make about the human world.

Finally, in the conclusion I reflect on the implications of Marx's theoretical project. My intent is in part to highlight the merits of that project and in part to highlight its lacunae and blind spots. I also intend to lead people to think about possible alternatives to Marx's approach. Marx's solutions to the problems of what is commonly called "capitalism," but what might better be called "economic modernity," have turned out to be unworkable. This study shows that the unworkability is deeply rooted in the theory (the theory in question was already in place by 1845–46). However, some of Marx's aims, some of his theoretical and critical instruments, and some, even, of his concrete conclusions remain valid, usable, and true today. Those aims, instruments, and conclusions can and ought to be deployed in the understanding, and reforming, of the contemporary world.

I originally intended to include in this book a study of Marx's *magnum opus, Capital*. I believe that *Capital* eminently confirms the claims that I make about a rationalist Marx intent on discovering essences so constituted that they will generate a necessary, universal, and predictive knowledge. *Capital* also reveals a Marx who was deeply involved in empirical research. Further, the work tells a dramatic story never previously told, the story of a conflict between Prometheus and the Vampires—a conflict, that is, between the creative force of human intelligence and dedication on the one hand, and the parasitic force of exploitation on the other. Especially in its long chapters on the working day, on machinery and large scale industry, and on capitalist accumulation, *Capital* vividly deploys the most important critical notion in the Marxian armamentarium. This is not, as Marx's sympathetic readers in the 1950s and 1960s thought, estrangement or alienation, but rather exploitation. This notion, which leads us to consider how the economic system itself, independently of any specific intentions, generates a surplus that gets distributed in nonrational ways, remains perennially valuable.

But I have decided to exclude an analysis of *Capital* from this book (of course, I do cite *Capital* on many occasions: it is not as if it makes no appearance between the covers of this book). If the analysis of *Capital* is to be carried out with a meticulous attention to the sources, it needs to be carried out at book length rather than at chapter length. In my opinion, no adequate historical study of *Capital* has yet been written. Until recently such a study could not have been written, because the manuscript sources (virtually illegible in their handwritten form) had not yet been published in anything like a textually adequate edition. Even now some of the manuscripts remain unpublished. However, it must be said the New *MEGA* is sufficiently advanced that new studies of Marx's later economics can indeed be carried out. I urge people to try. But the inclusion of Marx's later economics in this book would have made it far too long to be easily publishable and far too weighty to be widely read. Further, such a study, I estimate, would have required at least an additional five years of research and thinking on my part. Research and thinking (and teaching as well) are what I do, but I prefer to have something to show for my labors now. Perhaps the still-unwritten study, *Prometheus and the Vampires*, accompanied by a study of *Marx's Later Dialectics*, will be written by me, perhaps by someone else. In any case, these books are not to be found here.[12]

As befits a study of a theorist whose favorite occupation was critique, this is a critical study; but it is also written out of a sense of awe. What issued from Marx's mind and pen is stunning in its breadth and depth. It is amazing to consider the energy and intelligence that went into that thinking and writing, especially given the sometimes difficult conditions under which the work was done. Standing in Highgate Cemetery on March 17, 1883, three days after Marx's death, Friedrich Engels began his eulogy as follows: "On the 14th of March, at a quarter to three in the afternoon, the greatest living thinker ceased to think" (*MEGA2* 1.25: 407/*MECW* 24: 467/*MER* 681). Engels was right in his assessment of Marx's intellectual standing, although it was then unrecognized except within a narrow circle. Charles Darwin had died in 1882, John Stuart Mill in 1873. Marx's work stands before us as a monument of social theory. In its combination of blindness and insight it remains something from which we can learn. Above all, it stands as an example of a thinking that seeks to go beyond the extant social world and its dominant assumptions. It asks us to not simply accept what is given to us, but to arrive at our own conclusions—and not arbitrarily, but by the deepest and most serious thought.

A final point concerns something in this study that some readers may find disconcerting. I have more or less deliberately highlighted Marx's contradictoriness, and have then focused on one side of the contradiction.[13] In brief, I have pursued the "rationalist" (theoretical, scientific) Marx. I do not deny the existence of another Marx, whom we might variously characterize as empirical, revolutionary, and practical. Another, different study might well focus on that Marx. This study does not. Nor does this study try to show how science and revolution, theory and practice, are actually consistent with each other in the end—for I am suspicious of the claim that they are. In short, the present study does what it does, and not something else. In doing what it does it emphasizes something that is really there in Marx, namely, his rationalism. Marx's rationalism needs to be taken into consideration and, I believe, countered in any attempt to come to terms with what Marxism ought to mean for us, now.

Acknowledgments

I have incurred debts to many persons and to several institutions in the writing of this study. Collectively my greatest debt is to the students who, over a period of many years, heard me lecture on Marx at the University of Iowa, the Australian National University, and the University of Virginia. Their interest invariably has been stimulating and their feedback, in the form of questions, comments, essays, and exams, has often helped me to see new things and to approach old things in new ways. How wonderful it is that there exist educational institutions where the delivery and active reception of lectures continue to be taken seriously. A second debt of a collective sort is to my colleagues at the University of Iowa in the years 1980–1990. From such persons as John S. Nelson, Deirdre McCloskey, David Klemm, John Lyne, and others in the "rhetoric of inquiry" group there, I learned many things that I would not have come to know otherwise. My colleagues at Iowa helped me to think far more clearly about issues of objectivity, argument, and method than I would otherwise have managed, and they led me to pose questions to and about Marx that I would not have thought of otherwise. Even more important, they provided a model of scholarly interaction that I have not seen equaled anywhere: democratic in their dealings and in their aims, they knew how to listen and at the same time how to criticize and enlighten. To spend ten years in such an environment was a great privilege.

Although I have for the most part worked on this study on my own, trying it out mainly in my own classes, on a few occasions I have also presented parts of it in other venues. These include the Departments of Sociology and of Government and Foreign Affairs at the University of Virginia; the University of Virginia Roundtable; the Social Science History Association; the European Social Science History Convention; the University of Groningen; the

University of Iowa; the University of Jena; the Davis Center at Princeton University; Oregon State University; and the École des Hautes Études en Sciences Sociales, Paris. I am grateful to those who arranged these occasions. I carried out late revisions as a guest at the Institut für die Wissenschaften vom Menschen/Institute for Human Sciences, Vienna, where I made good use of the Institut's excellent social-science and philosophy reference library. I also used the Österreichische Nationalbibliothek and the libraries of the Wirtschaftsuniversität Wien and of the Universität Wien.

I cannot remember all the people who have enlightened me with their thoughts or who have helped me in other ways. Still, a list would include, among others, Frank Ankersmit, Mitchell Ash, Dorothe Bach, Alan Beyerchen, Tico Braun, Rob Chametsky, Alon Confino, Steven Cunningham, Vincent Descombes, Richard Drayton, Janusz Duzinkiewicz, Fernando Gil, Matthew Goldfeder, Carey Goodman, Michael B. Guenther, Malachi Hacohen, Robert Hariman, Joshua Himwich, John Holloran, Thomas (Tal) Howard, George Klosko, János Kovács, Michael Krätke, James Krueger, Chris Lorenz, Catalin Mamali, Deirdre McCloskey, Jason Megill, Erik Midelfort, Kelly Mulroney, Alan Nagel, Mark Notturno, Mary Jo Nye, Robert Nye, Derek Nystrom, Susan Peabody, Gianfranco Poggi, Philip Pomper, Sebastian Reinfeldt, Jürgen Rojahn, Richard Rorty, Jeffrey Rossman, Paul A. Roth, Tim Shiell, David N. Smith, Alan Spitzer, Andrew Starner, Bob Tanner, Mark Thomas, Richard Weikart, Hal Wells, Nick West, Brad Whitener, Perez Zagorin, Günter Zöller, and Olivier Zunz. No doubt some of these people will have forgotten how they helped me—but they did. In some cases people raised issues with me that I was simply not able to respond to adequately; in the standard phrase, they cannot be held responsible for what is to be found in this book. Finally, I cannot neglect to mention the late Eugene Kamenka, who headed the History of Ideas Unit, Research School of Social Sciences, Australian National University during my three years at that university, in 1977–79: he, and many of the visitors he invited to Canberra, introduced me to the world of Marx scholarship long before I had any thought of writing on Marx.

During the period when I was working on this study I received, in 1994, a Sesquicentennial Associateship granted by the Edgar F. Shannon, Jr., Center for Advanced Studies at the University of Virginia. Although little of my time during the fellowship semester was devoted to the Marx project, the released time from teaching that it provided allowed me to move forward in various other ways, clearing a space for this project and giving me infinitely better living and working arrangements. A second Sesquicentennial Associateship, held in spring semester 2000, was essential to the completion of the project. Also helpful were two grants, modest in size but valuable in effect, from the Bankard Fund for Political Economy; I am grateful for the generosity of the forward-looking donors, Mr. and Mrs. Merrill H. Bankard. Without the resources and staff of the University of Virginia's Alderman Library, especially its acquisitions, reference, and interlibrary loan departments, the project could not have been carried out. Kevin Coffey spent long hours and a clear and fresh intelligence helping to put two successive versions of the manuscript into good shape. His insightful memos often led me to see things that I would otherwise have missed. Particularly valuable was our mutual effort to make sense of Marx's dissertation. Michael Doak made some extremely important contributions to the writing of the historical materialism chapter, mainly by imparting some order to the recent literature on historical materialism. Brian Snyder made an equally weighty contribution to the politics chapter. Warren Breckman, himself the author of an important book on Marx, offered an exemplary detailed reading of a late draft of three-quarters of the manuscript. Some of his comments made their way into the book; others stand as reminders of the incompleteness of any interpretation of anything. John Holloran gave me the title. Other late-stage readers include: Malachi Hacohen, James Krueger, Mark Notturno, Bob Tanner, and Brad Whitener. I have inadequately responded to the comments of these and other critics. In the problems that I cannot resolve, I see occasion for continued scholarly work and public reflection. The two anonymous readers, generous of their time and erudition, who read the draft manuscript for Rowman & Littlefield contributed much to its improvement (one of these readers later identified himself to me: Harold Mah). It was a pleasure to work with Steve Wrinn, executive editor at Rowman & Littlefield and with his assistant, Mary Carpenter. All these people contributed in ways that transcended considerations of market, property, and economic calculation generally.

My partner Rita Felski has helped me in innumerable ways, as both friend and scholar. Maria Megill Felski has provided a fresh and ever-changing view of the world, and Jason, Jessica, and Jonathan Megill have been steadfast in their concern.

A German version of part of the argument of chapter 3 appeared as "Über die Grenzen einer gewissen Art von Sozialtheorie: Marx, der Rationalismus und der Markt," trans. Klaus-Michael Kodalle, in *Republik und Weltbürgerrecht. Kantische Anregungen zur Theorie politischer Ordnung nach dem Ende des Ost-West-Konflikts*, ed. Klaus Dicke and Klaus-Michael Kodalle (Köln: Böhlau, 1998), 363–98.

Chapter One

Marx's Rationalism: How the Dialectic Came from the History of Philosophy

> The truth is not to be found on the superficial plane of the senses; for, especially in subjects which claim a scientific status, reason must always remain alert, and conscious deliberation is indispensable. Whoever looks at the world rationally will find that it in turn assumes a rational aspect; the two exist in a reciprocal relationship.
>
> —G. W. F. Hegel, *Lectures on the Philosophy of World History: Introduction: Reason in History*, trans. H. B. Nisbet, with an introduction by Duncan Forbes (Cambridge: Cambridge University Press, 1975), 29.

My argument in this study is that Marx is best seen as a "rationalist," in a sense that I shall specify in this chapter and develop and illustrate as I proceed. Marx's commitment to rationalism had a massive impact on the positions he adopted and on the strategies he pursued over the course of his career. That commitment set up a sharp tension between his positions and strategies on the one hand and, on the other, the real world to which the positions and strategies were to be applied. The reader will come to see the precise dimensions and character of Marx's rationalism once we have worked our way through a number of important "problem areas" in his thinking. In this chapter I define Marx's rationalism and indicate how this orientation entered into his thought. In the three subsequent chapters I examine, respectively, Marx's encounter with politics; his encounter with the economic sphere and in particular with the market; and his attempt to offer a theory of history-in-general (his so-called historical materialism). In the conclusion I offer a general assessment, attempting to answer the question, What can be learned from Marx, for us, now?

EMBEDDED RATIONALITY

The term *rationalism* is by no means ideal for designating the orientation that I shall now describe. But no better term exists. The trouble with the word is that it comes to us loaded down with too many meanings. Some of the meanings are not congruent with what I have in mind in using the term. Conversely, some aspects of what I have in mind have usually been designated by other terms. But since there is no good alternative it is the term we must use, while being careful in our usage. Accordingly, I begin by surveying the customary meanings of *rationalism*, in order to point out which meanings are applicable here. Next, I offer a meaning of my own, albeit a meaning that is initially too abstract and general. I then proceed along two lines. I examine the specific criteria that enter into Marx's version of rationalism—namely, universality, necessity, predictivity, and progress by contradiction. And, I trace out the roots and connections of these criteria.

Marx's rationalism is Janus-faced. It has a Hegelian face and a natural scientific face. One might think of the two faces as looking back into the past and forward into the future. When one goes back far enough into the past, the two faces join, for Marx's thought is ultimately beholden to Aristotle's metaphysics, and Aristotle provides a common theoretical foundation for both Hegelianism and natural science. Marx's project led forward to science, and more especially to social science, but he was a philosopher before he was anything else. The particular orientation of his philosophy had an overwhelming impact on how he thought about the human world. Although he proclaimed, as early as 1845, that he had abandoned philosophy for science, the impact of his early philosophical training on his positions continued to be profound. I contend that always, until his death, Marx remained a philosopher, indentured to and sustained by the particular way of thinking that became his during his years as a student of philosophy, 1837–41.[1]

The word *rationalism* has commonly been used in four divergent ways. I can best highlight its meanings by contrasting it with four other terms: *empiricism, feeling* (or sentiment), *religion, historism*. The rationalism of the opposition "rationalism" versus "empiricism" is the best known. Here, "rationalism" is the view that knowledge comes ultimately from the mind's innate ideas or capacities, whereas "empiricism" is the view that knowledge comes ultimately from sense experience.[2] Next in order of prominence is the rationalism of the opposition "reason" versus "feeling," where "rationalism" means a resistance to the emotive aspects of human life.[3] Third, there is the rationalism of the opposition "rationalism" versus "religion," where "rationalism" means an attack on revealed religion in the name of philosophy or science.[4] Finally, one ought not forget the rationalism of the opposition "rationalism" versus "historism," where "rationalism" means commitment to the notion that there exist unchanging values graspable through reason (as manifested especially in doctrines of natural law or natural right), and "historism" means the view that everything is subject to historical change.[5]

Only two of these four senses of rationalism are readily applicable to Marx. First, Marx was more "rationalist" than "empiricist"; in other words, he was a rationalist in the sense that he aimed to discover underlying logical essences that, he claimed, could not be discovered merely by generalizing from empirical data. *Capital* (1867) is especially marked by rationalism in this sense. However, it must be emphasized that Marx did not see the search for logical essences as standing in opposition to empirical research; in any case, the contrast between rationalism and empiricism is a questionable one.[6] Second, Marx was a "rationalist" critic of religion, particularly near the beginning of his career: indeed, on one occasion he used the very term, *Rationalismus*, to refer to an antireligious orientation.[7] But contrary to what is often assumed, Marx was relatively uninterested in critiquing religion. After his 1843 essay, "On the Jewish Question," which, as we shall see, is ultimately not concerned with Judaism (or with religion) at all, Marx dealt with religion only in passing (Friedrich Engels devoted somewhat more attention to the subject).[8] Rationalism in the antireligious sense did not play an important role in Marx's theoretical project, although it was certainly not absent from his mind.

Accordingly, while a consideration of the conventional meanings of *rationalism* is a useful starting point for the present investigation, these meanings do not come close to embracing the full dimensions of what I intend by Marx's rationalism. A step back is required, opening up a broader horizon. What is this horizon? In brief, it is the horizon marked out by the claim that there is a logic or reason inherent in the world. Rationalism in this broad sense—which is the sense most relevant to Marx—amounts to adherence to a notion of what I call "embedded rationality." Embedded rationality is a rationality that is *in* the world; it is to be distinguished from a norm or standard standing outside the world. Many (although far from all) nineteenth-century intellectuals were rationalists in this sense. It is not simply Marx's view, although Marx's version of rationalism was distinctive and he adhered to it with uncommon rigor.

For example, one finds the notion of embedded rationality in natural theology, and specifically in its so-called argument from design. Natural theology, which flourished in the eighteenth century and continued to be taken seriously well into the second half of the nineteenth century, claimed to find proofs of God's existence in nature. Nature, it was claimed, everywhere shows evidence of intelligence. In other words, nature shows signs of having been designed by a rational being; consequently, God exists (for "God" is none other than this rational being). By the same token, if the world was indeed made by a rational and omnipotent God it must be rational, since a rational and omnipotent God would not have made an irrational world. Such was the argument, and although it had been demolished by Hume and Kant in the second half of the eighteenth century, it remained part of the mental furniture of many educated people throughout the nineteenth century.[9]

One overwhelming piece of evidence for the prevalence among nineteenth-century intellectuals of a belief in the fundamentally rational character of the world is provided by the reception of Darwin's *The Origin of Species* (1859). The theory that Darwin presented in *The Origin of Species* completely dispensed with the notion that nature has some sort of rationality embedded in it. But in part because Darwin himself attempted to conceal this fact with a certain amount of saccharine language, and in part because Darwin's readers were simply not able to recognize or acknowledge the view that no rational intention underlies nature, Darwinian evolution was widely misinterpreted: it was seen, not as showing how no rational intention is required for evolution to take place, but as both assuming an initial rational intention and as actually offering further support for that assumption (for how else could such a being as man have come into existence?). In short, evolution was widely taken to be a progressive, even providential, process leading from primitive organisms to the pinnacle of organic life, man.[10]

Of course, Marx had no truck with natural theology or with the argument from design. In no way did he accept the notion that there is a rational God outside the universe overseeing its functioning and thus guaranteeing its rational operation. But if anything, Marx's commitment to what we can think of as "world-rationality" was actually more intense than was the commitment of the natural theologians or of their later confrères, the providential evolutionists. The natural theologians did not see the rationality embedded in the world as self-subsistent: in their view it derived from God. For Marx, on the contrary, world-rationality did not require an external guarantee.

Within the philosophical tradition, the difference between the natural theologians and Marx is analogous to the difference between Leibniz and Spinoza, who in the late seventeenth and early eighteenth centuries wrote about God and the world. Leibniz posited a rational God who created the extant world because it was the best of all the possible worlds. Spinoza posited a rational God who turns out to be nothing other than the world itself: in Spinoza's words, *Deus, sive Natura*: "God or Nature." (The word *or* has two divergent meanings: the *or* of identity, as in "Virginia is a state or commonwealth", and the *or* of alternativity, as in "air freight can arrive via La Guardia or JFK." Here, Spinoza unequivocally intended the *or* of identity.) Thus, in Spinoza's view there is no source external to the world from which the world's rationality comes. Commitment to the rationality of the world becomes all the more intense in such a perspective, precisely because there is no external source of rationality. Marx's position, in this regard, has a close affinity with Spinoza's.

I am not arguing that Spinoza had a deep, direct influence on Marx, or that Leibniz did either. Marx was familiar with the account of Spinoza in Hegel's *Lectures on the History of Philosophy*. We know that in January–March 1841 Marx made excerpts from Spinoza's *Tractatus Theologico-Politicus* and from his letters, although the editors of *MEGA*2 also inform us that Marx apparently did not make use of the excerpts at any later time (*MEGA2* 4.1: 223–76, 773). Further, there are some affinities between Spinoza and Hegel: as the French Marxist philosopher and historian of philosophy Louis Althusser once remarked, "it is possible to describe Hegel as Spinoza set in motion."[11] Given the extent to which Marx was formed philosophically by Hegel, one should not be surprised to find him reinventing aspects of Spinoza's philosophy on his own. This is as much as to say that my argument at this point is more about affinity than it is about influence. Marx's intellectual training was as a philosopher, and he remained profoundly marked by this training throughout his career, even though, by 1845 at the latest, he rejected philosophy for science. In consequence, if we are to grasp Marx's problems, concepts, and methods we need to take account of the philosophical tradition out of which he came. In considering the problems that were important to him Marx arrived at his own solutions, but those solutions were not necessarily unprecedented.

Marx was a Spinozist in the sense that his fundamental conception of the world involved elements that are also to be found in Spinoza's world-conception.[12] Consider a striking passage in Marx's "Economic and Philosophical Manuscripts" (1844), in the section that its editors have entitled "Private Property and Communism." Here Marx writes that "since for socialist man the *whole of what is called world history* is nothing more than the creation of man through human labor, and the development of nature for man," socialist man has "palpable and incontrovertible proof of his self-mediated *birth* [*seiner* Geburt *durch sich selbst*]" (*MEGA2* 1.2: 398/*MECW* 3: 305/*EW* 357). Here Marx is portraying a world that requires nothing outside itself for its self-production. Such a world stands as a human, historicized analogue to Spinoza's world.

The Spinoza reference is illuminating, largely because it helps us to see more clearly the character of Marx's relation to Hegel, who *did* influence Marx—deeply. Two points in particular are worth noting: both have to do with the difference between Spinoza's commitment to embedded rationality and Hegel's commitment. It makes sense to compare Spinoza and Hegel, for their philosophies have a certain underlying similarity. Indeed, Hegel himself held, in his *Lectures on the History of Philosophy*, that Spinozism "is the essential beginning of all philosophizing," because Spinoza maintained that a single substance, which causes itself, makes up the universe; Spinoza thus articulated, according to Hegel, a unifying principle where other philosophers had failed to do so (*LHP* 3: 257). Both Spinoza and Hegel adhered to the notion of embedded rationality; both were also monists, holding that only the world exists, with no transcendent realm beyond it.[13]

It is equally necessary to attend to the differences between Spinoza and Hegel, for the differences help us to locate Marx more clearly in relation to the theoretical options available to him. The first point of difference is obvious, but it is not trivial: it concerns the *historical* character of Hegel's conception of embedded rationality. Hegel's best-known assertion of world-rationality is undoubtedly the following statement, which appears in the preface to his *Elements of the Philosophy of Right* (1820):

> What is rational is actual;
> and what is actual is rational.[14]

So far as it goes this statement is entirely congruent with Spinoza's conception of world-rationality. Not visible in it is the fact that Hegel's notion of embedded rationality took the form of a notion of embedded *progress*, for Hegel held that reason realizes itself—that is, becomes real, or "actual"—to an ever-greater degree as time passes. In another, less well-known statement in *The Philosophy of Right*, Hegel asserts that "the truth . . . is the momentous transition of the inner to the outer, that incorporation [*Einbildung*] of reason into reality which the whole of world history has worked to achieve."[15] Here, Hegel's commitment to the notion of embedded progress is entirely clear. Marx's conception of history came directly out of Hegel's; accordingly, I shall examine, below, the linkages between Marx and Hegel with respect to the notion that history manifests an embedded progress. Spinoza is completely outside this range of concerns; from a Hegelian perspective, Spinoza was entirely ahistorical.

Because Hegel's impact on Marx was massive, it is tempting to see Marx's rationalism as simply a version of Hegel's. The temptation needs to be resisted; the perspective opened up by Hegel's philosophy was broad, but Hegelianism had its limits too. Spinoza—or, more precisely, Spinoza's reception by other thinkers—helps us to grasp these limits. There are two ways of understanding Spinoza's ontology—his conception of what the world is. One can emphasize the *Deus* in Spinoza's *Deus, sive Natura*, or one can emphasize the *Natura*. Some of Spinoza's interpreters emphasized the first, and hence saw him as a pantheist; others emphasized the second, and saw him as an atheist. These two interpretations of Spinoza correspond to the two opposing sides of the Cartesian soul/body, spirit/matter dualism, within the ambit of which all modern philosophy is situated. The pantheistic Spinoza is an idealist, believing that spirit rules the world; the atheistic Spinoza is a materialist, believing that the world is ruled by physical forces alone.[16]

For his part, Hegel was understood by his contemporaries and successors, including Marx, to be an idealist. In other words, they saw Hegel as believing not only that ideas are important in human life and history, but also that everything in the world is spirit. In short, Hegel was seen as an ontological idealist (which is what we call someone who believes that the world is spirit or idea). Further, in the perspective of Hegelianism, to say that the world is rational is to say that it is structured in such a way that it can be fully understood by a fully developed mind. Since in Hegel's view, reality is indeed rationally structured, "logic," for him, was far more than simply a compendium of the rules of thinking; it amounts, rather, to ontology, to the science of being. Hegel's *Science of Logic* (1812–16) is an attempt to describe at its deepest level the logical structure of the world as it is known to us. The structure in question is a structure of thought. Famously, although somewhat misleadingly, Hegel tells us in the introduction to the *Science of Logic* that the content of logic is "the exposition of God as he is in his eternal essence before the creation. . . ."[17] But perhaps it is best to think of Hegel's God as nothing other than the world itself, and to think of his (or His) logic as the starting point for the process of thinking that, in Hegel's eyes, just is the world. So in Hegel's view, the world is rational. And Hegel further holds that the rationality is not simply *there*, as a finished object. Rather, the Hegelian world works out its rationality over time.

We are concerned finally with Marx, not Hegel. Insofar as Marx is at issue, there is more to be said about the world's rationality. The ambivalent character of Spinoza's philosophy, which is accurately reflected in the conflict between atheistic and pantheistic interpretations of Spinoza, reminds us that the idealist option is merely one of two possible ways of conceiving of the world as rational. One can think of the world as God (or idea, or spirit), or one can think of it as Nature (or matter). Correspondingly, there is logic (as Hegel understood it), and there is also natural science. One of the most striking features of Marx's theorizing is the presence in it of both idealism and naturalism, of an appeal to both Hegelian philosophy and natural science.[18] In this respect Marx's perspective was markedly broader than Hegel's. Hegel's interest in natural science was always secondary to his idealism. Indeed, in 1816, in his inaugural lecture as professor of philosophy at Heidelberg, he drew a contrast between philosophy and natural science, with the clear intent of portraying himself as philosophy's defender against the potential overextension of natural science:

> In other European countries, where the natural sciences and the cultivation of the scientific intellect [*Verstand*] has been pursued with enthusiasm and respect, philosophy,

except in name, has . . . perished, while the German nation has pursued it as a possession peculiarly its own.[19]

It is not for nothing that Hegel began his intellectual career at a theological seminary, the Tübingen Stift. Hegel's *Philosophy of Nature* confirms the claim that Hegel always remained focused on the idealist side of the spirit/matter divide, for the work completely subordinates nature and natural science to the notion of spirit.[20] Using the terms popularized by C. P. Snow in his notion of "the two cultures," one might portray Hegel as a defender of the humanities against science—were it not for the fact that for Hegel the name of *Wissenschaft* (science) applied to both the humanities and the natural sciences.[21]

In any case, whereas Hegel was far more attached to the "spirit" side of the spirit/matter opposition, Marx's attachment was two-fold. On the one hand, Marx was profoundly influenced by a Hegelian conception of rationality, in which logic equates to ontology and in which ontology thus equates to mind, or spirit, thinking. Hegel's ontologization of logic resonated in Marx's work throughout the whole of his intellectual career. It is thus an egregious error to think that Marx can be adequately characterized as a materialist, at least as the term *materialist* is normally used. In philosophy, the term normally designates an ontological view—a view, that is, as to how the world in general is ultimately constituted (it is material, and nothing more).

Yet on the other hand Marx was (or, more accurately, quickly became) far more deeply attached to the natural sciences of his time, and to theoretical perspectives emerging from natural science, than Hegel had been a half century earlier. Forty-eight years younger than Hegel, Marx became caught up, by the early 1840s, in the enthusiasm for natural science and its potential extension that marked nineteenth-century theory. (I shall return to Marx's interest in science, which is quite marked in the "Economic and Philosophical Manuscripts" [1844], later in this book.) It should be noted that the early Marx's interest in science was largely an interest in the *idea* of natural science, not an interest in its details. Consequently, to understand Marx we need to understand not only the idealist perspective (outwardly repudiated, but never abandoned) that came to him primarily from Hegel, but also the impact on him of intellectual expectations associated with natural science. Of considerable importance for Marx was the philosopher Ludwig Feuerbach (1802–1872), who by the early 1840s was insisting on the programmatic importance of natural science. Thus, in his "Preliminary Theses on the Reform of Philosophy," which Marx read in March 1843 right after its publication, Feuerbach proclaimed that "All science must be grounded in *nature. . . . Philosophy must again unite itself with natural science. . . .*"[22] Marx probably did not need Feuerbach to point him toward natural science, but his reading of Feuerbach does seem to have confirmed, and perhaps speeded up, a tendency in that direction.

THE CRITERIA OF RATIONALITY

I have suggested that both Hegel and Marx, like many other nineteenth-century thinkers, adhered to the notion of embedded rationality, and I have also suggested that both thinkers conceived of embedded rationality as an embedded progress. But I have said nothing about the content of the presumed rationality. "Reason" by itself is an empty term. When I say that Marx adhered to the notion of embedded rationality, what exactly do I mean?

It is hardly surprising that in order to grasp Marx's conception of rationality we must first look at Hegel's conception. But we cannot stop with Hegel; once more, we need to take a step back in the history of philosophy, this time to Aristotle. Aristotle was an important presence for Hegel, and largely because of this he was an important presence for Marx as well. Moreover, besides helping us to see what Hegel's and Marx's rationality criteria were and why Hegel and Marx adhered to these criteria, the connection to Aristotle also helps us get our hands on the meaning and significance of the Hegelian and Marxian dialectic, which is crucial if we are to understand Marx's conception of history. The dialectic connects all three philosophers: Aristotle, Hegel, Marx. In his 1878 book *Anti-Dühring* (or, to take its longer title, *Herr Eugen Dühring's Revolution in Science*), Engels called Aristotle "the Hegel of the ancient world," who "had already analyzed the most essential forms of dialectic thought" (*MEGA2* 1.27: 231/*MECW* 25: 21/*MER* 694; see also *MEGA2* 1.27: 97/*MECW* 25: 593).[23] Engels's characterization of Aristotle implies that the inverse is also true—that Hegel was the Aristotle of the modern world. In fact, in important respects, Hegel, who in his *Lectures on the History of Philosophy* called Aristotle "one of the richest and deepest of all the scientific geniuses that have as yet appeared," seems to have modeled his project on Aristotle's (*LHP* 2: 117).

The important point here, hitherto largely unexplored, is that Marx's rationality criteria owed much to Aristotle. More accurately, they owed much to "Aristotle," since Marx's Aristotle was not so much the Aristotle who lived in the fourth century B.C. as the Aristotle who lived between the covers of Hegel's *History of Philosophy*. I have already mentioned the four criteria that I claim were decisive for Marx, namely, universality, necessity, predictivity, and progress by contradiction. All of these criteria except for predictivity are derived directly from Hegel, and all three relate to Hegel's interpretation of Aristotle. As for predictivity, it is an implication of universality and necessity taken together; it can also be derived from notions of natural science.

Consider universality and necessity. Moderns or postmoderns tend to think of universality, and especially of necessity, in the light of Cartesian rationalism—as involving, that is, a deductive model of reasoning derived from mathematics. But Hegel's main inspiration in matters of universality and necessity was Aristotle, not Descartes. Hegel's discussion of Aristotle in his *History of Philosophy*—114 pages in the English translation—is the longest account of any single philosopher in the entire work, slightly longer than his account of Plato (almost 60 percent of the *History of Philosophy* is devoted to Greek philosophy, far exceeding the space devoted to philosophy from Descartes's time onward). Hegel deals with Aristotle's metaphysics, his philosophy of nature, his philosophy of spirit (psychology, ethics, politics), and his logic. He declares that Aristotle's logic stands as his greatest achievement: it does "the greatest honor to the deep thought of its discoverer and to the power of his abstraction" (*LHP* 2: 211).

In Hegel's view, the greatest merit of the "first period of Greek philosophy," which Hegel saw as reaching its peak in Aristotle, was that it introduced into philosophy a commitment to universality: "This demand for a universal . . . is henceforth present to knowledge" (*LHP* 2: 228, 231). But the defect, according to Hegel, was that Aristotle attained universality only by virtue of falling into abstractness: on the one hand, there was a universal Idea, stripped of particularity; on the other, a "long series of particular conceptions, which are external to one another, and in which a unifying principle . . . is wanting" (*LHP* 2: 229). Thus the greatest merit of Aristotle's philosophy was also, in Hegel's view, its greatest defect: Aristotle's logic achieved universality only by detaching itself from the concrete particularities of the empirical world and of history. In the syllogism "All men are mortal; Gaius is a man; therefore Gaius is mortal," the universals "manhood" and "mortality" are concepts that stand apart from the world. In Hegel's view, the problem with taking Aristotelian logic as the model for universal and necessary reasoning is that the universals, in such reasoning, are not in reality, but are only *posited* of it (*LHP* 2: 213–14).[24]

Hegel does declare that Aristotle made logic secure by "separating it from what is material": thus formalism was necessary for establishing logic (*LHP* 2: 211). But Hegel aimed to carry logic forward beyond Aristotle, superseding Aristotle's logic. For Hegel wanted two things that were not to be found in Aristotle. First, in Hegel's view, the principle governing philosophy as a whole needs to be the idea of self-reflective thought—the idea of a thought capable of contemplating itself. Hegel does not find such a conception in Aristotle, who in contrast to many philosophers from Descartes onward had not been concerned with subjectivity and consciousness. Second, Hegel wanted the unifying principle of philosophy to be "truly concrete": hence the philosophical principle should be present "in the particular" as well as in the conception of the whole (*LHP* 2: 230–31). Logic, in short, ought to take account of history. This is not a surprising view, for a serious thinker who in his youth and manhood had lived through the earthquake that was the French

Revolution—who had closely watched the amazing events that followed the storming of the Bastille on July 14, 1789, and who in 1806 had heard the thunder of the battle of Jena and had seen the victorious Napoleon on horseback.

But to return to the world of thought: Hegel held that Aristotle had been trapped at the level of "the logic of the understanding." In Hegel, "the understanding" (*Verstand*; also translatable as "intellect" or "scientific intellect") is concerned with the relation of finite things to other finite things. Hegel aimed for a higher-level logic—a logic not of "the understanding" but of "reason" (*Vernunft*) (*LHP* 2: 213). Such a logic would strive to bring otherwise disjunct parts into "a necessary systematic whole . . . in which each part is held to be a part, and the whole alone as such is true" (*LHP* 2: 223). As Hegel interpreted him, Aristotle had been right to strive for universal and necessary knowledge. But Hegel held that universality ought to be concrete and not merely formal and abstract. One arrives at a concrete universality, Hegel further held, only if logic is seen as working itself out, over time, within the world. In short, Hegel aspired to concretize—and historicize—the syllogism. No longer merely formal, rationality would be the working out of a necessity within history itself.[25]

The concern in the present study is not with Hegel but with Marx: from our point of view Hegel was simply Marx's most important forerunner. In some respects, Hegel was broader in his interests than was Marx; in other respects, Marx was the more compendious thinker. As already noted, one point of difference between Marx and Hegel is that Marx was intellectually and temperamentally closer to natural science. Hegel had an extensive knowledge of the natural sciences of his time, as his *Philosophy of Nature* shows, but it was not at all from the natural sciences that the deepest commitments of his thinking came.[26] In some ways he always remained the theology student that he had been long before, at the Tübingen Stift. Philosophically, this meant that throughout his life he stayed resolutely on the idealist side of the spirit/matter, idealist/naturalist divide that came out of Descartes. But Aristotle far preceded the idealist/naturalist division that has been such a fundamental part of modern philosophy, and partly in consequence we can see him, with a justified anachronism, as straddling the divide between the two modern camps of idealism on the one hand and of natural science, naturalism, materialism, or positivism on the other. In consequence, there were things that Aristotle (or "Aristotle") could offer to Marx that Hegel himself could not.

One relevant point is that Aristotle held that the primary object of scientific knowledge is universals, and likewise that scientific knowledge is necessary knowledge. A famous passage from the *Posterior Analytics* can be translated as follows: "There can be no *knowledge* of that which [exists or comes to be] by chance, for that which [exists or comes to be] by chance occurs neither necessarily nor in most cases. . . ."[27] Along a similar line, in his *Metaphysics* Aristotle held that:

> there is neither definition nor demonstration about particular perceptible substances . . . demonstrations and definitions that express knowledge are of necessary things.[28]

In other words, in Aristotle's view there could be no genuine knowledge of things that are mere particulars, or that are the consequence of accident (rather than of necessity). Shifting the focus to the modern period, one can link up Aristotle's privileging of universality and necessity both with idealism, which takes the process of thinking as the primary ontological reality, and with materialism or naturalism, which sees matter and its movements as the primary ontological reality. On the one hand, universality and necessity are attributes of the syllogism ("All men are mortal. . . ," etc.), and this fact establishes a connection with logic, with thinking, with spirit. On the other hand, universality and necessity were also to be found at work in Newtonian natural science, which strove to articulate universal and necessary laws of nature, of the type f=ma.

Hegel the idealist was committed to universality and necessity. However, to understand what the criteria of universality and necessity meant *for Marx*, one needs to think not only in idealist terms but also in terms of natural science. As noted already, the young Marx developed an interest in natural science, and this expanded over time. In an amazingly precocious letter to his father, written in November 1837, Marx claims that he had acquainted himself "to some extent" with natural science, as part of an attempt to resolve the conflicts between idealism and reality, mind and body, art and science (*MEGA2* 3.1: 16/*MECW* 1: 18). No doubt the claim needs to be discounted: at the age of 19 1/2 Marx was in part showing off to, and attempting to justify himself in the eyes of, his father. But it is probably not an accident that in his doctoral dissertation, toward which he began to work in 1839, Marx chose to focus on the philosophies of nature of two ancient philosophers. Already by the late 1830s Marx was aware, through progressive circles in Trier and through the Hegelian professor of law at Berlin, Eduard Gans, of Saint-Simonian social philosophy, which had a scientifically inflected side to it. His dissertation materials make it clear that, like many in the free-thinking tradition, he saw natural science (and philosophy) as standing in opposition to the obscurantism of religion. Further, in the early 1840s he was marked by Feuerbach's insistence on the importance of nature and natural science. This insistence became public and emphatic by early 1843, although it had already appeared in Feuerbach's work several years earlier. Further, in the wider world the expansion of the field of influence of the natural sciences was a notable feature of the times. After 1850 and especially after 1870 natural scientific discoveries came to have a sustained and highly visible impact on the conditions of everyday life. But the beginnings of this process were certainly already discernible by the late 1830s, although much more through the work of inspired tinkerers and engineers than through any results coming out of the brains of theoretical natural scientists.

But the question as to exactly when the young Marx became enamored of natural science, or under what promptings, is largely irrelevant to our concerns here. The crucial point is that Marx's commitment to natural science, and to naturalism, was in place by 1844 at the latest. In the "Economic and Philosophical Manuscripts" Marx insists repeatedly that "man" is "a *natural being*," and he asserts that "only naturalism is capable of comprehending the process of world history [*nur der Naturalismus fähig ist, den Akt der Weltgeschichte zu begreifen*]" (*MEGA2* 1.2: 408/*MECW* 3: 336/*EW* 389). One sees, here, something of a reversal of Hegel's *Lectures on the Philosophy of Nature*. Notoriously, in his *Philosophy of Nature*, Hegel had offered a spirit-oriented account of natural science: he had attempted to subordinate *Natur* to *Geist*, with unpersuasive results. Marx, on the other hand, insists that history, and hence the human world in general, needs to be understood in the light of an understanding of nature—and that means, in the light of natural science.

Marx's natural science was the natural science of what the historian of science Stephen Brush has called "the first scientific revolution." I take this "Newtonian" natural science to be an attempt to understand the world as a perfect machine functioning according to universal mechanical laws.[29] The phrase "scientific determinism" suggests the absolute necessity with which events follow laws in such a dispensation. Updating Aristotle with Kant, one might say that it is a "condition of possibility" of rational understanding that the fortuitous be excluded—and Newtonian natural science did indeed appear to exclude the fortuitous. Hegel's necessity was the offspring of the syllogism. Marx's necessity is more complex, for both the logical and the mechanistic notions of necessity were present in his mind from at least the early 1840s (and his work remained fundamentally uninfluenced by the notion of statistical laws, which emerged, very slowly, out of thermodynamics after 1850 or so). *How* notions of necessity were present in Marx is, of course, one of the things that I am most concerned with in the present study.

The third criterion of rationality, predictivity, follows from the criteria of universality and of necessity. The claim here is simple: if our assertions are universally valid they ought to generate predictions that will hold good. Conversely, if we are unable to make good predictions in any domain, we do not have a rational understanding of it. Hegel, it must be pointed out, put little or no emphasis on prediction as a criterion of rationality. Prediction involves an orientation toward the future. But Hegel tended to be past-oriented, or retrospective: that is, his emphasis was on explaining, or rationalizing, what had come into existence after it had done so. There is a metaphor in the preface to his *Philosophy of Right* that perfectly articulates this retrospective orientation: "The owl of Minerva [that is, philosophy] begins its flight only with the onset of dusk."[30] The generally contemplative cast of Hegel's thought does not fit well with an emphasis on prediction. Prediction is marginal even to his understanding of natural science. In his *Philosophy of Nature*, where he offers descriptive accounts of the natural science of his time, he seems correspondingly to view natural science as offering a (merely) descriptive account of nature. Hegel's emphasis is far more on the fact that natural science enables us to make sense of nature, comprehending it with our minds, than it is on the fact that natural science (or rather, *some* natural science) offers laws and theories having predictive power.

Whereas Hegel's orientation, at least in his later years, was overwhelmingly backward-looking, Marx's orientation was overwhelmingly forward-looking, or "promethean."[31] Marx was promethean in part because (for whatever reason) he was a radical, inclined throughout his life to want to change the existing order. Marx's third criterion of rationality is in principle present in Hegel, since universality and necessity do imply predictivity. It is far more manifestly present within Newtonian natural science. I am not saying that Marx *got* the predictivity criterion from Newtonian natural science, for it seems rather to have been a logical outcome of his stance as a forward-looking Hegelian. But the affinity with natural science was there at the start. Beginning in 1844 he evoked natural science in a serious way (for an early instance, see the EPM, at *MEGA2* 1.2: 425/*MECW* 3: 303/*EW* 355). As we shall see, the predictivity criterion had important consequences for the substance of Marx's thought: the French word *néfaste*, which bundles together the meanings suggested by the English words *ill-fated*, *mischievous*, and *pernicious*, is perhaps the best single term for characterizing the nature of these consequences.

The fourth criterion, progress by contradiction, is so closely tied up with Hegel's conception of history generally that we now need to turn to that subject.

HEGEL AND HISTORY: OR, WHERE IS HEGEL'S HISTORICAL DIALECTIC HIDING?

The notion of progress by contradiction—in a word, of dialectic—is central for understanding Hegel, and above all for understanding Hegel's conception of history. The notion of dialectic is equally important for understanding Marx's conception of history. And so one sets out with considerable eagerness to find answers to two questions: Where in Hegel's writings is his conception of history most fully presented and exemplified? and Where in Hegel's writings is his conception of a historical dialectic most fully presented and exemplified? But the question that I actually want to begin with is: Where does *Marx*'s dialectic come from? I propose, in short, to seek out the Hegelian dialectic and conception of history by first seeking out the roots of Marx's dialectic and conception of history. (Let us leave aside temporarily the problem of defining *dialectic* in a more specific way than simply "progress by contradiction," for a fuller definition will emerge as we proceed.)

It is surprising how little attention has been devoted to the question of how Marx came to the dialectic. Of course, in a certain sense everyone knows where Marx found the dialectic: he found it in Hegel. Consequently, most commentators do not find interesting the question Where did Marx's dialectic come from? because there is a basic agreement on the answer. The next question is: *Where* in Hegel's writings did Marx find the dialectic? Often, commentators have seen Marx's dialectic as rooted in Hegel generally, with little or no further specification. Often, they have seen the dialectic as rooted in specific works: either in the *Phenomenology of Spirit* (1807), or in the *Logic* (1812–16), or in both works (this last option quickly takes one back to the view that the dialectic comes from Hegel generally). But little investigation has actually been done into the matter.

Consider the views of a selection of commentators. For the "critical" Marxist (and one-time guru of the American New Left) Herbert Marcuse, the dialectic amounted simply to the principle of negation: in Marcuse's words, "the power of negative thinking is the driving power of dialectical thought."[32] Marcuse hearkens back, here, to a "left" Hegelian interpretation of Hegel (Hegel as a forward-looking radical *manqué*); indeed, in his classic study of the Marx-Hegel relation, *Reason and Revolution*, Marcuse sounds like a Left Hegelian transported into the twentieth century.[33] Marcuse had little interest in the question of how (as a matter of historical fact) Marx came to the dialectic: his interest was in promoting the dialectic as a critical instrument now (which led him to place great emphasis on the dialectic's moment of negation, and very little on its moment of synthesis). But insofar as Marcuse had a view on the question as to where, in Hegel, a critical, proto-Marxian dialectic is to be found, that view is clear: the dialectic is to be found *everywhere* in Hegel—or at any rate everywhere in Hegel from his "Jena system" of 1802–6 onward.

"Orthodox" Marxists, on the other hand, picked up on certain statements made by Marx and Engels in the 1850s and after that portrayed the Marxian dialectic as inspired, above all, by Hegel's *Science of Logic*. Engels was important in establishing the "orthodox" line of interpretation. In 1859, he became the first person to assert (in his review of Marx's *A Contribution to the Critique of Political Economy*, published the same year) that the relation of Marx's work to Hegel was decisive: and while Engels mentioned a number of Hegel's writings, he especially emphasized Marx's work "of extracting from the Hegelian logic the nucleus containing Hegel's real discoveries in this field" (*MEW* 13: 474/*MECW* 16: 474–75).[34] The later paladins of orthodox Marxism followed Engels in this regard. In his "Philosophical Notebooks" of 1914–16, which record his reading notes on Hegel's *Logic*, Lenin exclaims:

> *Aphorism*: It is impossible completely to understand Marx's *Capital*, and especially its first chapter, without having thoroughly studied and understood the *whole* of Hegel's *Logic*. Consequently, half a century later none of the Marxists understand Marx!

As for Trotsky, in a discussion of Marx's dialectic published not long before his death he emphasized such dialectical "laws" as "change of quantity into quality, development through contradictions, conflict of content and form, interruption of continuity, and the change of possibility into inevitability, etc.," all supposedly derived from the *Logic*.[35]

Consider a few more recent commentators. The term *dialectic* does not appear in the index of Shlomo Avineri's *Social and Political Thought of Karl Marx*. Fundamentally, Avineri is interested in social and political thought and not at all in abstract philosophy: his chapter on "the revolutionary dialectics of capitalist society" is not about dialectic but about Marx's account of the fate of the capitalist system.[36] Furnished with a promising title, the collection *Dialectics and Method*, cited earlier, brings together a number of authors who are certainly interested in the dialectic. However, the collection's focus is on tracing the dialectic back to "fundamental ontological issues"; how Marx actually arrived at the dialectic remains a question of little importance.[37] The philosopher Leszek Kolakowski begins the first volume of his *Main Currents of Marxism* with a long chapter on "The Origins of Dialectic." Kolakowski ranges widely, discussing Plotinus, Eriugena, Meister Eckhart, Jacob Böhme, and Angelus Silesius, among others. But when he reaches Hegel he seems to run out of gas, for he offers a general account of Hegel's philosophy (mentioning the *Phenomenology, Philosophy of History*, and *Philosophy of Right*) but says little about the dialectic in particular.[38]

In short, it remains unclear from the secondary literature where, in Hegel, a historical dialectic is to be found. One way of moving toward an answer to the question Where is Hegel's historical dialectic to be found? is by looking at the very early Marx. Which of Hegel's works did the early Marx read, and when? If we can see where *Marx* found the dialectic, we shall be closer to answering the question.

Among Marx's writings, the most obvious place to look first is the "Economic and Philosophical Manuscripts" (1844). In the section of the EPM that Marx's editors have titled "Critique of Hegel's Dialectic and General Philosophy," Marx mentions two of Hegel's works, *Phenomenology of Spirit* and *Encyclopedia of the Philosophical Sciences*; and Marx also wrote, in conjunction with the "Critique of Hegel's Dialectic" section, a separate "conspectus" (summary) of the *Phenomenology*'s last chapter (*MEGA2* 1.2: 399–418/*MECW* 3: 326–46/*EW* 379–400; *MEGA2* 1.2: 439–44 [Konspekt]). (The *Encyclopedia of the Philosophical Sciences* was Hegel's summary of his philosophical system. The first edition was published in 1817 as a guide for his students at the University of Heidelberg, and in 1827 and 1830 he published successively larger versions.[39]) In the "Critique of Hegel's Dialectic" Marx does not cite Hegel's "big" logic, the *Science of Logic* of 1812–16; instead, he cites the far shorter version contained in the 1830 edition of the *Encyclopedia*. Thus it was not the *Science of Logic* itself, but Hegel's so-called lesser Logic that was the basis for the account of Hegel's logic that Marx offers in the "Critique of Hegel's Dialectic."

So far as I know, there is no evidence that the young Marx read either the *Phenomenology of Spirit* or the *Science of Logic* attentively. To begin at the beginning: What did the Marx of the Berlin period (October 1836–April 1841) know about Hegel? In those decisively formative years I detect no serious engagement on Marx's part with either the *Phenomenology* or the *Science of Logic*. To be sure, the *Logic* and the *Phenomenology*, along with the entire Hegel corpus, would have been part of the oral tradition of the group of critically oriented Hegelians at Berlin, into whose informal "Doctors' Club" of young lecturers Marx was accepted around June–August 1837 (DRAP 1: 6). Further, in summer semester (May–August) 1838 Marx attended the logic lectures of the Hegelian Professor Gabler—"the colourless Gabler," David McLellan calls him.[40] Marx also attended two semesters of lectures by another, far more striking Hegelian, Eduard Gans, on criminal procedure in winter semester (October–March) 1836–37 and on Prussian law in summer semester 1837. Warren Breckman has suggested that Gans would have given Marx an important entry into Hegel's progressive potential.[41] In his letter to his father of November 1837, Marx claims that he had "got to know Hegel from beginning to end, together with most of his disciples" (*MEGA2* 3.1: 17/*MECW* 1: 19). Jerrold Seigel suggests that "it would not be unreasonable to suppose that Marx meant by this phrase ['beginning to end'] that he had read the only comprehensive summary of Hegel's whole philosophy, the *Encyclopedia of the Philosophical Sciences*."[42] I believe that Seigel is right.

I have seen nothing to persuade me that either the *Logic* or the *Phenomenology* had any deep impact on Marx at this time. Rather, I am inclined to think that Marx's knowledge of and enthusiasm for Hegel came mostly from other sources: quite likely from Gans; certainly from discussion with the Hegel enthusiasts of the Doctors' Club; from a serious reading of the short and convenient *Encyclopedia of the Philosophical Sciences*; and from one other work of Hegel's, rarely mentioned in the Marx literature, to which I shall turn below. Marx's engagement with Hegel then took on a new, slightly different focus beginning as early as September 1841, when he first began to think of offering a critique of Hegel's political philosophy, a project that he was to undertake in a sustained way in 1843: he was thus led, in 1843, to read seriously Hegel's *Elements of the Philosophy of Right*, a work that he had not been concerned with during his Berlin years.

As for Marx in 1844, the accounts of Hegel's *Phenomenology* and *Logic* that Marx offers in the "Critique of Hegel's Dialectic" do not suggest a deep or lengthy involvement with these works. Overall, Marx presents a rather formulaic reading of Hegel. The formula came from Feuerbach. Feuerbach's impact on the very early Marx is murky; his impact on Marx in 1843–44, less so. Suffice it to say that Marx may well have been "moved" by Feuerbach on two occasions. The earlier occasion was when he was conceptualizing his doctoral dissertation, "Difference between the Democritean and Epicurean Philosophy of Nature," in 1839. At this time Feuerbach, like several others at roughly the same time (notably the theologian Bruno Bauer, soon to become Marx's doctoral mentor, and the Polish philosopher August Cieszkowski) started asserting that Hegelian philosophy needed to be superseded. It is possible, and perhaps likely, that Feuerbach had some impact on Marx already at this early stage in his work. From 1839 onward, Feuerbach's attitude toward Hegel was in transition, culminating in essays published in 1843, in a dismissive identification of Hegelian philosophy with religion.[43] In March 1843 Marx read and was excited by the first of these essays, "Preliminary Theses on the Reform of Philosophy."[44] He became something of a Feuerbach enthusiast (although with reservations and only temporarily: Marx's enthusiasms were always conditional). In 1843 Marx found in Feuerbach two ideas that, although they were not original to Feuerbach and although they had been present in Feuerbach's work as early as 1839, were now expressed much more clearly and were applied much more broadly than before.

The ideas in question were, first, the notion of estrangement (*Entfremdung*) (or alienation [*Entäusserung*]—the two terms are nearly identical in meaning), and second, the notion that both religion and contemporary philosophy tend to maintain this estrangement by treating the estranged fragments of human life and culture as if they were not estranged fragments at all, but rather the very basis of the world. Marx had certainly encountered the notion of estrangement long before 1843: it was a commonplace in the literature and philosophy of the time.[45] It was much more Feuerbach's second notion—namely, that human cultural products tend to obscure the humanistic basis of culture—that came to Marx as a new revelation. It did so because Feuerbach "operationalized" (as we might say) this notion, by making it the basis for a "genetic-critical" method—a method that involved analyzing a conception or belief in such a way as to trace out its roots in experience. According to Feuerbach, when this is done, one often exposes an estrangement and subservience that were not previously visible, or that were previously misapprehended. This is how, in *The Essence of Christianity*, Feuerbach had approached dogmatic religion. In 1843 he now applied the same procedure to Hegelian philosophy in the same way, arguing that whereas Hegel took *Geist*, spirit, as the subject that governs human life, *Geist* is only an offshoot, a predicate, of Man. Accordingly, the task of the critical philosopher is to reverse the inversion and thus to transform or even transcend philosophy, placing everything on a humanistic basis, with Man as the subject.[46]

In 1844, in his "Critique of Hegel's Dialectic and General Philosophy" in the EPM, Marx applies Feuerbach's method to Hegel, while looking with only the most rapid eye at what Hegel actually wrote. Marx jots down the main headings of the *Phenomenology*'s table of contents. (Writing out such headings is a strong signal that the work itself has not been read.) He quotes various sentences from the *Encyclopedia*. He criticizes the final chapter of the *Phenomenology* ("Absolute Knowing").[47] Throughout, he substitutes bodily "man" for disembodied "spirit"—the Feuerbachian reversal of subject and predicate. Moveover, connecting with an activist, "Fichtean" tendency in Feuerbach, he emphasizes act, creation, and movement over what he sees as Hegel's too-great attachment to "*fixed thought-forms*" (*MEGA2* 1.2: 415/*MECW* 3: 343/*EW* 397). Finally and most importantly, Marx offers a "strong reading" (that is, a misreading) of the *Phenomenology* in particular.[48] In Marx's misreading, the *Phenomenology* is *really* about the role of labor in human life.

Here is the most striking sentence in Marx's "Critique of Hegel's Dialectic." It is difficult, and demands to be read several times:

> The greatness of Hegel's *Phenomenology* and its final result—the dialectic of negativity as the moving and producing principle—lies in the fact that Hegel conceives the self-creation [*Selbsterzeugung*] of man as a process, objectification [*Vergegenständlichung*] as loss of object [*Entgegenständlichung*], as alienation and as supersession of this alienation; that he therefore grasps the nature of *labor* and conceives of objective man—true, because real man—as the result of his *own labor*. (*MEGA2* 1.2: 404/*MECW* 3: 332–33/*EW* 385–86)

It is a daring and brilliant intellectual move that Marx makes here. The brilliance lies in Marx's linkage of two things. He links Hegel (or, more accurately, he links an imaginary philosopher, invented by himself, whom one might call "Hegel") with the notion of the estrangement, or alienation, of labor. Marx worked up the latter notion in the genially productive months of May/June–August 1844. During these months, using a Feuerbachian machete, he slashed his way through the writings of a number of economists, producing as a result the economic parts of the "Economic and Philosophical Manuscripts." In so doing, he came to see "modern political economy," and not religion or philosophy (Feuerbach's view), as the true locus of estrangement within the modern world (*MEGA2* 1.2: 405/*MECW* 3: 333/*EW* 386).

My concern remains the question of where the dialectic comes from. If one does not look at it too closely, the "Critique of Hegel's Dialectic" might well be taken as suggesting that Marx was most heavily influenced by Hegel's *Phenomenology*. This is especially the case if one interprets the laudatory side of Marx's account of the *Phenomenology* in the light of his discussion of labor elsewhere in the EPM, where he celebrates labor's creative power. In fact, there is a prometheanism—a dynamism—in Hegel's *Phenomenology* that is in line with Marx's insistence in the EPM on seeing history as a dynamic process that moves forward by dint of labor and industry. To put the point another way, the *Phenomenology* has an aura of radicalism about it that (*pace* Marcuse) cannot readily be found in the *Science of Logic*, the *Philosophy of Right*, the *Encyclopedia of the Philosophical Sciences*, or the posthumously published lecture courses.

One piece of evidence that might appear to support the view that Marx derived his dialectic from Hegel's *Phenomenology* is the fact that in its now famous "Lordship and Bondage" section Hegel wrote about labor—and did so dialectically. More precisely, Hegel wrote about the bondsman, who in working for the lord suffers an "alienated existence"—yet through his work the bondsman also "becomes conscious of what he truly is," and thus spirit is brought to a higher level.[49] The notion of labor as alienated calls to mind Marx's account of estranged labor in the "Estranged Labor and Private Property" section of the EPM. Further, Hegel portrays the relationship between lord and bondsman as quintessentially dialectical. It is a relationship in which the lord starts out with manifest advantages over the bondsman, but these very advantages allow the bondsman, because he is forced to work upon nature, to acquire "a mind of his own."[50] Little wonder, then, that some commentators have focused on the lord/bondsman discussion, given that it has an affinity with the position that Marx would later work out. The most famous of these commentators was Alexandre Kojève, who in his *Introduction to the Reading of Hegel*, expounded in lectures in Paris in the 1930s that were attended by a coterie of French intellectuals, dealt at considerable length with the *Phenomenology*'s account of lordship and bondage. In turn, other commentators after Kojève developed the lordship and bondage dialectic in various ways, as such historians of Hegelian thought as Michael Roth and Judith Butler have pointed out.[51]

But there are problems with the attempt to see Hegel's *Phenomenology* as the source of and model for Marx's dialectic. One point that should be noted is that labor is actually quite incidental to Hegel's discussion of lordship and bondage: his account centers on recognition and fear much more than it does on the bondsman's act of laboring. Another point is that, although the relationship of lord and bondsman is dialectical, the dialectic in question is hardly a historical dialectic, for the *Phenomenology* is not really a history. Rather, it offers a kind of theoretical reflection on the conditions required before "absolute knowing" can exist. (We might think of absolute knowing as a state combining self-knowledge with scientific objectivity.) Further, surprising though it may seem to aficionados of the Marx literature, Marx himself does not seem to have taken any special notice, anywhere, of Hegel's account of lordship and bondage.[52] While it is true that Marx discussed the *Phenomenology* in the "Economic and Philosophical Manuscripts," one must note that (a) this was in 1844, which was already late in Marx's formation as a theorist, and (b) as noted above, Marx discussed the work only briefly, and mainly in order to apply, rather unoriginally, a Feuerbachian transformative criticism to it.

In short, one does not find in the "Economic and Philosophical Manuscripts" adequate support for the view that the *Phenomenology* was an important source of Marx's dialectic. True, Kojève did articulate an eminently dialectical and supposedly Marxian interpretation of the *Phenomenology*. It is tempting to think that his brilliantly creative interpretation was already present in Marx himself. But it is not. If Marx had been sitting in the lecture room in the 1930s perhaps he would have found Kojève's interpretation interesting. But it was Kojève's interpretation, not Marx's. Moreover, it is equally plausible that Marx would have regarded Kojève's interpretation as dangerously idealist. Marx held that one needs to go *beyond* Hegel. Marxifying Hegel, Kojève makes Hegel appear more acceptable from a Marxian point of view than he deserves to be. Kojève underplays what in Marx did not derive from metaphysical idealism. Marx was deeply influenced by metaphysical idealism, but metaphysical idealism was not the only intellectual matrix out of which his theory emerged. On the contrary, as noted before, one also needs to take account of his connection to the naturalistic side of the idealism/naturalism split that he, like all post-Cartesian philosophers, faced.

Another consequence of the Kojévian view is that it makes the *Phenomenology* the most important link between Hegel and Marx. Kojève's "*Phenomenology*-oriented" view of Marx needs to be contrasted with the "*Logic*-oriented" view favored in Kojève's time by exponents of official, "orthodox" Marxism. As already noted, there is no evidence that the early Marx ever read Hegel's *Science of Logic* with any care and attentiveness. The earliest actual evidence we have of a reading by Marx of Hegel's logic is provided by the 1844 "Critique of Hegel's Dialectic": and here, as already noted, Marx read the highly condensed version of Hegel's logic to be found in Hegel's *Encyclopedia*, 1830 edition. A later episode in Marx's intellectual biography risks distorting our view of the early Marx. As is well known to specialists, in late 1857 and early 1858 Marx turned to a reading of Hegel's *Logic*, as he was working on a raw draft that, after many permutations, would eventually lead to *Capital* (the draft is generally known as the *Grundrisse* ["fundamental outlines"], from the title given to it by later editors). In a letter to Engels of January 16, 1858, Marx reported that he had "taken another look at Hegel's *Logic* [*Hegels "Logik" wiederdurchgeblättert hatte*] by mere accident" and had found the work to be "of great use . . . as regards the *method* of treatment" as he struggled to deal with economic issues. Indeed, he hoped to be able to write, sometime, an essay stating in simple language "what is rational in the method [*das Rationelle an der Methode*]," a matter that Hegel himself had rendered obscure (*MEW* 29: 260/*MECW* 40: 249). Famously, in the postface to the 1873 edition of *Capital*, Marx admitted having "coquetted" in *Capital* with Hegel's "mode of expression" (*MEGA2* 2.6: 709/*MECW* 35: 19/*CAP* 1: 103). But a look at *Capital* (especially at the conceptually important first chapter, on "The Commodity") shows that Hegel's *Logic* had a much deeper influence on Marx's conceptualization than Marx here acknowledged.

Engels, and Lenin after Engels, emphasized Hegel's *Logic* as important for Marxian dialectics. From their point of view, the *fundamental* Marxian work was *Capital*; they had no interest in the EPM, which Lenin presumably did not know about and certainly had never read, and which Engels could only have seen as a way station on the road to historical materialism. When in *Ludwig Feuerbach and the Outcome of Classical German Philosophy*, the later Engels defined Hegelian dialectics as "the self-development of the concept," he referred to the *Logic*, with its focus on the analysis of concepts (*MEW* 21: 292/*MECW* 26: 383). What Hegel did for Being in his *Logic*, Marx tried to do in *Capital* for the commodity: hence Lenin's claim, already cited, that "it is impossible completely to understand Marx's *Capital*, and especially its first chapter, without having thoroughly studied and understood the *whole* of Hegel's *Logic*."[53] The *Phenomenology*, by way of contrast, is almost completely absent from Lenin's view of Hegel and the dialectic, as it is from Engels's.

Commentators who assume that the *Phenomenology* or the *Logic*, or the two of them together, are the most important source for Marx's conception of the dialectic are starting in the wrong place, in two senses.[54] First, they begin too late, with the Marx of 1844 (or, even worse, with the Marx of 1857–58, if they emphasize the later Marx's reading of the *Logic*). But the Marx of

1844—to be sure, only twenty-six years old at the time—was already, in important respects, "later" Marx, already engaged in forgetting the earlier phases of his intellectual career. It is true that at the beginning of the EPM Marx suggests that the *Phenomenology* and the *Logic* contain, like Feuerbach's writings, "a real theoretical revolution" (*MEGA2* 1.2: 326/*MECW* 3: 232/*EW* 281). But the theoretical revolution in question was one that Marx himself did not perceive before his reading in 1843 of Feuerbach's "Preliminary Theses." Although Marx did read Feuerbach's most famous work, *The Essence of Christianity*, around July 1841 (DRAP 1: 10), he did not get a theoretical revolution from it. Only in the two essays of 1843, "Preliminary Theses" and "Principles of the Philosophy of the Future," did Feuerbach go beyond his concern with estrangement as such in order to articulate, clearly, a method by which estrangement might be unveiled wherever it is found. Writing in 1844, Marx deploys Feuerbach's method of subject-predicate reversal against Hegel's *Phenomenology* and *Logic*. Thus he argues that Hegel treats "spirit" as the active subject that creates all that exists, instead of acknowledging that "man" is the subject and "spirit" merely that which man creates. But this is a reading of the *Phenomenology* and the *Logic* that Marx did not have in mind before his March 1843 encounter with the "Preliminary Theses"; or, to put the matter more circumspectly, I am aware of no evidence that Marx, in earlier contacts with the *Phenomenology* and the *Logic*, saw anything like what he was able to see when, in May/June–August 1844, he composed the "Economic and Philosophical Manuscripts."[55]

DIALECTIC AND HISTORICAL DIALECTIC IN HEGEL

If one problem with previous attempts to specify the relation between Marx's dialectic and Hegel's is that commentators begin too late in Marx's intellectual development, a second problem is that such exegeses concentrate almost entirely on the Marx side of the connection, failing to attend to the various uncertainties on the Hegel side. The question Where in Hegel did Marx find the dialectic? leads back to the question posed earlier: Where in Hegel is the dialectic to be found? In order to discover where it is, we need to know what it is, for what it is is by no means obvious. Finding the dialectic turns out to be more difficult than one would think. The difficulty of finding it is one indication that the thing being sought is unclear.

What is the dialectic? If one's focus is on the *logical* dialectic, Engels's definition—"dialectics is the self-development of the concept"—is as good as any. The logical dialectic is central to Hegel's *Science of Logic*. Here Hegel engages in an analysis of the "first Notions of logic, being and nothing, and becoming." His analysis is aimed at teasing out the contradictions that arise as one begins to think out what being is.[56] Dialectic in this sense is also to be found in the *Phenomenology*, where, as Hans-Georg Gadamer has pointed out, "the chapters . . . are so constructed that, as a rule, the dialectical contradictions are . . . developed out of the concept which is being thematized at that particular moment. . . ."[57]

But there is nothing specifically historical about the dialectic so conceived. There is no reason to think that the self-development of the concept should unfold in a historical-temporal way. In his account of the dialectic in *Ludwig Feuerbach and the Outcome of Classical German Philosophy* Engels obscures this fact: as is well known, Engels had, on the one hand, a talent for clear exposition and, on the other, a tendency to ride roughshod over crucial distinctions and unresolved problems. In this instance, we are simply not told how it happens that the logical process through which Hegel goes in the *Science of Logic* "elaborates itself . . . in history" (*MEW* 21: 292/*MECW* 26: 383).

Clearly, our focus here needs to be on the dialectic, historically understood. What would such a dialectic look like? The notion of a historical dialectic is not entirely unfamiliar: it was a staple of potted expositions of Marxism (thesis, antithesis, synthesis . . .) throughout most of the twentieth century. In a historical dialectic one would expect to find a sequence of situations, with each situation arising out of a contradiction or contradictions in a preceding situation. There would be a movement from one situation (it could be called a "stage"), through a transition, to another situation, and the process would then repeat itself at a higher level. Each situation would need to be marked by two characteristics. First, each would need to possess an ultimate unity: each would need to be a totality, a coherent whole.[58] Each situation would need to be ultimately coherent, because it makes no sense to talk about a contradiction unless one assumes an overarching coherence that is, it seems, impaired by the contradiction, but still somehow present. For a contradiction is not the same as a mere difference or division: contradiction implies some sort of deep opposition to the extant situation, such that either the situation goes away or the contradiction goes away. In other words, a contradiction is more than a difference. Second, at least one contradiction would need to emerge *by necessity* out of the situation. In other words, the thing (whatever it is) that is contradictory to the very existence of the situation would need to arise from the situation as an unavoidable part of it. Otherwise the contradictory thing could be smoothed away and the situation thereby preserved.

In brief: one finds (a) a totality; (b) a contradiction that emerges necessarily from the totality and that cannot in the long run be contained within the totality; and (c) the emergence of a new totality from the ruins of the old. It is a well-known model, for it is found, or at least alluded to, in certain well-known Marxian texts—for example, *The Communist Manifesto* (1848), the preface to *A Contribution to the Critique of Political Economy* (1859), and *Socialism: Utopian and Scientific* (1880). Living flesh can be put on the dry Hegelian bones by borrowing from the Marx of 1845 and after. Feudalism, the story goes, generates within itself a contradiction between countryside and town, between landed interests and the bourgeoisie. Town and bourgeoisie are necessary if feudalism is to function, for they provide goods that cannot be produced in any other way and without which the system would collapse. The growth of towns and of the bourgeoisie is such that they cannot be contained within the feudal system. Meanwhile, the bourgeoisie in the towns generates the elements of capitalism, which eventually congeal into a new unified situation—a new totality, that already at its birth bears within itself the seeds of its future dissolution. This is the familiar Marxian model of the historical dialectic. For its part, the first chapter of *Capital*, with its analysis of the commodity, offers the best instance in Marx of the dialectic worked out logically.

The question remains: Where in Hegel is there a historical dialectic? It is surprisingly difficult to find. There is nothing like a historical dialectic in Hegel's *Science of Logic*: how could there be, given that Hegel seems to have conceived of the work as an account of God "in his eternal essence before the creation of nature and of a single finite spirit" (to quote more fully a passage that I earlier quoted in part).[59] There is certainly a dialectic in the *Logic*, for in it Hegel explores the conceptual transformations of a multitude of oppositions—between being and nothing, being and becoming, finitude and the infinite, the one and the many, repulsion and attraction, divisibility and indivisibility, essence and appearance, and so on. But the dialectic of the *Logic* is not stretched out over historical time. This is true even of the material in the second and third sections of volume two, where Hegel deals with such topics as mechanism, teleology, and life. At most the dialectic of the *Logic* might be a substructure for a possible historical dialectic, but it does not itself offer anything that looks like a sequence of historical transformations.

At first glance the *Phenomenology of Spirit* appears to offer what we are looking for. Consider again the lord-bondsman dialectic, noted earlier. The dialectic in question is logical or conceptual, but it is also temporal, in the sense that it describes a process that is stretched out over time. In the relationship between lord and bondsman, the lord seems at first to have the advantage, since he is able to force the bondsman to labor for him. But the bondsman's laboring allows him to test and improve his capacities in struggling against nature, and so the bondsman makes history whereas the lord is left behind. Moreover, the lord's standing as lord depends on the bondsman's recognizing him as lord, a recognition that the bondsman can withdraw at any moment—so in that sense the lord is dependent on the bondsman, rather than vice versa.

Such, in simplest terms, is Kojève's influential interpretation of the lord-bondsman dialectic. But while the dialectic of lord and bondsman is *temporal*, it is not *historical*, for, as noted above, it cannot be located at any identifiable point in human history.

If one could take the lord-bondsman dialectic, in Kojève's account of it, as typical of the *Phenomenology* as a whole, and if one could also think of that dialectic as one stage in a larger historical story, one would be right to see the *Phenomenology* as presenting a historical dialectic. But the *Phenomenology* as a whole is not like that. It is not a history, although Hegel does link certain of its themes to identifiable historical developments, such as the Enlightenment and the Terror. Hans-Georg Gadamer suggests that we should see the *Phenomenology* as giving an account of "a movement back and forth between that which our consciousness believes and that which is actually implied in what it says," a movement that generates a progression toward a better state of knowledge.[60] One can also think of the *Phenomenology* as one side of what Hegel, at the end of the *Phenomenology*, calls "comprehended History," the other side being History proper.[61] To put this as J. N. Findlay does, the *Phenomenology* would be "a fine blend of the contingently historical and the logically necessary" (although to my mind Findlay obscures the extent to which Hegelian history is purified of contingency, and turned into a necessary process).[62] Finally, the *Phenomenology* can also be interpreted as presenting various spiritual phenomena that are part of, but inadequate to, the fulfillment of Spirit that occurs in absolute knowing. Here the key issue is not the temporal relation of these phenomena to absolute knowing; rather, it is their adequacy (or not) to absolute knowing. In sum, the *Phenomenology* is certainly not in contradiction with a historical dialectic; it simply does not offer a historical dialectic.

Continuing the search for a Hegelian historical dialectic, one turns to Hegel's *Lectures on the Philosophy of History* (first published in the 1830s, like all Hegel's lecture series). A word is required concerning the misleading title of the *Philosophy of History*. By "philosophy of history," Hegel meant an attempt to arrive at a philosophical understanding of the historical process in general. In its actual content, however, the *Philosophy of History* is not an account of history in general. Rather, it is an attempt to write a generalized history of one aspect of history, the evolution of the state. But it is not very successful in providing such a history. As the political theorist Joshua Dienstag has pointed out, Hegel's account of history in the *Philosophy of History* is remarkably static, for it is entirely unclear how history moves from one civilization to the next. For example, nothing in Hegel's account of ancient China prepares the reader for the discussion of ancient India that follows. The bondsmen of one era never become the masters of the following era: servitude is simply condemned, with no silver lining for the bondsmen. In short, "historical stages appear as a succession of shapes—not as a series of transitions. . . ." As Dienstag also points out, Hegel's lectures on *Aesthetics* are likewise undialectical, a fact that allows us to skip over the *Aesthetics* without giving any further attention to them.[63]

So the question remains: Where, in Hegel, is there a historical dialectic? One is tempted to say: nowhere. But this is to move too quickly, for one of Hegel's historical works is quintessentially dialectical, offering a rational, progressive history of precisely the sort that the post-1844 Marx claimed to have found in the sphere of material production. The work in question is Hegel's *Lectures on the History of Philosophy* (not to be confused with his *Lectures on the Philosophy of History*). Unlike such works as the *Phenomenology of Spirit* and the *Philosophy of Right*, the *Lectures on the History of Philosophy* have not recently been fashionable in the wider intellectual world. (It should be noted, however, that the first edition sold out even before Hegel's *Werke* had been finished, and so a second edition of the *Lectures* was published within what was still the framework of the first edition of the *Werke*.) Serious aficionados of the history of philosophy are likely to have read it at some point in their careers, but no one else. The work has been largely neglected by Hegel scholars.[64] It has been neglected even more by Marx scholars.[65] Yet there is reason to think that the *Lectures on the History of Philosophy* had a far greater impact on Marx, both directly, and indirectly through other Hegelians, most notably Gans, who had been influenced by it, than did any other of Hegel's writings. Further, discerning its impact on Marx is crucial if one is to be clear about the assumptions that underlie historical materialism.

Before exploring the historical dialectic as it appears in the *History of Philosophy* one needs to ask the question: what, *historically*, was the dialectic? Working from a Marxian starting point, I have already given a description of dialectic as involving contradictions that force a transition to another, higher state—as when contradictions within feudalism bring about a transition to capitalism. In philosophy, however, dialectic first of all meant argument concerning matters that do not admit of certainty but that nonetheless are more than mere matters of opinion. In Aristotle's view, scientific knowledge (*epistēmē*) involves demonstration (*apodeixis*): that is, scientific knowledge involves the making of necessary inferences (we would call them "deductions") from premises that also need to be necessary.[66] Crucial, here, is the syllogism, a form of reasoning that Aristotle saw as based on absolutely certain premises that then generate absolutely certain conclusions (unlike modern writers, Aristotle did not consider the premises of a syllogism to be mere suppositions). Aristotle held that reasoning that is not necessary cannot be regarded as producing scientific knowledge. In other words, he held that in the domain of science, one attains certainty. Hence there is no room in science for argument.

Aristotle also held that not all matters admit of demonstrative certainty. For example, one cannot be certain of what happened in the past, although judicial bodies are asked all the time to come to decisions concerning such matters; similarly, the members of legislative assemblies cannot know for certain what the outcome of such-and-such a proposed course of action will be. Aristotle held that in domains where demonstrative certainty is not possible, rhetoric and dialectic come into play. In Aristotle's view, as articulated in his *Rhetoric*, neither rhetoric nor dialectic is "scientific knowledge of how any definite subject matter is"; rather, "both are capacities for finding arguments."[67] Aristotle defines rhetoric in particular not as a means for arriving at knowledge, but rather as "the capacity to observe the available means of persuasion on a given question."[68] In other words, even though one cannot reach certainty concerning such-and-such a matter, one can at least discover, through the craft of rhetoric, all the arguments for and against a given position.

Dialectic, in Aristotle's conception of it, comes come into play when it is possible to go a step further—when, although one cannot arrive at demonstrative certainty regarding an issue, one can at least approximate such certainty. Aristotle asserts in his *Topics*, which is a work that discusses dialectical methods and arguments, that dialectic does not start out from necessary premises; on the contrary, it starts out from commonly accepted beliefs. It then proceeds according to the method that Aristotle ascribed to Socrates in Plato's dialogues: significantly, *dialektikē* is cognate with *dialegesthai*, "discuss," and *dialogos*, "dialogue." Central to dialectical method is the exploration of contradictory opinions: indeed, Aristotle insists that common beliefs tend to generate puzzles (*aporiai*). Dialectic seeks to "expound" the puzzles on a given question; in doing so, it seeks to find solutions that resolve the puzzles while retaining the most important common beliefs.[69]

In two major respects Hegel's view of dialectic is different from what we find in the writings of Aristotle. First of all, in Hegel's eyes dialectic is not something that lies between demonstrative knowledge and mere opinion. On the contrary, Hegel took the characteristics that Aristotle had attributed to dialectic and attributed them to the process of reasoning in general. In effect, Hegel declared that there is no difference between the demonstrative reasoning that leads to *epistēmē* and the looser form of reasoning that prevails in dialectic. This is a radical divergence from Aristotle.[70] The implication of Hegel's expansion of dialectic is clear: all worthy thinking, in Hegel's view, is dialectical. According to Eckermann, in conversation with Goethe Hegel said that dialectic is "nothing more than the regulated and methodical cultivation of the spirit of contradiction, which is a gift common to everyone, and particularly valuable for distinguishing the true from the false."[71]

Second, it is not simply that Hegel came to see all systematic thinking as dialectical. He does more than this: he sees *the world itself* as dialectical. By this, I mean that he conceived of the world on the analogy of a dialectical argument among philosophers. One imagines, in such an argument, a particular position being stated, its complexities being sifted and explored, contrary positions being stated, and disputes arising between adherents of the contrary positions. As Hegel conceptualized it, this is the way that the process of history moves, and the process of history, he further claimed, *is* the world. At the end of the day, philosophers engaged in a dialectical argument will have succeeded in articulating the truth more fully than was the case at the beginning of the day. Similarly, in Hegel's view, history itself is a rational process—more accurately, it is *the* rational process—whereby truth manifests itself in an ever more articulate form over time, and at the end of the day philosophers are able to look back on and make sense of that process.[72]

Viewed from one angle, Hegel's dialectical conception of history reveals itself as a substantialization and historicization of the Aristotelian syllogism. (By *syllogism* I simply mean a valid deductive argument—that is, an argument in which the conclusion follows necessarily from the premises.[73] The syllogistic form with which we are familiar [All men are mortal, etc.] is inessential. Thus mathematical reasoning is syllogistic, in this sense.) In the *Lectures on the History of Philosophy*, Hegel finds Aristotle's logic to be defective, for in its formalism and in its focus on individual propositions it has no room for the "living organic whole, in which each part is held to be a part, and the whole alone as such is true" (*LHP* 2: 223 [chap. III.B §4 (Logic)]).[74] Viewed from another, slightly different angle, Hegel's dialectical conception of history can be interpreted as a historicization *and universalization* of Aristotle's notion of dialectic. We can most vividly comprehend Aristotle's dialectic if we call up an image of philosophers arguing among themselves in the Lyceum, and arriving by this means at a closer approximation to truth. Hegel's dialectic is far more ambitious: in Hegel, it is the world *itself* that, through conflict, brings about the progressively more complex and ramified manifestation of truth.

It was sheer madness on Hegel's part to see history as the working out of a (presumably very long) deductive argument and/or as a serious technical debate among philosophers. Why should we think that history, so dependent on such natural or partly natural forces as earthquakes, volcanic eruptions, droughts, hurricanes, blizzards, heat waves, global warmings, tsunamis, and epidemics, and with the presence in it of such unpredictable and apparently contingent events as wars, revolutions, assassinations, car accidents, airplane crashes, missed trains, broken condoms, love affairs, ill-timed suicides, marital disagreements, random murders, adulteries, fornications, and the like, proceeds like an argument among philosophers? Even more unlikely, why should we think that it proceeds like the working out of a deductive argument? Yet Hegel did think these things—or at any rate he said or wrote them, which is all that we have to go on, since, strictly speaking, we have no access to the inner workings of his mind.

I want to make two points with respect to the oddity, even madness, of Hegel's view of history.

First, there is a cunning ambiguity here. When Hegel suggests that history is a dialectical process—in a word, when he suggests that history is rational—what exactly does he mean by "history"? One reading of Hegel—which was surely the dominant reading among his contemporaries—is that by "history" he meant a past reality existing quite independently of our own interpretation of it. On this view, Hegel was claiming that history, *as it actually was*, is rational. But there is an alternative reading of Hegel's words that is equally plausible, and perhaps even more plausible, as a designation of what he meant to say. One *could* take Hegel to mean, by "history," events that happened in the past *as they are understood by us now*. In this view, "history" actually equates to something like "events that happened in the past, *once we have made sense of them*." But if we have made sense of them, they are *ipso facto* "rational." QED. The owl of Minerva has taken flight.

Accordingly, when Hegel states in the passage from the *Philosophy of History* that is the epigraph of the present chapter that "Whoever looks at the world rationally will find that it in turn assumes a rational aspect; the two exist in a reciprocal relationship," what does he mean?[75] He might mean that the world looks rational because it *is* rational; or he might mean that the world *looks* rational, because we look at it in a rational way. Similarly, consider the claim that Hegel makes in the passage from his *Science of Logic* that I have taken as one of the epigraphs of this book: "Ancient metaphysics had . . . a higher conception of thinking than is current today. For it based itself on the fact that the knowledge of things obtained through thinking is alone what is really true in them."[76] Here, too, Hegel appears to identify the world with our knowledge of the world. A question thus arises, which we might pose as follows: should Hegel be understood as an ontologist or as an phenomenologist? That is, is he telling us about the fundamental constitution of the world, or is he telling us the conditions of human life and knowledge? Overwhelmingly, he was taken to be an ontologist.

Marx came to reject the idealist ontology that he saw in Hegel. He argues against it explicitly in the "Critique of Hegel's Dialectic." He was already suspicious of it in his doctoral dissertation materials: *ontology*, as I am using the term here, is the quintessence of theory, whereas in his fifth "Notebook on Epicurean Philosophy" (most likely written in summer semester [April–August] 1839), Marx looks forward to a philosophy that would go beyond pure theory and instead turn into "a practical relationship toward reality" (*MEGA2* 4.1: 100/*MECW* 1: 491/*MER* 11). To be sure, Marx took no notice of Hegel's ambiguity in matters of ontology: pursuing single-mindedly his own arguments, he was rarely fair to his opponents, rarely sensitive to the subtleties of what they said. But while Marx rejected Hegel's supposed ontology, he accepted, in contrast, the Hegelian notion of embedded progress. Yet he did so without acknowledging what, in Hegel, gives this notion some standing—namely, the notion that what we think of as the world is the world *as we interpret it*, so that the rationality of the world mirrors back to us the rationality of human beings. In his hope and his activism, Marx was disinclined to notice such things. Thus, *qua* philosopher, Marx comes across as a Hegel lacking in second thoughts. But one can twist the kaleidoscope yet again, by asking the question: How seriously did Marx intend his general theoretical claims (in which embedded rationality emerged as an important assumption)? This is a question to which I shall turn with full force only toward the end of chapter 4.

My second point is that there is a good reason why the history of philosophy is the one Hegelian history that conforms to Hegel's dialectical model of history. Philosophy is the domain of human action that can most plausibly be seen as proceeding along the lines of a continuing dialectical argument—for that is what philosophy is. As Hegel defines it, philosophy is the enterprise that aims at the discovery and unfolding of truth. If one accepts the definition, it follows that the history of philosophy must be a rational history, if by "rational history" we mean a history whose *telos* is the progressive discovery and unfolding of truth. Of course, there are counterarguments to this Hegelian claim. One counterargument is that in actual fact philosophers have been motivated by many considerations—vanity, desire for fame, and such like—having nothing to do with the discovery of the truth. Another counterargument (put forward by none other than Marx himself, in 1845–46) is that philosophy is not a search for truth but is rather an ideologically driven attempt to conceal current social reality. But the counterarguments miss the tautological solidity of Hegel's assertion that the history of philosophy is a rational history—for remember, in Hegel's conception, philosophy aims at truth *by definition*. Consequently, everything in the past that did not conduce to philosophy's pursuit of truth—such as the vanity of philosophers, their search for fame, the fact that they were paid by the state and were expected to support it, and so on—is excluded from the history of philosophy. Consider, further, Hegel's broader assertion: that the world looks rational to those who look at it rationally. This holds preeminently for philosophy, for philosophy just is the pursuit of truth, and its history is in consequence a rational history. It is little wonder, then, that Hegel's account of the history of philosophy looks far more dialectical than do any other of his historical or quasihistorical writings.

In some measure, the *History of Philosophy* needs to be seen as Hegel's answer to Aristotle. Hegel objected that Aristotle's universality and necessity were purely formal in character, restricted to the abstract realm of the syllogism. In Hegel's view universality and necessity must be seen as working themselves out *within* the world (conceived of as a concrete totality, a unified and concrete whole), rather than as forms separated from the world. Hegel saw this totality as developing over time; it is not something that can be identified as existing at any particular moment in history separated from other moments. Further, Hegel regarded the development itself (and not merely its end or *telos*) as necessary—that is, as something from which all contingency, all chance, is excluded.

In the introduction to the *Lectures on the History of Philosophy*, and likewise in the brief concluding section ("Final Result") of the entire work, Hegel is eloquent in his insistence that a necessity runs through the history of philosophy. (*Mutatis mutandis*, the historical materialist Marx also claims to have discovered a necessary historical process.) Consider the following passage, from the second-last paragraph of the *History of Philosophy*:

> the history of philosophy is not a blind collection of fanciful ideas, nor a fortuitous progression. . . . I have . . . sought to show the necessary development of the successive philosophies from one another, so that the one of necessity presupposes another preceding it. . . . the succession of philosophic systems is not due to chance, but represents the necessary succession of stages in the development of this science. (*LHP* 3: 552)[77]

In a passage that appears in the introduction to the *History of Philosophy*, Hegel makes a similar set of claims:

> Philosophy is system in development; so is the history of philosophy; and this is the main point to be noted and the first principle to be dealt with in this treatise on that history. . . . the history of Philosophy . . . shows the different stages and moments in development in time, in manner of occurrence, in particular places, in particular people or political circumstances . . . in short, it shows us the empirical form. (*LHP* 1: 29–30/1833 ed., 13: 42)

From yet another passage taken from the introduction, we can begin to grasp how one gets from Aristotle's logical deduction (*sullogismos*) to Hegel's history. First, read the passage:

> The whole of the history of philosophy is a progression impelled by a progression [*Fortgang*] that is inherently [*in sich*] necessary and deductive [*consequent*]; it is inherently rational, determined by its Idea. Just as in philosophy the development of concepts is necessary, this is also the case in its history. The impelling force [*das Fortleitende*] is the inner dialectic of the forms. (*LHP* 1: 36–37/1833 ed., 13: 50)

Hegel's reference here to "the development of concepts" and to "the inner dialectic of the forms" are clues to the thinking that led him to conceptualize history as a necessary succession. For what Hegel is doing is this: he is projecting Aristotle's notion of logical deduction onto the history of philosophy (and also, I contend, onto history in general). Aristotle focused on the necessary movement from premises to conclusion. Hegel, for his part, reconceptualizes Aristotle's logical necessity in such a way that it becomes the backbone of the history of philosophy. In other words, Hegel portrays the transition from one moment in the history of philosophy to the next moment as analogous in its necessity to the transition from premises to conclusion in a logical deduction.

If a history is to be necessary, it must also be universal. In other words, the two most basic criteria of rationality, for Hegel and for Marx after him, go together necessarily. In the following passage at the beginning of the *Lectures on the History of Philosophy* Hegel is explicit about his wish to exclude particularity:

> The events and actions of this history are . . . such that personality and individual character do not enter to any large degree into its content and matter. . . . In Philosophy, the less attention [*Zurechnung*] and credit [*Verdienst*] are accorded to the particular individual, the better is what is produced [*die Hervorbringungen um so vortrefflicher sind*]. . . . (*LHP* 1: 1–2/1833 ed., 13: 12)

The reason Hegel wishes to focus on the universal and exclude particularity is clear: only in this way can the history be recounted as a process in which all the steps are necessary, for only in this way can the history appear as analogous to the syllogism, which likewise keeps particularities at bay and focuses instead on concepts. Thus in the syllogism "All men are mortal; Gaius is a man; therefore Gaius is mortal," one finds the universals "manhood" and "mortality"; and the particular man, Gaius, is considered only insofar as he possesses a generic manhood and not for his own particular characteristics, in just the way that Hegel claims he will exclude from consideration the personalities and individual characters of the philosophers entering into his history of philosophy. When one excludes what is inessential, one is able to see how "philosophy aris[es] of necessity from previous philosophy" (*LHP* 1: 4/13: 14).

Hegel is very clear about the analogy he wants between the syllogism and historical sequence. "The sequence [*Aufeinanderfolge*] of systems of philosophy in history," he tells us,

> is similar to the sequence in the logical deduction of the concept-determination in the Idea [*die Auseinanderfolge in der logischen Ableitung der Begriffsbestimmungen der*

> *Idee*]. . . . if the fundamental conceptions of the systems appearing in the history of philosophy be entirely divested of what regards their outward form, their relation to the particular and the like, the various stages in the determination of the Idea are found in their logical concept. Conversely in the logical progression taken for itself, there is, so far as its principal elements are concerned, the progression of historical manifestations. . . . (*LHP* 1: 30/13: 43)

At first glance it may seem strange that the fact that Hegel conceived of his rational history as analogous to the syllogism is not much noted in the scholarly literature. Perhaps the point was so obvious to Hegel's early students and readers—after all, Hegel states it explicitly himself—that it did not need to be emphasized.[78] As already noted, later readers have tended to direct their attention to other works than the *History of Philosophy*. In any case, there should be no doubt that Hegel conceived of history as a substantialization, and projection onto a temporal axis, of a necessity that previously was ahistorical and formal. Admittedly, the history of philosophy is an *ideal* history, and it is also a history that concerns itself with a rare and peculiar phenomenon in human life, the pure pursuit of truth. Hegel, sly realist that he was, knew perfectly well that real history—even the history of philosophy—is replete with particularities and contingencies. But it seems clear that the kind of history that he preferred was the kind that he limns in his *Lectures on the History of Philosophy*.[79]

Finally, the history of philosophy is a progressive history. After all, the aim of philosophy is the discovery of truth. Those who are truly philosophers—who are engaged in the disinterested search for truth—are constantly engaged in arguments intended to bring us closer to that end. (By definition, those who betray the enterprise of searching disinterestedly for truth are to that degree not part of the history of philosophy.) Thus it is not surprising that Hegel tells us in the *History of Philosophy* that "spirit alone is progress." "The labor [*Arbeit*] of the spirit, to know itself, to find itself, this activity [*Thätigkeit*] is spirit, the life of spirit itself." "Determinate philosophies . . . are an intellectual [*geistiges*], rational, forward advance [*Fortschreiten*]: they are of necessity one philosophy in its development" (*LHP* 3: 546–47/1836 ed., 15: 685–86). At the end of the *History of Philosophy*, Hegel also comments on certain moments of rapid movement:

> Often it [spirit] appears to have forgotten itself, to have lost itself; but, inwardly [*innerlich*] set at odds to itself, it inwardly works forward [*ist er innerliches Fortarbeiten*]—as Hamlet says of the ghost [*Geist*] of his father, "Well said, old mole! canst work i' the ground so fast?"—until, strengthened in itself, it shoves and bursts asunder the crust of earth that divides it from the sun, its concept. In such a time, when the crust of earth, like a soul-less, tottering building, falls away, it [spirit] has put on seven-league boots, and shows itself arrayed in new youth. (*LHP* 3: 546–47/1836 ed., 15: 685)

To readers familiar with Marx, this final passage will have a strangely familiar ring to it: it is nothing other than Marx's concept of revolutionary change, abstractly described.

MARX, EMBEDDED PROGRESS, AND THE HISTORY OF PHILOSOPHY

So far, I have indicated the main components of rationalism: universality, necessity, predictivity, and dialectic (or progress by contradiction). I have argued that the Hegelian form of this rationalism derived in large degree from Hegel's creative misreading of Aristotle's logic and dialectic, and I have claimed that the one text in which Hegel succeeded in projecting his rationalism onto a historical plane is his *Lectures on the History of Philosophy*. Finally, I have suggested—but *only* suggested—that the *History of Philosophy*, besides serving as a linchpin connecting Hegel back to Aristotle, connects Hegel to his great and impatient successor, Marx.

We must now examine the Marx side of this relation. I am making two connected claims here. My first claim is that the primary model for Marx's conception of history (which in large measure equates to his conception of dialectic) is Hegel's *History of Philosophy*. My second claim is that Marx's conception of rationality was heavily dependent on criteria that he drew from the *History of Philosophy*. (Marx's conception of history and his conception of rationality are closely intertwined, for, like Hegel, Marx envisaged a *rational history*.) But so far I have not provided any evidence from the Marx side for the truth of these claims. Moreover, there is a larger problem. It is a question of the Marx-Hegel relation seen *within the context of nineteenth-century theory*. In the present section I shall indicate how Marx is differently related to nineteenth-century theory than was Hegel before him. In the section that follows I shall look at two texts of the very early Marx that connect him back to Hegel.

It has sometimes been said that Marx was a synthesizer of ideas that came to him from elsewhere, and not an original thinker.[80] There is some justice to this claim. The difficulty is that the claim underrates the breadth and brilliance of the synthesis and the rigor of the thinking that went into it. A characteristic move of nineteenth-century theorists was to attempt to tie together in one way or another the disparate parts of human knowledge. The synthesizing project in nineteenth-century theory is best seen as a response to the sense on the part of many nineteenth-century intellectuals that the domain of secular knowledge, which until the late eighteenth century had seemed relatively unified, had now become so large and ramified that it no longer held together. In the seventeenth and eighteenth centuries it was still possible to think of all secular knowledge as falling under the single, portmanteau heading of "philosophy" (a term having a far larger ambit then than it does now), and in turn to see the general field of philosophy as divided into only two major subfields: moral philosophy (dealing with things human), and natural philosophy (dealing with nature). After about 1780 it became increasingly difficult to do this: in part because history, and change and diversity more generally, came to be a matter of central rather than of merely marginal concern to European thinkers; in part because the sheer volume of what was systematically known continued to increase from decade to decade; and in part because of a process of division of labor and specialization that bred disciplines and subdisciplines, each devoted to the systematic study of one or another slice of the human or natural world.[81]

It is unsurprising, then, that many of the most highly regarded nineteenth-century theorists aimed at carrying out a synthesis of one sort or another. Even among nineteenth-century literary figures, one can identify a comparable synthesizing concern in the projects of some writers—Honoré de Balzac comes most quickly to mind—to create stylistically unified and broad-ranging descriptions of the human world. Hegel was a preeminent synthesizer, and the synthesizing impulse played a preeminent role in his thought. Consider, for example, the very title of his *Encyclopedia of the Philosophical Sciences*: as the "circle" hidden in "encyclopedia" suggests, his aim was to create a unified and self-contained system of knowledge, with the premises leading to the conclusions and the conclusions leading back to the premises. Fichte and Schelling likewise strove to construct unified and compendious philosophical systems. One thinks also of the French positivist Auguste Comte, with his *Course of Positive Philosophy* and his later *System of Positive Politics*, and of the English positivist Herbert Spencer, with his projected (and largely completed) *Synthetic Philosophy*.[82] It would be possible to say much more about the synthesizing impulse in nineteenth-century theory, but what matters for our purposes is simply the fact that the impulse existed.

It was an impulse in which Marx shared. While the rigor of the theory at which he arrived by 1845 brought with it, at times, a quite terrifying narrowness of focus, one cannot in the least say that Marx was a narrow thinker. On the contrary, he was surely more brilliantly compendious than almost all of his contemporaries. Maurice Mandelbaum has suggested that, for all its multiplicity, nineteenth-century theory was dominated by two, and only two, philosophical schools: metaphysical idealism, and positivism.[83] Although the two schools might be better called "idealism" and "naturalism," Mandelbaum's suggestion is entirely correct. It is not surprising that it should be so, for the opposition between idealism and naturalism is simply a version of the fundamental Cartesian opposition between soul and body, spirit and matter.

It is part of Marx's genius that he was connected to both sides of the spirit-matter, idealism-naturalism opposition. In this respect Marx was a far more representative nineteenth-century thinker than was Hegel, for Hegel was unequivocally an idealist and not at all a naturalist.[84] In fact, in his Heidelberg inaugural lecture he came close to implying that there is an outright opposition between natural science and philosophy.[85] In some degree, Hegel seems to have seen himself as engaged in a defense of the "human, historical sciences" (the "*Geisteswissenschaften*," or "sciences of the spirit," to use a late-nineteenth-century term) against the encroachments of the *Naturwissenschaften*. Notoriously, his *Lectures on the Philosophy of Nature* crammed the phenomena of natural science into a Procrustean bed in which natural phenomena were subordinated to spirit.

The question that must be asked is *how* Marx put together idealism and naturalism. To begin to answer the question properly we must concern ourselves with what these two positions actually amounted to. To concern ourselves with what these positions amounted to requires that we distinguish among different possible areas of theoretical attention. We can divide the world into four areas of such attention (uncertain though the boundaries between them are), each with its own distinctive type of object: Being, Nature, Humanity, and Method. Figure 1.1 presents this idea in simple schematic form. As thinkers, we can concern ourselves with the ultimate nature of reality, with "Being." A concern with Being requires, by definition, that we go beyond what can be perceived by the senses, for it is the *ultimate* nature of reality that

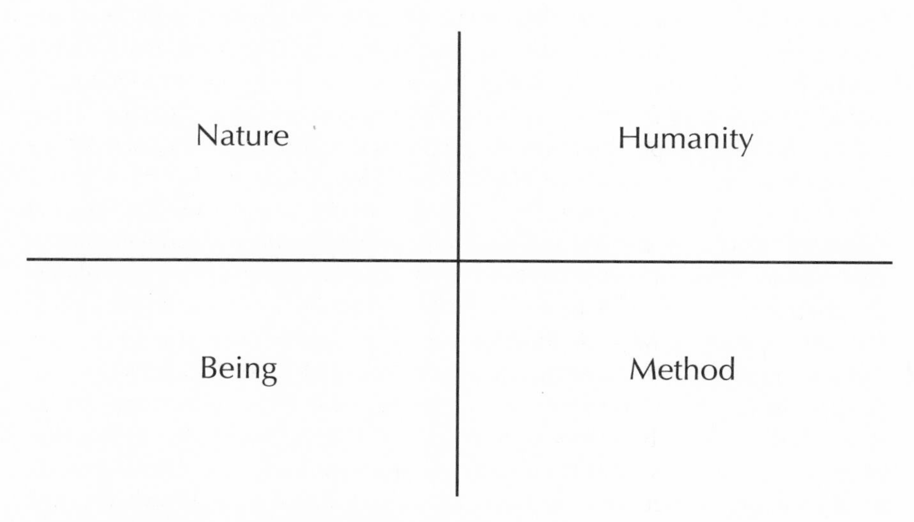

Figure 1.1. Four Areas of Theoretical Attention

the ontologist is concerned with, not its perceived nature. Second, we can concern ourselves with Nature, which for purposes of the present discussion we can define as that part of the world that we can perceive, but that is not *specifically* human: obviously, the boundary between what is natural and what is human is not exactly clear, but this is not a matter at issue here. Third, we can concern ourselves with the realm of Humanity. Finally, we can concern ourselves with issues of Method: the question that the methodologist asks is, How do we rightly go about the search for truth?

We do not need to concern ourselves with all of the above-noted matrix, for not all of the distinctions are relevant to the question of Marx's relation to the two philosophical positions of idealism and naturalism. In fact, to get at Marx's relation to these positions we need to focus on only two of the above-noted concerns: ontology and methodology. Ontology is the field of investigation that attempts to arrive at conclusions regarding the fundamental nature of reality (*onto* comes from the Greek word for "being"). Methodology is the sphere of investigation that attempts to arrive at conclusions as to which methods of investigation are most likely to lead to the discovery of truth. Both ontology and methodology were important areas of concern in nineteenth-century theory, although in the positivist "school" concern with ontology was often implicit rather than explicit.

Idealism is a view that holds, first, that reality is fundamentally ideal or spiritual in character, and, second, that insight into this fundamental reality is best obtained through an ideal or spiritual dimension existing within human beings themselves.[86] Thus, idealism was both an ontological and a methodological doctrine: it articulated both a view as to the ultimate nature of reality and a view as to which method of investigating reality is the best method. The "school" that opposed idealism likewise advanced both an ontological and a methodological doctrine. On the ontological level, the opposite of idealism is materialism, which is the view that reality ultimately consists of matter and nothing more. On the methodological level, the opposite of idealism is positivism. Positivism took its cue from the natural sciences. The method recommended by positivists was to gather observable facts and then to arrive inductively at regularities among those facts; these regularities were understood as laws, either of nature or of society. Positivism had ontological assumptions and implications, but strict positivists steered away from ontology on the grounds that there can be no scientific knowledge of things that are not observable (and the ultimate nature of the world is not an observable).[87]

If we are to grasp the overall character of Marx's synthesizing project as it emerged in 1844–46, we need to understand where Marx stood both ontologically and methodologically. What I am interested in here is Marx's position once he had arrived at a coherent and relatively stable position, which was the case in summer 1844 at the earliest. The earliest statement that is of interest for getting at the ontological position of the "mature," historical materialist Marx appears in the "Critique of Hegel's Dialectic and General Philosophy" in the "Economic and Philosophical Manuscripts." Here, after a quick Feuerbachian demolition of the "absolute knowing" chapter of the *Phenomenology*, Marx begins to articulate his own position. In an important passage, he suggests that:

> Here we see how consistent naturalism or humanism differs both from idealism and materialism and is at the same time their unifying truth. We also see that only naturalism is capable of comprehending the process of world history. (*MEGA2* 1.2: 408/*MECW* 3: 336/*EW* 389)

When Marx suggests that he is a naturalist and humanist, and likewise that he is neither an idealist nor a materialist (since he is beyond those positions, having arrived at the naturalistic-humanistic synthesis of them), what does he mean? The passage is confusing on its face, because in *The German Ideology*, within another year or so, he would present himself as a materialist. But the puzzle is only apparent: it is clear from the wider context surrounding the passage that Marx meant, here, that he was neither an *ontological* idealist nor an *ontological* materialist. In other words, Marx wished to take no position on the question What is the ultimate nature of the reality? Rather, his orientation was practical and pragmatic: he wished to address what really concerns human beings. What really concerns human beings is not What is the ultimate nature of reality? It is rather How are we to live within the social and natural world that surrounds us? To put the matter another way: Marx's fabled historical materialism (sketchily present in the EPM, then articulated in detail in *The German Ideology*) was not an ontological materialism, at least not in the normal sense of "ontological." It was much more specific and limited: a view of human history, not a view of reality-in-general.[88] The fact that Marx became a historical materialist gives us no warrant for thinking that he was an ontological materialist. And indeed, he was not an ontological materialist.[89]

On the methodological plane, on the other hand, it is a matter not of "neither/nor" (neither an idealist nor a materialist) but of "both/and." Methodologically, by the time that he wrote the "Economic and Philosophical Manuscripts" Marx had come to hold that a "science of man" will come into being that will be analogous to the (Newtonian) natural sciences, which, Marx points out, "have been prolifically active" (*MEGA2* 1.2: 395/*MECW* 3: 303/*MEW* 355). Marx was never a positivist, for although he came to share positivism's concern for the discovery of laws of nature and society, he did not hold, as nineteenth-century positivists did, that the way to discover laws is by the method of data collection and induction to regularities. However,

Marx did share with the positivists a deep attachment to natural science. The mid-century period was marked by the emergence of a larger, more ramified, and more self-conscious scientific community than had existed earlier. It was also marked by the emergence of an explicit school of scientific materialism.[90]

I have already noted Feuerbach's heralding of natural science in his "Preliminary Theses on the Reform of Philosophy" (1843), with its claim that "*philosophy must again unite itself with natural science. . . .*"[91] In 1840 Feuerbach was already saying similar things in his letters. In one letter he writes that "I consider no law of metaphysics valid unless I can prove it as a law of nature"; in another he suggests that philosophy has a close affinity with such empirical natural sciences as geology and mineralogy, and that, like the great paleontologist Cuvier, it "is able to recognize from the splinter the skeleton of the whole."[92] Feuerbach continued along this line the next year, stating in the foreword to *The Essence of Christianity* (1841) that the work addresses a content that is "pathological or physiological" and that it follows "the method of analytical chemistry." In the 1843 foreword to the work, he bills himself as "a natural scientist of the mind [*ein geistiger Naturforscher*].[93]

The impact of Feuerbach no doubt helps to explain the presence of a concern with natural science in the EPM. This presence is most striking in the passage, quoted briefly earlier, where Marx notes that "the *natural sciences* have been prolifically active and have gathered together an ever growing mass of material," and that, in particular, "natural science has intervened in and transformed human life . . . *practically* through industry." But one did not really need Feuerbach to be led to say such a thing: all one had to do was notice that railways were being constructed at great speed on the European continent.[94] With his high level of energy and his indefatigable curiosity, how could Marx *not* have attended to the impact of "practical" natural science on human life in his time? Thus, whereas Hegel the methodological idealist aimed to subsume natural science under philosophy, Marx in the EPM suggests an eventual mutual subsumption: "Natural science will in time subsume the science of man just as the science of man will subsume natural science: there will be one science" (*MEGA2* 1.2: 395–96/*MECW* 3: 303–4/*EW* 355). In a draft for his "Speech at the Graveside of Karl Marx," Engels wrote that "no man could feel a purer joy than [Marx] when a new scientific progress was secured anywhere, no matter whether practically applicable or not" (*MEGA2* 1.25: 403/*MECW* 24: 463). This is Engels's opinion, of course, but it rings true of the Marx of 1844 and after. Besides his commitment to Romantic poetry, one finds in Marx a deep commitment to the rosiest, most optimistic side of the Enlightenment.

Accordingly, in claiming that Hegel's *History of Philosophy* had a decisive impact on Marx's concept of rationality, I am not claiming that Marx, after

1844–45, remained within the ambit of Hegelian idealism. He did not. On the contrary, he ended up articulating a position that drew from both sides of the idealism/materialism split. But what is important at this point is the *location* of the idealism/materialism divide in Marx's work. What is important is that, very early, ontology seems to have stopped being an object of concern for Marx. He was fundamentally not interested in the question of the ultimate nature of the world. Accordingly, he ended up reconstituting the idealist/materialist split as *an empirical feature of humanity*: man has a material nature, but he also has a thinking nature. The split also appears within nature: nature is material, but when human beings work upon nature it comes to be marked by human projects and needs. Finally, the split makes its appearance within method: Marx's method involves a search for the *essential* features of a thing, not induction from particulars—but at the same time it involves extensive data collection, as recommended by the positivists.

The question of Marx's method is quite important. Marx's approach to solving scientific problems can be touched on only lightly here, since the present book is concerned with what underlies method more than it is with method as such.[95] Marx's approach is one of the prime markers of his dependence on Hegel. Fundamentally, Marx always remained Hegelian. One is struck by his obsessive collection of data, and yet he was anything but an empiricist in the way that he processed the data. In spite of everything, his characteristic approach to any problem was to articulate a concept (an "essence," if one wants to call it that) and then to derive consequences from the concept. When, in *The Holy Family* (written in late 1844 in collaboration with Engels), Marx attacked Hegelian method, he did so in terms that were deeply Hegelian. In a burlesquing passage, he criticizes what he takes to be the Hegelian notion of fruit, in which, allegedly, only the abstract notion, *the* fruit, is real, and individual fruits are not real; and he accuses "the speculative philosopher" of "presenting universally known qualities of the apple, the pear, etc., which exist in reality, as determining features *invented* by him, by giving the *names* of the real things . . . to abstract formulas of reason." As Brudney has pointed out, Marx (and Feuerbach) targeted Hegel's commitment to abstraction.[96] And yet Marx's attack, here, on the abstract character of the Hegelian concept, which he characterizes as an "empty, undifferentiated unity" detached from "the "diversity" of a concrete existence, reads very much like Hegel's own various attacks on an abstract, formal reasoning detached from the particularities of the real world (*MEW* 2: 59–62/*MECW* 4: 57–60).[97] Marx is trying to hoist Hegel on his own petard, but he does not seem to be aware that this is what he is doing.

Hegel's approach gave Marx universality and necessity. Marx also thought that it gave him predictivity. Hegel, I have contended, did not aim at predictivity. The *History of Philosophy*, like Hegel's other attempts to write history, was retrospective in its concerns, aimed at showing how the past has been fulfilled in the present or at least is on the verge of being fulfilled. Thus, the history of philosophy leads up to Hegel's presence, right now, in this lecture room, giving the last lecture of his course on the history of philosophy. Marx shifted perspective: Hegel's past-oriented perspective became, in Marx's hands, a future-oriented perspective. Here I am right now, and things are not as they should be, and the question is How are those things to be changed? This was a massive shift—although it was "always already" anticipated by Hegel himself, who acknowledged the road of activism but turned away from it. In short, Marx develops a possibility undeveloped by Hegel himself (Marx thought that he was seconded in doing so by natural science and by the technology deriving from natural science). What Marx does not alter, in altering Hegel, is the notion of a rational history. Marx's history may not look like the story of philosophers quarreling with each other, but, *mutatis mutandis*, that is what it is. It is now projected forward into the future, something that Hegel had declined to do.

THE VERY EARLY MARX: TWO KEY TEXTS

Up to now I have said almost nothing about the texts of the very early Marx—the Marx of 1837–41—that connect him to Hegel. Instead I started from the other direction, looking at Hegel's works with a view to seeing what, in Hegel, might plausibly have been a source for Marx's concept of rationality, and especially for his notion of dialectic (progress by contradiction). Now I want to reverse the procedure and look at what, in the very early Marx, plausibly connects him to Hegel.

I say "very early" for a reason. Although Marx's early writings (many of them previously unpublished) were made available in the old *Marx-Engels Gesamtausgabe* (*MEGA*), published in the years 1927–35, they came to be widely noticed only in the 1950s and 1960s. What people at that time found most interesting in the early writings was the notion of estrangement. This amounted to a fixation on the "Economic and Philosophical Manuscripts" (also known as the "Paris Manuscripts" and as the "1844 Manuscripts"). When people referred to the "early" Marx it was the Marx of 1844 that they had in mind. Enthusiasm for the early Marx met its opponent in the writings of the French Marxist philosopher, and Communist Party adherent, Louis Althusser, who argued vehemently that the humanistic Marx of 1844 was not yet the scientific Marx of 1845 and after.[98] A "problem" was thus generated: How does one reconcile the early Marx that is so strikingly visible in the EPM with the later Marx, the Marx of *Capital*? It was a problem that dominated discussion of Marx's work for a generation.[99]

The focusing of attention on the relation of the Marx of the EPM to the Marx of *Capital* obscured the earlier phases in Marx's intellectual career. To be sure, within the "early" Marx, commentators also frequently included, besides the EPM, writings going as far back as spring/summer 1843, when Marx began to articulate his Feuerbachian, transformative, humanistic criticisms of current political and economic theory. In that summer, just after his marriage, Marx made substantial progress on a critique of Hegel's political theory. He was picking up on, and continuing in a different register, a project that he had worked on intermittently between November 1841 and September 1842 (DRAP 2: 35, #204). Further, by the time he turned to the writing of "On the Jewish Question" in fall 1843 he was already beginning to head in the direction of a critique of the modern economy. For this reason, and because "On the Jewish Question" says some interesting things about politics, and also because in it Marx made a provocative and troubling use of anti-Semitic language, this essay has attracted much attention. But few commentators have looked seriously at Marx's writings prior to 1843. For most commentators, "early Marx" has meant the Marx of 1844, with some foreshadowings from 1843. That is as far back as they go. If they mention Marx's earlier writings they usually do so only in passing. They tend to view this earlier work (if they think about it at all) as insignificant compared with the Marx of 1843–44 (if one favors the "humanistic" Marx) or of 1845 (if one favors the "scientific" Marx).

However, Marx's intellectual career began long before the months in 1844 when he produced the "Economic and Philosophical Manuscripts," and long before the period from mid-March to the end of September 1843 when he produced the rather turgid manuscript variously known as "Critique of Hegel's Philosophy of Right" or "Critique of Hegel's Doctrine of the State" (*MEGA2* 1.2: 5–137/*MECW* 3: 3–129/*EW* 57–198). Marx's active intellectual career goes back to 1837, and includes the doctoral dissertation and associated notebooks (1839–41) and his initial journalism (1842–43). From these earlier attempts by Marx to learn how to think, things of great importance persist, from the humanism of 1844 through the historical materialism of 1845–46 to the end of Marx's career—although, to be sure, there were also changes. Marx turned twenty-five in May 1843, and when he wrote, at white heat, the amazing "Economic and Philosophical Manuscripts" he was only a bit older than twenty-six. But he was both energetic and amazingly precocious, and before 1843–44 he had already done much thinking, talking, and writing. His elders in the Doctors' Club, mostly young lecturers, thought highly of his abilities. A fellow Doctors' Club member (and history teacher in a Berlin secondary school), Karl Friedrich Köppen (1808–63), dedicated his 1840 book *Frederick the Great and His Opponents* to Marx, when Marx was a mere twenty-two years old (DRAP 3: 112). The Rhineland journalist and socialist (and future Zionist), Moses Hess (1812–75), even suggested in a letter written to a friend in September 1841, shortly after Hess had met Marx, that Marx was

> the greatest, perhaps the *only, genuine philosopher* now alive . . . soon, when he makes his public appearance (whether through writing or on the lecture platform), the eyes of Germany will be drawn to him . . . he unites the most cutting wit and the deepest philosophical seriousness [*er verbindet mit dem tiefsten philosophischen Ernst den schneidendsten Witz*]; think of Rousseau, Voltaire, Holbach, Lessing, Heine, and Hegel united, I mean *fused*, not thrown together—and you have Dr. Marx.[100]

While a testimonial like this doubtless needs to be toned down, it is nonetheless indicative of the impression that the young Marx (b. 1818) often made on the slightly older contemporaries with whom he associated. They thought of him as undeniably brilliant, as capable far beyond his years.

So it is not surprising that two of Marx's enterprises preceding 1843–44 call for our attention. First, before the well-known Marx of 1843–44, there was the Marx of 1842 and early 1843, who wrote journalism, primarily for the *Rheinische Zeitung*, a reform newspaper financed by a group of Rhineland businessmen and lawyers, that he edited between October 1842 and March 1843; in this period Marx also wrote articles critical of current policy that he published in other places. Marx's career as an editor was derailed in March 1843, when the hostile attitude of the Prussian censor forced his removal from the paper, and then, shortly thereafter, led to its banning. The often very revealing articles that Marx wrote during this phase have been almost entirely overlooked by Marx's students and commentators.[101] I shall turn to this material in the next chapter.

Second, before Marx became a journalist he was unequivocally a philosopher and a historian of philosophy. He began his serious study of philosophy in 1837, and until autumn 1842 he continued to hope that he would obtain a university post (DRAP 1: 10). The Marx of this period was a Hegelian philosopher (although a Hegelian philosopher of radical stripe). I shall now turn to his philosophically oriented writings of this period, for they cast much light on his relation to Hegel and on his rationalism generally. The writings in question are, first, the long and revealing letter that Marx wrote to his father in November 1837, and, second, the surviving text of his doctoral dissertation, along with notes written by Marx in the course of its preparation, a set of texts that Marx wrote during several spurts of activity from early 1839 through to December 1841 (DRAP 1: 7–10). These two sources are the only theoretically oriented texts by Marx that survive from the 1837–41 period.[102]

In October 1836 Marx had moved from the provincial University of Bonn to the University of Berlin, by far the weightiest university in Germany, and in the letter that he wrote to his father on the night of November 10–11, 1837, he sought to justify his course of studies over the preceding year and to lay out where he was tending for the future. His father was worried about how his son would support himself in life, especially since he had been engaged since January 1837 to Jenny von Westphalen—the daughter of Heinrich Marx's friend and former superior in the Prussian civil service in Trier, Baron Ludwig von Westphalen. Moreover, Heinrich Marx was in ill health, and knew it; he would die, of tuberculosis and liver ailments, in May 1838 (DRAP 1: 7).

The central theme of Marx's letter is that of transition. As Marx puts it in his first sentence, "there are moments in one's life which are like boundary posts marking the completion of a period but at the same time clearly indicating a new direction." And he continues:

> At such a moment of transition we feel compelled to view the past and the present with the eagle eye of thought in order to become conscious of our real position. Indeed, world history itself likes to look back in this way and take stock, which often gives it the appearance of retrogression or stagnation, while, as it were, it only throws itself into an armchair in order to grasp itself, to spiritually penetrate its own activity [*That*], which is that of spirit. (*MEGA2* 3.1: 9/*MECW* 1: 10)

What measure of irony are we to read into this beginning? The ludicrousness of the image—"world history" reclining in an armchair (*Lehnstuhl*)—suggests some degree of self-distancing, but who can be certain whether there actually is a self-distancing, or what significance such a self-distancing would have? Still, we *can* say that in evoking a "world history" that is concerned with grasping its own activity as "that of spirit," Marx casts his description of his life in terms that are borrowed from Hegel. To be more specific: Marx's world history does not so much resemble Hegel's world history as it resembles his history of philosophy. Only the history of philosophy has, as its *telos*, a reflective understanding of the sort that Marx appears to be alluding to here.

In the pages that follow, Marx goes on to describe his intellectual and emotional itinerary of the preceding year. He notes his love for Jenny von Westphalen. Turning self-critical, he declares that the three volumes of poetry that he had written for her (in 1835 and 1836) were marked by "complete opposition between what is and what ought to be." (He here writes on two levels, for he evokes both the conflict between reality and aspiration with respect to his plans to marry, and the conflict in Kantian philosophy between sensuous inclination and ethical duty.) (*MEGA2* 3.1: 10/*MECW* 1: 11/*MER* 7)

Marx also comments on his legal studies—a matter of deep concern to Heinrich Marx, given Heinrich Marx's own legal interests and his conviction that Karl's best possibility for earning a living was likely to be found in the law. Marx writes that in studying the law he had found that "the same opposition between what is and what ought to be, which is characteristic of idealism, stood out as a serious defect." He claims that, inspired in part by J. G. Fichte's *Foundations of Natural Law, according to the Principles of the Science of Knowledge* (1796–97) he had attempted to construct a metaphysics of law.[103] But he had been hindered—he declares—by the "unscientific form of mathematical dogmatism" that he says Fichte had affected, for the mathematical object (e.g., the triangle) "remains a mere abstract conception in space and does not develop into anything further." Marx's critique of what he sees as Fichte's abstract and unhistorical formalism is thoroughly Hegelian in spirit, for it clearly parallels Hegel's own criticisms of the abstract formalism of mathematical reasoning.

Here is what Marx wants instead of Fichte's approach. The passage is worth reading carefully:

> In the concrete expression of a living world of ideas, as exemplified by law, the state, nature, and philosophy as a whole, the object itself [*das Objekt selbst*] must be studied in its development . . . the rational character of the thing itself [*die Vernunft des Dinges selbst*] must develop as something imbued with contradictions in itself and find its unity in itself. (*MEGA2* 3.1:10–11/*MECW* 1: 12)

What the passage shows is that already, in November 1837, Marx had a conception of the historical dialectic—of progress by contradiction. Marx is also certainly asserting that history is a rational process. We know that in April 1837 Marx had turned to an intensive study of Hegel's philosophy and of the Hegelian school, and that he had made the acquaintance of the critical Hegelian circle at the University of Berlin (DRAP 1: 5). His reflections on how the philosophy of law ought to be carried out are clearly an outcome of his turn to Hegelian philosophy.

Marx tells his father that, in an effort to overcome the deficiencies of Fichte's philosophy of law, he had attempted to articulate his own philosophy of law, divided into the two sides of formal law and material law. This project, too, had proved abortive; but (conveniently) it had led Marx to the important conclusion that "there could be no headway without philosophy." And now he reveals to his father that he had turned to Hegelian philosophy. Previously, Marx writes, he had read fragments of Hegel, but Hegel's "grotesque craggy melody" had not appealed to him. But then, during a period of illness—which, we know, occurred in April 1837—he "got to know Hegel from beginning to end, together with most of his disciples." In Hegel he found something that he had not found in "the idealism of Kant and Fichte." Marx implies that Kant and Fichte regarded ideals or norms as existing in a transcendental realm detached from reality. Marx claims that Hegel, in contrast, had helped him to arrive

> at the point of seeking the idea in reality [*im Wirklichen*] itself. If previously the gods had dwelt above the earth, now they became its center. (*MEGA2* 3.1: 10–16/*MECW* 1: 12–19)

There could hardly be a better brief description of the notion of embedded rationality than this.

To be sure, one should not overemphasize the significance of a document written so quickly under circumstances of such calculation by an author so young. But the adolescent Marx was astoundingly bright and productive, the letter *is* revelatory, and its revelations are strongly in line with Marx's subsequent trajectory. The letter shows that Marx found three defects in the philosophies of Kant and Fichte. First, they sharply divide is and ought, real and ideal. (The is/ought separation is exemplified most strikingly in Kant's notion of the categorical imperative, which is a norm of pure duty totally detached from the sensuous, material world of human passions and desires). Second, they fall victim to an abstract formalism, appearing to impose distinctions *on* the world instead of deriving distinctions *from* it. Third, they fail to show any sort of process at work within the world: instead, they offer a static picture of reality.

On all these points Marx sees Hegelian philosophy as providing a contrasting view. Above all, Marx wishes to claim that rationality is something embedded in the world, not something to be imposed on it. Marx's commitment is to studying "the rational character of the thing *itself* [my italics]," by which he appears to mean a thing having some weight and density in the world. Further, Marx wishes to see this object as part of a single world-historical process. In all these respects he seems entirely in line with what Hegel aspired to. But there was an important difference here between Marx and Hegel. Hegel himself never articulated the *one* rational history of humanity that his general view required; and, among his specialized histories, only the history of philosophy was dialectical in fact. Marx was destined to be more daring, or more foolhardy, than Hegel had ever been.

Marx's doctoral dissertation, "Difference between the Democritean and Epicurean Philosophy of Nature," and the "Notebooks on Epicurean Philosophy" that were preparatory to the dissertation, give us a deeper entry into the philosophical position of the very young Marx.[104] Marx's decision to do a doctoral degree in philosophy rather than in law seems to have taken firm shape toward the end of 1838, when he obtained money from his mother (his father having died) to cover the requisite fees (*MEGA2* 1.1: 880; *MEGA2* 3.1: 334). His research and writing extended from early 1839 through early 1841, when he was between the ages of 20 and 23.[105] During this time Marx was closely connected with the Hegelian theologian Bruno Bauer. In 1838, in his book *The Religion of the Old Testament Presented in the Light of the Historical Development of Its Principles*, Bauer had declared that Christianity's emergence "was dependent on the power of the content that the classical spirit of antiquity produced." In Bauer's view the way to Christianity had been prepared by "the Roman spirit" and in particular by "the Roman religion of self-consciousness."[106] Marx's dissertation project quite obviously derives, in part, from Bauer's concern with ancient notions of self-consciousness. In the foreword (written March 1841) to his dissertation, Marx characterizes the dissertation as "only . . . the preliminary" to a "larger work" that would deal with "the cycle of Epicurean, Stoic, and Skeptic philosophy in their relation to the whole of Greek speculation." In describing "the subject of the treatise," Marx goes on to claim that "with the Epicureans, Stoics, and Skeptics all moments of self-consciousness are represented completely" (*MEGA2* 1.1: 13, 22/*MECW* 1: 29, 35). Marx's deeper debt—as well as Bauer's—is to Hegel's *Lectures on the History of Philosophy*, for it is in the *History of Philosophy* that Hegel presents these philosophies as constituting "the philosophy of the Roman world," a world where, faced by a "wave of adversities," people turned for respite to "man's inmost self" (*LHP* 2: 234–35/1833 ed., 14: 426–27). The difference between Hegel on the one hand and Bauer and Marx on the other is that Bauer and Marx believed that Hegel had too much preferred Plato and Aristotle to the later philosophers. In Marx's view, Hegel had missed the "great importance for the history of Greek philosophy and for the Greek mind [*Geist*] in general" of Epicurean, Stoic, and Skeptical philosophy (*MEGA2* 1.1: 14/*MECW* 1: 30). For Hegel had held that Epicureanism and Stoicism in particular amounted to "a philosophizing of the understanding [rather than of reason]," and that in this philosophizing "Plato's and Aristotle's speculative greatness is no longer present" (LHP 2: 232/1833 ed. 14: 423–24).

There is also a possible linkage of Marx to Feuerbach, although the link to Bauer was clearly much stronger at this stage. In his essay "Toward the Critique of 'Positive Philosophy,'" published in the *Hallische Jahrbücher* in late 1838, Feuerbach took up a theme that such contemporaries as August Cieszkowski and Bruno Bauer were also articulating, namely, the theme of "going beyond." Feuerbach contends that "philosophy . . . must proceed beyond Hegelian philosophy." Feuerbach observes that there was once a time when the work of Aristotle was considered "identical with philosophy and reason themselves." But to believe in "an actual incarnation of philosophy in a determinate historical manifestation," Feuerbach declares, is to fall into "speculative superstition." Such an error amounts to enclosing "within narrow boundaries of time and space, the eternally creating life of the spirit." Aristotle had been superseded; Hegel will be superseded too.[107] It is thus no accident that Marx's dissertation focuses on philosophy in the post-Aristotelian period. In this period the Aristotelian system was abandoned. In his fifth "Notebook on Epicurean Philosophy" (probably April–August 1839) Marx draws a parallel to philosophy's situation now, after Hegel. In the ancient world the transition from the Aristotelian system to the philosophy of self-consciousness had the character of a "turn-about [*Umschlagen*] of philosophy, its transubstantiation into flesh and blood." *Mutatis mutandis*, Marx was clearly looking for the same thing now—a movement beyond Hegelianism into a something else whose character, for the moment, he seems entirely unsure of. (*MEGA2* 4.1: 100–1/*MECW* 1: 491–93)

Still, Hegel remained Marx's basic point of reference in the dissertation materials. The *History of Philosophy* provides the overall framework within which Marx's dissertation fits. Yet Marx's account also takes implicit issue with Hegel. Betraying a pro-Aristotelian bias, Hegel regarded the philosophy of self-consciousness as a back eddy in the history of philosophy—as a flight from a public world to a private world. The abstract will of the (imperial) ruler reigned supreme, suppressing the distinctiveness of nations; meanwhile, individuals sought refuge within themselves (*LHP* 2: 235/1833 ed. 14: 426). Marx, on the contrary, saw the post-Aristotelian schools as advancing beyond Aristotle—just as, by 1839, Bauer, Feuerbach, Cieszkowski, and others were seeking to advance beyond Hegelian philosophy. But the degree to which Marx's project remains dependent on the conception of a progressive intellectual process that the *History of Philosophy* so clearly attempts to portray is striking.

In chapter 2 I shall address the dissertation and "Notebooks on Epicurean Philosophy" from the perspective of the young Marx's political interests. Here I simply want to indicate, briefly, how the dissertation materials manifest Marx's conception of rationality. Consider the following passage from the seventh "Notebook on Epicurean Philosophy," probably written between mid-October 1839 and mid-February 1840, where Marx discusses how one ought to go about doing the history of philosophy:

> Philosophical historiography [*philosophische Geschichtsschreibung*] is not concerned either with comprehending the personality, be it even the spiritual personality, of the philosopher, as, in a manner of speaking, the focus and the image of his system, or, still less, with indulging in psychological hairsplitting and point-scoring. Its concern is to distinguish in each system the determinations [*Bestimmungen*] themselves, the actual crystallizations pervading the whole system [*durchgehnden wirklichen Krystallisationen*], from the proofs, the justifications in argument, the self-presentation of the philosophers as they know themselves; to distinguish the

> silent, persevering mole of real philosophical knowledge [*den stumm fortwirkenden Maulwurf des wirklichen philosophischen Wissens*] from the voluble [*gesprächigen*], exoteric, multifariously behaving [*mannigfach gebährdenden*] phenomenological consciousness of the subject that is the vessel and energy of those developments. (*MEGA2* 4.1: 137/*MECW* 1: 506)[108]

This is an amazing passage, in what is a decidedly amazing paragraph. It does not appear in the dissertation itself in its extant form and there is no reason to think that it was in the submitted dissertation either. (I here quote only the first half of the paragraph; in the next chapter I quote and discuss the equally amazing second half, in which Marx develops the critical implications of the view of philosophy that he is here working toward.) For our present purposes, the most striking thing about the paragraph is Marx's claim (in the first sentence) that when one writes the history of philosophy one does not concern oneself with the individual personality of the philosopher. Rather, one attempts to latch onto the essence of the particular philosophical system that one is examining. One seeks the system's "determinations," which operate in a hidden, mole-like way, and which are to be distinguished from the chattering and all-too-visible multifariousness of philosophers' own individual consciousnesses.

In short, Marx insists on a de-individualized history of philosophy. Marx's commitment is to the writing of a history of philosophy that would focus unremittingly on the advance of "real philosophical knowledge." The focus should not be on what individual philosophers say *qua* individual philosophers. Rather, the focus should be on the logic of the ideas themselves, as they develop within the framework of the specific philosophical systems in question. This conception of the history of philosophy will be familiar to readers who have worked their way attentively through the present chapter. It is *Hegel's* conception of the history of philosophy, as stated at the beginning of his *Lectures on the History of Philosophy*, in a passage that I have already quoted:

> The events and actions of this history are . . . such that personality and individual character do not enter to any large degree into its content and matter. . . . In Philosophy, the less deserts and merits are accorded to the particular individual, the better is the history. . . ." (*LHP* 1: 1–2)

Marx's notebooks are largely taken up by quotations or paraphrases of the works that he is reading; a careful scholar, he usually provides page or section references also. He does not do so here. One can see the relation between the quotation from Marx that I have given and the passage from Hegel's *History of Philosophy*, but it is not a matter of mere copying. Rather, it seems clear that Marx has internalized Hegel's notion that a proper history focuses on the universal and necessary, leaving aside the particular and contingent.

The dissertation materials also bear witness to the fact that in Marx's view any investigation that claims the status of science must have a necessary foundation and necessary interrelations among its parts. As Hegel put it in *Lectures on the History of Philosophy*, "a mere collection of facts is not a science" (*LHP* 1: 31). Listen to what Marx writes in his dissertation in the course of comparing Epicurus with his predecessor, Democritus. According to Marx, in their philosophies of nature both philosophers started out from the same building blocks: atoms, and the void. But while in Marx's view Epicurus and Democritus taught "exactly the same science, in exactly the same way," Marx holds also that they "stand diametrically opposed in all that concerns truth, certainty, application of this science, and all that refers to the relationship between thought and reality in general" (*MEGA2* 1.1: 25/*MECW* 1: 38).

Particularly relevant for our purposes is the difference that Marx claims to find between Democritus' and Epicurus' respective conceptions of science, as well as between their conceptions of the objects with which science is supposed to deal. According to Marx, Democritus held that "the world of sensuous perception [*sinnlichen Wahrnehmung*]" is "the real and content-filled world." It is "the unique real object" of investigation, and "as such has value and significance." In consequence, Marx claims, Democritus is driven

> into *empirical observation*. Dissatisfied with philosophy, he throws himself into the arms of *positive knowledge*. . . . Cicero calls him a *vir eruditus* . . . the catalogue alone of his books given by Diogenes Laertius bears witness to his erudition. (*MEGA2* 1.1: 27/*MECW*: 1: 40)

Marx contends that Epicurus, on the other hand, "*has contempt for the positive sciences*" (*MEGA2* 1.1: 28/*MECW* 1: 41). (A "positive" science, in this context, is a science that focuses on what is immediately given—on whatever facts are lying about—and fails to get behind those facts to the rationality that underlies them). In Marx's view, the problem with empirical observation (and also with the erudition gained from reading a multitude of books) is that one's starting point is not a *necessary* starting point. Rather, one starts off from one's own particular observations, which are subject to all sorts of errors, or from erudition, which is simply a compendium of other people's opinions. According to Marx, Democritus' "*lust for knowledge*," combined with his "*dissatisfaction with true, i.e., philosophical, knowledge* . . . drives him far abroad," in search of whatever he might learn from "*Egyptian priests, Persian Chaldeans, and Indian gymnosophists.*" Epicurus, on the other hand, "leaves his garden in Athens scarcely two or three times," traveling only to visit friends. (*MEGA2* 1.1: 27–28/*MECW* 1: 41–42)

One's confidence in interpreting Marx is impaired by the fact that the chapter titled "General Difference in Principle between the Democritean and Epicurean

Philosophy of Nature" is missing from the extant dissertation manuscript. In that chapter Marx would presumably have dealt in more detail with the conflicting views of science that he saw in Democritus and Epicurus. But the general point seems clear. It is that Marx is committed to the notion that science pursues universal and necessary truth. The pursuit of universal and necessary truth requires that the investigator abstract himself away from mere particulars—not in order to enter a territory where "all cows are black," as Hegel once dismissively remarked of Schelling's notion of the Absolute, but rather to discern, in the form of "determinations" or "crystallizations" pervading an entire system, the necessity and universality that underlie those particulars. Thus, in the study of the history of philosophy one presumably does not *ignore* philosophers' personalities and self-presentations, but what one focuses on are the "determinations" that pervade each philosophical system. These determinations follow their own logic. Like a blind and silent mole burrowing through the ground, they are undeflected by the personalities of individual philosophers.

Marx's standards of universality and necessity were Hegel's standards (although in some ways Marx intensified the standards beyond Hegel).[109] It is my claim that these standards marked Marx's mind—in 1839–41 and throughout. The Hegel of the *History of Philosophy* lies behind Marx's dissertation, not only in regard to the content of the dissertation but in regard also to the criteria of rationality that it implicitly, and sometimes explicitly, recommends. Hegel's *Logic* is certainly present in what Marx writes in the dissertation materials (shades of his "extremely diligent attendance" *chez* Gabler in 1838), but the *Logic*, and everything else in Hegel, is filtered through the philosophical historiography that Marx had set himself the task of writing. For the *History of Philosophy* is the one dialectical history that Hegel wrote. There is no other. Hegel's rationality-criteria are displayed in his other works also, but only in this work did he come close to exemplifying these criteria in a historical work. As I shall show in chapter 4, the fact of Marx's affinity with this work casts light on the character of the so-called materialist conception of history that he (with Engels) articulated for the first time in 1845–46.

There are three points to be made here concerning Marxian history, all of them points of affinity between Marx and Hegel. They are important, I contend, for understanding Marx's project generally. They derive from Marx's (Hegelian) rationality-criteria:

1. All Marxian history has to be couched in universal terms. To quote a line from Marx's seventh "Notebook on Epicurean Philosophy": "Anyone who writes the history of philosophy separates essential from inessential. . . ."

(*MEGA2* 4.1: 137/*MECW* 1: 506). To "separate the essential from the inessential" is to push off to the side what is peculiar, local, marginal, strange. It is to highlight what is the same across boundaries of space and time. It is also to highlight those changing things that can be seen as fitting within a single overarching process. These are not objections to Marxian history—they are merely statements as to its character.

2. All Marxian history has to be couched in necessitarian terms. Hence, any element of chance has to be pushed off to the edges of the history. To be sure, particularly later in their careers, Marx (and Engels) were hardly unaware of chance (beginning in the 1850s, chance was becoming increasingly visible in contemporary science, e.g., in thermodynamics and in Darwinian evolution). But the thrust of Marxism was toward necessity.

   As I note elsewhere in this book, Marx had a deep commitment to freedom. It is hard to put together in a single coherent picture everything that Marx said and did. Perhaps the best that one can say here is that when Marx thought of freedom in relation to his theoretical concerns, he saw freedom as something that human beings achieve by becoming aware of the universal and necessary laws of nature and of society, and then actively using their knowledge of those laws to gain mastery over the natural and social world.

3. Perhaps most significant: Marx takes as his model for history-in-general a particular history that is rational by definition, since philosophy, which is the object of the history of philosophy, is itself aimed at the rational apprehension of reality. (Anything not so aimed—e.g., desire for fame, desire for riches, intellectual vanity, and personal peculiarities of whatever kind—is *not philosophy*, and hence is excluded from the history of philosophy in Hegel's understanding of the pursuit.) This had peculiar results, once Marx came to the conclusion (as he did by 1845–46) that the armature of history-in-general is the history of material production. For he was led, in advance, to conceptualize the history of material production as rational in the same sense that the history of philosophy is rational. (One might also claim that Marx's history is "teleological," but this is a claim that is only half true, as I shall try to show later.)

AGAINST ACCIDENT IN HISTORY

There is no need here to discuss the circumstances that made it utterly clear to Marx, in late 1841, that he would never have a career as a professor of philosophy. Suffice it to say that those circumstances pushed him out of philosophy before he had gotten at all far in his attempt to revise his dissertation for publication. It was in journalism that he landed, as we shall see in chapter 2. For the moment, though, I want to evoke a significant but now almost totally forgotten episode dating from much later in Marx's career, well beyond his intellectually formative years, an episode having to do with Charles Darwin. The incident gives us some sense of the continuing force of Marx's commitment to a necessitarian view of history.

Marx initially greeted Darwin's *The Origin of Species* (1859) with enthusiasm, suggesting to Engels in a letter of December 19, 1860, written right after his reading of the book, that it "contains the foundation in natural history for our view" (*MEW* 30: 131/*MECW* 41: 232). At least at first glance, Darwinian evolution does seem to bear some resemblance to Marx's notion of historical progress. But the impression is entirely false. Although some of Darwin's language in *The Origin of Species* suggests that there exists an evolutionary process in biology proceeding from lower forms to higher forms, these suggestions are window dressing: they conceal a theory that in no way supports the view that the Darwinian "transmutation of species" works in a progressive direction. The theory describes the survival or nonsurvival of biological variations that do not arise as a result of any inherent logic of nature. Further, the survival or nonsurvival of these variations is determined by whether the variations in question do or do not conduce to survival within the natural environment *as it exists at that moment*: whether the variations that survive conduce to the emergence of more beautiful or more complex biological forms is entirely irrelevant. For example, one could imagine a situation in which organisms highly resistant to nuclear radiation (say, cockroaches) survive, and almost all other organisms (including *homo sapiens*) are destroyed.

In short, the Darwinian mechanism of natural selection does not point in any particular direction, let alone from inferior forms to higher forms. Those passages in *The Origin of Species* that suggest such a progression (most notably in the final two paragraphs of the book) are more or less transparently connected to the view that a divine providence underlies the world—a view that Darwin himself privately rejected, although he was willing to deploy it if it would help make his theory more palatable to his contemporaries. Although Marx and Engels were willing to appeal to Darwinism for propagandistic purposes, Marx's attitude to Darwin was in fact ambivalent, as Richard Weikart has documented.[110] In particular, Marx viewed with suspicion the Darwinian "struggle for existence"—a notion that Darwin derived in part from his reading of the political economist Thomas Robert Malthus, whom Marx regarded as a blatant apologist for the existing order. But Marx and Engels did not publish their reservations concerning Darwin, and many Marxian socialists did try to adapt Darwinism to socialist use. It was relatively easy to do this because many commentators at the time did not grasp the more disturbing implications of Darwin's theory. Given Darwin's own language, it was easy to fit the theory into the framework of providentialism, with God superintending the evolutionary process. Such a view pulled the theory's fangs.[111] But Christian providentialism was anathema to Marx, and he was too smart to miss the fact that the implications of Darwin's theory went radically against basic assumptions underlying his own attempt to chart the collapse of capitalism and point the direction to the future.

Some of the limitations of Darwin, from Marx's point of view, are made startlingly clear by Marx's reaction to a book published in 1865, Pierre Trémaux's *Origin and Transformations of Man and Other Organisms*, which sought to revise Darwin's theory.[112] Trémaux and his book are now almost entirely forgotten, and deservedly so: the book, which tried to correlate biological evolution with different soil types, had absolutely no scientific value. Trémaux is relevant here for one reason alone: because Marx noticed and was attracted by his theory. As Weikart has pointed out, in a letter of August 7, 1866, Marx excitedly reported to Engels that Trémaux's book was not only "a very important work" but even "a *very important* advance over Darwin" (*MEW* 31: 248/*MECW* 42:304). Why was Marx so excited? In brief, it was because Trémaux held that "The perfection of organisms [*êtres*] is or becomes proportional to the degree of development [*élaboration*] of the ground [*sol*] on which they live" (Trémaux, 17–18). As Weikart notes, Trémaux's theory "dispensed with the Darwinian struggle for existence and natural selection," which Marx believed were projections of the conditions of bourgeois society back into nature: instead, evolution was attributed to the effect of the *sol* [ground, earth, soil]. But what is especially relevant here is that, as Weikart also notes, Trémaux's theory purported to explain evolution as "a necessary, lawful process," rather than as a process dependent on chance; or as Hervé Le Bras notes, Trémaux's theory allowed Marx to avoid "the chance character of evolution." Indeed, Marx was so taken by Trémaux that he seems to have still recommended the book even after Engels wrote to him insisting, correctly, that Trémaux's theory was nonsense.[113]

Admittedly, in the Marx of the 1860s there was a much more explicit appeal to natural science than can be found in the Marx of 1837–46. In the earlier period Marx's appeal to natural science was very unspecific. In the later period, in contrast, he explicitly evoked both biological evolution, as here, and physics, as in his evocations of "the law of economic motion" of modern society (preface to first edition of *Capital*, *MEGA2* 2.6: 67/*MECW* 35: 10/*CAP* 1: 92). Newtonian natural science had been highly successful in discovering laws of nature having an apparently universal validity and predictive force. The notion of natural-scientific necessity was consistent in some considerable degree with the Hegelian notion of a necessity of reason, and was thus something that Marx could easily graft onto the Hegelian notion. In both cases, chance is the enemy.

But Marx's Hegelian commitment was clearly more fundamental than his natural-scientific commitment. It was so not only because it came first but also, more important, because it underwrote the notion not just of an embedded rationality, but of an embedded *progress*, a necessary development toward something higher. The laws that Newtonian science discovered were not laws of development; on the contrary, they left no room for development, for they described the operations of an essentially unchanging system. In consequence, one has to say finally that the Hegelian commitment is the deeper one, for it was Hegel who offered Marx the vision of an embedded *historical* rationality, exemplified most clearly in the history of philosophy. Marx's commitment to such a rationality determined how he viewed History generally; underwrote his search for necessary laws in other, more limited domains of human life; and established the criteria by which he distinguished scientific knowledge from frivolous or ideologically driven opinion.

Chapter Two

Why Marx Rejected Politics

> All revolution—the *overthrow* of the existing ruling power and the *dissolution* of the old order—is a *political act*. But without revolution *socialism* cannot be made possible. It stands in need of this political act just as it stands in need of *destruction* and *dissolution*. But as soon as its *organizing activity* begins and its *goal*, its *soul* emerges, socialism throws its political mask aside.
>
> —Karl Marx, "Critical Marginal Notes on the Article 'The King of Prussia and Social Reform. By a Prussian'" (*MEGA2* 1.2: 463/*MECW* 3: 206/*EW* 420).

It is well known that Marx both called for and predicted the disappearance of politics and of what he called "the political state." Of course, *for now*, both the political state, and a politics that can be used in an attempt to overthrow the political state, decidedly do exist and are important. But Marx held that politics and the political state will not exist once socialism has been achieved. He made this claim for the first time in July 1844 in the article "Critical Marginal Notes on the Article 'The King of Prussia and Social Reform. By a Prussian'," in the passage that is cited in this chapter's epigraph. Marx writes: "as soon as [socialism's] *organizing activity* begins and its *goal*, its *soul* emerges," it "throws its *political* mask aside."

Similar claims appear in other writings. For example, in *The Communist Manifesto* (1848), Marx and Engels assert that after the proletarian revolution "the public power loses its political character" (*MEW* 4: 482/*MECW* 6: 505/*MER* 490/LPW 20). Marx makes a similar claim in *The Civil War in France* (1871). Although *The Civil War in France* is ostensibly an account of the failed Paris Commune of 1871, in light of its deficiencies as history or journalism it is perhaps better seen as an attempt on Marx's part to envisage a future socialism in more detail than he had done before. In *The Civil War in*

France Marx claims that under the Commune, the police force "was at once stripped of its political attributes"; police, judges, and other public servants were "responsible agents of society" rather than servants of the state (*MEW* 17: 339/*MECW* 22: 331/*LPW* 185). Here again Marx envisages a state, of sorts, under socialism—but a *nonpolitical* state. He returns to the theme in a polemical "conspectus," written in 1874–75, that deals with the anarchist Mikhail Bakunin's *Statism and Anarchy* (1873). In this piece of writing, Marx envisages the persistence of "government" within socialist society—but it will be a government in which the division of functions will take on "a business character [*ist Geschäftssache geworden*]"; in which there will be no "rulership [*Herrschaft*]"; in which elections will "completely lose their present political character"; and in which there will be "no state in the present political sense of the word" (*MEW* 18: 635/*MECW* 24: 519/*MER* 545).

The claim that Marx makes is that once things are set up aright, politics will no longer be needed. In Marx's lexicon and scale of values, politics is basically a bad thing. To be sure, from early in his career until late, he had an involvement with politics. He engaged in an almost unrelenting critique of political arrangements and policies in the present. He also engaged in a great deal of organizational, agitational, and propagandistic activity that could be called political. But he held that when the form of society that he looked forward to came into being, politics would disappear. Although Marx had various ends that he hoped, from time to time, to bring about *by means of* political action, he had no commitment to the processes of political deliberation, negotiation, and compromise as modes by which human beings, in the future socialist (communist) order, will decide what arrangements they are going to support and what actions they are going to undertake in their lives together as human beings.

Why did Marx reject politics (in the sense of excluding it from the future socialist order)? That is the question that the present chapter sets out to answer. The answer has a great deal to do with the Marxian rationalism explored in chapter 1. It is a two-pronged answer. First, Marx came to conclude, by 1844, that politics does not have an immanent rationality. Thus he concluded that politics is *defective*. Second, by 1845–46 Marx also concluded that science (natural and social) will tell us, unequivocally and without room for doubt or disagreement, what needs to be done. In other words, matters of state and administration can be so scientifically structured that deliberation will be unnecessary—the *machine*, which human beings will of course be directing, will function. Thus Marx concluded that politics is *unneeded*.

That is the short, rather peremptory answer to the question as to why Marx rejected politics. This chapter works out the answer in a more detailed way. It explores the impact of Marx's rationality-criteria, and of his commitment to embedded progress, on his apprehension of politics. It does so by following a certain Marxian trajectory. The trajectory begins with Marx's earliest philosophically significant piece of writing, namely, his November 1837 letter to his father. It considers thereafter his "Notebooks on Epicurean Philosophy" and doctoral dissertation, his journalism, and his attempts to critique Hegel's political theory and to write a political history of the French Revolution. These efforts led finally to Marx's conclusion that the mask of politics will eventually be cast aside. Of course, Marx's antipolitical trajectory cannot be viewed in isolation, for it connects in various ways with Marx's career in general and with the subsequent history of Marxism.

A COMBATIVE SPIRIT

Let us begin with the grounds for Marx's critical involvement with politics. Throughout all the phases of his life and career he displayed "an attitude"—an attitude of militancy. Marx's attitude quickly became visible to almost everyone who had significant contact with him. Marx himself recognized and acknowledged this aspect of his being from an early age. At the end of the long and deeply revealing letter of November 10–11, 1837, that Marx, in Berlin, wrote to his father in Trier, Marx refers to his "combative" or "militant" spirit (*kämpfende Geist*), which had often "overwhelmed" his heart and led him astray (*MEGA2* 3.1: 18/*MECW* 1: 21). It is hard to know where the militancy came from. Some commentators have suggested that it arose from a sense of alienation from his family, but the evidence for this claim is equivocal, and it can equally well be interpreted as an innate trait of character. What is undeniable is that an attitude of militancy was central to Marx's life, and to his work as well.[1]

Think of this militancy as having two components: a commitment to freedom and a commitment to critique. Given the tyrannical character of the regimes that were established in the twentieth century in Marx's name, the notion that Marx was committed to freedom may come as a surprise. And yet it is true: Marx's deepest commitment was indeed to freedom, which he unequivocally proclaimed to be his highest value. Freedom is a concern that arises again and again in his work, from earliest to latest. One might have thought that, as a socialist, he would also have had a powerful commitment to equality. But he did not. He sneered at those who, he thought, placed equality above freedom; in his eyes equality has value only insofar as it indicates the extension of an ever-greater degree of freedom to more and more people. It is interesting and characteristic that when in the mid-1860s, as part of a popular Victorian parlor game, his daughters induced him to answer a questionnaire describing his character traits and his favorite and least favorite things, he declared that the vice he most detested was servility.[2]

To say what Marx meant by freedom would require a book by itself. But the essential features of Marx's conception of freedom are clear. First, he was committed to what has sometimes been called "freedom from," or negative freedom. In other words, he opposed the imposition of external constraints upon the individual. Second and perhaps more important, he was committed to "freedom for," or positive freedom. In other words, people should not only not be interfered with. More than this, they should be able to go out into the world and engage in activities that they want to engage in, that fulfill their needs, and that enable them to become better, happier, more interesting, more highly developed persons than they were before. Note a famous passage in *The German Ideology* (1845–46) in which Marx looks forward to a time when, with "society" regulating "the general production," it becomes "possible for me to do one thing today and another tomorrow, to hunt in the morning, fish in the afternoon, rear cattle in the evening, criticize after dinner, just as I have a mind to" (*MEW* 3: 33/*MECW* 5: 47/*MER* 160). This is only one of dozens of passages in which Marx (and Engels) articulate their commitment to freedom. It is not at all wrong to suggest that the whole of their project was directed toward freedom's infinite unfolding.[3]

Second, throughout his career Marx was oriented in an adversarial way toward the existing social and political world. A fundamental discontent with the way things are marked both his work and his life. A negating impulse runs through his life: the only wholehearted exceptions were his relationships with his wife, née Jenny von Westphalen; with his daughters Jenny, Laura, and Eleanor; and with his amazingly tolerant, helpful, and upbeat collaborator Engels. From early in his career he was known for the vigor and power of his arguing. Usually he was engaged in a work of demolition. Particularly during the first half of the 1840s, when he was moving rapidly from one not entirely thought-out position to the next, it is striking how quickly he would repudiate philosophers and activists with whom, only a short while before, he had been closely associated. For example, he was closely connected with his doctoral mentor, the Hegelian theologian Bruno Bauer, in the years 1839–42, but he vehemently attacked Bauer in "On the Jewish Question" (published February 1844), in *The Holy Family* (published February 1845), and in *The German Ideology* (1845–46; not published). Equally striking is how in 1843–44 he used, in an imaginative and wide-ranging way, the critical humanist work of Feuerbach, and then rejected Feuerbach in 1845. Critique is significant for Marx in a broader sense as well. Robert C. Tucker has suggested that the "idea of *Kritik*" is "a great unifying theme running through the writings of classical Marxism . . . a key to the continuity of the thought of Marx and Engels. . . ." As Tucker notes, it is a theme explicitly signaled in the titles of many important Marx writings—among others, the introduction to "A Contribution to the Critique of Hegel's *Philosophy of Right*"; *A Contribution to the Critique of Political Economy*; *Capital: A Critique of Political Economy*; and, inimitably, *The Holy Family: A Critique of Critical Criticism* (*MER* xxvii–xxix).

Freedom and criticism, then, are leitmotifs of Marx's work. These concerns were already in place early in Marx's intellectual development: they are visible almost from the time of his acceptance, in summer 1837, into the "Doctors' Club" of critically minded Hegelians at the University of Berlin. Marx's letter to his father of November 1837 provides the first documentary indication of his stance in the wake of that involvement. Evolution toward freedom was a theme of Hegel's philosophy, and the group with which Marx was now connected aimed to assist this forward movement. By about 1840 this tendency had become an identifiable intellectual movement, the "Young Hegelians."[4] In the period up to 1844 Marx devoted much of his critical energy to the realm of politics. (Or rather, he *thought* that he was addressing politics. I shall try to indicate the extent to which he missed seeing what politics is about.)

Marx's tremendous concern for freedom and his tremendous love of criticizing go along with the rationality-criteria that I discussed in chapter 1—universality, necessity, predictivity, and progress by contradiction. Criticism requires standards. In the period up to 1844 Marx was intent on applying these rationality-criteria to politics. Marx's early wish seems to have been to give an *immanently rational* account of politics—that is, an account that would discover the rationality of politics on the level of politics itself. Such an account would then serve as a touchstone for the critique of politics. "Critical Marginal Notes on 'The King of Prussia and Social Reform'" signals the end of this theoretical effort. (To be sure, the "Critical Marginal Notes" do not signal the end of Marx's critique of current politics, for that critique continued unrelentingly, but with its rational foundation located at another, "deeper" level—that of economics.) The beginning of Marx's attempt to give an immanently rational account of politics is more difficult to date. But the attempt certainly has foreshadowings in Marx's doctoral dissertation, toward which he began to work in early 1839 (only in early 1842 did he wholly abandon the idea of revising it for publication). Even in his purely academic writing, Marx obviously hoped to have some influence on the actual course of political events; in this sense, his dissertation was already political.

Marx's conception of politics, I shall argue as we proceed, always remained indentured to the criteria of universality, necessity, and predictivity that came to him from philosophy. In this sense Marx never "left" philosophy, although he certainly attempted to do so (I allude to Brudney's memorable title, *Marx's Attempt to Leave Philosophy*). Marx thus lived in an intellectual world different from the one many of us know today. At least, this is how we must see Marx if we take seriously Michel Foucault's idea that "philosophy becomes modern by renouncing the effort to ground the transitory in the eternal."[5] Marx is not, in Foucault's sense of "modern," a modern philosopher at all, for despite everything, Marx emphatically did attempt to ground the transitory in the eternal.[6] Since for Marx this grounding had its roots in philosophy, we must turn now to consider how philosophy and the hope for change were connected in his thought. I shall then consider, in turn, four phases in Marx's engagement with politics, associated with Trier, with the radical Hegelianism of Berlin, with Marx's early journalism, and finally with a set of attempts on his part to theorize and to rationally narrativize politics. These phases were marked first by an alliance between political concerns and philosophy, and then by a detaching of the two, as Marx came to conclude that political events, practices, and institutions were not up to the level that a rational grasp of social reality demanded.

HEGELIANISM, RATIONALITY, AND THE HOPE FOR CHANGE

The question that centrally concerned Marx the theorist was How can we come to understand the world rationally? Understanding the world rationally involved, for him, a number of interconnected matters. At the broadest level it meant discovering the rationality that lies embedded in the world. More specifically, understanding the world rationally meant understanding the world in such a way as to conform to Marx's rationality-criteria. That is, the knowledge in question must be universal. It must unfold in a necessary way, akin to the unfolding of a syllogism or geometrical proof. Following from the criteria of universality and necessity, it must be predictive. Finally, it, and the movement that it describes, must be dialectical—it must be a matter of a historical progression that moves forward by contradictions. I showed in chapter 1 that Marx was deeply indebted to Hegel for these criteria (although Marx's attachment to the idea of natural science may have intensified the hold on him of predictivity in particular). I also showed that there is reason to think that the model for Marx's version of these criteria was Hegel's *Lectures on the History of Philosophy*, although, to be sure, the criteria are also manifested, albeit less clearly and fully, in Hegel's other writings.[7]

One might ask why Marx was attracted to Hegelian philosophy in the first place. The question cannot be answered in any definitive way; at the same time, a number of possibly true answers suggest themselves. One answer has to do with the sheer nerve, brilliance, and range of Hegel's work. Hegel's scientific project—for he certainly saw his project as scientific—was articulated in emulation of Descartes's project, by which modern philosophy was invented.[8] At greater distance, it seems also to have been articulated in rivalry with Aristotle, the ancient "master of those that know."

But the magnitude of Hegel's ambition is only part of the story, although an important part. More relevant here is the fact that Hegel's philosophy was something that social and political radicals, discontented with the existing order of things, could use for their own purposes. Already in his letter to his father of November 1837, Marx claimed that Hegelian philosophy offers, in contrast to the philosophies of Kant and Fichte, a way of overcoming the opposition "between what is and what ought to be" and of seeking "the Idea in the real [*im Wirklichen*] itself" (*MEGA2* 3.1: 10, 15–16/*MECW* 1: 11, 18/*MER* 7). It is not simply that Hegel saw the world as rational; more important is the fact that he saw the world's rationality as *developing over time*. For example, in the concluding section of his *Lectures on the History of Philosophy* Hegel declares that "spirit alone is progress," that it "inwardly works forward [*ist er innerliches Fortarbeiten*]," that it involves "an intellectual [*geistiges*], rational, forward advance [*Fortschreiten*]" (*LHP* 3: 546–47/1836 German ed., 15: 685 [for bibliographical data concerning the German edition see chapter 1, notes 64 and 77]). Hegel's notion that there is a progressive force embedded in the world makes his philosophy relevant to the stance of the radical intellectual. What better way to overcome the opposition between what is and what ought to be than by striving to bring the latter into existence—while knowing that one's efforts are authorized by history? For the possessor of a combative spirit, what better authorization could exist than this? Accordingly, very early in Marx's career, Hegelian philosophy satisfied a double imperative for him—the imperative of science and a still diffuse activist imperative to change the existing order of things.

Of course, this was not Hegel's view of his philosophy; at any rate, it was not the *older* Hegel's *publicly expressed* view. But Hegel was nothing if not ambiguous. In one of those striking *obiter dicta* that sometimes leap from his pages, Hegel declares in the preface to his *Philosophy of Right* (1820) that "the owl of Minerva [i.e., philosophy] begins its flight only with the onset of dusk." In other words, philosophy can sum up the day, but it cannot point the way forward to the next day.[9] Here we have a backward-looking, or "epimethean," view of philosophy. The later Hegel was not a radical—but he also was not a reactionary. On the one hand, he could be deeply cautious, indeed obsequious, in his dealings with governmental authorities. Thus in a note written on the occasion of his sending a copy of the newly published *Philosophy of Right* to the (formerly reformist) Prussian Chancellor Prince Hardenberg, he claims that his scientifically derived and theoretically presented account of "those principles generally required by the nature of the state" aims at

> showing agreement with the principle that the Prussian state—belonging to which necessarily gives me great satisfaction—has had the good fortune of having upheld and of still upholding. . . . Philosophy in its own sphere of action . . . may give immediate support to the Government's beneficent intentions. . . . Your Highness's most humble G. W. F. Hegel. . . .[10]

On the other hand, it is undeniable that Hegel felt constrained by the conservatism, and in particular by the censorship, of the Prussian state, and at times made his frustration known.[11]

The notion that philosophy comes at nightfall could evoke, further, not just reformist thoughts but the more radical thought, "promethean" in character, that a shape of life had grown old and needed replacing by something new.[12] Thus one can see philosophy less as summing up the past than as exposing and attacking the contradictions of the existing order, with the aim of destroying that order. Indeed, on occasion the younger Hegel himself saw things in precisely this way. Consider his assertion in an 1808 letter that "theoretical work . . . accomplishes more in the world than practical work. Once the realm of representations [*Vorstellungen*] is revolutionized, actuality will not hold out. . . ."[13] This is not philosophy as "the owl of Minerva"; this is philosophy taking a prompting role in pushing the world forward. As a Berlin professor in the 1820s Hegel would never have said such a thing: he was too comfortably installed in his professorial chair and too aware of the task that this civil service position imposed upon him—namely, to support the Prussian state. But the radical implications were there to be seen, whatever the austere garb of the Berlin professor. And after Hegel's death in 1831 it hardly mattered what Hegel *himself* had said: those radicals who found succor in his philosophy entered into it in their own radical spirit and delivered out radical conclusions from it. Characteristically, they did so by emphasizing the moment of contradiction within the dialectic, whereas moderates and conservatives in the Hegelian camp emphasized the degree to which the present order of things had brought about a resolution of previous contradictions.[14]

It was the poet Heinrich Heine who in three scattered statements made between 1834 and 1854 most brilliantly captured Hegel's capacity to appear in sharply different guises—as he indeed did to the various Hegelian camps present on the intellectual scene in the 1830s. John Toews amusingly juxtaposes three different yet connected Hegels, each of them pointed out in Heine's writing and each of them represented by an appropriate Heine quotation. There is the servile and accommodationist Hegel, who, Heine suggests, "bestowed on the existing order of church and state some all too dubious vindications." There is the critical and progressive Hegel, whom Heine characterizes as one among the "monks of atheism": this Hegel surreptitiously interprets the Hegelian dictum, "everything that is, is rational" to mean "everything that is rational must be." Finally, there is the revolutionary and transcendent Hegel, who (Heine writes, in the wake of the failure of the revolutions of 1848) incubated the eggs that hatched the birds that intoned a new music that was *not* the music of Hegelian philosophy itself.[15]

The literary scholar Margaret Rose has shown that from an early age Marx was attracted to Heine. Like Marx, Heine (b. 1797) was a Rhinelander. He was also a Jew, who opted for baptism in 1825 in order to avoid the professional disabilities. His lyricism, his irony, and his independence of mind were striking. Marx would also have noted the attempted banning of Heine's works, along with those of the other members of the "Young Germany" school, by the Federal German Diet in 1835.[16] In the second half of the 1830s a number of German intellectuals were working out for themselves the progressive possibilities that Hegelian philosophy seemed to offer. These possibilities were the critical and revolutionary ones observed and noted by Heine. One cannot say that Heine influenced Marx in the matter of Hegel interpretation: it is better to say that Heine and Marx were part of a common intellectual community and thus were aware of, and potentially open to, common influences and thoughts. Still, no one articulated the Hegel who counted for the very early Marx more insightfully or vividly than Heine did. Heine's two more radical versions of "Hegel"—the Hegel who wished to use philosophy as a critical weapon to expose the irrationality still existing within the world, and the Hegel who was incubating the eggs that would hatch the revolutionary and transcendent birds that would turn against philosophy itself—are both present in Marx in the period during which he was working toward his dissertation (1839–41).

The critical use of Hegelian philosophy was a hallmark of the work of Marx's doctoral mentor Bruno Bauer in the very late 1830s and early 1840s. In 1840 and 1841 Bauer and Marx were close to each other both intellectually and personally. Bauer, who in 1839 had gone to the University of Bonn to take up a lectureship in theology, urged Marx to obtain his doctorate promptly, with a view to obtaining, with Bauer's help, a lectureship in philosophy at Bonn. "The terrorism of true theory will clear the field," Bauer declares in a letter to Marx of March 28, 1841; in another letter of three days later he asserts that it would be "madness" (*Unsinn*) for Marx to devote himself "to a practical career," for "theory is now the most effective practice and we cannot yet predict in what a great manner it will become practical" (*MEGA2* 3.1: 353, 355).

In an attempt both to exemplify critical philosophy and to reveal Hegel to be a critical philosopher himself, Bauer wrote a short book, *The Trumpet of the Last Judgement against Hegel the Atheist and Antichrist*, published anonymously in November 1841. Here Bauer worked out the idea that behind the mask of the public Hegel, who presented himself as a defender of the existing order, there is a critical Hegel intent on undermining that order. He highlights this imagined critical Hegel by the puckish tactic of writing in the voice of a deeply offended Pietist who has discerned that, for all his professions of attachment to the state and to established religion, Hegel was actually (horror of horrors) an atheist in disguise.[17] The Pietist rejects "Hegel" because of this; Bauer's intent was of course to celebrate "Hegel's" supposed atheism. In August–September 1841, Marx helped Bauer in his work on the *The Trumpet of the Last Judgement*, and some thought that it was their joint work when it was published; and the two friends planned to collaborate on a sequel to *Trumpet*, to be called *Hegel's Hatred of Religious and Christian Art and His Destruction of All the Laws of the State*, but the work was never written (DRAP 1: 10).

Marx accepted the notion that philosophy can and should play a critical role in society. In his dissertation materials he is emphatic about this point. In a passage that appears in the extant dissertation manuscript, but that was probably not part of the version that was sent to the University of Jena in early April 1841, he writes that

> the practice of philosophy is itself *theoretical*. It is the *critique* that measures the individual existence by the essence, the particular reality by the Idea. (*MEGA2* 1.1: 68/*MECW* 1: 85/*MER* 10)

Marx continues with a contrast between what he calls the "liberal party," which is "the party of the concept," and another side, which he identifies as "positive philosophy," that is attached to the "*non-concept*, the moment of reality." The "liberal party" measures existing reality against the standards established by philosophy; thus it "maintains as its main determination the concept and the principle of philosophy." Since it has a critical standard that it can deploy against reality, "the liberal party achieves real progress," whereas positive philosophy, which merely accepts whatever exists, goes nowhere (*MEGA2* 1.1: 69/*MECW* 1: 86). In short, critical philosophy makes the world more rational; it is the means by which progress is made to occur.[18]

Yet, without at all rejecting the notion of a critical philosophy, by 1841 at the latest Marx also articulated the third of the stances that Heine identified, for he envisaged philosophy being transformed by its encounter with the world. (One might call these two positions—namely, philosophy criticizing and philosophy being transformed—"critical Hegelianism" and "transcending Hegelianism" respectively.) In this respect Marx went beyond his mentor Bauer, who, as Daniel Brudney notes, was "never hostile to (Hegelian) philosophy as such."[19] Marx's "transcending" of Hegelian philosophy is well known and needs no extended discussion here. Suffice it to say that Marx envisages something that already comes close to the notion of a transcending of philosophy as early as his fifth "Notebook on Epicurean Philosophy," which probably dates from summer semester (April–August) 1839 (*MEGA2* 4.1: 566). In the extant dissertation manuscript, in a passage that appears in close proximity to the passage quoted above, identifying philosophy as "the *critique* that measures . . . individual existence," there is a clear assertion that a critical philosophy will also be a philosophy that goes *beyond* philosophy. And the notion of an end to philosophy is reprised in a journalistic article of July 1842, to be noted below.

The most striking of this set of passages—because it comes first and thus has an aura of excited discovery about it—is the one appearing in the fifth "Notebook on Epicurean Philosophy" (misidentified as the sixth notebook in editions prior to *MEGA2*). The passage has something of the brilliance of the "Estranged Labor and Private Property" section of the "Economic and Philosophical Manuscripts" (1844), to which I shall turn in chapter 3; it is reminiscent also of Marx's "Theses on Feuerbach" (1845). The passage extends for several pages. Indeed, after his first substantive paragraph, Marx engages in a remarkable and, so far as I know, never-repeated exercise in intellectual exuberance, gratuitously translating almost everything in the paragraph into Latin—a two-finger exercise for Marx, but striking nonetheless. Elements of the 1839 passage reappear later in the dissertation manuscript, and they appear again in the 1842 newspaper article. Thus we have some reason to believe that Marx was particularly attached to the line of reflection that the passage offers.

The passage reads as follows. I quote it at some length, although I omit parts of it and break it off well before before its end:

> As in the history of philosophy [*Philosophiegeschichte*] there are nodal points [*Knotenpunkte*] that raise philosophy in itself to concretion [*Konkretion*], attend to abstract principles as a totality [*Totalität*], and thus break off the rectilineal process [*und so den Fortgang der graden Linie abbrechen*], so also there are moments when philosophy turns its eyes to the external world, and no longer conceptualizes it, but rather, in the manner of a practical person, weaves, as it were, intrigues with the world, emerges from the transparent kingdom of Amenthes [thoughtlessness] and throws itself on the breast of the worldly Siren. That is the carnival of philosophy, whether it disguises itself as a dog like the Cynic, in priestly vestments like the Alexandrian, or in fragrant spring array like the Epicurean. It is essential that philosophy should then wear character masks . . . just as Prometheus, having stolen fire from heaven, begins to build houses and to settle upon the earth, so philosophy, expanded to be the whole world, turns against the world of appearance [*die erscheinende Welt*]. So it is now with the philosophy of Hegel.

> While philosophy has sealed itself off to form a . . . total world, the determination of this totality is conditioned by the general development of philosophy . . . thus the totality of the world in general is divided within itself, and this division is carried to the extreme, for spiritual existence has been freed, has been enriched to universality. . . . The world confronting a philosophy total in itself is therefore a world torn apart.
>
> He who does not acknowledge this historical necessity must be consistent and deny that men can live at all after a total philosophy, or he must hold that the dialectic of measure as such is the highest category of the self-knowing spirit and assert, with some of the Hegelians who understand our master wrongly, that *mediocrity* is the normal manifestation of the absolute spirit. . . . (*MEGA2* 4.1: 99–100/*MECW* 1: 491/*MER* 10–11 [fragment])

There is much in what I have quoted that invites comment—for example, Marx's evocations of universality and necessity and his insistence that we need to intensify contradictions rather than muffle them. There is more in the rest of the fifth Notebook that deserves comment as well, including Marx's praise, moving in its seriousness, of Aristotle, Spinoza, Hegel, and other philosophers committed to the universal (as distinguished from what is limitedly empirical and specific), to rationality (including "the rationality of nature" [*MEGA2* 4.1: 104/*MECW* 1: 496]), and to science, and intent on expounding their principles with a consistency that reveals (rather than hides) the resulting contradictions.

Here I want to focus on only two points. First, note Marx's claim that from time to time philosophy, examining itself, manages to see how its own abstract principles are actually inseparable parts of a larger whole, a concrete totality. Hegel's concretization and historicization of Aristotelian logic, discussed in chapter 1, can be seen as arising from just such a turning of philosophy to an examination of itself—in the form, of course, of an examination of its own history, an examination sensitive to how specific facts can be seen as parts of larger wholes. Although the matter cannot be properly addressed in this book, it should at least be noted that Marx's investigation of capitalism would have been inconceivable without a similar methodological attentiveness to totality.

Second, note Marx's evocation of those moments "when philosophy turns its eyes to the external world." There is some danger of mistaking the character of this turn to the external world. It is easy to think that critique and the turn to the external world are simultaneous. But they are not: the first manifestation of critique is in philosophy's critical examination of the history of philosophy itself. This is made clear in another passage, in the seventh "Notebook on Epicurean Philosophy," where Marx alludes to the "critical element [*kritisches Moment*]" that is required if the history of philosophy is to be expounded scientifically (*MEGA2* 4.1: 137/*MECW* 1: 506).[20] Marx is *not* here envisaging a movement from a theoretical philosophy that focuses on intraphilosophical issues (e.g., on issues of ontology, or on the history of philosophy) to a critical philosophy that focuses on the world. On the contrary, in Marx's view philosophy that examines itself in the proper way is *already* critical. This is an important point, because it underscores the continuity between a philosophy that examines its own history and a philosophy that examines the world of social and political phenomena, including the history of those phenomena.

When critical philosophy "turns against the world of appearance" it does so in the name of an essence that philosophy alone has grasped. Philosophy measures the world against this essence and finds the world wanting. Philosophy alone is capable of grasping the essence—which is not something that philosophy imposes *on* the world, but something that it discovers *in* the world. Marx is here articulating a quintessentially activist conception of philosophy. Underlying the activism that is displayed here is Marx's deep commitment to the possibility of knowing the world in its essence.[21] Or perhaps it is the reverse: perhaps Marx's desire for change underlies his rationalism. In any case, the rationalism supports the activism, no matter which came first.

The long passage from the fifth "Notebook," quoted earlier, strongly suggests that Marx is at the very least a critical Hegelian, cunningly intent on masking himself in order to render his criticism more effective ("*Es ist . . . da wesentlich, Kharaktermasken anzulegen*" [*MEGA2* 4.1: 99/*MECW* 1: 491/*MER* 11]). Material in the dissertation manuscript itself (material possibly written in 1841) shows him in the guise of a transcending Hegelian as well. (Admittedly, the critical moment, in which one subjects philosophy to critique, and the "transcending" moment, in which one goes beyond philosophy, are not sharply divided from each other: the latter is little more than an intensification of the former.) For in the dissertation manuscript Marx holds not only that philosophy turns against "*die erscheinende Welt*" (thus repeating the terminology of the fifth "Notebook"), but also that the world turns against philosophy. The passage is well known to Marx specialists, but it is still worth quoting. It comes right after the passage, already quoted, where Marx asserts that "the practice of philosophy is itself *theoretical*." Critical philosophy, Marx continues, "turns itself as will against the world of appearance." In so doing it seeks to "realize" itself—that is, to "make itself real [*sich zu verwirklichen*]." But the consequence is not only that the world is changed in order to meet the critical demands of philosophy. On the contrary, it also happens

> that as the world becomes philosophical, philosophy also becomes worldly [*daß das Philosophisch-werden der Welt zugleich ein Weltlich-werden der Philosophie*], that

> its realization [*Verwirklichung*] is also its loss [*Verlust*], that what it struggles against on the outside is its own inner deficiency, that in the very struggle it falls precisely into those defects which it fights as defects in the opposite camp, and that it can only overcome these defects by falling into them. That which it opposes and that which it fights is always the same as itself, only with factors inverted. (*MEGA2* 1.1: 68/*MECW* 1: 85/*MER* 10)

In other words, philosophy changes the world; but the world also changes philosophy, and in doing so eliminates philosophy as a distinct enterprise.

To be sure, Marx continued to see himself as a philosopher, even though, to the extent that he was a transcending Hegelian, he paradoxically looked forward to the "loss" of philosophy. He had hoped since 1838 to obtain a university post in philosophy, although it is easy to see after the fact that success in this was improbable and perhaps impossible. Under the conservative regime of Friedrich Wilhelm IV, who came to the throne in June 1840, even ordinary Hegelians were unwelcome. Still, Marx's itinerary from 1838 through much of 1841 pointed in an academic direction. Indeed, he moved to Bonn in July 1841 in order to be close to Bauer and to the hoped-for position at the University of Bonn. Only in October–November 1841, when Bauer's atheism finally led to his suspension from the Bonn faculty, did Marx abandon his hope for a university post (DRAP 1: 10).

The point here is that when, in 1842, Marx turned to oppositional journalism he did so *faute de mieux*, as a second-best choice after his first choice had been withdrawn from him. His move to journalism, moreover, did not mean an abandonment of philosophy: essentially, it meant the continuation of his philosophical project. Thus Marx the journalist was still committed to a double operation, rooted in philosophy: the "becoming worldly" of philosophy and the "becoming philosophical" of the world. The philosophy in question was articulated in a universalistic and necessitarian way—an articulation made possible by the fact that its initial object was nothing other than the history of philosophy itself, defined as the pursuit of universal and necessary knowledge. It was such a philosophy that he now deployed in an effort to grasp, and also change, the world outside philosophy.

That Marx continued to see his project as philosophical after he had abandoned the possibility of an academic career is emphatically shown by one of his earliest journalistic articles, alluded to earlier, appearing in the *Rheinische Zeitung* in July 1842. Titled "The Leading Article in No. 179 of the *Kölnische Zeitung*," the article attacks the positive view that a Catholic newspaper, a rival to the *Rheinische Zeitung*, had taken of press censorship. Among other things Marx discusses a question that the *Kölnische Zeitung* had posed: "Ought philosophy to discuss religious matters also in newspaper articles?" The *Kölnische Zeitung* claimed that philosophy has no role to play in the discussion of public affairs. In his response Marx directly picks up on his line of thought in the passage in his dissertation manuscript quoted earlier, suggesting that when philosophy "comes into contact and interaction with the real world of its day" it becomes "the philosophy of the contemporary world [*die Philosophie der gegenwärtigen Welt*]." Repeating an idea that had appeared in his dissertation, he claims "that philosophy becomes worldly and the world becomes philosophical [*daß die Philosophie weltlich und die Welt philosophisch wird*]" when this happens. (*MEGA2* 1.1: 183/*MECW* 1: 195) Philosophy remained determinative for his project, even after he had left the official domain of philosophy, for the world that looked back at Marx when he looked at it through the lens of philosophical thinking was none other than a world potentially amenable to rational transformation. Insofar as some aspects of the world would never fit such a transformation, they were destined to disappear from sight.

MARX'S POLITICAL BEGINNINGS: TRIER

It makes sense to see the young Marx's engagement with politics as involving four moments or phases, which overlap in various ways. First, there is the *Rhenish* moment, which involves family and personal experience in Marx's hometown of Trier, as well as the complaints of progressives throughout the Rhineland against what they saw as retrogressive tendencies both in Berlin, far to the east, and among their conservative Catholic *confrères* in the Rhineland itself. Second, there is the *radical Hegelian* moment, associated above all with Marx's studies at the University of Berlin (October 1836–March 1841). Third, there is the *journalistic* moment, associated with his editing of the *Rheinische Zeitung* between October 1842 and March 1843, but also involving other journalistic work, into which Marx plunged as early as January 1842. Finally, there is the *theorizing* moment, which involved an attempt on Marx's part to understand politics as a (critical) philosopher. Marx's efforts along this line began as early as November 1841, when he began to think of critiquing Hegel's *Philosophy of Right*, but his journalistic activities brought those efforts to a halt. Then, between March 1843 (when the suppression of the *Rheinische Zeitung* gave him more free time) and August 1844, he devoted a great deal of effort to the attempt to understand politics philosophically. This attempt took two directions. First, he sought to apply, to political theory and to contemporary politics, the reductionist "genetic-critical" method (see chapter 1) that he had seen Feuerbach apply to religion and to Hegelian philosophy. And, as is less well known (because his efforts in this domain were completely abortive), he also attempted to come to an acceptable historical-theoretical understanding of by far the most momentous political event of his time, the great French Revolution of 1789 and after.

In the next few sections I shall look at these phases. They are central to answering the question Why did Marx reject politics? Of course, the narrative of Marx's life and career has been told many times before, most recently in the biography by Francis Wheen.[22] In this chapter, and throughout this book, I proceed topically more than I do narratively, presupposing the Marx narratives that have already been written. I give enough in the way of contextual fact to allow my argument to be followed; readers who want more information will usually find it in the earlier studies that I have copiously cited in this book's endnotes.

The established Marx narrative begins in Trier, a regional town pleasantly situated on the Moselle River, with a population of about 15,000 in 1818.[23] For the topic Marx and politics, two intertwined facts are of fundamental importance: Marx's Jewish origins, and the final defeat of Napoleon in 1815. Marx's father, Heinrich (Herschel) Marx, was a son of the rabbi of Trier, and his elder brother, Karl's uncle, served as rabbi of Trier until his death in 1829. Pursuing an unusual path for a Jew at this time, Heinrich Marx qualified as a lawyer by 1814. But in the wake of Napoleon's defeat in 1815 at Waterloo, the Rhineland came under the control of the conservative and bureaucratic Kingdom of Prussia, whereas it had previously been under the more detached administration of France.[24] This led to a problem, for the Prussians were serious about enforcing an edict of March 1812 that made it entirely explicit that Jews could not occupy positions in the legal system or other state offices (only recently had Jews begun even to *think* about occupying such positions; the edict was responding to a recently emerged impulse toward integration). After all, Prussia was a Christian state. It still claimed to be based on the divine right of kings. It had officially sanctioned Christian churches that were answerable to the King and his ministers. Heinrich Marx's associates considered him an honest and capable colleague, and would have been happy for him to continue serving in his post as a Jew. The edict did allow the possibility of exceptions. The President of the Provincial Supreme Court came through in April 1816, interviewed Heinrich Marx, and recommended to the Prussian Minister of Justice that an exception be made for him. But the Minister of Justice was against exceptions, and when the answer came back it was "no." Consequently, Heinrich Marx converted to the Evangelical [Lutheran] church in 1817 or 1818, and his children and wife were baptized later, in 1824 and 1825 respectively. As Karl Marx grew up, he would have become gradually more aware of the circumstances of the conversion.

By the time he reached adolescence, Marx would also have become aware of an important political issue in Trier and in the Rhineland generally in the

1830s. Aside from issues of religion, what drove Rhenish politics was the tension between some local notables, influenced by liberal political ideas and self-interest, who wanted liberal constitutional reforms and a greater sensitivity on the government's part to new commercial interests, and the Prussian civil and military establishment, which was as suspicious of Rhenish liberals as it was of Rhenish Catholics, and which was disinclined in any case to diminish the paternalistic power of the state. After the French revolution of 1830 overthrew the Bourbon monarchy there, a call for reform surfaced in Trier. Progressively oriented locals favored an increased measure of popular representation—in other words, a legislature with actual legislative powers—whereas the Prussian government wanted to be unhindered by such nuisances. Various local notables were influenced by Enlightenment ideas and by Kant and Schiller, as well as by the French Saint-Simonian movement with its attachment to freedom, science, and sensuality.

In January 1834 (when Karl was just short of sixteen) Heinrich Marx participated in a banquet in favor of representative government sponsored by a local social and cultural club. Indeed, he gave a brief talk—a toast, in fact—in which he referred to the provincial assemblies that the government had deigned to establish in the 1820s by the term *Volksvertretung* [representation of the people] rather than by the officially approved term, *Ständesversammlung* [assembly of estates]. *Volksvertretung* implied the equal representation of all citizens, and was thus anathema to the regime; *Ständesversammlung* left intact the traditional distinction between the noble *Stand* (estate) and everyone else.[25] This banquet, and a more radical banquet twelve days later at which Heinrich put in a brief appearance, attracted the unfavorable attention of the authorities, who made known their displeasure. In the face of official disapproval, Heinrich Marx and his friends foreswore involvement in any more banquets.

A full ten years later, Marx referred in "Critical Marginal Notes on 'The King of Prussia and Social Reform'" to an event that had occurred in July 1843. On this occasion, in the wake of a banquet in Düsseldorf honoring the Flemish Parliament (a pretext for some low-key liberal agitation), the Prussian government put forward an Order in Council forbidding state employees from participating in such banquets. Marx commented scathingly on the acquiescent local response to the order, noting that "the burning desire of the entire liberal bourgeoisie for freedom of the press and a constitution" had been "suppressed without the aid of *a single soldier*, in a country where passive obedience is the order of the day" (*MEGA2* 1.2: 446/*MECW* 3: 190/*EW* 403)
One cannot help but think that in writing "Critical Marginal Notes" K
Marx must have had in mind not only the events of 1843–44 but also the
1834. It is clear that one cannot use a text of 1844 to establish Marx's

mind in the 1830s. But already in November 1837 he had described his spirit as *kämpfend*, "combative." To be sure, he did not seem to have politics specifically in mind in this passage from his letter to his father. But given the circumstances of his family, his father's own (tentative) political sympathies, and his subsequent history, we are justified in inferring some measure of political concern on Marx's part already at the age of nineteen and a half.

EMBEDDED RATIONALITY DEFENDED: THE POLITICS OF MARX'S DOCTORAL DISSERTATION

In October 1835 Marx went off to study at the nearby University of Bonn, but he soon decided to transfer to the University of Berlin, to which he moved in October 1836. The University of Berlin, which the Prussian government had founded in 1810 in the wake of Prussia's defeat by France, was the best university in Germany, with more eminent professors than any other. On the consent form allowing the transfer, signed by Marx's father in July 1836, Heinrich Marx noted that the move to Berlin would be "for the purpose of continuing there his studies of Law and Cameralistics [governmental administration]" (*MEGA2* 4.1: 655/*MECW* 1: 655). Heinrich Marx's hope was that legal training would lead eventually to Marx's obtaining a secure position in the civil service. Heinrich Marx was not a wealthy man: his health was poor (he died in May 1838), and there would be a widow and other children who needed to be provided for. On the positive side, Heinrich was well regarded in the Prussian legal service, and he thought that this might help Karl obtain a position once he had the qualifications. Hence the fixation on law as Marx's field of study. But as noted already, Marx quickly fell in with the young, Hegelian-oriented lecturers at Berlin who were grouped together in the Doctors' Club. Marx's discovery of Hegel, and of a group of like-minded, progressively oriented Hegel enthusiasts, laid the basis for his entire intellectual career.

I have already discussed Marx's doctoral dissertation, "Difference between the Democritean and Epicurean Philosophy of Nature" (and the related "Notebooks on Epicurean Philosophy"), in two contexts: in chapter 1, where I showed how it highlighted the derivation of Marx's rationality-conception from the Hegelian history of philosophy, and earlier in the present chapter, where I noted the progressive, change-oriented, forward-looking impulse in the dissertation materials. Here our focus needs to shift again, for now the emphasis needs to be on how the dissertation materials fit into the development of Marx's concern with politics. In brief, there seems to be a politics to Marx's epistemology and ontology, manifested in a sympathy for those positions that, in Marx's view, would provide a rational justification for political activism.

In a letter written in 1857, almost twenty years later, Marx declared that he had studied Epicurus and other Greek philosophers more out of political than out of philosophical interest (letter of December 21, 1857, to Ferdinand Lasalle: *MEGA2* 3.8: 223/*MECW* 40: 226). One has to be cautious about this statement, for it can be seen as implying an opposition between political and philosophical concerns that did not exist for Marx in 1837–41. But the claim that the very early Marx had political concerns in mind seems justified by the texts themselves. Admittedly, it is not at all obvious how the dissertation, which offers an erudite account of the views on nature of Democritus, Epicurus, and various other writers, is political. It is true that toward the end of the extant dissertation manuscript Marx claims that philosophy is about to start criticizing the world (*MEGA2* 1.1: 67–68/*MECW* 1: 85–86/*MER* 9–10). But this was quite probably a late addition that would not have been part of the version of the dissertation that Marx submitted to the University of Jena, and it appears in any case to have little to do with most of the argument of the dissertation. So the question is: *how* is the dissertation political?

The key point is that Marx consistently attacks those philosophical positions that fail to recognize the full power of human reason and that deny that there is a rationality embedded in the world.[26] Consider the mythological figure who presides over the dissertation (and who recurs again and again in Marx's work), the semidivine Titan, Prometheus. Marx revered Prometheus as the patron saint of technology, for by stealing fire from the gods and giving it to men he opened the way to the development of productive forces that is the basic storyline of historical materialism. But although this view of Prometheus was certainly present in Marx's mind in 1839–41 (cf. chapter 1, note 31), in the dissertation Marx was much more interested in the figure who defied the gods than in the figure who initiated technology. In the foreword to his dissertation (drafted in March 1841, and not included in the manuscript that was submitted to Jena early the following month), Marx quotes Prometheus' declaration (from Aeschylus' *Prometheus Bound*), "In simple words, I hate the pack of gods" (*MEGA2* 1.1: 14/*MECW* 1: 30).

One needs to be clear here: Marx himself was never much interested in attacking religion as such (Engels was much more antireligious). Marx's mentor Bauer was a critical theologian—or rather, had become one by 1840.[27] Marx himself was not, although in late summer and early fall 1841 he had some brief involvement with Bauer's atheistical writing projects. In evoking Prometheus in his dissertation Marx was less interested in launching an attack on religion than he was in defending the scope and freedom of philosophy. Ever since, in 1723, the philosopher Christian Wolff was ordered on pain of death to leave Halle and its university, allegedly at the behest of Pietists active at court, the notion of a conflict between theology and philosophy had been an important theme in certain segments of German intellectual life.[28] In his dissertation Marx plays the role of the free-thinker who feels threatened by religion. In the foreword he declares that Prometheus is "the most eminent saint and martyr" of philosophy. The "theologizing intellect," represented in Marx's text by Plutarch, seeks to keep philosophy down; philosophy, with its "world-subduing, absolutely free heart," resists. (*MEGA2* 1.1: 14/*MECW* 1: 30)

"World-subduing [*weltbezwingend*]" needs to be taken in its full sense here. It is a matter of understanding the world clearly and thus of opposing the obscurities propagated by theologians, holding in check "the deep shadows of retrograde ghosts" (*MEGA2* 1.1: 12/*MECW* 1: 28). In the argument of the dissertation itself Marx emphasizes our continuing struggle to grasp the world in a rational way. His manifest focus of interest is on the epistemology, psychology, and implicit ontology of Epicurus. (The crucial passages for grasping Marx's account of these matters are *MEGA2* 4.1: 19–22, 24–40, 50–65, 135–36/*MECW* 1: 412–16, 417–32, 442–58, 504–6 [in Notebooks one, two, three, and seven]). According to Marx, Epicurus "asserts the absolute freedom of spirit" (*MEGA2* 4.1: 25/*MECW* 1: 418). He "is concerned only with freedom of consciousness" (*MEGA2* 4.1: 28/*MECW* 1: 421). Above all, Marx claims, Epicurus is obsessed by the problem posed to human beings by "meteors"—that is, by astronomical and atmospheric phenomena (*meteor* comes from the Greek *meteōron*, a thing in the air, from *meta*, beyond, and *aeirein*, to lift up). Such phenomena—which include weather generally, as well as comets, meteor showers, eclipses, and so on—are often surprising and difficult to explain. As Marx puts it, the problem is that "through the sensuous independence and mysterious remoteness of its existence, the object challenges consciousness. . . ." (*MEGA2* 4.1: 26/*MECW* 1: 419).

According to Marx, in response to this problem Epicurus posited an active consciousness. In Marx's account, Epicurus holds that "[consciousness's] whole activity [*Thun*] is only the struggle against the remoteness that, like a curse, shackles the whole of antiquity" (*MEGA2* 4.1: 27/*MECW* 1: 419–420). Consciousness overcomes the remote and apparently inexplicable character of meteors by affirming "that there is not one explanation, but many, that is, that any explanation will suffice: thus it acknowledges that its activity is active fiction" (*MEGA2* 4.1: 27/*MECW* 1: 420). As a result, accepting whatever explanation pleases it, consciousness is released from the worry caused by the existence of such phenomena. It is also liberated from any notion of "divine, teleological influence" at work in the world, for one no longer needs to see meteors as resulting from the actions of gods or spirits (*MEGA2* 4.1: 28/*MECW* 1: 422). Such is Epicurus' philosophy of consciousness.

But what of Epicurus' philosophy of nature, the alleged subject of the dissertation? It is primarily in this connection that Marx engages in his comparison of Epicurus and Democritus. (The most important passages for understanding Marx's account of the two philosophies of nature are to be found in part 2, chapter 1 of the dissertation and in the first and fourth Notebooks [*MEGA2* 1.1: 33–40, *MEGA2* 4.1: 9–22, 80–92/*MECW* 1: 46–53, 412–16, 469–78].) The classical writers who commented on Epicurus and Democritus, and who are pretty much our only sources for their views, assert that both philosophers were atomists.[29] They also assert that whereas in the universe as imagined by Democritus atoms are unfree, in the universe as imagined by Epicurus atoms "swerve"—that is, they deviate from strictly deterministic paths.

In Marx's interpretation, by endowing his atoms with swerves Epicurus gave them an "ideal" or spiritual side, a moment of self-determination. More than this, in attributing freedom to atoms Epicurus destroyed any possibility of thinking that the universe has an inherent, embedded rationality. After all, one finds here the arbitrary swerving of atoms, which means that the universe as conceptualized by Epicurus has an accidental look to it. Epicurus is delighted by the fact that looking at the world in this way frees the mind from the need to find the *one*, *correct* explanation of natural phenomena (cf. above). It also frees the mind from needing to worry about what happens: after all, things just happen ("shit happens," one might say in a later idiom; so why worry?). Epicurus' view frees us, finally, from needing to worry about the status of the soul. Toward the end of the first Notebook, Marx points out the "*accidental nature*" of the soul and of related notions in Epicurus' perspective. According to Marx, Epicurus held that the necessity of the existence of the soul "is not only not proved, but is even admitted to be not provable, only possible." (*MEGA2* 4.1: 21/*MECW* 1: 415)

In some respects Marx viewed Epicurus favorably. According to Marx, Epicurus freed the atom from natural determination and also, at a deeper level, from the necessity imposed by a divine creator. Simultaneously, he freed consciousness from subjection to a threatening universe. As Breckman puts it, this amounted to a liberating of both ontology and ethics from theology.[30] This is why Marx writes that Epicurus was "the greatest representative of Greek enlightenment [*der größte griechische Aufklärer*]" (*MEGA2* 1.1: 57/*MECW* 1: 73). But as Breckman also emphasizes, there was in addition a critical dimension to Marx's view of Epicurus—for Marx *rejected* Epicurus' philosophy, despite the significant praise that he gives it. In the draft of a new preface to the dissertation, written in late 1841 or early 1842, Marx characterizes the Epicureans, Stoics, and Skeptics as "*philosophers of self-consciousness*"—a view of these writers that was already present in Hegel and in Bauer, as we have seen (*MEGA2* 1.1: 92/*MECW* 1: 106). Breckman contends that Marx saw Epicurus' atomistic philosophy of nature as having affinities with German idealist philosophy, which also emphasized self-consciousness. Thus Epicurus' championing of the autonomy of the atom runs parallel to assertions of self-determination in idealist philosophy, which sought (Breckman's words) to raise "man as man" above the "blind dictates and uniformity of nature." For this reason Breckman argues—rightly, I believe—that Marx's criticism of Epicurean atomism is simultaneously a criticism of post-Hegelian subjective modes of thought. (Breckman 264–65, quotation at 264)

My aim here is not to rehearse the critique of subjectivist philosophy in Marx's dissertation materials. Rather, what is important for our purposes is to get at those elements in the dissertation materials that suggest the commitment to universality, necessity, predictivity, and embedded rationality that subsequently played a fundamental role in Marx's conceptions of politics and economics. I have already cited Marx's contrast between the "*liberal* party" or party of the concept, which we can identify with the Left Hegelians, and the party of the "nonconcept" represented by the "positive philosophy" (not to be confused with "positivism") of the conservative philosopher Schelling and his allies (*MEGA2* 1.1: 69/*MECW* 1: 86). In Marx's view, this opposition in contemporary philosophy had its forerunner in the opposition between Epicurus on the one hand and such theologizers as Plutarch, who criticized Epicurus for his impiety. In both conflicts (between the "liberal" party and the party of the nonconcept, and between Epicurus and Plutarch), Marx's claim is not that one side of the opposition is right and the other wrong. On the contrary, his claim is that the two sides are dialectically related: as Marx says of the present-day opposition, "Each of these parties does exactly what the other one wants to do and what it itself does not want to do." (*MEGA2* 1.1: 69/*MECW* 1: 86) What unites the two oppositions is that in each case both of the contending "parties" are subjective modes of thought. Thus Marx adheres to neither side, to the liberal/Epicurean side as little as to the conservative/Plutarchian side. Rather, he seeks to go beyond both.

For Marx's argument is that despite the manifest opposition between Epicurus and the theologizing intellect, Epicurean philosophy involves a separation between thought and being, and in this respect has an affinity with theology. As Breckman puts it, both Epicurean atomism and supernatural theism "consign reality to irrationality, arbitrariness, and 'premiselessness'" (267). How is this so? As Marx notes, Epicurus' atoms are *thought*, through reason; they have no existence outside thinking—no existence in immanent being, in actuality. Two passages in Marx's dissertation are worth quoting in this regard:

> The *true* principles are the atoms and the void, *everything else is opinion, semblance*. . . . The principles can therefore be perceived only through reason,

> since they are inaccessible to the sensuous eye if only because of their smallness. For this reason they are even called *ideas*. The sensuous appearance is, on the other hand, the only true object. (*MEGA2* 1.1: 25/*MECW* 1: 39)
>
> Abstract individuality [which is what the atoms are in essence] is freedom from being, not freedom in being. (*MEGA2* 1.1: 47/*MECW* 1: 62)

To gloss these statements: According to Marx, in Epicurean philosophy of nature there is a separation of thought from existence, for the metaphysical entities that atomists posit—namely, atoms—only acquire their existence in thought (since they cannot actually be observed). But because thought has thus not been reconciled with existence, one runs the risk of irrationality. In other words, Marx contends that in spite of the fact that Epicurean philosophy sees *thought* as something that can and must be constrained by reason, it ends up permitting any and all claims about *existence*, however irrational. In effect, free rein is given to all beliefs about the extant world. Marx's claim is that only when the reason that governs thought also governs existence will one overcome the risk of "superstitious and unfree mysticism" (*MEGA2* 1.1: 57/*MECW* 1: 73).

Here is how Marx summarizes Epicurus' alleged views on how the motions of the heavenly bodies ["meteors"] are to be explained:

> Their origin has no simple cause, and they have more than one category of essence corresponding to the phenomena. . . . It is constantly repeated that the meteors are not to be explained *haplos* . . . (simply, absolutely), but *pollachos* . . . (in many ways). This also holds for the rising and setting of the sun and the moon. . . [etc.].
>
> Every explanation is sufficient. Only the myth must be removed. It will be removed when we observe the phenomena and draw conclusions from them concerning the invisible. We must hold fast to the appearance, the sensation.

Marx goes on to claim that Epicurus' acceptance of multiplicity in explaining the motions of the heavenly bodies (such that he was willing to say that "every explanation is sufficient") arose from his concern to free human beings from an upsetting fear of heavenly omens. Epicurus wishes human beings to accept his view that heavenly bodies "may behave sometimes in one way, sometimes in another." Since "conforming to no law is the characteristic of [heavenly bodies'] reality," people will know that when strange things happen in the heavens there is nothing to fear. (*MEGA2* 1.1: 53–54/*MECW* 1: 68–69) To drive home the character of "Epicurus'" position here: Epicurus' view of the world is fundamentally subjective. Person A can explain such-and-such a phenomenon one way, and person B another way, and person C another way, and in Epicurus' view, as presented by Marx, this is fine.

Marx's account of Greek philosophy after Aristotle is remarkably similar in its basic storyline to Hegel's account in his *History of Philosophy*, where the essential development of Greek thought is also the development of philosophy's subjective side. One can see in both Marx and Hegel the association of Greek thought with wise men—a subjective connection. Epicurus' atomism is seen as a manifestation of Epicurus' own subjective orientation. Atomism is an orientation geared toward abstract individualism—the form, for Epicurus, of all existence whatsoever. Marx's argument is that abstract individualism, and hence subjective philosophy, must abstract itself away from the being (existence, world) that confronts it. This is why Epicurus' atoms swerve away from the straight line: the purpose of action is abstracting, swerving away, from pain in order to find respite in tranquillity. But in Marx's view, in abstracting away from what is *there* in the world subjective philosophy runs the risk, as Breckman puts it, of "sliding" into "irrationality and myth" (266).

The basic problem is that by denying that there is a unifying rationality embedded in the world (since the world consists of swerving atoms), and by approving of whatever beliefs make their holders feel good, "Epicurus" ends up justifying every wild worldview that comes along. If it makes you feel good to believe that the character of the world is X, it is fine to do so, no matter what the world is really like. Unfortunately, however,

> if abstract-individual self-consciousness is posited as an absolute principle . . . all true and real science is done away with [*aufgehoben*] inasmuch as individuality does not rule within the nature of things themselves. . . . On the other hand, if that self-consciousness . . . is raised to an absolute principle [i.e., to some sort of divinity], then the door is opened wide to superstitious and unfree mysticism. (*MEGA2* 1.1: 57/*MECW* 1: 72–73)

In short, Marx rejects subjective philosophy because (1) it will never be able to engage in "true and real science"; and because (2) it too easily degenerates into superstition and "unfree mysticism."

Marx's commitment to universal and necessary reason is clearly at work in his discussion of subjective philosophy. As Breckman points out, the Epicurean pursuit of *ataraxy*, or the serenity of the self, "required that the Epicureans deny any immanent rationality in being" (267). This is because, if the world were rational, this would limit the self-determination of individuals, who for Epicurus are analogous to swerving atoms. In a truly rational world individuals would not want or need to rise above the world, that is, to swerve out of its determinations. On the level of practical life, the fact that Epicureans do seek to rise above the world shows that they deny that the world is rational. On the theoretical level, Epicurus' denial of the rationality of the world is shown by his acceptance of explanations of the heavenly bodies offered *pollachos*, "in many ways." In this acceptance we can see that Epicurus has failed to bring together thought and being.

I have already quoted the passage in his dissertation where Marx refers to the world becoming philosophical and philosophy becoming worldly. Marx goes on to say that this process can be seen both in its objective and its subjective aspect. Objectively, what happens is the realization—that is, the becoming real—of philosophy. In other words, philosophy turns into something that is at work in the world itself, rather than locked away in an ivory tower. But there is also the subjective aspect of philosophy, which amounts to "*the relationship of the philosophical system* that is realized *to its intellectual carriers*, to the individual self-consciousness in which its progress appears" (*MEGA2* 1.1: 68/*MECW* 1: 85/*MER* 10). Because philosophy is rooted in the self-consciousness of individual philosophers, an adequately universal synthesis between the objective and the subjective side of philosophy does not exist. The carriers of philosophy prove inadequate to the philosophy that they are carrying. Implicitly, then, one has to go beyond philosophy. Marx at this point does not appear to know what one goes beyond *to*. But politics is certainly one potential candidate.

Notwithstanding his radicalism (albeit a radicalism not clearly focused on any specific field of action), Marx in his dissertation shows himself to be not at odds with Hegel's commitment to rationality. He agrees with Hegel that the world is rational, and he takes Hegel's rationality-criteria as his own. For Marx the problem is that the world's rationality is as yet unrealized. And this means that the world must be changed, so that it *will* be rational. Marx's "must" is both a logical imperative and an (untheorized) moral imperative. But it is a moral imperative that, *qua* moral imperative, actually has no visible place in Marx's conceptual universe. When Marx claims that "it is a psychological law that the theoretical mind, once liberated in itself, turns into practical energy" (*MEGA2* 1.1: 67/*MECW* 1: 85/*MER* 9), he means something close to a logical law, not a natural or moral law. A logical contradiction is discovered in the world. It must, and will, be resolved.

THE POLITICS OF MARX'S JOURNALISM, 1842–EARLY 1843

I noted at the beginning of this chapter that Marx excluded politics from the future socialist order. He held instead that the socialist state would be completely nonpolitical. The dealings of the socialist state would have "a business character," there would be no rulership, and elections would "completely lose" their political character (to cite again Marx's comments on Bakunin's *Statism and Anarchy*, *MEW* 18: 635/*MECW* 24: 519/*MER* 545). I also suggested that this was a view at which Marx arrived after a certain amount of thinking about these matters. By 1844 Marx had concluded that politics does not have an immanent rationality, and by 1845–46 at the latest he had concluded that if things were organized scientifically there would be no need for politics (for there would be no specifically political decisions left to make). He did not articulate these conclusions before 1844–46.

It is thus a matter of examining how he reached them. In my view there was a fundamental disjunction *from the beginning* between Marx's rationality-criteria on the one hand and the phenomena of politics on the other. It took Marx several years, however, to reach the antipolitical conclusions to which his rationality-criteria tended. The criteria left little room for politics. In looking at his journalism of 1842–early 1843 we can begin to see how this is so. In his early journalism the young philosopher was subjected for the first time to the shock of confronting, and writing about, the extant social and political world. The journalism is important from our perspective because in it we can observe the encounter between Marx's way of thinking, on the one hand, and the various areas of human concern that he confronted, on the other. In his dissertation materials Marx had applied a philosophical mode of thinking to a philosophical subject matter. As a journalist he was obliged to apply a philosophical mode of thinking to nonphilosophical subject matters. For this reason the peculiarities of his philosophical approach are more clearly visible in the journalism than they are in the dissertation materials.

As noted above, by fall 1841 the possibility of Marx's having an academic career had completely disappeared. Fortunately for Marx, at about the same time an interesting opportunity surfaced. From September 1841 onward he was drawn more and more deeply into the work of a new, liberally and commercially oriented newspaper, the *Rheinische Zeitung für Politik, Handel und Gewerbe* [Rhineland Times for Politics, Trade, and Industry] (DRAP 1: 10). The newspaper was established by a group of Rhineland business and professional men. The promoters of the paper intended that it would follow a line favorable to political liberalization and to business interests. The Prussian government was willing to allow the new venture, in spite of its liberal cast, partly (it seems) as a goodwill gesture to a group of influential Rhinelanders, partly because it might be good for business, and partly because it would serve as a counterweight to the provincialist and Catholic-ultramontane views of the existing Cologne paper, the *Kölnische Zeitung*.[31]

Precisely what did Marx the journalist find himself writing about? Famously, in the history of his opinions that he offered in one of his best-known pieces of writing, the preface to *A Contribution to the Critique of Political Economy* (1859), Marx remarked that "in 1842–43, as editor of the *Rheinische Zeitung*," he had "experienced for the first time the embarrassment of having to discuss so-called material interests" (*MEW* 13: 7/*MECW* 29: 261–62 /*MER* 3). In short, in the 1859 preface, Marx presented his work on the *Rheinische Zeitung* as pointing forward to the full-fledged historical materialism that he was to adopt in 1845–46. But this statement is a retrospective smoothing out of an intellectual evolution that was far more uncertain and contingent. Marx *did* address "material interests" in the early journalistic phase of his career. But it was invariably within the context of state policy that he did so. Politics was uppermost in Marx's mind in this period, and economics followed in politics' train.[32]

Some analysis of the content of Marx's journalism is in order. In the appendix, I list under topical headings Marx's journalistic articles in the *Rheinische Zeitung* period; I also indicate the length, to the nearest half-page in *MEGA2*, of each article. The listing is more than most readers will want, which is why I place it in an appendix. Table 2.1 distills the essence, indicating the topics covered by the articles and the percentage of space devoted to each topic.

The table needs some commentary. Between January 1842 and March 1843 Marx wrote thirty-two articles.[33] Except for four of the articles (one of which Marx seems to have decided not to finish), all appeared in the *Rheinische Zeitung*. In fact, the only significant piece to be published other than in the *Rheinische Zeitung* was "Comments on the Latest Prussian Censorship Instruction," which because of the censorship could not be published in Germany. Instead it appeared in a collection published in Switzerland and edited by the radical journalist and editor Arnold Ruge, *Anekdota zur neuesten deutschen Philosophie und Publicistik*, the first section of which was devoted to the censorship question.

The rationale for the topic divisions will not be immediately obvious. But the essential point is clear—namely, that Marx *qua* journalist was concerned mainly with political matters. The manifestly political topics of censorship, assemblies/oppositional political activity, political theory, and state administration

Table 2.1. Topics Addressed in Marx's Journalism of January 1842–March 1843

Topic	*Space Devoted to Topic* %
censorship/freedom of the press	40
property rights/economic policy/relations of production	33
assemblies/oppositional political activities	10
political theory	6
state affairs/administration	5
theology	3
divorce law	2
newspaper polemics	2

Total is 101 percent because of rounding off. See the appendix for a list of the articles, length of each, total number of pages in each category, and total number of pages overall.

amount to 61 percent of Marx's journalistic output in 1842–43. Divorce and theology might seem to be anomalies. But divorce too was a political issue, and was being widely discussed at the time: it was a question of the relationship between state law on the one hand and marriage as a religiously sanctioned institution on the other, a question particularly difficult in a state where three religions (Evangelical [Lutheran], Reform [Calvinist], and Catholic) uneasily coexisted. As for the two articles on theology, one was a direct defense and the other an indirect defense of critical theology (represented by Bruno Bauer, and more distantly by David Friedrich Strauss and Ludwig Feuerbach) in the face of a government that excluded critical theology and critical Hegelian philosophy from the universities.

The content of the one-third of the journalistic writing concerned with "property rights/economic policy/relations of production" deserves some discussion. The existence of these articles led Marx, in 1859, to find the beginnings of his historical materialist outlook in his *Rheinische Zeitung* work. There are five articles under this category. Two are far more substantial than the others. The longest, thirty-seven pages long in the *MEGA2* printing, deals with the debate in the Sixth Provincial Assembly of the Rhine Province on the wood-theft law. The other long article, twenty-seven pages in the *MEGA2* printing, discusses economic distress in the Mosel wine region. What is striking about all Marx's articles in this category is how deeply state- and policy-related they are.

Marx's unfinished *magnum opus, Capital*, is best seen as concerned with penetrating the surface features of economic modernity in order to get at the true conditions of production. To use Marx's later terminology, this meant dealing with "relations of production," with "forces of production," and with the relations between them. The Marx of the *Rheinische Zeitung* was not yet thinking in that way, however. In his economic discussions in the *RZ*, productive forces are very much in the background. Marx focuses instead on productive relations, emphasizing the interaction of these relations with law, policy, and the state (he would later place law, policy, and the state under the general heading of "legal and political superstructure").

Consider, for example, the article on the debates on the wood-theft law (*MEGA2* 1.1: 199–236/*MECW* 1: 224–63 [Oct.–Nov. 1842]). Here Marx was addressing productive relations and the legal and political superstructure that ratifies and protects those relations. By custom, there existed a communal right, going back for centuries, to glean dead wood in forests (the right to glean had biblical precedent: see Ruth 2.2–17). By the nineteenth century the right to glean was a legal anomaly. Forest lands that in the early modern period had not been systematically harvested for their wood, or that had been regarded as communal property (in part because they weren't being systematically harvested), were now under the ownership of individuals who wanted an income from the forest, just as they would have wanted an income from cleared land. Further, population had risen; there were more people around. Finally, forest wardens and other authorities had difficulty distinguishing between dead wood gleaned from the forest and wood illegitimately taken from living trees or from trees deliberately damaged so that they would die. How, under these circumstances, were property rights to be protected? The answer that most appealed to the established state and its bureaucrats, and to many liberals, was: by abolishing the customary right. This was the set of issues that Marx addressed in his wood-theft article. His focus was not on the conflict between the relations of production and the forces of production, or on the conflict between outmoded relations of production and new relations of production: these would be his concern in *Capital*. Rather, his focus is on what he takes to be the absurdity of current legal arrangements and of the various proposals being made to reform those arrangements.

Marx's article on the conditions facing wine-growers in the Mosel, titled "Vindication of the Correspondent from the Mosel," does focus on a branch of material production (*MEGA2* 1.1: 296–323/*MECW* 1: 332–58 [written and published January 1843]; *MEGA2* 1.1: 324–27 [written January 1843, censor refused publication in *RZ*, published 1845]). But here too the issue was less a matter of material production than of governmental policy. In brief: what should state policy be with regard to the vinegrowers in the Mosel, who at the time were severely pressed by competition? Indeed, Marx's article was itself prompted by governmental action—otherwise he would probably not have written on the subject. A correspondent for the *Rheinische Zeitung*, in an article that the paper published in December 1842, had made certain claims about conditions in the Mosel district that the government had then challenged. Since the *Rheinische Zeitung* was under threat of being banned because of this allegedly error-ridden article, Marx felt obliged to defend the piece in an attempt to show that it was not blatantly false and that its publication was no justification for banning the paper.

In short, in Marx's journalism of 1842–March 1843, there is a focus on politically related issues. It is clear that this focus arose in considerable measure out of the demands of the situation within which Marx found himself. For example, he wrote eighty-seven pages (by *MEGA2* count) on censorship and freedom of the press. His emphasis on the subject had much to do with the fact that he was a radical journalist who wanted to get his writings published in Germany and who did not want the *Rheinische Zeitung* to be censored or banned. Marx wrote on other political topics because these, too, were up for discussion at the time. In writing on these issues he had to have some sensitivity to what would or would not be acceptable to the government, to his employers, and presumably to his readers. Yet it would be wrong to discount these journalistic writings because of their situational character. They were not *simply* occasional pieces, done for hire. In the first place, even at the age of twenty-four, Marx's force of personality was legendary, and he did manage to impose his own radicalism on the *Rheinische Zeitung*. We know that he did so because some of the shareholders were upset by the paper's radical tone—as is shown by the minutes of a remarkable six-hour shareholders' meeting, held in February 1843, where the threat that the paper might be closed was extensively discussed.[34]

Second and more important, although we are better informed about what Marx wrote than about what he "really believed," the distinction between the two is rather artificial. Insofar as what Marx wrote (and did) had a coherent structure, one might want to say that Marx believed such and such. I am persuaded that at a deep level there was indeed a structure to what Marx said and did. We might call this structure a belief-system. Marx's belief-system had two main points: commitment to rationality and commitment to freedom. One might want to think of Marx's belief-system in a pragmatic way—as amounting to patterns, or habits, of action.[35] One might also want to think of Marx as playing a set of roles, roles that were variants of one another: the firebrand student; the would-be radical professor; the radical journalist; the revolutionary activist. (There were other roles as well, as Francis Wheen and others have shown: the wild son; the enamored husband; the doting father; the slightly crazed émigré; the scheming organizer.) Marx was especially good at playing the activist. In this book we are exploring the theoretical coherence behind the activist role, and the limits of that coherence. The coherence is to be found less in a subject matter than in a way of approaching all subject matters, some of which were more amenable to the approach in question than were others. We need to examine more closely the character of this coherence.

It is striking that Marx's journalistic pieces of the *Rheinische Zeitung* period are all arguments against one or another opponent. But there are different ways of arguing. In these pieces Marx argues like a philosopher—tightly, logically. It is not surprising to see him arguing in this way in his philosophical writings. It is surprising to find such a style of thinking so fully deployed in the journalism. I have already noted Marx's insistence, in his article of July 1842 attacking the *Kölnische Zeitung*, that philosophy needs to become "the philosophy of the contemporary world" (*MEGA2* 1.1: 183/*MECW* 1: 195). Marx's articles of 1842–early 1843 show that this was no mere *boutade*. Rather, Marx the journalist brought his philosophical training to the public discussion of public issues.[36]

Four intellectual "moves" are particularly striking in the journalism of 1842–43. The moves stand out all the more clearly because they occur within a context that is not that of technical philosophy. The key question, to which I shall turn later, is to what extent they are compatible with the reality of politics. The most basic move that Marx makes is to point out that his opponents engage in a begging of the question, assuming what needs to be proved. For example, one of the contributors to the assembly debate on freedom of the press had argued for restrictions on the press on the grounds that "man, individually and in the mass, is always one and the same. He is by nature imperfect and immature." But as Marx points out, this "thesis of the permanent immaturity of the human race" is precisely what needs to be argued for (*MEGA2* 1.1: 140–41/*MECW* 1: 152–53). Marx's move here is tied up with his philosophical commitment to the notion that all starting points need to be necessary starting points. The notion appeared in his doctoral dissertation materials earlier; it appears in his critique of political economy later.[37]

Second, Marx characteristically points out contradictions within the positions that he is attacking. He does this time and time again. It would be boring to list a large number of instances: a few will suffice.

For example, in his article on the censorship instruction issued by the Prussian government on December 24, 1841, Marx notes that the instruction claimed to recognize "the value and need of frank and decent publicity [*freimüthigen und anständigen Publicität*]." The instruction thus presented itself as concerned "to free the press from improper restrictions" and to free writers from "any undue constraint" (*MEGA2* 1.1: 97/*MECW* 1: 109). Yet it was a *censorship* instruction, not an instruction on freedom of the press.

Similarly, in his article on the Rhine assembly debates on freedom of the press Marx notes that the opponents of freedom of the press "doubt mankind in general," since they see mankind as likely to be led astray by a free press. But these same opponents "canonize individuals," namely, the censors responsible for determining what ought or ought not to be printed. (*MEGA2* 1.1: 157/*MECW* 1: 169)

Likewise, in "The Leading Article in No. 179 of the *Kölnische Zeitung*" Marx points out that the assertion by the *KZ*'s editor, Karl Hermes, that "to spread philosophical and religious views by means of the newspapers, or to combat them in the newspapers, we consider equally impermissible," was contradicted by the fact that Hermes' own article spread religious views and combated philosophical views. In the same article Hermes had declared himself to be in favor of "the freedom of scientific research": "In our day, *scientific research* is rightly allowed the widest, most unrestricted scope." Accordingly, Hermes had claimed that a "sharp distinction must be drawn between the requirements of freedom of scientific research . . . and what lies outside the limits of scientific research." But the drawing of this boundary, Marx holds, surely belongs to science itself. Hermes, on the contrary, believed that the line should be drawn by an "official reason," possessed not by scientists but by the censor. Finally, Hermes had portrayed a Christianity that is "sure of its victory" in the great struggle with error—but "not so sure of it as to spurn the aid of the police," Marx adds. (*MEGA2* 1.1: 173, 196, 179/*MECW* 1: 185–86, 188, 191)

Marx's third characteristic move is to point out contradictions not simply within an opponent's position but *within an existing situation*. This move ties in with the forward-looking interpretation of Hegelian philosophy that the Left Hegelians recommended and practiced. In Hegel's words in the preface to the *Phenomenology*, already quoted: "spirit is indeed never at rest but always engaged in moving forward" (§11, p. 6). Spirit moves forward by contradiction: one thing comes into contradiction with another thing, leading to a need for resolution that pushes the argument, and reality, forward. Given their adherence to this view of how the world operates, the Left Hegelians, including Marx, were intent on finding contradictions within the existing situation. Thus one finds on Marx's part a marked tendency to bifurcate, or dichotomize, any situation that he is attending to.[38]

In Marx's early journalism this tendency is most obviously manifested in his insistence that the political world is being contested between two diametrically opposed parties—one progressive and the other retrograde, one attached to "the concept" and the other attached to the way things are now, one party guided by (critical) philosophy, the other guided by dogma and authority. The later Marx looks for contradiction within and between the spheres of productive forces and productive relations and pays little attention to "the legal and political superstructure." But Marx's bifurcating tendency remains entirely in place.[39]

Finally, these moves point toward a fourth feature of Marx's project: his commitment to what he refers to as the "rational character [*rationalen Charakter*]" of criticism ("Freedom of the Press," *MEGA2* 1.1: 147/*MECW* 1: 159). Beyond this, the journalistic Marx also appears to have a faith in the underlying rational character not only of criticism but also of the world. The two—commitment to rational criticism and faith in the rational character of the world—go together; they *require* each other. Marx professed to believe in the power of criticism, which in his view is "the true censorship, grounded in the essence of the freedom of the press itself" (*MEGA2* 1.1: 147/*MECW* 1: 159). The professed character of this commitment can be seen in the way that Marx addressed the arguments of one of the defenders of press freedom, who had held in the assembly debates that press freedom is a species of the genus freedom of trade, and that the press therefore ought to be allowed to function in accordance with the laws of freedom of trade. Marx, on the contrary, contends that "*the primary freedom of the press consists in its not being a busi-*

ness [Die erste Freiheit der Presse besteht darin, kein Gewerbe zu sein]" (*MEGA2* 1.1: 163/*MECW* 1: 175). It is above the marketplace, Marx implies, because it is finally a spiritual enterprise. "The press is the most general way by which individuals can communicate their spiritual existence [*geistiges Dasein*]. It knows no respect for persons, but only respect for intelligence [*Intelligenz*]" (*MEGA2* 1.1: 165/*MECW* 1: 177). In short, it appears that journalism, in Marx's eyes, was a spirit-oriented enterprise.

We see here a Hegelian faith in reason rendered in a Left Hegelian key. I have in mind the Hegel who wanted philosophy to advance from "*love* of knowing" to "*actual* knowing."[40] This faith expresses itself concretely in Marx's high confidence in the power of rational criticism. In the journalism of 1842–43 it is seen most clearly in his article criticizing the *Kölnische Zeitung*, where he speaks glowingly of those ages when philosophy penetrates "into salons, priests' studies, editorial offices of newspapers and court antechambers, into the love and the hate of contemporaries," and where he alludes scornfully to philosophy's enemies, who utter "wild shouts for help against the fiery ardor of ideas" (*MEGA2* 1.1: 182–84/*MECW* 1: 195–96). To all appearances Marx retained this rational faith throughout his career. An assumption underlies the faith, an assumption that is most tellingly revealed by the third "move," the seeking out of contradictions within existing situations. It is the assumption of an underlying rational coherence to the world; for only such an assumption can warrant the claim that there is an impulsion for contradiction to resolve itself into unity at a higher level. This assumption is fundamental to Hegel's world view, from which Marx borrows. It is tied up with the notion of final cause that Hegel, borrowing from Aristotle, deploys globally rather than only locally. It is also tied up with Hegel's perhaps unwitting secularization of certain neo-Platonic aspects of Christian theology.[41] Marx is the heir of this rationalist assumption of unity. It is the glue holding his project together. When the glue dissolves, the different parts of his project must go their separate ways. At this point it is no longer the Marxian project. It becomes something less than Marx intended—a heuristics, rather than a global theory. But a heuristics is not something negligible. Quite the contrary: it is an important starting point for productive thought.

Besides showing a continuation of the rationalist commitment of the doctoral dissertation materials, Marx's journalism also shows a transfer of attention from one domain of interest to another. I suggested in chapter 1 that Marx was connected to both sides of the spirit-matter, idealism-naturalism opposition that dominated modern philosophy from Descartes onward. The spirit-matter opposition can be seen as operating in four different domains of theoretical attention: the domains of ontology, nature, human society, and method (cf. figure 1.1). In his dissertation Marx still paid considerable attention to the classic domain of the spirit-matter opposition, the domain of ontology. (For present purposes, *ontology* refers to any attempt to come to an understanding of a level of reality underlying, and putatively more real than, nature and society. Whether such an enterprise is even *possible* is not a question that can be pursued here.) In addressing the Democritean and Epicurean philosophies of nature, Marx was actually addressing the ontologies implicit in these philosophies. Marx the dissertator was fascinated by the idea of somehow reconciling freedom and determinism—categories that in modern philosophy map onto the ontological fields of spirit and matter respectively. This is why he was so interested in Epicurus' emphasis on the "swerve" of atoms. Marx identified the "swerve" as what allowed Epicurus to accommodate both freedom and determinism. Hence Marx discerned in Epicurean atomism an attempt—albeit a failed attempt—at a synthesis of spirit and matter, idealism and naturalism.

In Marx's journalism of 1842–early 1843 there is a parallel concern. But the concern operates within a different domain, that of humanity. Within this domain Marx attempts to take account of the sphere of unfreedom (the sphere of material interests and needs), while subjecting this sphere to the claims of reason. In other words, in the journalism of 1842–early 1843, as in the dissertation materials, we find an attempt to address the problem of freedom. But the problem is no longer addressed on the ontological plane. Marx now wants to bring together "matter" and "spirit" within the human domain, in such a way that freedom is preserved. This can only be done, so Marx appears to be suggesting, within the context of the state and politics.

Consider, for example, Marx's article on "the Estates-Committees in Prussia," published in two parts in December 1842. Although its subject is a proposal to establish a general Prussian legislative assembly based on the old Estates system, Marx begins with a few comments on the press (not surprising, since by December 1842 the *Rheinische Zeitung* was already in trouble with the censorship). Marx writes:

> What makes the press the most powerful lever for promoting culture and the spiritual education of the people [*geistigen Volksbildung*] is precisely the fact that it transforms the material struggle into an ideal struggle [*den stofflichen Kampf in einen ideellen Kampf*], the struggle of flesh and blood into a struggle of minds [*Geister-Kampf*], the struggle of need, desire, and the empirical into a struggle of theory, knowledge [*Verstand*], and form. (*MEGA2* 1.1: 272/*MECW* 1: 292)

This is the language of a thinker who has internalized the Hegelian notion that history is a process by which humankind moves from "nature" to "spirit."[42] It is the language, further, of a thinker who sees debate over politics as involving an actual sifting of positions, leading to truth. Finally, it is the language of a thinker committed to a broadly Hegelian conception of the state. In such a conception, the state is not primarily a forum within which negotiation is carried out between competing social interests and through which compromises are then achieved. Rather, the state is primarily the embodiment of reason (although in Marx's view the reason is still very far from having been adequately realized).[43]

Marx's "rational" conception of the state is particularly prominent in a passage at the end of the "Estates-Committees" article, where he suggests that in a "true state [*wahren Staate*]" material interests are so permeated by "*spiritual powers* [geistige Mächte]" that "there is no landed property, no industry, no material thing that as a raw element of this kind could make a bargain [*Abkommen treffen*] with the state." On the contrary, in such a situation "the state pervades the whole of nature with spiritual nerves." In consequence, "nature without the state" is no longer dominant; one has only "the nature of the state" (*Staatsnatur*); and "the free human being [*Mensch*]" will dominate "the unfree object" (*MEGA2* 1.1: 285/*MECW* 1: 306). Such a conception is far from the late twentieth-century liberal conception of "interest" politics. It is even further from Marx's historical-materialist conception (after 1845) of the state as either the governing committee of the ruling class or the device by which a political-bureaucratic clique can attain a seemingly independent (although actually parasitic) power over the social order.

One might wonder whether Marx really believed, *in foro interno*, that there is an "organic state reason [*organische Staatsvernunft*]" that can and will supersede "the pressing need of private interests [*die Nothdurft der Privatinteressen*]" (*MEGA2* 1.1: 283/*MECW* 1: 303). After all, in this article he was constructing with his left hand a case for the continued existence of the *Rheinische Zeitung*, as an organ that would elevate material struggles to an ideal level. As I have suggested, questions of the Did he really believe . . . ? type need to be reframed in terms of consistency. What is important at the most fundamental level is that throughout his career, beginning in the second half of 1841 at the latest, Marx consistently maintained two personae: Marx the theorist and scientist and Marx the activist and revolutionary.[44] (As I have noted, there were other personae as well, but they are of less interest to us in the present book.) Commitment to some sort of notion of a rational state is consistent with Marx's underlying commitment to rational theory. And it is surely significant that he returned to the notion of a rational state in his "Critique of Hegel's Doctrine of the State" (summer 1843; to be discussed below).[45] As long as there is going to be *any* theory of the state, the state would need, by Marx's lights, to have within it some sort of embedded rationality.

The "Estates-Committees" passage is paralleled by other, slightly later assertions in Marx's writings on political theory (see the next section). Marx in this period still carried with him the philosopher's commitment to "the concept and principle of philosophy" (*MEGA2* 1.1: 69/*MECW* 1: 86 [doctoral dissertation]). His "spiritualizing" of material interests—not by denying them, but by integrating them into a rational framework—is entirely in line with this philosophical commitment. *Nota bene*: I do not claim that Marx had a clear idea as to what would be involved in such a state and politics. I claim only that he had a broad rational commitment that underwrote particular commitments to rationality. The wider commitment was to the rational penetrability of the world. The particular part of the world that Marx's journalistic and editorial duties led him to focus on was politics, and so his instinct in 1842–early 1843 was to attempt to show the rationalizability of that subdomain of human concern.

Consider Marx's article of August 1842 attacking the Göttingen law professor Gustav Hugo (1764–1844), a "forefather and creator" of the so-called historical school of law, which held that law should be based on tradition. For Marx, former student of the conceptualizing and universalizing Hegelian law professor Eduard Gans (1797 or 1798–1839), such a view was anathema. Marx portrays Hugo as a misinterpreter of Kant, who had developed in an unfortunate direction Kant's already unfortunate claim that we cannot grasp the essence of things. According to Marx, Hugo had made himself into a skeptic with regard to our capacity to know "the *necessary essence* of things [nothwendige Wesen *der Dinge*]," in order to be a "*courtier* [Hoffmann]" as regards the "*accidental appearance* [zufällige Erscheinung]" of things. That is to say, Hugo had claimed (according to Marx) that "no rational necessity [*vernünftige Nothwendigkeit*] animates [*beseelt*] positive institutions, e.g., property, the constitution, marriage, etc." (*MEGA2* 1.1: 192/*MECW* 1: 204). This being the case, the nonrationality of those institutions is no argument against them, and we might as well accept them since they exist. In Marx's view, then, Hugo is "the *complete skeptic*. . . . With him, the *eighteenth-century skepticism* against the *rationality of what exists* [*die* Vernunft des Bestehenden] appears as *skepticism* against the *existence of rationality* [*das* Bestehen der Vernunft]" (*MEGA2* 1.1: 193/*MECW* 1: 205). With Marx, on the other hand, commitment to the notion that the world is at base rational (and that human beings can discover this rationality) seems to be the precondition for any and all political engagement.

To put the matter another way: this and similar passages show that in 1842–early 1843 Marx viewed politics under the guise of *Wissenschaft* (science). I take *Wissenschaft* in Marx's sense of the term, which is both extensive and restrictive. It is restrictive in that it imposes severe rationality-criteria. It is extensive in at least two ways. First, it is a sense of science that—totally in the spirit of Hegel—includes philosophy, and indeed (for the moment) takes philosophy to be the highest form of science. Second, it is extensive in that, more so than was the case with Hegel, it takes account of natural science. (In chapter 1, I attempted to identify what prompted Marx's interest in and commitment to natural science. Among relevant considerations are: Marx's belief that respect for and investigation of natural science tend to hold religious obscurantism in check; his noticing of Feuerbach's commitment to nature; and his dawning awareness—first made explicit in the "Economic and Philosophical Manuscripts" [1844])—of the growing relevance of natural scientific investigation to human society.)

We can see indications of Marx's extensive view of science at various places in his journalism of 1842–early 1843, but nowhere more obviously than in his two articles on the divorce bill, proposed by the Prussian government in 1842, that envisaged making the dissolution of marriage more difficult. As in his discussion of Hugo and the historical school of law, Marx insists, in his November 1842 article on the divorce bill, that "the consistent legislator" must be guided by "the essence of things [*dem Wesen der Dinge*]"—that is, he must grasp "the essence of marriage in and for itself." Without such guidance, legislation becomes an arbitrary imposition. Marx complains that the current Prussian law on divorce is "based on an intellectual abstraction which . . . conceived the natural, legal, moral content as external matter which in itself knows no laws." The law that the legislators have constructed attempts to arrange the matter of divorce "in accordance with an external aim. It treats the objective world not in accordance with its innate [*eingebornen*] laws, but in accordance with arbitrary, subjective ideas. . . ." (*MEGA2* 1.1: 263/*MECW* 1: 275) In a follow-up article on the same subject published in December 1842, Marx continues along the same line, going so far as to claim that the legislator "should regard himself as a natural scientist [*Naturforscher*]. He does not *make* the laws, he does not invent them, he only formulates them, expressing in conscious, positive laws the inner laws of spiritual relations" (*MEGA2* 1.1: 288/*MECW* 1: 308).[46]

It is clear that Marx is not appealing here only to the material laws of nature (laws that are certainly relevant to marriage, since one important aspect of marriage is the satisfaction of sexual desire). He is appealing also (as the reference to "spiritual relations" makes clear) to a moral or spiritual dimension in the world. As he notes in the final line of the December 1842 article, he recommends "conscious subordination to moral and natural forces" (*MEGA2* 1.1: 290/*MECW* 1: 310). The combined appeal to moral forces and to natural forces is not at all surprising. A common aspect of nineteenth-century intellectuals' conceptions of nature was their tendency to see nature as having an ideal dimension. This was most often expressed in the oft-repeated claim that the laws of nature had ultimately been put into nature by God. This was not Marx's view, but a similar conception of the coherence and rationality of nature does underpin his theoretical project.

The journalism of 1842–early 1843 shows Marx's philosophical preoccupations, and the machinery attaching to those preoccupations, in full operation. It is quite surprising to the first-time reader of these articles how deeply philosophical the early journalism is. But in his journalism Marx could address only fragmented parts of the general territory of the state and politics. With his resignation as editor of the *Rheinische Zeitung* in March 1843 he finally had time to undertake a systematic investigation of political theory.

MARX'S ATTEMPT TO THEORIZE POLITICS, 1841–LATE 1843

Why was Marx interested in politics? The answer is obvious: because he had nothing but contempt for the unfreedom that pervaded German society, and because he believed that political change was needed if Germany was to be liberated. In short, Marx had a pragmatic, practical interest in politics—an interest that persisted until the end of his life. But Marx was not simply an activist: he also wanted to have a coherent *understanding* of politics. As early as September 1841 he had already thought of critiquing Hegel's political theory, and in the period between November 1841 and September 1842 he apparently drafted a "Critique of Hegel's Theory of Natural Law [*Naturrecht*]" that is no longer extant (DRAP 1: 10; 2: 35, #204).

In Marx's early journalism one finds some observations that are relevant to political theory, including his references to the rational state. But only after the *Rheinische Zeitung* adventure ended was Marx able to turn to political theory in a sustained way. From May through October 1843 he lived in the spa town of Kreuznach, near Mainz, where Jenny von Westphalen's mother had a house. Indeed, at Kreuznach, on June 19, 1843, Marx married Jenny, who was to be his loving and—one must say it—heroic wife until her death in December 1881, a little more than a year before Marx's death. When in October 1843 the couple moved to Paris, Marx's interests took a different turn. But before the move to Paris he engaged in several months of serious investigation into political theory, producing a lengthy critique of the "doctrine of the state" that Hegel offers in his *Philosophy of Right*.

The fragmentary and rather glancing attempts at political theory in Marx's journalism of 1842–early 1843, and the more sustained effort visible in the "Critique of Hegel's Doctrine of the State" (summer 1843) are parts of a single effort by Marx to arrive at some sort of coherent theory of politics and the state.[47] This attempt was centered on two distinct poles, which we can call "Hegelian" and "Feuerbachian." The Hegelian pole dominated first. After

March 1843 the Feuerbachian pole dominated. But Marx's Hegel-inflected rationality-criteria remained in place even in the "Feuerbach" period: Marx never adopted what he must have thought of as Feuerbach's rather flaccid empiricism. By the time he began to distance himself from Feuerbach (early 1845), his concern with articulating an account of politics that would show it to have an *immanent* rationality had come to an end. He had already concluded, by July 1844—see "The King of Prussia and Social Reform," cited at the beginning of this chapter—that there would be no politics under socialism.

Let us consider first the political theory embedded in the writings of Marx's *Rheinische Zeitung* period. It is completely in line with his continued Hegelianism in this period that he depicts the state as a "true," rational entity (at least potentially). Marx repeatedly insists—a Rousseauian, Kantian, and Hegelian point—that the state should represent the general or universal, as opposed to the particular. The universal is rational and the rational is universal. In "Comments on the Latest Prussian Censorship Instruction" he observes that the "Christian state" is defective, because it unavoidably introduces religious particularity into an institution that ought to be "the realization of political and juridical reason." In "Leading Article in No. 179 of the *Kölnische Zeitung*" he argues that the "questions of the time" need to be discussed by philosophers, in "the clarifying language of public reason," rather than in "the obscure language of private opinion." As for the state, "the question . . . is not whether there should be any philosophizing about the state, but whether this should be done well or badly." Similarly, Marx attacks as defective the "estate system," that is, the system in which each of the different traditional orders in the state (e.g., the nobility) elects its own legislative representatives, because the system aims at the representation of *particular* interests. Thus in an article draft of February 1843 he contrasts "estate unreason" with "civic reason." (*MEGA2* 1.1: 105–6, 186, 351–52/*MECW* 1: 117–18, 198, 363)

Marx in his journalism grants to philosophers—in the broad sense of those persons who have learned how to think universally—an important role in politics. The term *Intelligenz*, which can mean both "intelligence" and "intelligentsia," comes up several times, and the *idea* of *Intelligenz* is persistently present. In "Communal Reform and the *Kölnische Zeitung*," Marx attacks a proposal to separate urban and rural communities in the Rhine Province for purposes of state administration. In Marx's view, such a change would "separate the province from its own reason [*Vernunft*]"; clearly, those capable of recognizing Vernunft when they see it live primarily in urban communities (*MEGA2* 1.1: 252/*MECW* 1: 267).[48] Marx saw, or at least claimed to see, the intelligence of the state as something that is especially embodied in its well-educated citizens—perhaps people like Oppenheim and Jung, who had brought him on board the *Rheinische Zeitung* and had supported his radical editorial line. Similarly, in "On the Estates-Committees in Prussia" he calls for "conscious representation of the intelligence of the people [*Volksintelligenz*], a representation that does not seek to assert individual needs against the state, but . . . to assert that state itself. . ." (*MEGA2* 1.1: 285/*MECW* 1: 305–6). There is more than a hint in Marx of the notion that Karl Mannheim made explicit in *Ideology and Utopia* (first edition, 1929), that of the free-floating intellectual who is able to see the world as it really is because he has no *particular* attachment in it.[49]

Another feature, beyond universality, that was important in Marx's early arguments concerning politics and the state is his insistence on what we might call the "specificity" of the political. At this point in his thinking Marx does not yet reduce politics to some other sphere that would presumably be more fundamental. To be sure, Marx's defense of the autonomy of politics and the state had a pragmatic dimension to it: he was trying to raise a barricade against theocratic influences, given the religious inclinations of Friedrich Wilhelm IV. For example, in "Comments on the Latest Prussian Censorship Instruction" Marx reveals his annoyance at the fact that "the specifically Christian legislator *cannot recognize morality* as an independent sphere that is sacrosanct in itself" (*MEGA2* 1.1: 106/*MECW* 1: 118). The Christian legislator falls into the same error with regard to the political state. For Marx, the specificity of the political lies in its attempt to represent the universal within society, rising above special interests and eschewing logrolling and wheeling and dealing.

Indeed, in "On the Estates-Committees in Prussia," Marx goes so far as to declare that in the "true state"

> there is no landed property, no industry, no material thing, which as a crude element of this kind could make a bargain with the state; in it there are only *spiritual forces*, and only in their state form of resurrection, in their political rebirth, are natural forces entitled to a voice in the state. (*MEGA2* 1.1: 285/*MECW* 1: 306)

It is hard to know what to make of this statement, which appears to out-idealize Hegel.[50] Did Marx "really believe" what he wrote here? But the general point is clear: in Marx's early journalism we are getting something sharply different from what is to be found in the historical materialist Marx (chapter 4). When Marx writes in the 1859 preface that in his work for the *Rheinische Zeitung* he "experienced for the first time the embarrassment of having to discuss so-called material interests," he puts an after-the-fact, historical-materialist "spin" on his journalistic experience. If we are to take it at face value, much of what he wrote at the time was aimed at preserving some measure of distance between material interest (which is necessarily particular, not universal) and the state.

After March 1843, Marx's conception of politics and the state changed, in part because in that event-laden month Marx read Feuerbach's brief and hard-hitting "Preliminary Theses on the Reform of Philosophy." In his widely noticed *The Essence of Christianity* (1841) Feuerbach had critiqued Christianity, applying to it a "genetic-critical" method that aimed to expose the actual foundation of Christianity, which he saw as alienated and alienating. This foundation turns out to be "Man." Feuerbach's argument with regard to Christianity was that whereas Christianity puts God in the position of active subject and man in the position of passive object created by God, in fact man is the active subject and God is only an idea created by man, the repository for human qualities from which man has unfortunately become separated or "estranged." Feuerbachian critique involved a double move—returning the predicate to its true subject (Man), but then criticizing the abstract, hypostatized form of that subject (in this case, the isolated, atomized person versus the "species-individual," who is connected by loving bonds to humanity generally). According to Feuerbach, Christianity is a disguised, imaginary humanism. It impairs the manifestation in the world of a *real* humanism embodied in the "species-being," Man. The task of the critical theologian is to unveil the true essence of Christianity, namely, its concealed humanism, and thus to open the way to the real love of human beings for each other and for humankind generally.

The Essence of Christianity reverberated like a thunderclap through German intellectual life, but it had relatively little impact on Marx. Marx had never had a deep attachment to Christianity or to any other religion. In consequence, unlike many other educated Germans of the time he had no reason to find Feuerbach's book either shocking or liberating. But it was a different matter with Feuerbach's "Preliminary Theses." For in the "Preliminary Theses" Feuerbach applied the method of subject-object reversal to Hegelian philosophy, to which Marx still had a deep attachment. Just as, in critiquing religion, Feuerbach tried to show that "God" is really man in disguise, in critiquing Hegelian philosophy, he sought to make the same point concerning "Spirit [*Geist*]." In reading the "Preliminary Theses" Marx seems to have been immediately struck by the potential usability of Feuerbach's genetic-critical method for his own theoretical aims. During a period of about six months following March 1843 Marx's aims were unequivocally focused on politics. In a letter to Arnold Ruge of March 13, 1843, Marx wrote that "Feuerbach's aphorisms seem to me incorrect only in one respect, that he refers too much to nature and too little to politics" (*MEGA2* 3.1: 45/*MECW* 1: 400). Marx in 1843 seems to have wanted to correct this defect in Feuerbach's thinking.

When, after his departure from the *Rheinische Zeitung*, Marx finally managed to concentrate on a critique of Hegel's political theory, he did so in direct imitation of Feuerbach's critique of Christianity and of Feuerbach's proposed critique of philosophy. Feuerbach's mode of critique deeply influenced Marx's view of the state. In December 1842 Marx had still felt able to refer to "the nature of the state [*Staatsnatur*]." In contrast, in the "Critique of Hegel's Doctrine of the State" Marx denies that the state *has* a nature. The basic move will be familiar to anyone who has read Feuerbach's *Essence of Christianity*—or who has dipped into Marx's "Economic and Philosophical Manuscripts," where Marx moves beyond a Feuerbachian critique of politics to a Feuerbachian critique of the current economic system. According to Marx, Hegel goes wrong in making the political state into the subject, with man the mere object of state action. In Hegel as interpreted by Marx, man is taken to be a "predicate of the Idea [of the State]"—whereas man is actually the creator of that Idea. Or to put the matter more concretely, "the constitution does not make the people, but the people makes the constitution." In Marx's account, Hegel, through sleight of hand, gives to his argument "the illusion of logical sequence, of deduction and development [*der Schein eines Consequenz, einer Ableitung und Entwicklung*]." But, claims Marx, Hegel's "general definitions [*Bestimmungen*]" generate no conclusions. (Note that Marx's objection is not at all to rigor, deductiveness, and the unfolding [*Ent-wicklung*] of an argument from its premises. Rather, Marx is offended by Hegel's deceptive simulation of such rigor). In short, Hegel engages in a "logical, pantheistic mysticism" in his investigation of the state; he starts out not from "a political Idea" but from an "abstract Idea" that he erroneously represents as political. (*MEGA2* 1.2: 7–19, 31, quotes at 15, 13, 8, 12/*MECW* 3: 7–18, 29–30, quotes at 14, 12, 7, 12/*EW*, 61–74, 87–88, quotes at 69, 67, 61, 66)

Marx's Feuerbachian move—his adoption of Feuerbach's notion that everything comes down, finally, to "Man"—amounts to a rejection on Marx's part of political theory *as an independent enterprise*. Political theory needs, rather, to be part of a general anthropological investigation. But Marx did not at this point reject political theory as such, nor did he reject politics as such. There is no reason to think that Marx had concluded, at this point, that it is not possible to articulate a theory or narrative of politics that would show politics to have an immanent rationality (so that it can be made sense of in its own terms, and not just as a variable dependent on something else). At this point, far from rejecting politics as such, he seems to have rejected only a politics that, subservient to the established state, fails to attack that subservience by agitating for the subordination of politics and the state to "Man." (In summer 1843 the meaning of a putting of "Man" in the subject position remained relatively unclear; only in 1844 [see chapter 3] did Marx begin to fill in this notion with some measure of actual content.) When Marx finally did articulate his theoretical rejection of politics, in 1844, it was on grounds that were

Hegelian rather than Feuerbachian. But before turning to this rejection, we need to broach an important question: Was Marx ever committed to politics, even at the beginning of his political-philosophical trajectory?

WAS MARX EVER COMMITTED TO (DEMOCRATIC) POLITICS?

Was Marx ever committed to politics—more specifically, was he ever committed to *democratic* politics—as something that is good or rational in itself? Because there might appear to be some attachment to politics in the writings of the *Rheinische Zeitung* period, and to a democratic politics in particular in the writings that Marx produced in 1843 after the suppression of the *Rheinische Zeitung*, the question needs to be addressed.

The *locus classicus* of apparent commitment on Marx's part to politics is to be found in a programmatic letter dated May 1843 and addressed from Marx to Arnold Ruge (1802–80). At the time, Ruge and Marx were planning to co-edit an oppositional journal, the *Deutsch-Französische Jahrbücher*.[51] It was to be published outside Germany in the hope of escaping the reach of the Prussian censors, and would contain, the editors hoped, contributions from French leftists as well as from Germans. The May 1843 letter, along with two others dated March and September 1843, were published in the first (and only) issue of the *Jahrbücher*. The letter identifies an ideal to be realized, namely, "a democratic state [*einen demokratischen Staat*]." This ideal is characterized as "a community of human beings [*Gemeinschaft der Menschen*] united for their highest aims." More fully:

> The self-confidence [*Selbstgefühl*] of the human being, freedom, has first of all to be aroused again in the hearts of these people [i.e., present-day Germans]. Only this feeling, which vanished from the world with the Greeks, and under Christianity disappeared into the blue mist of the heavens, can again transform society into a community of human beings united for their highest aims, into a democratic state.

The letter goes on to proclaim that the Germans must stop being slaves and must become human beings instead. Furthermore: "Human beings—that means spiritual beings, free men—that means republicans [*Menschen, das wären geistige Wesen, freie Männer Republikaner*]" (*MEGA2* 1.2: 475–76/*MECW* 3: 134/*EW* 201).

Words like these suggest that in May 1843 Marx was committed to "republicanism" as a goal, and hence, presumably, to a politics that would persist beyond the despotic backwardness of the present age (since republicanism involves seeing politics as an essential part of human existence).[52] But the letter is textually questionable, for we now know that Ruge heavily rewrote the *Deutsch-Französische Jahrbücher* letters (we do not have the original manuscripts but only the text published in the *D-FJ*).[53] In 1843 Ruge was a proponent of "republicanism," even of "humanist republicanism."[54] In consequence, we cannot be sure to what extent the passages quoted here were actually Marx's. In particular, the "*Republikaner*" reference appears in no other writings by Marx. Since Ruge did rewrite the letters and since it is known that Ruge was committed to "republicanism," any claim for a "republican" commitment on Marx's part at any point in his career is highly questionable.

On the other hand, Marx's appeal to democracy is paralleled elsewhere in his writings of 1843 (although nowhere else in the Marx corpus). Specifically, Marx discusses democracy in the "Critique of Hegel's Doctrine of the State," and there is also a reference to "the democratic state" in "On the Jewish Question" (October–December 1843).[55] In these texts Marx situates his thinking about democracy and politics within a (Hegelian) framework of dialectical contradiction and resolution that he sees as leading to an *Aufhebung* of the political state.[56] *Aufhebung* is a tricky term, derived from Hegelian dialectics: it simultaneously means abolition, transcendence, and preservation; it can also be translated as "supersession" and as "sublation."

As the term *Aufhebung* suggests, Marx claims in these writings that the political state is destined to be surpassed. In one important passage in the "Critique," Marx analogizes democracy to Christianity, claiming that the relation of democracy to "all other political forms" is "in certain respects" similar to Christianity's relation to all other religions (*MEGA2* 1.2: 31/*MECW* 3: 29–30/*EW* 87–88). There is a subtext here, derived from Feuerbach, who in *The Essence of Christianity* had portrayed Christianity, the (flawed) religion of love, as an advance over Judaism, which he saw as "the religion of the most narrow-hearted egotism."[57] But Feuerbach also claimed that Christianity itself must and will be superseded, to be replaced by a humanism that would see man, not God, as the active and creative subject. Marx's implication seems to be that the democratic political state is destined to be superseded, just as Christianity is about to be superseded by humanism.

This interpretation is confirmed by another passage in "Critique of Hegel's Doctrine of the State," where Marx claims that the instituting of universal suffrage will lead to the dissolution of the state. One needs to understand the view of modern history underlying Marx's general argument here. Marx maintained that in the wake of the French Revolution a sharp division had emerged between civil society (which for Marx is the sphere of concrete, material, selfish individualism, a sphere dominated, in his view, by market-based economic activity) and the (political) state, which he saw as involving an abstract, formal commitment to universalism and to the human community.

Thus Marx holds that the (political) state and (civil) society stand in contradiction to each other.[58] When universal suffrage comes, this means that civil society will have

> raised itself [*sich erhoben*] to the point of abstraction from itself, to the *political* existence which constitutes its true, universal, essential existence. But the perfection [*Vollendung*] of this abstraction is also its transcendence [*Aufhebung*]. . . . And with the demise of the one, the other, its opposite collapses also. Therefore, *electoral reform in the abstract political state* is the equivalent to a demand for its *dissolution* [*Auflösung*] and this in turn implies the *dissolution of civil society*. (*MEGA2* 1.2: 130–31/*MECW* 3: 121/*EW* 191)[59]

In short: the political state will disappear.

Admittedly, one must be cautious in attributing a specific, concrete meaning to Marx's statements of 1843 to the effect that there will be a dissolution, sublation, or movement beyond the political state and politics. His statements have more to do with the formal application of radical dialectics to Hegel's political theory than they do with any thinking about how a post-*Aufhebung* situation would actually function. One point that needs to be made is that what is superseded is less the political state itself than the allegedly sharp division between the political state and civil society. Marx does write, in the "Critique," that civil society will have "*really* raised itself . . . to the *political* existence that constitutes its true, universal, essential existence" (*MEGA2* 1.2: 130/*MECW* 3: 121/*EW* 191). So *in some sense* politics remains. But in what sense? This is not entirely clear from these 1843 texts.

Thus we are left not quite knowing what Marx's position concerning politics and the state actually was in 1843. His attempt to theorize about politics does not generate any real insight into how he thought politics would actually operate in the future—if it was to operate at all. It is not clear what unification at a higher level would actually *mean* for a possible future politics or state. One has the impression that Marx was moving about in semidarkness—that he did not know what an *Aufhebung* of the present situation would bring with it. One also has the impression that he knew that he did not know.

An important reason for Marx's vagueness on matters of politics is surely that *from the beginning* he really had no conceptual space for politics, given the tightness of his rationality-criteria. By *politics* I mean, again, those practices of deliberation, negotiation, and compromise by which human beings decide how to organize their lives together.

In Marx's view, however, deliberation, negotiation, and compromise were simply not "on" in the future society. If Marx had no commitment to political deliberation he had even less commitment to democratic political deliberation. Such matters were not of fundamental interest to him, because in his view science will show us what needs to be done. The results of scientific investigation are not open to discussion—they are simply true. Already in a newspaper article published in July 1842, Marx made clear his hope that philosophy would do "in the political sphere" what "physics, mathematics, medicine, and every science" have each done "in their respective spheres." The thought here seems to be that philosophy ought to be able to articulate the same sort of rational account of the political sphere that physics articulates of the world of matter and motion. ("Leading Article . . . of *Kölnische Zeitung*," *MEGA2* 1.1: 188/*MECW* 1: 201) This would be an account that every rational person would accept, once he or she understood it. Hence politics would be unneeded and democracy irrelevant. Below, I shall discuss this antipolitical tendency further, in the section titled "The Main Failing of Marx's View of Politics."

MARX'S ROAD OUT OF POLITICS: THE ROLE OF HISTORY, LATE 1843–44

Marx's theoretical rejection of politics was the unHegelian product of his Hegelianism. How did Marx in 1844 find *Hegelian* grounds for excluding politics and the political state from the future socialist order? The answer to this question has to do with the historical aspect of Marx's Hegelian rationality-criteria. Consider again Marx's letter to his father of November 1837. In this letter Marx points out that the philosopher is charged with unveiling "the rationality of the thing itself [*die Vernunft des Dinges selbst*]." At greater length:

> In the concrete expression of a living world of ideas, as exemplified by law, the state, nature, and philosophy as a whole, the object itself [*das Objekt selbst*] must be studied in its development . . . the rationality of the thing itself must develop as something imbued with contradictions in itself and find its unity in itself. (*MEGA2* 3.1: 10–11/*MECW* 1: 12)

In other words, in order to have rational understanding of an object, one must understand how it developed historically.

Feuerbach made no attempt at all to outline the rational development of the objects he studied. For a Hegelian this had to be a grave deficiency. Feuerbach looked for unity, but his unity had the character of a more or less instant reduction of one entity to another: of theistic religion to humanism; of philosophy to humanism. There was no attempt on Feuerbach's part to unveil a necessary development of the object, such that its contradictions at a lower and earlier level get resolved into unity at later and higher levels. It was not

Feuerbach who was decisive for Marx's rejection of politics, but Hegel himself. More precisely, the rationality-criteria that Marx derived from Hegel were decisive.

How so? Since Marx, following Hegel, held that a rational understanding of anything requires that one study it "in its development," to have a rational understanding of politics one must have a rational, developmental understanding of its history. "Truth includes not only the result but also the path to it," as Marx opined, Hegelianly, in his article on the Prussian government's censorship instruction (*MEGA2* 1.1: 101/*MECW* 1: 113). Marx the journalist claimed to see a political evolution in the modern world. As he put it in his article on the banning of the *Leipziger Allgemeine Zeitung*, in Germany "the press is *young*, the popular spirit also is *young*"—and so "the political thinking of an only just awakening popular spirit" is "less mature, more shapeless and hasty" than the political thinking to be found in England and France, where "the popular spirit . . . has become great, strong, and self-confident in the course of political struggles" (*MEGA2* 1.1: 292/*MECW* 1: 312). In "On the Jewish Question" and in the introduction to "A Contribution to the Critique of Hegel's Philosophy of Right," both published in the *Deutsch-Französische Jahrbücher* in February 1844, Marx continued to suggest that a political evolution was taking place in modern Europe, with Western Europe leading the way for Germany.

The question, then, is What would be the characteristics of an adequate history of politics? In chapter 1, I suggested that Hegel's *Lectures on the History of Philosophy* gave him his model for a proper history. Above all, a truly scientific history should focus on what is of universal significance, casting aside mere idiosyncrasy, and it should describe a progression that is a necessary progression. In a characteristic passage, Hegel writes, concerning the history of philosophy, that

> only as a succession of phenomena established through reason, and having as content just what is reason and revealing it, does this history show that it is rational; it shows that the events recorded are in reason . . . that faith must surely be the more rational in which chance is not made ruler over human affairs. (*LHP* 1: 31)

Lest one think that Hegel held these criteria to be applicable only to the history of philosophy, he made essentially the same claim in the introduction to his (much better known) *Lectures on the Philosophy of History*. Here Hegel tells us that "the Idea is truly the leader of nations and of the world; and it is the spirit, with its rational and necessary will, that has directed and continues to direct the events of world history." He asserts that, philosophically considered, history is to be seen as *inherently* necessary, rather than as contingent. For "the sole aim of philosophical enquiry is *to eliminate the contingent*," and "*contingency is the same as external necessity, that is, a necessity that originates in causes that are themselves no more than external circumstances*." Thus the historical necessity to which Hegel refers is an *internal, immanent* necessity. He declares that "the history of the world is a rational process, the rational and necessary evolution of the world spirit." And he notes the need "to recognize the universal and the rational" in history.[60]

I suggested in chapter 1 that one can more readily see the history of philosophy as adhering to these criteria than the histories of other entities. Indeed, I contended that Hegel's *History of Philosophy* was Hegel's *only* properly dialectical history: not surprising, since Hegelian dialectic was modeled on dialectic as described by Aristotle, where it is argument among philosophers. Thus it seems appropriate that a history of philosophy, which amounts to a history of the arguments that philosophers test out on each other in the course of their search for truth, would turn out to be itself dialectical. But can there be a comparable history of politics? Marx would have been aware of the sharp contrast between the history of philosophy and the history of politics that Hegel poses near the beginning of the *History of Philosophy*. Here Hegel declares that because the history of philosophy shows us "a succession of noble minds" who have "penetrated into the being of things, of nature, and of spirit" and have "won for us . . . the treasure of reasoned knowledge," it comes about that "personality and individual character do not enter in any large degree" into the content and matter of this history; so that "in philosophy, the less deserts and merits are accorded to the particular individual, the better is the history." Hegel claims, however, that it is quite different with "political history, in which the individual, according to the peculiarity of his disposition, talents, affections, the strength or weakness of his character, and in general, according to that through which he is this individual, is the subject of actions and events" (*LHP* 1: 1–2). In short, Hegel, at this moment in his thinking, considered the history of politics to be largely governed, not by universality and necessity, but by particularity and contingency. To be sure, his *Lectures on the Philosophy of History* do amount to a history of politics; but as I noted in chapter 1 it is an unsatisfactory history, in which the transitions from one form of the state to the next are left completely unclear. In contrast, as Hegel says near the end of his *History of Philosophy*, "the succession of philosophic systems is not due to chance, but represents the necessary succession of stages in the development of this science" (*LHP* 3: 552).

Given that, to all appearances, the early Marx accepted Hegel's notion that to understand a thing one must understand its history, and given that he also adhered to rigorous criteria of rationality derived mainly from Hegel, he had reason, on Hegelian and not simply on Feuerbachian grounds, to find the political domain a challenging one to accommodate to scientific knowledge. I am persuaded that by October 1843, if not earlier, there was in Marx's mind something approaching a conscious awareness of the need to construct a history of politics. I have already noted how Marx's "Critique of Hegel's Doctrine of the State," written during the Kreuznach interlude, implies a Feuerbachian reductionism, with the state disappearing into the conceptual maw of "Man." Far less widely known than Marx's Feuerbachianism of March 1843–44 is the fact that, beginning in summer 1843 and continuing until summer 1844, he studied, and planned to write a history of, the French Revolution. During summer 1843, while he was still in Kreuznach, he began to read on the French Revolution. After his move to Paris in October 1843 he "began an intensive study of the history of the French Revolution, with the idea of writing a history of the Convention," as Hal Draper notes (DRAP 1: 13–15, at 15).[61] His concern, that is, was with political affairs in France in the years 1792–95, a turbulent period that included the Reign of Terror and much else.

Meanwhile, toward the end of 1843 or early in 1844 Marx read Friedrich Engels's essay, "Outlines of a Critique of Political Economy," which was published in the *Deutsch-Französische Jahrbücher* along with Marx's two pieces. Engels's essay had a profound impact on Marx's thinking; in its wake, he turned to a serious reading of political economy, focusing on such writers as Adam Smith, David Ricardo, Jean-Baptiste Say, and James Mill, to name the most important. One of my claims in the present study is that there was a negative interplay between Marx's reading in economics and his reading in political history. The economists whom he read—primarily English and French writers—were oriented in a theoretical rather than in a descriptive and historical direction. They aimed to articulate what they thought of as universally valid theory. In contrast, many of the German writers within the general field of economic science were more interested in describing, analyzing, and providing solutions to particular economic problems than they were in discovering universal laws on a Newtonian model—for them, economics was much more a *practical* than a *theoretical* science.[62] I believe that Marx's reading of the political economists noted here helped him to see how he himself might arrive at valid theory. In contrast, his reading of political history generated no theoretical (universal and necessary) propositions, and this was a substantial part of the reason why in 1844 Marx was to turn from politics to economics.

I have already noted Marx's Feuerbachian argument, in "Critique of Hegel's Doctrine of the State," against the alleged "logical, pantheistic mysticism" of Hegel's political theory. Also running through the "Critique" is a historical narrative that is Marx's own: it follows the pattern of unity—contradiction—unity at a higher level that is prominent in Left Hegelian dialectics. The story begins with the Middle Ages, when the entities that we now think of as "the state" and "civil society" were allegedly jumbled together. Over time the state emerged as an institution distinct from society generally, and simultaneously a complex economy also emerged. As a good Left Hegelian, Marx held that the state and civil society currently exist in a situation of radical opposition to each other. Marx suggests that the French Revolution marked the beginning of this radical opposition, which he contends is definitive of what he calls "the modern world" or "the modern age." In the wake of the French Revolution the state projects an abstract notion of universality (universal political rights, the general welfare), while on the other hand civil society arises as the sphere of particularity and dog-eat-dog competition. Marx looks forward to the future reintegration of what is today divided, a reintegration in which the real world of civil society—but a civil society somehow transformed into a community—would have priority.[63]

It is of course obvious that Marx's historical narrative here is deeply abstract and schematic. It is true that criticisms that he made in his "Mosel" piece (January 1843) of the detachment of Prussian bureaucrats from actual conditions on the ground in the Mosel region give some concreteness to his general notion that the extant state is detached from real life (*MEGA2* 1.1: 312/*MECW* 1: 347–48). But, overall, his allusions in "Critique of Hegel's Doctrine of the State" (and subsequently in "On the Jewish Question") to the historical role of the French Revolution begged for further development—especially since Marx clearly found the French Revolution fascinating, not least because it was the best revolution in sight.[64]

"Critique of Hegel's Doctrine of the State" clearly opened up two directions for further inquiry. One was the economic direction, to be addressed in chapter 3. The other was the political direction. Marx in 1843 saw the pursuit of both sides as justified. Pursuit of the civil society side of the split was justified, in Marx's eyes, by the centrality of property and social class in the world that he saw around him (see, e.g., *MEGA2* 1.2: 89–90, 118–19, 123/*MECW* 3: 79–81, 109, 113–14/*EW* 146–47, 178, 183). (However, in 1843 Marx does not seem to have held, yet, that economics serves as the *basis* of the state.) Pursuit of the political side was justified by the fact that the most momentous historical event for Marx's time was the French Revolution, and by the further fact that the struggles that interested Marx and that caught the attention and commitment of many in his generation were those struggles taking place in England, France, Germany, and elsewhere that concerned the political system, and that were focused especially on issues of political representation and legislative power. The struggles in question were all residues of the French Revolution. So it is not surprising that Marx should have attempted to write the history of the crucial period of the Revolution extending from September 1792 to October 1795, when France was governed by the Convention, a body that combined legislative, executive, and judicial functions. Such a history would presumably offer, in a concrete way and with a certain measure of detail, an account of precisely how the radical bifurcation of state and civil society that, Marx insisted, was connected with the Revolution, had come to be.

Marx wrote no such history, beyond the making of sometimes rather detailed and digressive reading notes.[65] The omission was not for want of trying. Marx's friends and acquaintances were well aware of his historiographical plans. Ruge is our main source here. In three letters, of May 15, 1844 to Feuerbach and of May 20 and July 9, 1844 to a friend, Karl Moritz Fleischer, he referred to Marx's efforts. In the May 15 letter to Feuerbach, Ruge writes:

> Marx . . . wants to write the history of the Convention and to that end he has accumulated material and has made some very fruitful historical points. He again lays aside the critique of Hegel's Philosophy of Right. He wants to make use of the Paris stay for this work, which is entirely right.[66]

In the July 9 letter to Fleischer there is a significant shift of tense. Here Ruge reports to Fleischer that Marx "wanted to write the history of the Convention and to that end has read enormously. Now that too seems to be again laid aside [*Jetzt scheint auch das wieder zu liegen*]."[67]

In reproducing Marx's reading notes of this period the "New *MEGA*" shows how seriously he pursued the history of the Revolution (see *MEGA2* 4.2: 9–217).[68] These notes show that Marx was interested in both revolutionary events and political structures. He read Rousseau's *Social Contract* and was interested in Rousseau's views on equality and universality as conditions for democracy (*MEGA2* 4.2: 93, 100). In Jacques-Charles Bailleul's *Critical Examination of a Posthumous Work by M. la Baronne de Staël*, he notes Bailleul's assertion that the nobility under the old regime had failed to serve as a *corps intermédiaire* between king and people, as well as Bailleux's views on the desirability of property qualifications for legislative deputies (*MEGA2* 4.2: 103). From Henry Brougham's book on Poland he gleaned several matters of political interest, especially the consequences of the absolute veto that had prevailed in the Polish state (*MEGA2* 4.2: 104–5). In his reading of Montesquieu's *Spirit of the Laws* he concludes from Montesquieu's account that the main cause of the downfall of the Roman republic was to be found in the fact that the knights, who originally formed the Roman cavalry, became "tax-collectors [*Plusmacher*], men of business" (*MEGA2* 4.2: 111; see *Spirit of the Laws*, Bk. 11, chaps. 18, 19). He took notes from Machiavelli's *Discourses* on the relations between nobles and people and on the connection of equality and inequality to the freedom and stability of the state (*MEGA2* 4.2: 276–78).

Overall, we see in this reading a concern on Marx's part with getting at the structure of political institutions. This concern embraced an interest in class and property relations. To use his later, historical materialist terminology (chapter 4): Marx was interested in "relations of production"—but relations of production considered primarily in their connection to what the historical materialist Marx would call "the legal and political superstructure." At this point Marx showed little interest in the connection of the relations of production to the "forces of production" (that is, to the raw materials, physical labor, productive machinery, and science and technology that are deployed in producing commodities).

As a Hegelian, Marx had to attend not simply to the structure of political institutions but also to their development. Getting at the development of political institutions requires investigation at subinstitutional levels as well. As Marx's notebooks make clear, he was often led to make notes on matters having a purely "*événementiel*" [event-like] character (to use the terminology of the French *Annales* school of historiography). The notes often have an "annals-like" character as well, with little in the way of connection from one item to the next. In other words, little (even nothing) that looks like a rational process of development appears. This is not to suggest that in reading the works that he read Marx could have been expected to work up a coherent picture of, say, the history of France in the Middle Ages (on which he took detailed notes, from C. G. Heinrich's *History of France* [*MEGA2* 4.2: 64–83]). It is merely to suggest the magnitude of the challenge facing a thinker who believed that an adequate history is universal and necessary in its development. The challenge was that of giving some sort of rational order to the kinds of facts that are conventionally to be found in political histories. Starting out from such source materials as Lord John Russell's *History of the English Government and Constitution*, Lancizolle's *On the Causes, Character, and Consequences of the July Days*, Wachsmuth's *History of France in the Age of Revolution*, and Ranke's *German History in the Age of the Reformation*, how was Marx to generate a scientifically justified history of politics?

The most significant evidence concerning Marx's projected study of the Convention are his excerpts from, and notes on, the *Memoirs* of an old Jacobin, René Levasseur de la Sarthe (1747–1834), published in Paris in 1829 (Marx made these notes end 1843—beginning 1844 [*MEGA2* 4.2: 725]). Levasseur was a surgeon (specializing in the delivery of babies) who was elected to the Estates-General in 1789 and to the Convention in 1792. In his account of the Convention Levasseur focuses on the conflicts between different political factions and on the way in which the factions were either overtaken by, or were able to take advantage of, the unprecedented events of the time. Marx read Levasseur's account of the Revolution carefully, constructing an epitome of it composed partly of quotations and partly of Marx's own summary (*MEGA2* 4.2: 281–99/*MECW* 3: 361–74).[69] For example, Marx quotes the following passage from Levasseur:

> The only force which existed in France during the interregnum which began on August 10 [1792] was popular élan, insurrection, anarchy. . . . The only means of salvation still remaining was, therefore, to make use of the resources offered by anarchy and to direct against our enemies the brute force which it aroused. (*MEGA2* 4.2: 284/*MECW* 3:362; from Levasseur, *Mémoires* [1989 edition], 81)

Levasseur portrays the revolutionary situation as one in which people were often ignorant of the conditions within which they were making decisions. Such ignorance prevailed even within the Convention itself. Swirling around the legislators was a changeable public opinion; for a time, "the Jacobin club was . . . the thermometer" of this opinion (Levasseur, 87). It was a situation, moreover, wherein much depended on the resoluteness of the contending parties. Thus the (moderate) Girondists gave way to other, more radical elements in the revolution because they turned "feeble and irresolute" once "the helm of the state was indisputably in their hands" (*MEGA2* 4.2: 285/*MECW* 3: 363). Unpredictability held sway. For example, Marat "would never have exercised the least influence" had the Girondists not chosen to engage in personal attacks on him, which allowed him to display "the calmness, constancy, *sang-froid*, and contempt for insults characteristic of real conviction and devotion" (*MEGA2* 4.2: 286–87/*MECW* 3: 364). In general, Levasseur's accounts of debates in and around the Convention describe, not a dialectical deliberative process of the type that Marx envisaged in his pieces extolling freedom of the press—a process that supposedly leads, through a sifting of rival views, to a further unfolding of truth—but a contingent process frequently sidetracked by accidents. Events happened to turn out in the way they did, but they could just as easily have turned out another way. This was not a description that fit well with Marx's rationality-criteria of universality, necessity, and predictivity.

In fact, Hegel himself could have predicted the failure of Marx's project of a political history of the French Revolution. As noted above, at the beginning of his *Lectures on the History of Philosophy*, Hegel contrasted the history of philosophy with the history of politics. Since, in Hegel's reading of it, the history of philosophy has to do with "noble minds" engaged in the serious search for truth, "personality and individual character do not enter in any large degree" into this history, so that "the less deserts and merits are accorded to the particular individual, the better is the history." But things are quite different with the history of politics, for here individuals actually matter: "the individual, according to the peculiarity of his disposition, talents, affections, the strength or weakness of his character, and in general, according to that through which he is this individual, is the subject of actions and events" (*LHP* 1: 1–2).

How, then, can one write a *scientific* history of politics—especially if one's concern is with the disorderly events of a revolution? In what seems to have been the last, belated gasp of Marx's French Revolution project, an untitled, 150-word, nine-point outline, probably written in November 1844, Marx jotted down some ideas about "*the history of the origin of the modern state* or the *French Revolution*." But Marx seems to have envisaged, here, a history of the *end* of politics and of the state, for his outline moves from "the self-conceit of the political sphere" which, Marx claims, had "mistake[n] itself for the ancient state" to "the *abolition* [Aufhebung] of the state and of civil society" (*MEW* 3: 537/*MECW* 4: 666). As François Furet has shown, Marx returned again and again to the Revolution, obsessed as he was by the question of how a new, socialist revolution might come about, and encouraged by the periodic re-eruptions of the revolutionary spirit in France, the country that was "the preferred terrain of political tremors" in nineteenth-century Europe. Furet also observes that by 1850 Marx had written "all he would ever write about the French Revolution as such—its origins, its history, its interpretation." Furet might well have said: "by 1844," for his repeated brief allusions to the Revolution in the late 1840s add nothing to his earlier views.[70]

IMPLICATIONS OF MARX'S ENCOUNTER WITH THE FRENCH REVOLUTION

The first thing that needs to be noted, as we move toward a critique of Marx's conception of politics, is that there is a profound difference between, on the one hand, the conception of politics that we can infer from Marx's journalism of 1842–early 1843 (discussed in the section, "The Politics of Marx's Journalism") and, on the other, the account of political machinations in the French Revolution that Levasseur offers in his *Mémoires*, discussed above. In the journalism of 1842–early 1843 we observe a Marx who seeks to enter into a *dialectical* political debate. He appears to equate political debate with a philosophy seminar. In other words, he appears to regard political debate as dialectical in the strict sense of the word (see chapter 1), involving a defining and sifting of concepts, a testing of them against each other, responses to the testing, counterarguments, and so on. Further, as noted above, in his July 1842 article criticizing the views of the rival *Kölnische Zeitung* he goes so far as to suggest that "philosophy" can and ought to do "in the political sphere" what "physics, mathematics, medicine, and every science have . . . done in their respective spheres." Here he seems to envisage philosophy/science offering *authoritative* judgments—that is, judgments that will be accepted by all informed persons of good will. He evokes the tradition of political philosophers, from Machiavelli to Hobbes, who have discovered "the law of gravitation of the state" and who are able "to deduce [*entwickeln*] its natural laws from reason and experience"

(*MEGA2* 1.1: 188–89/*MECW* 1: 201). Surely their discoveries ought then to be followed by all of us.

There is nothing like Marx's image of a dialectical politics, based, somehow, on (political) science, in the Convention as described by Levasseur. There is conflict in Levasseur's Convention, but it is not a matter of the conflict and testing of opinions through the dialectical clash of opposites. It is not a *dialectical* conflict, because it does not turn on the philosophical sifting of opposing views. It turns on other things. So-called real conviction—a resoluteness and calmness in acting—is likely to win out over indecision irrespective of the merits of the opposing cases. Events turned out the way they did, but they could also have turned out differently. For example, if the Girondists had not engaged in personal attacks on Marat, or if they had acted resolutely once they were in power, they might never have fallen to the Jacobins. And beyond the discussions taking place in the legislature, there were also the contingencies imposed by events on the streets of Paris and the battlefields of Europe.

If these are the circumstances that prevail in politics, political events cannot be predicted. They are too contingent, too dependent on accidents of personality, mood, the state of someone's digestion, and happenstance of various kinds (assassinations, assignations, assignats, adulteries, and the like). More than this, it is not possible to "postdict" political events either. In other words—forgetting now about prediction—it is impossible to construct a rational history of politics *after the fact*, if "politics" is understood to include the vicissitudes of actual political struggle and if a "rational history" is understood to be one that conforms to Marx's rationality-criteria. It is my inference that Marx reached this conclusion by July 1844, by which time he would have decided that he could not write a political history of the French Revolution that would satisfy his rationality-criteria. We do know that by July 1844 Marx had laid aside his project of a political history of the Convention. It is my further inference that Marx's failure with his Convention project would have led him to conclude, more broadly, that in order to make sense of politics at all one has to make sense of it *by appeal to a level of reality more rational than is the level of politics itself*. And this means that by July 1844 the stage was set for historical materialism, historical materialism being, among other things, an attempt to lay out a deeply rational level of social reality, namely, the level of material production, in terms of which the conditions and movements of other, less rational levels of reality might be explained.

In his *Lectures on the History of Philosophy* Hegel tells us what constitutes a "rational" history:

> Only . . . as a succession of phenomena established through reason, and having as content just what is reason and revealing it, does . . . history show that it is rational: it shows that the events recorded are in reason. . . . That faith must surely be the more rational in which chance is not made ruler over human affairs. (*LHP* 1: 31)

It is true that Hegel speaks here of the history *of philosophy*, not of history in general. But as I contend in chapter 1, it was precisely in *this* Hegelian history that Marx found his primary model for history generally (and for his dialectic as well).[71]

Still, Hegel's commitment to a necessitarian and universalistic understanding of history, high though it was, did not hold a candle to Marx's commitment. The difference has to do with Marx's more discontented, more forward-looking orientation. As Hegel puts it near the beginning of his *History of Philosophy*, "particular kinds of knowledge cannot yet be attained. . . ." (*LHP* 1: 36). But Hegel—and this is of course the older, rather conservative Hegel—emphasizes that we "ought to feel no disappointment" at the fact that our knowledge is incomplete, for it is simply a fact that "in the history of the world progression is slow [*gehen die Fortschritte langsam*]." Here Hegel's equanimity, his Olympian perspective, shows itself. For Hegel, "contingency [*Zufälligkeit*] must vanish on the appearance of Philosophy" (*LHP* 1: 36–37). But philosophy will take full flight only when the time is ripe for it. Hegel is patient, Marx not.[72]

For Marx, waiting would not do. To the later Hegel's epimetheanism we need to juxtapose Marx's prometheanism. To be sure, Marx recognized that there are things that cannot be known, or at any rate cannot be known now. Hence he usually refused to speculate about the shape of the future order. But the general feeling in Marx is one of immense epistemological confidence. Marx's evident hope is for an understanding of the necessary, and not just contingent, character of the historical development of the human world generally, just as Hegel had sought to unveil the necessary development of philosophy. This hope for a necessary history of the human world appears for the first time in certain passages in the "Economic and Philosophical Manuscripts" (1844) (see chapter 3), and it is then worked out in the historical materialism of *The German Ideology* (1845–46) and related writings (chapter 4). One can see how the notion of a necessary historical process would have attracted Marx, a radical intellectual living in what he regarded as a backward country—for if one can come to understand the nature of the necessity by which history moves, one has the possibility of taking that process in hand and helping it move forward.[73] One likewise sees how Marxism had the same appeal for many people in less-developed countries over the course of the twentieth century.

Yet at the same time Marx mitigated the necessitarianism of his concept of history. Consider the passage in Marx's fifth "Notebook on Epicurean Philosophy," already quoted, where he declares that "in the history of philosophy there are nodal points that raise philosophy itself to concretion, apprehend abstract principles in a totality, and thus break off the rectilinear process [*den*

Fortgang der graden Linie abbrechen]" (*MEGA2* 4.1: 99/*MECW* 1: 491/*MER* 10). Here Marx is both echoing Hegel's *Lectures on the History of Philosophy* and foreshadowing his own notion of revolution. For, on the one hand, Marx saw history as a necessitarian process. On the other hand, he did not. In the first half of the nineteenth century there was a muted polemic between Hegel, who subordinated the contingent and particular in history to the necessary and the universal, and the historian Leopold von Ranke, who reveled in the contingent and particular (while looking forward to God's eventual revelation of the necessary and universal). With respect to Marxism, the dialectic between necessity and contingency is in fact *an internal debate within Marxian theory itself*. Marx most particularly places the contingent within the "nodal points" that "break off the rectilinear process"; and these nodal points are nothing other than revolution.

In short, the necessitarianism of Marx's theoretical history of humankind is counterbalanced by the contingent element that he finds in revolution. Accordingly, Marx could have a theory of such-and-such social system, and he could also have something that at least passed for a theory of history generally. But, by his own standards as to what is required to have an adequate theory, he could not have a theory of revolution, because what characterizes revolution is precisely its unpredictability (within the larger necessitarian framework imposed by the mode of production). So in Marx one finds a *doctrine* of revolution, and one can also find Marx practicing, and articulating at least to some degree, possible *tactics* of revolution (e.g., the notion that a "dictatorship of the proletariat" would be required in the transitional period between the collapse of capitalism and fully developed socialism). But one cannot find a Marxian *theory* of revolution. One should also note that, taken together, Marxian theory and Marxian doctrine had a tremendous breadth of psychological resonance—appealing both to the intellectual desire for an apparently powerful theory and to the emotional desire for the apparent freedom and spontaneity of revolutionary activity.

THE MAIN FAILING OF MARX'S VIEW OF POLITICS

The main failing of Marx's view of politics is that his rationality-criteria were too stringent for the political realm. For example, in his journalism of 1842–early 1843 Marx was inclined to attack opponents on the grounds that their premises were not adequately supported—were not *necessary*. This is a line of attack that would persist in Marx's work: for example, at the beginning of the "Estranged Labor and Private Property" section of the "Economic and Philosophical Manuscripts" he attacks political economy because it "proceeds from the fact of private property. It does not explain it" (*MEGA2* 1.2: 363/*MECW* 3: 270/*EW* 322). Such a mode of attack has some justification on the plane of science, where it amounts to a call for care and rigor. It seems to me not to be justified on the plane of politics, where very little is susceptible to apodictic certainty.

To put the matter in Aristotelian terms, Marx fails to grasp the degree to which political debate is unavoidably enthymematic. An enthymeme is a defective syllogism. In Aristotle's view, the premises of a syllogism are *necessarily* true. (This is not the modern view. In the modern view, the premises of a syllogism are only *hypothetically* true, so that, although the conclusions of a syllogism follow necessarily from the syllogism's premises, this does not necessarily mean that they are true.) In the enthymeme, the premises of the argument are constituted by commonly accepted opinion rather than by things known necessarily to be true. Aristotle knew perfectly well that political debate does not live up to the high logical standards of the syllogism. But there is no room for such looseness in Marx. When he observes a political debate (or, more accurately, when he observes an opponent in a political debate), he sees out-and-out illogicality. In his early journalism he does not acknowledge the difficulty of arriving at a foundation of apodictic certainty within the political realm. He proceeds as if the political realm were the realm of philosophy.

To be sure, in his journalism of 1842–early 1843 Marx addressed only incidentally the question of how politics is to be rationally understood. What he focused on, rather, were the specific issues that came his way—freedom of the press, political representation, economic policy, and so on. But given his theoretical drive, his commitment to philosophy, it would have been surprising had he not *tried* to articulate a theoretical perspective on politics. And indeed this is what he attempted in the "Critique of Hegel's Doctrine of the State," discussed above. This and related works show that the whole thrust of Marx's theorizing drive, with respect to politics, was to go *beyond* politics.

"Critique of Hegel's Doctrine of the State," never published by Marx, needs to be seen in conjunction with two subsequent works that were published: "On the Jewish Question" and the introduction to "A Contribution to the Critique of Hegel's Philosophy of Right," both of which were written in late 1843 and appeared in the *Deutsch-Französische Jahrbücher* in February 1844. I shall discuss "On the Jewish Question" from another point of view in chapter 3. For the moment, what is significant about the work is its incisive articulation of the state/civil society distinction. According to Marx, the state in its most fully "*perfected* [vollendete]" form is defined by an "abstract universality" that is most clearly discernible in the state's championing of the universal rights of man and citizen (*MEGA2* 1.2: 151, 155–63/*MECW* 3: 156, 160–68/*EW* 223, 227–34). "Civil society," on the other hand, is the sphere of individualism, which is most fully present within the economic sphere.

Marx sees this alleged sharp opposition between state and civil society as pointing forward to an *Aufhebung* or transcending of the opposition. So in some sense the state and politics disappear into the larger maw of whatever is to succeed these forms. To the extent that this happens, any rationale for the articulation of a theory of politics disappears also. What we see here is a Feuerbachian drive toward the reduction of politics to something else. In Feuerbach's terms, that would be a reduction of politics to the poorly defined Feuerbachian Man. But that is not the way that things turn out for Marx. It is not that politics and economics get reduced to Man; rather, politics gets reduced to economics, understood in a very broad sense, as human productive activity. If one wants to think of the outcome of the state/civil society clash as (nonetheless) a synthesis, the economic aspect dominates the synthesis. Marx's move is unquestionably a move to economics broadly defined. I attribute this outcome to the impact of Marx's rationalism, which did not accommodate politics, but which did accommodate certain aspects of economics—as we shall see in chapter 3.

How did Marx's rationalism not accommodate politics? Here it is useful to consider the relation of Marx's approach to politics to the conception of politics that is to be found in Bruno Bauer's short book of 1843, *The Jewish Question*—to which Marx's "On the Jewish Question" was a response. In "On the Jewish Question" Marx subjects Bauer's treatment of the "Jewish question" to withering attack, and in the book of late 1844 that he co-authored with Engels, *The Holy Family*, or *Critique of Critical Criticism: Against Bruno Bauer & Co.*, the two authors took up the cudgels again. *The Holy Family* targeted Bruno Bauer and a short-lived Berlin-based group, "the Free Ones" (*die Freien*), that Bauer was associated with. (The group had come together in early 1842 and included, among others, Bruno's brother Edgar Bauer.) In *The Holy Family*, Marx and Engels brand Bauer and his friends as complete fools, practitioners of a supposedly ultraradical criticism that actually supports the existing order of things.

The circumstances of Marx's attack on Bauer and on *die Freien* need to be understood. By fall 1842 Marx was editing the *Rheinische Zeitung* and was acutely conscious of the danger that the paper would be suppressed. Accordingly, he was alarmed by the polemics of *die Freien*, particularly their atheistic sallies. Marx complained about the group in a letter to Ruge of November 30, 1842. Here he contended, against them, that "religion should be criticized in the framework of political conditions . . . religion in itself is without content, it owes its being not to heaven but to the earth" (*MEGA2* 3.1: 38/*MECW* 1: 394–95). Meanwhile, in a letter to Marx of December 13, 1842, Bauer supported *die Freien* (*MEGA2* 3.1: 386–87). The fact that in March 1843 the *Rheinische Zeitung* actually *was* suppressed cannot have helped relations between Marx and Bauer. The breach between them that opened up in December 1842 is placed on display in Marx's "On the Jewish Question."[74]

But what is obscured in Marx's attack on Bauer is how Bauer-like Marx remained. What we have in Bauer's *The Jewish Question* is a rigorist application of a radical Hegelian dialectic to a political question, namely, the question as to whether Jews can be good citizens. In chapter 1, I characterized dialectic as involving "progress by contradiction." Bauer's dialectic might be better characterized as progress by the *elimination* of contradiction. One might imagine, in reading Marx's swingeing attacks on Bauer in "On the Jewish Question," that Marx definitively separated himself from Bauer. Marx himself no doubt thought so. But Marx retains Bauer's deeply uncompromising conception of the dialectic, a conception of the dialectic that becomes problematic in its application to the human world. This is perhaps most clearly visible in Bauer's discussion in *The Jewish Question* of the legal and political status of French Jews under the contemporary July Monarchy in France.

How did the July Monarchy deal with "the Jewish problem"? In regard to the participation of Jews in the political system, the French had arrived at a moderate compromise. This compromise was part of a more general attitude, that of the "*juste milieu*" [moderate middle]. The attitude of the *juste milieu* infuriated Bauer, who wanted what he himself characterized as an "extreme" solution to the Jewish question. In essence, the Jewish "question" was as follows: Can a people that sees itself as the chosen people, set apart from all others, legitimately claim the right to participate in the politics of the non-Jewish majority? Bauer's answer was that it cannot. Bauer held that the solution to the Jewish problem would come about only when all dogmatic religion, Christianity as well as Judaism, is abandoned. Or, as Bauer put it, the "one remedy" is "complete disbelief in servitude, belief in freedom and humanity."[75]

This was not the solution to the Jewish question that the French had adopted. They had instead adopted what Bauer regarded as an indefensible compromise between two incompatible positions. On the one hand, Bauer claimed that the revolution of July 1830, which founded the July Monarchy, "was directed against privileges, therefore, also against the state church."[76] But on the other hand, the French had lacked "the courage to profess the liberty that the revolution had conquered." Thus, when the assembly debated a law that would establish Sunday as the statutory day of rest, an amendment was rejected that would have removed any mention of a specific day (Bauer, 71, 68–69). In other words, the French were not up to the level of their principles. The *juste milieu* was a reaction against the Christian state—against religious and clerical privilege—but "it does not yet go all out for liberty, against all religious norms. It stops half-way."(75) The *juste milieu* "has freedom in theory," since it ignores religious differences in France and thus separates the state from religion; but "in practice . . . it is unfree and sacrifices the minority to the majority." It ignores the conflict between religious interests on the one hand and civil and state interests on the other, and instead claims that "the minority is so small that a wrong done to it can hardly be called a wrong."(76)

Summing up the situation, Bauer argues that

> the technique of the *juste milieu* is to let things go as they may, ignores the contradiction between theory and real life, and if a conflict occurs one tries to shove it up, hoping that there will not be another too soon. . . . The *juste milieu* is full of contradictions. It has freedom in theory but in practice disavows it, and it has freedom in practice which in theory, in the law, is ignored. (77)

One can see why Bauer was so upset. In his view, progress occurs by the clash of opposites, and the opposites here refused to clash. This is why, in Bauer's conceptual universe, moderation is bad and extremity is good.

But what Bauer describes in attacking the *juste milieu* is the practice of most properly functioning politics most of the time. Bauer's response to the willingness of politicians to compromise—his response to their "faint-heartedness," as he calls it (77)—was to abandon political engagement for the pursuit of pure theory, detached from the unresponsive masses of humankind. Marx's response, too, was to abandon politics, and on a similar ground—that it does not follow the dictates of reason. However, whereas Bauer left the domain of human action for a world of pure theory, Marx's response was different. Unlike Bauer, Marx remained an activist, concerned with transforming the human order. At the same time, Marx also remained a rationalist—but a rationalist who would find the rationality of the world in the economic, rather than in the political, sphere.[77]

* * *

Terrell Carver has rightly noted that Marx "did not write a comprehensive or even exemplary work of political theory." Carver continues:

> Instead [Marx] addressed himself as a political agent to a politics of democratic constitutionalism and revolutionary communism, and to a detailed critique of the economics of the day. It is from those works that his contributions to political theory can be constructed and assessed.[78]

Carver is also right in pointing out Marx's role "as a political agent." Marx the political agent certainly did support the struggle in his day for constitutional democracy—meaning, in brief, the instituting of as wide a voting franchise as possible and the subordination of the executive to the legislature.

But how committed was Marx to "democratic constitutionalism"? I contend that Marx was not committed to democracy at all. His real commitment was to a "revolutionary communism," a.k.a. socialism, that would be realized after the "liberal" and "bourgeois" struggle for political reform had succeeded. The revolution would establish a *nonpolitical* state within which the course of action to be pursued would be determined scientifically and not through a process of political deliberation and debate. Or, as Engels put it in his widely disseminated pamphlet, *Socialism: Utopian and Scientific* (1880), after the socialist revolution

> state interference in social relations becomes, in one domain after another, superfluous, and then tails off [*schläft ein*] of itself; the government of persons is replaced by the administration of things [*Sachen*] and by the direction [*Leitung*] of processes of production. (*MEGA2* 1.27: 620/*MECW* 24: 321/*MER* 713)

The processes of political deliberation, let alone those of democratic deliberation, would not exist in such an environment. Within such an environment political theory would be irrelevant. It is thus not surprising that Marx did not write "a comprehensive or even exemplary work of political theory."[79]

The position that Engels articulates is not only a "late," "Engelsian" position. Even in the Marx of 1842–44 notions of democracy and of political deliberation are essentially absent. As Brian Snyder has pointed out in an unpublished paper, over the course of his career Marx put forward four different (although sometimes overlapping) conceptions of politics and the state. We have already encountered some of them. First, there is Marx's conception of the "true state," where "rational freedom" is realized, a conception that Marx first articulated, as we have seen, in his journalism of 1842. (Marx also refers to this as the "democratic state," although we never really learn what, concretely, the "democracy" consists of.) Second, there is his conception of the state as the sphere of abstract, illusory universality, standing in opposition to the particularity, egotism, and concreteness of civil society, which surfaces in his writings of 1843. Third, there is his conception of the state as superstructure, arising from the economic base, which is one aspect of his historical materialism. Fourth, there is his conception of the state as an instrument of class oppression, with politics equivalent to class activity (struggle), which can be found in *The Communist Manifesto* and elsewhere. Snyder shows that by late 1843, the only positive sense of the state—namely, the notion of the "true" or "democratic" state—disappears from Marx's work.[80] But how "democratic" was "the democratic state" (to which, as noted above, the early Marx refers only once or twice)?[81] In fact, we have every reason to think that the early Marx viewed the term *democratic* as an empty, redundant placeholder, meaning nothing more than "true" or "rational."[82]

Carver evokes Marx the political agent, the activist. The close relation between Marx's activism and his theory needs to be noted. One of the main points of the present book, and one that in some measure surprised me, is the extent to which the notion of activity was persistently important for Marx. Activity tends to get obscured in the later Marx, in the historical materialism in particular, but when one looks under the conceptual structures that Marx was wont to build one finds the notion that human beings are *active* beings. For a long time I tended to think of this commitment to activity as a residue, in Marx, of Fichte. Activity is crucial in Fichte's philosophy, and indeed (see chapter 3) there is a passage in Fichte's *Science of Knowledge* (*Wissenschaftslehre*) that reads like a schematic draft of Marx's account of the estrangement of activity in the "Estranged Labor and Private Property" section of the EPM (although there is no reason to think that Marx paid any particular attention to the *Science of Knowledge*).

There are other ways, also, of trying to find the roots of Marx's emphasis on activity. In addition to Fichte, one can also mention Feuerbach. In his "Theses on Feuerbach" (early 1845) Marx refers explicitly to the emphasis on "human activity" in Feuerbach's work, only objecting that Feuerbach restricted this activity to the abstract realm of ideas (*MEW* 3: 5/*MECW* 5: 3/*EW* 421–22). There is also Kant. Many years ago, one of the first scholars to comment on Marx's dissertation, the historian of philosophy Norman Livergood, presented Marx as a philosopher seeking to articulate a new kind of materialism that would overcome the defects of mechanistic materialism, which left no room for freedom. Livergood also saw Marx as articulating an epistemology aimed at correcting Kant's epistemology—taking over from Kant the notion that the mind actively participates in the construction of knowledge rather than being merely a passive receiver, but then arguing against Kant that active participation in knowledge *does* involve a grasp of reality as it actually is.[83]

But to evoke these possible philosophical influences on Marx is perhaps to miss the point. One is tempted to say that Marx's activism is as deeply rooted as his rationalism, to such a degree that any attempt to *explain* the activism—that is, to say what caused Marx's project to be oriented toward activity—risks underestimating the extent to which activism is *essential* to the project. Similarly, while one can find analogues to and promptings for Marx's rationalism, his rationalizing project is finally his alone, and to imagine the project without the rationalism is to imagine away the project. All talk of Hegel's influence on Marx needs to be seen in this light.

Does Marx's activism arise from his personality? From his life-experiences (estrangement, etc.)? From his reading of other philosophers? My inclination is to say both "all" and "none" of the above. If one's focus is on the relation between Marx's project and his life-experiences, one can show how his activism comes to him from the familial and political context of Trier—from the liberalism there, from the repression, perhaps also from the petty humiliations of Jewish integration. If one's focus is on the history of philosophy one can show how there is an activist dimension in Fichte—and also, in different ways, in Kant, Hegel, and Feuerbach.

Here the focus is on the shape and articulation of Marx's theoretical project itself. When this is the focus one sees a symbiotic relationship between Marx's rationalism and his activism, such that, the more rigorous the requirements that theory imposes, the more one is driven to activism. Marx, *qua* theorist, is seeking to articulate a theory that will be universal, necessary, and predictive. This means that he must find a reality that is amenable to such a theorization. But no current reality is. Consequently, the realizing of the theory is pushed off into the future. Thus Marx's theoreticism and his revolutionary communism go together. From a *theoretical* point of view, the aim of revolutionary communism is to produce a reality that will be amenable to theorization. Of course, from a *practical* point of view the aim is a different one: it is to produce a free and humane society. The two aims are not entirely congruent, for it is not at all clear that the means that will be required to achieve a society amenable to theorization will also conduce to freedom and humanity.

In any case, Marx's activism was clearly central to his project. And throughout much of his life he was a *political* activist. But for all this, I do not see him as providing the *disjecta membra* of a political theory that he never quite put together. Certain aspects of Marx's theorizing—particularly his emphasis on class—do need to be taken account of in current political theory. But the most striking thing about Marx's attitude toward politics remains his wish to get beyond it. He was the figure of an antipolitical political activist. Proximately, Marxian theory holds that politics (now) is the epiphenomenon of the forces and relations of production. It also holds that (more distantly) politics will disappear from human society.

When Marxian socialism puts its political mask aside, what face is revealed? It is the face of science that stares back at us. At this point, we reach the "degree zero" of political theory. I shall turn back to this matter in the conclusion. What I cannot hold back here is my sense that we reach, at this point, a key error in Marx (I would suggest that, at the level of general theory, there are only two such errors: this is one of them). The error is the product of Marx's own scientific rigor, misapplied to the political domain.

MARXIAN HISTORY AND THE POLITICS OF THE PRESENT

Marx's exclusion of politics from the future socialist order does not mean that he failed to notice the politics of his own or preceding times. Quite the contrary, particularly in the wake of the failure of the revolutions of 1848 to establish democratic constitutionalism—let alone bring any success to revolutionary communism—Marx was driven to reflect on an extant politics that had so much disappointed his hopes.[84] What is evident from Marx's forays into contemporary history (as well as from Engels's forays into the roots of German politics) is their deep awareness of the failure of politics to follow in any clear way the progressive outline that they had charted out for history generally.[85] Their claim is that *fundamentally* there is a progressive movement embedded in history. They also recognize that the empirical history that they observe does not conform in any simple way to that progressive movement. But they still insist that, for all its contingencies, politics is determined by class and class ultimately by the productive forces of society.

One could devote an entire book to Marx's and Engels's historical writings alone. Here I want to call attention to only one of these writings, *The Eighteenth Brumaire of Louis Bonaparte. The Eighteenth Brumaire*, written between December 1851 and March 1852, is an account of French politics from 1848 through 1851—from the outbreak of the Revolution of 1848 on February 24 of that year to Louis Bonaparte's declaring himself emperor on December 2, 1851. If the reader wants to get the feel of one Marxian work of history, this is the work to read (*MEW* 8: 111–207/*MECW* 11: 99–197/*LPW* 31–127/*MER* 594–617 [excerpts only]).

The Eighteenth Brumaire's first few lines are among the most famous in the entire Marx corpus:

> Hegel observes somewhere that all the great events and characters of world history occur twice, so to speak. He forgot to add: the first time as high tragedy, the second time as low farce. Caussidière after Danton, Louis Blanc after Robespierre, the *montagne* [democratic socialists] of 1848–51 after the *montagne* [Jacobin democrats] of 1793–95, and then the London constable [Louis Bonaparte], with a dozen of the best debt-ridden lieutenants, after the little corporal [Napoleon Bonaparte], with his roundtable of military marshals! The eighteenth Brumaire of the fool after the eighteenth Brumaire of the genius! (*MEW* 8: 115/*MECW* 11: 103/*MER* 594/*LPW* 31 [Carver translation])

As Terrell Carver remarks, *The Eighteenth Brumaire* is "Marx's most sustained mature effort at satire, parody, and invective" (*LPW* xii). And precisely this quality of the work has given it a considerable attractive force: it is indeed a marvelous piece of satire.

But what is Marx satirizing? In part he is satirizing the political actors of 1848–51. This is obvious: in *The Eighteenth Brumaire* all the actors of 1848–51, from Louis Bonaparte on down, are seen as inferior to their predecessors of 1789–95. But I want to suggest that Marx is also satirizing the idea of a Marxian political history itself. Marx's target is not just (political) history in the sense of "what happened"; it is also the genre of writing that attempts to describe and explain such history. To put this another way: *The Eighteenth Brumaire* is both a *parody* (of Louis Bonaparte and everything he represented) and a *self-parody* (undermining its own implicit theoretical hopes). Its resulting concern with heterogeneity and nondeterminacy (insofar as actual political events are concerned) helps to explain the attraction that it held for poststructuralist literary critics in the late twentieth century.[86]

Marx *qua* theorist is a reductionist insofar as politics is concerned. This is first of all true in an explanatory sense: failing to make adequate sense of a set of phenomena on the level of the phenomena themselves, Marx tries to make sense of them by reference to another, "deeper," more rational level of reality. He largely fails, and is aware of his failure (at least so his turn to parody suggests). It is, second, true in a *real, historical* sense—for, failing to explain politics in terms congruent with his rationality-criteria, he decided that politics is something that needs to be superseded in reality itself. Politics will be reduced to nothing, disappearing from the scene, political man giving way to social man. *The Eighteenth Brumaire* both highlights the rationalist pretensions that are in play here (by insisting so much on the existence of an underlying, rational, economic history) and calls those pretensions into question.

It is no accident that by the time Marx wrote *The Eighteenth Brumaire* he had already turned to a study of the modern economy that would be far more searching than anything he had done before. (Already in June 1850 he had obtained his admission card to the British Museum's Reading Room, which was to be the site of much of this research [DRAP 1: 50, #24].) We might see *The Eighteenth Brumaire* as marking the final end of a trajectory: the trajectory of Marx's *theoretical* concern with politics (of course, it did not mark the end of his practical concern with politics; that continued throughout his life). *The Eighteenth Brumaire* also calls attention to the resumption of another trajectory: the trajectory of his analysis of capitalism, of *economic* rather than of *political* modernity. One misses the broader significance of *The Eighteenth Brumaire* if one fails to see it within the context of Marx's shift to economic analysis.

Chapter Three

Why Marx Rejected Private Property and the Market

We, on the contrary, desire nectar and ambrosia, purple mantles, costly perfumes, luxury and splendor, dances of laughing nymphs, music and comedies.

—Heinrich Heine, *Religion and Philosophy in Germany: A Fragment*, trans. John Snodgrass, foreword by Dennis J. Schmidt (Albany: State University of New York Press, 1986), 2d part, 79.

From 1844 onward Marx insisted repeatedly that in the future socialist (communist) society there would be no market and no private property.[1] There would be no buying and selling, no trading, no bartering even. Such activities would be absolutely excluded from socialism as Marx defined it. There would be no money either. Money's primary function is to facilitate buying and selling, but buying and selling would no longer exist. If by "private property" we mean possessions that individuals or groups of individuals have the right to dispose of as they wish, including disposal by sale or trade, it follows from the abolition of exchange that there would be no private property either. If one attributes to money the secondary function of allowing individuals to store value and pass it on to others—say, to their descendants—this function, too, would disappear from the future socialist order, since all material goods would be held by the human community in general.

Marx also maintained that once communism is fully established individuals will have use of whatever objects in the world they need. They might need an object in order to produce some other needed object, or for self-development, or for simple enjoyment, or for a combination of all three purposes. For example, let us imagine George and Erica, who are first-rate engineers and production managers. They and the volunteer team that they are directing are building a bridge that will establish a better link between two towns. They have access to all the machinery and raw materials that are required to carry out this task in an efficient manner. These are of the highest quality, yet George, Erica, and their team have been able to suggest some improvements, which are about to be published in a technical journal read by people interested in construction engineering. Let us also conjure up Sophie, who has been a pianist for a quarter of a century. From the time she started to play there has been a piano in the house where she lives, and when her true talent began to show she suddenly found that a fine Steinway had been provided for her use. Every week or so she gives a concert—*gives* it; she also does some teaching. Let us finally conjure up Elliott, who likes to pilot a small airplane on weekends, just for relaxation and for the joy of seeing the landscape spread out below him; he, too, has always had the equipment that he needed to pursue this interest of his, from the time that he first went out to qualify as a pilot.

In Marx's vision of the future (which he expressed most clearly in the "Economic and Philosophical Manuscripts" [1844] and *The German Ideology* [1845], but which he seems to have never abandoned), these same conditions will prevail throughout the socialist (communist) order. Wherever there is a human need, the satisfaction of which requires the making of some thing, everything required for the production of that thing will be provided from the general stock of equipment, raw materials, and labor available in the society as a whole. (To be sure, there may well be production constraints that will persist for a very long time, but the point is that the very best will be done at any given moment to see that all human needs are satisfied.) Within this future society, nothing is ever bought, sold, or traded in exchange for something else. No money changes hands: there *is* no money. One should note further that "human need," in this society, is not a fixed category. On the contrary, both human needs and the productive system that has the aim of satisfying those needs are constantly developing. Inputs—raw materials, equipment, the knowledge, skill, and exertions of the workers—are always being improved, and the new goods that are produced as a result call forth more refined needs on the part of the population. All of this occurs without the presence of markets, money, or private property. Such is communism (socialism) as Marx envisaged it (I shall document this assertion in the sections that follow).

In this chapter I ask one very specific question concerning this imagined and hoped-for future society: Why did Marx exclude from it exchange, private property, money, competition, and everything connected with these? I ask this question *historically*, which means that I resist the tendency to "improve" Marx in the hope of making him more usable for present purposes. This tendency is widespread. For example, it underpins the so-called analytical Marxism that first emerged in the late 1970s. People often want to "tweak" the theories of past thinkers, fixing a weak link here, correcting a logical error there, and in general bringing the benefit of subsequent experience to bear upon the theorist's proposals.[2] In a distanced way (by pointing out deficiencies), that is one part of what I do here. But I subordinate such improving efforts to the historical project of getting at the fundamental features of the theory itself as it was articulated—albeit while highlighting some features to make them stand out more clearly. In answering the question as to why Marx rejected private property and the market, I shall reveal some unaccustomed features of Marx's project—features that his commentators almost always miss.

DID MARX REALLY REJECT PRIVATE PROPERTY AND THE MARKET?

It is first necessary to establish that Marx really *did* exclude the market from his vision of a future socialism, for there is a definite tendency in the literature to soften his antimarket claims.[3] Consider some passages relevant to the issue.

In the *Manifesto of the Communist Party* (1848) Marx and Engels contend that the distinguishing feature of communism is "the abolition [*Abschaffung*] of bourgeois property." They also contend that since "bourgeois private property is the final and most complete expression of the system of producing and appropriating products that is based on class antagonisms," it follows that "the theory of the communists may be summed up in the single sentence: The transcending [*Aufhebung*] of private property."[4] Marx and Engels make the further point that if there is no private property, there will also be no selling and buying. As they put it, "under the present-day bourgeois relations of production, freedom means free trade [*den freien Handel*], free buying and selling [*den freien Kauf und Verkauf*]." But "if bargaining [*Schacher*] disappears, so also does free bargaining." They continue: "Talk about free bargaining [*freie Schacher*] and all the other boasts about freedom by our bourgeoisie have a meaning, if any, only in contrast with restricted bargaining [*gebundenen Schacher*], with the servile burghers of the middle ages, but have no meaning when contrasted to the communist abolition [*Aufhebung*] of bargaining" (*MEW* 4: 475, 476/*MECW* 6: 498, 499–500/*MER* 484, 486/*LPW* 13, 15).

Similarly, in the economic manuscript known as the *Grundrisse*, which Marx worked on between July 1857 and May/June 1858 (DRAP 1: 84, 88), and which was an initial raw draft for what eventually became *Capital* (1867), Marx states that "exchange corresponds to the bourgeois organization of society" (*MEGA2* 2.1.1: 70/*MECW* 28: 72/*GRUND* 134). Since Marx hotly desired the abolition of the bourgeois organization of society, it follows that he wants the abolition of exchange.

Marx articulates the same position in the 1875 "Critique of the Gotha Programme," where he attacks the proposed program of the new German Socialist Workers' Party for being insufficiently critical of capitalism and of the existing German state. Here he asserts that "within a co-operatively organized society based on common ownership in the means of production the producers do not exchange their products" (*MEGA2* 1.25: 13/*MECW* 24: 85/*LPW* 213).

Engels, in his *Socialism: Utopian and Scientific,* originally written in 1876–78, emphasizes that under socialism "anarchy in social production," which he and Marx saw as inseparable from the market, would be replaced by a system in which production would be conducted "upon a predetermined plan" (*MEGA2* 1.27: 625/*MECW* 25: 642/*MER* 717).

Finally, one needs to look at a little-known text that Engels published in 1845. The text in question is the published version of a speech that Engels had delivered on February 8, 1845, at a meeting that he helped organize in Elberfeld, adjacent to his home town of Barmen in Westphalia's Wupper valley. Three of these meetings, which were devoted to discussing socialist ideas, were held before the local authorities banned any further such gatherings: the last of the three attracted as many as 200 people. Engels declared in an excited letter to Marx that "all of Elberfeld and Barmen, from the financial aristocracy to small shopkeepers, was represented, the proletariat being the only exception" (letter of February 22–March 7, 1845, in *MEGA2* 3.1: 267/*MECW* 38: 22–23). Engels published the worked-up text of his speech in the *Rheinische Jahrbücher zur gesellschaftlichen Reform* [Rhineland Yearbooks on Social Reform] in August 1845. As a matter of principle Marx and Engels avoided discussing how postcapitalist society would be organized. Hence their rare accounts of the matter tend to be fragmentary and elliptical. Sometimes these accounts are indirect as well, as in *The Civil War in France*, which ostensibly describes the brief and tragic history of the Paris Commune (1871), but which actually has more to do with Marx's vision of the postcapitalist order. Consequently, it turns out that in the Elberfeld speech Engels says more about postcapitalist society than he or Marx would ever say again.

The speech is an attack on the "world of free competition [*freien Konkurrenz*]" that Engels sees around him. In such a society, Engels suggests, "it is impossible to speak of a rational organization [*vernünftigen Organisation*], of an allocation of jobs." Engels suggests further that "such an unregulated economic system [*unregelte Wirtschaft*] must in the long run lead to the most disastrous results for society; the disorder that lies at its basis, the neglect of true, general well-being, must sooner or later make itself felt in the most striking fashion." Engels goes on to paint in broad outline what in his opinion are the characteristics and outcome of free competition. One result, according to Engels, is economic polarization: the rich get richer, the poor poorer, and there are fewer rich people and more poor people. Engels suggests that "[this] contradiction will develop more and more sharply until finally neediness forces society to a reorganization on more rational principles [*vernünftigeren Prinzipien*]." But economic polarization is not the only problem with "free competition." Another problem is the sheer disorderliness of production. "Since each man produces and consumes on his own without attending much to what others are producing and consuming, a crying disproportion between production and consumption must, of necessity, quickly develop." Further, since the distribution of goods is entrusted to "merchants, speculators, and shopkeepers, each one of whom has only his own advantage in mind," distribution will manifest "the same disproportion." The upshot is an economic system marked by a great deal of waste and by recurrent trade crises. (*MEW* 2: 536–38/*MECW* 4: 243–45)

Engels emphasizes that under communism things will be completely different. The present arrangement of society is "the most irrational and impractical that we can possibly conceive of." Communist society, in contrast, will be "rationally organized." "In communist society, where the interests of individuals are not opposed to one another but, on the contrary, are united, competition is eliminated." "Private gain, the aim of the individual to enrich himself on his own, disappears from the production and distribution of the goods necessary for life. . . ." (*MEW* 2: 539–40/*MECW* 4: 246–48) How, then, will production decisions be made? Engels suggests that production will be socially regulated. One is reminded of *The German Ideology*, which Marx and Engels began writing in fall 1845. Here we are told that under communism, "society regulates the general production" (*MEW* 3: 33/*MECW* 5: 47/*MER* 160).

But how will society regulate production? In *The German Ideology* Marx and Engels offer no illumination on this question. In the Elberfeld speech Engels is far more forthcoming. He suggests that:

> Since we know how much, on average, a person needs, it is easy to calculate how much is needed by a given number of individuals, and since production is no longer in the hands of private producers but in those of the community and its administrative bodies, it is a trifling matter *to regulate production according to needs* [*so ist es eine Kleinigkeit*, die Produktion nach den Bedürfnissen zu regeln].

Thus there will be no trade. Engels—scion of a textile manufacturer—asks us to think about "cotton or manufactured cotton goods":

> In the rationally organized society . . . it will be . . . easy for the central authority to determine how much all the villages and townships in the country need. Once such statistics have been worked out . . . average annual consumption will only change in

> proportion to the increasing population; it is therefore easy at the appropriate time to determine in advance what amount of each particular article the people will need—the entire great amount will be ordered direct from the source of supply. . . . (*MEW* 2: 539/*MECW* 4: 246–47)

Engels here offers the most detailed direct account, anywhere in the Marx-Engels corpus, of the economic organization of the future socialist society. Obviously, the account does not tell us much. But it does make the general outlines of Engels's view, *anno* 1845, clear. It is surely significant that the account is to be found in something written by Engels rather than in any of Marx's writings.[5] But absolutely nothing in Marx's writings contradicts Engels's account in the Elberfield speech of how postcapitalist society would operate, and a great deal in Marx is actively consistent with it. On the basis of the textual evidence, then, one has to conclude that Marx and Engels held that in socialist society there would be no market, and hence no private property. (I define "private property" as Marx did. In Marx's eyes, something is private property only if one can sell one's ownership rights on the market. I say more on this matter below, in the section titled "Marx's Unitarism and the Private Property—Market Relation.")

To be sure, not all commentators agree that Marx and Engels were so resolutely opposed to the market as I am contending. Beginning around 1900 and continuing until the present, commentators of various ideological stripes, writing with various concrete situations in mind, have obscured or denied the nonmarket character of Marxian socialism. This lengthy tradition of misinterpretation has been exposed and demolished by the intellectual historian and sociologist David Ramsay Steele, who, in *From Marx to Mises: Post-Capitalist Society and the Challenge of Economic Calculation*, rightly observes that "Marxian communism necessarily entails the absence of any buying and selling."[6] Steele points out that the obscuring of Marx's antimarket position resulted from a number of factors. One important consideration was that Marxists, beginning with Marx himself, held that socialism would come about as a result of the movement of historical and social forces. Since socialism is destined to arrive in any case, discussion of the details of the future socialist order is both unnecessary, and a possible distraction from the immediate struggle (Steele, 28–29).

A second consideration has to do with the practical situations within which late-nineteenth- and early-twentieth-century Marxist political movements operated. In Germany, the Social Democratic Party was the largest party by 1912. Its leadership was Marxian in inspiration (the socialist movement in Germany had not yet split into separate Social Democratic and Communist Party wings). But the Marxism in question was a toned-down, "revisionist" Marxism. Acting like regular politicians, the party leadership did not focus its attentions on the delights that would arrive after capitalism collapsed. Instead, it campaigned for reforms that would help the party's electoral supporters, the workers, within the existing system. Few people, either among the leadership or among supporters, thought that abolition of private property and of the market was a realistic goal in the foreseeable future, and so they did not invoke such matters.

In Russia, it is true, adherents of a revolutionary version of Marxism came into power in 1917. During the civil war that broke out following the Bolshevik seizure of power, paper money essentially lost all value. Once this began to happen some radicals in the party heralded the collapse of paper money as an important weapon in the war against capitalism, and even as a harbinger of socialism itself. In 1919–20, when it became clear that the Bolsheviks would prevail over their opponents, they actually attempted to stamp out petty trade, and force was used to prevent peasants and workers from exchanging foodstuffs for manufactured goods. But the result of this war on the market was mounting social discontent. Faced with outright rebellion, the regime legalized petty trade again and ended the requisition of grain from the peasantry. Had the Bolsheviks not retreated they would surely have lost their hold on power very quickly.

In short, two major wings of the twentieth-century Marxist movement found it expedient for practical reasons to diverge from Marx's uncompromisingly antimarket position. Self-proclaimed Marxists, particularly of the revolutionary sort, did not go so far as to say that Marx had made a mistake in opposing the market, competition, money, private property, and the like. To all indications they did not *believe* that Marx had made a mistake, and they certainly avoided confronting any tensions between what Marx argued for and what, in the immediate practical situation, they found desirable to carry out as policy. As Steele has shown, they avoided going head-to-head with these tensions by deferring (and thereby softening) Marx's antimarketism.

For example, in *Capital*, volumes 1 and 2, and in "Critique of the Gotha Programme," Marx suggests that after the collapse of capitalism, labor-vouchers, representing time worked, might be used as instruments for rationing out consumer goods (*Capital* 1, 2: *MEGA2* 2.6: 109, *MEW* 24: 358 /*MECW* 35: 89–90, 36: 356/*CAP* 1: 172, *CAP* 2: 434. "Critique . . .": *MEGA2* 1.25: 13–14/*MECW* 24: 87–88/*LPW* 213). Some commentators (e.g., Peter Kropotkin, cited by Steele, 31) have claimed that Marx's labor-vouchers are tantamount to money, even though Marx asserted that labor-vouchers would not circulate (and hence cannot be considered money). Thus it is made to seem as though Marx did not advocate the *immediate* abolition of money, once socialism was established.

Another feature of Marx exegesis that allowed a deferral of the abolition of the market is the still widely asserted claim that Marx held that there are two distinct stages in postcapitalist development: socialism, and communism. The first person to advance this view was Lenin, in his influential treatise, *The State and Revolution* (1917).[7] The distinction was later picked up by Stalin and others, and is often still thought to have substantial support in Marx's own writing. It does not. Its basis is an offhanded passage in "Critique of the Gotha Programme" where Marx speculates on the transition from a communism still "stamped with the birthmarks" of capitalism to a communism that has eliminated those birthmarks. Marx suggests that in the first period after capitalism workers would be given goods in proportion to their work and that only later would people be given goods in proportion to their needs. Elevated into a distinction between "socialism" and "communism," this suggestion was useful to a party trying to implement a Marxist system in an economically backward country. If the USSR was, by Lenin's definition, no more than "socialist," then it was legitimate to pay workers based on their production, and it was likewise legitimate to have rubles (identified with Marx's labor-vouchers) to pay them with.

In these softenings and deferrals of Marx's antimarket position (which I shall explore in detail in the sections that follow), we see an impulse to make Marx more usable. In other words, there is an impulse to make him, in the interpreter's eyes, more immediately applicable to the current situation. Marx's early-twentieth-century adherents had a hard time seeing how property or the market could be abolished any time soon. Instead of concluding that Marx had been wrong, they found it easier to deny that Marx had been as vigorously and immediately opposed to private property as he was.

On the one hand, the wish to make past theory immediately useful for the present and the future is legitimate. On the other hand, it is necessary to grasp the limits of such a procedure. To modify an author's theory in this way is to scant its historical otherness. Continuities and commonalities between past and present need to be argued for rather than simply assumed. One of the functions of historical research is to highlight those places where the conceptual space of the past is precisely *not* our conceptual space. When we find honest and intelligent commentators systematically distorting the material of the past, we have the right to suppose that we have discovered a discontinuity between different conceptual spaces.[8]

ROOTS OF THE PROBLEM: THE EARLY MARX

We have lost sight of how surprising Marx's rejection of private property and the market actually is. Although their numbers have dwindled, some people do still see Marx's rejection of the market, private property, competition, and so on as thoroughly justified. Anyone who shares Marx's antimarket position will feel a diminished need to explain why Marx rejected the market, for an answer to the question comes quickly to mind: because this is the correct position to adopt. Others, by attenuating Marx's antimarket position (see the previous section), tend to make that position disappear as something that would need to be explained. Still others, one suspects, would see Marx's antimarket position as so much a part of what Marxist theory is that they would find it odd to abstract it out as something in need of any *particular* explanation. Finally, there are those who assert that Marx was unequivocally a totalitarian: for them, Marx's rejection of private property and the market likewise does not stand in need of explanation, for it can be seen as consistent with his supposed hatred of freedom generally.

Contrary to those who have found a totalitarian Marx, Marx's primary and overwhelming value was nothing other than freedom (see chapter 2). The point is so important that it deserves all the repetition it can get. Thus there is a pathos in Marx, that a philosophical-scientific project articulated in the interests of greater freedom for human beings should have unintendedly contributed to servitude. But the fact of Marx's commitment to freedom is unequivocal. Already on August 12, 1835, in an examination essay entitled "Reflections of a Young Man on the Choice of a Profession," Marx made the Kantian point that "worth can be assured only by a profession in which we are not servile tools, but in which we act independently in our own sphere" (*MEGA2* 1.1: 456/*MECW* 1: 7). If this sentiment were not consistent with much else that Marx wrote and with many details of his activity, we could write it off as examination fluff. But all the evidence suggests that Marx retained his commitment to freedom until the day he died. As a young man he was attracted not only by the rational ways of philosophy but also by its "absolutely free heart" (*MEGA2* 1.1: 14/*MECW* 1: 30 [doctoral dissertation]). When in 1844–45 he rejected philosophy for science, it was a science that would tell us the laws of nature and of humankind and hence would allow us, he believed, to take control of the world, rising above both necessity and contingency.

Marxism's twentieth-century history puts Marx's commitment to freedom in danger of being forgotten. For fifty years and more the "official" West repeatedly proclaimed that Marxism was *the* enemy of freedom. And indeed, the regimes that ruled under the banner of Marxism ranged from barely acceptable to horrendously brutal. Attempts to portray such regimes as, for example, Stalin's Russia, as if it were barely distinguishable from Chicago under Mayor Daley senior or Québec under the premiership of Maurice Duplessis are politically and ethically obtuse. There was something deeply wrong with these regimes. But the fact that most of them, most of the time, were enemies of freedom does not mean that Marx was an enemy of freedom.

I do not hold that the Communist regimes that emerged in the twentieth century were implementations of Marx's vision of socialism. They were not. Yet Marx's theory was closely connected with these regimes, and in consequence their historical existence raises a problem that needs to be considered in the interpretation and assessment of the theory. Given that Marx saw himself as a champion of freedom, the problem is to get at what may have been wrong in a theory that lent itself too readily to totalitarian use. (The other, much larger problem, that of assessing the regimes themselves, is beyond my capacities to address: it is a problem fitted to keep an army of historians, political theorists, and philosophers busy for years, if not forever.[9]) I believe that there was something wrong in the theory, namely, a kind of rationalist quasitotalitarianism that wrongly assumed that an ethical basis for human action exists embedded already in a world somehow coordinated to human needs; that scorned the *juste milieu* and compromise generally, thus failing to appreciate the peculiarities of the political order; and that underrated the extent to which a loose, *a posteriori*, experimental attitude is required for the best functioning of the economic order.

One aspect of human freedom is the freedom of individuals to take up and use parts of the material world. The right of private property is the legal recognition of such a freedom. Marx was no dyspeptic, intent on reducing everyone to the eating of communal gruel. On the contrary, he was all in favor of the sensuous delights that the material world has to offer. In his "Critical Marginal Notes on 'The King of Prussia and Social Reform'" (July 1844) he rejected Robespierre's wish "to establish a universal *Spartan* frugality" (*MEGA2* 1.2: 457/*MECW* 3: 199/*EW* 413). More forcefully, he wrote in the "Economic and Philosophical Manuscripts," sometime in the period May/June–August 1844, that "the society that is *fully developed* produces man in all the richness of his being, the *rich* man who is *profoundly and abundantly endowed with all the senses*" (*MEGA2* 1.2: 394/*MECW* 3: 302/*EW* 354). These are not the words of someone who would have rejected private property because he did not care for the material things that the world has to offer. Like his friend, the poet Heinrich Heine (see the epigraph of this chapter), Marx embraced the notion that the world exists to be enjoyed; like Heine, he was all in favor of purple mantles, costly perfumes, luxury and splendor, nectar, and ambrosia (he also loved cigars, lemonade, arguing, storytelling, sociability, drinking in bars, and doting on and being doted on by the women in his family). Yet Marx *did* reject private property. He explicitly distanced himself from the views of "piecemeal reformers [*Reformatoren en détail*]," who, assuming in their proposals the continuation of private property,

> either want to *raise* wages and thereby improve the situation of the working class, or—like Proudhon—see *equality* of wages as the goal of social revolution. (*MEGA2* 1.2: 333/*MECW* 3: 241/*EW* 289)

In Marx's view, this sort of approach simply does not address the underlying defects of the existing order of things.

Marx's position with regard to private property was not generally shared by radicals of his time. For example, "associationism," a form of social thought that argued for the right of bourgeois, workers, and others to associate together in pursuit of the common interests of their class or group, flourished in Germany in the late 1830s and early 1840s. As Warren Breckman has shown, associationism was promoted by one of the teachers who most influenced Marx, the Hegelian philosopher of law Eduard Gans (1797–1839).[10] But neither German associationists, nor schools or theorists that influenced them (the Saint-Simonians, Charles Fourier), nor such counterparts as Pierre-Josèphe Proudhon, argued for the abolition of private property. In short, for most radical theorists of Marx's generation and earlier, a social, communitarian concern did not entail an attack on private property as such.[11] And yet, in spite of his highly developed concern for freedom—including individual freedom, including even the freedom of the individual creative genius—Marx came to reject private property outright. Once more we get back to the thing to be explained.

I have already said that I am not interested in offering yet another intellectual biography of Marx: I *presuppose* the narrative of Marx's life and thinking more than I tell it.[12] Yet historical sequence cannot be rejected out of hand. This is because in the real world there are trajectories, not instant arrivals at positions. In its account of the trajectory that brought Marx to his rejection of the market, the present chapter is both parallel to and a continuation of chapter 2, on Marx's antipolitical trajectory. Marx saw in the two instances a common set of issues coming out of a common problematic. The antipolitical trajectory began earlier than the antiprivate property antimarket trajectory, and gave it a certain stimulus. Marx came to look for on the economic level something that by summer 1844 he knew he could not find on the political level, namely, necessity, universality, and predictivity. To be sure, the distinction between the two trajectories is somewhat artificial. I impose it on the material in the interests of attaining a clarity that conventional narratives of Marx's intellectual evolution cannot offer.

The period covered in this chapter runs from late October 1843 to fall 1844. This was Marx's *annus mirabilis*. The miraculous year began when Marx and the former Jenny von Westphalen, who on June 19, 1843, became Jenny Marx, moved from Germany to Paris and took up residence close to other German expatriates, in the Faubourg Saint-Germain on the Left Bank. Within a year of arriving in Paris Marx had worked his way through a strategic selection of writings on political economy and had articulated a critique of the market. It was almost certainly the most intellectually productive single year in his entire life.[13] It is no accident that when Marx's early writings first came to be widely noticed (in the 1950s and 1960s) the writings of this year most caught people's attention. This was so to such a degree that "Marx of 1844," and the "Economic and Philosophical Manuscripts" in particular, became shorthand for the early Marx generally. The "Estranged Labor and Private Property" section of the EPM, as well as some other parts of that brilliant, stimulating outpouring, is justly famous—but now, perhaps, wrongly neglected in the face of Marxism's collapse. The EPM laid the basis for the entirety of Marx's subsequent intellectual career. Especially in articulating the notion of the estrangement of labor, the EPM offers food for thought and suggests a line of criticism against the existing order that retains some validity. Marx changed his emphasis after 1844, but he never abandoned his conclusions of that year.

My concern here is both historical and theoretical. Most important, I offer an account of how Marx arrived at his antimarket position—which means that I offer a historical account. It is not that a single, tightly woven argument led ineluctably to his rejection of the market. Rather, two quite different arguments went together. I shall call them the "estrangement" argument and the "irrationality" argument. Each generated a justification for rejecting the market. Only the first of these arguments is well known to Marx's commentators. Both arguments inclined Marx against the market, but the irrationality argument was by far the more decisive of the two, for reasons that I shall lay out below.

The works that we are concerned with here are theoretical works—that is, they are works that strive to offer universal claims about the territory with which they are concerned. If one is to approach these works with a proper sensitivity to what they are, one must approach them with both historical and theoretical ends in mind. To be sure, I cannot claim to make fully justified theoretical judgments concerning the objects of Marx's attention: that is more the work of philosophers, social theorists, and economists than it is of historians. Nonetheless, I do claim to go part of the way toward such judgments. I can and do make suggestions concerning the legitimacy of Marx's claims regarding the market and regarding politics, even though in this book, which is primarily historical, I cannot establish these claims with certainty.

MARX'S UNITARISM AND THE PRIVATE PROPERTY–MARKET RELATION

It is important to hold onto the fact that Marx's rejection of private property and his rejection of the market amount to virtually the same thing. Marx all but identified these two terms: thus private property = the market. There is a theoretical argument in favor of this equation that is well known to economists: let us first look at the theoretical argument, and then let us look at the text in which Marx most clearly offers this argument back to us.

The argument is embarrassingly simple, for the interdependence of the market and private property can be established on purely *a priori* grounds, through an analysis of concepts. Begin with the concept of private property. What does it mean to have ownership rights over a piece of property? In brief, to own something means to have the right to dispose of it as one will.[14] Disposing of property as one will includes exchanging it for other goods. But what is exchange? It is the trading of goods, or more precisely of *rights* to goods, over which one has a property claim. Without such trading there is no market. Indeed, the carrying out of exchange *is* the market. Consequently, private property entails a market. Where markets do not exist, private property does not exist either. *Quod erat demonstrandam*.

The converse is also true: that is, the market entails private property, or at least a close functional equivalent of private property (no private property, no market). This is because a real market exists only if there are buyers and sellers eager to maximize their own material well-being. Where sellers do not actually own what they bring to market, or when they own what they bring to market but do not care whether they get a good price, there is no market. There might be gift-giving (as among family and friends or within tightly knit communities generally), or there might be a giveaway (as when war booty is distributed to one's friends and associates), but these do not equate to a market.[15] Where buyers and sellers have an actual stake in what is bought or sold—that is, where they own what is bought or sold—there is generally an incentive to get a good price. Imagine bureaucrats selling off government-owned enterprises in a situation where they are under no enforced fiduciary responsibility to get the highest price that the enterprises can fetch. Imagine, as well, the pseudo-markets that prevailed in the Soviet Union and other countries within the Soviet orbit during much of the twentieth century. Without private property there is no prevailing incentive to allocate what is being disposed of to the bidder who puts the highest value on it. Instead, people tend to pass out goods to their friends and cronies. And what could it possibly mean to bid on an item if one cannot offer property or a promise of property (commonly known as money) in return? Consequently, markets presuppose private property, or its functional equivalent (such as when the buying and selling agents of collective entities are put under an adequately enforced fiduciary obligation to trade in the best interests of the entities that they represent).

None of this ought to be controversial. It was indeed Marx's own position and that of the political economists of his time. In *The German Ideology* (1845–46) [sect. 6.B], Marx (with Engels) writes:

> In reality I possess private property only insofar as I have something saleable [*Verschacherbares*] . . . . My frock-coat is private property for me only so long as I can

> barter, pawn or sell it [*verschachern, versetzen oder verkaufen*]. . . . If it loses that feature, if it becomes tattered [*zerlumpt*], it can still have a number of features which make it valuable *for me*, it may even become a feature of me and turn me into a tatterdemalion [*zerlumpten Individuum*]. But no economist would think of classing it as my private property, since it does not enable me to command any, even the smallest, amount of other people's labor. (*MEW* 3: 211–12/*MECW* 5: 230)

In short, Marx accepted the view that something can be considered private property only if it can be sold on the market. His aim in the pages from which I have taken this quotation is to demolish an attack that the proto-anarchist Max Stirner had made (in *The Individual and His Own*, 1844) on "the communist abolition [*Aufhebung*] of private property" (*MEW* 3: 211/*MECW* 5: 229). Contra Stirner, Marx insists that private property must be abolished. Why? He claims on these pages that "private property estranges [*entfremdet*] the individuality" of people and of things. He continues: "how little connection there is between money, the most general form of property, and personal peculiarity. . . ." (*MEW* 3: 212/*MECW* 5: 230). Marx's focus here is on private property because that was Stirner's focus. He articulates a rather unpersuasive, Romantic-sounding argument against private property, for *all* general yardsticks abstract away from "personal peculiarity." Thus the argument cuts too wide to be taken seriously. But by the time that Marx (or Engels) wrote this passage, Marx had already articulated an argument about the "estranging" character of the existing system that deserves to be taken more seriously: I shall examine it in detail below.

To this point I have been approaching the market–private property relation in Marx on the level only of a thinking through of economic issues. But the interdependence that Marx saw between private property and the market had a deeper root in his thinking. Marx had a strong inclination to want to see apparently distinct (even opposing) entities as aspects of a larger whole. When he turned to economics, from his earlier studies in philosophy and politics, he very quickly came to regard private property, the market, exchange, money, and the like as really *the same thing* from slightly different points of view. Marx's treating of these concepts as aspects of a larger whole is one manifestation of a tendency in his thought that I call *unitarism*. By "unitarism," I mean an inclination toward the dissolving of *specific*, *circumscribed* concepts or regions of concern into a totality that eliminates or at least minimizes the differences between them.

Marx's unitarist tendency is closely connected with the Hegelian notion of progress by contradiction. Radical Hegelians followed the tactic of searching out the contradictions within a given reality. They assumed that contradictions are markers of instability, and they made this assumption on the basis of a further assumption, deep and unexamined, that reality itself is ultimately unified and harmonious—that there is not, as the French philosopher Jacques Derrida would say, a *différance* [originary difference] in the constituting of the world. The radical Hegelians' forward-driving prometheanism tended, as a result, to grant privilege to unification over diversification. One can see this in, for example, Bruno Bauer's attack (discussed in chapter 2) on the *juste milieu* in politics. In Bauer's eyes, the crime of the *juste milieu* was that it was willing to live with contradiction. For example, it was willing to hold that Jews should have exactly the same rights as everyone else, while also holding that in some respects they could have privileges peculiar to their status as Jews. This sort of stance deeply offended Bauer, who believed that the task of the intellectual is to point out and overcome contradiction.

The first Hegelian was Hegel. But Hegel's unitarist tendencies were held in check by his tremendous sensitivity to the stark reality of what is *there* in the world.[16] One of the things that strikes any serious reader of Hegel is his factual heaviness, his insistence on delivering over to us a tremendous body of information concerning whatever he is talking about. This is Hegel the realist speaking. One thinks of his *Philosophy of Right*, his *Lectures on the Philosophy of Nature*, and his *Lectures on the History of Philosophy* (and not quite so much, perhaps, of his *Phenomenology of Spirit* and *Science of Logic*). It is noteworthy, for example, that Hegel never wrote a history of the-world-in-general, but only "special" histories, and one suspects that this was in part because the writing of a single history would have entailed riding roughshod over too much reality. Further, from 1818 onward, Hegel's status as a servant of the Prussian state limited what he could say by way of divergence from the existing institutions of that state, and must surely have accentuated his realistic tendencies.

The *very* early Marx was likewise disinclined to dissolve away particular extant institutions into a unified whole. Possibly inspired by Eduard Gans's project of writing a rational history of law, Marx wrote, in his November 1837 letter to his father, that "in the concrete expression of a living world of ideas, as exemplified by law, the state, nature, and philosophy as a whole, the object itself [*das Objekt selbst*] must be studied in its development. . ." (*MEGA2* 3.1: 11/*MECW* 1: 12). If we are justified in making an inference from this passage, written at white heat near the beginning of Marx's intellectual career, it would be that a focus on "the object itself" would tend to prompt the investigator to concentrate on the particular specialized territory within which the object is to be found—and thus that Marx would not have wanted to dissolve, say, "law," "the state," "nature," and the like into some other, all-embracing category. Certainly, as late as 1842, in his articles on the historical school of law and on divorce, Marx was still willing to see specific institutions as the proper object of scientific investigation. Thus he condemns the "historical school" philosopher of law Gustav Hugo for holding that "no rational necessity [*vernünftige Nothwendigkeit*] pervades [*beseelt*] positive institutions, e.g., property, the state constitution, marriage, etc." (*MEGA2* 1.1: 192/*MECW* 1: 204). This seems to imply that *Marx* would find a rational necessity in each of those institutions: at any rate, he does not reject the possibility.

But in 1843 there seems to be a shift in Marx's position. It was now a matter of seeing all particular institutions as destined to be dissolved into a totality. One suspects that Marx's shift was more or less the direct consequence of his reading of Feuerbach's "Preliminary Theses on the Reform of Philosophy" in March 1843, but for our purposes the cause of the shift is less important than the simple fact that it occurred. Thus, in "Critique of Hegel's Doctrine of the State" and "On the Jewish Question," both written in 1843, perhaps the most striking theme is the notion that man and citizen, and civil society and state, which Marx claims are presently in contradiction with each other, are destined to disappear into a unified humanity. As Marx puts it in "On the Jewish Question," "All emancipation is a *bringing back* [Zurückführung] of the human world and of relationships to *man himself*" (*MEGA2* 1.2: 162/*MECW* 3: 168/*EW* 234). Marx articulates exactly the same "bringing back" in the "Private Property and Communism" section of the "Economic and Philosophical Manuscripts." Here Marx looks forward to a time when "the positive supersession of *private property*" will have occurred. According to Marx, this supersession amounts to

> the positive supersession of all estrangement, and the return [*Rückkehr*] of man from religion, the family, the state, etc., to his *human*, i.e. *social* existence. (*MEGA2* 1.2: 390/*MECW* 3: 297/*EW* 349)

In short, in his writings of 1843 and 1844 Marx offers an (admittedly abstract) picture of an ideal future society in which no *particular* institutions exist. The only institution is social humanity, society as a whole. Implicitly, one mode of rationality applies to all aspects of the future social order. In dissolving rather than regionalizing, Marx forecloses the possibility that there might be different standards of operation and evaluation appropriate to different spheres of life. What is most relevant for the present chapter is that he forecloses the possibility that certain aspects of economic life might require abrogating, or at least holding in suspension, the concept of rationality that he deploys. (To recur to the topic of chapter 2: Marx also forecloses the possibility that if politics is to be rationally understood it might require a different rationality than that permitted by the standards of universality, necessity, and predictivity.)

Marx's encounter with private property and the market needs to be seen against the background of his unitarism. Marx's unitarist inclination meant first of all that he saw the different elements in the economic system (as described in the writings of the economists) as aspects of a single unified system. His unitarism meant second that there was no way that he could rely on a conception of countervailing forces in his account of the human world. Within politics, he could not have a conception of political checks and balances (of judiciary vs. executive vs. legislature, of government vs. opposition, of federal vs. state vs. regional government, and so on). The continued existence of institutions capable of checking each other went against his notion that contradiction always tends to "abolish" itself in some higher synthesis. But of course, it is not simply that he could not countenance persisting oppositions within the political sphere—he also could not countenance the continued existence of the political sphere itself. And this meant that, at this moment in his thinking, Marx had to reject the notion that a democratic polity might be willing and able to intervene in society with the intention of correcting undesirable consequences flowing from the market (yet without in any way wishing to demolish the market, or even in any fundamental way wishing to hinder its operations).[17]

WHY IT IS IMPORTANT TO ASK WHY MARX REJECTED THE MARKET

I did not think to ask the question Why did Marx reject the market? until the great mutation of 1989–91, when first the "German Democratic Republic," then Soviet Russia, melted into air, with attendant changes throughout central and eastern Europe. The collapse of the USSR surprised almost everyone by its rapidity. As for the People's Republic of China, it turned ever further away from any pretense of having a socialist economy. Changes of such magnitude give occasion for reflection. The events of 1989–91 confirmed what had become increasingly clear to serious observers over the course of the preceding twenty years, namely, that the various Soviet regimes were generally failing in their attempts to establish and sustain productive economies, let alone productive economies that were geared to the needs of their citizens. By a massive deployment of material resources and human talent the Soviet Union managed to put people into orbit around the Earth, but it could not produce food efficiently, it could not produce electricity safely, environmental protection was laughable, it lacked a properly functioning telephone system, its air travel system operated on a wing and a prayer, it could not produce a decent automobile, and it was hopelessly behind in the design and production of computers and software.

Many things went wrong with the twentieth-century attempt to model societies on Marx's theory. The best single overview of the economic problems that arose is probably still the account offered by Ferenc Fehér, Agnes Heller, and György Márkus in their book *Dictatorship over Needs*, published well before the collapse, in 1983.[18] But, as noted already, my focus in the current book is not on the history and fate of the Soviet regimes but rather on the question that they raise concerning Marx's theory—namely, what, within this theory, which was put forward in the interests of human freedom and with freedom as its foremost value, connected it to these despotic systems.

I have long been struck by the existence of inconsistencies in Marx's system of thought: Marx strove mightily for consistency but he did not attain it.[19] From this recognition, one does not need to go very far to arrive at the notion of imagining how parts of the theoretical system might be articulated differently. I was never attracted to Marx by the psychology of the convert, and so I never had the feeling that the system ought to be taken as a whole. Rather, I was attracted to Marx by the seriousness of his thinking and by the striking metaphors, representations, and insights to be found in his work. It was more than anything else the vigor of his mind that led me for years to read and teach his work. Then 1989–91 turned Marx into history. Meanwhile, in the years following my first reading and teaching of Marx the "New MEGA" had made the basic formative texts of Marxism available in a textually legitimate form. In contrast, the historian could never wholly trust *MEW* and *MECW*, for these editions were influenced by pedagogical and propagandistic considerations that obscured actual historical connections.

Abandonment of any desire to see Marx's system of thought as internally consistent encourages the question: Can one save Marx from himself? That is, can one discard the weaker aspects of his thinking and highlight those aspects that still have critical and illuminative power? In large degree I believe that one can. What remains is not Marxism, but it does have an identifiable relation to Marxism. Remember that the aged Carlos himself declared, "*je ne suis pas marxiste*."[20] One can conclude that the very category "Marxism" is itself questionable and hence is all the more open to revisionary understanding. The notion of a revisionary understanding of Marx might seem to conflict with the idea of getting at Marx's theory "as it actually was." But the historian's work involves not only the descriptive task of showing what was "there" in the putative past. It also involves the interpretive task of addressing the significance of the putative past for us, now (while always keeping in mind the gulf between the past and us).[21] From such a perspective it makes entire sense to revisit the past starting out from our new, changed standpoint, in order to see, both in the past that actually existed and in the unchosen corridors of the past, what we were not able to see before.

Besides description and interpretation, the historian also has a responsibility to explain, or at least to attempt to explain. In other words, besides asking the questions "What was the case?" and "What is the significance of the past for us, now?," the historian also needs to ask the question, "What caused things to be as they were?" The historian's explanatory task, like her interpretive task, authorizes a shaking up of the past (although it does not authorize the misuse of evidence). As is well known, all talk of explanation (in the sense of making assertions as to what caused something) presupposes counterfactual reasoning: for example, to say that imperialism caused World War I is to say that, all other things being equal, if imperialism had not existed World War I would not have occurred. In other words, in order to make causal claims in history one has to imagine how things might have been different. This is unavoidable: it is part of the logic of historical investigation. Accordingly, answering the question, What led Marx to reject the market? requires imagining a Marx who might have come to a position different from the one that he actually came to. And this means that we need to look closely at that point in Marx's career at which his conception of the market took shape and his decision was made.

In short, we need to ask the question, How and why did Marx arrive at the conclusion that the market does not have a legitimate place in a fully human society? As a preliminary matter, note that the question being posed here can be understood in two divergent ways. It can be understood as asking either about Marx's theoretical (logical, scientific) justification for rejecting the market, or about causal (psychological) factors leading him to that rejection. The two questions—or, rather, their answers—overlap. For a thinker can be led to the discovery of a theoretical justification for a position by factors that are not theoretical. These would be factors that, from a theoretical point of view, are accidents of personality and situation, lacking any determining force *as justifications* for the position arrived at. And yet such factors could very well lead the thinker up to the point where he or she finds, and adopts, a justification for the position. We legitimately view such factors as "causes" for the thinker's holding the position in question. On the other hand, once a thinker arrives at a justification for a position, the justification *also* stands as a cause for his holding that position, since we can—and most likely will—be led to adhere to a position by arguments leading us to think that the position says something correct about the world.[22]

In what follows I shall proceed through three explanations for Marx's rejection of the market. I shall begin by suggesting a *cause* for Marx's rejection of the market. To put this more precisely: I shall begin by suggesting a *cause that is not a justification*—that is, a cause that serves as a (possible) motive for Marx's rejection of the market, but that does not have theoretical standing. The motive is a certain social disdain for the market, the outlines of which I shall explore in a moment. I shall then turn to examine a *justification* for Marx's rejection of the market—that is, I shall examine a cause for his rejection of the market that does have theoretical standing, a cause that one can argue about on a theoretical level. According to this justification, which was the *first* justification Marx came to, the market is of questionable standing because it is involved in a system that estranges, or alienates, human beings. Finally, I shall turn to Marx's *second* justification for rejecting the market, according to which the market ought to be rejected because it is irrational. The two justifications are connected to each other, and the second justification in particular is connected to Marx's social disdain for the market, yet at the same time they are all quite distinct, and need to be considered separately.[23]

MARX'S DISDAIN FOR THE MARKET: WAS "JEWISH SELF-HATRED" A FACTOR?

One plausible explanation for Marx's rejection of the market is that he felt a disdain for its operations—that he saw those operations as beneath the dignity of man and beneath the standards of proper social behavior. "Disdain" is less a reason than a cause, less a justification than a prejudice. A prejudice is not an argument, and from a theoretical perspective "disdain" is thus not very interesting. But we are interested here not just in the theoretical position at which Marx arrived, but in how he arrived at that position. Since it is my claim that a prejudice against the market may have brought him to the brink of what I consider to be the more important of his two arguments against the market, it is relevant to consider that prejudice.

Marx's disdain for the market first comes out clearly in an essay that is notorious in the annals of Marxism, namely, his "On the Jewish Question" (which I discussed from another point of view in chapter 2).[24] Marx wrote "On the Jewish Question" in the period from mid-October to mid-December 1843 and published it in the first (and last) issue of the *Deutsch-Französische Jahrbücher* in February 1844 (*MEGA2* 1.2: 141–69/*MECW* 3: 146–74/*EW* 211–41). "On the Jewish Question" is the first writing by Marx in which he addresses the issue of market relations. In Germany in the first half of the nineteenth century the so-called Jewish question went something like this: Given that the existing states in Germany are Christian states, closely allied with Christianity and having established state churches (Evangelical [Lutheran], Reform [Calvinist], and Catholic), what role in public life should Jews be allowed to play, now that they are increasingly eager to move out from the narrow confines of the Jewish community into the gentile world?

However, in spite of its title, Marx's essay is not centrally about "the Jewish question" at all. Marx's real concern in the essay was to attack the sociopolitical views of his former mentor, Bruno Bauer, from whom Marx had begun to distance himself in late 1842–early 1843, while he was editor of the *Rheinische Zeitung*. At the time, Bauer was connected with a Berlin club, *die Freien*, whose members adopted a provocative tone that in Marx's view pointlessly increased the likelihood of a government crackdown on, among other things, the *Rheinische Zeitung*. In 1843 Bauer published a short book and an essay on the Jewish question. Marx found much to disagree with in these writings.[25] The first part of Marx's "On the Jewish Question" was prompted by the book, the second part by the essay.

The central theme of Marx's essay is the theme of freedom. In the first and longer part of the essay Marx distinguishes between "political emancipation" and "human emancipation" (the German term that I render as "emancipation" is *Befreiung*, which can also be translated as "liberation"). By political emancipation, Marx meant the granting of rights of political participation to one or another group within society—for example, to Jews. By human emancipation, he meant a freedom that would go beyond simply the possession of political rights—a freedom that would involve a wide exercise of self-determination on the part of human beings. In the second part of "On the Jewish Question," Marx contends that human liberation involves, as a primary element, emancipation from the market.

I shall now quote the passages in "On the Jewish Question" that are the culmination of Marx's account of the market. Their tone is shocking, for Marx uses the word *Judenthum* (Judaism, the Jewish people) as a synonym for the greedy and utterly self-interested behavior that he sees as endemic in modern society, and the word "Jew" (*Jude*) to designate those who engage in such behavior.

Marx writes as follows:

> Let us consider . . . the *everyday Jew* . . . .
> What is the worldly basis of Judaism? *Practical* need, self-interest.
> What is the worldly worship of the Jew? *Haggling* [Schacher]. What is his worldly God? *Money*.
> Well then! Emancipation from *haggling* [Schacher] and from *money* . . . would be the same as the self-emancipation of our age. (*MEGA2* 1.2: 164/*MECW* 3: 169–70/*EW* 236)

I have truncated Marx's discussion, which continues in similar vein. But a further passage, which concludes the essay, must be quoted, because it envisages a movement beyond the market:

> As soon as society succeeds in abolishing the *empirical* essence of Judaism—haggling [*Schacher*] and the conditions that give rise to it—the Jew will have become *impossible*, for his consciousness will no longer have an object, the subjective basis

> of Judaism—practical need—will have become humanized and the conflict between man's individual sensuous existence and his species-existence will have been superseded.
>
> The *social* emancipation of the Jew is the *emancipation of society from Judaism*. (*MEGA2* 1.2: 169/*MECW* 3: 174/*EW* 241)

I again emphasize that when Marx uses the terms *Judaism* and *Jew* in these passages he does not intend either the religion, Judaism, or the Jewish community. Instead, he means something close to what the Canadian political theorist C. B. Macpherson meant when he coined the phrase "possessive individualism"—namely, an attitude in which the acquisition of private property becomes the central reality of social life.[26] Marx's *Alltagsjude* (everyday Jew) is a general character type in modern commercial and industrial society, not the adherent of a particular religion or the member of a particular ethnic group. As Marx uses the word, the Christian inhabitant of New England is as much a Jew as persons who happen to be ethnically or religiously Jewish.[27] We catch whiffs in Marx's language of a later, deeply threatening, symbolic order. With our richer and more troubled historical experience we can see that he was entering into equivocal territory. We have every right to regret the language, and every obligation to remind ourselves that words can acquire a dismissive power of quite shocking force. But even while regretting Marx's language we should not attribute to it meanings that only became powerful later, in the twentieth century. An anti-Semitic discourse existed in Europe in 1843 and Marx plugged into it. Something like such a discourse existed in German philosophy: for example, because Hegelians believed in a historical progression, it was more or less a given in German philosophy in the first half of the nineteenth century that Judaism, the earlier religion, was inferior to Christianity, the later religion.[28] Presumably, Marx used the language he did in "On the Jewish Question" because he thought that it would make his argument more vivid and compelling to his audience.

I do not believe that Marx was driven by so-called *jüdischer Selbsthaß*.[29] Nor do I believe that anti-Semitism sustained Marx in his antimarket position. (By "anti-Semitism," I mean both a prejudice against the Jewish religion and its adherents, and a prejudice against social practices allegedly engaged in by persons having a Jewish ethnic and cultural identity.) Yet I also find it quite likely that some degree of stereotyped anti-Semitic social prejudice helped lead Marx *to* his antimarket position. It is difficult to get at the motivation of historical agents, at least when one is concerned with matters as complex, charged, and hidden as this. Still, it is well known that Marx was not above making anti-Semitic comments, particularly about ideological opponents: for example, he did so against Ferdinand Lassalle, who was a rival for leadership of the German workers' movement until his death in 1864.[30] However, notwithstanding Marx's impulse toward anti-

Semitic language in polemical contexts, it is hard to see him as in any serious sense anti-Semitic, and it is ludicrous to see him as self-hating. He disdained Judaism as a religion, and he disdained what he saw as the provinciality of a closed Jewish community; but he also disdained religion generally, and provinciality generally.

One is struck, for example, by Marx's comments in a letter to Arnold Ruge of March 13, 1843, where he tells Ruge that "some priests and other enemies of mine" in "my own family" were agitating against his plan to marry Jenny von Westphalen. Marx does not bother to mention one reason why they must have been upset, namely, that Karl's children by Jenny would not be members of the Jewish community, since in Jewish law descent is matrilineal. Marx's use of the word *Priester* instead of *Rabbiner*, and his even-handed complaint against Jenny von Westphalen's "pietistic aristocratic relatives," show that Marx's complaint was against the retrograde character of religion in general and not against Judaism as such. (The Christian relatives were no doubt disturbed by the thought that Jenny's marriage to Karl Marx, an insincerely converted and, as shown by the *Rheinische Zeitung* episode, troublemaking Jew, endangered the immortal souls of the prospective children.) Indeed, in the same letter Marx tells Ruge that the head of the Jewish community in Cologne had visited him and had asked him to write a petition on the community's behalf to the Rhine Province Assembly, and Marx says that he was willing to do so (with the expectation that the petition would be turned down and that the petitioners would feel "embitterment" toward the government). Clearly, Marx had no difficulty dealing with the Jewish community, and the Jewish community, for its part, was willing to ask this bright young man, nephew of one former rabbi of Trier and grandson of another, for help, even though he had no connection to the synagogue. (*MEGA2* 3.1: 45–46/*MECW* 1: 399–400) Accordingly, Marx's disdain for various aspects of Jewish existence (adherence to religion, a certain provinciality) is not evidence of Jewish self-hatred. There was nothing complicated in Marx's relation to his own Jewish background. He saw himself as having opted for secularism and for universality, rather than for a passé religious affiliation and narrow ethnic affiliation. And that was that.

I do, however, believe that Marx's antimarket position was in part supported by something more general than anti-Semitism, yet related to it: it was supported by a disdain on his part for a certain type of behavior that he saw as connected to the market. It was behavior that Marx found suspect because it was, by his lights, irregular, in the literal sense of the term. That is, it was behavior that did not conform to rational, universal rules. (In his personal life Marx was often strikingly irregular—but we are talking here of a domain over which Marx wanted to obtain theoretical mastery.) In "On the Jewish Question" Marx identifies markets with a certain type of social behavior—namely, the grasping attempt to maximize, at each moment, by whatever means possible, one's own gain. In the gentile European imagination of the nineteenth century (and earlier) such behavior was strongly associated with Jews. As generations of German Christians "knew," when Jesus threw the buyers, sellers, money-changers, and pigeon-dealers out of the Temple (Matt. 21: 12) he was showing his displeasure at Jewish addiction to commerce.[31] But Marx's focus was on the behavior, not on Jews or even on Jewish participation in the behavior. His comments on the quintessential land of go-getting, the United States, make this clear: since "the pious and politically free inhabitant of New England" stands as Marx's prime example of the everyday Jew, we can see that he does not mean "Jew" in the normal sense of the term (*MEGA2* 1.2: 165/*MECW* 3: 170/*EW* 237).

An important clue to the character of the behavior that Marx disdained is to be found in the word that he uses to name market behavior: *Schacher*. In "On the Jewish Question" he uses *Schacher* six times, and in addition he uses its past participial form, *verschachert*, once ("Das Weib wird verschachert [Woman is put on the market]") (*MEGA2* 1.2: 164–65, 167, 169/*MECW* 3: 170–71, 172, 174/*EW* 236–37, 239, 241). He does not use the word *Markt* [market] at all. *Schacher* was a pejorative term, in German generally and for Marx in particular. It is a word of Hebrew origin (the Hebrew word, *sachar*, means "trade"), also used in Yiddish. In neither Hebrew nor Yiddish did the word have pejorative connotations; indeed, in modern Hebrew its derivate, *mischar*, forms part of the name of the Israeli Ministry of Trade and Industry (the equivalent word, *mas'chara*, is also found in Arabic). In passing from Yiddish to German, *Schacher* acquired the connotation of dishonest trading practices.[32] Given the word's origins it is easy to read *Schacher* in a narrowly anti-Semitic light.

In my view, however, Marx's objection to the market in "On the Jewish Question" was primarily to the mode of social behavior that he saw in *Schacher* and not to anything specifically Jewish. The problem with *Schacher*, from Marx's point of view, seems to have been that it was irregular—that it did not accommodate itself to a publicly available and generally known set of rules.[33] The relevant issue here is the commitment of German philosophy and of the German bureaucratic state to rules and to universality.[34] By dint of hard, intelligent, and reliable work Marx's father became a respected attorney in the Prussian civil service. Heinrich [born Herschel] Marx detached himself not only from the long rabbinical tradition that had prevailed in the Marx family for generations, but also, it seems, from any suspicion of personal avarice or dishonesty.[35] As is well known, Heinrich Marx embraced with enthusiasm the universalist ideology of the Enlightenment.[36] Marx thus grew up within the stratum of civil servants, the most important part of the German *Bildungsbürgertum*. In principle, at least, one qualified for positions in the civil service through education. In the more advanced of the German states the task of the bureaucrat and lawyer was to apply fixed legal and administrative rules to the particular cases that came before him: as the historian Hans Rosenberg pointed out, the Prussian state in particular had long been the locus of an "unremitting struggle" on the part of the state bureaucrats "for replacing arbitrary royal powers and whimsical interference with general legal rules."[37]

To be sure, by 1843 Marx was no fan of the German state (not that he had ever been). But what the early Marx objected to in the German state was its failure to live up to the universal norms by which, he claimed, it ought to operate. He had obviously had to deal with the German state's particularity and arbitrariness in his journalistic work. In his May 1842 article, "Debates on Freedom of the Press," he evokes the particularity and case-by-case arbitrariness of the censorship authority—a reality that he would soon confront head-on as editor of the *Rheinische Zeitung* from October to March 1843. He asserts, in "Debates on Freedom of the Press," that a censorship law is a "preventive law [*Präventivgesetz*]." As such, it "has within it no *measure*, no *rational rule* [*vernünftige Regel*]; its boundary is determined [*gesetzt*] not by necessity, but by the fortuitousness of arbitrariness [*durch den Zufall der Willkühr*], as the censorship daily demonstrates ad oculos" (*MEGA2* 1. 1: 151/*MECW* 1: 163).

I hypothesize that, with his commitment to universality, Marx was predisposed to dislike *Schacher*. Such would be especially so, given that he also saw a close relationship between law and freedom. He was deeply committed to the general value of human self-determination. But so long as human beings are subjected to any institution that is ruled by chance and arbitrariness, self-determination is impossible. Marx had made this argument in his journalism of 1842—in relation, however, to law and the state, not in relation to the market.[38] Admittedly, there is no indication that when Marx wrote "On the Jewish Question" in late 1843 he had a fully worked out argument against the market. At most there seems to have been a prejudice—against *Schacher*. But within a year, by late 1844, an antimarket argument is to be found in Marx. The argument is connected with his talk of *Schacher* and is consistent with his earlier reflections on law and self-determination. As I have already suggested, the argument is that the market is irrational. In other words, Marx concluded that it is impossible to understand the market *qua* market in terms of the rationality-criteria of necessity, universality, and predictivity. Only by dialectically transcending the market and moving on to a different level can one attain rational understanding. And since—Marx would argue—the market *qua* market cannot be rationally understood, it follows that the market as such is an irrational institution. I shall work out this argument in detail in subsequent sections.

WHY DID MARX REJECT THE MARKET? THE ROLE OF ESTRANGEMENT

However, Marx articulated his "irrationality" justification for rejecting the market only after some delay. Before doing so, he articulated the "estrangement" argument—according to which the current economic system (and the market, which is part of that system) is estranging. (For the term *estranging* one could justifiably substitute *dehumanizing*, both because it is closer to current parlance and because it signals the close relationship of the estrangement argument to Feuerbach's humanistic philosophy). Marx already suggests the "estrangement" argument in one of the final paragraphs of "On the Jewish Question." Here he tells us that "selling is the praxis of alienation [*Die Veräusserung ist die Praxis der Entäusserung*]," and that, "when under the sway of egoistic need," man can produce objects "only by making his products and his activity subordinate to an alien substance"—namely, money (*MEGA2* 1.2: 168/*MECW* 3: 174/*EW* 241). But he first worked out the estrangement argument in the "Economic and Philosophical Manuscripts," with much of the argument concentrated in the "Estranged Labor and Private Property" section (*MEGA2* 1.2: 363–75/*MECW* 3: 270–82/*EW* 322–34).[39]

When the EPM was "discovered" by the learned world in the 1950s, it was Marx's discussion of estrangement (or alienation) that captured people's attention. Consequently, in its general outlines Marx's "estrangement" argument is well known—at least to people who know Marx.[40] Most of us have experienced work that is unfulfilling. Those of us who have found work that *is* fulfilling are well aware that many people around us are not so lucky. To this extent the notion of estrangement speaks directly to us. But the question that I am concerned with here is: to what extent does the fact of estrangement justify abolishing the market? My claim will be that Marx's "estrangement" argument turns out to be less persuasive as a critical argument against the market *per se* than it is as a critical argument against the way work is organized. In his unfinished masterpiece, *Capital*, Marx makes three arguments against the existing system: that it is estranging, that it is exploitative, and that it is irrational. It is my claim that only one of those three arguments, the "irrationality" argument, can be seen as an unequivocal argument against the market (and this is so only if one accepts Marx's rationality-criteria as in fact applicable in this case).

What exactly *is* estrangement, then, in Marx's conception of it? Famously, in the "Estranged Labor and Private Property" section Marx identifies estrangement's four aspects. In Marx's order of exposition, they are as follows:

1. *estrangement from the product of labor*. Marx claims that within a social system dominated by private property workers are estranged from the products of their labor, for these products are taken from them and sold (*MEGA2* 1.2: 364–68/*MECW* 3: 271–75/*EW* 323–27).
2. *estrangement from the act of labor*. Marx holds that workers are estranged from "the *act of production* within *labor* [*zum* Akt der Production, *innerhalb der* Arbeit]." In other words, the workers do not like the work: they feel miserable and unfulfilled in it. (*MEGA2* 1.2: 367–70, quote at 368/*MECW* 3: 274–78, at 275/*EW* 326–29, at 327)
3. *estrangement from "species-being."* Workers are estranged from what Marx, following Feuerbach, calls their "species-being" (*Gattungswesen*). Marx meant, by this term, the potentialities of human nature. In his view, in an unestranged existence people simultaneously and reciprocally "naturalize" and "humanize" themselves in confronting the objective world of nature. In "humanizing" nature—that is, in transforming nature so that it better satisfies human needs (e.g., building bridges over gorges)—people at the same time develop the potentialities slumbering within humanity—such as, for example, the technological and scientific capacities that get developed as human beings strive to bend nature to human ends. In present-day society, however, people are estranged from the possibility of developing their full potentialities, and are to this degree "dehumanized." (*MEGA2* 1.2: 369–70/MECW 3: 276–77/*EW* 328–29)
4. *estrangement from other human beings*. Marx claims that:

> When man confronts himself, he also confronts other men. What is true of man's relationship to his labor, to the product of his labor, and to himself, is also true of his relationship to other men, and to the labor and the object of the labor of other men.

In short, Marx here claims that the first three forms of estrangement—from the product of labor, from the act of labor, and from human potential—are accompanied by the estrangement of human beings from one another. (*MEGA2* 1.2: 370/*MECW* 3: 277–78/*EW* 329–30)

Such, in summary, is Marx's account of the forms of estrangement. The account raises a compelling question, one that is deeply relevant to the matter of Marx's attitude toward private property and the market: What are the relations among the different forms of estrangement? More specifically: what *causal* relations prevail among the different forms of estrangement?

The question is difficult to answer. The problem is that Marx is often ambiguous as to whether he wants to say "X causes Y," or whether, on the contrary, he wants to say "Y is an instance of X." As shown in chapter 1, Marx took necessity to be a criterion of rationality. In consequence, he was strongly inclined toward an analytic process of reasoning, in which conclusions turn out to be already contained within the relevant premises.[41] Marx's approach, rigorously followed, makes Y an instance of X and makes it sound odd to think of X as *causing* Y. (A persistent problem in Marx—which I shall touch on in chapter 4—is that he leaves little if any room for the counterfactuality that is the hidden side of any claim about causation. The lack of room for counterfactuality is intimately tied up with Marx's necessitarian view of history.)

Still, Marx's text certainly suggests causal claims. The apparently causal aspect of Marx's account of estrangement is important to pursue, whatever the underlying conceptual difficulties, because it is relevant to Marx's attitude toward private property. Recall the order in which Marx discusses estrangement:

1. estrangement from the product of labor,
2. estrangement from the act of production,
3. estrangement from species-being, or human potential, and
4. estrangement from other human beings.

Judging from Marx's order of exposition, one might think that his argument would be that estrangement from the product of labor causes the other forms of estrangement, such that

1. estrangement from the product leads to
2. estrangement from the laboring involved in producing that product; which thwarts
3. the development of human potential, since the estrangement of the worker from his (her) work prevents the worker from developing new powers *through* the work.

Further, Marx's claim seems also to be that (1), (2), and (3) together thwart

4. the relations of human beings to each other.

Thus: estrangement from the product of labor (which presumably means: from private property) would be the root cause of the other estrangements. Readers who are especially keen might want to work their way through Marx's text in order to check my account of it. They should, however, be forewarned that the text is difficult, containing many traps for the unwary.

The question of what, in Marx's view, causes what is important for analyzing Marx's position. On the answer to the question In Marx's view, what is the root cause of estrangement? hangs the answer to another question: In Marx's view, what, primarily, would need to be changed for estrangement to be overcome? Let us suppose that Marx's position is that estrangement from the product is indeed the cause of estrangement generally (this is not Marx's position, but we need first of all to consider what the implications would be if it were). Marx does appear to contend, at one point, that the worker's estrangement from the product of his [her] labor is a consequence of the existence of private property. As Marx puts it:

> If the product of labor does not belong to the worker, and if it confronts him as an alien power, this is only possible because it belongs to *a man other than the worker*. (*MEGA2* 1.2: 371/*MECW* 3: 278/*EW* 330)

It would then follow that for estrangement to be overcome the fundamental thing that would have to occur would be the abolition of private property. The abolition of private property would end the estrangement of the worker from the product, and presumably the other forms of estrangement as well. So interpreted, the claims in this passage, if true, would provide a theoretical justification for insisting on the abolition of private property.

But what is interesting, and at first glance puzzling, is that Marx does not claim that estrangement from the product causes estrangement from the act of production. His claim is the reverse: that estrangement from the act of production causes estrangement from the product. To be sure, Marx is not always crystal clear on this point, but he is clear enough. Consider the following two passages. Here is the first passage:

> Although private property *appears* [my italics] as the basis, as the cause [*als Grund, als Ursache*] of alienated labor, it is in fact its consequence, just as the gods were

> *originally* not the cause but the effect of confusion in men's minds. Later, however, this relationship becomes reciprocal.
>
> It is only when the development of private property reaches its ultimate point of culmination that this its secret re-emerges, namely, on the one hand that it is the *product* of alienated labor and, secondly, that it is the *means* through which labor alienates itself, the *making real* [Realisation] *of this alienation*. (*MEGA2* 1.2: 372–73/*MECW* 3: 279–80/*EW* 332)

This passage is clear on one point, namely, that in Marx's view private property is not the cause of estrangement/alienation—although private property does "later" become a support of "alienated labor." Concerning another point the passage is ambiguous, as any reader who cares to reread the quotation and think about it for a while will be able to see; for it is not clear from the passage itself what Marx intends by "alienated labor [*entäusserte Arbeit*]" (the phrase could equally well be translated as "externalized labor"). Does he mean the *act* of labor, external to the worker's true being, or does he mean the *product* of labor, which exists "externally" to the worker and which one might consider by that very fact to be estranged? Perhaps the weight of the passage is on the second possibility—but this is not clear from the passage. "Externalized labor" could equally well mean, not the object created by labor that then exists outside the labor, but the act of laboring, which has nothing to do with—and is consequently external to—the worker him[her]self.

The second passage, occurring a few pages before the one just quoted, is a (rhetorical) question that addresses the ambiguity:

> How could the product of the worker's activity confront him as something alien if it were not for the fact that in the act of production he was estranging himself from himself? . . . If the product of labor is alienation, production itself must be active alienation, the alienation of activity, the activity of alienation [*thätige Entäusserung, die Entäusserung der Thätigkeit, die Thätigkeit der Entäusserung*]. (*MEGA2* 1.2: 367/*MECW* 3: 274/*EW* 326)

In the previously quoted passage it is ambiguous whether "alienated labor" means labor's estrangement from the act of production or from the product. But the present passage is clear on this point: it portrays the worker's estrangement from the act of production as primary, for it presents estrangement from the act of production as (somehow) causing estrangement from the product.[42]

In the light of the German philosophical tradition, it is not surprising that Marx should have been inclined to prioritize estrangement from the act of production over estrangement from the product. As I suggested in chapter 1, there was an "activist" tendency in German philosophy. Marx was closely connected to this tendency. Although it is slightly misleading to do so, one might call this tendency "Fichtean," since Johann Gottlieb Fichte's philosophy was fixated on "act" (*Tathandlung*), and in particular on the "activity" (*Tätigkeit*) of the *Ich*, the "I" or self or ego, which in the course of its activity falls into an alienation (*Entäusserung, Entäusserns*) of itself from itself. Indeed, Fichte's discussion in his *Science of Knowledge* (1794–95) of the self's "activity of alienation" (*Tätigkeit des Entäusserns*) sounds almost like a schematic version of Marx's discussion of estranged labor in the "Economic and Philosophical Manuscripts."[43] But the activist tendency is also Hegelian: consider Hegel's assertion in his *Lectures on the History of Philosophy* that "The labor [*Arbeit*] of the spirit, to know itself, to find itself, this activity [*Thätigkeit*] is spirit, the life of spirit itself" (*LHP* 3: 546–47/1836 ed., 15: 685–86). Stereotypically, one might think of Hegel as a logicist and Fichte as an activist—Hegel adhering to the slogans "Im Anfang war das Wort" and "Im Anfang war der Sinn" (In the beginning was the Word, and Meaning), Fichte adhering to the slogans "Im Anfang war die Kraft!" and "Im Anfang war die Tat!" (In the beginning was Power, and the Deed).[44] But it is more exact to say that Hegel, the all-embracer, was *both* an activist and a logicist.

And the activism was picked up by the Left Hegelians. This was true of Feuerbach (as noted in chapter 1). It was especially true of Moses Hess, like Marx a Jewish journalist from the Rhineland. Marx had occasion to deal with both writers in connection with the notion of activity. He cites Hess's essay, "The Philosophy of the Act," twice in the EPM. The more interesting citation occurs in the context of a discussion by Marx of the active, creative, almost aesthetic character of the human senses (*MEGA2* 1.2: 326, 393/*MECW* 3: 232, 300/*EW* 281, 352).[45] Further, in his justly celebrated "Theses on Feuerbach" (spring 1845), Marx laid great emphasis on the role played by the notion of activity in Feuerbach's philosophy—to be sure, by this time Marx was persuaded that Feuerbach's activity was in the wrong place (attached to idealism rather than to materialism) (*M*EW 3: 5–7/*MECW* 5: 3–5/*EW* 441–42). Indeed, the general emphasis among the Left Hegelians on the need to move from theory to "praxis" can be seen as part of a larger focus on activity.

In any case, the point that I am making is clear: the character of the philosophical tradition out of which Marx came makes it unsurprising that for Marx the dominant consideration in his account of estrangement would have been estrangement from the act of production. If it is indeed true that Marx held that estrangement from the act of production is the primary form of estrangement, it makes sense not only that he would have held (as seems to be the case in the second indented passage that I quoted above) that estrangement from the act of production causes estrangement from the product, but also that he would have held that private property is the consequence rather than the cause of estrangement. For Marx connects estrangement from the product very closely with private property. It is again not surprising that he should do so: after all, the product from which the worker is estranged is an object that the capitalist owns as property and that he takes and sells on the market. Further, in the light of what Marx says in the second indented passage above, it is likewise unsurprising to find him contending, in a statement that appears a few lines before the first passage quoted above, that private property is "the product, result, and necessary consequence of *alienated labor*."[46]

Our concern here is not so much exegetical as it is explanatory: we want to know why Marx made the decision, fateful for socialism, of rejecting private property and the market. I defer for treatment in chapter 4 the thorny question of the status of Marx's causal statements.[47] But one puzzle arising from the text needs to be dealt with here. In brief: given that Marx appears to regard estrangement from the act of production as causing estrangement from the product, why, in the "Estranged Labor and Private Property" section, does he begin his discussion of estrangement with estrangement from the product? After all, one would normally expect that in listing a number of categories an attentive writer would put the most important category first.

In fact, Marx had two strong reasons for discussing estrangement from the product first—reasons that have nothing to do with any wish on his part to attribute causal primacy to estrangement from the product. First, much of the "Economic and Philosophical Manuscripts" is the record of Marx's confrontation with the existing literature on political economy (today we call the field simply "economics"). The "Estranged Labor and Private Property" section follows on the heels of an extensive discussion by Marx of contemporary political economy. It is an effective argumentative procedure to begin by accepting, or at least by feigning to accept, the premises held by one's opponents, and then, *on the basis of those very premises*, to seek to demonstrate that undesirable conclusions, or at least contradictory ones, follow. Such a critique is generally known as an "immanent" or "internal" critique. Marx's pursuit of an immanent critique of political economy leads him to begin by provisionally accepting the premises of the political economists. Marx could find a model for this "immanent" way of attacking political economy in Engels's "Outlines of a Critique of Political Economy." Since Engels's essay was published, in February 1844, in the *Deutsch-Französische Jahrbücher*, co-edited by Marx and Arnold Ruge, which contained Marx's own "On the Jewish Question" and introduction to "A Contribution to the Critique of Hegel's Philosophy of Right," it seems safe to assume that Marx must have read "Outlines" by early 1844, if not earlier. In any case, we know that he read it, or more likely reread it, in summer 1844, since he made some brief notes on it at the time (*MEGA2* 4.2: 485–86/*MECW* 3: 418–43).[48]

The first sentence of the "Estranged Labor and Private Property" section acknowledges the "immanent" aspect of Marx's critique of political economy: "We have started out from the premises of political economy. We have accepted its language and its laws" (*MEGA2* 1.2: 363/*MECW* 3: 270/*EW* 322). The basic premise of political economy, in Marx's view, is private property: as Marx writes, a few lines later: "Political economy proceeds from the fact of private property" (*MEGA2* 1.2: 363/*MECW* 3: 270/*EW* 322). Accordingly, in his immanent critique of political economy Marx was driven to begin with private property as well. But as already noted, private property and estrangement from the product are closely connected: after all, it is as the property of someone else that the product is taken away from the worker who made it. Thus Marx was led to begin his account of estrangement with estrangement from the product. Marx's layout here had two things to recommend it: first, one's audience can better grasp one's argument if one begins with familiar material; and second, there is no argument stronger than an argument that arises from one's opponent's own premises. Potentially such an argument has a conclusive force to it, analytically and hence necessarily working out conclusions that the opponent has failed to grasp.

Second, we also find here in the EPM the outlines of another argumentative procedure on Marx's part, one that would be decisive for *Capital*. The procedure in question became more important to Marx in the 1850s, when, shaken by the disappointing results of the revolutionary movement of 1848, he came to engage in an attempt to unveil what he clearly saw as the modern bourgeois order's deep structure. The procedure involves an attempt on the part of the analyst and critic (and for Marx the two were the same) to move from the level of superficial appearance to the level of underlying essence. In other words, in one's exposition of any sphere of reality one begins with things that people can actually see, and then one tries to show that what people see is misleading—that there is another, truer reality behind or below the appearances. Moreover, there is a historical story that Marx connects with the relation between appearance and essence. The gist of the story is that at first things were clear, then they were made obscure, and now, as historical development continues, the obscure reemerges into visibility. In short, appearances deceive. And so Marx was driven to display appearances first, in order to set the stage for his revelation of the hidden and hence unfamiliar essence.

These two considerations allow us to offer complementary explanations as to why Marx begins his account of estrangement with a discussion of estrangement from the product, before moving on to estrangement from the act of production—even though Marx's view seems to be that estrangement from the act somehow precedes or gives rise to estrangement from the product, and not vice versa. In the first place, the product is estranged from the worker in the form of private property, and private property is the basic, although unjustified, premise of the political economists whom Marx is attacking; in the second place, estrangement from the product is more outwardly visible than estrangement from the act of production. Reading *through* the confusions that Marx heedlessly sows in the EPM, we can readily see that he regards estrangement from the act of production as primary. In the light of Marx's connection to the activist strand in German philosophy, it is hardly surprising that he should have reached such a conclusion.

The matter can be looked at from yet another angle. To see estrangement from the act of production as primary was by the same token to reject the notion that estrangement from the product is primary. Marx may well have been inclined against taking estrangement from the product as primary because this would have put him close to a false position that he attributed to Hegel. In brief, by 1844, Marx attributed to Hegel the view that there is a gulf between spirit on the one hand and the material and natural world on the other, such that when human beings create, through their ingenuity, material objects, the material objects, *because* they are material, amount to an estrangement of that ingenuity. In other words, Marx claimed that Hegel wrongly identified "objectification" (*Vergegenständlichung*), that is, the making of objects, with estrangement (*Entfremdung*) (*MEGA2* 1.2: 414/*MECW* 3: 342–43/*EW* 396). It was precisely such a view that Marx wished to attack: for he envisaged a future society in which the making of material objects would not be an estrangement of human beings, but would rather give them pleasure and would enable them to develop their capacities.

In fact, Marx misrepresents Hegel's position; here, as elsewhere, Marx cannot be trusted to give a fair and accurate account of the positions of those he attacks.[49] Marx's attack on Hegel at this point is really about something much broader than Hegel's alleged views concerning the production of material objects. What Marx is criticizing is a central orientation of the idealist tradition. As I suggested in chapter 1, one of the distinctive features of Marx's project is that it connects with both sides of the great divide in nineteenth-century thought (and indeed in all post-Cartesian thought), namely, the divide between spirit and matter. Deeply influenced by both sides of that opposition, Marx seeks to get beyond the spirit/matter chasm. What this means is that Marx *could not be an ontologist in the traditional sense*, for within the ontological project of philosophical modernism (that is, within its attempt to get at the underlying constitution of the world) the spirit/matter chasm is unavoidable.[50] (Further, Marx was unprepared to be a critic of philosophical modernism itself—unprepared, that is, to be a Heidegger *avant la lettre*.) A move to the study of humanity solved the problem, by allowing Marx to leave aside the entire ontological issue in its traditional sense. This fact reveals itself in the "Economic and Philosophical Manuscripts," where Marx's response to Hegel's alleged identification of objectification with estrangement is to situate both objectification and estrangement within the context of a particular social order—and also within a particular activity, that of material production. This amounts to a de-ontologization of the spirit/matter problem. In 1844, to be sure, the details remained to be worked out: that working out is to be found first of all in the historical materialism that Marx articulated in 1845–46, and later in his theory of capitalist society itself.

To stick with 1844: it seems clear that when he wrote the "Estranged Labor and Private Property" section Marx was persuaded that the central defect of the current economic order was that, in it, the worker is estranged in (and from) the act of production. But if the fundamental problem with modern bourgeois society is that the worker is estranged from the act of production, why not focus on *that* as the problem to be solved? Why not seek to improve the work environment—by legislation, by explicit attention to the workplace, by the increasing application of worker-friendly technology, and the like?[51] One can imagine a political system that would make laws designed to encourage the continual improvement of the work environment—laws that all businesses would have to obey, so that none would obtain an unfair advantage over its competitors. In short, one can imagine a well-functioning social democracy. In such a political system, the conclusion would have been reached that, overall, the market and private property offer the best way of producing material goods. But the conclusion would also have been reached that private property and the market do not necessarily conduce to wider social needs, and that legislation is required in order to correct what citizens, through their deliberations, will have decided are undesirable consequences of the workings of the market alone. And thus the effort would be made to improve the scene of work—and also to mitigate other alienating aspects of society, aspects that do not enter into Marx's focus, in the EPM, on the estrangement of labor in the production process.

One can imagine such a system, but Marx did not. The statement, quoted earlier, that Marx and Engels made in *The Communist Manifesto*, to the effect that "the theory of the communists may be summed up in the single sentence: Abolition of private property" is not to be explained as a polemical sally (*MEW* 4: 475/*MECW* 6: 498/*MER* 484/*LPW* 13). On the contrary, from 1844 onward Marx always insisted that private property needs to be abolished. Yet Marx had no hostility to the individual use and enjoyment of things. It is also clear that, for Marx, private property as such is not the root of what is wrong with the present-day economic order. On the contrary, insofar as one can get a clear account out of the EPM—and I emphasize again that there are deep ambiguities in it—his argument seems to be that the fundamental problem in the existing order is that the worker is estranged from the act of production. According to Marx, the worker is also estranged from the product that is produced, which is taken away from the worker in the form of private property.

But this second aspect of estrangement appears to be secondary in his eyes to the estrangement that arises within the scene of production itself.

In short, although some uncertainty is created by Marx's tendency to see related concepts as merely aspects of each other, it seems clear that he did not attribute to the market a causal role in the estrangement of labor. Admittedly, the complex "private property/money/exchange" might be seen as worsening a situation that already exists because of estrangement from the act of production. Marx suggests as much, noting that alienated labor gave rise to private property, but that "Later . . . this relationship becomes reciprocal [*schlägt . . . in Wechselwirkung um*]" (*MEGA2* 1.2: 373/*MECW* 3: 280/*EW* 332). But Marx does not hold that this complex is at the root of the problem.[52]

Nor, if we think about these matters on our own, does there seem to be any compelling reason for seeing the market/private property *as such* as being estranging. On the contrary, consulting their own experience, many readers will conclude that *in the absence of dire poverty*, having the right to buy and sell things on the market, and to say of particular objects, "This thing belongs to me," are anything but estranging. For example, from a very early age children love to claim ownership of things, and from a slightly later age they love to be able to spend money, even if only a pittance, to buy things. And many adult persons also find ownership, as well as buying (bargaining, shopping), far more pleasurable than unpleasurable.

Accordingly, we return to the intertwined questions posed at the beginning of this chapter, but with a deeper sense of the puzzlement that they raise: Why did Marx reject private property? Why did he reject the market? Surely he should have focused on the abolition of "act" estrangement, subordinating everything else to this aim. Or, to pose the question in yet another way: why did a Marx who was concerned with getting rid of estranged labor, and who was hostile to private property and the market only insofar as they blocked the unfolding of the full possibilities of humankind, not appear on the scene?

A MATTER OF *DENKSTIL*: INDIVIDUALISM AND HOLISM IN MARX

The French Marxist philosopher Louis Althusser (1918–1990) would have rejected this question out of hand, on the grounds that the notion of estrangement—and, even more, the notion of act-estrangement—was something that Marx abandoned when, in 1845–46, he turned to historical materialism. The Marx of 1844, Althusser claimed, was the immature, *humanist* Marx, whom the mature, *scientific* Marx left behind in 1845. In Althusser's view, there is an "epistemological break"—a "*coupure épistémologique*"—dividing the

"Economic and Philosophical Manuscripts" from the later Marx.[53] In Althusser's view, the scientific Marx was concerned with the structure of capitalist society, and not with such trivialities as whether workers feel good about their work.

As is widely recognized, Althusser's claim that there is a radical break between the early and the late Marx is vastly overstated. It is true that the Marx of the EPM had not yet articulated the materialist conception of history, something that Marx and Engels would do for the first time only in *The German Ideology* (apparently written between November 1845 and August 1846 [DRAP 2: 9]). But elements of the materialist conception of history are certainly present in the EPM, even though in the EPM Marx did not work out that conception in detail but only noted that he needed to do so.[54] Nor is it true that there is a *methodological* break between Marx in 1844 and Marx in 1845–46—the entire argument of the present book goes against such a claim. Nonetheless, there are tensions in Marx. But the tensions are less between the early Marx and the later Marx than they are within Marx's project at every moment. Why is this so?

What we have, in Marx, is a philosopher deeply concerned with arriving at a unified understanding of the world, and at the same time a philosopher whose bent is to pursue every problem to its nth degree. As I have argued, he was a "unitarist," looking forward to the ultimate resolution or "bringing back" of all conflicting entities to one. He was also, at least in part, a holist, inclined to look for and find totalities, each of whose components reflects and is integrally connected with all its other components. One commentator, Bertell Ollman, has gone so far as to see Marx as adhering to a Leibnizian "philosophy of internal relations," according to which every element within the world is simply an aspect of the larger totality that is the world as a whole. Ollman's claims are overstated, but they are far from being wrong. For the fact is, Ollman identifies an important feature of Marx's thought, although it is a feature that I link much more to a historicized version of Aristotelian syllogistic reasoning (see chapter 1) than to Leibniz.[55]

If we were to think of Marx as a kind of thinking machine, it would be a machine that in its very search for consistency (coherence) generates inconsistencies (incoherence). Marx insisted on finding or inventing wholes or totalities; relatedly, he insisted on trying to bring unity to the contradictions to be found in any particular situation. Intelligent attempts to see the human world as a unified whole tend to bring to light those places where the world cannot (or cannot yet) be seen in this way. Marx *qua* theorist was engaged in trying to see the human world as a unified whole. Time and again his analyses bring to light, even generate, tensions—for example, between necessity and freedom; between labor as burden, labor as gratification, and labor as self-development; between agency and structure; between rationality and democracy; between administration and democracy; between the intended and the unintended; between science and activism; between rationality and freedom. This is part of the reason why the tensions in Marx need to be seen as simultaneous and not just as successive. The fact that Marx contradicts himself is less a defect than an indication of the seriousness of his thinking. Not every thinker who contradicts him[her]self is worth attending to, but Marx is worth attending to because of the rigor of his thinking and because of his attentiveness to real developments in modern society.

As I have suggested, one difficulty that emerges in Marx's work is that of disentangling which elements in any given situation Marx sees as causes and which he sees as effects. Marx has a strong tendency to want to describe the world as if the total system (e.g., capitalism), *qua* system, rather than any specific part of the system, is causative. I do not think that this difficulty in Marx can be gotten round without misrepresenting him in lesser or greater degree. To be sure, one can always cut the Gordian knot, by ignoring Marx's holist commitments and approaching him with an eye to specific features of his project, specific claims and mechanisms. One can even treat Marx's work as a kind of handyman's box—a box containing nuts, bolts, and other devices from which one picks and chooses as one goes about trying to construct social theories. I do not approach Marx in these ways because I am mainly engaged in a different game, the game of trying to arrive at a historical understanding of Marx. I see Marx's contribution to our own current understanding of the human world as much more indirect than such approaches suppose. These pragmatic approaches skip a step. *First* we need to see the theoretical project as it was. *Then* we can think of how to proceed forward from that project.

I suspect that Marx does not make the move from seeing estrangement from the act of production as primary, to concluding that the defectiveness of the modern economic order can be overcome if that estrangement is overcome, because his fixation on the system *as a whole* precludes such an approach. Such an approach would be "piecemeal" (to quote Marx's rebuke to such reformers as Proudhon [*MEGA2* 1.2: 333/*MECW* 3: 241/*EW* 289]). What Marx wants is an *Aufhebung* (transcendence, going beyond) of the system as a whole. Indeed, it is not just that he *wants* such a transcendence: it is that the parts of the system are, in his conception, so interconnected that it is hard to see how one part could be transformed without a transformation of the other parts.

The language of the "Economic and Philosophical Manuscripts" highlights this interconnectedness. Thus Marx refers to the current economic system as both the "rule of private property" and as the "*money* system"; he also refers to it as "this entire estrangement [*diese ganze Entfremdung*]." Marx writes, indeed, that there is an

> essential connection between private property, greed, the separation of labor, capital and landed property, exchange [*Austausch*] and competition, value and the devaluation of man, monopoly and competition, etc.—the connection between this entire estrangement [*diese ganze Entfremdung*] and the *money* system. (*MEGA2* 1.2: 359, 364/*MECW* 3: 266, 271/*EW* 318, 323)

Exchange (*Austausch*) is the term that Marx almost always employs to refer to the market. Except in quoting or paraphrasing other writers, he rarely uses the term *Markt*, in the EPM or elsewhere: his emphasis, rather, is on the activity that defines the market, which, obviously, is the activity of exchange.[56] The "essential connection" that Marx sees between private property and exchange comes close to looking like an identity. Insofar as we actually take it to *be* an identity, then we have a chicken–egg problem. Does Marx castigate private property because it leads to exchange, or does he castigate exchange because it leads to private property? From such a passage as this it is impossible to tell. Indeed, slightly later, in *The German Ideology*, Marx and Engels assert that "division of labor and private property are . . . identical expressions," with the division of labor referring to the activity of production, and private property to the product of that activity (*MEW* 3: 32/ *MECW* 5: 46/*MER* 160).[57] In any case, whatever their precise relations, it is clear that Marx views the categories of labor, market (which makes the division of labor possible), and private property as, at the very least, intimately connected.[58]

One thus finds oneself asking whether private property is simply exchange viewed from a different perspective. Or, are private property and exchange two *different*, but connected, entities? However, the ambiguity need not detain us, for all we need to know is that Marx saw private property and the market as so closely interrelated that insofar as Marx's attitude toward the market is negative, his attitude toward private property must be negative also. The argument is extensible: insofar as private property is the "objective" side of what appears in its "subjective" side as estrangement from the act of production, then private property remains an issue.

My contention, for which I shall present specific evidence in the following sections, is that the market plays a special role in this network of interrelated categories. Marx could not accept the approach of seeking to end estrangement from the act of production (without worrying very much about private property) because, I contend, private property is intimately interrelated with the market, and, as I shall establish below, Marx saw the market as generating confusion and irrationality. This is why concentrating on the ending of act-estrangement was, for Marx, a nonstarter. Rather, in Marx's view abolition of the market, and of private property (since the latter is inseparable from the market), are what is primarily required.

Thus the "Estranged Labor and Private Property" section of the "Economic and Philosophical Manuscripts" helps us see two things. First, it helps us see how deeply the Marx of 1844 was focused on estrangement. To be sure, Marx also sees the existing economic order as exploitative, but, although he acknowledges and points to exploitation he does not thematize it, and he rejects out of hand Proudhon's proposal to counter exploitation by imposing equality of wages. Second, this section of the EPM helps us to discern a tension in Marx's position—given that, on the one hand, he saw estrangement from the act of production as the fundamental cause of the problems of the current system, while, on the other hand, he looked at the existing order in such a systemic way that he found it impossible to focus on any one element of that system as being the cause of the system's defectiveness. What this means is that the estrangement argument is only ambiguously an argument against the market: it is much more an argument against the system as a whole, with the emphasis being placed, if on anything, then on the context of production rather than on the context of exchange. However, shortly after writing the EPM, Marx articulated his "irrationality" argument, which is much more directly focused on the market, and which goes much further in explaining Marx's abiding wish for the market's abolition.

WHY DID MARX REJECT THE MARKET? THE MARKET AS IRRATIONAL

Marx himself never used the term *irrational* to characterize the market, but it is a legitimate term for designating what he seems to have had in mind. In chapter 1, I canvassed Marx's conception of rationality and its intellectual origins. As was pointed out, the Hegelian notion that a truly rational knowledge is a necessary knowledge, in which nothing is contingent, was of great importance to Marx. In Hegel's view it is philosophically unacceptable to ground an intellectual system in a mere assumption; one's starting point has to be established as *necessarily* true by the results of the intellectual field itself. Hence, knowledge is in a literal sense encyclopedic: the end point of a field of knowledge "cycles back" and establishes the necessity of the beginning.[59] Further, when such specialized sciences as law, natural history, and medicine descend into details, "the idea of nature dissolves into contingencies," and the "descriptions of reality" that these sciences offer end up being determined "not . . . by reason but rather by chance and by games"—a weakness, in Hegel's view.[60] Marx was profoundly influenced by this necessitarianism.

Subsidiary to Hegel's impact on Marx was the generalized impact of natural science. Initially, Marx seems to have been led to take an interest in nature partly by his own curiosity and partly by the notion that natural science is a good antidote to religious obscurantism. Feuerbach's evocations of natural science also must have influenced Marx. Further, by the early 1840s it was commonplace to note the way in which the landscape was being altered by such technological and scientific marvels as railways—a topic on which Ruge wrote in 1840 (chapter 4). Finally, as Marx read his way into the political economists in 1844 he must have noticed that David Ricardo and especially James Mill saw political economy as engaged in the discovery of laws of economics, analogous to the Newtonian laws of nature. Consequently, by summer 1844, in the "Economic and Philosophical Manuscripts," Marx portrays a natural science that had "intervened in and transformed human life . . . through industry," and envisages an eventual unification of natural science with the science of man (*MEGA2* 1.2: 272/*MECW* 3: 303–4/*EW* 355). None of this required much specific knowledge of natural science, and the early Marx certainly did not have such knowledge. The *idea* of natural science was sufficient.

If one takes the Newtonian laws of nature as truly universal, the implication seems clear: everything is determined, and hence everything is predictable. In the most famous assertion of this view, the French mathematician Pierre Laplace declared that an intellect capable of knowing all the forces and positions at work within nature, and capable of subjecting these data to analysis, "would embrace in the same formula the movements of the greatest bodies of the universe and those of the lightest atom: nothing would be uncertain for it, and the future, like the past, would be present before its eyes."[61] By implication from Newtonian physics, a mark of *all* scientific knowledge is that it articulates laws that are predictive. By the early nineteenth century such a view was influential in the incipient science of economics. In Adam Smith, the origins of economics in an earlier tradition of moral philosophy are still visible, whereas in such works as Ricardo's *Principles of Political Economy and Taxation* (1817) and James Mill's *Elements of Political Economy* (1821), Smith's broad moral vision gives way to a Newtonian view. For example, Mill seeks to discover the laws regulating production, distribution, exchange, and consumption in a way that evokes natural-scientific laws.[62] And the Ricardian "iron law of wages" (holding that wages cannot rise significantly above a subsistence level) likewise has the air of a natural-scientific law imposed on human beings. Hence we are not surprised when we see that in the "Economic and Philosophical Manuscripts" Marx glosses Ricardo as holding that "Economic laws rule the world blindly" (*MEGA2* 1.2: 348/*MECW* 3: 256/*EW* 306).

How do the notions of necessity and of scientific law connect with Marx's rejection of the market? I have already canvassed and rejected the notion that Marx rejected the market either out of Jewish self-hatred or out of some more generalized disdain of market behavior. And, as I also argued above, the "estrangement" argument is not exactly adequate either, for it is hardly an argument against the market specifically. Only when we add the "irrationality" argument—arrived at by late summer or fall 1844—do we see why he came to be such an uncompromising opponent of the market.

To put the matter briefly: by summer or fall 1844 Marx came to hold that the market is not rationally understandable—that it is not accessible to scientific understanding. At the time of his writing of "On the Jewish Question" (late 1843), Marx had not yet seriously studied political economy and he does not seem to have had any clearly articulated argument concerning the rationality either of political economy in general or of the market in particular. In "On the Jewish Question" one certainly finds a social prejudice against market activity—against *Schacher*—but there is no *argument* against the market.

However, by February 1844 at the latest Marx was able to read Engels's essay, "Outlines of a Critique of Political Economy." At this point Marx had not yet connected personally with Engels—that would occur only in August–September 1844—and Engels's essay seems to have come to the *Deutsch-Französische Jahrbücher* quite late and completely independently of Marx (inference from editorial discussion in *MEGA2* 1.3: 1109–12). Hence there is no reason to think that Marx collaborated in any way in the content of the "Outlines," nor, so far as I can see, is there reason to think that the "Outlines" had any influence on Marx's "On the Jewish Question." "Outlines of a Critique of Political Economy" is a characteristically Engelsian exercise in polemical journalism. It was the product of a rapid (and very shrewd) glance at contemporary political economy rather than the result of profound and lengthy study. Nonetheless, it operated like a time bomb on Marx's work, stimulating him to embark on his own study of political economy.

But what is striking in the present context is something rather more specific. In the first sentence of his "Outlines" Engels uses two crucial words: *Schacher* and *Wissenschaft*. I quote Engels, whom we already find in full polemical flight:

> Political economy arose as a natural consequence of the extension of trade, and with its appearance elementary, unscientific *Schacher* was replaced by a developed system of authorized [*erlaubte*] fraud, a complete [*komplete*] science of enrichment. (*MEGA2* 1.3: 467–94, at 467/*MECW* 3: 418–43, at 418)

Two points should be noted here. First, Engels explicitly declares that *Schacher*, haggling, is unscientific (*unwissenschaftlich*).[63] In "On the Jewish

Question" Marx himself makes no such claim. One suspects that the idea that *Schacher* is unscientific was lurking in his mind at the time, but he did not say it: Engels seems to have been first to do so. Second, Engels makes another claim—this, in contrast, a claim that Marx would shortly reject. As the passage makes clear, Engels situates *Schacher* in the past. He sets up an opposition between unscientific, passé *Schacher* and the modern science of political economy, which is both "a developed system of authorized fraud" and a "complete science of enrichment." Thus, implicitly, Engels accepts the claim made by Ricardo, James Mill, and the like that they were articulating a science—although in Engels's eyes it was not a disinterested science. More important, in contrast to Marx's view as articulated in "On the Jewish Question," Engels sees unscientific *Schacher* as belonging to an *earlier* system, not to the current economic order.

Already in 1842 Marx had paid some glancing attention to the political economy literature, but from 1842 to about May 1844 Marx's main intellectual efforts were directed elsewhere: to a primarily journalistic engagement with the political issues of the day; to the study and critique of political theory, especially Hegel's political theory; and to his historical study of the French Revolution. (I discuss these efforts in chapter 2.) Marx's plan, articulated in late 1843 or early 1844, to write a history of the French National Convention of 1792–95 was one aspect of this engagement with political issues. Even as late as May/June–August 1844 he still had in mind the idea of writing on jurisprudence and political theory, as we know from the preface to the "Economic and Philosophical Manuscripts" (*MEGA2* 1.2: 325/*MECW* 3: 231/*EW* 280–81). However, sometime in the first half of 1844 Marx turned seriously to the study of political economy. He appears to have done so *after* his reading of Levasseur on the French Revolution (*MEGA2* 4.2: 727). His reading in political economy—more intensive than extensive—included works, or economically relevant parts of works, by Jean-Baptiste Say, Fryderyk Skarbek, Adam Smith, Xenophon, David Ricardo, James Mill, John Ramsay MacCulloch, Guillaume Prevost, Engels (the "Outlines"), Antoine-Claude Destutt de Tracy, C. W. C. Schülz, Friedrich List, Heinrich Friedrich Osiander, and Eugène Buret (*MEGA2* 4.2: 7*–8* [Inhalt]).

In the course of this reading Marx came to two "discoveries." The first of these, already discussed, was his discovery of the estrangement of human beings in labor. In brief, Marx condemns the existing economic system for being dehumanizing, and he condemns the science of political economy for failing to confront this fact. Marx's discovery of the estrangement of labor has been well known for half a century. The coming to light of Marx's interest in estrangement generated what was seen in the 1950s and 1960s as the "problem" of relating the "early" Marx (that is, the Marx of 1844) to the "later"

Marx.[64] Even now estrangement and "Marx in 1844" are often seen as all but synonymous.

Marx's second discovery of 1844, which I shall now finally lay out, was his discovery of the irrationality of the market. So far as I know this Marxian discovery has not been noticed at all. Yet this second discovery is immensely important for our understanding of why Marx's socialism—that is, his vision of the future society—excludes the market. Imagine a Marx less stringently committed to the rationality-criteria laid out in chapter 1. Imagine, in short, a Marx more willing to follow the lead of his own specific researches, his own empirical observations.[65] It is my claim that a more empirical, less stringently rationalistic Marx would not have been driven to exclude market relations from his vision of the future socialist (communist) society. Other types of socialism allowed a place for the market; Marxian socialism did not. I contend, further, that this fact, along with Marx's related rejection of politics in favor of a supposedly scientific administration, meant that there was no real possibility of Marx's model attaining, in the real world, the end—namely, maximization of human freedom—that it set for itself.

At first glance it might seem surprising that commentators have not noticed Marx's discovery that the market is irrational, for the excerpts and notes in which Marx articulated his "irrationality" argument were first published years ago, in the "old" *Marx/Engels Gesamtausgabe* (*MEGA*), in 1932.[66] But when one thinks about it one can readily see why commentators overlooked this argument. First, the writings are sometimes difficult. Second, the upheavals of the time—above all the rise to power of the National Socialists in Germany and the consolidation of Stalinist tyranny in the Soviet Union, followed by World War II—helped to delay serious and widespread consideration of Marx's early texts until the 1950s. The original printing of *MEGA* was not exactly widely available, given the forced move of the operation from Germany to the USSR in 1933 and Stalin's killing of the edition (and its editor) after 1935. But even if the edition had been more readily available, people were not much interested in what it contained. In the 1930s and 1940s serious study of Marx usually meant study of Marx's mature economic theories, as put forward in *Capital*. With rare exceptions, it did not mean the study of Marx's early writings.[67]

Second, once Marx's early writings did become readily available, what grabbed people's attention was the notion of estrangement, for this notion appeared to open the way to a Marxism more fruitful and progressive than the version sponsored by the Soviet Union. Estrangement offered a way for "western Marxists" to articulate a Marxism different from Soviet-style dialectical materialism, which emphasized the inexorable forward movement of the juggernaut of history (spearheaded by the USSR), and counted worker estrangement as simply the price one pays for rapid industrialization. In contrast, Marx's "irrationality" argument, which must surely have been *noticed* by some readers even though no one (to my knowledge) took the trouble to write about it, offered no readily discernible explanatory or ideological payoff.

Finally, it should be noted that the *MEGA* edition of Marx's excerpts and notes, although a considerable editorial achievement for its time, was incomplete, and its editorial quality is inferior to that of *MEGA2*. And the volumes of *MEGA2* most relevant to the "irrationality" argument were published only in 1981 and 1982.[68] Consider only two points: the editors of *MEGA2* indicate to readers the markings that Marx made on his manuscripts (e.g., strokes in colored pencil in the margins [see *MEGA2* 4.2: 48*]); and, as we shall see shortly, they correct the sequence of two important early writings. As a result, it was more difficult to see the irrationality argument and its significance in Marx's excerpts and notes as they were published in the earlier, inferior "Old *MEGA*" version than it is to see them in the *MEGA2* version. With *MEGA*, the historian always has the uneasy feeling that, for all their illegibility and inaccessibility, one would still need to consult the original Marx manuscripts in order to be sure about any conclusions that one arrived at. With *MEGA2*'s presentation of Marx's manuscripts, the historian no longer feels the worried need to go back to the originals, which are, in fact, all but illegible. Instead, he or she can concentrate on the gloriously legible printed texts.[69]

Marx's claim that the market is irrational arose directly from his critical examination of a debate in early nineteenth-century political economy concerning the nature of value. The texts in which Marx first articulated this line of argument are the excerpts and notes that he wrote in the course of his reading of the French translations of Ricardo's *Principles of Political Economy and Taxation* and James Mill's *Elements of Political Economy*. Marx seems to have made his excerpts and notes of Ricardo and Mill in summer/fall 1844, *after* writing, in May/June–August 1844, the "Economic and Philosophical Manuscripts." The Ricardo and Mill excerpts mark a subtle and, it seems, hitherto undiscussed turn in Marx's conception of the economic world. The *MEGA2* editors note that the manuscript of the Ricardo excerpts shows physical traces of repeated subsequent consultation (lines in the margin, underlinings in the text) (*MEGA2* 4.2: 759). As I shall show below, this is no accident: the contents of these manuscripts, and of the Ricardo manuscript in particular, mark a crucial step in Marx's intellectual evolution.

Already in early 1844 Marx clearly had some idea that the science of political economy is fraught with contradiction, for this was the central argument of Engels's "Outlines of the Critique of Political Economy." Engels devotes one section of the "Outlines" to a discussion of, among other matters, the political economists' contradictory views on value (*MEGA2* 1.3:

475–78/*MECW* 3: 424–27). In spring 1844 Marx himself turned to a detailed reading of Adam Smith's *Wealth of Nations* and of two economic works by the French political economist and republican, whom Marx regarded as Smith's disciple, Jean-Baptiste Say.[70] In his "Say" excerpts Marx makes the Hegelian observation, concerning political economy, that "The whole of political economy rests . . . on a fact without necessity"—that fact being private property, whose fundamental status political economy fails to justify (*MEGA2* 4.2: 319: "*Die ganze Nationalökonomie beruht . . . auf einem factum ohne Nothwendigkeit. . .*"). Marx likewise complains, in both his Smith and his Say excerpts, that at crucial points these economists offered inadequate definitions of their concepts: thus, Say was confused in his definition of value, and Smith fell into a vicious circle in his attempt to establish what the relations are between exchange and the division of labor (*MEGA2* 4.2: 319, 336).

But Marx seems to have arrived at his argument concerning the irrationality of the market only in reading and making excerpts from David Ricardo and James Mill. Marx excerpted Ricardo and Mill only after excerpting Say and Smith. It also seems likely, as noted above, that he did his careful reading of Ricardo and Mill only after writing the "Economic and Philosophical Manuscripts" themselves.[71] The irrationality argument is not to be found in the EPM. The EPM is dominated, rather, by the estrangement argument. Words that suggest that Marx is thinking about the rationality, or not, of the current economic system appear infrequently: *fluctuation* once, *chance* once, *fortuitous* three times, *accident(al)* four times. In contrast, *alien* and its cognates appear 148 times, and *estrange* and its cognates 149 times. Estrangement or alienation is always rooted in an activity that comes to be divided from itself or its ends—and "activity" and its cognates appear 103 times in the EPM.[72]

In fact, Marx worked out his irrationality argument in the course of reflecting on the competing views of Ricardo and Say concerning "natural price," a notion that had been important in classical economics from Adam Smith onward.[73] The Ricardo-Say confrontation is not yet present in the EPM. Ricardo believed in the notion of natural price, whereas Say did not. The confrontation between Ricardo and Say was particularly easy to make, since the translation of Ricardo that Marx used included critical notes by Say.[74] It is also worth noting that in his "Outlines" Engels gave a brief account of the Ricardo–Say opposition, contrasting their views on what determines value (*MEGA2* 1.3: 475–77/*MECW* 3: 424–26), and that in summer 1844 Marx read and made notes on Engels's essay (*MEGA2* 4.2: 485–86).

Whereas in the "Economic and Philosophical Manuscripts," Marx does not bring Ricardo and Say into any kind of confrontation with each other, in his excerpts and notes on Ricardo he does do this. (This is an additional reason in favor of the editorial view that Marx made his Ricardo excerpts only after writing the "Economic and Philosophical Manuscripts".)[75] But whereas in his "Outlines" Engels (entirely characteristically) used the Ricardo–Say opposition as an occasion for making an easy polemical point against political economy, Marx drew from this opposition a theoretical conclusion of great importance and generality.

Marx observes in his Ricardo excerpts that Ricardo wrote that the "exchangeable value" of a commodity is determined by the quantity of labor used in its production (*MEGA2* 4.2: 392–427, at 392).[76] Obviously, if that is what "exchangeable value" is, it cannot quite be the market price of a commodity, which may well change from one minute to the next. Rather, Marx holds that when Ricardo uses the term *exchangeable value* he always means "the natural price, abstracted from the accidents of competition [*den Accidenzen der Concurrenz*], which he designates as some temporary or accidental cause"—that is, it is some sort of *ideal* value (*MEGA2* 4.2: 405).[77] Say, on the other hand, attacked the notion of natural price. In Say's view, Ricardo's economic reasoning was too abstract—too detached from actual experience. Say insists that one cannot find natural price in the real world: in Say's words, quoted by Marx: "the natural price . . . appears to be . . . chimerical. In economics there are only current prices [*le prix naturel . . . paraît être . . . chimérique. Il n'y a que des prix courans en économie politique*]" (*MEGA2* 4.2: 405).

Indeed, in Marx's eyes Say offers a persuasive argument against Ricardo's definition of natural price, with its reliance on cost of production as the factor that determines the natural price of a commodity. If we assume that cost of production determines natural price, then if the cost of production of a commodity rises, the natural price will rise proportionately. But Say points out that Ricardo's claim involves a *certeris paribus* assumption: that is, Ricardo assumes that the rise in the costs of production of a commodity, and hence of the natural price, would not be accompanied by any change in the relation between demand and supply. Yet for the price on the market to rise in line with a rise in production costs, so that it would track the Ricardian natural price, the demand for the commodity would also have to rise. But that would not be the case. All other things being equal, demand falls in the face of a rise in production costs: this is because people tend to buy fewer units of a given commodity if the price of the commodity rises. Thus, price on the market cannot be assumed to track production costs. Accordingly, instead of basing value on production costs, Say contends that what determines value is a combination of the usefulness of the commodity and its production costs, with more weight to the former.[78] In Say's view, the usefulness of a commodity is represented by the demand for it, and its production costs are represented by supply (*MEGA2* 4.2: 392). In short, the market is the measure of value at any given moment. Thus Say denies that there is an invariant measure of value (*MEGA2* 4.2: 395). For example, if silk suddenly becomes more fashionable and wool less, the value of these commodities changes, in Say's view—whereas Ricardo held that their natural price remains the same, because the quantity of labor necessary for producing them has not changed (*MEGA2* 4.2: 405).

Marx takes a position that is distanced from both Say and Ricardo, but that nonetheless remains fundamentally Ricardian in spirit. Marx agrees with Say's claim that Ricardo's economic reasoning is too abstract. In Marx's view, political economy as conceptualized by Ricardo purchases lawfulness, consistency, and determination at the price of substituting abstraction for reality. In Marx's words: "Political economy [in Ricardo's understanding of it], in order to give its laws a certain measure of consistency and determinateness, must suppose that reality is accidental and that abstraction is real" (*MEGA2* 4.2: 405). Marx unequivocally agrees with Ricardo's conviction that it is important to get away from what is accidental and to cultivate instead law, determinateness, and consistency. The point of disagreement is that whereas Ricardo wants to contend that, in spite of all the "accidents of competition" that operate, the market somehow tracks an ideal rational realm inhabited by natural prices and having the regularity of law, Marx wants to deny this. Marx's attitude toward Ricardo is double: on the one hand, in Marx's view Ricardo reveals the irrationality of the market in his very attempt to go beyond the "accidents of competition"; on the other hand, Ricardo obscures the irrationality of the market by assuming that market price somehow reflects and manifests natural price.

Say's move—namely, abandonment of the widely held notion in political economy that commodities have a "natural price"—was a daring way of disposing of the tangles that surrounded this concept, a Gordian solution. But Marx rejected Say's move. A thinker differently constituted than Marx might well have been able to tolerate a theory in which "current price" (*prix courant*) is all that there is, but Marx could not. Contingency is not necessity. Thus Marx comments that if it is only a matter of the "current price" and nothing else—as Say held—then "objects are no longer seen in connection to their costs of production, nor their costs of production in connection to human beings, but, on the contrary, the whole of production is seen in connection to *Schacher* [. . . *werden die Sachen nicht mehr in Bezug auf ihre Productionskosten und die Productionskosten nicht mehr in Bezug auf die Menschen, sondern die ganze Production in Bezug auf den Schacher betrachtet*]" (*MEGA2* 4.2: 406).

Thus, in Marx's excerpts and notes on Ricardo the famous *Schacher* again appears. Can anything be worse than *Schacher*? Marx could easily have used a neutral term, such as *Kauf und Verkauf* (buying and selling).[79] But it is now obvious that the key issue is not social disdain, let alone anti-Semitism. Rather, the problem with *Schacher* is theoretical/intellectual/philosophical. *Schacher* provides no firm and determinate basis for the observable fluctuations (*Schwanken, Schwankungen*) of market price. In consequence, it allows nothing rational to be seen. In Marx's eyes, Ricardo was right in his recognition of, and desire to get away from, the accidents of competition, although he was wrong on other matters. Marx recognized and recoiled from the high level of unpredictability of market price, and he recoiled even more from a position that would allow nothing but those fluctuations. This is why, fundamentally, Marx remained a Ricardian.[80]

THE IRRATIONALITY ARGUMENT NAILED DOWN

It appears that almost immediately after reading Ricardo's *Principles of Political Economy and Taxation*, Marx turned to a reading of James Mill's *Elements of Political Economy* ("Aus James Mill," *MEGA2* 4.2: 428–70). The Mill excerpts are significant because in them Marx nails down the irrationality argument for the first time. The crucial passage appears at that point in the Mill excerpts where Marx ceases excerpting Mill and begins a sustained commentary. I shall quote the passage *in extenso* and then I shall comment on it:

> Mill succumbs to the error, committed by the entire Ricardo school, of defining an *abstract law* without mentioning the fluctuations or the continual suspension through which it comes into being. If . . . it is an *invariable* law that in the last analysis—or rather in the sporadic/accidental [*zufällig*] congruence [*Deckung*] of supply and demand—the cost of production determines price/value, then it is no less an *invariable law* that these relations do not obtain, i.e., that value and the cost of production do not stand in any necessary relation. Indeed, thanks to a previous fluctuation [*Schwanken*] in supply and demand, to the disparity [*Mißverhältniß*] between the cost of production and exchange value, supply and demand always coincide only momentarily. And in like fashion, the momentary congruence is succeeded by the same fluctuating [*Schwankung*] and the same disparity. This is the *real* movement, then, and the above-mentioned law is no more than an abstract, accidental [*zufälliges*], and one-sided moment in it. Yet modern political economy dismisses it as accident [*Accidenz*], as inessential. Why? Because if the economists were to attempt to fix this movement in the sharp and precise terms [*Formeln*] to which they reduce the whole of economics this would produce the following basic formula [*Grundformel*]: laws in economics are determined by their opposite, lawlessness. The true law of economics is *chance* [Zufall], out of whose movement we learned people [*Wissenschaftlichen*] arbitrarily seize on a few moments and establish them as laws. (*MEGA2* 4.2: 447/*EW* 259–60)[81]

This is an amazing passage, and I do not expect the reader to grasp it in a single quick reading. Suffice it to say that the passage continues preoccupations that are already present in the "Economic and Philosophical Manuscripts" and, far more clearly, in the "Excerpts from David Ricardo." Its continuity with the Ricardo excerpts is obvious. In noting Mill's (and Ricardo's) view that value is determined by the costs of production, and then adducing the alternation or fluctuation (*Wechsel, Schwanken*) of market prices that makes it impossible to come up with a determinate figure for production costs, it tersely restates the "value" argument in the earlier excerpts. Less clear is its continuity with the EPM, where only hints of the irrationality argument are visible. But at a number of places in the EPM Marx does evoke the themes of chance and necessity that are crucial to the irrationality argument. Several times he notes, and implicitly deplores, the workings of chance within the capitalist economy: "the sudden chance fluctuations in market price . . ."; "nothing is more subject to chance than the price of labor, nothing is exposed to greater fluctuations"; "chance causes can raise the profit on capital"; "the producer is . . . the plaything of chance"; "exchange itself appears in political economy as an accidental fact" (*MEGA2* 1.2: 328, 332, 341, 348, 364/*MECW* 3: 236, 240, 249, 255, 271/*EW* 283, 287, 297, 305–6, 323).

Conversely, Marx also makes it clear in the EPM that he wants to see before his eyes a world in which chance has ceded to universality and necessity: "It is inevitable that . . . landed property . . . should be drawn entirely into the orbit of private property . . ."; "it is inevitable that immovable monopoly should become mobile and restless monopoly . . ."; "it is inevitable . . . that landed property, in the form of capital, should manifest its domination . . ."; "competition is frequently . . . explained in terms of external circumstances . . . these external and apparently accidental circumstances are only the expression of a necessary development"; "the necessary *development* of labor is liberated *industry*"; "the real course of development (to be inserted here) leads necessarily to the victory of the capitalist"; "it (political economy) develops a *cosmopolitan*, universal energy that breaks through every limitation and bond"; and so on (*MEGA2* 1.2: 360, 364, 378–79, 381, 291/*MECW* 3: 267, 286, 288, 291/*EW* 319, 323, 337, 340, 342). Quoting the economist C. Pecqueur, Marx implies that much of the chaos of the economy results from the fact that in the market "supply is ignorant of demand, and demand of supply" (*MEGA2* 1.2: 348/*MECW* 3: 256/*EW* 306). How much better it would be if universal knowledge could prevail, Marx wants to suggest.

But neither in the "Economic and Philosophical Manuscripts" nor in the "Excerpts from David Ricardo" does Marx take the step that he takes in "Excerpts from James Mill." That step was to reflect on the market in the light of a particular conception of science. In the passage that I have quoted, Marx sees political economy as doing what, in a Galilean-Newtonian conception of science, natural scientists do: that is, it finds (or tries to find) laws, on the model of f = ma.[82] Starting out from this conception of science, Marx distinguished between phenomena subsumable under laws and phenomena not subsumable under laws. Phenomena that have been subsumed under laws are predictable, while those that have not been subsumed under laws are unpredictable. Hence such phenomena are "accidental" or "zufällig": for an accident (from L. *accidere*, to fall), or *Zufall*, is an event that falls upon us, without the possibility of our seeing it in advance.

Marx's claim here is that in the real world (as distinguished from the formal abstractions of the political economists) the market is not, and cannot be, subsumed under laws. This is why Marx writes that "the true law of [existing] economics is chance." Economics takes the market as its focus and foundation, but by its very nature the market cannot be predicted. However, Marx's conviction that the fluctuations of the market cannot be subsumed under laws did not lead him to reject, or even to qualify, the notion that the task of economic science is to subsume phenomena under laws. Rather, for Marx the nonaccordance between the fluctuations of the market and the task of economic science is an indicator of the market's irrationality.[83] (Of course, he would later try to subject even the market's irrationality to scientific explanation, and show how this irrationality would of necessity be overcome and lead to a rational system—without the market.)

THREE ESSENTIAL POINTS CONCERNING MARX AND THE MARKET

In the present context it is perhaps not necessary to develop in total detail the connections and significance of the position that Marx arrived at in 1844. But three points do seem crucial.

First, for a Left Hegelian, the claim that a given entity is irrational has a clear and obvious implication. Famously, Hegel proclaimed in his *Philosophy of Right* that "what is rational is actual, and what is actual is rational."[84] Right Hegelians contended that what exists must therefore be rational; Left Hegelians contended that anything existing that critical examination shows to be irrational ought to be rejected.[85] Accordingly, Marx held that the market's irrationality meant that it ought to be rejected.[86] Hence the future socialist society must have nothing to do with the market. Economic life in socialist society must be organized on a nonmarket basis. The rejection of the market was a fateful move for Marx to make. It clearly finds its theoretical justification in Marx's discovery in 1844 that the rise and fall of market prices is not in accord with the necessity and predictivity that he believed were central to scientific understanding.

Second, Marx in 1844 was able to identify the fact of market contingency, but he did not yet have in hand a well-developed explanation for this fact. Clearly, to hammer the nail in completely and thus to confirm his rejection of the market, he needed an explanation for the fact. I shall turn to Marx's explanation for market contingency in a moment.

Third, Marx implies in the "Economic and Philosophical Manuscripts" that the true task of theory is to show how "apparently accidental circumstances are only the expression of a necessary development" (*MEGA2* 1.2: 364/*MECW* 3: 371/*EW* 323). In Marx's view, this was what theory cannot do with regard to the market. Thus the market ought to be rejected. Nonetheless, it would seem a reasonable conclusion that one cannot rightly reject the market unless one has available some other sphere within which things proceed in a more regular, less capricious way. The way is thus open, here, to historical materialism, which attempted to find the needed regularity in a history that would focus on the sphere of production, and which suggested that the capricious sphere of the market would ultimately be *aufgehoben* by socialism.

The text in which Marx explains why the rise and fall of market prices cannot be predicted, and where he offered at least some justification for thinking that the sphere of production, unlike the sphere of the market, is dominated by necessity, is his *Poverty of Philosophy: Reply to* The Philosophy of Poverty *by M. Proudhon* (1847). As the title indicates, *The Poverty of Philosophy* was Marx's rejoinder to Proudhon's *System of Economic Contradictions; or, Philosophy of Poverty* (1846).[87] Proudhon was the perfect goad and foil to Marx, for Proudhon emphasized aspects of economic life that Marx himself wanted to emphasize, while at the same time falling into what Marx could only consider to be egregious and easily refutable errors.

The first major topic that Proudhon addresses in *The Philosophy of Poverty* is value, and this includes a discussion of the opposition between use value and exchange value—hence a discussion of the market.[88] Among other things, Proudhon was eager to insist that "the free will of man" plays a central role in economics. In Proudhon's account, the market is the place where "the free buyer" and "the free producer" meet. The buyer is judge of his own need, judge of the suitability of the object to his purposes, and judge of how much he wishes to pay for the object. For his part, the producer is master of how the work is to be carried out and thus has the capacity to reduce his expenses. In consequence, Proudhon holds, "arbitrariness necessarily enters into value, and causes it to oscillate between utility and opinion."[89] Indeed, Proudhon goes so far as to contend that

> the rise and fall of the prices of commodities is independent of the quantity of labor expended in their production; and their greater or less cost does not explain in the

least the variations of the price index [*les variations de la mercuriale*]. Value is as capricious as freedom.[90]

Marx, in his *Poverty of Philosophy*, rips Proudhon apart, showing how his understanding of basic economic categories was hopelessly confused. We are not interested here in Marx's overall critique of Proudhon, but only in the observations concerning necessity and contingency in the economic order that Marx's reading of Proudhon occasioned. Marx argues that within the context of a modern economy, where the division of labor dominates and where there is, in consequence, a high level of interdependence, it is nonsense to speak of buyers and producers as being free. The crucial passage is worth quoting at some length:

> The producer, the moment he produces in a society founded on the division of labor and on exchange (and that is M. Proudhon's hypothesis), is forced to sell. M. Proudhon makes the producer master of the means of production; but he will agree with us that his means of production do not depend on *free will* [libre arbitre]. Moreover, many of these means of production are products which he gets from the outside, and in modern production he is not even free to produce the amount he wants. The extant degree of development of the productive forces compels him to produce on such and such a scale.
>
> The consumer is no freer than the producer. His estimation depends on his means and his needs. Both of these are determined by his social position, which itself depends on the whole social organization. True, the worker who buys potatoes and the kept woman who buys lace both follow their respective estimations. But the difference in their estimations is explained by the difference in the positions which they occupy in society, and which themselves are the product of social organization. (*MEW* 4: 75/*MECW* 6: 118–19)

In brief: Marx claims that in the modern economy production and consumption are determined. Marx's claim is that, possessing knowledge of the level of technology and the conditions of production within a particular industry, one could predict how the producer will "decide" to order his productive activity. What is especially striking is that Marx holds that the same determinism holds true on the consumption side as well.[91] The image here is of buyers and sellers locked into a deterministic, and hence predictable, economic system.

However, Marx did not conclude, from the alleged fact that production and consumption can be predicted, that the workings of the market can be predicted. Indeed, in the course of an attack on Proudhon's pursuit of fairness in pricing, Marx offers a coherent argument why the rise and fall of market price is unpredictable. Proudhon held that there exists a "law of the proportionality of values," according to which "labor is the principle of the proportionality of values." The workings of this law would somehow lead to a situation in which commodities would be produced in the correct proportions, in which they would be exchanged at their correct value (proportionate to the labor time required to produce them), and in which relative economic equality ("equality of conditions") among producers would prevail.[92] Marx proceeds to demolish not only Proudhon's lack of a coherent argument at this point, but also the very idea of a "relationship of proportionality [*Proportionalitätverhältnis*]" among commodities. In Marx's view, the "correct proportion between supply and demand" envisaged by Proudhon had "ceased long ago to exist":

> This correct proportion between supply and demand, which is beginning once more to be the object of so many wishes, ceased long ago to exist. It has passed into the stage of senility. It was possible only at a time when the means of production were limited, when exchange took place within very restricted bounds. With the birth of large-scale industry this correct proportion had to come to an end, and production is inevitably compelled to pass in continuous succession through vicissitudes of prosperity, depression, crisis, stagnation, renewed prosperity, and so on. . . .
>
> What kept production in correct, or more or less correct, proportions? It was demand that dominated supply, that preceded it. Production followed close on the heels of consumption. Large-scale industry, forced by the very instruments at its disposal to produce on an ever-increasing scale, can no longer wait for demand. Production precedes consumption, supply compels demand.
>
> In present-day society, in industry based on individual exchange, anarchy of production, which is the source of so much misery, is at the same time the source of all progress. (*MEW* 4: 97/*MECW* 6: 137)

Proudhon had contended that "the operations of commerce are essentially irregular."[93] This was exactly what Marx himself had concluded in 1844. Marx now offers an explicit—and correct—explanation as to why this is so. According to Marx, where production follows consumption—that is, where a certain commodity is produced only when it is noticed that the cupboard is becoming bare of that commodity—predictability may well reign. But when producers are forced to anticipate a demand that *may or may not arise in the expected volume*, oscillations are likely to set in. If the producers perfectly anticipate demand, there is no problem. But even a minor misanticipation will begin to generate unanticipatable loops, with prices rising and falling unpredictably, with consumers shifting from one product to a different product in response to price, and so on. Marx does not fill in this picture, which is generally accepted by present-day economists, but he so clearly states the basic point that there seems to be no doubt that he had the point clearly in mind.[94] Proudhon thought that the "arbitrariness" of the market resulted from the freedom of buyer and seller. Marx was too good a Hegelian, and too good a thinker generally, to confuse arbitrariness with freedom, and he was too good an observer of the realities of economic life beyond the market to see its participants as "free" in the sense that Proudhon thought them to be.

Through benefit of hindsight, we can see that it was a fateful mistake on Marx's part to reject the market. This is not a paean to the "free market," which is free only in a limited sense; is not self-regulating; brings with it much vulgarity; and, in sum, does not automatically conduce to the public good. I shall turn in my conclusion to a discussion of the "calculation problem" (pointed out in 1920 by Ludwig von Mises) that arises in the absence of markets, and that was clearly a bugbear in the vast socialist experiments undertaken under Soviet auspices. I shall also turn there to the "discovery" function of the market (emphasized by Israel Kirzner and others) that likewise had no equivalent under socialism. One does not need to accept the radical libertarianism that is often associated with the so-called Austrian school of economics in order to see the correctness of the "calculation" and "discovery" arguments. I do not see *laissez-faire*, or anything like *laissez-faire*, as at all justified. Marx was right in seeing that the market is guided by no invisible hand and that it does not automatically conduce to the satisfaction of human needs. He was only wrong in his insistence on abolishing it.

It is clear that the early Marx deployed two sets of criteria in judging the current economic order: rationality-criteria; and criteria having to do with humanism and aiming at the full flowering of an unalienated humankind. I have focused on Marx's "rationality" argument because, unlike the "estrangement" argument, it is virtually unknown, and because it goes much further than the "estrangement" argument does in explaining both Marx's own conclusions and what was made of his theory in the twentieth century.[95] It would have been better had Marx either loosened his rationality-criteria or not deployed them at all.

In fact, aspects of Marx's own position militate against his rejection of the market. Consider the following passage from Engels's Elberfeld speech, already quoted toward the beginning of this chapter:

> Since we know how much, on the average, a person needs, it is easy to calculate how much is needed by a given number of individuals, and since production is no longer in the hands of private producers but in those of the community and its administrative bodies, it is a trifling matter *to regulate production according to needs* [*so ist es eine Kleinigkeit*, die Produktion nach den Bedürfnissen zu regeln]. (*MEW* 2: 539/*MECW* 4: 246)

Such a claim—namely, that human needs can readily be calculated in advance—presupposes a static social order. But that is precisely *not* what Marx envisaged. He saw the social order as existing in a constant state of development. Human needs, too, develop, along with everything else. Indeed, Marx *praised* the development, and further development, of human needs. So how is one to know with any exactitude what human needs are, or are going to be?

The answer is obvious: only in an *a posteriori*, and not (alas) in an *a priori* manner. All testing is *a posteriori*, experimental. Planning—or, perhaps better, endeavoring—can be nothing more than an educated shot in the dark. This is why wholesale social engineering does not make sense; the only kind of social engineering that conduces to human needs is what Karl Popper and others have referred to as "piecemeal social engineering," which allows for corrective feedback mechanisms.[96] No bureaucrat, no scientist or technician with a theory in hand, can decree for us what we will want. When such personages attempt to decree our wants, they generate what Fehér, Heller, and Márkus call "the dictatorship over needs," which is a form of tyranny and of impoverishment. But Marx emphatically rejected the *a posteriori* mode.[97] The unintended result is that Marxian rationalism triumphs over Marxian humanism and empiricism.

How does the *a posteriori* discovery of needs get carried out? Again, we can look to the Engels of 1845. In the same Elberfeld speech, Engels asks:

> How is the manufacturer to discover how much of his products are needed in this or that market, and even if he could discover this, how could he get to know how much his competitors are sending to each of these markets? How can he—who in most cases does not even know where the goods he is just producing will go—possibly know how much his foreign competitors will send to each of the markets in question? He knows nothing about all this; like his competitors, he manufactures on spec [*ins Blaue hinein*] and consoles himself with the thought that the others must do likewise. He has no other guide than the constantly fluctuating level of prices [*ewig schwankenden Stand der Preise*] which, in the case of distant markets, is quite different at the moment when he dispatches his goods from what it was when the letter informing him about it was written, and which again is different at the time the goods arrive from what it was when they were dispatched. Where you have such irregularity of production it is also quite natural that at every moment there are interruptions to trade. . . . (*MEW* 2: 537–38/*MECW* 4: 244–45)

The answer is already contained in Engels's question. The maker of commodities discovers how much people want his products by whether they are willing to buy them, in what quantities, at what price. In short, Engels is (mostly) right, although in a different sense than he intended: the manufacturer "has no other guide than the constantly fluctuating level of prices."

* * *

Why, then, did Marx reject the market? One can certainly see Marx as having been predisposed to such a rejection by his social disdain for market behavior. But the deeper ground for his rejection of the market was conceptual and theoretical. Marx aimed to articulate a *scientific* account of social processes, and by his lights such an account required predictability. In the wake of Henri Poincaré and much subsequent theorizing along a similar line, we are well familiar with systems wherein the effects of a particular change cannot be predicted. Weather is the classic example. Meteorologists once had high hopes of devising models that would deliver accurate and detailed long-range weather predictions. Those hopes have been dashed, for it has become clear that a trivial variation in the initial state of a system (e.g., a butterfly flapping its wings in Brazil) can lead to dramatically different effects later on (e.g., tornadoes in Texas).[98] But the post-Poincaré model of science was unavailable to Marx.

To be sure, Marx (and Engels) eventually came to recognize the existence of areas of unpredictability in the scientific world—most obviously, at the point of change-of-state from one system to another. But as theorists they were never able to deal satisfactorily with unpredictability in general, or with the unpredictability of market prices in particular, given that market prices are subject to feedback effects derived from the attempts of buyers and sellers to adjust their behavior in the light of the manifestation on the market of the results of previous misanticipations. As *The Poverty of Philosophy* indicates, Marx was aware of this phenomenon, but he did not know how to deal with it conceptually. Accordingly, because he could not think of a way to make the market look rational, he theorized it out of existence.

Marx correctly saw that the rise and fall of market prices is unpredictable not, as Proudhon thought, because of the supposed free will of buyers and sellers, but because of the nature of the market itself. Thus Marx hated the market on intellectual grounds. But the market is inseparable from "modern bourgeois" production. A Marx who was *only* opposed to estrangement might well have envisaged an overcoming *within the capitalist system* of the basic form of estrangement, estrangement from the act of production. But if one needs to get beyond the market because it is irrational, one must get beyond capitalism. *Kapital delendam esse censit.*

Marx's rejection of the market derives, in short, from his attempt to apply to the market a conception of rationality (derived from Aristotle, and influenced by dominant nineteenth-century notions of natural scientific predictability) that are inappropriate to such a sphere. As shown in chapter 2, Marx encountered similar difficulties when he attempted to apply his conception of rationality to politics. Rejecting both politics and the market, he attempted instead to find rationality in the history of production. But the history of production as Marx conceptualized it—a history driven by "social and material productive forces"—likewise underplayed the role of the unpredictable in human material progress. It is my claim that the basic defect of Marxian theory *in general* lies in its all-too-global application of an all-too-restrictive conception of rationality. Everything else pales before this defect.

In insisting, in his hyper-Enlightenment way, on a general rationalizability, Marx followed one tendency—a very strong one—in European thought in his time. Challenges to this position arose in the second half of the nineteenth century, but by that time Marx's position—let us say, his *official* position—was already solidly in place. In chapter 4 I turn to this position, which goes under the name of "historical materialism" or "the materialist conception of history." The materialist conception of history is, to be sure, a relic—but it is an illuminating relic, showing Marx the systematic theorist at work. However, Marx was nothing if not intelligent, and in the midst of his attempts to lay out a rational history of production that would be determinative of history in general, one finds a good deal of evidence suggesting that he was his own greatest skeptic.

Chapter Four

The Character and Limits of Marx's Unified Rational History of Humankind

1. In the social production of their life, men enter into definite relations that are indispensable and independent of their will, relations of production which correspond to a definite stage of development of their material productive forces. **2.** The sum total of these relations of production constitutes the economic structure of society, the real base [*Basis*], on which rises a legal and political superstructure, and to which correspond definite forms of social consciousness. **3.** The mode of production of material life conditions the social, political, and intellectual life process in general. **4.** It is not the consciousness of men that determines their being, but, on the contrary, their social being that determines their consciousness. **5.** At a certain stage of their development, the material productive forces of society come into conflict with the existing relations of production, or—what is but a legal expression for the same thing—with the property relations within which they have been at work hitherto. **6.** From forms of development of the productive forces these relations turn into their fetters. **7.** Then begins an epoch of social revolution. **8.** With the change of the economic foundation [*Grundlage*] the entire immense superstructure is more or less rapidly transformed. **9.** In considering such transformations a distinction should always be made between the material transformation of the economic conditions of production, which can be established with the accuracy of natural science [*der materiellen, naturwissenschaftlich treu zu konstatierenden Umwälzung in den ökonomischen Produktionsbedingungen*], and the legal, political, religious, aesthetic or philosophic—in short, ideological forms in which men become conscious of this conflict and fight it out. **10.** Just as our opinion of an individual is not based on what he thinks of himself, so can we not judge of such a period of transformation by its own consciousness; on the contrary, this consciousness must be explained rather from the contradictions of material life, from the existing conflict between the social productive forces and the relations of production. **11.** No social order ever perishes before all the productive forces for which there is room in it have developed; and new, higher relations of production never appear before the material conditions of their existence have matured in the womb of the old society

> itself. **12.** Therefore mankind always sets itself only such tasks as it can solve; since, looking at the matter more closely, it will always be found that the task itself arises only when the material conditions of its solution already exist or are at least in the process of formation. **13.** In broad outlines Asiatic, ancient, feudal, and modern bourgeois modes of production can be designated as progressive epochs in the economic formation of society. **14.** The bourgeois relations of production are the last antagonistic form of the social process of production—antagonistic not in the sense of individual antagonism, but of one arising from the social conditions of life of the individuals; at the same time the productive forces developing in the womb of bourgeois society create the material conditions for the solution of that antagonism. **15.** This social formation brings, therefore, the prehistory of human society to a close.
>
> —Karl Marx, preface to *A Contribution to the Critique of Political Economy* (*MEW* 13: 8–9/*MECW* 29: 263–64/*MER* 4–5).

Today, after the collapse of Marxism as an ideology and as a serious political program, two things are still known about Marx. First, Marx was a revolutionary. Of all things known about Marx, this is the best known. Engels set the tone. In his speech at Marx's graveside, on March 17, 1883, he declared: "Marx was above all else a revolutionary" (*MEGA2* 1.25: 408/*MECW* 24: 464/*MER* 682).[1] Engels was right. But to stop at this point is to be stuck with something that has become a banal cliché. In the present book I have emphasized, on the contrary, something that is *not* well known about Marx: his rationalism. But the rationalism and the revolutionism are related to each other. Indeed, they are twins, one the obverse of the other. Marx's revolutionism, with its insistence on a moment of radically negating spontaneity within the historical process, is both the "other" of his commitment to a rational, necessitarian history and the inevitable consequence of that commitment. To fail to take account of his rationalism is to consign him to the dismissive category of "infantile leftism"—that is, to opposition merely for the sake of opposition, without analysis or reflection. But that is not Marx. When Marx declared in the "Theses on Feuerbach" (April–May 1845), that "philosophers have only *interpreted* the world, in various ways; the point, however, is to change it," he was not saying that we can dispense with understanding the world (*MEW* 3: 7/*MECW* 5: 8/*MER* 145). Rather, he was saying that we need to understand the world in the one true and comprehensive way—in short, we need to understand the world *scientifically*.

The second-best known thing about Marx is that he was a "historical materialist," an adherent of "the materialist conception of history" (the terms are basically synonymous).[2] The materialist conception of history was tied up with Marx's claim to have understood history and society scientifically. Let us listen once more to Engels in his speech at Marx's graveside: he begins his account of

Marx's achievements by asserting that "just as Darwin discovered the law of development of organic nature, so Marx discovered the law of development of human history" (*MEW* 19: 333/*MECW* 24: 463/*MER* 681).[3] In other texts—most notably *Socialism: Utopian and Scientific* (1880)—Engels asserted at greater length his claim that Marx had offered a scientific account of human history. Partly as a result of Engels's accounts of Marx's work and partly for other reasons, after Marx's death the historical materialist Marx became as widely known as the revolutionary Marx. As one late twentieth-century British commentator, Paul Hirst, noted in 1985, "most Marxists have considered the centrepiece of Marx's achievement to be 'historical materialism,' a science of history."[4]

Insistence on the crucial importance of historical materialism/the materialist conception of history for Marx's project goes well beyond the Marxian camp, for—with some exceptions—it is *generally* regarded as the core of Marx's project, or at least as one of its two great pillars. And in a certain sense this is true. But here, too, as with his revolutionism, one needs to look at historical materialism in relation to his rationalism. In particular, the materialist conception of history gave Marx the rational substratum that he believed he needed if he was to be able to theorize about the human world. Fundamentally, this substratum came to Marx from Hegel. However, contrary to Marx's (and Engels's) self-presentations, the materialist conception of history was—as we shall see—far less a matter of *inverting* Hegelian philosophy than it was a matter of *continuing* it. Marx continued Hegel's commitment to a notion of embedded progress. Marx's difference with Hegel was that he displaced this progress from the realm of intellectual production (as exemplified above all in the history of philosophy) into the realm of material production.[5]

From a historical point of view, Marx's "discovery" of the materialist conception of history (in 1845) was the counterpart to his discovery (in 1844) of the irrationality of politics and the market. Indeed, it rescued Marx from these discoveries, for without it the human world would have had no solid foundation, but only *Schacher* [haggling] and its political equivalent. The materialist conception of history thus puts into relief the fact that Marx was a deeply committed foundationalist. Moreover, unless one examines close up the materialist conception of history it is impossible to see how Marx's position relates to the position of his philosophical predecessor, or, more broadly, how it relates to the sense of cosmic optimism that gripped so many other nineteenth-century intellectuals. These historical issues have, in addition, a theoretical significance. Bringing historical materialism down to its essential components and underlying assumptions amounts to a dismantling of it, and it is my contention that a dismantling of the materialist conception of history—while still holding on to the crucial role it played within Marx's theorizing—is a precondition for being able to get anything useful out of Marx's theoretical project.

WHAT WAS HISTORICAL MATERIALISM?

A small library of books exists, all focused on the exegetical question What was [Marx's] historical materialism?[6] Beyond this question is the broader question, the question of the truth (or not) of historical materialism. We might pose this as: To what extent does the materialist conception of history actually illuminate the human world? It is a global question, impossible to answer in any definitive way and certainly not apt to be well answered in a chapter. Here I engage in the more local enterprise of clarifying what Marx's historical materialism a.k.a. materialist conception of history actually was. This enterprise can surely contribute to discussion of the global question. Indeed, to ask the global question without having first clarified what historical materialism meant for its formulators would be an extremely foolish way of proceeding.

In view of the fact that historical materialism looms large in our image of Marxism, it is striking, and at first glance rather surprising, that Marx (and Engels) rarely focused on it as a direct topic of concern. In fact, in only three works did they centrally and directly engage in laying out what historical materialism actually involved. One is *The German Ideology*, which was written jointly by Marx and Engels, apparently between November 1845 and July 1846 (DRAP 2: 9). A second "work" consists of fifteen sentences in the preface to Marx's *A Contribution to the Critique of Political Economy*, published in 1859 (these sentences make up the epigraph of the present chapter). A third work is one part of Engels's *The Anti-Dühring*, first published in 1877–78. This last account is more widely known in the version that appeared as the third part of Engels's *Socialism: Utopian and Scientific*. Additionally, there are a number of letters in which Marx and Engels comment on the materialist conception of history.[7] To be sure, the materialist conception of history—or, rather, some of its elements—is present in all of Marx's important works. But the actual laying out of what it was occurs very infrequently.

One question that has been much debated in the Marx literature is the question of the compatibility of Marx's and Engels's different presentations of historical materialism.[8] To the degree that the different presentations are not compatible it becomes an important matter which of them to take as the initial basis for one's account of their views on the subject. Here I shall be rather peremptory. Marx's and Engels's main accounts of historical materialism—those of 1845–46, 1859, and 1880, as well as the shadowy historical materialism of the "Economic and Philosophical Manuscripts" (1844)—are indeed compatible with each other. Where it is a matter of contradictions, the contradictions are mostly not between Marx's (and Engels's) different presentations of historical materialism. Rather, they are *within the materialist conception of history itself*. As a result, the task of describing Marx's historical

Marx & Engels' accounts of historical materialism are congruent; the issue w historical materialism is in historical materialism

materialism is simplified—at least insofar as an initial presentation is concerned. For we do not need to focus on how the 1845–46, 1859, and 1880 presentations are different. Instead, we can simplify matters by taking *one* of these accounts as the basis for a description of the materialist conception of history, without doing any great violence to the overall view. We can look at differences between them later, as well as at various modifications, reservations, and second thoughts concerning the very project of articulating such a general view of history.[9]

For convenience, I do want to make a choice among the three main presentations. The account of the materialist conception of history that appears in Marx and Engels's *The German Ideology* is the most important of the three. It was the first working out of historical materialism. It is closer to the actual roots of historical materialism than are the other, later accounts. It is also the lengthiest of the three. The account that appears in Engels's *Socialism: Utopian and Scientific* was the most widely circulated, since *Socialism* long served as a primer of scientific socialism. But I turn aside from *The German Ideology* and from *Socialism: Utopian and Scientific* and focus instead on the account in the 1859 preface. (I shall of course also draw on *The German Ideology*, *Socialism*, and other Marxian writings when they cast light on the 1859 preface and on Marx's views generally).

Why focus on the 1859 preface? First, because of its greater compression it is a more apt candidate for explication than are *The German Ideology* or *Socialism*. Second, the compression brings to light fissures in the historical materialist view that are not so readily visible in the other, more leisurely accounts. Finally, unlike *The German Ideology*, which Marx and Engels wrote in the first flush of enthusiasm for their new worldview, and unlike *Socialism*, which is marked by Engels's characteristic tendency to sweep difficulties under the rug, the 1859 preface gives evidence of a certain distancing on Marx's part from the view that he is articulating; indeed, in the preface he carefully characterizes the view that he reached in 1845 as "a guiding thread for my studies," not claiming it to be absolute Truth (*MEW* 13: 8/*MECW* 29: 262/*MER* 4). Marx's sometimes well-hidden ambivalence about historical materialism needs to be held in view—partly for the sake of a proper estimation of his genius and partly for the sake of our own attempt to grasp what is living and what is dead in his theoretical project.

The broadest and simplest definition of *historical materialism* is the one that Engels offers at the beginning of the third part of *Socialism*, where he says that the materialist conception of history "starts from the proposition that the production of the means to support human life and, next to production, the exchange of things produced, is the basis of all social structure. . ." (*MEGA2* 1.27: 608/*MECW* 24: 306/*MER* 700). I would proceed further with what Engels has to say about historical materialism in the remaining seventeen pages of *Socialism* were it not for the fact that what Marx says in the 1859 preface is more interesting. Marx's brief account is more interesting than Engels's long one because, in his attempt at analytical rigor, Marx brings out much more clearly than Engels does the *fragility* of the materialist conception of history. For the first thing that needs to be noted about historical materialism is that it begins to fall apart almost as soon as it is subjected to critical examination. The later Engels, writing after Marx's death, as good as admitted this fact (in, for example, the letters by Engels listed in note 7 of this chapter). Marx himself diverged from important tenets of the materialist conception of history when he thought it justified to do so and when it suited his purposes. Marx was certainly aware of some of the limitations of the materialist conception of history when he wrote the 1859 preface. But this does not relieve us of the task of laying out its central features in a brief and simple way. We can then proceed to bring to light some of the problems that it raises.

We need to proceed analytically: that is, we need to carve up historical materialism so that we can see its component parts. Because the 1859 preface lays out these parts in little more than a paragraph, it makes this task relatively easy.[10] Marx gives us four closely related things in the preface. First, he gives us a *set of social categories*, including a not very well-developed indication as to the relations among these categories and as to how they move through time. Second, he gives us a *theory as to how human history proceeds* (I use the term *theory*, here, in the sense of a generalized description, rather than in the more rigorous sense of a device for explanation and prediction). Third, he gives us a *metaphysic of history*—by which I mean a pattern that purportedly underlies all historical movement. Finally, he gives us an *expression of faith in the benign character of history*. In my account of historical materialism I shall concentrate on the set of social categories, of which figure 4.1 serves as a simple visual representation.

To grasp adequately an account that—for all its brevity—is quite complex, conceptual tools are required. One important tool is a distinction between two ways of viewing the relation of the social order to time. On the one hand, an observer can seek to make sense of society as it exists at some (any) given moment in time. Here the observer views the social order as if it were frozen *in* time, existing in a kind of ideal, continuous present. This "synchronic" or "social statics" view focuses on *structure*. On the other hand, an observer can focus on the movement of the social order *through* time. In simplest terms, this "diachronic" or "social dynamics" view is concerned with *process*.[11] Note that one needs to keep in mind the purely conceptual character of the distinction between statics and dynamics and between structure and process. The claim is not that structure and process are separate *in reality*; the claim is

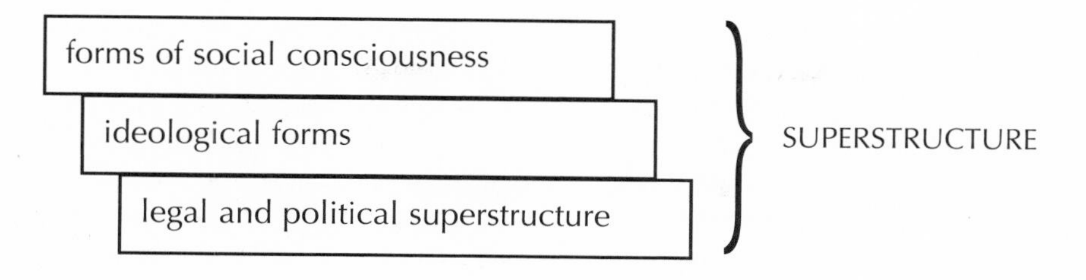

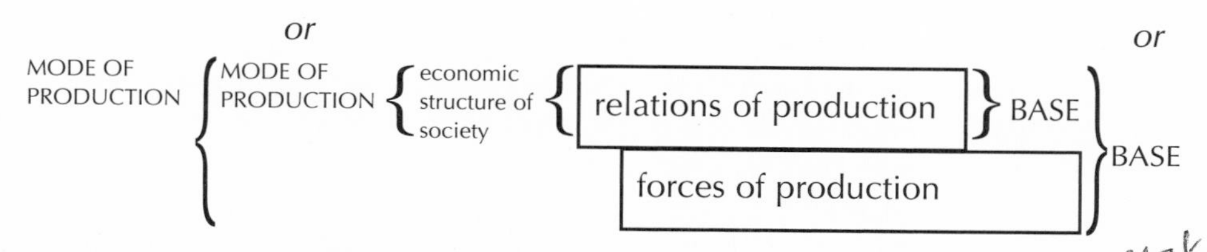

Figure 4.1. Historical Materialism: The Social Categories

rather that one can distinguish them on the level of thinking, and moreover that it is often illuminating, and sometimes indispensable, to do so.

Although, for purposes of the present book, the most important aspect of Marx's 1859 account is the set of social categories, the theory of history and the metaphysic of history also need to be held in mind. Marx's theory of history offers a concrete, although very schematic, description of historical change: in essence, it holds that historical change is the product of conflict between "productive forces" and "productive relations" (categories to be discussed in a moment). According to Marx, in every instance up to now the conflict between these two could not be resolved within the existing social order. In consequence, each previous "mode of production"—Asiatic, ancient, feudal, and bourgeois—has collapsed, giving way to the next mode. Ultimately, however, a new social formation, socialism, will arise, which will be nonconflictual in character (see sentences 5–8, 11, and 13–14 of this chapter's epigraph). As for Marx's metaphysic of history, it amounts to an account of the *form* of the historical progression in question. That form is dialectical: in other words, it involves progress by contradiction (see the same sentences).

The social categories, as presented schematically in figure 4.1, are interesting because they enable us both to articulate in short compass the core of historical materialism and to highlight important ambiguities in Marx's account.[12] Figure 4.1 is useful first of all because it puts in visual form the classical Marxian distinction, emphasized in the 1859 preface, between superstructure (*Überbau*) and base or foundation (*Basis, Grundlage*). The superstructure of the social order, in this conceptualization, consists of the "legal and political superstructure" (sentence 2), plus other aspects of the social order that are also not directly involved in production—identified in figure 4.1 as "ideological forms" and "forms of social consciousness." It seems pretty clear that Marx regarded all three of these elements as superstructural, not just the legal and political aspect.

But there is an ambiguity with regard to the "base." I cannot pursue all the textual evidence and other arguments relevant to this ambiguity; I can do little more than identify it. On the one hand, there is some reason to think that "base" and "mode of production" embrace both productive relations and productive forces. I have tried to suggest this view in figure 4.1 by marking a separation between the forces and relations of production, taken together, and the legal and political superstructure. On the other hand, there is also some reason to think that Marx intended the "base" to embrace only the relations of production and not the productive forces, and that he likewise intended "mode of production" to embrace only the relations of production. (Marx also uses the term *mode of production* to designate the entirety of social systems or historical epochs, as when, in sentence 13, he refers to the Asiatic, ancient, feudal, and modern bourgeois modes of production, but I am not concerned here with this other sense of the term.)

The ambiguity between the two interpretations is a genuine one, unequivocally present in Marx's text. It is a *significant* ambiguity, not a mere triviality. What it signifies is the intertwining, in Marx's thinking, of the "material" and the "social" aspects of the productive forces (alluded to in sentences 5 and 10 respectively). In the logic of Marx's view, there is no sharp division between the relations of production (which one might inaccurately want to characterize as "social") and the forces of production (which one might inaccurately want to characterize as "material"). The most critical point here is that one ought to resist the tendency to think of the forces of production as *material*; on the contrary, they are material *and* social. I am persuaded that this is the best way of thinking of productive forces, considered as a category of social analysis, and also that this was in fact Marx's own view. Hence, it does not make sense to posit the sharp division between forces and relations of production that is implied by an unequivocal exclusion of the forces of production from the "real base" of society. Yet Marx could not bring himself to simply meld together the material and the social, or the material and the mental or intellectual. This is because he never quite got over his need, perhaps born of a certain insecurity and desire to maintain his originality vis-à-vis Hegel, to distance himself from his beginnings as a Hegelian philosopher. Hegelian philosophy, Marx held after he had stopped being a left-Hegelian philosopher, is excessively concerned with ideas, thought, spirit. I am persuaded that, because of this, in conceptualizing the history of production Marx was led to his heavy emphasis on production's *material* character. Yet Marx was too good a thinker to forget that production rests also on an ideational foundation, that is, on science in the broadest sense of the term.[13]

In the layout given in figure 4.1 the forces of production are represented as the category underpinning all the others. It seems appropriate to begin with this category. The question as to the relationship of the material and the social emerges directly out of Marx's language. The term *Produktivkräfte* (productive forces) appears three times in the 1859 preface: twice the *Produktivkräfte* are characterized as *materielle* (material), and once as *soziale* (social) (sentences 1, 5, and 10 in the epigraph). Awareness of the decisions that need to be made when one translates from the original German highlights an important interpretive question. In brief: are the words "material" and "social" intended to modify "forces," *or* are they intended to modify "production," *or* are they ambiguously intended to modify both? The phrase *materielle Produktivkräfte* can be translated into English as "material forces of production," or as "forces of material production," or as "material productive forces." By opting for the last of the three translations, as in the version here, the translator avoids having to make an explicit interpretive choice (although the choice of this translation over the others is itself an interpretive choice). "Material productive forces" leaves to the reader the task of deciding what "material" modifies.

What should the reader's choice be? That is, in "material productive forces," what is "material"? Does Marx want to say that the forces are material, or does he want to say that what is produced is material? The 1859 preface does not offer a clear answer. However, an answer readily appears when one examines Marx's writings more generally. From the "Economic and Philosophical Manuscripts" through to *Capital*, Marx is consistent in characterizing the objects being produced as material. This is obvious in, for example, Marx's analysis in the EPM of estranged labor (discussed in chapter 3), where the workers' estrangement from the product is keyed to the idea that the products in question are material objects that can be separated from the workers who produce them. To my knowledge, Marx never suggests that the forces doing the production are *solely* material, nor does he suggest that it would somehow make sense to fixate on "material" forces of production while leaving aside "nonmaterial" forces.

Alternatively, we can turn away from Marx's text and simply think about the concrete issue at hand: production. The question, What is "material" in the "material productive forces?," is in a certain sense analytic in character, for it is a matter of deciding what ought to be included in the category "productive forces" given the way that the world operates. When one thinks about the category long enough and in the right way, one is likely to conclude that three things need to be included among the forces of production. First, for production to take place there must be raw materials, which are then subjected to some sort of transformation in the production process. Second, except at the most primitive level some sort of machinery will be required, even if only a hoe or shovel. Third, there needs to be labor: that is, somebody has to *do* something.

Raw materials and machinery are certainly material in character: they consist of material objects existing in the world. Labor is a more complicated matter. It is not a physical object, but it does involve the application of physical force to the material world. However, labor also includes a mental or intellectual component: it normally involves thinking, and the more complex the labor the more refined the knowledge that is involved. Thus at least one of the three sorts of productive force, labor, includes a nonmaterial aspect. This observation leads us to the conclusion that *materielle Produktivkräfte* really means "forces of material production." What is material are the things that are being produced.[14] The forces of production, on the other hand, are both material and nonmaterial. Machinery is material, but it also embodies human ideas. So-called raw materials are likewise bound up with human ideas: even something so "natural" as a lump of coal can become a productive force only when human beings have arrived at the idea that it can be used to produce heat.

The analysis that I have just given skips over a number of important issues, but it is not misleading, and it seems unnecessary to repeat work that has been done by such writers as John McMurtry, in *The Structure of Marx's World-View* (note 6). Nor is it necessary to survey *all* the categories to be found in the 1859 preface. It is clear, however, that we cannot avoid considering "relations of production" (or "productive relations"). There is nothing in the 1859 preface that tells us what productive relations are, but we know from other texts that Marx thought of them as being relations among people (or, more accurately, among classes of people) that arise from the operation of the productive forces.[15] At an individual level (which did not much interest Marx), persons have relations to other persons by virtue of the roles they play in the productive process. The captain of a fishing vessel, the first mate, the cabin boy, the people who tend the nets, and so on play roles determined by their functions within the forces of production, in this case represented by the fishing vessel (I draw this example from McMurtry, 11–12). At a structural level, the class of capitalists and the class of workers likewise stand in a certain kind of relation to each other by virtue of their roles in the operation of the productive machinery, broadly considered, of society.

It is significant that the category of productive relations goes in two quite different directions. The example of the personnel on a fishing boat playing roles that are determined by the technology of fishing embraces only one side of productive relations as Marx appears to conceptualize them. McMurtry, and G. A. Cohen even more, in his *Karl Marx's Theory of History: A Defence* (note 8), point also to another side of productive relations, represented by ownership and market relations. The language of the 1859 preface signals Marx's ambiguity as between these two aspects of productive relations. He tells us that the productive relations prevailing in a society "correspond to" the "material productive forces" of the given stage of development of the society (sentence 1 of the epigraph). The German term for "correspond to" is *entsprechen*. One is tempted to render *entsprechen* into English as "correlate to": *correlation* is the term commonly used in contemporary social science when there is not sufficient evidence to justify the assertion that the relation between one set of phenomena and another set is causal. (For example, there could well be no causal relation between polo-playing among a certain subset of fifteen-year-olds and the presence of an unusually high percentage of these people in the top category of wealth-holders twenty-five years later. That is, there is a correlation between these two sets, but playing polo at fifteen is not what caused these people to be wealthy twenty-five years later.)

However, Marx seems to have had more than mere correlation in mind. He seems to have thought that in some sense the productive forces *cause* the corresponding productive relations. We might think of the productive forces as equating to the technology deployed in a given society. Thus, to restate the matter, Marx seems to have held that a society's deployed technology *gives rise to* its productive relations, and to the social structure generally. Why else would he have written (sentence 6) that the productive relations can "fetter" the productive forces (thus suggesting that the productive forces are the dynamic and hence the determining element, albeit being temporarily held back by the productive relations)?

But Marx also seems to have thought that a society's productive relations do *not* arise from its productive forces. He implies (sentence 11) that the productive forces are only the "material conditions" for the emergence of "higher" relations of production—and this seems to suggest that they are not the impetus for that emergence. Also, he writes that "at a certain stage of their development, the material productive forces of society come into conflict with the existing relations of production" (sentence 5). Presumably, such a conflict could not emerge if productive relations were nothing but a reflex of the productive forces. How, then, are we to conceptualize productive forces and productive relations in such a way that we are able to offer an explanation for why Marx thinks that he is justified in claiming that forces and relations come into conflict with each other? This is a troublesome question, but it points us toward an understanding of what underpinned and, in Marx's eyes, initially justified the materialist conception of history.

WHAT MOVES HISTORY FORWARD?

If we restate the issue we can see the thinking that underlies the conflict between the forces and the relations of production in Marx's conception of history. For the question as to what brings forces and relations into conflict with each other is closely related to another question: what, in Marx's historical materialist model, moves history forward?

As I have depicted them so far, Marx's social categories (productive forces, productive relations, and so on) are atemporal in character. Clearly, one has to introduce the dimension of time into the picture. Marx obviously holds that *in some sense* the categories remain the same over time, for otherwise they would not continue to *be* "productive forces," "productive relations," and so on. Yet it is also obvious that what fills these categories—the empirical, historical *examples* of productive forces, productive relations, and so on—changes. The productive forces develop—they continually move forward. And subsequent to the development of the productive forces, changes also occur in the productive relations and in the entire superstructure of society. How else could it be, given the movement postulated in sentences 5–8 of the epigraph?

At first glance it might seem that some causal agent other than the productive forces is needed if one is to account for the emergence of conflict between "forces" and "relations." For one cannot immediately see how productive relations would come into conflict with the productive forces, unless the relations are somehow being influenced by a cause other than the productive forces. But the notion that some other causal agent, standing apart from the productive forces, is at work within the system would undermine my claim that, in line with his general commitment to the rationalism that I described in chapter 1, Marx's conception of history had a unified, analytic, self-contained character to it.[16]

It is my (unprovable) assumption that total self-consistency is impossible, and that the attempt at self-consistency inevitably runs up against its limits, against a *différance* that finally causes it to unravel. So I am not arguing that Marx *achieved* a unitary theory or model; I am arguing only that Marx *aimed toward* such a model. Admittedly, we are on tricky ground here. I am suggesting that in some sense Marx intended a unified theory, and one has to note the considerable difficulty attaching to notions of historical intention. Unlike statements, intentions are not readily subject to observation. Beyond this basic difficulty, I am also persuaded that Marx's intentions, whatever his hopes or Engels's claims, were not exactly single and unified. Nonetheless, there is substantial textual material that supports the claim that Marx was trying for a unitary theory. The material is not to be found in the 1859 preface, which is too elliptical to offer such support. It is to be found, rather, in other texts. For example, as shown in chapters 2 and 3, Marx displayed a "unitarist" tendency to reduce competing elements, concepts, institutions, and so on, to unity, and this tendency is entirely consistent with an attempt on his part to assert a single, unified, theory of history.

Consider now the conflict that arises in Marx's model between forces and relations of production. According to Marx, this conflict ultimately causes a given mode of production to fissure and collapse. My claim is that Marx did not see the forces/relations conflict as having its source in the existence of some other, separate force, contradictory to the productive forces. There is no hidden planet perturbing the orbits of the known planets, no intervention from outside the closed system of forces and relations. To put this another way, Marx did not have recourse to some sort of *deus ex machina* or unacknowledged *conatus* toward a goal that would make history move, and in so doing would generate tensions within the system. Instead, he was persuaded that there was an *internal* principle moving history forward.

Some commentators—most notably Jon Elster, in his *Making Sense of Marx*—have claimed, on the contrary, that Marx adhered to a "teleological" conception of history, by which they mean a conception of history in which appeal is made to an *external* principle moving history forward.[17] Elster suggests that in the absence of an intrahistorical principle or causal mechanism that would explain how or why history moves from A to B to C to Z, we have to assume that Marx surreptitously postulated some sort of *intention toward an end* that would drive it forward, but without that intention being located *in any identifiable intending agent*. In Marx's conception of history, according to Elster, things occur because they are required if such-and-such a historical endpoint is to be achieved. And indeed, on occasion Marx *appears* to suggest that such-and-such a development takes place in capitalist society because the development in question has the "historical and social function" of moving humankind forward to socialism.[18] Clearly, if this is what Marx is *actually* suggesting, it would be as if an intending agent were arranging developments under capitalism. And if this were so, then Marx would indeed be putting forward a teleological conception of history in Elster's sense. (Alternatively, a teleological conception of history might simply be one in which a particular end or *telos*, for example, socialism, is posited as desirable, without any suggestion being made that events happen *because* of this end, or *because* an external intending force is at work. However, in the following discussion I am referring to a teleological conception of history in the sense of an appeal to an external principle.)

The question as to whether Marx adhered to a teleological conception of history and employed a teleological mode of explanation is closely tied up with the question as to what, in Marx's view, moves history forward. Insofar as Marx was a teleologist of history, we get an immediate answer to the question, "What moves history forward?" History moves forward because it is the intention of an abstract, disembodied intending agent (perhaps History, perhaps Reason) that it should do so. Socialism is the desirable outcome of history, and so everything in history is moving in socialism's direction.

I agree with Elster that there are assertions in Marx that have a teleological ring to them. But I attribute the presence of such assertions to propagandistic considerations that sometimes muddy Marx's reasoning *qua* theorist and scientist. Marx the propagandist wished to fortify the working class and its would-be allies against the rigors and disappointments that he believed were still to come. Thus his inclination was to claim, without evidence, that the darkest part of the night is just before the dawn. (The *locus classicus* of this line of thinking is to be found in Marx's introduction to "A Contribution to the Critique of Hegel's Philosophy of Right" [published early 1844], where he suggests that the worse off the revolutionary class is, the more advanced will be the revolution [*MEGA2* 1. 2: 181–82/*MECW* 3: 186/*EW* 256].) Since evidence that would support Marx's linkage of deep and generalized suffering with stunning victory is lacking, this claim *sounds* teleological.

However, without denying Marx's tendency, on occasion, to fall into teleological-sounding language, I have to insist that Marx's conception of history was not teleological (to make unjustified claims is not the same thing as having a teleology). Note that I am not claiming that Marx's conception of history is *correct*; I am only claiming that it is not teleological (in Elster's sense). Nor is it functionalist (that is, it does not postulate that things happen *because* they will lead to such-and-such a desired end).[19] In this respect, it is helpful to contrast Marx with another writer, also influenced by Hegel, who most decidedly was a teleologist: the eschatologically oriented Polish philosopher August von Cieszkowski (1814–1894). Cieszkowski's *Prolegomena zur Historiosophie*, published in 1838, offers some affinities with the thought of the radical Hegelians with whom Marx associated.[20] In particular, in his *Prolegomena* Cieszkowski depicts a historical movement from theoretical philosophy to a "philosophy of *praxis*" in which action (*That, Thätigkeit*) has priority over mere thought and reflection.[21] Marx's sometime colleague Moses Hess, a fellow Rhinelander, Jew, and journalist, picked up on Cieszkowski—most notably in his 1843 essay, "The Philosophy of the Act," which Marx cites in the "Economic and Philosophical Manuscripts."[22] However, in the present context what strikes one is how different Cieszkowski's view of history is from Marx's. Cieszkowski draws his conception of history not from Hegel's *Lectures on the History of Philosophy*, as Marx primarily did, but from the *Lectures on the Philosophy of History*. As shown in chapter 1, Hegel's *Philosophy of History* does not offer a proper historical dialectic, with the contradictions in one stage generating a movement on to the next stage: for example, there is no visible process of transition leading from China, to India, to the modern German world.

The upshot is that Cieszkowski really does offer an idealist, teleological conception of history. Cieszkowski's history is driven by the *Weltgeist* (world spirit) rather than by identifiable historical agents. Indeed, Cieszkowski *proclaims* his commitment to teleology: Cieszkowski's final (third) chapter is titled "teleology of world history." Cieszkowski's offering of a teleological view of history is almost a rational necessity. For given the blatant absence from Hegel's *Philosophy of History* of any account of the transitions from one stage to the next stage in history, anyone who wished to build a philosophy of history on the basis of that Hegelian work had little choice but to attribute the transitions to some sort of overarching intention driving the process forward. Consequently, in Cieszkowski we see what a teleological view of history actually looks like.

Marx was at a higher intellectual level than this. One defect of an approach to Marx influenced by analytic philosophy and by present-day social science theory is that it tends to fillet away the conceptual and imaginative armature of his work. Thus one loses sight of those aspects of Marx's project that are not reducible to what he had to say about this or that particular aspect of the world. Analytic philosophy has much to teach us about the world and about thinking, but there is a tendency in it to miss what Marx's *project*—as distinguished from the specific discrete propositions that he put forward—actually was. Accordingly, one has to applaud intelligent, analytic readings of Marx, while at the same time recognizing their limits. When one looks at Marx's work in the light of the intellectual background out of which it came, things look far less "teleological" than they do when the background is omitted. This is not to say that Marx's position suddenly becomes justified. It is only to say that the problems with Marx's view have little to do with his allegedly teleological orientation.

So what is the conceptual armature of the materialist conception of history? By the time one gets to the 1859 preface that armature is heavily concealed. The armature is difficult enough to uncover even in *The German Ideology*. Although residues of Marx's earlier perspective do remain in that work, one must go back further in his intellectual development if one is to discern historical materialism's actual conceptual underpinnings. Having looked at the very early Marx, one can then proceed forward in time with some hope of seeing how Marx's later statements of the materialist conception of history are grounded in an earlier, philosophical view.

A good place to begin is with some assertions to be found in an essay by Arnold Ruge that appeared in October 1840 in the journal that Ruge was editing at the time, the *Hallische Jahrbücher*. Ruge is not Marx. But Ruge, like Marx, was in the Left Hegelian circle, and the two men later worked in collaboration with each other (most important, on the *Deutsch-Französische Jahrbücher* in 1843 and early 1844). The essay in question comments on the memoirs of the poet and historian Ernst Moritz Arndt, *Erinnerungen aus dem äußeren Leben* [Recollections from the External Life].[23] Arndt (1769–1860) had been an ardent German patriot and critic of Napoleon during the period of the Napoleonic Wars and he remained an important source of German nationalist thinking. In 1818 he had been appointed professor of modern history at the newly founded University of Bonn, only to be barred from lecturing in 1819 because of his advocacy of political reform—constitutionalism, popular assemblies, freedom of the press. However, his traditionalist and patriotic bent meant that he was of interest to the Prussian Crown Prince, and when the latter came to the throne in June 1840 as Friedrich Wilhelm IV Arndt was rehabilitated, and resumed lecturing at Bonn.

Ruge approaches Arndt from a liberal Hegelian perspective. This is significant, for it was clear that the new king, with his conservative, Romanticist, and pietistic leanings, might not be well disposed toward Hegelian philosophy. In passing, Ruge defends Hegel against two sets of opponents. First, he defends Hegel against those who would see him as having betrayed the radical implications of his philosophy by selling out to the established, conservative order. Ruge declares, on the contrary, that in Hegel's writings there is "infinitely more freedom than in all the works of all the most rabid shriekers against his servility." Second, Ruge defends Hegel against those attacking him from the opposite, conservative side of the political spectrum—critics who, as Ruge would have it, wanted to throw away not only "philosophical cultivation [*philosophische Bildung*]," but also what is related to philosophical cultivation, namely, "liberalism, rationalism, and critique." Ruge declares, further, that philosophy

> comes to its true power, position, and self-recognition in no other way than when it implements idealism, and also recognizes practical idealism . . . as its own deepest [*eigenstes*] essence, as the reality of its ideality, as the living actuality of the dialectic and of the method of intellectual [*geistigen*] movement in the world and in history.

Accordingly, in Ruge's eyes Hegel was "a better idealist than the Old Germans [*Altdeutschen*]"—better, that is, than those who wanted to go back to a supposedly better German past. The reactionaries thought that social reality is fundamentally static, or at least that it can be made static. Hegel emphatically disagreed. (Ruge, 180–81)

Although Ruge honors Arndt's person, and his activity in the German liberation movement against Napoleon, he finds Arndt's views concerning the present and future less admirable, too tied up with "a dark cloud of romantic idées fixes." He laments that, currently in Prussia, the "kingdom of visibly existing things derived from a dead past" dominates "the invisible kingdom of thought, in which the future is modeled." He contends against "the movement of reaction" that is "presently our politics." He evokes "the struggle for intellectual and political freedom, the idealism of the present against the idealism of the past." He suggests that "science [*Wissenschaft*], and specifically . . . the rigorous school of Hegelian philosophy" makes it possible to go beyond the "raw, dogmatic pathos of the wars of liberation" and to recognize "the inner, spiritual [*geistige*] freedom of the dialectic, and, in it, the true principle of freedom itself." (Ruge, 173, 178–79)

Ruge thus evokes an intellectual progress. But it is an intellectual progress that, in Ruge's view, has been changing in character. In Ruge's account, "the hitherto existing spirit was contained within the mind; through comprehension itself, it became already other than itself; the stream of history passes right through the mind of the philosopher [*Der bisherige Geist ist in seinen Geist hineingelegt und mit dem Begreifen selbst bereits ein anderer geworden, der Strom der Geschichte geht mitten durch den Geist des Philosophen*]." While it may appear unexciting that history has proceeded so, Ruge insists that:

> This is no kingdom of gray, bloodless shadows that has nothing to do with the world; rather, it is the entire energetic, living movement [of history] itself. Philosophical comprehension is the most essential result of history, the most consequential and most pregnant historical existence, the truly justified "ought" of [historical] development [*das wahrhaft berechtigte Sollen der Entwicklung*]; and no one would have understood this more clearly than Hegel himself, whose concept of the dialectic in general, and therefore also of the praxis of history, is simply that the certainty [*Bestimmtheit*] on which we stand comes to be recognized in its innermost truth; that the self-recognition of one stage is always the next stage; and that a new self, a new spirit, is thus born. (Ruge, 180)

Ruge suggests further that (Hegelian) philosophy has negated religious and political orthodoxy and has brought "the thinking person [*der denkende Geist*]" to the insight "that everything that is positive is not outside of himself, but on the contrary lies within his own existence and present—that everything that is and that persists does so only through him. . . ." (181–82). (It was precisely this sort of interpretation of Hegel that led some critics to suggest that Hegel's position was tantamount to atheism.)

In essence, Ruge offers us a variant of the view (common in the late 1830s and early 1840s among radical Hegelians) that when theory reaches its culmination it turns into *praxis*. This view, expressed by, among others, Cieszkowski, Hess, and Marx himself, gave a radical twist to Hegel's backward-looking notion that philosophy comes to understand a world only when that world is near to its end ("the owl of Minerva begins its flight only with the onset of dusk").[24] In the eyes of these thinkers, the epimethean, apparently conservative, perception that philosophy has to content itself with making sense of what has already happened justifies a promethean leap forward beyond philosophy. After all, if philosophy can survey and grasp the present age, this surely means that it is near its end. In the Hegelian imagining of the history of absolute spirit, there is a progression from art, through religion, to philosophy. Art, which reached its height at the time of the Greeks, gave way to religion, which reached its height with the Christian incarnation, which in turn gave way to philosophy, which reached its height with Hegelian philosophy. But the completion (*Vollendung*) of philosophy in Hegel's system can also be seen as the *ending* of philosophy, which now gives way to *praxis*.

Ruge's evocation of a turn from theory to *praxis* is thus familiar stuff. What is unfamiliar, and quite surprising, is that Ruge asserts in his review of Arndt that the *praxis* in question will manifest itself in modern industry. Here Ruge takes up a position sharply opposed to Arndt's. Arndt had long been known for his defense of the peasantry against any and all forces that would impair it.[25] Ruge, on the other hand, praises the industrial development that in 1840 was only barely beginning to put its mark on Germany. The "stream of history," Ruge suggests, has migrated from philosophers' minds to industry. In Ruge's words: "Industry has no other meaning than does the work of the spirit generally; its goal is in no way what is material, and its principle is none other than that of idealism itself. [*Die Industrie hat keinen andern Sinn als die Arbeit des Geistes überhaupt, ihr Zweck ist keineswegs das Materielle und ihr Prinzip nicht anderes als der Idealismus selbst*]" (184). Ruge evokes the most striking technological innovation of the age, steam power: "With and without steam, spirit has taken on the work of subjecting more and more the rawness of land and peoples, of mountain and valley, of peasant and nobleman, of the rich and poor rabble [*Pöbel*]."

Further, Ruge rejects Arndt's complaint, common among conservatives at the time, that industry destroys the quality of the people:

> No one is rabble [*Pöbel*] who *labors* in the service of spirit, and all labor takes place in the service of spirit and works toward one great result, that we become master over the sluggish nature that is within us and outside us; and if the conjoining [*Kombination*] of steam wagons spares our legs, this conjoining, because it is a labor of spirit [*geistige Arbeit*], is no less labor than journeys on foot and the isolated exhaustions [*Strapaze*] of men under a patriarchal regime . . . on the contrary, it eliminates a monstrous sum of idleness, since it stimulates men to industrious labor, to spiritual movement, to a realization [*Umsatz*] of thoughts, and is finally in no way a "broodhen of the rabble," for, through the immediate participation of the poor in a

widened forming of the world, popular apathy, renunciation of the right of spirit and of the right of man to be lord and master [*Herrenrecht*], are immediately broken; not a few noble people are thereby created, and all of humankind, through such a development [*durch ein solches Institut*] is ennobled. (183–84)[26]

In short, we can easily see what in *Ruge*'s view moves history forward: history is moved forward by the power of human intelligence, by the labor of spirit. Previously, this intelligence was deployed to greatest effect in theoretical philosophy; today, according to Ruge, it is deployed to greatest effect in the transformation of the world through industry. Again: Ruge was not Marx. But isn't the same motive force, human intelligence, at work in Marx's materialist conception of history? The answer to this question is "yes." Now let us see how this is so.

HISTORICAL MATERIALISM AS HISTORY OF SCIENCE

There is no more misleading term in Marxism than *historical materialism*, or the related term, *materialist conception of history*. The terms are misleading because they invite a deep misunderstanding of the character of Marx's conception of history. The terms first of all invite a misunderstanding of the relation of Marx's conception of history to Hegel's conception, and to Hegel's thought generally. Because of this, we need to look once more at the Marx-Hegel relation.

As noted already, one view of the Marx-Hegel relation is manifested in the opinion that the materialist conception of history is an inversion of Hegel's "idealist conception of history." This was certainly the official, authorized, Marx-Engels view of the matter. For example, Marx wrote in the postface to the second edition of *Capital* (1873) that, with Hegel, the dialectic "is standing on its head. It must be inverted, in order to discover the rational kernel within the mystical shell." (*MEGA2* 2.6: 709/*MECW* 35: 19/*CAP* 1: 103) Engels offers the "inversion" view in *Socialism: Utopian and Scientific* (*MEGA2* 1.27: 589–90, 604–5/*MECW* 24: 285–86, 302/*MER* 683–84, 698). He repeats the claim in his late essay, *Ludwig Feuerbach and the Outcome of Classical German Philosophy* (1888).[27]

A variant of the "inversion" view is the view that, whereas Hegel was engaged in doing philosophy, Marx was engaged in doing science. This view likewise has support in Marx's and Engels's own writings. The crucial passage is to be found in *The German Ideology*:

Where speculation ends—in real life—there real, positive science begins: the representation of the practical activity, of the practical process of development of men.

> Empty talk about consciousness ceases, and real knowledge has to take its place. When reality is depicted, philosophy as an independent branch of knowledge loses its medium of existence. (*MEW* 3: 27/*MECW* 5: 37/*MER* 155)

How seriously should the "inversion" view be taken? One has to say: not very. The "inversion" view is rooted in Marx's polemic of 1843–46 against idealist philosophy. It has a lot to do with Marx's overinsistent need to establish his own originality in relation to Hegel. It also has much to do with Feuerbach. A key text is the "Critique of Hegel's Dialectic" section of the "Economic and Philosophical Manuscripts," where Marx applies Feuerbach's method of subject-predicate reversal to Hegel's logic and to his philosophy in general (*MEGA2* 1.2: 399–418/*MECW* 3: 326–46/*EW* 379–400). This text was preceded by the manuscript "Critique of Hegel's Doctrine of the State," written in 1843, which subjected Hegel's political theory to subject-predicate reversal (for a crucial passage, see *MEGA2* 1.2: 12/*MECW* 3: 12/*EW* 66). But before Marx's enthusiastic taking up of Feuerbach's critical method, which occurred in or shortly after March 1843, nothing of the "inversion" view is to be found in his work. Rather, the very early Marx aligned himself with two other views concerning Hegel, both of which I noted in chapter 2. One view emphasized the need to develop the *externally critical* potential of Hegelian philosophy—that is, its usefulness at measuring, and critiquing, "the individual existence by the essence, the particular reality by the Idea" (*MEGA2* 1.1: 68/*MECW* 1: 85/*MER* 10 [doctoral dissertation]). The other emphasized the need to develop Hegelian philosophy's *self-transcending* potential, pointing the way beyond philosophy (we have just seen this view taken up by Ruge in 1840).

Consider, for example, the question of the relation between philosophy and science. So far as I can see, until 1845 Marx accepted the Hegelian notion that there is no difference between properly conducted philosophy and properly conducted *Wissenschaft* generally (a view manifested in, for example, Ruge's 1840 reference to "science, and specifically . . . the rigorous school of Hegelian philosophy"). The sharp opposition between philosophy and science that Marx and Engels parade in *The German Ideology* does not correspond to Marx's view prior to the "Critique of Hegel's Dialectic." At this point in the present book there is no need to engage in extensive quotation, since it is hardly in dispute that, earlier in his career, Marx equated philosophical activity and scientific activity. One passage will serve: in his fifth "Notebook on Epicurean Philosophy" (probably written April–August 1839), Marx ranks Spinoza, along with Aristotle and Hegel, as standing higher than Plato, on the grounds that "the inspiration of Plato culminates in [religious] ecstasy," whereas the inspiration of Aristotle, Spinoza, and Hegel "burns on as the pure ideal flame of science." Moreover, Marx adds that this inspiration serves as "the animating spirit of world-historical developments" (*MEGA2* 4.1: 104/*MECW* 1: 496). Here there is a clear continuity, in Marx's conception, between the history of philosophy and the history of science. Only in 1843 did this continuity begin to break down, and only in 1845 did Marx deny it entirely.

We are concerned here with the Marx of 1845–46 and after—the Marx who had explicitly articulated the materialist conception of history. How much of Hegel remains in *this* Marx? The question cannot be adequately answered unless one is aware of Marx's relation to the history of philosophy. In chapter 1 I argued that the primary "suture" between Hegel and Marx was provided by Hegel's *Lectures on the History of Philosophy*. Here I propose to elaborate on this claim, now directing attention to the materialist conception of history, which I did not discuss in chapter 1.

Consider Elster's account, in *Making Sense of Marx*, of the Marx-Hegel relation. It is an account that, although mistaken, nonetheless identifies a crucial problem. Elster writes:

> Hegel, disastrously, retained the idea that history had a goal, yet did not invoke any intentional agent whose actions were guided by that goal. Hegel's philosophy of history is a secular theodicy, which is to say that it is nonsense. His *Lectures on the Philosophy of History* and (to a much smaller extent) the *Phenomenology of Spirit* rest on disembodied intentions, actions in search of an actor, verbs that are attached to no subject. . . . In his notes on the neo-Confucian philosophers, Leibniz observed that if they believe in an orderly universe, they must also believe in a divine creator. 'I strongly doubt whether they have the vain subtlety of admitting sagacity without admitting also a sage.' This, however, is exactly what Hegel did, and I shall argue that Marx to some extent took over this pattern of thought. They remained imprisoned in a halfway house, between a fully religious and a fully secular view of history.[28]

But Elster has failed to notice that Marx's primary model for the materialist conception of history is a work in which there are, in fact, identifiable human agents at work. (As for the agents implied in the materialist conception of history itself, they are no longer identifiable—at least not in the sense of all being nameable—but we know who they are *in general*: they are human beings engaged in the effort of wresting their needs from a recalcitrant nature.) Nor is it helpful to think of Marx (hyper-Enlightenment rationalist) as "imprisoned in a halfway house . . . between a fully religious and a fully secular view of history." Marx is not some sort of halfway theologian. On the contrary, his view of history is deeply secular. The defects of the materialist conception of history do not have to do with Marx's somehow being indentured to a covertly religious set of assumptions. Quite the contrary, the problems that dog the materialist conception of history emerge from two quite different deep failings. First, there is the problem of Marx's science itself—a science that is too necessitarian in character, insufficiently attuned to the *disorder* of things. Second, there is Marx's insistence on offering a *single* theory that would attempt to explain everything—at least, everything *worth* explaining—in the human world.

The first thing that must be said in response to the claim that Marx's conception of history is teleological is that the materialist conception of history has, at its base, the actions of human beings as they apply their intelligence to the problem of producing whatever is required if human needs are to be satisfied. To be sure, the statement that I have just made will seem at least somewhat discongruent with the image I have offered of the productive forces driving society forward (figure 4.1). But what must be understood is that for Marx the crucial productive force is human activity applied to the material world. This fact is obscured by Marx's focusing on the bourgeois mode of production—that is, on capitalism, economic modernity. One of the things that characterizes the bourgeois mode of production, in Marx's view, is that in it machinery dominates the worker, thus concealing human activity's crucially important role in transforming the world. As Marx puts it in a passage in the *Grundrisse* (the manuscript of 1857–58 that is the initial, very raw draft that eventually resulted in *Capital*):

> The worker's activity [*Thätigkeit*], reduced to a mere abstraction of activity, is determined and regulated on all sides by the movement of the machinery, and not the opposite. The science that compels the inanimate limbs of the machinery, by their construction, to act purposefully, as an automaton, does not exist in the worker's consciousness, but rather acts upon him through the machine as an alien power, as the power of the machine itself. (*MEGA2* 2.1.2: 572/*MECW* 29: 82–83/*GRUND* 693/*MER* 279)

But Marx held that the domination of machinery, and of an estranged science, over the worker—that is, the domination of *material* productive forces over *social, human* productive forces—is only temporary. (As I argued in chapter 3, Marx held that this domination is either a consequence of the estrangement of labor from its own activity, or is so closely tied up with that estrangement as to be indistinguishable from it.) For Marx, human activity is *always* at the root of the productive forces, even when this fact is obscured by the way the social order is configured. This means that, for Marx, history is not teleological in the metaphysical sense of the term. Individuals and groups of human beings have ends, *teloi*, but History has none. What drives history forward is not some overarching force. What drives history forward is something inherent in the productive forces themselves. Because Marx thinks that this "something" will bring about continuing progress, he does not need an *external* driving force for history.

Although we are approaching the ballpark, we have not yet uncovered exactly what this "something" is. But let us be patient. For the moment, note that Marx explicitly rejected the view that history is driven forward by any sort of overarching force, whether it be the overarching force of History itself, or some force lying outside History and somehow encompassing it. An early passage—perhaps the earliest—to this effect appears in *The Holy Family*, which Marx and Engels co-authored in late 1844, shortly after Marx's writing of the "Economic and Philosophical Manuscripts." This was before Marx's formulation of the materialist conception of history, but at a time when he had already tagged the notion (in the EPM) as something to be developed. Here we find an attack on a version of Hegelianism that was indeed teleological in Elster's sense:

> *History* does *nothing*, it "possesses *no* immense wealth," it "wages *no* battles." It is *man*, real living man who does all that, who possesses and fights; "history" is not, as it were, a person apart, using man as a means to achieve its own aims; history is *nothing but* the activity of man pursing his aims." (*MEW* 2: 98/*MECW* 4: 93)[29]

Marx makes the same point in a letter of December 28, 1846, to a Russian journalist who had asked him his opinion of Proudhon's recently published *Philosophy of Poverty*. Proudhon had attempted in *The Philosophy of Poverty* to apply Hegel, whose work he did not understand, to economic issues. This attempt had included the claim on Proudhon's part that there is a "universal reason," independent of human beings themselves, that somehow governs history. Marx suggests in opposition to Proudhon that "the productive forces," which are "the result of man's practical energy," determine history. He suggests, further, that "the social history of men is *never anything but* the history of their *individual* development, whether they are conscious of this or not." (*MEGA2* 3.2: 70–71/*MECW* 38: 95–96/*MER* 137 [my italics]) Marx then developed this point in *The Poverty of Philosophy*, where he insists that human beings need to be seen as "the actors and authors [*Schausteller und Verfasser*] of their own history" (*MEW* 4: 135/*MECW* 6: 170 [chapter II, §1, 5th observation]).

Although Marx is not always to be trusted when he characterizes his own position, there is good reason for accepting his self-characterizations here. He really did reject the notion of a History that is somehow a great metaphysical force, or is moved by such a force. But we still do not know what, in his conception, *does* move history forward, nor do we know why he sees conflict of a fundamental sort arising within the system.

We can gain clarification on these matters by viewing historical materialism in the light of the pre-1843 Marx. In a passage from his journalism of 1842 that I quoted in chapter 2 to a different purpose, Marx writes that "the same spirit that constructs railways with the hands of workers, constructs philosophical systems in the brains of philosophers" (*MEGA2* 1.1: 183/*MECW* 1: 195). The point is easily reversed: the same spirit that constructs philosophical systems in the brains of philosophers constructs railways with the hands of workers. This is precisely what Ruge had contended in 1840. Both Ruge and Marx were clearly alluding to the Hegelian conception of philosophical progress. In the *History of Philosophy* (whatever its particular defects) Hegel offers a history of how specific, identifiable agents attempted to solve philosophical problems. Their collective activity generated the progress of philosophy. Whatever the defects of Marx's conception of history—and it *is* defective, in various important ways—we need to do Marx the honor of understanding what that conception actually was. This makes a great deal of difference to our understanding of the character and limits of Marx's thought generally.

Let us take the first question first: What moves history forward? The terms *materialist conception of history* and *historical materialism* have persistently been taken as indicating that Marx elevates "matter" over "idea," that he sees "idea" as a mere reflection of "matter," and that in Marx's view the motive force that leads to human progress must somehow be located in "matter," with "matter" defined as something standing outside human control. Such a conceptualization of Marx's view leads very quickly either to the notion that Marx held that there is some sort of force embedded within matter that leads history forward, or to the notion that, given the clearly unjustified character of the first notion, he must be unwittingly activating some sort of external teleology.[30] But in fact, Marx held that historical progress will happen because of the workings of the intellectual powers of humankind. People need to rid their minds of the notion that Marx was committed to an all-embracing metaphysical materialism. As I noted previously, there is no reason to think that he was committed to metaphysical (that is, ontological, or philosophical) materialism at all.

"Ideas" were important for Marx. But the ideas in question are not located "in the mystical womb of the absolute Idea"—as Marx, castigating Proudhon's all too teleological interpretation of Hegel, says in his letter to Annenkov (*MEGA2* 3.2: 72/*MECW* 38: 97/*MER* 138). Rather, from 1844–45 onward Marx held that the only ideas that truly count are the ideas of human beings confronting their material and social environments. And these are the ideas of science. This point already comes out clearly in the "Private Property and Communism" section of the "Economic and Philosophical Manuscripts." Here Marx contends that "natural science has intervened in and transformed human life . . . practically through industry and has prepared the conditions for human emancipation" (*MEGA2* 1.2: 395–96/*MECW* 3: 303/*EW* 355). This passage identifies the practical intellectual powers of humankind as crucial to what was soon to become historical materialism. Marx's notion of practice, here, equates with humankind's down-to-earth struggle to wrest from nature the means for satisfying its needs.

Less than a year later, Marx noted the epistemological implications of this practice in his "Theses on Feuerbach." In the second of the theses, which we might well title "on the practical testing of truth," Marx tells us that:

> The question whether objective truth can be attributed to human thinking is not a question of theory but is a *practical* question. Man must prove the truth, i.e., the reality and power, the this-sidedness of his thinking in practice. The dispute over the reality or non-reality of thinking that is isolated from practice is a purely *scholastic* question. (*MEW* 3: 5/*MECW* 5: 3/*EW* 422)

Here Marx links science and practice. Scientific claims are tested in and by the attempt to apply them to the real world. If they fail to produce adequate results they must be rejected. This is a step beyond the Hegelian history of philosophy, where, Marx now implies, ideas are only tested against other ideas. But Marx's concern with the testing of truth-claims is clearly a continuation of the project of philosophy. The crucial difference with philosophy, in Marx's view, is that the search for truth now moves down into the realm of actual human life and activity. The testing process that Marx envisages involves—indeed, absolutely requires—an encounter with reality itself.

Marx held that this encounter, which we might think of as a dialectical encounter between theory and reality, has progress as its implication. After all, testing leads to correction, which leads to the testing of the new hypothesis, which leads to the further advance of scientific knowledge. Admittedly, in the "Theses on Feuerbach" there is no portrayal of a process of historical advance. Still, it is clear that progress follows from thesis two: it is *built into* the scientific testing that Marx envisages. Admittedly, Marx also does not say in the "Theses on Feuerbach" where the practice to which he refers is situated. In *The German Ideology*, part 1, he and Engels fill in these gaps. They there portray a process of advance and situate that process in the sphere of material production. The materialist conception of history is thus a working out of the implications of thesis two. More broadly, it is a rewriting of Hegel's *History of Philosophy*, which is Marx's model for conceptualizing the history of science.[31] Of course, in the *History of Philosophy* Hegel covers only one part of the history of science—the more theoretical, abstract, and universal part, concerned with the general structure of the world rather than with particular localizable problems. But the appropriate larger category for the *History of Philosophy*—the larger genre of which it is a part—is indeed the history of science.

The materialist conception of history bears at its beginning the marks of two competing (but in Marx's mind intimately connected) tendencies. It bears, first, the mark of an essentialist, analytic, quasisyllogistic approach to knowledge that is ultimately rooted (via Hegel) in Aristotle's metaphysics. Thus Marx and Engels refer, at a number of points in *The German Ideology*, to the "premises" of history, as if everything else in history will follow therefrom: "The premises from which we begin are not arbitrary ones. . . ." "The first premise of all human history is. . . ." "This method of approach is not devoid of premises. . . ." "We must begin by stating the first premise of all human existence. . . ." (*MEW* 3: 20, 27, 28/*MECW* 5: 31, 37, 41/*MER* 149, 149, 155, 155). Yet, second, Marx also emphasizes that empirical research can and should be done: he declares that "these premises can . . . be verified in a purely empirical way," and he recommends "empirical observation" (*MEW* 3: 20, 25/*MECW* 5: 31, 35/*MER* 149, 154). It is striking how close the analytic and empirical tendencies stand to each other. The materialist conception of history embodies a dual methodological commitment. Marx possesses in high measure both a theorizing impulse and the drive to collect data to support his theorizing.

In any case, the important point is clear, and this is that the materialist conception of history amounts to a schematic history of science. Its closest Hegelian model is Hegel's history of one of the sciences, namely, the science that Hegel regarded as the highest science, philosophy. It is also history of science in the pragmatic and empirical sense suggested by the second of the "Theses on Feuerbach," where testing is at issue. But I am not suggesting that the two faces of Marx's project can be harmonized. How, after all, can one reconcile thesis two's emphasis on practical testing with the necessitarian and unitarian Marx I describe in much of this book? I am suggesting, rather, that they persist as opposing "rationalist" and "empiricist" moments in his thinking (cf. chapter 1). The balance between the two is different at different times in Marx's career, mainly, I suspect, as a response on his part to the different situations within which he found himself.[32] But the two tendencies are always present, at least after 1844.

The second, empirical face of the materialist conception of history enables us to answer the question, "What, in Marx's eyes, moves history forward?" In Marx's historical materialist view, history, which has its initial impulse in the confrontation between humans' needs and nature's paltriness, moves forward by means of the self-correcting mechanism that is scientific testing. Society progresses by virtue of the fact that human beings come to a better and better knowledge of nature and society, and are thus increasingly able to control nature and society. In other words, social progress equates to the necessary advance of science. No intervention from outside the system is required. This is the essence of the so-called materialist conception of history. It is what leads Engels to declare, at the end of *Socialism: Utopian and Scientific*, that "Man, at last the master of his own form of social organization, becomes at the same time the lord over Nature, his own master—free" (*MEGA2* 1.27: 625/*MECW* 24: 325/*MER* 717). The freedom in question is characterized by conscious human mastery over nature and over the social order.

In short, the insistence, so obvious in the 1859 preface, that historical materialism involves humankind's movement upward has its roots in Marx's underlying commitment to the power of human intellect. I have located the model for Marx's working out of this view in Hegel, but it is important not to lose sight of its wider connections. The belief that scientific knowledge has a strong tendency to advance was present in late-Enlightenment thought and was very common among nineteenth-century Enlightenment-inflected theorists. One thinks of the account of progress that Condorcet presented in his *Sketch for a Historical Picture of the Progress of the Human Mind* (1795), written while he was in hiding from the guillotine. One finds a stronger form of the commitment to progress-through-constantly-increasing-knowledge in the writings of Saint-Simon and in the progressive positivism of Auguste Comte. Commitment to this sort of progress is also to be found in the writings of John Stuart Mill (although, as *On Liberty* [1859] shows, Mill was assailed by worries about progress's continuation). In other words, properly understood, the so-called materialist conception of history was not a great new invention. It was a variant of a widespread nineteenth-century (Enlightenment and post-Enlightenment) view.[33] In the J. S. Mill variant, the progress of science (knowledge) is what makes progress possible. The so-called materialist conception of history is also about the progress of science, understood in its widest possible meaning.

Let us now return to the forces of production. As I noted earlier, the productive forces are made up of raw materials, machinery, and labor. But there is another way of slicing the productive forces, and this is by distinguishing between what is active and what is passive in them. The driving force of history is clearly *thought*—more specifically, it is the dimension of thought that is concerned with mastering nature with a view to satisfying human beings' needs. Beginning with *The German Ideology*, Marx distinguishes between *material* labor and *intellectual* labor (see *MEW* 3: 31–32/*MECW* 5: 44–45/*MER* 158–59). In its intellectual aspect, labor involves the application of knowledge to the productive process. Marx sees production as more than simply the locus for producing what is needed to satisfy human needs. It is also the locus wherein scientific knowledge emerges and is tested. Material production moves forward by virtue of the fact that, through this practice and testing, human beings come to know nature, and thus to control nature, to an ever-greater degree. And the knowledge is cumulative, being passed on from one person to the next and from one generation to the next.

Imagine a team of engineers and construction workers engaged in the task of designing and building a bridge. Imagine, in particular, George, Erica, and their colleagues, whom we met at the beginning of chapter 3. The team is attempting to build a bridge over a previously untraversed gorge—a bridge that will not break under the weight of the vehicles using it, will not resonate dangerously in the wind, and will not be destroyed by metal fatigue. The team does not rely on unsystematic experience as it goes about its work. On the contrary, it relies on a body of scientific knowledge that, to a considerable degree, the members of the team will have internalized. Indeed, the internalization of scientific knowledge is a Marxian ideal.

Moreover, this is not simply an internalization of knowledge *about objects in the external world*; it is the internalization of a way of thinking—a way of thinking that Marx regards as one of the highest developments of human nature. In a famous passage at the beginning of chapter 7 of *Capital*, Marx describes what goes on in the production process as

> a process between man and nature, a process by which man, through his own actions, mediates, regulates, and controls the metabolism between himself and nature . . . he acts upon external nature and changes it, and in this way he simultaneously changes his own nature. (*MEGA2* 2.5: 129/*MECW* 35: 187/*CAP* 1: 283)

To gloss this passage: In doing such things as building bridges, human beings "humanize" nature: that is, they transform nature, accommodating it to human needs; and at the same time, in the course of engaging in the effort required in this process of humanizing nature, they also "naturalize" themselves—that is, they develop the potentials slumbering within their own human natures.[34]

The knowledge that is gained in the course of study and practice leads to the building of a bridge, and then perhaps to a better bridge, and then perhaps to a still better one (and built more efficiently than before). The knowledge in question is thus obviously a force of production. In other words, forces of production involve not only inert, lumpish material things, but an entire dimension of intellectual input and output, obtained through human cooperation in productive work, through study (including study of the traditions of socially maintained and socially transmitted knowledge that we call "science" and "technology"), and through the challenges of the moment and the activities that take place in an attempt to meet those challenges. This knowledge is the source of history's dynamism, in Marx's view. It is knowledge (science) that offers us reason for believing that human history is a series of "progressive epochs in the economic formation of society" (sentence 13). The belief that this is so seems a wager on Marx's part (a faith; a hope). Further, I am inclined to believe that it was a conscious wager—one that Marx knew he was making.[35]

As for the conflict between the forces and relations of production, this amounts to a conflict between what is more advanced and what is less advanced. That is, it is a conflict between, on the one hand, the most recently developed level of technology and, on the other, arrangements that emerged out of an earlier technology and that now persist through a kind of historical inertia. Indeed, there is a "stickiness" or retarding friction that is to be found all the way up the line, from productive forces, to productive relations, to legal and political superstructure, to ideology, to forms of social consciousness (see again figure 4.1). In Marx's model, this friction holds back (but only temporarily) the movement of the higher-level social categories. Conflict in the social order results from a disjunction between the material/social productive forces, where the impulsion to forward movement is *alone* located, according to the theory, and the relations of production, legal and political superstructure, ideological forms, and forms of social consciousness, which are not imbued with this impulsion but instead merely "follow along." They follow along, but in doing so they are retarded by the fact that there are people who do not recognize, or who refuse to accept, the reality being imposed upon them by the movement forward of the productive forces.

One can think of these different categories as subject to different temporalities. The temporality of the forces of production is the temporality of a present that is moving forward into the future. The temporality of everything else is the temporality of something from the past that persists in the present, by the weight of existing social interests—by the weight of social inertia, one might say. There is a famous passage near the beginning of Marx's *Eighteenth Brumaire of Louis Bonaparte* (1852) in which Marx gives lapidary expression to this idea: "Tradition from all the dead generations weighs like a nightmare on the brain of the living" (*MEW* 8: 115/*MECW* 11: 103/*MER* 595/*LPW* 32). The idea in the 1859 preface is that in an earlier time the productive relations that now exist would have been the appropriate relations for the productive forces that then existed; but the productive forces have moved forward and the productive relations have failed to keep up. Similarly, the current legal and political superstructure, which is not adequate to the existing forces and relations of production, would have suited an earlier socio-economic order. Marx's conceptualization suggests that generally speaking there is a kind of progressive retardation within the social order. That is, productive relations lag behind productive forces; the legal-political superstructure lags even further behind, ideology is even more antiquated, and forms of social consciousness (which Marx no more than mentions) are (usually) the most antiquated of all.[36] Admittedly, to my knowledge Marx never actually makes the claim that the higher-level categories are quite as I portray them in figure 4.1—that is, progressively more retrograde than the lower-level categories; it is thus only a *possible* interpretation of his view, and not one that we can definitely say has his approval.[37] But it is an interpretation that is consistent with the generally rationalist tendency of Marx's thinking.

AN EXCURSUS ON COHEN, ELSTER, AND CAUSATION

How would one go about accommodating the materialist conception of history to present-day social science and history? The question is worth asking, and it can be best pursued by considering further some points arising from Elster's *Making Sense of Marx*. Elster's concern is to rescue Marx for a methodologically individualistic, rational-choice-oriented social science. The rescue is carried out against an analytic defender of Marx, G. A. Cohen, who in *Karl Marx's Theory of History: A Defence* attributes to Marx a commitment to "functional explanation." A functional explanation is an explanation of something not in terms of its background or origin but in terms, rather, of its consequences. *An example:* Why do birds have hollow bones? Answer: They have hollow bones because hollow bones are lighter than solid bones and thus facilitate flight. Similarly: Why do social tensions intensify under capitalism? Because their intensification leads to the collapse of capitalism and hence to socialism.[38] In short, functional explanation attempts to explain things or events on grounds of their being functional for (conducive to) the bringing about or maintenance of some particular state of affairs. Such explanations do not explain things or events either as arising from the actions of agents or as arising from the operation of laws.

The main question that concerns me here is whether Marx was in fact committed to functional explanation. In the present context the question as to whether functional explanation is a legitimate form of explanation is secondary. Nonetheless, one cannot entirely avoid the question. My own view, which I cannot defend in detail,[39] is that functional explanation as such is not legitimate. In essence, Cohen seeks to argue in *Karl Marx's Theory of History* that to show that X had beneficial consequences is to explain X. But in the absence of particular factors (mechanisms or actions) that bring X about, this surely cannot be true. For example, it seems inadequate to answer the question, "Why do birds have hollow bones?" as it was answered earlier. In contrast, two examples of legitimate explanations are: (1) God gave birds hollow bones because he intended them to fly, and (2) Light-boned birds have a greater survival propensity than heavy-boned birds, since they can take to the air more easily, so that the Darwinian mechanism of natural selection led to birds being hollow boned. In both cases, we see that it is not the consequences of X that explain X, but rather something that precedes X. This, it seems to me, is the way that explanation ought to proceed.

The question thus arises why Cohen was led to spend time arguing for a bad form of explanation. The reason for this is actually quite clear. He intended his book as a defense of Marx's historical materialism—or rather, as a defense of Marx's historical materialism in Cohen's construction of it. For Cohen, defending the materialist conception of history means making it available for use in social science now. Cohen is entirely clear on this point. He tells us early in the book that, whereas "Hegel's reading of history as a whole and of particular societies is just that, a *reading*," Marx

> offers not only a reading but also the beginnings of something more rigorous. . . . The ensuing chapters attempt a reconstruction of parts of historical materialism as a theory or infant science. (Cohen, 27)

Since social science is deeply involved in the task of explaining things, if one is to show that historical materialism is social science *in nuce* one has to show how it is explanatory.

As I have done here, Cohen in *Karl Marx's Theory of History* focuses his attention on the 1859 preface. Thus the categories with which he works are precisely the categories that I have been discussing in this chapter. In his chapter X, "Functional Explanation: In Marxism," Cohen attempts to lay out the explanatory relationship between two sets of categories: first, between the productive forces and the "economic structure of society" (that is, the relations of production as a whole), and second, between the economic structure of society and the superstructure. What is the nature of the causal relations between these different entities? Cohen argues that the level of development of the productive forces in a society explains the nature of its economic structure in the functional sense of explanation, for "the economic structure has the function of developing the productive forces." Similarly, the economic structure of society explains the superstructure, for "the superstructure of society is responsible for the stability of its economic structure."[40] But it is not immediately evident how one could consider these two alleged explanations to be explanatory at all. Cohen works back from alleged effect to alleged cause, but there seems to be no account of how the cause *leads to* the effect—which is what we normally want to see in an explanation (at least as the term *explanation* is normally understood in philosophy and social science). But consider, again, the first of the two explanations. Cohen holds that if it is the case that the economic structure of society has the function of developing the productive forces, this implies that one can predict that when the productive forces *do* progress, there will be "massive transformations of social structure," since "institutions and society itself are explained as serving a development of power that prevails against forms of society resisting it" (Cohen, 285).

We thus see how functional explanation can be stated in such a way as to have at least the *form* of explanation, as explanation is usually understood. The problem is that Cohen identifies no specific mechanisms or actions that would allow us to see how or why the relations of production have the function of developing the productive forces, and how or why the superstructure has the function of stabilizing the economic structure. Indeed, it seems rather the opposite, namely, that existing productive relations *retard* the progress of the productive forces, and so on up the line (figure 4.1). I wish to suggest that Cohen was most likely led to attribute a functionally explanatory intent to Marx because it is difficult to grasp how the materialist conception of history could be seen to be explanatory in any other sense of explanation. Consequently, to see historical materialism as functionally explanatory seemed to be the only way to see it as explanatory at all.

Functional explanation has often been associated with a view known as "holism," as Cohen notes (although he denies that the association is a necessary one). For example, the anthropologists Bronislaw Malinowski and A. R. Radcliffe-Browne held to some or all of the following theses: that all elements in social life are interconnected; that these elements support or reinforce one another; and that each element is as it is *because* of its contribution to the whole. (Cohen, 283–85). The question as to how the materialist conception of history is explanatory quickly gets tied up with the question of whether, to what extent, and in what sense or senses Marx was a "holist." With regard to this issue Marx's writings are substantially ambiguous. One might say that there are contradictory positions that he adheres to, and it is useful to try to untangle where, exactly, the contradictions are located.

In considering the question as to whether Marx was a holist, it is helpful to bear in mind four positions, which we might think of in relation to figure 4.2. In brief, I want to suggest that we ought to think of individualism and holism in both a *methodological* and an *ontological* sense (cf. my less detailed discussion in chapter 3). An *ontological* holist is someone who holds that wholes are greater than the sum of the parts and relations of which they are made up. The ontological individualist maintains that a whole is made up of a collection of parts and of the relations among those parts, and of nothing else besides. The ontological holist maintains, in short, that there is some sort of *je ne sais quoi* that the whole has *in addition* to the parts and relations making it up. To put this another way, the ontological holist maintains that there exist *simple qualities of wholes.* These are qualities that attach to the whole *qua*

Methodological Individualism	Methodological Holism
Ontological Individualism	Ontological Holism

Figure 4.2. Individualism and Holism

whole—say, to the Proletariat, or to Capitalism. Conversely, an ontological individualist is someone who is not committed to the notion that there are simple qualities of wholes. Going to the methodological level, then, a methodological holist would be someone who, in seeking to explain things, treats wholes *as if* they have simple qualities, and a methodological individualist would be someone who, in seeking to explain things, does not proceed as if wholes have simple qualities.[41]

Where, then, does Marx stand on these matters? An important point to note is that since the conceptualization that I have just offered was articulated only in the twentieth century it raises issues and questions to which Marx, as a nineteenth-century writer, did not need to, and indeed could not, respond. Thus we are forced to be somewhat speculative, attempting to discern where Marx stands in part by referring to categories that Marx did have available to him—most obviously, the categories of the deductive and the inductive and of appearance and essence. As I have already noted, Marx tends to waver on such issues from one period in his intellectual development to another. (I disagree, however, with commentators who find Marx moving from one fixed and definite position to another fixed and definite position: his positions, and his movements from one position to another, strike me as much more uncertain and contingent than that.) Thus it is commonly agreed that in *The German Ideology* Marx was about as empirically inclined as he was ever to be (although, as I have argued, even in *The German Ideology* there was also an analytic side to his thinking). As for the distinction between appearance and essence, Marx in *The German Ideology* and for several years after that work seems to have seen appearance and reality as quite close to each other, whereas in the *Grundrisse* (1857–58) and in *Capital* (1867), he suggests that the difference between appearance and essence is great and that much work is required to get from the former to the latter.[42]

But notwithstanding the wafflings, Marx's position with regard to methodological and ontological individualism and holism seems to me to be relatively clear. The first thing to note is that there is no reason to think that Marx was an ontological holist. On the contrary, insofar as we can attribute any position at all to him on this issue, he has to be seen as an ontological individualist. Two clarifications are here required, however. One is that Marx's ontological individualism tends to be an ontological individualism by default rather than a consistently actually articulated position. In other words, because he never articulated an ontological holism, because on occasion he does seem to put forward an ontological individualism, and because he was not one of those thinkers who consciously seeks to put forward contradictory positions (e.g., Emerson, Whitman, Nietzsche), we pretty much have to see him as an ontological individualist generally. For example, unlike some thinkers in his time, he did not adhere to an organicist view of society; organic metaphors are extremely rare in his work. Organicism has an affinity with ontological holism, since the living organism does seem to possess a *je ne sais quoi* such that, although we can dissect the family dog, we cannot put all its parts back together again and expect it to get up again and bark.

I note also, in passing, that Marx should not be equated with his intellectual mentor Hegel, whose holist and organicist tendencies are much more pronounced. "*Das Wahre ist das Ganze* [the true is the whole]," Hegel proclaims in the *Phenomenology of Spirit*.[43] But this does not seem to be Marx's position, for he *rejected* what he saw as Hegel's attachment to totalizing entities. For example, in the "Critique of Hegel's Dialectic and General Philosophy" in the EPM, as well as in his manuscript "Critique of Hegel's Doctrine of the State" of a year earlier, he is vehement in attacking what he sees as Hegel's tendency toward the hypostatization of such entities as Spirit, Absolute Knowledge, and the State.

My second clarification has to do with terminology. Following Tim Shiell in "On Marx's Holism" (cited in note 41), I distinguish, as noted previously and as indicated in figure 4.2, among *four* positions: ontological and methodological holism and ontological and methodological individualism. For the most part, those who discuss the question as to whether Marx was a holist or an individualist articulate only a single-line distinction, between methodological individualism on the one hand and holism *tout court* on the other. But this is a mistake. One needs to distinguish between kinds of individualism and holism, and the most obvious distinction to be made, in this context, is the distinction between ontology (being) and method (cf. figure 1.1 and the associated discussion). Martin Jay hints at the need for such distinction when he poses the following question in his important study of twentieth-century Marxism, *Marxism and Totality*:

> Did Marx share with the organic tradition a belief in the ontological priority of the whole over the parts, or was his holism merely methodological and without ontological intent?[44]

But in most of the literature the distinction is passed over, and this means that commentators sometimes do not say with precision what their own researches show they ought to say.

For example, in *Making Sense of Marx* Elster observes that "one should not forget that Marx . . . was committed to methodological individualism, at least intermittently" (7). Elster *should* have said something like "one should not forget that Marx was committed to ontological individualism, although, methodologically, he very often looks like a holist." First, let us take up Marx's ontological individualism. Here Marx seems to me to be a responsible and clear-minded thinker, far from obfuscation and close to the ideals of a clarifying social science. Consider the following assertion from Marx's 1846 letter to Annenkov, quoted previously: "the social history of men is never anything but the history of their individual development. . . ." (*MEGA2* 3.2: 71/*MECW* 38: 96/*MER* 137). One finds no hint here of a Humanity, World Soul, Geist, or any other totalizing entity that is somehow presented as having a life of its own. Marx's claim is that human history is simply what human beings, all added up together, do. He appears to be asserting an ontological individualism in this passage. One ought not to say that he is asserting a methodological individualism here, because no methodological claim is in evidence.

However, individualism is far from being the whole story about Marx. This point comes out clearly in Elster, for *Making Sense of Marx* is in part a search-and-destroy mission aimed at the elements of holism and teleology in Marx. The presence of both individualist and holist elements in Marx is also suggested by the shape of the secondary literature dealing with these issues in Marx. As Shiell notes, "commentators on Marx commonly argue (or assume) that Marx held some form of holism or 'organicism'": Shiell mentions Georg Lukács, Bertell Ollman, and Melvin Rader. Shiell also notes that "on the other hand, a few commentators argue that Marx held to some forms of individualism": he mentions Carol Gould, Louis Dumont, and Laird Addis (235). Following Shiell, I find that at a methodological level Marx is heavily inclined toward holism. That is, Marx proceeds *as if* collective entities have simple properties—as if capitalism, for example, is something more than the sum of its parts and relations. Thus, notoriously, Marx contends that capitalism *itself* needs to be destroyed—the mere reform of its parts and relations is not adequate. His whole analysis of capitalism is premised on capitalism's existence as a systemic order, in which "an immense collection of commodities" circulate

(*MEGA2* 2.6: 69/*MECW* 35: 45/*CAP* 1: 125). Yet on the other hand he never suggests that what is to be destroyed is some sort of ontological essence.

How is one to account for Marx's noncommitment to ontological holism, but his commitment to methodological holism? Shiell suggests that Marx's methodological holism can be accounted for by his absolute hostility to the existing order. Marx is committed to *radical* change. As Shiell puts it, "Marx is not interested in merely changing the relation between the worker and the machine, or the bank loan officer and the potential home owner, or in changing only the worker's class-consciousness." Of course, he does want to change these things, but "it is the overturning of the whole existing order that interests Marx." However, "methodological individualism . . . provides only the simple determinations, the thin abstractions"—and hence "cannot provide the sense of radical change which emerges from the full conception of the whole" (244–45). Thus, in Shiell's account, Marx's methodological holism arises from his stance of radical opposition to the existing order of things.[45]

I find this explanation only partly persuasive. Two other factors might also help account for the holistic tendency in Marx's thought. One of these is an obvious suggestion, given the general trend of the present book. Marx was deeply influenced by Hegel's commitment to universality and to necessity, and by the deductive, quasisyllogistic tendencies of that thinker. Marx's connection back, ultimately, to the ancient syllogism goes along with methodological holism. It stands in tension with methodological individualism, the bent of which is to work up universal conclusions by induction from particulars. Marx's own quasisyllogistic inclination—as manifested in, for example, the "Estranged Labor and Private Property" section of the EPM—tends to generate a kind of holism (wherein, for example, private property, estrangement, the division of labor, and so on, appear as modifications or variants of each other [see discussion in chapter 3]).

A second factor involves what I propose to call "the holism of explanatory failure." This is a holism, or an *appearance* of holism, that emerges when an explanation is inadequate. For example, Marx was intent on showing how the inner laws of capitalism lead inevitably to the collapse of capitalism. But he never actually managed to show, in persuasive detail, how this would be the case. In the absence of an adequate explanation, with an adequate chain of particular causes and effects laid out, it looks as though Marx is saying that something inherent *in capitalism as a whole* is leading to its collapse. One might propose, rather snidely, the following motto: "If you cannot explain how a hoped-for effect will occur, just assume that the system as a whole will bring it about." This would be the general form of the holism of explanatory failure. Note that explanations of this type might well have a functionalist weighting—cf. my discussion of Cohen, previously—since the argument could be that capitalism as a whole brings about its own collapse, because it is written into history that socialism will come, and the collapse of capitalism conduces to socialism's arrival.

It is in any case clear that when one focuses on issues of explanation and causation, a palpable disjunction emerges between the materialist conception of history and present-day history and social science. Analytical and "rational choice" interpreters of Marx certainly attempt to find causal statements in Marx. But the question is really whether, at least when Marx is working on a "grand" level—that is, when he is trying to give an account of the social system in general—he offers any room for causal claims at all.[46] In chapter 3, I noted ambiguities with regard to causation in Marx's discussion of the relation between estrangement and private property. A different sort of ambiguity comes up in the 1859 preface, where Marx writes (in sentences 2, 3, and 4) that certain things "rise" from, "correspond" to, "condition," or "determine" certain other things, but neither in the preface nor elsewhere does Marx clarify what he means by these claims. Nor does he offer anything that looks like adequate justification for whatever he is claiming. How, in social scientific terms, is one to make sense of such ambiguities?

Some of the problems that surround Marx and causation come out in a passage from Marx's *Poverty of Philosophy* (1847) that Cohen analyzes:

> Social relations are closely bound up with productive forces. In acquiring new productive forces men change their mode of production; and in changing their mode of production, in changing their way of earning a living, they change all their social relations. The hand-mill gives you society with the feudal lord; the steam-mill, society with the industrial capitalist. (Cohen, 143–44; *MEW* 4: 130/*MECW* 6: 166 [chapter II, §1, 2d Observation])

But what exactly does the claim "the hand-mill gives you society with the feudal lord . . . ." mean? Does it mean that the hand-mill is a *necessary condition* of feudalism, so that one could say, "If no hand-mill, no feudalism"? Or does it mean that the hand-mill is a *sufficient condition* of feudalism, so that one could say, "If hand-mill, then feudalism"? Or does it mean that the hand-mill is a necessary *and* sufficient condition of feudalism, in which case the hand-mill might well be so intimately related to feudalism that one could not separate out the two in such a way as to say that one is the cause and the other the effect? Or does it mean something else altogether?

In fact, I do not think that Marx's general theory is amenable to this type of questioning. (It is possible that some of his specific analyses of economic modernity *are* so amenable, but this is a matter that needs to be left aside from the present book: I invite others to pursue it.) In my opinion, the difficulty of seeing precisely what is meant by the various apparently causal claims that

Marx makes in articulating the materialist conception of history is a blinking red light that should indicate to us that historical materialism is not a collection of explanatory propositions. (Additionally, if one takes the word *theory* in the sense in which it is usually taken in analytic philosophy and in social science, to mean a set of propositions that can be used to explain something, then the materialist conception of history should not be regarded as a theory. Rather, it should be regarded as a view or perspective.) Again: historical materialism is not an explanatory theory—at least not in Marx's version of historical materialism.

For I think that what we basically have here is a deductive structure. Consider again the problem of the relation between productive relations and productive forces, or between the two of these together and the legal and political superstructure. In the context of Marx's general theory (if that is what it is), it looks as though we ought to be hunting for the mechanisms by which the forces of production give rise to the relations of production, and by which the forces and relations together give rise to the superstructure. But although figure 4.1 makes it look as though, for example, forces of production and relations of production are two different entities, between which, one would then assume, a causal relation might apply, it is much more in keeping with the cast of Marx's mind to think of them as two aspects or faces of the same totality, hence not as separate entities between which causal relations would have the possibility of arising.[47]

In short, we should first of all think of the different categories that Marx notes in the 1859 preface not as separate entities, but as different aspects of a totality. They all arise from, or are modifications of, human productive activity, even in the case of those categories that Marx sees as *hindering* productive activity. One should note that Marx, *qua* theorist, tended to view everything in human life as one variety or other of productive activity: hence the quotations, from 1844 and 1845–46, already given earlier, that all but identify "labor, *life activity*, productive life" with each other, and that declare that "what they [individuals] are therefore coincides with their production [*Was sie* [*Individuen*] *sind, fällt also zusammen mit ihrer Produktion*]" (*MEGA2* 1.2: 369/*MECW* 3: 276/*EW* 328; *MEW* 3: 21/*MECW* 5: 30–31/*MER* 150).

As I noted earlier, the higher-level categories become "retarded" with respect to the productive forces, but this does not mean that Marx envisages some external causal force operating on the productive forces and slowing them down. On the contrary, Marx seems to be holding that the ongoing thrust of innovation at the basic, technological level—a thrust that is powerful and relentless—carries the forces of production forward, while the relations of production, legal and political superstructure, ideological forms, and forms of social consciousness, although they come out of the same basic acts of production, remain weighted down and slowed by residues from the past ("the weight of all the dead generations . . ."). As a result, the latter offer resistance, in an almost mechanical sense, to structural change. Conflict arises between backward relations of production and the more advanced productive forces, but this seems more an artifact of Marx's dialectical need to find conflict *somewhere*, than it is an indication that there are two or more separable entities capable of being related as cause and effect.

One needs, moreover, to ask this question: In the light of what model should one talk about causation/explanation? By far the most illuminating model operates in terms of counterfactuals. In a counterfactual analysis, a "cause" simply is something, C, without which something else, E, would not have arisen, all other things being equal. If we say that imperialistic rivalries between the Great Powers of Europe caused World War I, what we mean is that in the absence of imperialistic rivalries, World War I would not have occurred, all other things being equal.[48] This way of thinking about causation (and hence about explanation) requires us to imagine other possibilities than the possibilities that actually eventuated—indeed, they require us to imagine, one might even say, alternative *worlds*: for example, a world in which there were no imperialistic rivalries between the Great Powers and in which World War I did not take place.

But there is nothing in Marx's theorizing that accommodates counterfactual analysis. Marx's commitment to necessity rises to a level that all but excludes alternative possibilities. On the one hand, Marx seems to want to make a causal claim, with estrangement from the act of labor generating estrangement from the product that is produced. In other words, he seems to want to say that because workers are estranged and alienated in the car factory, they are estranged and alienated from the cars that they are turning out. Yet when Marx adds that "the product is simply the résumé of the activity. . . . The estrangement of the object of labor merely summarizes the estrangement, the alienation in the activity of labor itself," the causal argument is undermined, for now it seems that the cars that come off the assembly line are not anything different from the workers' labor, but are, in fact, only the workers' labor summarized and brought together (*MEGA2* 1.2: 367/*MECW* 3: 274/*EW* 326).

Mutatis mutandis, the same conclusion applies to Marx's apparently causal claims in the context of his accounts of historical materialism. In other words, there is no change of method between 1844, when he wrote of the estrangement of labor, and 1845–46 and later, when he offered (rarely) the general view that is the materialist conception of history. True, some of the things that Marx says, in his articulations of historical materialism itself and in passages where he seems to want to apply historical materialism (e.g., "the hand-mill gives you society with the feudal lord") do have some of the outward marks of causal claims. But such assertions are better seen as analytic statements telling us about subdivisions within a larger category. Thus the "hand-mill" statement could be rewritten as: "Feudal society is marked by the presence within it of much bodily labor unassisted by mechanical power, such as the labor needed to operate hand-mills." In "On the Jewish Question" (1843) Marx writes: "To formulate a question is to answer it" (*MEGA2* 1.2: 143/*MECW* 3: 147/*EW* 213). In the "Economic and Philosophical Manuscripts" this comes out as "This new way of formulating the problem already contains its solution" (*MEGA2* 1.2: 374/*MECW* 3: 281/*EW* 333). There is a parallel in the 1859 preface, where Marx writes (sentence 12 of the epigraph) that "mankind always sets itself only such tasks as it can solve": that is, if one can set a task, already contained in the setting of the task is the solution to it.[49] Here Marx's analytic tendency links up with his faith in the benign character of history.

THE DECONSTRUCTION OF HISTORICAL MATERIALISM

Am I right to devote a substantial chapter to the materialist conception of history? After all, Marx and Engels did not publish *The German Ideology*; Marx's presentation of historical materialism in the 1859 preface is very brief; and *Socialism: Utopian and Scientific* was Engels's work rather than Marx's. In the tremendous mass of his writing Marx concerned himself only in exceedingly rare instances with a general conception of history. His focus was almost always on one or another specific issue or situation. Above all, he came to be concerned with the structure of the modern bourgeois mode of production, a.k.a. capitalism. He also concerned himself with issues of revolutionary tactics and strategy. With the materialist conception of history he concerned himself hardly at all.

Some of Marx's commentators have argued that the materialist conception of history has been overemphasized. No doubt many other commentators have thought the thought without making the claim. Years ago, in a little-known article, Arthur M. Prinz asserted that "Marx nowhere in all his works gives us anything that could pass even as an effort at systematic exposition of his 'economic' or 'materialistic' interpretation." Prinz went on to argue that the short presentation of the materialistic conception of history in the 1859 preface was part of an attempt on Marx's part to clothe himself in the prestigious garb of science, as a way, first, of getting *A Contribution to the Critique of Political Economy* past the Prussian censor and, second, of supporting his claim to leadership of the German working-class movement. Although Prinz certainly underrates *The German Ideology*, part 1, there is more than a grain of truth to his assertions. In essence, his argument is that the materialist conception of history, as presented in the 1859 preface, is little more than a cunning facade that Marx put up in order to conceal his real aims and intentions.[50]

A more recent Marx scholar, Terrell Carver, has likewise argued that excessive emphasis has been placed on the "propositional generalisations" that Marx offers in the 1859 preface. As Carver points out, *A Contribution to the Critique of Political Economy* was "never widely circulated." Much of the material in it was incorporated in different form into *Capital*; the material in its preface was not. Carver also notes that "one person . . . was gripped" by Marx's text, namely, Engels. Engels's reading of the preface's generalizations as "scientific laws, or law-like tendencies" came to be seen as authoritative by Marxists and non-Marxists alike. In the process, much else in Marx that did not fit these generalizations was scanted. "Historical materialism" came to stand for Marx's thought as a whole, and everything else within the Marx corpus—"the better-illustrated discussions of the *Manifesto*, the more intensely political analysis in *The Eighteenth Brumaire*, and the more exploratory conceptual studies in the economic works"—was judged in its light (*LPW* xiv–xv).

One needs to take the views of these commentators seriously. One also needs to distinguish between making Marx useful and understanding what his project was. The historian's perspective that is deployed in the present book requires that one lay out what was *there* in Marx's work, whether useful or not. The historian's concern is also to gain some clarity about how and why things happened as they did—thus, how and why Marx arrived at his positions. Historical investigation is different from the attempt to rescue that which, in the past, is most worthy of being taken up by us, now. To be sure, the two concerns are not entirely distinct: if one is to see what is valuable in Marx, one must understand what is there in the project and why it is there. Only in this way can one embark with some confidence on a direction that learns from Marx, while avoiding his mistakes.

There is certainly an element of shock value to thinking of historical materialism, as Prinz does, as basically a facade intended to impart to Marx's views a more impressive scientific veneer than they would otherwise have had. Prinz's interpretation of the materialist conception of history is by no means something to be quickly rejected. It is clear, for example, that the materialist conception of history—and Engels's dialectical materialist elaboration of it—*did* catch the attention of the large number of intellectuals, activists, and operatives who, in the fifty years after Engels's death, turned Marx's views into the ideology of "scientific socialism."[51] It is equally clear that Marx—in the spirit of "*je ne suis pas marxiste*"—held himself at a distance from such views; and so did Engels, at least some of the time. Thus there is certainly *some* justification for the view that historical materialism was, in Marx's eyes, a kind of facade. Overall, however, I think that one has to regard Prinz's reading of the 1859 preface as interesting, but not quite justified. For it underrates the role that the materialist conception of history played in allowing Marx to become the kind of theorist that he became.

Indeed, there is reason to think that the project of analyzing the capitalist mode of production, revealing both its rationality and its irrationality, would not have been possible without Marx's passage through historical materialism. First, the materialist conception of history was the bridge that led Marx from philosophy to social science. In the 1859 preface Marx asserts that the unnamed manuscript that we know as *The German Ideology*—the work in which Marx walked over that bridge—had fulfilled two functions for his thinking. Marx asserts first that the work represented his and Engels's settling of accounts with their "former philosophical conscience" (*MEW* 13: 10/*MECW* 29: 264/*MER* 5). Historical materialism was certainly part of this settling of accounts: it was a set of assertions designed to highlight the general insufficiency of the thinking of the left-Hegelian philosophers from whom Marx and Engels were taking their leave. To this degree historical materialism functioned, in *The German Ideology*, as a weapon in debate, tied up with a dismantling of Feuerbach's philosophy but aimed also at Bauer and his friends. If Prinz is right, historical materialism played a somewhat similar role in the 1859 preface as well.

Marx also writes that the unnamed manuscript had been important for the "self-clarification" that it offered. This is a more positive view of the materialist conception of history: it not only gave him a weapon by which to attack former views, but also led him forward. We can see that it clarified his still inchoate project in at least two ways. First, it allowed him to carry over his Hegelian commitment to embedded rationality—indeed, to embedded *progress*—into the project of a critical social science. He could not have done this without having an account of rational progress comparable to Hegel's account (but embracing the history of humankind generally and not only the history of philosophers). Given Marx's presence within an *episteme* where the notion of historical development was accorded great importance, the project of a critical social science surely would have foundered without such a guarantee. The whole structure of Marx's thinking depended on the rationality-criteria that he had inherited from Hegel, and these criteria had a historical (dialectical) dimension. Unless the criteria were satisfied, it is hard to see what would have been left—aside, perhaps, from revolutionary agitation ungrounded in theory.

Second, adherence to the materialist conception of history allowed Marx to leave aside a number of questions that would surely have diffused—and defused—both his theoretical project and his revolutionism. Some of these questions were ones that the materialist conception of history put out of the way by answering. No doubt the answers were very schematic, but they were adequate enough to allow the analysis of the capitalist mode of production to go forward. Most important, in its diachronic dimension the materialist conception of history situated the capitalist mode of production neatly between feudalism and socialism, giving capitalism both a starting point and an ending point. Without such a division, how could there even be a concept, capitalism, to be offered up to analysis? Admittedly, the confident succession that Marx stakes out in the 1859 preface —Asiatic, ancient, feudal, modern bourgeois, to be followed by socialism—is something that already, before 1859, Marx had begun to call into question. But the 1859 preface's locating of the capitalist mode of production within historical time was good enough for the immediate purpose, in the sense that it allowed Marx's analysis of the existing economic order to be carried out on the assumption that this order would have a determinate end, just as it had had a determinate beginning.

Another type of question that Marx did not have to deal with has to do with what I have identified as the "synchronic" dimension of the materialist conception of history. Once Marx had articulated the materialist conception of history, he no longer needed to be puzzled as to what the basic element is in any particular social order. The basic element in all societies known up to now is the economic element—perhaps also including technology. Thus the fundamental problems of the present are defined as all having to do with the economic order. The analysis of modern society *must* be articulated as an analysis of the modern bourgeois mode of production, and not, say, as an analysis of bourgeois politics or bourgeois culture.

Recall the point that I made in chapter 2 in connection with Marx's attempt to come to a scientific understanding of politics. Marx held that in order to have a scientific understanding of anything at all one needs to understand that thing in relation to its history. Hence Marx's inability to see how one could write a political history of the French Revolution that would conform to his rationality-criteria was, for him, a strong signal that something is wrong with the political domain itself. At the same time that Marx was signing off from his attempt to write a history of the Convention, he was getting engaged by the political economy literature. But what is sauce for the goose is also sauce for the gander. It is not enough to confront the modern economy as it exists now. Marx's rationality-criteria required that he be able to appeal to a coherent, rational history of production—a "dialectical" history, in which there is progress-by-contradiction. And this is what Marx and Engels set out to provide in the crucial part 1 of *The German Ideology* (*MEW* 3: 17–77/*MECW* 5: 27–93/*MER* 146–200).

Marx's attempt at a unified understanding of human productive life time and again came up against its own internal tensions and contradictions. One tension emerges from the notion of a materialist conception of history. Even though he did not use the term *historical materialism*, there is a line of thinking in Marx according to which what is material is conceived of as foundational and what is intellectual is conceived of as superstructural. This line of thinking conflicts with that other line of thinking in Marx according to which the driving force of history is human intelligence as it is applied to the real world. Let us see how this tension works itself out in Marx's conceptualization of the social categories (productive forces, productive relations, legal and political superstructure, ideology, forms of social consciousness).

This conceptualization is marked by what we can think of as a "metaphoric of verticality." By this I mean that those things that are supposedly least decisive are seen as superficial and those that are supposedly most decisive are seen as fundamental. Further, the process of understanding is conceptualized as a process of going from the superficial to the fundamental. But Marx's metaphoric of verticality quickly deconstructs itself. Consider the elevated, "superficial" categories, ideology and social consciousness. As already noted, Marx tells us next to nothing about social consciousness, but he does tell us what sorts of ideas are included in ideology—namely, legal, political, religious, aesthetic, and philosophical ideas (epigraph, sentence 9). Marx also makes it clear that he sees ideology as retrograde. In short, ideology, in Marx's conception, is a residue from the past, a matter of "the tradition of all the dead generations" still lying upon our heads. President Ronald Reagan in the 1980s often sounded, in his public pronouncements, like a belated version of nineteenth-century liberalism. A few years earlier the adviser for national security affairs under presidents Nixon and Ford, the German-Jewish émigré Henry Kissinger, remarked in an interview that Americans love the figure of the lone lawman who rides into town and cleans it up, and suggested that he tried to operate in a way that played to this American prejudice. Here are two instances of how Marx's "retrograde" model of ideology hooks on to something that can be seen in the real world.[52]

How does Marx explain, on a theoretical level, the existence of such retrograde forms? Of course, Marx does offer a straightforwardly pragmatic explanation for ideology—namely, that it serves the interests of the ruling class. As he and Engels write, famously, in *The Communist Manifesto*: "The ruling ideas of an age were always but the ideas of the ruling class" (*MEW* 4: 480/*MECW* 6: 503/*LPW* 18/*MER* 489). But why does the justification of the ruling class, once it has been in power for a while, tend to take the form of retrograde ideas? To my knowledge Marx never explicitly tells us, but one can easily construct an account of the matter once one notices a peculiar absence from Marx's set of social categories, namely, science. One might have expected that a set of social categories so apparently comprehensive would have allowed an explicit place for science. After all, science is the contrary term to Marx's "ideology"—yet there is no place where science is located within the model as schematized in figure 4.1. Science surely ought to be there—especially since Marx is so insistent in the preface (and also earlier, in *The German Ideology*) on science's importance. Thus Marx refers to "the accuracy of natural science" (sentence 9), and he concludes the 1859 preface with a stirring evocation of the authority that, in his view, science ought to have ("Here all mistrust must be abandoned/And here must perish every craven thought") (*MEW* 13: 11/*MECW* 29: 265/*MER* 6).

So why is science absent from Marx's set of social categories, which define, as they do, historical materialism in its synchronic dimension? The answer is that science is not absent. To be sure, there is no *explicit* place for science in the materialist conception of history. But this is because the materialist conception of history is nothing other than *the history of science properly construed*. In other words, science cannot have a particular place within the model because science *is* the model.

Consider a relevant passage from *The German Ideology*, which acquires significance in the light of the 1859 preface. Here Marx declares that mistaken ideas do not have a history:

> Morality, religion, metaphysics, all the rest of ideology and their corresponding forms of consciousness . . . no longer retain the semblance of independence. They have no history, no development. . . . (*MER* 3: 26–27/*MECW* 5: 36–37/*MER* 154–55)

And why not? What distinguishes these mistaken ideas is that they are cut off from the "real life-process" of "real, active men" (*MEW* 3: 26/*MECW* 5: 36/*MER* 154). Conversely, we know from Marx's "Theses on Feuerbach," thesis two, that "the truth of a theory is tested in practice," as noted earlier. Consequently, if it is truth that we are talking about, there must be the possibility of putting ideas into conflict with reality, theory into conflict with practice. Ideas that are not in the realm of science are not part of this dialectical process of testing, which, through contradiction (which is another way to think of testing), generates progress. Ideological ideas, which in Marx's view are "phantoms [*Nebelbildungen*] in the human brain" (*MER* 3: 26/*MECW* 5: 36/*MER* 154), are excluded from the process of dialectical testing because they do not have sufficient contact with reality to allow testing to take place. It is because of this that they have "no history, no development."[53] For Marx, only *rational* history is *real* history ("the real is the rational . . .": but Marx was far less tolerant of contingency than Hegel was). Conversely, ideas that are tested in practice do have a history, because what defines proper history, for Marx, is the presence of a dialectical process, generating progress by contradiction (in this case the contradiction is between idea and matter, theory and fact). In Marx's eyes, anything else is not real history, even though it may extend itself out over historical time.

The presumed fact that ideas that are not tested are not part of the historical process has a further and not generally noticed implication—namely, that the framework of social categories that Marx gives us in the 1859 preface collapses down upon itself. (To be sure, the 1859 preface is only one Marxian text, and a very short one at that. In the wider scheme of things it is not very important. But the same framework of categories that Marx articulates in the 1859 preface is also present in *The German Ideology* and is assumed in *The Poverty of Philosophy*, *The Communist Manifesto*, and many other of Marx's writings.) One can look at the collapse from at least two different perspectives. The category of "legal and political superstructure" collapses because, as I argued in chapter 2, Marx holds that there will be no politics in the future socialist order. The category of ideology likewise collapses, for ideology is a set of ideas justifying the existing political order (in the future there will be no "ruling class" and hence no "ruling ideas"). As for the notion of social consciousness, it too disappears, at least as something distinct from a correct, scientific, apprehension of and engagement with the world. In short, the social categories that Marx gives us are in his view valid for the analysis of past and present social orders. But Marx quite evidently sees them as irrelevant to any analysis of the *future* social order, socialism. What we will be left with are productive relations and productive forces—and it is not at all clear that the former will be distinguishable from the latter, for Marx envisages an integration of the material and the social, the natural and the human. One might say that everything collapses down into the mode of production.

In Marx's view, science is centrally related to this collapse. Marx makes it clear at various points in his writing that he envisages human beings' internalization (more precisely: *workers'* internalization) of a scientific way of thinking. Consider again the sentence from the *Grundrisse* quoted in an earlier section:

> The science that compels the inanimate limbs of the machinery, by their construction, to act purposefully, as an automaton, *does not exist in the worker's consciousness*, but rather acts upon him through the machine as an alien power, as the power of the machine itself. (*MEGA2* 2.1.2: 572/*MECW* 29: 83/*GRUND* 693/*MER* 279 [my italics])

What we have here is an assertion on Marx's part that in the present-day economic world, science is something that stands apart from—is outside—the workers. Since science, for Marx from 1845 onward, is always something that is tested in practice (thesis two), and since the practice in question equates above all to productive activity (for it is in seeking to wrest the means for satisfying their needs from nature that human beings' ideas are most compellingly tested), one of the things that Marx is saying here is that, as things stand now, workers are estranged from their productive activity. (They were less estranged before the advent of capitalism, but by the same token science was less developed.)

In other words, Marx is repeating the claim that he made, although without any reference to science, in the "Estranged Labor and Private Property" section of the "Economic and Philosophical Manuscripts," namely, that under the present economic dispensation workers are estranged, alienated (among other things, they are estranged and alienated from science). Since the movement to socialism is a movement by which human beings become *dis*alienated, Marx is contending that in socialist society science will not stand outside the consciousness of the workers but will be integrated into it. Under socialism, science will be at one with the workers. Science will be the workers' intelligence. This intelligence, which is the primary force of production, will drive the historical process forward in a systematic and efficient way, as opposed to the grossly inefficient way that has prevailed up to now. Of course, capitalism already points the way to socialism, and Marx did in fact claim to find the beginnings of such an internalized scientific consciousness within workers now.[54]

Another way of looking at the self-deconstruction of the materialist conception of history is through the lens of Marx's unitarism. In relation to science, unitarism amounts to the notion that knowledge of reality is not separate from reality itself. Concretely put: Marx envisages a unifying of social theory and social practice (one could say a unifying of theory and practice *tout court*, for in Marx's view *all* theory and *all* practice are social). For Marx, science under socialism is not something separate from practice. Rather, science will be a *systematically successful practice*. Indeed, it is a systematically successful practice that will ultimately disappear as a separate enterprise, for it will be identical with good practice generally.[55]

Consider what happens to Marx's category of consciousness when one looks at it in the light of his unitarism. Marx's most important reflections on this matter occur in *The German Ideology*. I shall quote only one important sentence:

> Consciousness can never be anything else than conscious existence [*das bewußte Sein*: "cognized being"] and the existence of human beings is their actual life-process. (*MEW* 3: 26/*MECW* 5: 36/*MER* 158)

In essence, Marx here equates consciousness with existence. In a situation of estrangement (chapter 3), consciousness stands aside and apart from the real existence of human beings. But in a situation of nonestrangement, where human beings are in control of the conditions of their lives, consciousness is not something separate from existence, in Marx's view. Indeed, in *The German Ideology* Marx and Engels posit a process of initial unity, followed by division, followed by reunification at a higher level. As they put it, "the production of ideas, conceptions, of consciousness, is *at first* directly interwoven with the material activity and the material intercourse of men, the language of real life" (*MEW* 3: 26/*MECW* 5: 36/*MER* 154 [my italics]). Later, with the emergence of a division between mental and physical labor, they diverged. Now there is the possibility, indeed the necessity, of conceptualizations and material reality coming together again.

How is this coming together marked out? Consider "ideology," which, as noted earlier, Marx characterizes as offering distorted representations of the existing order of things. Obviously, when distorted representation disappears, ideology disappears. Ideology's opposite is science. Marx and Engels envisage, in *The German Ideology*, the disappearance of philosophy and of all other distorted representations, and their replacement by the true representation that is science. As they write:

> Where speculation ends—in real life—there real, positive science begins—the representation of the practical activity, of the practical process of development of men. Empty talk about consciousness ceases, and real knowledge has to take its place. When reality is depicted, philosophy as an independent branch of knowledge loses its medium of existence. (*MEW* 3: 27/*MECW* 5: 37/*MER* 155)

Thus, everything on the level of estranged consciousness disappears. Only the forces and relations of production remain. So, once again, the conceptual structure schematized in figure 4.1 disappears, with production alone remaining. Moreover, it is not only the synchronic aspect of historical materialism that collapses, but the diachronic aspect as well. In *The Communist Manifesto* Marx and Engels announce that "the history of all society up to now is the history of class struggles" (*MEW* 4: 462/*MECW* 6: 482/*LPW* 18/*MER* 473). In the "de-revolutionized" 1859 preface, the struggle is between forces and relations. But Marx tells us in the 1859 preface (sentence 14) that "the bourgeois relations of production are the last antagonistic form of the social process of production." In other words, the materialist conception of history, as laid out in the 1859 preface, applies only to human society up to now. It does not apply to the society of the future. In sentence 15, further, Marx tells us that the bourgeois social formation "brings . . . the prehistory of human society to a close." In other words, the materialist conception of history is actually, by Marx's usage here, a conception of the *pre*history of human society. Insofar as there will be conflict in the future society, it will not be between human beings. Rather, it will be between human beings acting collectively, on the one hand, and, on the other, a nature from which they will wrest the means for satisfying their ever more developed needs.

The self-deconstruction of the materialist conception of history helps to illuminate the relation that Marx and Engels saw between history and freedom. It has repeatedly been claimed that the materialist conception of history offers a deterministic view of human history and society, and that the primacy of the productive forces, in particular, implies that Marx held that human beings are necessarily subordinate to the material conditions within which they live. These claims are simply wrong. It is true that in an estranged social order, where human beings do not *possess* knowledge (in the sense of having internalized it), they are indeed subordinated to forces outside themselves, in Marx's view. But Marx and Engels, as I have made clear, envisage a time in the future when human beings will have taken control of their lives. And they will take control of their lives by the knowledge they have of the laws of production and of society.

The laws that Marx and Engels assume are deterministic, Newtonian laws. But precisely their necessary character allows human beings who understand them, who grasp them from the inside, to take control over the natural and social environments within which they live. Marx and Engels write, near the end of part 1 of *The German Ideology*, that "the transformation, through the division of labor, of personal powers (relationships) [*Mächte* (*Verhältnisse*)] into material forces . . . can only be abolished [*aufgehoben*] by individuals again subjecting these material forces to themselves. . . ." (*MEW* 3: 74/*MECW* 5: 77–78/*MER* 197). As human beings, we rise above material constraints. Or as Engels puts it, at the end of *Socialism: Utopian and Scientific*: "Man, at last the master of his own form of social organization, becomes at the same time lord over nature, his own master, free" (*MEGA2* 1.27: 580/*MECW* 24: 325/*MER* 717).

These outcomes will only be achieved through scientific knowledge of the laws of nature and of society. The materialist conception of history is really a materialist-idealist conception of history, for it maintains that material forces can and will be subjected to a human consciousness that is scientific, and that this consciousness is scientific because it is constantly tested against material reality. Alternatively, we might rename the materialist conception of history the *productivist* conception of history, since production is the privileged venue (the only venue?) for this testing.

A CROSSING OF THE BORDER

In the first of his "Theses on the Philosophy of History" (completed 1940, published 1950), the heterodox Marxist Walter Benjamin, writing a few months before his suicide on the Franco-Spanish frontier as he was fleeing the Nazi juggernaut, observes that:

> The story is told of an automaton constructed in such a way that it could play a winning game of chess, answering each move of an opponent with a countermove. A puppet in Turkish attire and with a hookah in its mouth sat before a chessboard placed on a large table. A system of mirrors created the illusion that this table was transparent from all sides. Actually, a little hunchback who was an expert chess player sat inside and guided the puppet's hand by means of strings. One can imagine a philosophical counterpart to this device. The puppet called "historical materialism" is to win all the time. It can easily be a match for anyone if it enlists the services of theology, which today, as we know, is wizened and has to keep out of sight.[56]

Quite so. This is what historical materialism became in Stalinist hands in the 1930s. It became an iron theory of history, ready to be trotted out to justify every atrocity, every egg broken in the alleged interests of the revolutionary omelet.

That is not how historical materialism began. It began as a rope bridge, or as a ladder, over which Marx climbed in order to get where he needed to go. What he needed was a rational underpinning for his analysis and critique of the existing order, which he abominated. He was interested in *one* socio-economic order, namely, the present one, the bourgeois mode of production, capitalism. The historical sequence laid out in the materialist conception of history was not required for analyzing and criticizing this order. It was only required for Marx's journey out of philosophy and into economic analysis. Once having made this traverse, Marx would have done better had he tossed the rope bridge into the gorge—had he *heaved* the ladder away, rather than simply dropping it where it could be picked up again by *marxistes*.[57]

Marx tried to flesh out what, in the world, is necessary; and the contingent, the accidental, tended to fall through the theoretical grid, to be lost from sight. *Of course* Marx, like Hegel, recognized contingency (recognized, that is, the limits of theory). But his unitarism, more intense than any comparable drive in Hegel, made him less tolerant of contingency than Hegel had been. Whatever Marx's intentions, a necessitarian *theory* of history tended to gain dominance over the specifics of the real world, even though he himself was deeply interested in those specifics. Theory of history replaced history.

The great historical irony is that Marx's abiding concern, with regard to the human world, was with human activity. Again and again he insists that human beings' own actions make history. This theme runs throughout his work, even though in certain phases his claims for activity tend to become obscured, because he is, after all, largely engaged in describing a socio-economic system wherein, in his view, human beings have been subjected to overwhelming domination by the machine.

To a certain extent Marx played into the Stalinist (and far from *only* Stalinist) misreading of his work. Marx himself tended to conceal the activist roots and implications of historical materialism. His activism, to be sure, is clear in the "Economic and Philosophical Manuscripts," where he emphasizes the "*real, active* relation [*Verhalten*] of man to himself," his "act of self-creation [*Selbsterzeugungsakt*]" (*MEGA2* 1.2: 414/*MECW* 3: 333, 342/*EW*, 386, 396). It is equally clear in *The German Ideology*, where he defines history as a series of historical *acts*:

1. First historical act (*Tat*): production of the means to satisfy human needs (which equates to the production of tools).
2. Second historical act: production of new needs.
3. Third historical act: production of the family.
4. Fourth historical act: production of co-operation (which is itself a force of production). (*MEW* 3: 28–30/*MECW* 5: 42–43/*MER* 156–57)

But when we get to the 1859 preface the activist underpinnings are obscured. Marx takes productive force as his basic analytical category, without pointing out that productive force is neither a puppet nor a god, above all not an overarching necessity, but is human beings actively making their own lives. The result is the appearance of a contrast between Marx's claims at different periods in his career. I say *appearance* of a contrast not in order to deny that there are actual differences between what Marx wrote about history at different phases of his career, but only to suggest that the differences are less great than they might seem at first glance.

In *Marxism and History*, the philosopher Helmut Fleischer identifies three views of history in Marx's work—views that he sees as quite distinct from each other. First, in Marx's 1844 Manuscripts, Fleischer finds an "anthropological" view of history: here history is conceptualized as "a process directed toward man's becoming fully man in the full wealth of his being, harmoniously united with his like and with a nature that has been humanized, though by way of the negativity of 'alienation.'" This is a view that I have especially touched on in chapter 3. Second, in the 1859 preface Fleischer finds a "nomological" or law-governed view, where history is seen as a process wherein productive forces and relations develop, "governed by the objective laws of a logic of social relations uninfluenced by human intentions." Finally, in *The German Ideology* Fleischer finds a "praxis-oriented" or "pragmatological" view of history, free of what Fleischer considers to be the excessively metaphysical view of history put forward in the "Economic and Philosophical Manuscripts" and the obscuring of human agency in the 1859 preface (and in certain aspects of *Capital*). In short, Fleischer sees three Marxian approaches to history, addressed variously to "the meaning of history as a whole, the way it works in practice, and its underlying laws."[58]

Fleischer usefully identifies three *tendencies* in Marx's conception of history. But I think it largely a mistake to regard them as three separate views, for this makes the differences between them too definite and absolute. It is true that after 1844 Marx diverged from the Feuerbachian version of humanism to be found in the EPM—but the notion of estrangement is still to be found in *Capital*. It is true that in *The German Ideology* Marx and Engels refer to their view as a "practical" materialism, but the notion of activity is already present in the EPM. It is true, finally, that human agency appears to be absent from the view of historical materialism put forward in the 1859 preface, but we see from what Marx writes in the *Grundrisse* and in *Capital* that this is *only* an appearance, generated by the fact that under capitalism workers lack effective control over the productive forces.

What, then, are we to make of the materialist conception of history—that rather changeable collection of views that are probably best exemplified in the 1859 preface, the piece of writing that prompted Engels to invent the phrase? Is historical materialism a brilliant set of analytic categories, rather abstract and schematic in their presentation, but nonetheless laying the basis for a possible social science? Is it a residue of Marx's battle with philosophy, revealing both his persisting need to challenge philosophy and his hidden dependence on it? Or is it, as Prinz suggests, essentially a ploy, designed to conceal Marx's real intentions and to give him a certain amount of scientific prestige?

It seems clear that we cannot take historical materialism seriously as any sort of *general theory*. We first of all know this because of Marx's and Engels's own willingness to diverge from important aspects of historical materialism, whether considered diachronically, as an account of historical sequence, or synchronically, as a statement as to which aspects of society are most fundamental.

One thinks, for example, of Marx's (and Engels's) notions of "oriental despotism" and of "the Asiatic mode of production," which they began theorizing about in 1853 in the course of considering British policy in India, and which they returned to repeatedly thereafter. In essence, the "Asiatic mode of production" was one in which private property, especially in land, was lacking, and in which the state, and a political elite attached to the state, came to acquire inordinate power as a result of its control over public works (e.g., irrigation systems).[59]

One thinks of Marx's persistent later interest in anthropological investigation, generating his "ethnological notebooks," where it is clear that he is far from the straight-line ordering of societies (Asiatic, ancient, feudal, modern bourgeois, socialist) that one finds in the 1859 preface.[60]

One thinks also of his deep interest in Russia (from 1873 onward), which led him, in a now famous letter of March 8, 1881 to the Russian revolutionary Vera Zasulich, to suggest that the peasant commune might provide a route to socialism in Russia that would bypass the bourgeois stage (*MEGA2* 1.25: 241–42/*MECW* 24: 370–71/*MER* 675 [excerpt]).[61]

One thinks of sections of *Capital* itself. As one Marx commentator, the philosopher Richard Miller, points out, in *Capital* Marx "discusses the reciprocal impact of power struggles and market mechanisms," dealing with such issues as the struggle to shorten the working day and the way in which mechanization was being used to increase labor discipline."[62] These are *political* matters, diverging from the alleged working out of iron, necessitarian laws.

Finally, one thinks of the various letters written by the later Engels, in which he tries to rein in the historical materialism of some of Marx's followers (see note 7 of this chapter for a list of these letters). Engels was particularly concerned in these later letters with the interplay in history between necessity and accident. He insisted that "according to the materialist conception of history, the *ultimately* determining element [*das* in letzter Instanz *bestimmende Moment*] in history is the production and reproduction of real life." But along the way there is an "interaction" between economics and politics, law, philosophical theories, religious views, and so on—an "endless host of accidents" that deeply influence what happens (letter to Joseph Bloch, September 21–22, 1890, *MEW* 37: 462/*MER* 760). Of course, these letters came after Marx's death. We cannot be sure how much they reflect the aged Marx's own views. But there is no reason to think that they are divergent from what Marx's own views were, or would have been.

In short, I think it fair to conclude that Marx was not committed to the materialist conception of history in any deep and doctrinaire way. It is also obvious that Marx modified his views on history and on social structure when confronted by what he took to be new evidence. He was, after all, a great scholar and researcher, a man who surely devoted more time to the empirical study of human society than did anyone else in the nineteenth century. *Of course* he was sensitive to data. *Of course* he could see, very often, how the data contradicted his theory. On some such occasions Marx changed his *views*. That is very clear. But we should not read more into this fact than it deserves. For the real question is: did Marx change his *theory*? So far as I can see, he did not.[63]

I suspect that when Marx went to that wonderful scholarly treasure-house, the Reading Room of the British Museum, or when he sat at his work table at home and wrote, his focus was not on any overall theoretical view but rather on the particular problem that confronted him at that particular moment. I suspect that this was generally true of his work: so that when he writes, as he (and Engels) do in *The German Ideology*, that what individuals are "coincides with their production, both with *what* they produce and with *how* they produce"—a statement that obviously leaves out a great deal of human life—he is writing those words because, at that particular moment, that was what he was moved to write (*MEW* 3: 21/*MECW* 5: 31–32/*MER* 150). Had he found himself needing to respond to a critic of such a conception of human life, he would then have gone on to write something else. But he did not have to respond to such a critic. His absolute obsession was with the struggle against the bourgeoisie, and to this struggle everything was subordinated.

What we finally need to carry away from Marx is surely not a general theory. What we need to carry away is rather the image of a deep and serious thinker and critic, unwilling to allow himself to be complacent about a world that, although it offered him much, did not offer him redemption. What we need to question, but not too deeply, is the cosmic optimist. Perhaps we know enough now to know that the world never offers us redemption—that mankind, *pace* the 1859 preface, does not always set for itself only such tasks as it can solve. What tasks, then, at Auschwitz? Rather, there is irredeemable finitude in the world. Imagine a children's birthday party. How many of those children, so happy now at the age of three, will find what they want in the world? How many will turn sour? How many will die before their time? How many will kill themselves?

In Marx's view, they all *should* find what they want, and in a rightly ordered, materially productive society, they all would. But there is something missing from such an image of the world—if Auschwitz taught us anything, it is that. We are fortunate in being able to see the deficiency, for we are as a result less likely to suffer an excess of distress or cynicism at the disappointments that the world offers us. Recognizing the limits of Marx's view is not the same as saying, "reject Marx." Rather, we should accept, and indeed adhere to and honor, a Marx corrected. But the task of correction is only just beginning.

Conclusion

For and Against Marxism

> Freedom as an inner capacity of man is identical with the capacity to begin, just as freedom as a political reality is identical with a space of movement between men. Over the beginning, no logic, no cogent deduction can have any power, because its chain presupposes, in the form of a premise, the beginning.
>
> —Hannah Arendt, *The Origins of Totalitarianism*, new ed. with added prefaces (New York: Harcourt Brace Jovanovich, 1973 [orig. 1951]), 473.

I have no intention of saying the last word on Marx; I want instead to start a debate. In spite of everything, Marx is not a finished chapter in our social, political, and intellectual life. The implications and relevance of his work are so wide that a full assessment would stretch out into infinity. I can hope only to provide, in this conclusion and in the book as a whole, some stimulus toward a rethinking of Marx's place in our tradition and in our time. No doubt much of what I say will be challenged and some things may be controverted. Such is the dialectic that is philosophical debate.

In the present book I have focused on Marx the rationalist philosopher. Further, I have concentrated my efforts on Marx's rationalism in its early manifestations. I have looked especially at Marx's engagement, in the period from 1837 through 1846, with Hegelian philosophy, with politics, and with economics. Marx died on March 14, 1883; he was intellectually active until two months before his death. Thus I have taken a limited swath of his work. In doing this I have always been attentive to Marx's later, "mature" writings, as well as to his activist and empirical commitments. But I have had to leave out much that in principle I would have preferred to include.

Emphasizing Marx's universalizing side, I have said little about his work as a student of the particular and the specific. I have noted but not pursued the activist Marx who was willing to modify the materialist conception of history when it got in the way of his immediate hopes and aims. Nor have I pursued the empirical Marx who was willing to abandon some aspects of historical materialism when they did not fit the facts that he was seeing. I have likewise left out an account of the later Marx's analysis of capitalism. Given the number and complexity of Marx's manuscripts on capitalism, to have examined them in a serious way would have stretched out the length of this study inordinately, in pages and in years. Such an examination would give us a fuller picture of the tension and interplay between Marx's rationalism on the one hand and his empirical sensitivity on the other, and would help us to better gauge the workings of his mind.

Yet this book nonetheless covers a great deal. It gets at an essential and profoundly neglected feature of Marx's thinking. This feature is central to his project and to its later fate, and it also connects with realities lying well beyond the reach of Marxism itself. For example, there is an affinity between Marx's rationalist side and the work of many social scientists today. Marx's commitment to the notion that necessity rules the social world, so that there are no accidental occurrences worth considering but only irrational remnants that have not yet been eliminated, has been and still is a powerful notion in some quarters. The belief that nothing is accidental is a wonderful heuristic principle, a magnificent spur to the project of explaining things. It is also dangerous, to the degree that it wishes to form the social order in its own image and to scant whatever does not fit.

The present study reaches out to embrace the entirety of a world that has now almost vanished—the world of would-be Marxian socialism, 1917–91. Perhaps it also embraces future worlds in which other theoretical views valorizing necessity and predictivity might come to the fore and attempt to make a recalcitrant humanity conform to its predictions. It is obvious that such worlds are too large to be "covered" by the present book. Recognizing this fact, I offer some conclusions that cannot be fully supported by the evidence that this book provides, although they are in part supported by it. In short, I have here chosen to speculate, at least to some degree. I do this in order to lay some important issues on the table. In doing so, I hope to stimulate further thinking about them. My more speculative suggestions will quickly be submitted to criticism. They will be corrected where they need correction and amplified where they need amplification. This, precisely, is the way that scholarship and science ought to operate: as a process of conjecture, response, and correction.

I hope that this book will help to dynamite apart the conceptual ice jam that surrounds Marx and that vitiates discussion of his work and effects. Most discussions of Marx, whether generally positive or generally negative, operate at a quite superficial level. In studying Marx's theoretical project I have tried to get down to the most basic level I could find. I found this basic level in Marx's rationalism. I have examined Marx's unfolding of his rationalism in the course of his early attempts to confront politics and the market. I have also looked at how his general conceptions of history and society are related to this rationalism. I hope that my charting of the outlines of Marx's rationalism will generate a renewed discussion of the role of Marxism in modern history. I hope that it will also help those of us who honor this amazing man, and who are attached to many of the things that he valued, to better discern what is living and what is dead in his theoretical project, what is worth preserving and carrying forward and what ought to be cut away.

I seek to offer something quite different from the eulogistic or dyslogistic responses to Marxism's collapse that have cluttered public discourse since the collapse of the Soviet Union and its empire. In the wake of the Soviet Union's collapse in fall 1991, I heard much discussion that I found utterly inadequate to the events that had occurred. Much of the discussion seems inadequate to me still. Instead of offering a eulogy or dyslogy of Marxism, I have sought to offer an autopsy. An autopsy is first of all a looking at something to see it for oneself.[1] This I have tried to do, by looking at the evidence of Marx's text and by declining all allegiances except for an allegiance to historical investigation. An autopsy is secondarily the examination of a corpse. Here I have tried to be a modern coroner, one attentive to discerning what in the body ought not to be harvested and what, on the contrary, might still be apt for use. Marx's project suffers from some major defects. Aspects of the project need to be deep-sixed, and one must guard against a romantic sentimentalism that declines to recognize this fact. But I also believe that there are things that can be salvaged from the body. Some of its bones and organs are useful still. Some of Marx's aspirations deserve to be emulated.

I have proceeded in this book in a largely negative vein. But this is only because previous aficionados of Marx's work have failed to see crucial defects that are there. It would be welcome if my exposure of these defects stimulates others to rethink its more positive aspects. Let me begin by listing the things that in my view we ought *not* to take from Marx: his method; his rejection of the market; his rejection of politics; and his underplaying of the dangerous sphere of human intimacy and anxiety. Let us now consider each of these matters in turn. I shall then turn to the project's more positive features.

MARXIAN METHOD

In the present book I have not dwelt on issues of method. I have instead focused on assumptions that underpin Marx's project in general, and they of course also underpin his method (or methods). But questions of method cannot be avoided. It is often suggested that Marx's method was one of his great theoretical contributions. This seems to me a mistake—at least if *method* means more than simply adopting an alert and critical stance toward reality.

Marx's most important discussion of method appears in "Notebook M" of the *Grundrisse* (Notebook M was written in late August–mid-September 1857). The most compelling context for addressing the method articulated in the *Grundrisse* would be in a discussion of Marx's analysis of capitalism. There is a study to be written examining the relation between Marx's methodological statements and the actual investigations that he carried out in *Capital* and in the large body of manuscript material connected to *Capital*. In the absence of such a study, there are still some important things that can and ought to be said about issues of method in Marx.

What *was* Marx's method (at any rate, what was the method articulated in Notebook M)? Some readers might wish to begin by puzzling out Marx's method on their own, by reading the key text from the *Grundrisse* and then trying to figure out for themselves what Marx's words mean (editions are plentifully available: *MEGA2* 2.1.1: 35–43/*MECW* 28: 37–45/*GRUND* 100–8/*LPW* 145–57/*MER* 236–44). However, as a substitute for such a reading, I summarize Marx's (late) method as follows.[2]

Influenced by Marx's reading of Hegel's *Logic*, the method that is limned in the *Grundrisse* aimed to uncover theoretical categories that are simultaneously universal and concrete. If one is to discover such concrete universal categories, one needs to grasp the essence (*Wesen*) of the larger entity—the system or structure—within which those categories are situated. That is, one cannot have a *concrete* universal category unless one understands the system of which it is a part and its particular relations to that system. (According to Marx, previous economists had failed to grasp this point. They had based their theories on concepts of labor, private property, and the like that they assumed were applicable to all human history, but that were actually applicable only to the bourgeois mode of production and derived their meaning from that mode.) If one is to grasp essences, one has to think of the systems within which those essences are located as wholes or totalities, rising or falling on the basis of certain essential features of the totality, and hence as not being definable by induction from particulars.

The above summary requires some clarification. Compare Marx's method to classic positivist method. Positivism in its main nineteenth-century forms articulated three basic tenets, which we can call, respectively, phenomenalism, correlationism, and physicism.[3] The first tenet is that only things that can be observed are relevant to scientific knowledge (we call these things *phenomena*, which comes from the Greek word for "appearance"). Nineteenth-century positivists held that the first task of scientific investigation is to go out and collect the observable facts that are relevant to whatever problem one is investigating. They held that the second task of scientific investigation is to order the data points to see how they correlate to each other. Finally, they held that physics is the highest science, and hence they also held that a field of investigation is more scientific the more it emulates physics. Positivists thus maintained that the correlations that investigators discover ought to take the form of universal laws (e.g., f = ma), which are to be arrived at inductively from the data.

Marx's method is precisely *not* positivist: indeed, it is in some respects the direct reverse of positivism. Why did Marx in 1857–58 find a method adapted from Hegel's *Logic* appealing? I believe it was because Marx was already deeply committed to the dual claims that capitalism *ought* to be destroyed (because it estranges and exploits human beings, and because it is not an adequately rational system) and that it is *doomed* to be destroyed (by the workings of its own internal contradictions). Marx had committed himself to these claims as early as 1843, as we can see from his essay "On the Jewish Question" and especially from the introduction to his projected *Contribution to the Critique of Hegel's Philosophy of Right* (both published in February 1844). Until the failure of the revolutions of 1848, Marx placed most of his hope for the destruction of the current system in the hands of insurgent radicals, who he believed would soon engage in the revolutionary overthrow of the existing order, beginning with France. Hence his claim, in the 1843 introduction, that "the *day of German resurrection* will be heralded by the *crowing of the Gallic cock*" (*MEGA2* 1.2: 183/*MECW* 3: 187/*EW* 257). But when the revolutions of 1848 failed to destroy any of the things that he so fervently hoped would be destroyed, he was forced to concentrate his hopes more on the notion that the underlying structural features of capitalism would bring about its destruction, and less on the prospect that an insurrection would take place the day after tomorrow.

In other words, in his examination of the capitalist system, Marx wanted to be able to discern the doom of capitalism in the workings of capitalism itself. But it was clear to Marx that the articulation of correlations among phenomena was not going to generate that sort of account of capitalism. After all, the "bourgeois" political economists whom Marx attacked were unable to discern, through *their* work, the future destruction of capitalism. Instead, they saw a functioning market that was always tending toward equilibrium if it wasn't actually at equilibrium. Marx insisted that the periodic recessions that occurred under capitalism were harbingers of its eventual collapse; his fellow economists saw them as periods of mild readjustment at most.

Given the difficulty of finding the imminent collapse of capitalism proclaimed by its surface workings (the only workings that positivism attended to), Marx needed some other method than positivist method if he was to establish his case. He needed a method that would allow him to dig down to a deeper level than the empirically observable. This is precisely what Hegel's *Logic*, with its distinction between a surface level of appearance (*Erscheinung*) and a deeper level of essence (*Wesen*), gave him. In effect, Marx picked up where Hegel left off, transforming an intellectual process that leads to increasing truth into a labor process that leads to the increasing mastery of the material world.

Further, Marx had a compelling need to conceive of the existing order as a totality, a unified whole. I suspect, following a suggestion by Tim Shiell (chapter 4), that he had this need in part because he was unremittingly hostile to the existing order. His hostility to the existing order long preceded any investigation on his part of the economic system: already in 1837 his father called him a "negating genius" (Heinrich Marx, letter of December 9, 1837 [*MEGA2* 3.1: 325/*MECW* 1: 688]). Accordingly, he was not at all satisfied with the idea that the existing order should be reformed in a piecemeal way. It was anathema to him that a sequence of additive changes in the existing order might make it acceptable after all. He was inclined to think of the flaws of capitalism as pertaining, not just to specific defects within capitalism, but to capitalism *itself*, considered as a whole. Hence he adopted a *methodological* holism, which proceeded *as if* there are emergent qualities of wholes, even though he had no *ontological* commitment to such a view.

But the method that Marx articulated and tried to follow is not adequate to what I take to be the proper end of method, which is to minimize the chances of arriving at erroneous conclusions. In fact, it is perhaps better not to call Marx's method a method at all: it is much more an *approach to the material*, a pre-established interpretive perspective. It is an approach that "always already" contains within itself a certain conviction about capitalism, namely, that capitalism is doomed to destroy itself. Marx's abstractionism—an abstractionism that is in some tension with his massive curiosity and his eye for vivid and telling detail—gave him a convenient opportunity to save, and then to save again, his intended conclusions. If at the level of exchange value one cannot find those conclusions manifesting themselves, one goes down to the level of Value with a capital V; if one cannot find that the labor theory of value is justified when one attends to the actual labor concretely carried out by specific persons or categories of persons, one goes down to the level of an Abstract Labor that does not correspond to any labor that is actually done. No wonder that one of Marx's best-known critics, the economist and sometime finance minister of Austria, Eugen von Böhm-Bawerk (1851–1914), wrote that in *Capital* "the system runs in one direction, the facts go in another."[4] Certain habits of mind that are manifested in *Capital* are worthy of emulation. These habits include Marx's concern with conceptualization, and his related concern with always keeping in mind the broad significance of the specific details under examination at any given moment in his analysis. But Marxian method as a whole ought not to be emulated, for it puts the testing of propositions at too great a distance from the investigation itself, and for this reason is too likely to encourage self-deception and obfuscation.

MARX'S REJECTION OF THE MARKET

We ought also to stand aside from Marx's uncompromising rejection of market relations. Some of Marx's conclusions with regard to the market give every appearance of being correct. For example, there was hardly anything that Marx rejected more vehemently than the claim that the market is self-equilibrating: this is one reason for the scorn he heaped on the economist Jean-Baptiste Say, who famously maintained that supply creates its own demand, so that the market naturally clears itself.[5] It also appears that Marx was right in his claim that no theory can accurately predict the rise and fall of market prices. To turn attention from markets in particular to the capitalist system as a whole, it likewise appears that Marx was right in holding that a dynamism permeates capitalism (for this theme, see especially the famous paragraphs of *The Communist Manifesto* where Marx and Engels sing a hymn of praise to the bourgeoisie for having played "a highly revolutionary role in history" [*MEW* 4: 464–67/*MECW* 6: 486–90/*LPW* 3–7/*MER* 475–78]). Many other economists of Marx's time failed to see this dynamism, for they insisted on other factors—such as population pressure, resource limitations, and the supposed using up of investment opportunities—that were contrary to any such dynamism; at the same time, they underestimated the power of human creativity and inventiveness. Finally, one can even suggest that, in the *very* long term, Marx's labor theory of value might well turn out to be correct, anticipating a time when, because of mechanization, automation, and the capacity to synthesize previously scarce natural resources, the only scarce resource—on account of the finitude of human life and the diversity of human desires—would be the labor of planning and guidance required to keep the machinery of production moving forward.

But in his rejection of markets Marx was wrong (chapter 3). Here Marx applied a rationality-criterion, predictivity, that could not—and cannot—be satisfied on the level of the market itself. Anyone who succeeded in doing so would have the wealth of Croesus at his command by the next day. But it is impossible: there are reasons why any theory predicting the rise and fall of market prices would almost instantly be disconfirmed. Marx was right in seeing that the institution of the market cannot live up to his rationality-criteria.

His error was in concluding that markets therefore need to be judged as ultimately irrational. What he should have seen was that the fact that the workings of markets cannot be adequately understood within the ambit of his theory spoke more to the limits of the theory than to the limits of the phenomena he was trying to understand.

In rejecting markets Marx failed to come up to the level of some of his other, better insights. For example, rejection of markets stands in some tension with Marx's insight into the dynamic character of capitalism. Marx saw this dynamism as having a human as well as a structural dimension. Already in the "Economic and Philosophical Manuscripts" he held that human needs should not be seen as fixed and unchanging. On contrary, he held that needs develop over time. It is not for nothing that he and Engels proclaimed in *The German Ideology* (1845–46) that the production of new needs is the first historical act (*MER* 3: 28/*MECW* 5: 42/*MER* 156).

To be sure, a Spartan Marxism, or even only a *restrained* Marxism, would hold that there is indeed a basic roster of needs, and that there is something wrong with going beyond this roster unless everyone in the society goes beyond it, and goes beyond it to the same degree. In theory, such an egalitarianism was widely honored in twentieth-century Communist regimes (in practice, the *nomenklatura* were usually able to enjoy goods far beyond the basic roster of needs). Certainly, one can see the rationale for articulating and then enforcing some sort of social minimum below which no one in a society would be permitted to fall, and a social maximum above which no one would be permitted to rise. Everybody would at least have "enough," although none would be wealthy.

But a restrained Marxism, committed more to equality than to freedom, was clearly not Marx's preference. On the contrary, Marx held to the dynamism of need—to the "wealth of *human* need," as he put it in the "Economic and Philosophical Manuscripts." Although he was scathing about those who speculate on creating new needs in others, his objection was only to oppression and exploitation and not to the production of new needs as such. He adored "the *rich man*"; he looked forward to the creation of whole new human senses (*MEGA2* 1.2: 394, 396–97/*MECW* 3: 301–2, 304/*EW* 353–54, 356). In short, he reveled in the expansion of need. But Marx's dynamism of needs creates a serious problem for his theory—although he does not seem to have recognized the problem, and he certainly did not confront it.

Let us look first at the "Spartan" case, where needs are assumed to be static. Let us suppose that a social minimum is decreed, and that, corresponding to this, a set limit is established as to what any one person is allowed to consume. Within a socialist society thus organized it would be clear, within narrow limits, what the sum total of needs within that society would be for a given period. It would be a simple matter of totaling up the needs. One would then organize production so that exactly those goods that would satisfy the needs in question would be produced. At first glance, it would be a relatively simple matter to arrange the production and distribution of these goods. This, at any rate, was the claim that Engels made as early as 1846, in his Elberfeld speech, discussed in chapter 3. Although it is a mistaken claim, let us accept it for the sake of the argument.

Now let us look at the case that Marx preferred, where needs develop. This is the situation that Marx envisaged would prevail under socialism/communism. But if needs develop, the organization of production becomes far more difficult than it is in a situation where there is a pre-established minimum and maximum. Admittedly, if one could predict needs, the problem would be solved: one could now have a *planned* development of needs. But it is difficult to see how, once needs have been set in motion, their satisfaction can be planned out in any detailed way. Some human needs are obvious (a starving person blatantly needs food). But needs beyond the basic level are not obvious, and their nonobviousness becomes the greater the more "developed" they are. One thinks of the need for bicycles, for example. This can become a need for three-speed bicycles, for ten-speed bicycles, and for various other refinements and specializations of bicycles—which might be paralleled by the need for in-line roller skates and scooters. Who would decide what precise combination of products to produce? It would be beyond the powers of any bureaucrat or industry administrator to plan such matters intelligently.

Against the argument that I have just made, it might be argued that bicycles, in-line skates, or scooters are either frivolous needs or are not needs at all, and hence ought not to be countenanced in the future socialist order. One then has to ask whether listening to Beethoven string quartets is a real need or only a frivolity. If being able to listen to Beethoven string quartets is a real need, how would one choose between that need and the need for tickets to a concert by the Dave Matthews Band or R.E.M.? How would one decide between Beethoven string quartets and performances of Shakespeare? How, further, would one decide between the production of one new play and another, different one, or between one new movie and a multitude of other possible movies?

One could object that all the above-noted needs are at best frivolous and at worst not needs at all: who *needs* Shakespeare or Beethoven? But it seems unlikely that Marx would have held to such a view, given that (in the "Economic and Philosophical Manuscripts") he insists on "the wealth of subjective *human* sensitivity—a musical ear, an eye for the beauty of form, in short, *senses* capable of human gratification" (*MEGA2* 1.2: 394/*MECW* 3: 301/*EW* 353). So, how is all this to be organized according to a plan? It seems impossible.

Marx also suggests in the EPM that "the idea of *one* basis for life and another for *science* is from the very outset a lie"—in short, he articulates a "unitarism," under scientific auspices (*MEGA2* 1.2: 396/*MECW* 3: 303/*EW* 355). But there seems to be no scientific answer to questions such as the ones that I am posing here.

Consider needs that are more clearly *material* needs, rather than intellectual or aesthetic needs that merely require some sort of material substratum (such as instruments, workers [musicians], venues, publicity, and so on). Imagine a world completely made up of socialist societies, with no nonsocialist society in existence. Imagine that the World Socialist Order has one thing in common with the former German Democratic Republic: its most commonly available automobile is the Trabant (a heavily polluting, rattletrap putt-putt of an automobile). In the GDR it was possible to discern that the Trabant was not a great, popularly priced automobile, because East Germans knew perfectly well that Western Europeans drove a variety of popularly priced automobiles, all of them markedly better than the Trabant. But in the World Socialist Order, how would one *know* this? The Trabant could be hailed as a technological marvel and few would be in a position to know that this was not so. The general point is that, intuitively, a socialist economy seems likely to be better at producing material goods it already knows about than at figuring out how to produce improved goods. I shall pursue this matter further below.

For the moment, let us go back to the simpler case, where a society has been organized around the notion of a social minimum and maximum (with an emphasis thus placed on tried-and-true goods that large numbers of people need—in short, on the staples of everyday life). Adherence to the social minimum would largely solve the problem of which goods to produce, among a potentially infinite number of possibilities. But it would not solve the problem of *how to produce them*. For characteristically there are many different ways of producing a good that will satisfy such-and-such a need or bundle of needs. One can produce the good with more wood and less steel or less wood and more steel, with more energy and less labor or more labor and less energy, in a few large factories widely separated from each other or in many small local factories, and so on. One or more of the ways of producing the "same" product would be optimal; other ways would be suboptimal. But how would the corps of administrators in this society (where "the administration of things" has replaced "the government of men") decide among all the different production options? Alas, they would have no nonarbitrary way of making these decisions. How is this so?

I invoke here the so-called calculation problem, pointed out by the Austrian economist Ludwig von Mises in a classic paper published in 1920, "Economic Calculation in the Socialist Commonwealth." As von Mises showed, in the absence of a price system it is all but impossible to make rational choices between one way of producing a product and another. Indeed, one cannot even tell for sure whether, in producing a product, one is creating value or destroying it, for one cannot know what it costs to produce the product, nor can one know how much people value it in comparison with other products. It is conceivable that the product could actually be worth less than the inputs used in making it, but in the absence of markets it would be difficult to discern this.[6] For example, in the German Democratic Republic, planners had a hard time figuring out whether the GDR's export goods were a net gain or a net loss for the national economy. This was because planners could never be quite sure whether, for example, the precision optical goods that the GDR exported were priced above or below their cost of production—for in the absence of real prices within the GDR the cost of production was not known.

The calculation problem is not the end of the difficulty with Marx's antimarket position. Consider, again, the dynamism of needs. The question that arises in response to Marx's position is: given the dynamism of needs, are needs predictable? Clearly, some needs—the relatively nondynamic ones—are predictable within quite close tolerances. Planners will pretty much know how much toilet paper and table salt will be needed in Karl Marx Stadt next year, absent any dramatic change in habits. But other needs are not so predictable. These are the needs that are less dependent on humans' physical constitutions and *longue durée* cultural habits and more dependent on factors that are relatively changeable.

Marx himself insists on the reciprocal character of the relationship between need and the objects that satisfy those needs. In the "Economic and Philosophical Manuscripts" he declares that need is dependent on the existence of a capacity for the need. For example, the need for music depends on the existence of a musical capacity, such that "the most beautiful music has *no* sense for the unmusical ear" (*MEGA2* 1.2: 394/ *MECW* 3: 301/*EW* 353). In the EPM passage Marx is particularly concerned to keep in mind the restricted conditions of the oppressed working class, and so his emphasis is on what is missing—receptivity to the most beautiful music. Elsewhere he emphasizes the other side of the reciprocal relation, namely, the dependence of the need on the object. Just as he claims that there can be no need without the existence in human beings of a capacity for the need, he also asserts that there can be no need without the existence in the world of the object or objects that will satisfy the need. This is perhaps an overstatement—we needed a preventative for polio before that preventative existed, just as we need cures for various cancers and for AIDS now. But it is not a gross overstatement: it is largely because people think that a cure for AIDS is *possible* that curing AIDS registers as a need. Otherwise, AIDS would be viewed as a stark fatality, like plague in 1350.

Consider the following pregnant passage in the *Grundrisse*, where Marx expatiates on the reciprocal relation between need and object, between consumption and production:

> The need which consumption feels for the object is created by the perception of it. . . . Production thus not only creates an object for the subject, but also a subject for the object. Thus production produces consumption (1) by creating the material for it; (2) by determining the manner of consumption; and (3) by creating the products, initially posited by it as objects, in the form of a need felt by the consumer. It thus produces the object of consumption. Consumption likewise produces the producer's *inclination* by beckoning to him as an aim-determined need. (*MEGA2* 2.1.1: 29/*MECW* 28: 30/*GRUND* 92/*MER* 230)

In other words, there would be no need for Beethoven string quartets if there were no Beethoven string quartets. Before Beethoven had composed and put on display the first few of his string quartets, how could one have known that such an object is needed in the world? Before at least a few quartets existed it was a pure wager that *any* of them would be needed. Until a few people had actually discovered their need for them, no one could know for sure that they would fulfill a social need. Rather, they would be nothing more than markers of the possibly neurotic need of a weird eccentric to compose string quartets.

Let us bring matters back to material products again. It is clear that people do not necessarily know that they need a particular material product before the product has actually been produced. No doubt there are many material products whose prospective use would be so obvious that people would say, sight unseen, "that is something I need"—just as there are some products of which people would say, "I would certainly never need that." But there are also many products that many people would not identify in advance as satisfying a need that they have. The need would be of the sort that only emerges once one has been told that something that can satisfy it exists. To what extent was there a clear need for typewriters when typewriters were invented, given the superiority of a good penman over early typewriters? There was at most only the possibility of a need—a possibility that was activated and increased only as typewriters were improved and began to overtake and then surpass the capacities of the well-trained human hand. Further, to what extent was there a need for personal computers in 1974? The technical capacity to produce personal computers existed in 1974, but few people knew that they needed a personal computer. Only after Steven Wozniak created the prototype of the original Apple I in March 1976, and after Hewlett Packard and Atari decided that they were not interested in producing the machine, and after Wozniak and Steven Jobs began producing the Apple I (first out of a bedroom in Jobs's parents' house and then out of their garage), was there much of a hint that many people might find such devices interesting. When Wozniak and Jobs tried to interest Commodore Business Machines in the more impressive Apple II in fall 1976 they got nowhere. The dimensions of the need started to become visible only when the Apple II machine took the computer industry by storm after its introduction in April 1977.[7] At the beginning of the twenty-first century hundreds of millions of people, if not billions, need personal computers. Before the thought, "I need a personal computer," could be articulated, people had to know of the possibility—and, in practical terms, they also needed to know whether it would be available at a price that made it reasonable for them to consider buying it. What was not practically conceivable at $10,000 per unit was conceivable at $2,000 per unit.

The point here is that there was no prior theory, no algorithm, that would have allowed an administrator or bureaucrat to conclude, "now people need personal computers and we had better start producing them." The need arose *a posteriori*, not *a priori*. If there had been a pre-existing theory that could predict the need for personal computers, then most likely IBM or some other large corporation already dominant in the computer industry would have brought out personal computers first. Instead, two nerds working on a shoestring made a bet that, unlike most launchings of new products, paid off for them and had a deep impact on the culture of the time.

There are thus *two* problems with Marx's rejection of the market. The first problem is that economic calculation is impossible without well-functioning markets. In the absence of prices it is impossible to calculate the cost of producing a given object. It is also impossible to figure out how badly people want the product. This is because in a socialist economy goods are *given* away. As a result, consumers do not need to make a calculated choice, related to price and hence in some rough way to production costs, between, say, different station wagons produced, respectively, by Ford, Subaru, Volkswagen, or Mercedes, or between a station wagon and other modes of transportation, such as traveling by bicycle or bus or rail. In fact, they *can't* make a cost-based choice, for the information required to make the calculation is not available.[8] Thus socialism (in Marx's meaning of the term, where socialism is *nonmarket* socialism) suffers from the *calculation defect* that von Mises pointed out.

Nonmarket socialism also suffers from a *discovery defect*. For the market is not simply a mechanism that, by making it possible to calculate costs, encourages the efficient satisfaction of needs. It is also, as the above line of reflection suggests, an instrument for discovering what people need and do not need. Consider the choices that consumers make as they decide (or not) to purchase an automobile (or a motorized scooter; or a bicycle). In making such choices consumers produce information that markets register. For example, years ago they made it known through the market that they preferred other automobiles to the Ford Edsel. Without the market, this information would have been either completely unavailable or available only in crude, cumbersome, or unreliable forms (e.g., through surveys or focus groups), and there would have been nothing enforcing its application. A socialist Ford Motor Company in a World Socialist Order might still be producing Edsels today.

The insight that markets are information-producing devices is already implicit in von Mises's "Economic Calculation in the Socialist Commonwealth." Von Mises's argument, after all, was that absence of markets entails an inability to calculate. In other words, socialism suffers from a knowledge deficit. But whereas von Mises focused on the economic weakness of socialism, two subsequent economists belonging, like von Mises, to the "Austrian" tradition, Friedrich von Hayek and Israel Kirzner, have focused on the epistemological advantage of markets. Their argument, stripped to its essentials, is that the market is a knowledge-producing mechanism.[9]

How is the market a knowledge-producing mechanism (a "discovery" mechanism)? Most obviously, the market helps people to discover what it is that they need. Consider again the decision of Jobs and Wozniak to begin producing personal computers. No theory predicted that there existed a vast untapped demand for personal computers. Nor would empirical survey research have shown such a demand either, because practically no one knew that devices of this sort could be produced at a relatively low price (or even produced at all). Consequently, hardly anyone had occasion to imagine such a device. Only when actual personal computers appeared on the horizon did people begin to see that they might indeed have a need for them. Jobs and Wozniak brought something that previously had been only a conceptual, theoretical reality, known to a small number of engineers, into the material world, where it could be seen in action.

The market is both a *display* device, showing people something that they probably would not see otherwise, and a *feedback* device, designed to register success and failure. Together, the display function and the feedback function produce knowledge. Of course, I assume the existence of a society in which both technical expertise and excess material resources exist: without these, there would be no novel application of technical expertise. I also assume a culture that allows some people to try out a new and unproved idea. (Such tryouts are tolerated by the private property system, which offers latitude for the floating of outlandish projects.) Some of these outlandish ideas turn out to be wildly successful, winning over even the most jaundiced and conservative of minds. The market mechanism allows such successes to be registered, displayed, and acted upon. Thus it discovers to us the fact that people see these products as satisfying some of their needs. The market has thus increased the store of information available within that society.

I am not arguing that the market, in and of itself, is a sufficient mechanism for the satisfying of human needs. On the contrary, there are many situations where the market does not conduce to need-satisfaction. For example, a drug has been invented that will keep a certain disease under control, but the disease is so rare that it is not profitable for any drug company to produce and market the drug. One can also observe the vulgarity, the commonness, and even the lethal character of many products that the ever expanding market brings to us. For example, one thinks of the rise of "fast food," which is increasing the rate of obesity in the United States, as well as the spread of cigarette consumption, a cause of lung cancer, to new customers in Asia and elsewhere. My claim is only that, under proper civic conditions, *in general* markets conduce to well-being—not that they do so universally. They enable us to calculate costs. They allow experimentation to take place. They enable us to see new products that we would not otherwise see, and thus they enable us to reflect on whether these new products will satisfy needs that we have, or might develop. Markets register failure as well as success, cutting the flow of resources into the making of products that do not sell well, and allowing resources to flow into other uses.

They do all this without the labor-intensive and epistemologically deprived central direction that is required if even the semblance of a working economy is to exist under socialism. At the end of *Socialism: Utopian and Scientific* Engels suggests that "anarchy in social production" will vanish under future socialism, to be replaced by "socialized production upon a predetermined plan" (*MEGA2* 1.27: 580/*MECW* 24: 325/*MER* 717). But Marx and Engels overestimated the capacity of scientific planning and underestimated the need for a certain amount of "anarchy" in production. Unless we can algorithmically predict when people are going to want/need personal computers, or digital watches, or ten-speed bikes, or hiking boots of a certain design, or castles in Spain, or pools where they can do lap swimming, or anything else, we *require* the market: at least, we require the market if Marx's *own* vision is to be actualized, namely, the vision of a society in which human nature and human needs develop over time and in which human beings are free.

The point that I am making goes beyond "the market" as we normally understand it. It is not only a matter of the various apparatuses for buying and selling that exist in capitalism. Rather, more generally, it is a matter of the existence (or not) of institutions within a society that both encourage experimentation and in one way or another discipline it. In order to satisfy Marx's own commitment to freedom as self-development, one needs to live in a society where experimentation is not only allowed but subtly encouraged. Marxian planning, *a priori* in character, is not adequate to Marx's own conception of human nature and its freedom. Human beings are creatures filled with possibilities that are to a considerable degree unpredictable. Indeed, an individual may not even know her possibilities until a situation has arisen in which the possibilities are drawn out and developed. Possibilities (and the needs attendant on those possibilities) are not even well known to persons themselves from moment to moment. How can they be known to economic planners?

Admittedly, certain gross features of human society are predictable over the short to medium term. Classic is the instance that much struck the positivist historian Henry Thomas Buckle, as well as other nineteenth-century proponents of a science of society, namely, the fact that on the basis of past data one can pretty much predict how many people will commit suicide month by month within a given population. But much of human life is contingent, and the contingencies seem crucial to the general tenor of the social order. Who predicted that Lenin would succeed in imposing his rule on Russia? Who predicted that Hitler, who in the late 1920s was considered a minor Bavarian politician and political journalist,[10] would construct the Third Reich? What theory of the early 1980s predicted that the Soviet Union would collapse in 1991, or any time near 1991? To my knowledge, the answer to all of these questions is in the negative. It is an answer that we ought to attend to.

Let us not fixate too much on the market as such. A better term than *market society* might be *experimental society*, for experiment is what is really at issue here. "Experiment" does not imply doing whatever one feels like: rather, it involves the testing of hypotheses (not just proposing them, and not just living them out either). A market, if it exists within a civil society where certain basic rules of morality and ethics are adhered to, serves as a device for what the philosopher Karl Popper called "conjecture" and "refutation."[11] That is, ideas are proposed, and then tested.

To be sure, one can imagine a very sophisticated computer program and communication network, which would be combined with mechanisms for the display of possibilities and for the registering of preferences, that would replace the market. Such a system would be set up with a view to overcoming what is perhaps the greatest defect of Marx's nonmarket, nonpolitical socialism, namely, the difficulty it has in gathering information as to what people want and need. Mikhail Gorbachev, the last president of the Soviet Union, no doubt had this defect in mind when he proclaimed *glasnost*, openness, one of the two basic principles (along with *perestroika* [restructuring]) of his attempt to make Communism work better.[12]

Let us imagine that a major Communist state still existed (none currently does, since the People's Republic of China hardly qualifies as a nonmarket system). The administrators of such a system would no doubt be looking, at this very moment, at the information-gathering possibilities of the World Wide Web, having discerned that the Web could be far more efficient at eliciting information than even the most obtrusive secret police. Can one imagine, then, a computerized information-gathering system that would render the market unnecessary? I think not. It is a question of the quality of the information gathered. One suspects that a system set up in such a way as to maximize the quality of the information would turn out to be *another form of the market*.

For how would one guarantee the authenticity and seriousness of individuals' stated preferences on the Web questionnaires that they would repeatedly be asked to answer? Indeed, how would the authenticity and seriousness of the questionnaires themselves be guaranteed? An answer suggests itself: require that people "put their money" (or rather, their labor-vouchers) "where their mouths are" (and require the same of the administrators formulating the questionnaires). But now the socialist World Wide Web would begin to look like—a market. The closer it would get to the kind of productive experimentation that markets, under conditions of adequate social and political freedom, encourage, the less the system would look like socialism. Instead of answering questions on the Web, people would begin to buy things on the Web. Thus, out of a socialism attempting to correct its information deficit, a market system would emerge, and a political state would then be required in the hope of correcting the market's defects.

Typically, twentieth-century advocates of central planning as a possible replacement for the market assumed a set of needs too static to be generally plausible. Consider one classic of the genre, *An Essay on Economic Growth and Planning* (1960), by the British Marxist economist Maurice Dobb. In Dobb's view, planners would be faced by the need to make choices and establish plans with regard to three general matters: choice of technique in the consumer goods sector; choice of technique in the investment sector; and distribution of investment between sectors.[13] There seems to be an implicit assumption on Dobb's part that consumer needs will be so obvious that bureaucrats sitting in offices will be able to readily see what they are. Dobb does not appear to recognize just how quickly planning would be rendered obsolete by the dynamism of needs. One suspects that, perhaps without quite recognizing it, Dobb was over-generalizing from the situation of Britain in the period 1930–60. It is true that if the society is one in which many people still find it difficult to obtain basic food, shelter, and clothing, planning might not yet have to hit the moving target of dynamic needs. Britain in those years, and most continental European countries as well, were still recovering from the waste of depression and the depredation of war. But Marxism is also about the production of *new* needs, and this side of Marxism is scanted by planning. Only the market, or some functional equivalent of the market, seems capable of accommodating the unpredictability of new needs. In short, there seems to be no way around the conclusion that we need to reject Marx's rejection of the market.

MARX'S REJECTION OF POLITICS

If we are to reject Marx's rejection of the market, we also need to reject his rejection of politics. These two rejections go together—although it must also be said that there are reasons for the existence of a vigorous political order that transcend specifically economic issues. To say that the market is required if needs, and the satisfaction of needs, are to develop over time in any kind of cumulative way is not to say that the market is self-regulating. On the contrary, there is no guarantee that markets will operate in a stable manner—no "invisible hand" guides the market's operations.[14] Nor does anything in the market mechanism *guarantee* that it will produce socially desirable outcomes in all instances. On these points Marx was right; he was only wrong in thinking that the proper conclusion is that exchange should be abolished and replaced by a planned economy.

Given that we have no reason to think that the market is guided by an invisible hand, it has to be regulated from somewhere outside itself. But where will that regulation come from? On what will it be grounded? One possible answer is: on an authoritative and absolutely objective science. But it is precisely the notion of an authoritative and absolutely objective science that is in question here. The regulating of a market economy certainly needs to be carried out on the basis of reliable data and with some help from scientific formalizations of the economic system and of its various components. But there would still remain an extremely large space for decisions that would not be determinable on the basis of scientifically authorized conclusions—to take one example, what kinds of schools to build and where to build them. Such decisions could only legitimately be made on the basis of political discussion and judgment. In other words, while the "irrationality" of the market does not justify its abolition, it does justify its enclosure within the wider frame of politics. One thus has to reject the Marxian rejection of politics, and at the same time one also has to reject the rejection, or at least the sharp minimization, of political intervention into the economic sphere by adherents of the view that markets alone will generate virtually all the desirable outcomes that one would wish to find within human society.

The theoretical perspective of the early twentieth-century economist John Maynard Keynes, author of the *General Theory of Employment, Interest, and Money* (1938), provides an important contrast case to Marx. As Keynes's biographer, Robert Skidelsky, notes in the first sentence of his short "Past Masters" book on Keynes, "Keynes's fundamental insight was that we do not know—cannot calculate—what the future will bring."[15] Quite so; and this is precisely the difference between Keynes and Marx. Given that we cannot calculate the future in any precise way, socialist planning is out, but in Keynes's view the application by governments of fiscal and monetary policy is not. On the contrary, Keynes, who had an almost Marxian sense of the volatility of unmanaged economies, held that capitalism *cannot survive* without such interventions.

As Skidelsky also points out, there is no magic formula that establishes precisely what interventions ought to be made. Skidelsky suggests that the Keynesian emphasis on fiscal policy (in which governments engage in supposedly contracyclical deficit spending) may have helped the major Western economies in the 1950s but that it made things worse from the mid-1960s onward. The emphasis that more conservative economists have put on monetary policy (in which governments manipulate the size of the money supply) has also had its failures. The upshot, Skidelsky suggests, is that economics has been more successful as an organized method of thinking about economic reality than as a guide to action (Skidelsky, 127–28). Skidelsky's point underscores the claim that I am making here, namely, that political deliberation is unavoidable—for Keynesian (and likewise post-Keynesian) economics is no more successful than Marx was in giving us a theory that will offer unequivocal guidance as to what we should do. Politics has to take up the slack; this fact cannot be gotten round.

It is not simply that we are not justified in holding that unregulated markets will be naturally stable. It is also that, even when efforts to alternately dampen and stimulate markets prove successful in keeping the economic system on an even keel, there is no guarantee whatever that this stabilized system will generate the human outcomes one would wish. For example, there are no grounds for thinking that the market alone will generate an adequate income for all persons, and hence no reason to believe that such things as education, health care, parks and recreation, cultural institutions, and the like will be adequately distributed within the society by virtue of the market's operation. Nor, indeed, are there grounds for thinking that the market will produce in adequate quantity and quality all goods that are needed within a society.

For example, in the United States a number of great libraries exist. These libraries serve as repositories for the documents of our cultural tradition (and for the documents of other cultural traditions as well). When contemplating such great scholarly libraries as, for example, Princeton University's Firestone Library or the New York Public Library, or any of a dozen others in the United States, one has to say that such institutions were created both *outside* and *inside* the market. The same applies to a number of great universities as well. For these cultural institutions were built up largely on the basis of wealth that had been produced by the workings of a market economy. But since such institutions rarely produce "customer revenue" commensurate with the costs of operating and maintaining them, their construction, building up, and maintenance require a detachment from market considerations—they require, in short, philanthropy and endowments.

The same applies to many other educational, cultural, and (in general) public-oriented institutions within society. Some of these institutions—for example, colleges and hospitals—are sometimes capable of functioning by market criteria, producing a positive balance at the end of a fiscal year. But the fact that such an institution may be able to function as a market unit does not mean that it is maximally desirable, or even that it is possible, that it should do so in its entirety. The college or hospital that relies on collected fees *alone* to run its operation is unlikely to reach the highest level of distinction in its practice. It is also likely to exclude from its clientele persons without the money to pay for its services. It is safe to say that every distinguished university and college in the United States has benefited from massive influxes of money from persons other than its "customers." The presence of this money—whether it comes from wealthy individuals, from foundations, from churches, or from governments—means that none of these institutions works in a purely market environment. The same is true, or ought to be true, of other institutions dispensing public benefits.

Thus the market needs to be supplemented and corrected in various ways. Obviously, some of the supplementation can come about as a result of private charitable efforts, for example, through the siphoning off of some of the richest takings into foundations having charitable, educational, artistic, and similar ends, and through the existence of churches and other voluntary associations that have social welfare as one of their aims. But there is no reason to believe that such corrections will be sufficient to make up for the inadequacy of the market, and so, in addition to public-spirited activities and benefactions on the part of citizens, one has to have the possibility of state action. In short, welfare-state mechanisms need to be in place within a society if benefit is to be maximized.[16] And this means that, contra Marx, there must be politics and there must be a political state.

Marx agreed as to the ends implied in the previous paragraph. Although he was not committed to equality as such, his commitment to maximum freedom meant a commitment to the maximum extension of freedom throughout the human community, and such an extension can be seen as tending toward, and indeed as requiring, a goodly measure of equality. Marx certainly would have agreed that the sorts of goods noted earlier, for example, health care and education, ought to be maximally available. There is an offshoot in Marx of the Kantian categorical imperative, with its insistence on the universal value of every human (moral) being, but it has to be stated that its presence is residual, and divested of any hint of ethical judgment or decision making.[17] It is the claim of this book that Marx was strongly driven toward the view that all decisions regarding what is to be done within the social order ought to be derivable from scientific investigation. As I read him, Marx held to the view that with an adequate theory of society and with adequate data one can derive all needed social solutions, as out of a computer. Properly speaking, no *decision* would have to be made—and certainly no *political* decision. We do not make a decision when we acknowledge that two plus two equals four. Rather, we accede to Truth. No state, no politics, is required for this to occur. But Marx was surely wrong in thinking that science will offer us all the social answers that we need (here Max Weber, with his insistence that science can inform us about means, but that we ourselves need to decide what ends we prefer, was closer to the truth than was Marx). Contra Marx, politics and a state are required for arriving at and implementing decisions concerning matters where science leaves us in the dark. Where should we put that road, if we want to build it at all? What kinds of schools do we want? Where should we put them? These, and a million other questions of the same sort, oblige us to make decisions as to how we want to live our social lives. The answers that we give to these questions cannot be arrived at scientifically, although what science tells us may well be relevant to our decision-making process.

There are also other grounds for rejecting Marx's rejection of politics. Note first of all that there is an underlying similarity between the views of the state that Marx articulated and the views articulated in his own time by classical liberals and by liberal-egalitarian radicals. All saw the state as, in one way or another, emerging out of the structural defects of society. Marx held that these structural defects can be overcome, and that when they are fully overcome the political state will disappear (human beings will still be faced by problems, but they won't be *political* problems). Classical liberals held (and still hold) that society itself can handle all tasks except for defense, police, justice, and the enforcement of contracts. Because of the persistence of these latter tasks a state will always be required, but it should be a minimal state.[18] Finally, liberal-egalitarians likewise see the state as making up for the defects of society, but the defects that they see are much more extensive and persistent than those that classical liberals find. Hence they end up regarding the state as much more persistently important than do either classical liberals (the state as minimally important) or Marx (the state as something that will disappear).[19]

Beyond the views on politics and the state of Marx, of classical liberals, and of liberal-egalitarians, there is another view, which we might legitimately call "republican," represented most strikingly by the political thought of Hannah Arendt. In the present book I cannot hope to address the complexities of Arendtian political theory. Suffice it to say that in *The Human Condition* and other of her works, Arendt, writing explicitly in response to Marx, advances a conception of politics in which political activity is seen as neither reducible to, nor an adjunct of, the domain of the social. Profoundly influenced by an image of the Greek polis, Arendt sees politics as the sphere within which human beings are most fully human. In this sphere they appear, and speak, on a public stage. It is a sphere where principle is appealed to, where deliberation takes place, where judgment is exercised, and where excellence is made manifest.[20]

There is no room for any such thing in Marx, as we saw especially in chapters 1 and 2. First, the early Marx's Feuerbachian reductionist tendencies worked against the notion of a distinct political sphere. Hence the Marxian "return of religion, the family, the state, etc.," to man's "*human*, i.e., *social* existence" does not countenance the existence of a politics independent of "social existence" (EPM, in *MEGA2* 1.2: 390/*MECW* 3: 297/*EW* 349). Second, Marx's scientism offers no room for deliberation and judgment of the sort that Arendt had in mind. The Marxian thought—articulated in 1844 and never abandoned—that "natural science will in time subsume the science of man just as the science of man will subsume natural science: there will be one science" holds out a promise that can never be fulfilled, except at the cost of eliminating what does not fit. Marx's idea of a *single* basis, for life and for science both, moves in the same direction (see *MEGA2* 1.2: 395–96/*MECW* 3: 303–4/*EW* 355).

Yet it seems clear that political deliberation and judgment are essential if there is to exist a well-ordered society. Looking at the world at the start of the twenty-first century, one finds that it is precisely the absence or defect of a political space that stands at the core of many of its social ills. In the absence or defect of such a space, troubling social problems are not addressed. In the worst cases, political order breaks down into a social and civil strife that destroys the lives of a large part of the population. One of Marx's complaints against the existing order is that it is exploitative (his two other complaints are that it is estranging and that it is irrational). It is surely correct that the economic order is not transparent to its participants and that, in the absence of transparency, exploitation, often in major degree, occurs. But a problem that may well be of equal importance is the absence or defect of a (democratic) political space, for without the existence of such a space it is hard to see how such exploitation can be successfully countered. Furthermore, when the political space breaks down completely (as in situations of war) the costs in human happiness and fulfillment turn out to be even higher than those imposed by economic exploitation. Nor do I think that it can be persuasively argued that these conflicts are *simply*—or even only *mainly*—the result of economic exploitation. There do seem to be political defects additional to economic ones.

As is well known, Marx envisaged workers coming together into a unified body in the scene of work. Consider the following statement from the "Fetishism of the Commodity" section of *Capital*, volume 1, chapter 1:

> Let us . . . imagine . . . an association of free men, working with the means of production held in common, and expending their many different forms of labor-power in full self-awareness as one single social labor force. (*MEGA2* 2.6: 109/*MECW* 35: 89/*CAP* 1: 171)

Consider also this statement from Marx's incisive, and even rather moving, chapter on "Cooperation":

> When the worker co-operates in a planned way with others, he strips off the fetters from his individuality, and develops the capabilities of his species. (*MEGA2* 2.6: 326/*MECW* 35: 334/*CAP* 1: 447)

But note that Marx's image in these passages is of workers engaged in a common scientific-technical task. In Marx's view, the task itself keeps the workers together, for he sees the workers as focused on a common aim, and science tells them how best to pursue this aim. These are workers who have internalized "the intellectual potentialities [*geistige Potenzen*] of the material process of production." Alas, under capitalism, which in the form of "large-scale industry" for the first time "makes science [*Wissenschaft*] a potentiality for production," this potentiality "is distinct from labor," for large-scale industry presses science "into the service of capital." (*MEGA2* 2.6: 355/*MECW* 35: 366/*CAP* 1: 482; chapter on "division of labor and manufacture") In the future socialist order, on the contrary, science will be with the workers—indeed, science will all but equate to their knowledge of productive processes. Under these circumstances the question "What is to be done?" will be answered by the work itself. Or, to recycle a phrase that Marx uses in the "machinery and large-scale industry" chapter of *Capital*, one does not need to disagree on the answer to the question "What is to be done?" for what is to be done will be "a technical necessity dictated by the very nature of the instrument of labor" (*MEGA2* 2.6: 376/*MECW* 35: 389/*CAP* 1: 508).

In these passages, and in Marx's thinking generally, there is no sense of the possibility that disputes might come up that could not be resolved by the dictates of science. What would the situation look like if the production in question were being carried out by Catholics and Protestants in a conflicted northern Ireland, Jews and Arabs in a conflicted Israel, or blacks and whites in a segregated southern United States? Marx's expectation, of course, is that such divisions would not exist under socialism. "Workers have no nation of their own," Marx and Engels declare in *The Communist Manifesto* (*MEW* 4: 479/*MECW* 6: 502/*LPW* 17/*MER* 488). It is a noble hope and he and Engels ought to be honored for it. But historical experience since 1848 contradicts the intended implication—namely, that politics is dispensable. There are real divisions and disagreements—"culture wars" in the broadest sense—that cooperative engagement in work does not overcome.

In short, contra Marx, it seems unlikely that work will unite us in the thorough way he hoped. On the contrary, "culture wars" always exist—*nothing* can overcome them, because different people, and groups of people, have different thoughts, feelings, and preferences as to how to live their lives. So the coming together of all does not occur. Instead we are left with disagreement. This means that there must be a way of dealing with disagreement. There must be some way of acknowledging it, recognizing its place, and then working around it. This is where the political plays its most important role. The politics in question needs to be not simply a mechanism for the compromising of differences and interests, but must also involve some sort of ethical commitment to the community in question. I see no room for such a thing in Marx's theory.

INTIMACY AND ANXIETY

Fourth, there is the sphere of intimacy, and the anxieties related to that sphere, which Marx also excludes from his social theory. In a terse critique of Marx, Habermas has objected that Marx reduces everything in human life to labor, thereby scanting two other aspects of life: social interaction, in which human beings relate to each other for purposes other than producing material objects, and the linguistic and aesthetic dimension of symbolic representation, which is likewise detached from the task of material production.[21] But Arendt is a sharper and more compelling foil to Marx than is Habermas. An important feature of the account of modernity that Arendt offers in *The Human Condition* is her distinction between the private realm, or sphere of intimacy; the social realm, which includes all of human beings' utility-oriented, economic interrelations with each other; and the public, or political, sphere. Her main focus of attention is on the relation between the social and the political, and her main complaint is that "society" has expanded at the expense of the public, political sphere. The private realm attracts her attention in lesser degree. Yet what she says about the private realm, and about the intimacy that is attached to it, is relevant to Marx's theory.

Arendt contends that our private lives are deeply influenced by the character of the public realm within which we find ourselves: "even the twilight which illuminates our private and intimate lives is ultimately derived from the much harsher light of the public realm." Arendt is suspicious of the effect that this harsh light has on intimacy: "For instance, love, in distinction from friendship, is killed, or rather extinguished, the moment it is displayed in public."[22] And so there is very much the sense, in her political theory, that a distance must be maintained between intimacy on the one hand and the social and political realms on the other. Although her concern as a political theorist is mainly with the destructive effect that, in her view, the inflating of "the social" [= the socio-*economic*] has had on the political sphere, the sphere of intimate life is nonetheless far from absent from her thinking about society and politics. It is not for nothing that her doctoral dissertation was on the theme of love (*caritas*) in the work of Saint Augustine, and in the 1930s she worked on a biographical study of the Berlin Jewess and *salonnière*, Rahel Varnhagen (1771–1833).[23] Arendt's concern in these works with charity, desire, memory, the neighbor, and the intimate and personal does not disappear from her political thought. On the contrary, these issues remain present in the background as important preoccupations informing her conception of politics.

With Marx the matter is very different. To be sure, Marx too was interested in the intimate sphere, especially in issues of family, love, and gender relations. These issues existed first of all as elements in Marx's personal life, in his relationships with his wife, Jenny von Westphalen, and with his children. Already in his November 1837 letter to his father, Marx wrote in adoring terms about Jenny. The couple married in June 1843 and in spite of many difficulties remained bonded for the rest of their lives.[24] But while personal concerns do come up in Marx's writings, they do so only around the edges of his social thought. In 1836 he wrote three notebooks of love poems for Jenny (*MEGA2* 1.1: 477–553/*MECW* 1: 517–27 [excerpts]). In the "Economic and Philosophical Manuscripts" there is a striking passage on gender relations, and another on the sadness of unrequited love.[25] In late 1845 he wrote a little-known text on suicide, focusing mainly on female suicide. It was ostensibly merely a translation of observations on suicide in early-nineteenth-century Paris drawn from the memoirs of a French police administrator, but it also includes Marx's own observations, and the existence of the text is indicative of Marx's interest in the subject.[26] It is also significant that in 1880–82 Marx made extensive notes on the writings of Lewis Henry Morgan and other anthropologists, in which he shows considerable interest in family and gender relations.[27]

But Marx's interest in the realm of intimacy exists outside his general theory. This is one of a number of instances of Marx acknowledging at a specific, empirical level realities that, at a theoretical level, he had no place for. Arendt's main complaint against Marx was that he reduced the political to the social. But intimacy, family, and the like undergo a similar reduction. This is such a persistent tendency in his thinking that it is hard to know where to begin. The reduction is most crucially asserted in his more generally oriented works, and then is assumed in his other, more focused works. In the "Economic and Philosophical Manuscripts" Marx contends, in a brilliant rewriting of Hegel, that labor is "the *essence*, the self-confirming essence, of man" (with Hegel making the mistake of seeing labor only as *mental* labor) (*MEGA2* 1.2: 405/*MECW* 3: 333/*EW* 386). The focus on labor persists in *The German Ideology*, where Marx and Engels tell us that what human beings are "coincides with their production, both with *what* they produce and with *how* they produce" (*MEW* 3: 21/*MECW* 5: 31–32/*MER* 150). When Marx and Engels go on to claim that the division of labor "was originally nothing but the division of labor in the sexual act," they are likewise conceptually subordinating the intimate to the socio-economic (*MEW* 3: 31/*MECW* 5: 44/*MER* 151). An allied line of thought is to be found in the *Grundrisse*, where Marx asserts that the human being is "not merely a gregarious [*geselliges*] animal, but an animal that can individuate itself [*sich vereinzeln*] *only* in the midst of society" (*MEGA2* 2.1.1: 22/*MECW* 28: 18/*GRUND* 84/*MER* 223 [my italics]). In all these passages, the sphere of intimacy is being passed over. Consider, for example, the last of this sequence of quotations. Admittedly, it is *partly* true that individuation takes place within society: what would the violinist Isaac Stern have become without the highly developed institution of the symphony orchestra? But much of our individuation is carried out in private or in intimate or anonymous groups, which is why young people tend to go into hiding, away from the snooping eyes of their parents, during their teenage years, and why love affairs are usually not carried out in public view. Can we really become who we are without being shielded from the too norm-imposing, too-revealing, too-embarrassing gaze of "society"? For most of us, I think, the answer is "no."

One question that deserves to be asked is why Marx reduced the intimate to the socio-economic. This book has explored at great length Marx's reduction of politics to economics, pointing out how in Marx's eyes politics cannot be rationally understood, whereas production can. But the reduction of the intimate to the social has not been discussed. Marx was familiar with the realm of intimate life, and valued it. Why identify it with production, then? Why not simply consign intimate life to the realm of the subjective, and leave matters at that? Part of the answer to this question is that there is, as we have seen, a "unitarist" impulse in Marx's thought that is quite overwhelming. Marx really *did* want to see the entirety of the human world in terms of a single theory (albeit a theory that, for specific, practical purposes, he was willing again and again to set aside).

But perhaps a more compelling point is that, fundamentally, Marx saw the domain of the intimate as unproblematic. Thus it could be safely ignored (whereas politics and the market, in contrast, had to be subjected to attack). In Marx's eyes there was a single, unquestionable model for true intimacy, namely, the relationship between man and woman. As Marx writes, in a stellar passage in the "Economic and Philosophical Manuscripts":

> The immediate, natural, necessary relation of human being to human being is the *relationship* of *man* to *woman*. . . . It is possible to judge from this relationship the entire level of development of humankind." (*MEGA2* 1.2: 388/*MECW* 1: 295–96/*EW* 347)

It is plausible to suggest that Marx's deep commitment to this single model must have contributed to his general nonattention to the intimate part of human life (it was something that could simply be *assumed*). In spite of his apparent lapse of fall 1850 (see note 24), Marx was enthusiastically committed to his own marital relationship. As for Engels, beginning sometime in the 1850s he lived in a common-law relationship with a working-class Irishwoman, Mary Burns, whom he had first met in Manchester in 1842 or shortly thereafter. Although he never married her, the relationship was functionally a marriage. After Mary died, unexpectedly and to Engels's great distress, in 1863, he entered into a similar relationship with Mary's sister, Lizzy Burns, whom he married in a legal ceremony in 1878, on the day before she died, satisfying one of her last requests.[28]

Marx appears to have universalized the model of monogamous heterosexuality early in his career, although he wrote very little about the matter. The closest we get to a general theoretical statement comes from Engels. After Marx died, Engels, inspired and guided by Marx's ethnological notebooks, quickly wrote *The Origin of the Family, Private Property, and State* (1884), and then produced an expanded edition in 1891. Here Engels portrays a succession of family forms (consanguine, punaluan, pairing) leading up to the present form, monogamous marriage. He declares that the "decisive victory" of the monogamous family is "one of the signs that civilization is beginning." He concedes that, to date, monogamous marriage remains "monogamy *for the woman only*, but not for the man," and he discusses at length the breaches of marital regularity that occur within the system of bourgeois marriage, where the husband's philandering is countered by the secret adulteries of the wife. Looking at present-day proletarian relationships, he envisages, for the future, the coming together of one man and one woman into a coupled relationship, which will be an *exclusive* relationship, since "sexual love is by its nature exclusive." Brought about without benefit of a marriage contract, these relationships will persist as long as affection persists, and will be dissolved "if affection definitely comes to an end or is supplanted by a new passionate love." He also suggests that equality for women "will tend infinitely more to make men really monogamous than to make women polyandrous." (*MEGA2* 1.29: 150–94, at 176, 177, 193/*MECW* 26: 139–90, at 170, 171, 188, 189 [chapter II, "The Family"])[29]

There is no reason to think that Marx would have diverged from Engels's elevating of the heterosexual monogamous relationship, based on mutual love and affection and dissoluble when love no longer continues, to the status of the highest form of intimate human relationship. For Marx's (and Engels's) commitment to monogamous heterosexuality is really only one aspect of a much larger Marxian commitment, namely, to the notion that there is a rationality embedded in the world. The rationality in question clearly includes, for Marx, an implicit moral-ethical dimension. In other words, for Marx the ethical character of the world is unproblematic—although I must hasten to add that Marx's scientism prevents him from ever saying "here I am making a moral-ethical point." In Marx's eyes, male-female love arises out of the natural constitution of the world. Love comes from nature itself. It is a position that Marx already adhered to in his articles of 1842 on the divorce bill, discussed in chapter 2, where he held that legislators, in dealing with marriage and divorce, need to treat the "objective world" in accordance with "its innate [*eingebornen*] laws" (*MEGA2* 1.1: 263/*MECW* 1: 275).

Moreover, the *eros* that Marx sees as naturally arising between man and woman seems continuous with *phileo*, the fellow-feeling and friendly concern that he sees as central to socialism—central, that is, to the socio-economic world once it has come to function in accordance with its fullest potentialities. There are various points in the Marx corpus where the conception of a socialist *phileo* comes through. Perhaps most striking is the passage in the EPM where Marx describes the "gatherings of French socialist workers" that he has observed in Paris. Among these workers

> smoking, eating and drinking, etc., are no longer means of creating links between people. Company, association, conversation, which in its turn has society as its goal, is enough for them. The brotherhood of man is not a hollow phrase, it is a reality, and the nobility of man shines forth upon us from their work-worn figures. (*MEGA2* 1.2: 425/*MECW* 3: 313/*EW* 365)

At the end of Marx's excerpts from James Mill's *Elements of Political Economy*, probably written shortly after the EPM, there is an amazing passage in which this sort of fellow-concern is placed squarely within the scene of production. Here he asserts that once people begin to produce "as human beings," they will mutually affirm each other in their production:

> In the individual expression of my own life I would have brought about the immediate expression of your life, and so in my individual activity I would have directly *confirmed* and *realized* my authentic nature, my *human, communal* nature.
>
> Our productions would be as many mirrors from which our natures would shine forth.
>
> This relation would be mutual: what applies to me would also apply to you. . . . (*MEGA2* 4.2: 465/*MECW* 3: 228/*EW* 277–78)

A GENERAL ASSESSMENT

Many people will find many aspects of Marx's vision of the future extremely attractive. The question is whether it is as realistic as it ought to be. One must say with sadness, after the historical experience of the twentieth century, that certain aspects of his vision of human life seem all too plain-vanilla and optimistic. It is clear that in many respects Marx is an adherent of Enlightenment optimism in its purest form, a kind of hyper-Enlightenment thinker (for no eighteenth-century *philosophe* was as confident about science and progress as he was—most, in fact, were rather dark in their view of history, humankind, and the future). There is no sense in Marx of the twisted reaches of the human psyche, no sense of neurosis, mental illness, clinical depression, anxiety, and so on, or of how such things might have an impact on human beings' lives in common, no sense, as in Arendt, that "the human heart . . . is a very dark place."[30]

There is also an assumption in Marx that the moral-ethical dimension of human life can look after itself. It is instructive to consider a line from one of the great monuments of twentieth-century Marxian art, Bertolt Brecht's *Three-Penny Opera*: "First comes grub, then comes morality [*Erst kommt das Fressen, dann kommt die Moral*]."[31] In his disabused cynicism Brecht shows himself to be a half-Marxist (although perhaps a complete Stalinist). First of all, this line, and the *Three-Penny Opera* as a whole, suggest that until the socio-economic needs of human beings have been looked after they cannot live moral lives. In contrast, Marx held that the workers can be moral long before the socialist revolution takes place: see his evocation of French socialist workers, above.[32] But second, the line also implies that once people's material needs are satisfied, they will live moral lives. Here, Brecht is surely conveying Marx's own view.

But is this view true? We have a good deal of justification for thinking that it is not. Recall that I am evoking, here, three spheres of human life, which we can think of as:

the sphere of intimacy	the socio-economic sphere	the political sphere

This is not Marx's conceptualization, for he expands the sphere of the socio-economic so that it ends up embracing everything in human life: "for socialist man the *whole of what is called world history* is nothing more than the creation of man through human labor" [EPM, *MEGA2* 1.2: 398/*MECW* 3: 305/*EW* 357). Accordingly, everything ends up being judged in socio-economic terms. When Marx, envisaging the future socialist society, writes of "the return of man from religion, the family, the state, etc., to his *human*, i.e. *social* existence," he is really referring to the expansion of the socio-economic sphere to embrace everything.

This includes morality. In the nobility of his view—and it is a noble view—Marx holds that in the future socialist society, in which human needs are satisfied or at least (since human needs are potentially infinite in their ambit) in which everyone knows that a great deal of effort is being devoted to ensuring that needs will be satisfied to the maximum degree possible throughout the society, then everyone will be moral. Marx has an expansive conception of human needs—need is a matter not only of material needs, but also of higher, spiritual needs beyond material need, such as the need for the best music and art. But it is also true that material need is the basis for the other needs, in Marx's view. And we know enough, now, to see that even in communities where no one starves and where everyone is reasonably well off, ethical behavior cannot be counted upon.

What I want to suggest here is that Marx underestimates the complexity and obscurity of the sphere of intimacy—the difficulty of obtaining satisfaction in that sphere, the challenges posed by the finitude and particularity of human life. In Marx's view, death "*appears as* [*erscheint als*] the harsh victory of the species over the particular individual, and seemingly contradicts their unity" (*MEGA2* 1.2: 392/*MECW* 3: 299/*EW* 351 [my emphasis]). But surely the issue is more difficult than that. Marx and Engels assert in *The German Ideology* that life is fundamentally a matter of labor and that what human beings are "coincides with their production." What this seems to suggest is that there are no *fundamental* problems on the intimate level. All we need is the social. Then, if human beings' social and material needs are satisfied, as they ultimately will be, there will be no fundamental problems left.

But such a view omits the difficulty and anxiety of intimate life and the harshness of the interplay between the intimate, the social, and the political. Here the history of Yugoslavia during the 1990s stands as an interesting and salutary warning. Yugoslavia was once *the* model Communist state, the state that, in declaring independence from both Stalinism and capitalism, seemed to have carved out a third way between Stalinist tyranny and rapacious capitalist greed. Under Tito, Yugoslavia apparently submerged the ethnic and religious differences within its population and embarked on the creation of a workers' state. Yet in the years after 1989 the basis of that state collapsed. It did so, I wish to suggest, because the anxieties of human beings at an intimate level came together with the desire of some Yugoslavs for political power. Gender, sexual, and other anxieties could be relieved by adherence to ethnic myths. Politicians seeking to obtain and hold onto power could propagate and rely on those myths in their political efforts. This sort of end run around the well-ordered and smoothly functioning sphere of the social and economic is something that Marx did not anticipate.

In short, one has to reject Marx's method; one has to reject his rejection of the market and of politics; and one has to reject his too-optimistic, too-uncomplicated view of human life.

But there are also things in Marx that ought not to be rejected. The great temptation is to reject Marx out of hand, given the crimes that were carried out in his name in the twentieth century. The temptation needs to be resisted, because elements of Marxian theory are true, and useful and even essential at the present time, which (at least as I write) is a time of capitalist economic triumph. Economic modernity has transformed the world—or, more accurately, it has transformed important aspects of the world (other aspects of the world—and here religion is the great instance—have proved resistant to what Marx thought was capitalism's universal tendency to dissolve away everything fixed and feudal).

First, some aspects of the materialist conception of history need to be retained. Admittedly, Marx's tendency to universalize historical materialism—his tendency to see *everything* in the human world as dependent on the movement of productive forces—must go. It is an arrogant claim, a quasitheological claim in fact. Absent a divine revelation of the course of history it can in no way find adequate support. But one does not need to follow Marx in his claim that human beings ultimately set for themselves *only* socioeconomic tasks (which they invariably solve) in order to be persuaded that, in its general outlines, historical materialism offers an extremely important approach to human society and history. Engels is right when he claims in *Socialism* that "the production of the means to support human life" is the fundamental basis of all social structure and of all history (*MEGA2* 1.27: 608/*MECW* 24: 306/*MER* 700). It is just not the *only* basis.

It might be imagined that Engels's observation is an obvious one, too obvious to require any emphasis at all. But I am struck by the extent to which, especially in America, I hear accounts of the world being offered that are blatant in their ignoring of material realities. In the United States *The Little Engine That Could* has long been the governing social myth, overshadowing all others, and wealth is known to sprout unbidden from the ground. The assumed fairness of the competition is seen as justifying the often grossly unequal outcomes that eventuate, to such a degree that use of the state's taxation power to slightly mitigate these outcomes is generally seen as an exercise in tyranny. Prevailing ideology takes an idealist stance, pointing to formerly disadvantaged persons who have managed to do well in spite of their disadvantages. And it is obviously true that certain habits of mind and action conduce to material success, while other habits conduce to failure. But it is a mistake to take this fact as demonstrating that, with sufficient will and determination, people can always bootstrap themselves upward.

In short, although one needs to reject any tendency to turn historical materialism into an all-explaining theory of history, historical materialism does make sense as a reminder and as a kind of heuristic test. In fact, it is more than a heuristic test: for, seen in the light of Marx's notion that needs are not static but instead develop, it is a standard of evaluation by which one can judge the adequacy of the way that people live. Is this a pleasant neighborhood? Is the air in this city polluted? Is there excessive noise? Are these freeways beautiful? Does it really make sense to commute twenty miles to work? And: how well can someone live on that wage? These are materialist questions, ones that focus on realities that, in the broader reaches of American politics, are often scanted in favor of other questions and concerns that have much less to do with how people actually live their lives. Especially in the context of a country where, with its longstanding ideology of rights, the significance of conditions is often underrated, the pared-down version of historical materialism that I am evoking here—we might better call it *social* materialism—is a useful corrective.

Second, Marx is surely right in emphasizing the dynamic character of economic modernity—and right, too, in fundamentally accepting this dynamism. In 1980 I did not know that I needed a personal computer; now I know that I do. Between these two dates lies a vast evolution, largely unpredicted by anyone in 1980. And for the most part it has been an improvement. Are the needs that economic modernity creates "false needs" that have been imposed upon us by capitalist advertising? It is true, of course, that the "new and improved" products that are put before us often aren't. It is also true that the relentless sellers' search to maximize the perceived "value added" of the products they are selling sometimes leads to the "dis-improving" of products—so that what originally was simple and well adapted to its intended use becomes overladen with conflicting uses. In general, however, the technology gets better. The deployment of the technology develops "the *open* book of the essential powers of man." It creates "an extended wealth of human needs" that amounts to an extension of the possibilities of human nature. Thus one can look toward a "fully developed" society that "produces man in all the richness of his being, the rich man who is *profoundly and abundantly endowed with all the senses*." (*MEGA2* 1.2: 394–95/*MECW* 3: 302/*EW* 354)

I find nothing basically wrong with this vision. It need only be remembered that this is not the whole of human life. Marx's vision leaves aside the difficulties of intimate life and the dangers of political life. People can be well endowed with material goods and yet, because of their own deep unhappiness and their failure to connect at an intimate level with other human beings, they can also be completely despicable, and dangerous, in their social behavior. And the political sphere, where man "shows himself," as Arendt puts it, can become a sphere where manipulation holds sway. Both spheres, quite beyond anyone's intention, can come to be pervaded by mistrust and even by terror. Marx does not acknowledge these facts in his theory. But I do not see that anyone has better described the specifically *economic* dynamic.

Third, Marx is useful in his pointing out of the costs of modern productive life. I am not thinking so much of Marx's theory of estrangement. For it seems to me that the theory of estrangement, although useful as a rough-and-ready critical tool, is excessively dependent on an assumption that is closely connected to Marx's rationalism, namely, the assumption that contradiction ought to resolve into unity. On this assumption, it is *ipso facto* troublesome that the worker does not feel at one with his work and that the product of the worker's labor is owned by another. But the assumption is remarkably weak. It is highly questionable to think that the ideal state of human nature is unity with itself. On the contrary, it can plausibly be argued that it is precisely in being estranged, and in maintaining estrangement, that human beings become the varied and interesting beings that they are. Marx's theory of estrangement does bring to the fore some of the dissatisfactions that human beings have with work, but it is overrated as a theoretical contribution.

The crucial issue is not whether work is estranging, failing to allow human beings to enjoy themselves and at the same time to develop their potentialities to the full. Realistically, most work most of the time will not live up to these standards. Crucial, rather, are the issues of exploitation and of control. As noted already, Marx condemns capitalism on three grounds: because it is estranging, because it is irrational, and because it is exploitative. The third objection is by far the most powerful. Admittedly, Marx's particular *theory* of exploitation—the theory of "surplus value," which he worked out for the first time in the 1850s—is less than fully persuasive. But Marx's *descriptions* of exploitation are powerful. One thinks especially of those large chunks of

Capital where Marx (often relying on reports written by factory inspectors, public health officials, and commissioners of inquiry into the exploitation of women and children) describes the horrendous working and living conditions that prevailed in many parts of the British industrial economy in his time. We owe these descriptions to Marx's astounding empirical attentiveness and sensitivity.

The question for Marx is where the way out is to be found. In revolution, first of all. But we can no longer be attracted to something so prone to failure. Marx's other answer, which he thought parallel to the first, was: in science. Here I think that Marx was right. In *Capital*, in the chapter on the division of labor and manufacturing, he suggests that when labor comes to be concentrated in workshops and factories, knowledge, judgment, and will are lost by the workers and come to be concentrated in capital. Thus "the intellectual potentialities of the material process of production" turn into a power that rules over the worker: science becomes "a potentiality for production that is distinct from labor" (*MEGA2* 2.6: 355/*MECW* 35: 366/*CAP* 1: 482). Here is perhaps the most frightening aspect of capitalism in Marx's eyes—it is not simply that the machinery of production is arrayed against the worker; it is that knowledge is arrayed against the worker as well. Marx's solution is the destruction of capitalism. That cannot be our solution, and so the problem to which Marx here points remains. That problem is: How are people to counteract the negative effects of the concentration of knowledge in the hands of persons and institutions already powerful by virtue of their places within the economic system?

Finally, I believe that Marx was right in his high valuation of freedom. To deal in detail with Marx's conception of freedom would require another book. Suffice it to say that he despised the servile and the uncritical. Contrariwise, he admired the "practical human energy" that he saw underlying the productive forces of society (December 28, 1846, letter to Annenkov, *MEGA2* 3.2: 71/*MECW* 38: 96/*MER* 137). How can one live, he seems to ask us, if one simply accepts the situation in which one finds oneself? One must criticize, and one must criticize again. Even his love poems to Jenny, he tells his father in 1837, are filled with "attacks on our times" (letter of November 10–11, 1837, *MEGA2* 3.1: 10/*MECW* 1: 11/*MER* 7). But freedom for Marx is not a matter of criticism only. It is a matter also of self-development and of connections with and sympathies to other human beings. Further, Marx contends for the maximal extension of freedom, and so freedom requires a high degree of equality within society, although equality as such is not, in Marx's eyes, a value. Freedom must have a material basis but it is far more than a material issue.

There are certainly things that Marx underestimates. Freedom for the axe murderer, the child molester, the thief, the liar? Freedom for the demagogic politician? Perhaps most insidious: freedom for the unhappy to spread their unhappiness to others? Of course not. But it is not that Marx denies freedom to such characters. Rather, Marx denies that such characters could possibly exist in the redeemed, socialist society of the future. And there he is surely wrong. But one can think of worse hopes, and of worse ways of being wrong. Rather than dismiss Marx—the dominant tendency now—we ought to hew to his hopes, and follow the example he gave us of the critical application of thinking to precisely such dominant tendencies. At the same time we need to discern where his analyses went wrong, and to consider how we might do better in the future.

17 August 2001

Appendix

A Topically Organized List of Marx's Journalistic Writings of 1842–43

This is a list of Marx's journalistic works of 1842–43; see the discussion in chapter 2, and in particular table 2.1: *Topics Addressed in Marx's Journalism of January 1842–March 1843,* which gives the percentage of space devoted to each topic. The percentages are based on a page count of the *MEGA2* printing of the articles. One purpose of this appendix is to provide the data supporting table 2.1. Another is to offer a more concrete sense of what Marx was writing about in 1842–43 than can be given in the text. Of course, to fully get the flavor of Marx's early journalism, one would need to read it (see *MEGA2* 1.1: 97–366; in English, the early journalism is to be found in *MECW* 1: 109–376). In some cases the editors of *MEGA2* have corrected the conclusions of previous editors concerning what was or was not written by Marx. One suspects that the *MEGA2* verdict is definitive; in any case, previous editions have been superseded for scholarly purposes. Note also that the topic divisions, below, are in some measure debatable. The English versions of the article titles have usually been taken over from *MECW*. Except where noted, all articles were published in the *Rheinische Zeitung*.

Censorship/freedom of the press. 13 items, 87 pp. total

"Comments on the Latest Prussian Censorship Instruction," *MEGA2* 1.1: 97–118/*MECW* 1: 109–31, written between January 15 and February 10, 1842, published in *Anekdota zur neuesten deutschen Philosophie und Publicistik*, 1 (February 1843). 22 pp.

"Proceedings of the Sixth Rhine Province Assembly. First Article. Debates on Freedom of the Press and Publication of the Proceedings of the Assembly of the Estates," *MEGA2* 1.1: 121–69/*MECW* 1: 132–81, written April 1842, published May 1842. 48.5 pp.

"The Leading Article in No. 179 of the *Kölnische Zeitung*" [criticizes a Catholic newspaper for supporting censorship by the government], *MEGA2* 1.1: 172–190/*MECW* 1: 184–202, written and published June–July 1842. 18 pp.

"Cabinet Order on the Daily Press" [the order, signed by Frederick William IV, made known the king's desire that newspapers be required to publish all factual corrections sent to them by the government], *MEGA2* 1.1: 264–65/*MECW* 1: 280–81, written and published November 1842. 1.5 pp.

"The Ban on the *Leipziger Allgemeine Zeitung* within the Prussian State" [regrets the banning from Prussia of the Leipzig (Saxony) paper], *MEGA2* 1.1: 291–93/*MECW* 1: 311–13, written and published December 1842. 2 pp.

"The *Kölnische Zeitung* and the Ban on the *Leipziger Allgemeine Zeitung*," *MEGA2* 1.1: 328–29/*MECW* 1: 313–14, written and published January 1843. 1 p.

"The Good and the Bad Press," *MEGA2* 1.1: 330/*MECW* 1: 314–15, written and published January 1843. 1 p.

"Reply to the Attack of a 'Moderate' Newspaper," *MEGA2* 1.1: 331–33/*MECW* 1: 315–18, written and published January 1843. 2.5 pp.

"Reply to the Denunciation of a 'Neighboring' Paper," *MEGA2* 1.1: 334–37/*MECW* 1: 318–21, written and published January 1843. 3 pp.

"Concerning the Polemic of the Augsburg *Allgemeine Zeitung*" [spat with a rival newspaper], *MEGA2* 1.1: 294/*MECW* 1: 359, written and published January 1843. 0.5 p.

"Reply to an Afterword of the Augsburg *Allgemeine Zeitung*: Editorial Note," *MEGA2* 1.1: 338–39/*MECW* 1: 359–60, written and published January 1843. 1 p.

"The Denunciation of the *Kölnische Zeitung* and the Polemic of the *Rhein- und Mosel-Zeitung*," *MEGA2* 1.1: 340–46/*MECW* 1: 322–28, written and published January 1843. 6.5 pp.

"The *Rhein- und Mosel-Zeitung*," *MEGA2* 1.1: 347–48/*MECW* 1: 328–30, written and published January 1843. 1.5 pp.

Assemblies/oppositional political activities. 4 items, 21 pp. total

"In Connection with the Article 'Failures of the Liberal Opposition in Hanover': Editorial Note" [comments briefly on conflicts in Hanover over the powers of the assembly there], *MEGA2* 1.1: 249–50 *MECW* 1: 264–65, written and published November 1842. 1 p.

"The Supplement to Nos. 335 and 336 of the Augsburg *Allgemeine Zeitung* on the Estates-Committees in Prussia," *MEGA2* 1.1: 272–85/*MECW* 1:

292–306 [comments on a proposal for a general Prussian assembly based on the old Estates system], written and published December 1842. 14 pp.

"The Local Election of Deputies to the Provincial Assembly," *MEGA2* 1.1: 355–59/*MECW* 1: 366–69, written and published March 1843. 4 pp.

"Stylistic Exercises of the *Rhein- und Mosel-Zeitung*" [on the local elections of deputies to the Rhineland provincial assembly], *MEGA2* 1.1: 363–65/*MECW* 1: 366–69, written and published March 1843. 2 pp.

State affairs/administration. 3 items, 10 pp. total

"The Question of Centralization in Itself and with Regard to the Supplement to No. 137 of the *Rheinische Zeitung*, Tuesday, May 17, 1842" [attacks an essay by Moses Hess on the question of centralization vs. provincial autonomy], *MEGA2* 1.1: 170–71/*MECW* 1: 182–83, written May 1842, unfinished, not published. 1.5 pp.

"Communal Reform and the *Kölnische Zeitung*" [attacks the government's plan to revise regional government in the Rhine Province, eliminating reforms instituted in the Revolutionary and Napoleonic periods and bringing the Rhine Province more into line with administration in Prussia itself], *MEGA2* 1.1: 251–59/*MECW* 1: 266–73, written and published November 1842. 6.5 pp.

"A Correspondent of the *Kölnische Zeitung* vs. the *Rheinische Zeitung*" [on "communal reform," again], *MEGA2* 1.1: 266–67/*MECW* 1: 277–79, written and published November 1842. 2 pp.

Divorce law. 2 items, 5 pp. total

"The Divorce Bill: Editorial Note: Criticism of a Criticism" [on a proposed reform of divorce law], *MEGA2* 1.1: 260–63/*MECW* 1: 274–76, written and published November 1842. 2 pp.

"The Divorce Bill," *MEGA2* 1.1: 287–90/*MECW* 1: 307–10, written and published December 1842. 3 pp.

Political theory. 2 items, 12 pp. total

"The Philosophical Manifesto of the Historical School of Law" [attacks the work of the jurist Gustav Hugo, an early exponent of "the historical school of law"], *MEGA2* 1.1: 191–98/*MECW* 1: 203–10, written and published August 1842, with the exception of one section deleted by the censor. 7.5 pp.

"Marginal Notes to the Accusations of the Ministerial Rescript" [defends the *Rheinische Zeitung* from the charge of attacking "the basis of the state constitution"], *MEGA2* 1.1: 349–53/*MECW* 1: 361–65, written February 1843, unpublished. 4.5 pp.

Newspaper polemics. 1 item, 3.5 pp. total

"The Polemical Tactics of the Augsburg Newspaper" [a rather pointless polemic with the Augsburg *Allgemeine Zeitung*], *MEGA2* 1.1: 268–71/ *MECW* 1: 288–91, written and published November 1842. 3.5 pp.

Property rights/economic policy/relations of production. 5 items, 72 pp. total

"Communism and the Augsburg *Allgemeine Zeitung*" [Marx's first discussion of "the social question"], *MEGA2* 1.1: 237–40/*MECW* 1: 215–21, written and published October 1842. 3.5 pp.

"Concerning the Polemic over Communism: Editorial Note" [the "social question" again, largely submerged in a polemic between newspapers], *MEGA2* 1.1: 241–42/*MECW* 1: 222–23, written and published October 1842. 1 p.

"Proceedings of the Sixth Rhine Province Assembly, Third Article: Debates on the Wood-Theft Law" [on the conflict that arose between the traditional right of peasants to glean fallen wood in forests, and the growing tendency to eliminate such communal property rights in favor of individual private property; the article also serves as a commentary on the legislative qualities of the Rhine Province Assembly, and thus could be classified as concerned with politics rather than with property rights], *MEGA2* 1.1: 199–236/*MECW* 1: 224–63, written and published October and November 1842. 37 pp.

"Vindication of the Correspondent from the Mosel," parts A and B [Marx defends the claims of a *Rheinische Zeitung* correspondent concerning economic distress in the Mosel vine-growing region], *MEGA2* 1.1: 296–323/*MECW* 1: 332–58, written and published January 1843. 27 pp.

"Vindication of the Correspondent from the Mosel," fragment of part C, "Cankers of the Moselle Region," *MEGA2* 1.1: 324–27 (written January 1843, published in Karl Heinzen, *Die preussische Büreaukratie* [Darmstadt, 1845], without mentioning Marx as author). 3.5 pp.

Theology. 2 items, 5.5 pp. total

"Yet another Word on *Bruno Bauer und die Akademische Lehrfreiheit* by Dr. O. F. Gruppe, Berlin, 1842" [attacks a critic of Marx's teacher, Bruno Bauer], *MEGA2* 1.1: 245–48/*MECW* 1: 211–14, probably written end of October/beginning of November 1842, published in the journal *Deutsche Jahrbücher für Wissenschaft und Kunst*, November 1842. 3.5 pp.

"The *Rhein- und Mosel-Zeitung* As Grand Inquisitor" [on the theological views of the recently deceased poet Friedrich von Sallet, which were close to those of David Friedrich Strauss, Ludwig Feuerbach, and Bruno Bauer], *MEGA2* 1.1: 360–62/*MECW* 1: 370–72, written and published March 1843. 2 pp.

Brief announcements [not included in the page count]

"On Adolph Stahr: Editorial Note," *MEGA2* 1.1: 286 [correction of an editorial error], written and published December 1942.

"Announcement of the 'Justification of the Correspondent from the Mosel'" [announces that a defense of the Mosel correspondent will appear the next week], *MEGA2* 1.1: 295/*MECW* 1: 331, written and published January 1843.

"Declaration" [Marx announces his resignation as editor of the *Rheinische Zeitung*], *MEGA2* 1.1: 366/*MECW* 1: 376, written March 17, 1843, published March 18, 1843.

Total number of pages: 216

Notes

PREFACE

1. Friedrich Nietzsche, *Twilight of the Idols*, "Morality As Anti-Nature," §3, in Nietzsche, *The Portable Nietzsche*, trans. Walter Kaufmann (New York: Viking Press, 1968) (translation altered).

2. Michel Foucault, *The Order of Things: An Archaeology of the Human Sciences*, trans. anon. (New York: Random House, 1970), 262.

3. For two accounts, the first sharply negative, the second critically sympathetic, see Leszek Kolakowski, *Main Currents of Marxism: Its Origins, Growth and Dissolution* (3 vols.; Oxford: Oxford University Press, 1978), vol. 2, *The Golden Age*, and vol. 3, *The Breakdown*; and Martin Jay, *Marxism and Totality: The Adventures of a Concept from Lukács to Habermas* (Berkeley and Los Angeles: University of California Press, 1984).

4. See Werner Blumenberg, *Portrait of Marx: An Illustrated Biography*, trans. Douglas Scott (New York: Herder & Herder, 1962) for a short and reliable study with a lot of pictures. Readers who are looking for an intellectual biography of a *gründlich* sort should consult Jerrold E. Seigel, *Marx's Fate: The Shape of a Life* (University Park: Pennsylvania State University Press, 1993 [orig. ed. 1978]), although Francis Wheen's lively biography, *Karl Marx* (London: Fourth Estate, 1999), is more vivid and readable. David McLellan, *Karl Marx: His Life and Thought* (New York: Harper & Row, 1973)—not to be confused with the many other books on Marx that McLellan has written—juxtaposes in an illuminating way explications of Marx's writings with accounts of what was going on in his life.

5. No magisterial account of Marx's thought has ever been written. Magisteriality was impossible when Marx was the foremost of *engaged* philosophers and seems largely pointless now. Still, for something close to magisteriality, one can consult Leszek Kolakowski, *Main Currents of Marxism*, vol. 1: *The Founders*, which offers a negatively inflected survey of the work of Marx (and of Engels); and Andrzej Walicki, *Marxism and the Leap to the Kingdom of Freedom: The Rise and Fall of the Communist Utopia* (Stanford: Stanford University Press, 1995), which offers a wide-ranging assessment after the collapse. For a modestly proportioned, rather sympathetic synthesis, somewhat outdated but still very

helpful after many years, see Shlomo Avineri, *The Social and Political Thought of Karl Marx* (Cambridge: Cambridge University Press, 1968).

6. Alvin W. Gouldner, *The Two Marxisms* (New York: Oxford University Press, 1980), 32.

7. For a brief, balanced account, not devoid of criticism, of the most important current school of contextualist intellectual history, see Knud Haakonssen, *Natural Law and Moral Philosophy: From Grotius to the Scottish Enlightenment* (New York: Cambridge University Press, 1996), 8–14.

8. Indeed, de Certeau repeatedly insisted that such a break is constitutive of modern historiography: see Michel de Certeau, *The Writing of History*, trans. Tom Conley (New York: Columbia University Press, 1988), xxv–xxvi, 46–47, 85, 99–102, 218–26, and passim.

9. On the publishing history of Marx's works, see Hal Draper, *The Marx-Engels Cyclopedia* (3 vols.; New York: Schocken, 1985), vol. 2: *The Marx-Engels Register: A Complete Bibliography of Marx and Engels' Individual Writings*; the publications of 1927–41 (and the 1953 East German edition of the *Grundrisse*) are mainly discussed on pp. 47, 48, and 203–4. One of the early students of the *Grundrisse*, Roman Rosdolsky, claims, probably correctly, that "only three or four copies" of the Moscow edition were available in the West: the East German edition was a photomechanical reproduction, in one volume, of the two-volume Moscow edition. Roman Rosdolsky, *The Making of Marx's "Capital,"* trans. Peter Burgess (London: Pluto Press, 1977; orig. German ed., 1968), xi.

10. Among other early works introducing the "Economic and Philosophical Manuscripts" (EPM), see Galvano della Volpe, "The Posthumously-published Philosophical Works of 1843 and 1844 (The Materialist Critique of the *A Priori*)" (1955), in della Volpe, *Rousseau and Marx and Other Writings*, trans. John Fraser (Atlantic Highlands, N.J.: Humanities Press, 1979), 161–73. Many of the essays in Iring Fetscher et al., *Marxismusstudien* (Tübingen: J. C. B. Mohr [Paul Siebeck], 1954–68) focus on the early Marx; a few attend in particular to the EPM. In the 1950s and early 1960s Yugoslav philosophers made a particularly important contribution to working out the early Marx/late Marx relation: see, for example, the essays, written in the early 1960s, in Gajo Petrović, *Marx in the Mid-Twentieth Century: A Yugoslav Philosopher Considers Karl Marx's Writings* (Garden City, N.Y.: Doubleday Anchor, 1967). The EPM first became widely known in the United States under the guise of a book by the psychoanalyst Erich Fromm: Erich Fromm, *Marx's Concept of Man*, with a translation from Marx's *Economic and Philosophical Manuscripts* by T. B. Bottomore (New York: Frederick Ungar, 1961). Remarkably, the publisher seems to have thought that in the America of 1961 the book would do better if Fromm, rather than Marx, were billed as its author. Published in the same year, Robert C. Tucker's *Philosophy and Myth in Karl Marx* (Cambridge: Cambridge University Press, 1961) also dealt extensively with the EPM and was noticed by academics. An edition of Milligan's translation of the EPM appeared three years later: Karl Marx, *Economic and Philosophic Manuscripts of 1844*, trans. Martin Milligan, ed. and with an introduction by Dirk J. Struik (New York: International Publishers, 1964). An excellent collection focused on Marx's early writings is *Marx's Socialism*, ed. Shlomo Avineri (New York: Lieber-Atherton, 1973): its various essays, originally published between 1959 and 1968, convey something of the excitement that the uncovering of the early Marx generated at the time. The same is true of the Petrović volume: in Yugoslavia in the 1950s and 1960s there was a concern among intellectuals with carving out a "third way" between the USSR and the USA, and the recovery of a humanistic Marx was part of that effort.

11. A useful point of entry to the literature on a multitude of topics in Marx's work is provided by *A Dictionary of Marxist Thought*, ed. Tom Bottomore, 2d, rev. ed. (Cambridge: Harvard University Press, 1991). David McLellan's modestly proportioned *The Thought of Karl Marx: An Introduction*, 3d ed. (London: Pan Books, 1995) gives both a chronological commentary on Marx and a thematic commentary (on such themes as alienation, historical materialism, ideology, class, and the party), along with very brief excerpts from Marx's (and Engels's) own writings.

12. Readers interested in *Capital* might well explore Moishe Postone's forcefully argued *Time, Labor, and Social Domination: A Reinterpretation of Marx's Critical Theory* (New York: Cambridge University Press, 1996). An older explication of *Capital*, still useful as a starting point, is Paul M. Sweezy, *The Theory of Capitalist Development: Principles of Marxian Political Economy* (New York: Oxford University Press, 1942). Of course, our view of Marx's analysis of capitalism may well change significantly, once all the later economic manuscripts currently appearing in *Abteilung* II of the New *MEGA* have been published and absorbed.

Only after finishing the present book did I become aware of the trilogy of books on Marx's later economics by the Argentinian scholar Enrique Dussel, which is the first work to rest on "a comprehensive reading from start to finish of all Marx's economic manuscripts" (Fred Moseley, "Introduction to 'The Four Drafts of *Capital*: Toward a New Interpretation of the Dialectical Thought of Marx,' by Enrique Dussel," *Rethinking Marxism* 13: 1 [Spring 2001]: 1–9, at 2). See Enrique Dussel, *La producción teórica de Marx: un comentario a los "Grundrisse"; Hacia un Marx descondido: un comentario de los Manuscritos del 1861–63*; and *Ultimo Marx (1863–1882) y la liberación latinoamericana: un comentario a la tercera y a la cuarta redacción de "El Capital"* (Mexico City: Siglo XXI, 1985, 1988, 1990). The second of these volumes has been translated into English: Dussel, *Towards an Unknown Marx: A Commentary on the Manuscripts of 1861–63* (New York: Routledge, 2001). For an overview of Dussel's interpretation of Marx, see Dussel, "The Four Drafts of *Capital*: Toward a New Interpretation of the Dialectical Thought of Marx," *Rethinking Marxism* 13: 1 (Spring 2001): 10–26.

13. I thus emulate my approach in an earlier book, *Prophets of Extremity: Nietzsche, Heidegger, Foucault, Derrida* (Berkeley and Los Angeles: University of California Press, 1985). In *Prophets* I distinguished between Nietzsche's "naturalism" and his "aestheticism" and focused on the latter, pursuing it as a theme through the writings of Nietzsche's successors as well.

CHAPTER 1

1. I make this claim while taking full account of Marx's *attempt* to leave philosophy; see Daniel Brudney, *Marx's Attempt to Leave Philosophy* (Cambridge: Harvard University Press, 1998). As we shall see in chapters 3 and 4, the Marx of circa 1844–45 did attempt to leave the German philosophical tradition, in which he had been a deeply committed participant, and in the "Economic and Philosophical Manuscripts" (1844) and *The German Ideology* (1845–46) there are appeals to the empirical and to the everyday that are at odds with important aspects of Hegelianism in particular. However, my contention is that the underlying "rationalism" of the Hegelian tradition nonetheless remained with Marx always;

it certainly continues to be visible in the putatively scientific (and hence supposedly not philosophical) historical materialism that he articulated in 1845–46. See also Harold Mah, *The End of Philosophy, the Origin of "Ideology": Karl Marx and the Crisis of the Young Hegelians* (Berkeley and Los Angeles: University of California Press, 1987), who likewise works the "leaving philosophy" theme. For a brief statement as to how Brudney and Mah differ from each other, see Brudney, *Marx's Attempt*, 367–68.

2. This sense is the preeminent one among philosophers: see Bernard Williams, "Rationalism," in *Encyclopedia of Philosophy*, ed. Paul Edwards (8 vols.; New York: Macmillan, 1967), 7: 69–75, and Alan Lacey, "Rationalism," in *Oxford Companion to Philosophy*, ed. Ted Honderich (Oxford: Oxford University Press, 1995), 741–44.

3. Jean-Jacques Rousseau embodies the rationalism/feeling opposition in the contradictory parts of his project—the "rationalist" Rousseau hewing to reason and duty, the "sentimental" Rousseau to natural inclination. Ernst Cassirer sketched out this opposition in several works: see Cassirer, *Rousseau, Kant, Goethe: Two Essays*, trans. James Gutmann, Paul Oskar Kristeller, and John Herman Randall Jr. (Princeton: Princeton University Press, 1947), 11–16, 57–59; and Cassirer, *The Question of Jean-Jacques Rousseau*, trans. and ed. Peter Gay (Bloomington: Indiana University Press, 1967), 39 and passim. For one reading of the "rationalist" Rousseau, see Robert Derathé, *Le Rationalisme de Jean-Jacques Rousseau* (Paris: Presses universitaires de France, 1948).

4. For a classic use of "rationalism" in this sense, see W. E. H. Lecky, *History of the Rise and Influence of the Spirit of Rationalism in Europe* (New York: Braziller, 1955; orig. 1865).

5. For one account of historism in this sense, see Friedrich Meinecke, *Historism: The Rise of a New Historical Outlook*, trans. J. E. Anderson, with a foreword by Sir Isaiah Berlin (London: Routledge and Kegan Paul, 1972; orig. German ed., 1936); at a number of points Meinecke opposes "historism" to "reason" and to "rationalism" (see, e.g., 4, 105).

In my list of meanings of the term, I leave aside the sociologist Max Weber's well-known distinction between instrumental rationality (*Zweckrationalität*) and value rationality (*Wertrationalität*). The Weberian actor imposes his own values on the world (*Wertrationalität*), calculating which means will best cause those values to be realized (*Zweckrationalität*). Relatedly, Weber sees a process of "rationalization" at work in the human world, since means are ever more efficiently being fitted to ends. As Julien Freund points out, Weber's "rationalization" is not to be confused with "the notion of the rationality of history." Most post-Weberian evocations of "rationality"—at any rate, those within social science—have a similar lack of relation to any notion of an *embedded* rationality: on "embedded rationality," see below. There is a massive literature on Weber, but see, briefly, Freund, *The Sociology of Max Weber*, trans. Mary Ilford (New York: Pantheon Books, Random House, 1968), 17–24, quotation at 18, and, for the broader context in Weber's thought, Reinhard Bendix's still useful *Max Weber: An Intellectual Portrait*, with an introduction to the new edition by Guenther Roth (Berkeley and Los Angeles: University of California Press, 1977).

6. As Richard Rorty and Hans Aarsleff have pointed out in very different ways: see Rorty, *Philosophy and the Mirror of Nature* (Princeton: Princeton University Press, 1979), especially chapter 1, "The Invention of the Mind," 17–69; and Aarsleff, *From Locke to Saussure: Essays on the Study of Language and Intellectual History* (Minneapolis: University of Minnesota Press, 1982), 9, 11, 283–84, and passim. Famously, at the beginning of the "Economic and Philosophical Manuscripts" Marx claims to have arrived at his conclusions "through an entirely empirical analysis based on an exhaustive critical study of political economy" (*MEGA2* 1.2: 325/*MECW* 3: 231/*EW* 281).

7. In his "Comments on the Latest Prussian Censorship Instruction" (written January–February 1842; published February 1843), Marx refers to the *Rationalismus* of the Prussian censorship decree of 1819, which (to quote Marx quoting the decree) opposed "fanatical transference of religious articles of faith into politics and the *confusion of ideas* resulting therefrom," and thus, in Marx's view, was superior to the censorship instruction issued by the religiously inclined government of Friedrich Wilhelm IV in December 1841 (*MEGA2* 1.1: 105–6/*MECW* 1: 117–18).

8. For a brief survey of Marx's and Engels's treatments of religion, see V. G. Kiernan, "Religion," in *A Dictionary of Marxist Thought*, ed. Tom Bottomore, 2d, rev. ed. (Cambridge: Harvard University Press, 1991), 465–68, at 465–66. David McLellan discusses Marx's and Engels's views on religion at greater length, in his *Marxism and Religion: A Description and Assessment of the Marxist Critique of Christianity* (New York: Harper & Row, 1987), 7–57.

9. The most pellucid statement of the "argument from design" was offered by William Paley in his *Natural Theology*, first published in 1802 and reprinted many times: see William Paley, *Natural Theology*, or, *Evidences of the Existence and Attributes of the Deity Collected from the Appearances of Nature* (Philadelphia, 1814). For Kant's demolition of the argument, see Immanuel Kant, *Critique of Judgment*, trans. Werner S. Pluhar, with a foreword by Mary J. Gregor (Indianapolis: Hackett, 1987), §85, "On Physicotheology," 324–30 (436–32 in the *Akademie* pagination).

10. For a brief account of the tensions in *The Origin of Species* and in Darwin, see David Kohn, "Darwin's Ambiguity: The Secularization of Biological Meaning," *British Journal for the History of Science* 22 (1989): 215–39. On the misinterpretation of Darwin's theory in a rationalizing, progressivist, developmental direction, see Peter J. Bowler, *The Non-Darwinian Revolution: Reinterpreting a Historical Myth* (Baltimore: Johns Hopkins University Press, 1988), especially chapter 1, "The Myth of the Darwinian Revolution," and chapter 3, "The Impact of the *Origin*," 1–19, 47–71.

11. Louis Althusser, "From *Capital* to Marx's Philosophy," in Louis Althusser and Étienne Balibar, *Reading Capital*, trans. Ben Brewster (London: Verso, 1997), 92. To be sure, Althusser somewhat distances himself from this description, and emphasizes instead the affinities between Spinoza and Marx in *contrast* to Hegel (see Althusser, "From *Capital*. . . ," 40, and "The Errors of Classical Economics: Outline of a Concept of Historical Time," in *Reading Capital*, 102–3). But this is no denial of the affinity to which I am pointing here, namely, Spinoza's and Hegel's common commitment to an *immanent* rationality—that is, to a rationality that is *in* the world. Hegel took issue with Spinoza on various points, but G. H. R. Parkinson has argued that Hegel's criticism of Spinoza was mistaken, in part because he too quickly assimilated Spinoza to an "oriental intuition" of universal substance, and because his reading was distorted by his disagreement with Schelling, whose nature philosophy Hegel projected onto Spinoza (G. H. R. Parkinson, "Hegel, Pantheism, and Spinoza," *Journal of the History of Ideas* 38 [1977]: 449–59). It should be noted that Hegel engaged with Spinoza as early as 1790, in the wake of a raging conflict among German intellectuals concerning the nature and implications of Spinoza's philosophy.

12. Again, I am not claiming that Spinoza directly influenced Marx (it would be reassuring to tell a continuous narrative of the sort "*first* Marx read Spinoza, then . . . ," but I cannot; it is not supported by the evidence). Note, however, that Marx's mentor Bruno Bauer, writing anonymously in the guise of an offended religious believer, lays great emphasis on Spinoza in a work, published in 1841, that Marx helped with: *The Trumpet of the Last Judgement against Hegel the Atheist and Antichrist: An Ultimatum*, trans. Lawrence

Stepelevich (Lewiston, N.Y.: E. Mellen, 1989), 118–19. The pseudo-pietistic author of *Trumpet* cites Hegel's claims that "all philosophy is pantheistic" and that "Spinoza is the high point of recent philosophy: either Spinozism or no philosophy" (see G. W. F. Hegel, *Lectures on the History of Philosophy*, trans. E. S. Haldane and Frances H. Simson [3 vols.; London: Routledge and Kegan Paul, 1955 (1892)], 3: 244, 283). Warren Breckman argues, persuasively, that pantheism played a significant role in progressive German thought in the 1830s, and that, in particular, Heinrich Heine and Moses Hess were inspired by Spinoza (Breckman, *Marx, the Young Hegelians, and the Origins of Radical Social Theory: Dethroning the Self* [New York: Cambridge University Press, 1999], chapter 5, "Pantheism, Social Question, and the Third Age," 177–220). Brief selections from *Trumpet* are available in *The Young Hegelians*, ed. Lawrence S. Stepelevich (Cambridge: Cambridge University Press, 1983), 177–86. For Marx's assisting of Bauer with *Trumpet*, see DRAP 1: 10.

13. On the crucial role that Hegel attributed to Spinoza in the history of thought, see Quentin Lauer, "Hegel As Historian of Philosophy," in *Hegel and the History of Philosophy: Proceedings of the 1972 Hegel Society of America Conference*, ed. Joseph J. O'Malley, K. W. Algozin, and Frederick G. Weiss (The Hague: Martinus Nijhoff, 1974), 21–46, at 34. Hegel's views on Spinoza are actually more complex than is relevant for us to consider here: see especially the densely dialectical "Remark" comparing Spinoza and Leibniz in Hegel, *Science of Logic* (originally published 1812–16), trans. A. V. Miller, foreword by J. N. Findlay (London: George Allen & Unwin, 1969), book two, section three, chapter 1, pp. 536–40. It is interesting that in his fifth "Notebook on Epicurean Philosophy" Marx ranks Spinoza, along with Aristotle and Hegel, as standing higher than Plato, on the grounds that "the inspiration of Plato culminates in [religious] ecstasy," while the inspiration of the other philosophers "burns on as the pure ideal flame of science," in consequence serving as "the animating spirit of world-historical developments" (*MEGA2* 4.1: 104/*MECW* 1: 496). According to the *MEGA2* editors the fifth Notebook likely dates from summer semester (April–August) 1839 (*MEGA2* 4.1: 566).

14. G. W. F. Hegel, *Elements of the Philosophy of Right*, ed. Allen W. Wood, trans. H. B. Nisbet (Cambridge: Cambridge University Press, 1991), 20: "Was vernünftig ist, das ist wirklich; und was wirklich ist, das ist vernünftig."

15. Hegel, *Elements of the Philosophy of Right*, §270, 293–94.

16. Hegel notes the competing "atheistic" and "pantheistic" interpretations of Spinoza in G. W. F. Hegel, *Lectures on the History of Philosophy* 3: 280–82. Ludwig Feuerbach, in his "Principles of the Philosophy of the Future" (1843), claimed Spinoza as "the Moses of modern freethinkers and materialists" (Ludwig Feuerbach, *Principles of the Philosophy of the Future*, trans. Manfred Vogel, introduced by Thomas E. Wartenberg [Indianapolis: Hackett, 1986], §15, 24).

17. Hegel, *Science of Logic*, 50.

18. John Mepham and David-Hillel Ruben note that "Marxist philosophy, since its inception, has been driven between the Scylla of positivism and the Charybdis of idealism (usually of a 'humanist' variety)" (John Mepham and David-Hillel Ruben, *Issues in Marxist Philosophy*, vol. 1: *Dialectics and Method* [Brighton, Sussex: Harvester Press, 1979], "General Introduction," x.) Given that Marx had connections to both natural science and idealist philosophy, it is far from surprising that there should exist a comparable tension among his followers and interpreters. It should be noted, however, that the early Marx's appeal to natural science was largely an appeal to the *idea* of natural science; at the time, his knowledge of recent scientific developments was not great.

Further comments concerning Brudney's *Marx's Attempt to Leave Philosophy* (note 1) are in order here. Brudney argues that Marx (with Feuerbach) was concerned to leave behind the philosophical framework of dualism. Here I believe that he is absolutely correct. But I find that Brudney overemphasizes what he identifies as Marx's rejection of abstraction. I also find that he tends to attribute to Marx a problem that is more our problem than his—namely, the problem of providing a normative justification for critiquing capitalism. Brudney sees Marx as still tied to philosophy because "apparently only a philosophical theory could provide" a justification for the critique of capitalism (Brudney, 21; also 7, 19, 360–61, and passim). My argument in this book is that Marx's attachment to philosophy goes much deeper than that. It cannot be accounted for by his alleged need for a way of justifying his critique of capitalism (Marx was not the sort of thinker to wait anxiously on justifications; he was not a professor of philosophy). Brudney's overwhelming focus is on the Marx of 1844–46, which amounts to a limited range of writings having a very Feuerbachian character. This is true even of *The German Ideology* (1845–46), which has a much more empirical "feel" to it than most of Marx's other writings—Feuerbach was always wanting to trace things back to empirical experience. Thus the actual roots and character of Marx's commitment to philosophy are missed. A look at Marx's earlier writings (and at some of the later writings as well) changes the picture considerably.

19. G. W. F. Hegel, "Inaugural Lecture at Heidelberg, 28 October 1816," in Hegel, *Introduction to the Lectures on the History of Philosophy*, trans T. M. Knox and A. V. Miller (Oxford: Oxford University Press, 1985), 1–2.

20. G. W. F. Hegel, *Philosophy of Nature*, ed. and trans. M. J. Petry (3 vols.; London: George Allen & Unwin, 1970).

21. C. P. Snow, *The Two Cultures and the Scientific Revolution* (Cambridge: Cambridge University Press, 1959).

22. Ludwig Feuerbach, "Preliminary Theses on the Reform of Philosophy" (1843), in Ludwig Feuerbach, *The Fiery Brook: Selected Writings*, trans. with an introduction by Zawar Hanfi (Garden City, N.Y.: Doubleday Anchor, 1972), 153–73, at 172. Feuerbach's essay appeared in an anthology edited by Arnold Ruge and published in Zurich (to escape the German censorship), *Anekdota zur neuesten deutschen Philosophie und Publicistik* (2 vols.; Zurich, 1843 [rpt., Glashütten im Taunus: Detlev Auvermann, 1971]), in which Marx's article, "Comments on the Latest Prussian Censorship Instruction" also appeared, credited to "a Rhinelander." In a letter to Ruge dated March 13, 1843 Marx declared that "Feuerbach's aphorisms seem to me incorrect only in one respect, that he refers too much to nature and too little to politics" (*MEGA2* 3.1: 45/*MECW* 3: 400). But this is an objection to Feuerbach's neglect of politics, with which Marx himself was deeply concerned at the time (see chapter 2), and not an objection to the attention Feuerbach gave to nature and to natural science.

23. Marx himself referred to Aristotle as "the greatest thinker of antiquity," *Capital*, vol. 1 (1867), chapter 15, "Machinery and Large-Scale Industry" (*MEGA2* 2.6: 396/*MECW* 35: 411/*CAP* 1: 532). It needs to be noted that Marx, as distinguished from Engels, rarely used the term *dialectic* to refer to his approach toward understanding the world. One needs to be reticent in applying the term to Marx—especially since its use leads too easily to the wrong assumption that Marx was committed to something called "dialectical materialism." Nonetheless, if we understand Marxian dialectic as simply a commitment to the view that history progresses through a process of conflict, there is no harm, and some good, in using the term.

24. See also Hegel, *Science of Logic*, vol. 2, section 1, chapter 3, "The Syllogism," 664–704, especially 664–69 and 704.

25. The notion of a historicization of deductive logic is pervasive in Hegel's work, and I shall return to the matter below. At least in principle, when Hegel "did" history he aimed to show how a logical necessity manifests itself in history; of course, historical actors may well be unaware of the necessity. Note the following passage in the *Lectures on the History of Philosophy*:

> Thus we see that Philosophy is system in development; the history of Philosophy is the same; and this is the main point to be noted and the first principle to be dealt with in this treatise on that history . . . the progression of the various stages in the advance of thought may occur with the consciousness of necessity, in which case each in succession deduces itself. . . . Or else it may come about without this consciousness as does a natural and apparently accidental process, so that while inwardly, indeed, the Notion brings about its results consistently, this consistency is not made manifest . . . the history of Philosophy . . . shows the different stages and moments in development in time, in manner of occurrence, in particular places, in particular people or political circumstances . . . in short, it shows us the empirical form. (*LHP* 1: 29–30)

This idea of history was exemplified in the work of various Hegelians, including that of Marx's teacher the law professor Eduard Gans, Marx's doctoral mentor the theologian Bruno Bauer, and Marx himself.

26. In the introduction and notes to his translation into English of the work, M. J. Petry massively demonstrates the extent of Hegel's knowledge.

27. Aristotle, *Posterior Analytics*, trans. Hippocrates Apostle (Grinnell, Iowa: The Peripatetic Press, 1981), 87b, 19–20 (*Posterior Analytics*, Bk. I: 30), 42. A more familiar translation is: "There can be no demonstrative knowledge of the fortuitous" (Aristotle, *Posterior Analytics*, trans. Hugh Tredennick, in Aristotle, *"Posterior Analytics" and "Topica"* [Cambridge: Harvard University Press, 1989]), 157).

28. See Aristotle, *Metaphysics*, 1039b27–1040a27, in Aristotle, *Selections*, trans., with introduction, notes, and glossary, by Terence Irwin and Gail Fine (Indianapolis: Hackett, 1995), 309. Cf. the famous passage in the *Poetics*, 1451b 5–12, where Aristotle denies to history the capacity to speak of what is universal and necessary (in Aristotle, *Selections*, 549).

29. Stephen G. Brush, *The History of Modern Science: A Guide to the Second Scientific Revolution* (Ames: Iowa State University Press, 1988), 3–6. Brush notes that Newton himself did not adhere to the "'clockwork-universe' paradigm," according to which the world is a perfect machine that never wears out or runs down and that follows deterministic laws. Brush thus prefers to call this paradigm "mechanistic" rather than "Newtonian." Cf. also Brush's suggestive and somewhat controversial account of the emergence (*after* Marx had formed his basic position) of indeterminism: Brush, "Irreversibility and Indeterminism: Fourier to Heisenberg," *Journal of the History of Ideas* 37 (1976): 603–30.

30. Hegel, *Elements of the Philosophy of Right*, 23.

31. Marx took Prometheus—the demigod who stole fire from the gods and gave it to man—as a hero, characterizing him in the final sentence of the foreword (dated March 1841) to his doctoral dissertation as "the most eminent saint and martyr in the philosophical calendar" (*MEGA2* 1.1: 15/*MECW* 1: 31); see also the "Notebooks on Epicurean Philosophy," where Marx analogizes the current, praxis-oriented state of philosophy with the Prometheus who, having stolen fire from heaven, "begins to build houses and to settle upon the earth" (*MEGA2* 4.1: 99/*MECW* 1: 491/*MER* 11). Taken back to the original Greek, the name *Prometheus*, with its putting together of *pro* [forward, before, in front of]

and *metheus* suggesting thought or mind, evokes a character who thinks things out deeply and tries to anticipate the future.

Marx evokes the opposite, backward-looking view of history most clearly in his "A Contribution to the Critique of Hegel's Philosophy of Right: Introduction" (1844): here he alludes to the historical school of law, to whom history "shows nothing but its *a posteriori*, as did the God of Israel to his Servant Moses" (*MEGA2* 1.2: 172/*MECW* 3: 177/*EW* 245, referring to Exodus 33: 23). He evokes the forward-looking view of history in the "Needs, Production and Division of Labor" section of the "Economic and Philosophical Manuscripts," where he asserts that we "already know *in thought*" that "history" will give rise to "*real* communist activity," and although this will be a "very difficult and protracted process," we already have "an awareness of the limits as well as the goal of this historical movement and are *in a position to see beyond it*" (*MEGA2* 1.2: 425/*MECW* 3: 313/*EW* 365 [last italics are mine]).

32. Marcuse, "A Note on Dialectic," in *The Essential Frankfurt School Reader*, ed. Andrew Arato and Eike Gebhardt, with an introduction by Paul Piccone (New York: Continuum, 1982), 444–51.

33. Herbert Marcuse, *Reason and Revolution: Hegel and the Rise of Social Theory*, 2d ed. with a supplementary chapter (London: Routledge and Kegan Paul, 1955 [original edition, 1941]). The dividing of Hegelians into left, center, and right derived from the third essay of the theologian David Friedrich Strauss's *Polemical Writings* (1837): Strauss, *Streitschriften zur Verteidigung meiner Schrift über das Leben Jesu und zur Charakteristik der gegenwärtigen Theologie*, 3 Hefte in 1 Band (rpt. Hildesheim: Olms, 1980), drittes Heft: *Die evangelische Kirchenzeitung* . . . (Tübingen: Osiander, 1837), III. Teil, "Verschiedene Richtungen innerhalb der Hegel'schen Schule in Betreff der Christologie," 95, 101–20. (For a not entirely satisfactory translation of the relevant part, see Strauss, *In Defense of My "Life of Jesus" against the Hegelians*, trans. Marilyn Chapin Massey [Hamden, Conn.: Archon, 1983], 38–66.) The split itself first emerged into visibility in the wake of the publication of Strauss's *Life of Jesus* (1835–36). David McLellan's concise study, *The Young Hegelians and Karl Marx* (New York: Praeger, 1969), remains the best initial entry to "young" or "left" Hegelianism (the two terms are essentially equivalent). However, it needs to be supplemented by such later, richly detailed works as Zvi Rosen, *Bruno Bauer and Karl Marx: The Influence of Bruno Bauer on Marx's Thought* (The Hague: Nijhoff, 1977); John E. Toews, *Hegelianism: The Path toward Dialectical Humanism, 1805–1841* (Cambridge: Cambridge University Press, 1980); and Warren Breckman, *Marx, the Young Hegelians, and the Origins of Radical Social Theory: Dethroning the Self* (note 12).

34. Engels made similar claims in other works as well—for example, in discussing dialectic in chapter 4 of *Ludwig Feuerbach and the Outcome of Classical German Philosophy* (1888) he again evoked the *Logic* (*MEW* 21: 292/*MECW* 26: 383).

35. V. I. Lenin, *Philosophical Notebooks*, trans. Clemens Dutt, ed. Stewart Smith, in Lenin, *Collected Works*, vol. 38 (Moscow: Progress, 1961), 180, and Leon Trotsky, *In Defense of Marxism (against the Petty-Bourgeois Opposition)* (New York: Merit Publishers, 1965), 51. For a popularized and polemical Trotskyist rendition of the "orthodox" view on dialectics, see George Novack, *An Introduction to the Logic of Marxism*, 5th ed. (New York: Merit Publishers, 1969), 54–126.

36. Shlomo Avineri, *The Social and Political Thought of Karl Marx* (Cambridge: Cambridge University Press, 1968), 150–84 and passim.

37. Mepham and Ruben, eds., *Dialectics and Method*, 1.

38. Leszek Kolakowski, *Main Currents of Marxism: Its Origins, Growth and Dissolution* (3 vols.; Oxford: Oxford University Press, 1978), 1: 8–80; on Hegel specifically, see 56–80.

39. The most reliable English translation, which is of the short, 1817 version, is G. W. F. Hegel, *Encyclopedia of the Philosophical Sciences in Outline*, trans. Steven A. Taubeneck, in Hegel, "*Encyclopedia of the Philosophical Sciences in Outline*" and "*Critical Writings*," ed. Ernst Behler (New York: Continuum, 1990).

40. McLellan, *The Young Hegelians and Karl Marx*, 3. At the end of the course Gabler officially attested to Marx's "extremely diligent attendance" (*MECW* 1: 700, 704; German original in Karl Marx and Friedrich Engels, *Gesamtausgabe* (*MEGA*) [12 vols.; Frankfurt, Berlin, Moscow: Marx-Engels-Verlag and others, 1927–35], 1. Abt., 1. Bd., 2. Halbband, 248).

41. Warren Breckman, "Eduard Gans and the Crisis of Hegelianism: Associationism, Civil Society, and the Social Question," *Journal of the History of Ideas* 62 (2001): 543–64; see also, more briefly, Breckman, *Marx, the Young Hegelians, and the Origins of Radical Social Theory*, 260. On Marx's studies at Berlin, see DRAP 1: 4–9; a list of courses taken is to be found in *MECW* 1: 699–700, German original in *Gesamtausgabe* (*MEGA*) 1. Abt., 1. Bd., 2. Halbband., 247–48.

42. Jerrold Seigel, *Marx's Fate: The Shape of a Life* (University Park: Pennsylvania State University Press, 1993), 63.

43. On Feuerbach's radicalization and eventual rejection of Hegelian philosophy, see Breckman, *Marx, the Young Hegelians, and the Origins of Radical Social Theory*, especially chapter 3, "Ludwig Feuerbach and Christian Civil Society," 90–130; on a possible influence of Feuerbach on Marx at the time of the doctoral dissertation, see 261–62.

44. "Preliminary Theses on the Reform of Philosophy" is available in English in Feuerbach, *The Fiery Brook* (note 22), 153–73, which also contains Feuerbach's second essay of 1843, "Principles of the Philosophy of the Future," 175–245 (for the latter work, the Vogel translation [note 16, above] is to be preferred, however). Standard studies of Feuerbach in English are Eugene Kamenka, *The Philosophy of Ludwig Feuerbach* (New York: Praeger, 1970) and especially Marx W. Wartofsky, *Feuerbach* (Cambridge: Cambridge University Press, 1977).

45. For example, estrangement or alienation appears in Letter 6 of Friedrich Schiller's immensely influential *On the Aesthetic Education of Man* (1794–95, 1801), where Schiller contrasts the unified character of Greek humanity with the divided character under which we moderns suffer: see Friedrich Schiller, *On the Aesthetic Education of Man in a Series of Letters*, trans. and ed. Elizabeth M. Wilkinson and L. A. Willoughby (Oxford: Oxford University Press, 1967), Sixth Letter, 31–43. The notion is also present (as are the terms *entäussern* and *Entäusserung*) in J. G. Fichte's *Wissenschaftslehre* (1794): see Johann Gottlieb Fichte, *Science of Knowledge*, trans. and ed. Peter Heath and John Lachs (New York: Appleton-Century-Crofts, 1970), 154 (1: 165), 233–34 (1: 264). More generally, the notion was a staple of late Enlightenment and Romantic literature and theory from Rousseau onward. I shall turn to Marx's development of the notion, in relation to labor, in chapter 3.

46. On Feuerbach's genetic-critical method, see Kamenka, *The Philosophy of Ludwig Feuerbach*, 3–4. In *The Social and Political Thought of Karl Marx*, 11–12, Avineri dubs it the "transformative method."

47. This is the only chapter of the *Phenomenology* on which Marx seems to have taken notes (dating from August 1844): see *MEGA2* 1.2: 439–44, 918.

48. On "strong" reading: Harold Bloom, *The Anxiety of Influence: A Theory of Poetry* (New York: Oxford University Press, 1973).

49. G. W. F. Hegel, *Phenomenology of Spirit*, trans. A. V. Miller, with analysis of the text and foreword by J. N. Findlay (Oxford: Oxford University Press, 1977), B.IV.A. "Independence and Dependence of Self-Consciousness; Lordship and Bondage," §§195, 196, 117–19. "Lord" (*Herr*) and "bondsman" (Knecht) have often been rendered into English, less accurately, as "master" and "slave."

50. Hegel, *Phenomenology of Spirit*, §196, 119.

51. Alexandre Kojève, *Introduction to the Reading of Hegel: Lectures on the Phenomenology of Spirit*, assembled by Raymond Queneau, ed. Allan Bloom, trans. James H. Nichols, Jr. (Ithaca, N.Y.: Cornell University Press, 1969; original French edition, 1947), 39–70. See also Michael S. Roth, *Knowing and History: Appropriations of Hegel in Twentieth-Century France* (Ithaca, N.Y.: Cornell University Press, 1988), 99–119 and passim; and Judith P. Butler, *Subjects of Desire: Hegelian Reflections in Twentieth-Century France* (New York: Columbia University Press, 1987), 77, 177–80, and passim.

52. Consider Hans-Georg Gadamer's claim that Marx misunderstood and misused Hegel's "master-servant dialectic." Among other things, Gadamer points out that "Hegel, in his dialectic, does not describe the wage worker, but principally the farmer and handworker in bondage." Quite so. But while it is clear that Marx repeatedly "misused" Hegel (as he did all his intellectual predecessors), my claim is that Marx did not *misunderstand* the lord-bondsman dialectic: on the contrary, he paid no attention to it at all. See Hans-Georg Gadamer, "Hegel's Dialectic of Self-Consciousness," in Gadamer, *Hegel's Dialectic: Five Hermeneutical Studies*, trans. and with an introduction by P. Christopher Smith (New Haven, Conn.: Yale University Press, 1976), 54–74, at 73.

53. V. I. Lenin, *Philosophical Notebooks*, in *Collected Works* 38: 180. For a surprisingly interesting recent study of a figure who is often seen as utterly without philosophical interest, see Kevin Anderson, *Lenin, Hegel, and Western Marxism: A Critical Study* [Urbana and Chicago: University of Illinois Press, 1995], especially part 1, "Lenin on Hegel and Dialectics," 3–119: see in particular 96–97, summarizing Lenin's view of Hegel's *Logic*.

54. Marcuse emphasized the *Phenomenology* and the *Logic* more or less equally in the run-up to Marx, but his preference was clearly for the forward-looking Hegel of the *Phenomenology*. His brilliant Left Hegelian interpretation of Hegel was intended to counter those commentators of the late 1930s and early 1940s who saw Hegel as contributing to an authoritarianism that led ultimately "into Fascist theory and practice." While Marcuse was correct in pointing out the distance between Hegel and fascism, Hegel was certainly not the proponent of the uniformly critical "negative philosophy" that Marcuse portrays. See Marcuse, *Reason and Revolution*, vii; on "negative philosophy" generally, see especially 91–168.

55. In the "Critique of Hegel's Dialectic" Marx is clear about what he finds important in the *Phenomenology* and in the *Logic* respectively: in both cases he emphasizes estrangement. Above, I cited Marx's account of "the greatness of Hegel's *Phenomenology*" (*MEGA2* 1.2: 404/*MECW* 3: 332–33/*EW* 385–86). As for the *Logic*: "Hegel's positive achievement in his speculative logic is to present *determinate concepts*, the universal *fixed thought-forms* in their independence of nature and mind, as a necessary result of the universal estrangement of human existence, and thus also of human thought, and to comprehend them as moments in the process of abstraction" (*MEGA2* 1.2: 415/*MECW* 3: 343/*EW*

397). To underscore a point made in my text: these are accounts that Marx offered only *after* his enthusiastic absorption, in 1843, of Feuerbach's "*positive* humanistic and naturalistic criticism," with its great emphasis on the need to overcome estrangement (*MEGA2* 1.2: 326/*MECW* 3: 232/*EW* 281).

56. Hegel, *Science of Logic*, preface to the second edition, 41.

57. Gadamer, "The Idea of Hegel's Logic," in Gadamer, *Hegel's Dialectic*, 75–99, at 83. Unfortunately, how one then gets from one chapter to the next chapter is not clear at all; see Robert B. Pippin, "You Can't Get There from Here: Transition Problems in Hegel's *Phenomenology of Spirit*," in *The Cambridge Companion to Hegel*, ed. Frederick C. Beiser (Cambridge: Cambridge University Press, 1993), 52–85, at 54, 57, 78 and passim.

58. The question of totality runs through the Marx corpus, as a problem that confronts his serious readers. Philosophically, the basic question is: did Marx adhere to, or did he reject, the notion that there can be "simple qualities of wholes"—that is, did he hold that there exist qualities that pertain to wholes themselves, and not simply to the parts or relations that make up these wholes? For a modest and clear attempt to sort out the issues, see Timothy Shiell, "On Marx's Holism," *History of Philosophy Quarterly* 4 (1987): 235–46. The most vigorous attempt to argue that Marx was a holist (rather than the opposite, a methodological individualist) is to be found in Bertell Ollman, *Alienation: Marx's Conception of Man in Capitalist Society*, 2d ed. (Cambridge: Cambridge University Press, 1976 [1st ed., 1971]). My own view, which is similar to Shiell's, is that Marx was most decidedly a holist in his approach to problems, but that the claim that he was an *ontological* holist cannot be sustained. Totality is a central theme in Martin Jay's magisterial account of twentieth-century Western Marxism, *Marxism and Totality: The Adventures of a Concept from Lukács to Habermas* (Berkeley and Los Angeles: University of California Press, 1984), although the notion is comprehensively displayed rather than deeply analyzed.

59. Hegel, *Science of Logic*, 50.

60. Gadamer, "The Idea of Hegel's Logic," 84.

61. Hegel, *Phenomenology of Spirit*, §808, 493.

62. J. N. Findlay, foreword to *Phenomenology of Spirit*, by Hegel, vii. Another, less positive view is the one articulated by Rudolf Haym in the 1850s, namely, that the *Phenomenology* is "*a psychology brought into confusion and disorder through a history, and a history brought to ruin through a psychology*" (Rudolf Haym, *Hegel und seine Zeit: Vorlesungen über Entstehung und Entwicklung, Wesen und Wert der Hegel'schen Philosophie* [Berlin: Gaertner, 1857], 243).

63. Joshua Dienstag, *"Dancing in Chains": Narrative and Memory in Political Theory* (Stanford: Stanford University Press, 1997), 152–53, 142–43. Dienstag's analysis of Hegel's *Philosophy of History* accords with an old and not inaccurate graduate school truism, namely, that whereas in Kant the transitions are clear and the states that they link are unclear, in Hegel, the allegedly dialectical thinker, the states are clear and the transitions are unclear. Dienstag also notes that in the *Philosophy of History* Hegel makes only one reference, an entirely glancing one, to bondage; this fact contrasts with Kojève's attempt to read an entire Marxian history into the lordship and bondage section of the *Phenomenology*. See G. W. F. Hegel, *The Philosophy of History*, trans. J. Sibree, with a new introduction by Carl J. Friedrich (New York: Dover, 1956), 407.

64. Quentin Lauer noted commentators' relative lack of interest in Hegel's *History of Philosophy*, in Lauer, "Hegel As Historian of Philosophy," in *Hegel and the History of Philosophy: Proceedings of the 1972 Hegel Society of America Conference*, ed. Joseph J.

O'Malley, K. W. Algozin, and Frederick G. Weiss (The Hague: Martinus Nijhoff, 1974), 21–46, at 21. This still seems true of the 1993 *Cambridge Companion to Hegel*, excellent though it is in many respects.

Note that the publishing history of Hegel's *Lectures on the History of Philosophy* is complex, and there is some difficulty knowing which variants to take as "definitive." The lectures were first published only after Hegel's death, and Hegel's editors had available to them a variety of lecture transcripts but no single text authorized by Hegel himself. In general, Marx would most likely have relied on oral tradition and on the edition of Hegel's *Vorlesungen über die Geschichte der Philosophie* published in 1833–36 as vols. 13–15 of Hegel's *Werke* (18 vols., Berlin, 1832–45). Generally, I cite the Haldane and Simson translation, *Lectures on the History of Philosophy* (note 12), which is based on the revised edition of Hegel's *Vorlesungen* that appeared in the *Werke* in 1840–44. So far as I can see, the textual variants have no significance insofar as my interpretation of Marx's work is concerned. For a modern edition of the *Vorlesungen*, see G. W. F. Hegel, *Vorlesungen über die Geschichte der Philosophie*, ed. Pierre Garniron und Walter Jaeschke (4 vols.; Hamburg: Felix Meiner, 1986–1996). Garniron and Jaeschke thoroughly discuss textual issues in vol. 1: xxxvii–xlviii; for a briefer account of the different editions, see G. W. F. Hegel, *Lectures on the History of Philosophy: The Lectures of 1825–26*, vol. 3, *Medieval and Modern Philosophy*, ed. Robert F. Brown, trans. R. F. Brown and J. M. Stewart, with the assistance of H. S. Harris (Berkeley and Los Angeles: University of California Press, 1990), 3–10.

65. I am aware of only two allusions in the Marx literature to any impact of the *Lectures on the History of Philosophy* on Marx's work. First, in his review of Marx's *A Contribution to the Critique of Political Economy*, Engels mentions the *LHP*, along with the *Phenomenology* and the *Aesthetics*, as showing Hegel's commitment to the view that there is "an evolution, an intrinsic coherence in history" (*MEW* 13: 474/*MECW* 16: 474). Second, the editors of *MEGA2* have noted the importance of Hegel's *History of Philosophy* for Marx's doctoral dissertation: "Above all, one can see the influence of Hegel's *Lectures on the History of Philosophy*, which was first published in 1833–35 and which soon became the object of lively ideological discussion" (*MEGA2* 4.1: 15*). To be sure, the literature is vast, and there are surely discussions of the relation of the *History of Philosophy* to Marx's project that I have overlooked. I would be grateful to be made aware of them.

66. A crucial text is Aristotle, *Posterior Analytics*, 71b10–25, in Aristotle, *Selections*, 39–40; see also the editors' comments in Aristotle, *Selections*, at note 14, 39–40, and in their glossary, s.v. "Demonstration," 576–77.

67. Aristotle, *Politics* 1356a30, in Aristotle, *Selections*, 524.

68. Aristotle, *Politics* 1355b25, in Aristotle, *Selections*, 522.

69. See Aristotle, *Selections*, "Glossary," s.v. "Dialectic, *dialektikē*, where the editors have provided a clear and compact discussion of dialectic, including references to a number of places in Aristotle's corpus where dialectic is discussed. For a basic definition, see *Topics*, 100a 18–30, 69. Aristotle insists that dialectic surveys opposing sides concerning an issue; quite frequently, he exemplifies the practice of doing so: see *Topics* 101a 34–36, 71, and (for an exemplification) *Posterior Analytics* 72b 5–19, 43, where, considering the question of how knowledge is possible, he begins by addressing two opposing positions—that no knowledge is possible, since there is an infinite regress that prevents demonstration from taking place, and that it is possible to demonstrate everything.

70. Or perhaps not. Aristotle's distinction between scientific knowledge and dialectical thinking appears to be ambiguous. On the one hand, Aristotle holds that *epistēmē* is

characterized by demonstration (*apodeixis*). On the other hand, he asserts that not all *epistēmē* is demonstrative—for there is the possibility of infinite regress, and when the regress stops the immediate premises that lie before one will not have been demonstrated (see Aristotle, *Posterior Analytics* 72b 20–25, in *Selections*, 43). In short, there appears to be a (dialectical) contradiction at this point in Aristotle's argument.

71. Quoted by M. J. Petry in his introduction to *Philosophy of Nature*, by Hegel, 96, citing F. von Biedermann, *Goethe's Gespräche* (5 vols.; Leipzig, 1909–11) 3: 477–78 (conversation of October 18, 1827).

72. My account differs from those of Hans-Georg Gadamer and Manfred Baum, both of whom greatly emphasize the relation of Hegel's dialectic to Plato, and especially to *Parmenides*. Gadamer in particular sees Hegel's supposed derivation of his dialectic from Plato as being based on "a total misunderstanding of passage 259b in the *Sophist*" (Gadamer, "Hegel and the Dialectic of the Ancient Philosophers," in Gadamer, *Hegel's Dialectic*, 5–34, at 22; Manfred Baum, "Begriffsgeschichte der Hegelschen Dialektik," in Baum, *Die Entstehung der Hegelschen Dialectik* [Bonn: Bouvier Verlag Herbert Grundmann, 1986], 6–28). But the question that needs to be raised is: How seriously ought we to take the derivation of the dialectic from *Parmenides* and from Plato's other "truly speculative" dialogues (Gadamer, *Hegel's Dialectic*, 7)? The attempt to root Hegel's dialectic in the more speculative Platonic dialogues strikes me as obfuscatory: we ought to attend to Hegel the realist, whose "morning prayer," he once remarked, was the reading of the newspaper, and who insisted, as we saw above, that dialectic is "nothing more than the regulated and methodical cultivation of the spirit of contradiction" (for the "morning prayer" quotation, see G. W. F. Hegel, "Aphorismen aus der Jenenser Zeit," no. 31, in *Dokumente zu Hegels Entwicklung*, ed. Johannes Hoffmeister [Stuttgart-Bad Cannstatt: Frommann, 1974 (reprint of 1936 ed.)], 360). Hegel's logical dialectic—worked out in his *Science of Logic*—may well owe some debt to the dialectical oppositions of Plato's *Parmenides* and related dialogues, but the notion of a historical process involving progress through contradiction seems more especially to be a development—and correction—of Aristotle. In general terms, G. R. G. Mure's observation that Hegel is indebted to both Plato and Aristotle, but that "in respect of its detailed content Hegel's philosophy . . . owes far more to Aristotle," seems well justified (G. R. G. Mure, *An Introduction to Hegel* [Oxford: Oxford University Press, 1940], xi–xii). The passing reference to *Parmenides* at the end of the Preface to the *Phenomenology* does not have probative force (Hegel, *Phenomenology of Spirit*, §71, 44).

73. See Aristotle, *Prior Analytics*, 24b18–20, in Aristotle, *Selections*, 30; passages of similar bent appear in *Posterior Analytics*, *Topics*, and *Rhetoric*.

74. Cf. Hegel's famous statement in the Preface to the *Phenomenology* that "the True is the whole [*das Wahre ist das Ganze*]" (Hegel, *Phenomenology*, Preface, §20, 11).

75. Hegel, *Lectures on the Philosophy of World History: Introduction: Reason in History*, 29.

76. Hegel, *Science of Logic*, 45.

77. Technically, the passage in question is from the second-last paragraph of the version of the *Vorlesungen über die Geschichte der Philosophie* that was published in 1840, 1842, and 1844 as volumes 13, 14, and 15 of Hegel's *Werke*: see Hegel, *Werke*, ed. Philipp Marheineke et al. (18 vols.; Berlin: Duncker und Humblot, 1832–45). It is this version of the *Vorlesungen* that Haldane and Simson translated into English. This is somewhat different from the version of the *Vorlesungen* published in 1833–36 in the *original* publica-

tion of volumes 13, 14, and 15 (which evidently sold well enough to justify a second edition). The passage cited here does not appear in the 1833–36 version. This is the version that the very early Marx consulted. Since I happen to have the 1833–36 version on hand, I have used it in order to indicate, at times, the first-published German text, modifying the Haldane and Simson translation in minor ways. As I observe in note 64, above, nothing of significance for Marx interpretation seems to hang on the difference of editions.

78. For example, when in his *Polemical Writings* (1837) the theologian David Friedrich Strauss distinguished between right, center, and left Hegelians according to whether they thought that the *entire* Gospel narrative is deducible from the idea [of "the unity of the divine and human natures"], that only a *part* of it is, or that *none* of it is, he was clearly evoking Hegel's notion of a rational, deductive history. See David Friedrich Strauss, *Streitschriften* (note 33), drittes Heft, III. Teil, "Verschiedene Richtungen innerhalb der Hegel'schen Schule in Betreff der Christologie," 95.

79. There is a tension, even a contradiction, between Hegel's notion of history as the working out of logical deduction and his notion of history as a dialectical sifting of truth through argument and debate. Can one reconcile these two Hegelian models of history? I do not think so. The point here is to display the edifice that is Hegel's conception of history in order to understand better the assumptions underlying Marx's project; it is not to deconstruct Hegel, although no thinker is better suited to deconstruction than he.

80. A classic statement of this view is Jacques Barzun, *Darwin, Marx, Wagner: Critique of a Heritage* (Boston: Little, Brown, 1946 [originally 1841]), 186–87.

81. No single study canvasses all of these developments. The closest approximation is the classic (and much neglected) study by the historian of philosophy Maurice Mandelbaum, *History, Man, and Reason: A Study in Nineteenth-Century Thought* (Baltimore: Johns Hopkins University Press, 1971).

82. Auguste Comte, *Cours de philosophie positive* (6 vols.; Paris: Bachelier, 1830–42); Comte, *System of Positive Polity* (4 vols.; New York: Franklin, 1967 [reprint of 1851–54 ed.]); Herbert Spencer, *First Principles*, 4th ed. (New York: Appleton, 1891 [1st ed., 1862]), and subsequent volumes.

83. Mandelbaum, *History, Man, and Reason*, 5.

84. In another respect Marx was not at all typical of nineteenth-century thought, for, as Hayden White has shown, Marx's radicalism put him off to the margins (Hayden White, *Metahistory: The Historical Imagination in Nineteenth-Century Europe* [Baltimore: Johns Hopkins University Press, 1973], 276–80, 284–85, 310, 329). Here it is perhaps useful to introduce a distinction between Marx's political radicalism and his intellectual radicalism. Politically, Marx rejected completely the Liberal-Conservative consensus to which most nineteenth-century intellectuals adhered. Intellectually, however, Marx's radicalism was a matter not of *rejecting* but of *going deeper*. In respect to his intellectual radicalism, one can usefully compare him to Friedrich Nietzsche (cf. White, *Metahistory*, 276–80). Whereas Nietzsche radicalized by attempting to reject completely the tendencies underlying the thought of his own time, Marx radicalized by *intensifying* those tendencies. Marx thus remains a characteristically nineteenth-century thinker, whereas one could never say this of Nietzsche.

85. G. W. F. Hegel, "Inaugural Lecture at Heidelberg, 28 October 1816" (note 19), 1–2.

86. For a more extended account, see Mandelbaum, *History, Man, and Reason*, 6–10.

87. Mandelbaum provides clear accounts of positivism and of materialism in *History, Man, and Reason*, 10–20 and 20–28.

88. A trickier question is: How does *Hegel* connect with ontology? The Marx of 1844 and after saw Hegel (or, more accurately, *claimed* to see Hegel) as an ontological idealist, that is, as an adherent of the view that the world, in its fundamental constitution, is idea or spirit. But in fact, Hegel was only ambiguously an ontological idealist, if he was an ontological idealist at all. Clearly, he was an idealist with regard to method (he favored, as a universal method, one that was honed on human cultural products); with regard to nature (the only nature that counted for him was the nature that has been processed through the human understanding); and with regard to humanity (the *telos* of all social order is the full flowering of human cultural knowledge). But did Hegel hold that the world fundamentally is spirit, or was his claim rather that the only access that we have to the world is through our thinking? I believe that the latter reading of Hegel is the more plausible. Note, for example, Frederick Beiser's argument that Hegel's philosophy of history is best seen as "nonmetaphysical" (that is, nonontological). Beiser points out that there are passages where Hegel "tells us most emphatically that spirit by itself is only an abstraction and comes into existence only through the activity of finite agents." (Frederick C. Beiser, "Hegel's Historicism," in *The Cambridge Companion to Hegel*, 270–300, at 291).

89. This is not an original point, but is in fact well known to people who know the Marx literature. I shall return to this and related points in chapter 4.

90. See Frederick Gregory, *Scientific Materialism in Nineteenth-Century Germany* (Dordrecht: Reidel, 1977), ix–xi, 1–10, and passim.

91. Feuerbach, "Preliminary Theses," 172.

92. Feuerbach, letters to Christian Kapp, February 3, 1840, and April 7, 1840, in Ludwig Feuerbach, *Briefwechsel II* (1840–1844) (Berlin: Akademie-Verlag, 1988 [Feuerbach, *Gesammelte Werke*, ed. Werner Schuffenhauer, vol. 18]), 4, 13.

93. Ludwig Feuerbach, *Das Wesen des Christentums*, ed. Werner Schuffenhauer and Wolfgang Harich (Berlin: Akademie-Verlag, 1973) (*Gesammelte Werke*, ed. Werner Schuffenhauer, vol. 5), "Vorwort" (1841), 6, 8. The first-edition foreword was omitted from George Eliot's widely known English translation of the work in favor of the foreword of the second edition (1843)—where Feuerbach characterizes himself as "a natural scientist of the mind" (Ludwig Feuerbach, *The Essence of Christianity*, trans. George Eliot [Buffalo, N.Y.: Prometheus Books, 1989], xiv). Feuerbach's natural-scientific bent is discussed by Brudney, *Marx's Attempt to Leave Philosophy*, 54–57.

94. The first steam-powered freight and passenger service began in England in 1825, with the building of the Stockton and Darlington Railway. The first German railway, 6 kilometers long, opened in 1835; by 1840 there were 462 kilometers of track, by 1850, 5,875, and by 1860, 11,157. Already before 1840 it was widely recognized that something dramatically new had come into being. For the figures, and a brief, meaty discussion, see Sheehan, *German History, 1770–1866*, 466–70.

95. A useful entry to questions of method in the later Marx (where methodological issues become important) is provided by Karl Marx, *Texts on Method*, trans. and ed. Terrell Carver (Oxford: Blackwell, 1975). This contains a translation of, and a helpful commentary on, two important methodologically oriented texts by Marx: his introduction (1857) to the *Grundrisse* [the first, very raw draft of what would eventually become *Capital*], and his critical *Notes on Adolph Wagner* [a contemporary economist] (1879–80). For a sophisticated attempt to unearth the logic, and hence by extension the method, of *Capital*, see Jindřich Zelený, *The Logic of Marx*, trans. and ed. Terrell Carver (Oxford: Blackwell, 1980), 9–114. However, a truly satisfactory account of Marx's method can emerge only

from a full examination of all Marx's later economic writings—at least if one adheres to the view that method can be properly studied only in relation to the particular subject matter being investigated.

96. Brudney, *Marx's Attempt to Leave Philosophy*, 7–8.

97. Hegel's attack on such reasoning has its first extensive appearance in the preface to his *Phenomenology of Spirit*, where he points out at great length the abstract and formal character of mathematics, and contends that philosophy, in contrast, has an "element and content [that] is not the abstract or nonactual, but the *actual*, that which posits itself and is alive within itself. . . ." See Hegel, *Phenomenology of Spirit*, Preface, §§42–52, 24–31, quotation at §47, 27. The *Holy Family* passage hearkens back to Marx's attack on Hegel's abstractionism in his "Critique of Hegel's Dialectic" in the "Economic and Philosophical Manuscripts," written some months earlier: see *MEGA2* 1.2: 403–5/*MECW* 3: 31–33/*EW* 384–86.

98. In *For Marx* (New York: Vintage, 1970), which contains articles dating from the early 1960s, Louis Althusser explores and sharpens the early Marx/late Marx contrast. Althusser's steely, hard-line, neo-orthodox Marxism contrasts with the friendly, humane, sensitive Marxism presented by the psychoanalyst, and aficionado of the 1844 Marx, Erich Fromm, in Erich Fromm, *Marx's Concept of Man*, with a translation from Marx's *Economic and Philosophical Manuscripts* by T. B. Bottomore (New York: Frederick Ungar, 1961). Reading Althusser and Fromm together gives much food for thought.

99. For a collection of articles centering on this problem, see *Marx's Socialism*, ed. Shlomo Avineri (New York: Lieber-Atherton, 1972).

100. Letter from Moses Hess to Berthold Auerbach, September 2, 1841, in Moses Hess, *Briefwechsel*, ed. Edmund Silberner with the cooperation of Werner Blumenberg (The Hague: Mouton, 1959), 79–80.

101. There are exceptions. These include, among others, David McLellan, *Marx before Marxism*, 2d ed. (London: Macmillan, 1980), chapter 4, "Marx the Journalist," 72–101; Harold Mah, *The End of Philosophy, the Origin of 'Ideology'* (note 1), 181–86; Warren Breckman, *Marx, the Young Hegelians, and the Origins of Radical Social Theory*, the section titled "From Atomism to Prussian Individualism: Marx's Philosophical Journalism," 272–79; and the pioneering essay by Arthur F. McGovern, "Karl Marx' First Political Writings: The *Rheinische Zeitung*, 1842–43," in *Demythologizing Marxism: A Series of Studies on Marxism*, ed. Frederick J. Adelmann (The Hague: Martinus Nijhoff, 1969), 19–63.

102. There is another, massive body of writing by the very early Marx—writing that is little known and less read—namely, his Romantically inclined "literary experiments" of 1835–37, consisting of love poems, a poetic drama, a comic novel, satiric epigrams, and other works (see *MEGA2* 1.1: 481–858; an incomplete assemblage is to be found in *MECW* 1: 515–632). These writings do not directly bear on Marx's conception of rationality, although they are important for other subjects. Interestingly, one can see *both* Marx's literary experiments and his philosophy as displaced attempts to pursue the goal of achieving a free society—displaced because, for intellectuals of Marx's generation, censorship and other forms of repression made the direct expression of political demands too dangerous to engage in. For a persuasive argument to the effect that, contrary to what has sometimes been said, Marx's literary works were not conservative in orientation, but in fact, through parody, satire, irony, and veiled evocations of authors out of favor with the government, manifested a critical spirit, see Margaret A. Rose, *Reading the Young Marx and Engels: Poetry, Parody and the Censor* (London: Croom Helm, 1978), especially 33–53.

See also S. S. Prawer's substantial study, *Karl Marx and World Literature* (Oxford: Oxford University Press, 1976), especially chapter 1, "Prometheus," which deals with Marx's literary interests up to 1841.

103. See Johann Gottlieb Fichte, *Grundlage des Naturrechts nach Principien der Wissenschaftslehre*, in Fichte, *Sämmtliche Werke* (8 vols.; Berlin: Veit, 1845–46), 3: 1–385.

104. I shall sometimes refer to the dissertation plus the "Notebooks" as the "dissertation materials." They have not been much written about. But see, *inter alia*, Eric Voegelin, "The Formation of the Marxian Revolutionary Idea," *Review of Politics* 12 (1950): 275–302, at 275–78; Franz Mehring, "La Thèse de Karl Marx sur Démocrite et Épicure," *La nouvelle Critique* 61 (janvier 1955): 17–29; Sannwald, *Marx und die Antike* (Zurich: Polygraphischer Verlag, 1957), especially 78–125 (the first substantial study); Norman D. Livergood, *Activity in Marx's Philosophy* (The Hague: Martinus Nijhoff, 1967), 7–53; Zwi Rosen, *Bruno Bauer and Karl Marx* (The Hague: Nijhoff, 1977), part 2, chapter 3, "Bauer's Influence on Marx's Dissertation," 148–61; and, embodying the best recent research, Breckman, *Marx, the Young Hegelians, and the Origins of Radical Social Theory*, 262–71.

105. In fact, we do not actually have the dissertation, titled "On the Difference between the Democritean and Epicurean Philosophy of Nature," that Marx submitted to the University of Jena in early April 1841. (Marx never studied at Jena and there is not a shred of evidence that he ever set foot in the town. He did not submit the dissertation to Berlin, it seems, because it would have been anathema to the philosophers there: the new king, Friedrich Wilhelm IV, had just called the elderly philosopher Schelling [1775–1854] to Berlin to strengthen true religion in its struggle against the impiety of Hegelian philosophy. At Jena procedures for obtaining the doctorate were so simple that it was possible, as in this case, to submit one's dissertation and obtain one's "promotion" by mail; and Jena had the further advantage of being outside Prussian territory.) There does exist an incomplete copy of the dissertation, which also includes elements that would not have been in the version that was submitted to Jena. For the dissertation, see *MEGA2* 1.1: 5–92; the work of the *MEGA2* editors, especially their discussion of the "emergence and provenance" of the dissertation (*MEGA2* 1.1: 879–87), is essential. The "Notebooks on Epicurean Philosophy" and associated fragments are to be found in *MEGA2* 4.1: 5–152, with an important discussion of "emergence and provenance" at *MEGA2* 4.1: 563–75. The editors offer a quite specific dating of the "Notebooks" on p. 566; they suggest that Marx began writing the dissertation itself around mid-1840 (p. 567). For English versions of the dissertation and "Notebooks," respectively, see *MECW* 1: 25–106 and 403–509. The *MEGA2* editors have shown that previous editors made some significant mistakes in putting together the German text that was the basis for the *MECW* translation. Accordingly, only the *MEGA2* text is authoritative, but none of the differences affect my reading of this material, either here or in chapter 2.

106. Bruno Bauer, *Die Religion des Alten Testamentes in der geschichtlichen Entwicklung ihrer Principien* (2 vols.; Berlin: Dümmler, 1838; rpt. Aaalen: Scientia Verlag, 1983) 1: lxxvii–lxxviii. Rosen, *Bruno Bauer and Karl Marx*, 149–51 notes the connection between Bauer's book and Marx's doctoral dissertation, as do the *MEGA2* editors, *MEGA2* 1.1: 880.

107. Ludwig Feuerbach, "Zur Kritik der 'positiven Philosophie,'" in Feuerbach, *Kleinere Schriften I (1835–1839)* , 2., durchgesehene Aufl., ed. Wolfgang Harich (Berlin: Akademie-Verlag, 1969 [*Gesammelte Werke*, ed. Werner Schuffenhauer, Bd. 8]), 181–207,

at 207. "Positive philosophy" refers to the philosophy of F. W. J. Schelling and related conservative writers, who were accused of simply accepting as legitimate, without critical examination, whatever exists—whatever is already "given" or "posited." It is not to be confused with the "positivist" philosophy of Auguste Comte and related writers.

108. Where does the *stumm fortwirkende Maulwurf* come from? For it is odd that this blind subterranean animal should stand as a metaphor for philosophical knowledge. It comes from *Hamlet*, act 1, scene 5, where Hamlet says of the ghost of his father, "Well said, old mole! canst work i' the ground so fast?" Marx was a great aficionado of Shakespeare, even at this very early age (it is noteworthy that Shakespeare was much adored in his fiancée's family). But this particular allusion is surely inspired by Hegel, who (as we have already seen) in the final section of his *Lectures on the History of Philosophy*, in the midst of a passage describing the forward-driving force of spirit, thinks to introduce Shakespeare's fast-working beast (see *LHP* 3: 546–47/1836 ed., 15: 685).

109. As noted above, Marx was much more deeply committed than Hegel was to the notion that there ought to be *one* universal and necessary history. Marx actually attempted to construct a history-in-general (as we shall especially see in chapter 4) whereas Hegel only pointed vaguely in its direction. Perhaps Hegel was finally too much of a realist for such a history: it would have required him to slay too many facts and walk through too many all-black fields at night for his own comfort. He would have felt himself a mythmaker: a Schelling. So he did not do it. Even if he had not died in 1831, but had instead lived ten years longer, in all likelihood he still would not have produced such a history.

110. See Richard Weikart, *Socialist Darwinism: Evolution in German Socialist Thought from Marx to Bernstein* (San Francisco: International Scholars Publications, 1999), chapter 1, "Karl Marx's Ambivalence toward Darwinism," 15–51. Incidentally, it used to be thought that Marx wrote to Darwin asking for permission to dedicate *Capital* to him, but it has been known since the 1970s that this is false: a letter from Darwin to Marx's son-in-law, Edward Aveling, who had wanted to dedicate his book, *The Student's Darwin*, to Darwin, ended up in the Marx archive and was misidentified as a letter to Marx (Weikart, *Socialist Darwinism*, 17).

111. The most prominent exponent of providential evolutionism was Alfred Russel Wallace, the co-discoverer of the theory: see his *Contributions to the Theory of Natural Selection* (New York, 1871 [original edition 1870]). Cf. my brief discussion of Darwin earlier in this chapter, and Peter J. Bowler's *The Non-Darwinian Revolution*, chapter 1 (note 10).

112. Pierre Trémaux, *Origine et transformations de l'homme et des autres êtres* (Paris, 1865). I owe my awareness of Trémaux to Richard Weikart, *Socialist Darwinism*, 29–30, 35–36. The French historian Hervé Le Bras also discusses Trémaux and Marx in "La Métaphore interdite: Karl Marx et André Siegfried entre histoire et géologie," in *Alter histoire: Essais d'histoire expérimentale*, ed. Daniel S. Milo and Alain Boureau (Paris: Les belles lettres, 1991), 63–84, at 80–82.

113. Weikart, *Socialist Darwinism*, 29; Le Bras, "La Métaphore interdite," 81. Marx writes in his letter to Engels of August 7, 1866, that: "Progress, which Darwin regards as purely accidental, is essential here [in Trémaux's theory] on the basis of the stages of the earth's development, degeneration, which Darwin cannot explain, is straightforward here . . . the gaps in palaeontology, which Darwin finds disturbing, are necessary here. Ditto the fixity of the species, once established, which is explained as a necessary law. . . ." (*MEW* 31: 248/*MECW* 42: 304–5). Engels pointed out how bad Trémaux's book was in letters to Marx of October 2 and October 5, 1866; in a letter of October 9, 1866, to Ludwig Kugelmann,

which may have been written after Marx's receipt of Engels's second letter, Marx still claims that Trémaux was "an advance over Darwin" (*MEW* 31: 256, 259–60, 530/*MECW* 42: 320, 323–24, 327).

CHAPTER 2

1. A sense of Marx's militancy, as well as other of his personal characteristics, comes out in a set of seven reminiscences of Marx by various people that David McLellan assembles at the end of his *Karl Marx: His Life and Thought* (New York: Harper & Row, 1973), 452–56 (this brief selection is more manageable than the nearly complete set of reminiscences to be found in *Karl Marx: Interviews and Recollections*, ed. McLellan [London: Macmillan, 1981]). Also revealing are some of the comments by Heinrich Marx in letters to young Karl. In a letter of March 2, 1837, Heinrich suggests that Karl's heart "is obviously animated and governed by a demon not granted to all men," and asks: "is that demon heavenly or Faustian?" In a letter of December 9, 1837, Heinrich implies that Marx is an "uncivilized stripling" (*verwilderten Burschen*), a "negating genius" (*negirenden Genie*) who needs to become more orderly, more practical, and more tactful (*MEGA2* 3.1: 308, 325/*MECW* 1: 670, 688).

2. *Karl Marx: Interviews and Recollections*, 167. The document in question is said to come from Laura Marx's album book. According to Jerrold Seigel, *Marx's Fate: The Shape of a Life* (University Park: Pennsylvania State University Press, 1993), 427 n. 30, it appears in *Mohr und General: Erinnerungen an Marx und Engels*, 2., durchgesehene Aufl. (Berlin: Institut für Marxismus-Leninismus beim ZK der SED, 1965). As Seigel notes, another version, dated "Zalt-Bommel, Apr. 1, 1865," that Marx did for a relative in Holland is reprinted in Werner Blumenberg, "Ein unbekanntes Kapitel aus Marx' Leben: Briefe an die holländischen Verwandten," *International Review of Social History* 1 (1956): 54–110, at 107–8. Finally, a third version, which appeared in Marx's daughter Jenny's album, is to be found in *MEW* 31: 596.

3. On this point, I disagree with Andrzej Walicki's otherwise rewarding essay, "Marx and Freedom," *New York Review of Books*, November 24, 1983, 50+. Walicki sees Marx as wanting to subordinate individual freedom to the collective emancipation of humanity. Marx's alleged wish to subordinate individual freedom to collective freedom might help explain the antifreedom character of Marxian regimes in the twentieth century. But I find that it is a mistake to claim that Marx wanted to subordinate individual freedom to collective freedom. On the contrary, he greatly valued individuality and looked forward to a time when all individuals would be free and when the unfolding of the individuality of each would conduce to the unfolding of the individuality of all. One might suggest as an instance of this a great symphony orchestra on a very good evening, where the skill and brilliance of each player makes possible a collective expression of freedom that would never be possible for individuals working alone. In my view, the antifreedom side of Marx's thought does not derive from any wish on his part to subordinate individuals to the collectivity. Rather, it derives from his excessive faith in the capacity of science to generate absolutely authoritative prescriptions and treatment protocols for the human world.

Marx's attitude toward freedom thus needs to be distinguished from the cramped, small-minded, malicious authoritarianism, hateful of anything that might allow individuals to stand out from the crowd, that was so often found in Communist regimes. Marx did not aim at such a mindset. He did not share such a mindset. It was not any impulse in his theory to subordinate the individual to the collectivity that led to its association with tyranny. Rather, that association was an inadvertent result of the theory's scientism. The obstinate failure of the social world to live up to the theory's rational-scientific hopes all but invited attempts to make the social world conform to the theory anyway. These attempts developed, inevitably, a tyrannical character.

In *Marxism and the Leap to the Kingdom of Freedom: The Rise and Fall of the Communist Utopia* (Stanford: Stanford University Press, 1995) Walicki deals compendiously with both the conceptions of freedom of Marx and of Engels and with the later fate of their ideas. See also David W. Lovell, *From Marx to Lenin: An Evaluation of Marx's Responsibility for Soviet Authoritarianism* (Cambridge: Cambridge University Press, 1984).

4. David McLellan, *The Young Hegelians and Karl Marx* (New York: Praeger, 1969) still offers the best initial orientation, but McLellan's book needs to be supplemented by such subsequent works as John E. Toews, *Hegelianism: The Path toward Dialectical Humanism, 1805–1841* (Cambridge: Cambridge University Press, 1980), Harold Mah, *The End of Philosophy, the Origin of "Ideology": Karl Marx and the Crisis of the Young Hegelians* (Berkeley and Los Angeles: University of California Press, 1987), Daniel Brudney, *Marx's Attempt to Leave Philosophy* (Cambridge: Harvard University Press, 1998), and Warren Breckman, *Marx, the Young Hegelians, and the Origins of Radical Social Theory: Dethroning the Self* (New York: Cambridge University Press, 1999).

5. I here quote Vincent Descombes' characterization of Foucault's position: Descombes, *The Barometer of Modern Reason: On the Philosophies of Current Events*, trans. Stephen Adam Schwartz (New York: Oxford University Press, 1993), 9. Descombes alludes to a line of thought in the late Foucault where Kant is (mis)interpreted as a philosopher who focused on contemporary reality above everything else: see, for example, Foucault, "What Is Enlightenment?," in Foucault, *Ethics: Subjectivity and Truth*, trans. Robert Hurley and others, ed. Paul Rabinow (*The Essential Works of Michel Foucault, 1954–1984*, vol. 1) (New York : New Press, 1998), 303–19, especially 308–9.

6. Many would say, contrary to Foucault, that the attempt to ground the transitory in the eternal is precisely what defines the modern. For example, something like Marx's preference for universal and necessary categories remains powerfully present in "modern" social science. Foucault might then be seen as envisaging a kind of postmodern postphilosophy. The carrier of such a postphilosophy would be the imaginatively powerful bearer of witness (one thinks of Alexander Solzhenitsyn or Wole Soyinka), not the rational critic. On reflection, one would then have to admit that elements of the novelistic and dramatic imagination are to be found in Marx, too—as any attentive reader of *Capital*, or even only of *The Communist Manifesto*, will quickly see. In short, the categories "modern" and "postmodern" begin to blur. But this is no denial of their temporary usefulness.

7. In general terms, Marx's dependence on Hegel is perhaps the best-known fact about his work: that dependence was first pointed out in 1859 by Friedrich Engels in his review of Marx's *A Contribution to the Critique of Political Economy*, published earlier the same year (*MEW* 13: 472–74/*MECW* 16: 472–75). My claim is that the character of the Marx–Hegel relation has been largely misunderstood. For more, see chapter 1.

8. In an insightful article, Frederick G. Weiss has pointed out how in his *Phenomenology of Spirit* Hegel, like Descartes in his *Meditations on First Philosophy* earlier, was concerned with laying down a certain foundation for knowledge (Frederick G. Weiss, "Cartesian Doubt

and Hegelian Negation," in *Hegel and the History of Philosophy: Proceedings of the 1972 Hegel Society of America Conference*, ed. Joseph J. O'Malley, K. W. Algozin, and Frederick G. Weiss [The Hague: Martinus Nijhoff, 1974], 83–94). One should note, further, that both Hegel and Descartes articulated their philosophies as, in part, responses to the disorders that they saw around them—in Descartes' case, disorders deriving from the wars that followed upon the Protestant Reformation; in Hegel's case, disorders deriving from the French Revolution and its aftermath. Disorder in the real world provides a powerful stimulus to the construction of philosophical systems aiming at certainty.

9. G. W. F. Hegel, *Elements of the Philosophy of Right*, ed. Allen W. Wood, trans. H. B. Nisbet (Cambridge: Cambridge University Press, 1991), 23.

10. G. W. F. Hegel, *Briefe von und an Hegel*, Bd. II: 1813–1822, 3., durchgesehene Aufl., ed. Johannes Hoffmeister (Hamburg: Felix Meiner, 1969), draft of letter from Hegel to Hardenberg, mid-October 1820, 241–42 (English trans. in Hegel, *The Letters*, trans. Clark Butler and Christiane Seiler, with a commentary by Clark Butler [Bloomington: Indiana University Press, 1984], 459).

11. As Shlomo Avineri points out, *Hegel's Theory of the Modern State* (Cambridge: Cambridge University Press, 1972), 117. Avineri is mistaken, however, in stating that in the note to Hardenberg Hegel remarked that the *Philosophy of Right* "may help the minister to see the relationship between the theory of the state and the Prussian state as it is and *as it may still develop* [Avineri's italics]." Hegel may well have *thought* this, but he certainly did not say it in this letter.

12. The contrast, derived from classical mythology, between Epimetheus (literally: afterthought) and Prometheus (forethought) seems appropriate here, although it was introduced only in 1880–81 by the Swiss writer Carl Spitteler in his epic poem *Prometheus und Epimetheus: ein Gleichnis* (Jena: E. Diederich, 1923). Epimetheus, who created the animals, was the simple-minded brother of Prometheus, who not only created humankind but also brought fire to man and thus made technology possible. Unfortunately, Epimetheus married the charming, curious, and deceitful Pandora, whom he allowed to open the eponymous box that Zeus had forbidden her to open.

From a later perspective, one might interpret the difference between Prometheus and Epimetheus as one between an ethic of production and an ethic of consumption. Pandora would then be the first shopper. Pandora and Epimetheus wander the shopping malls at this very moment. From a strict Marxian perspective, heavy on productivism, they have opted out from the male task of building the future: they really ought to be welders in Magnitogorsk, building more steel mills. For Marx on Prometheus, see chapter 1, note 31.

13. Hegel to Friedrich Immanuel Niethammer, October 28, 1808, in G. W. F. Hegel, *The Letters*, trans. Butler and Seiler, 179. Hegel's statement in the letter can be regarded as a concretization of his assertion in the preface to the *Phenomenology* that "spirit is indeed never at rest but always engaged in moving forward" (Hegel, *Phenomenology of Spirit*, trans. A. V. Miller, foreword by J. N. Findlay [Oxford: Oxford University Press, 1977], §11, p. 6). In the letter, abstract "spirit" turns into the flesh-and-blood theorist—Hegel—carrying out his scientific work.

14. Thus both Bauer and Feuerbach characterized themselves as occupying an "extreme" position—an accurate characterization (especially of Bauer), since their intent was to identify and then accentuate the contradictions that they perceived in the present order of things. Bauer proclaims that "Only truth is extreme [*extrem*]"; Feuerbach declares that "only the final, uttermost degree, only the *extreme*, is always the truth." Bruno Bauer, re-

view of Theodor Kliesoth, *Einleitung in die Dogmengeschichte*, in *Anekdota zur neuesten deutschen Philosophie und Publicistik*, ed. Arnold Ruge (2 vols.; Zurich, 1843 [rpt., Glashütten im Taunus: Detlev Auvermann, 1971]), 2: 135–59, at 155; and Ludwig Feuerbach, *Das Wesen des Glaubens im Sinne Luthers: Ein Beitrag zum "Wesen des Christentums"* (1844), in Feuerbach, *Kleinere Schriften II: (1839–1846)* , 2., durchgesehene Aufl., ed. Wolfgang Harich (Berlin: Akademie-Verlag, 1982 [*Gesammelte Werke*, ed. Werner Schuffenhauer, vol. 9]), 356. (I was led to these two statements by Brudney, *Marx's Attempt to Leave Philosophy*, 110, 385.)

15. Heinrich Heine, *Sämtliche Werke*, ed. Jonas Fränkel and others (11 vols.; Leipzig: Insel, 1910–20), 7: 344 (*Zur Geschichte der Religion und Philosophie in Deutschland* [1834–35]); 9: 484 ("Briefe über Deutschland" [unfinished, posthumously published]); and 10: 171 ("Geständnisse" [1854]), passages quoted and discussed in Toews, *Hegelianism*, 95–97.

16. See Margaret A. Rose, *Reading the Young Marx and Engels: Poetry, Parody, and the Censor* (London: Croom Helm, 1978), 20, 24, 27–28, 38–39, and passim. Rose suggests that as early as 1837, in his love poetry, Marx took Heine as his poetic model. Pointedly, Heine was not included in the amnesty that was subsequently granted to the Young Germans (Rose, 21, 24). Heine had been living in Paris since 1831; as Draper notes, during Marx's time in Paris (October 1843–January 1845) the two associated closely with each other, "with Heine often visiting the Marx family to go over his poems" (DRAP 3: 90–91).

17. Bruno Bauer, *The Trumpet of the Last Judgement against Hegel the Atheist and Antichrist*, trans. Lawrence Stepelevich (Lewiston, N.Y.: E. Mellen, 1988); excerpts from Bauer's *Trumpet* are to be found in *The Young Hegelians*, ed. Lawrence S. Stepelevich (Cambridge: Cambridge University Press, 1983), 177–86.

18. The entire passage (*MEGA2* 1. 1: 66–70/*MECW* 1: 84–87) appears, incongruously, as the second note to the missing section IV ("General Difference in Principle Between the Democritean and Epicurean Philosophy of Nature") of the Erster Teil of the dissertation. The passage is out of keeping with the eleven notes that follow it, which really are notes. For this reason, and because the explicitly radical tone and content of the passage also do not accord with most of the rest of the dissertation manuscript, I assume, but do not know with certainty, that the passage did not form part of the submitted dissertation.

19. Brudney, *Marx's Attempt to Leave Philosophy*, 110.

20. I here quote from Marx's passage on philosophical historiography (*philosophische Geschichtsschreibung*), also discussed in chapter 1. It is no accident that these crucial passages occur in relation to Marx's discussions of the "history of philosophy [*Philosophiegeschichte*]" and of "philosophical historiography." That they do underscores my claim for the primacy of the history of philosophy in Marx's understanding of the rationality of the world. As the editors of *MEGA2* point out, the notion of "nodal points" (*Knoten*) in the history of philosophy is to be found in Hegel's *Lectures on the History of Philosophy* (see *LHP* 2: 13–14/1833 ed., 14: 182).

21. In a significant passage that appears in Marx's second "Notebook on Epicurean Philosophy" (written April–August 1839), Marx refers to "the Kantians" (who believe that there exists a noumenon that is inaccessible to human knowing) in the following terms: "The Kantians . . . are, so to speak, the appointed priests of unknowing [*die angestellten Priester des Nichtwissens*]; their daily business is to say the rosary over their own impotence and the potency of things" (*MEGA2* 4.1: 36–37/*MECW* 1: 428–29).

22. Francis Wheen, *Karl Marx* (London: Fourth Estate, 1999).

23. David Felix, *Marx As Politician* (Carbondale: Southern Illinois University Press, 1983) offers a short, opinionated, unsympathetic, but clear and pointed account of the young Marx's political engagement with his own time and place: pp. 1–19 take Marx from his beginnings to the date of his resignation from the editorship of the *Rheinische Zeitung*, March 17, 1843. Jerrold E. Seigel, *Marx's Fate: The Shape of a Life* (University Park: Pennsylvania State University Press, 1993 [orig. ed. 1978]), 1–119, offers a far more searching and detailed account of Marx's life up to October 1843; he deals, of course, with much more than politics. A medium between Felix and Seigel is David McLellan, *Karl Marx: His Life and Thought* (New York, Harper & Row, 1973), chapter 1, "Trier, Bonn and Berlin," 1–61. For Trier specifically, Heinz Monz, *Karl Marx: Grundlagen der Entwicklung zu Leben und Werk*, expanded 2d ed. of *Karl Marx und Trier* (Trier: NCO–Verlag, 1973) is comprehensive and authoritative. One should also not forget the month-by-month, even day-by-day, chronology provided in Hal Draper's *Marx-Engels Chronicle* (DRAP 1). The most readable biography is Wheen's, noted above; the most serious, Seigel's.

24. While a detailed knowledge of the political, social, and cultural context of Germany in this period is not required for an understanding of the present book, the subject is inherently interesting, and a reliable and comprehensive account is to be found in James J. Sheehan, *German History, 1770–1866* (Oxford: Oxford University Press, 1989), part three, "The Limits of Restoration, 1815–1848," 389–653.

25. Seigel, *Marx's Fate*, 39–40; for a more detailed account of the political situation in Trier in the 1830s, see Monz, *Karl Marx*, 126–38.

26. More could be said about the dissertation than I hazard here or in the previous chapter. Particularly valuable is Breckman's discussion of "Marx's Dissertation: Atomism and the Theological Intellect," in Breckman, *Marx, the Young Hegelians, and the Origins of Radical Social Theory*, 259–72, an account that I have found essential for my own attempt to understand the dissertation materials. Discussion with Kevin Coffey, and a memo by him, were equally important in helping me to crack the nut of Marx's dissertation, which I initially found close to unbreakable.

27. See Mah, *The End of Philosophy*, 59–62.

28. Wolff's expulsion from Halle came to be elevated into an almost mythic event, with the Pietists playing the role of villain (in his "Leading Article in No. 179 of the *Kölnische Zeitung*," published in July 1842, Marx himself alludes to the conflict between Wolff and his religious opponents [*MEGA2* 1.1: 189/*MECW* 1: 201]). What actually happened was much more interesting and complex, as John Robert Holloran, "Professors of Enlightenment at the University of Halle, 1690–1730" (unpublished Ph.D. dissertation, University of Virginia, 2000), shows.

29. We actually know almost nothing directly about what either Epicurus or Democritus wrote. None of Democritus' writings survive. Out of an alleged 300 manuscripts by Epicurus, only three letters and a number of short fragments survive. In short, practically everything we know about the doctrines of these two writers come to us at second hand. Thus Marx's conclusions are best regarded as a brilliant spinning out of inferences from a tiny body of source material. This is one reason why the dissertation ought to be seen more as an allegorical commentary by Marx on the state of critical philosophy circa 1840 than as a treatise in the history of philosophy.

30. Breckman, *Marx, the Young Hegelians, and the Origins of Radical Social Theory*, 264.

31. Felix, *Marx As Politician*, 13–18, offers a vivid brief account of Marx's involvement with the *Rheinische Zeitung*. The earliest substantial account of Marx's journalism

that I am aware of is Arthur F. McGovern's little-known paper, "Karl Marx' First Political Writings: The *Rheinische Zeitung*, 1842–43," in *Demythologizing Marxism: A Series of Studies on Marxism*, ed. Frederick J. Adelmann (The Hague: Martinus Nijhoff, 1969), 19–63. A large number of documents relevant to the *Rheinische Zeitung* are to be found in *Rheinische Briefe und Akten zur Geschichte der politischen Bewegung 1830–1850*, ed. Joseph Hansen (Essen: Baedeker, 1919), 1: *1830–1845*, 401–506 and passim. Felix suggests that Marx was helped in establishing his authority over the *Rheinische Zeitung* by the fact that two directors of the paper, Georg Jung and Dagobert Oppenheim, both of them lawyers, both bankers' sons, had been members of the Doctors' Club and were friends of Marx (13). We do know that, in a letter of October 18, 1841, to Arnold Ruge, Jung wrote of Marx that "although he is a desperate revolutionary [*ein ganz verzweifelter Revolutionär*]" he had "one of the sharpest minds [*schärfsten Köpfe*] that I know" (Karl Marx and Friedrich Engels, *Gesamtausgabe (MEGA)* [12 vols.; Frankfurt, Berlin, Moscow: Marx-Engels-Verlag and others, 1927–35], I. Abteilung, Bd. 1, *Marx: Werke und Schriften bis Anfang 1844* [Berlin, 1929; rpt. Glashütten im Taunus: Detlev Auvermann, 1970], 2. Halbbd., *Jugendarbeit, Nachträge, Briefe und Dokumente*, 261–62, at 262). Except for the fact that Marx eventually brought the hand of the government down upon the paper, he proved to be a highly capable editor.

32. In a letter of April 15, 1895, to Richard Fischer, Engels gave an account of the shift in Marx's interests that is broadly congruent with the account offered in the 1859 preface. Engels reports that Marx had told him that having to deal, as editor of the *RZ*, with conditions in the Moselle wine-growing region and with the law on theft of wood had caused him "to be pointed from mere politics [*bloßen Politik*] to economic relations [*ökonomische Verhältnisse*] and so to have come to socialism" (*MEW* 39: 466). There is no question that Marx's experience with the *Rheinische Zeitung* led him to think more about economic issues than previously. My argument, to be worked out in the rest of this chapter and in chapter 3, is that Marx's shift to historical materialism involved at least two additional moments: the conclusion that politics is not amenable to Marx's rationality-criteria, and the conclusion that material production (but not the market) *is* amenable to these criteria.

33. In addition to the thirty-two articles listed in the appendix and taken account of in table 2.1, *MEGA2* includes among Marx's articles three brief announcements that are of no intellectual significance and which I have excluded from the page count.

34. The document in question, "Minutes of the General Meeting of the Shareholders of the *Rheinische Zeitung*. February 12, 1843" is amazing. It records a conflict between those who deplored the paper's "blunt tone" and "caustic and sarcastic language" and proposed that the paper take a tamer line, and those who held that it had been established as a "partisan newspaper" to "represent a definite trend," namely, "the liberal tendency in Germany." Supporters of the latter position went so far as to argue that it would be better for the paper to be banned than have it betray the principles on which it had been founded (see *MEGA2* 1.1: 434–43, at 437–39, 442, and passim/*MECW* 1: 712–24, at 717–19, 724, and passim). A petition to the king asking that the paper not be suppressed was signed by 911 citizens. There is no doubt that the *Rheinische Zeitung* had come to be widely noticed: in January 1843, shortly before its banning, its circulation was 3,300–3,400, very substantial for the time, although still under the *Kölnische Zeitung*'s circulation of 9,000 (*Rheinische Briefe* 1: 410, 411).

35. I allude to Alexander Bain's deflationary proposal that "the genuine, unmistakable criterion of belief" is "preparedness to act," a proposal that, famously, was taken up by C.

S. Peirce and then, largely through Peirce's stimulus, by William James. See: Alexander Bain, *The Emotions and the Will*, 3d ed. (New York: Appleton, 1876 [1st ed., 1859]), 505ff.; C. S. Peirce's fragment, "Pragmatism Made Easy" (1906), quoted in Joseph Brent, *C. S. Peirce: A Life* (Bloomington: Indiana University Press, 1993), 85; and James's brilliant and provocative paper, "The Will to Believe," in William James, *The Will to Believe and Other Essays in Popular Philosophy* (New York: Longmans Green, 1897; rpt. New York: Dover, 1990), 1–31. Our concern here is not to define belief but rather to think intelligently about what Marx believed. Let us assume, in a Peircean spirit, that if Marx acted in ways congruent with a certain set of beliefs, he really did adhere to those beliefs.

36. This fact was observed by the *Mannheimer Abendzeitung* in an article of February 28, 1843. Alluding to Marx's articles on press censorship (May 1842) and on the wood-theft law (October–November 1842), the *Mannheimer Abendzeitung* declares that:

> the reader of these long articles still remembers very well the sharp, incisive understanding, the truly admirable dialectic, with which the author tore apart the empty remarks of the deputies and then annihilated them from the inside out; rarely has the critical understanding been seen to operate with such an eagerly destructive virtuosity, never has it more brilliantly shown its hatred of the so-called "positive," which it has caught and crushed in its own virulent propaganda.

Quoted in *MEGA2* 1.1: 1021. The *MEGA2* editors do not identify the author, but it must surely have been Karl Ludwig Bernays, the editor of the *Abendzeitung*, who fled to Paris in 1843 under threat of arrest for his writings. There he collaborated with Marx and Ruge on the *Deutsch-Französische Jahrbücher*, to whose only issue he contributed two articles. He also edited the radical émigré journal *Vorwarts!*, in which Marx published "Critical Marginal Notes on 'The King of Prussia and Social Reform.'" On Bernays: DRAP 3: 20.

37. For example, in his second "Notebook on Epicurean Philosophy" Marx observes, critically, that ancient philosophy "knows that ideas [*Vorstellungen*] are in consciousness, but . . . does not know their boundary, their principle, their necessity" (*MEGA2* 4.1: 31/*MECW* 1: 425). Similarly, at the beginning of the "Estranged Labor and Private Property" section of the "Economic and Philosophical Manuscripts" (1844), Marx observes that "political economy proceeds from the [contingent] fact of private property. It does not explain it" (*MEGA2* 1.2: 363/*MECW* 3: 270/*EW* 322).

38. Often this is the thing to look for when one wants to consider the question of how plausibly Marx is portraying whatever situation he is attending to. It can safely be said, as a rule, that Marx over-bifurcates. Marx's portrayal of capitalism offers the most massive instance of this.

39. Marx's bifurcatory tendency is repeatedly signaled on the stylistic level by the tropes of antithesis and inversion. Especially in his early writing he is addicted to the particular type of inversion known as chiasmus (which has the form "the A of the B . . . the B of the A"). See, for example: "The *censorship of tendency* and the *tendency of censorship* are a *gift of the new liberal instruction*;" "His fear of the bad [press] is seen to be fear of the good [press]"; "The press law punishes the abuse of freedom. The censorship law punishes freedom as an abuse" (*MEGA2* 1.1: 110, 145, 150/*MECW* 1: 123, 157, 161). A multitude of other examples could equally well be cited. Chiasmus (from the Greek letter chi, the Greek alphabet's equivalent of X) serves to highlight a thing or situation that is apparently centered and unified, but that has within it radically opposed possibilities.

40. Hegel, *Phenomenology of Spirit* (note 13, above), preface, §5, 3.

41. On the neo-Platonic motif of the "circuitous journey" from unity, through division, to unity at a higher level, see M. H. Abrams, *Natural Supernaturalism: Tradition and Revolution in Romantic Literature* (New York: Norton, 1971), 169–95 and passim.

42. This fact is completely obscured when *MECW* mistranslates "ideal struggle" as "ideological struggle." The mistranslation is presumably intended to show that the Marx of December 1842 was already very close to being a historical materialist. It seems clear that the Marx of 1842 did not have a clearly defined conception of what political debate is, if it is not simply philosophical-scientific reasoning applied to the human order. But it is equally clear that he had not yet made his reductionist move—he had not yet reduced political debate to something that is "merely" ideological.

43. This is a point that Arthur F. McGovern particularly emphasizes, among previous commentators. Admittedly, in this period "the state," for Marx, meant the whole life of the nation and not simply its political life, for he had not yet articulated his later sharp distinction between state and civil society. See McGovern, "Karl Marx' First Political Writings: The *Rheinische Zeitung*, 1842–43," 60–63.

44. Why think of the second half of 1841 as the time by which Marx had constructed his theoretical and revolutionary personae? Because by that time there is clear documentary evidence that Marx was impressing these personae on his contemporaries. I have in mind Moses Hess's letter of September 2 praising Marx's philosophical abilities to the skies and Georg Jung's letter of October 18 identifying Marx as both a "desperate revolutionary" and as "one of the sharpest minds I know" (letters cited at chapter 1, note 100 and this chapter, note 31).

45. "If by the constitution we mean the universal, fundamental determinants of the rational will [*des vernünftigen Willens*], it follows that every people (state) must have this as its premise. . . . This is actually a matter of knowledge [*Wissens*] rather than will. The will of a people may not overstep the laws of reason [*die Gesetze der Vernunft*]. . . . In the case of an irrational people we cannot speak of a rational organization of the state" [*vernünftigen Staatsorganisation*]. (*MEGA2* 1.2: 61–62/*MECW* 3: 58/*EW* 120)

46. In the "Critique of Hegel's Doctrine of the State" Marx repeats the point about discovering, rather than making, laws: "The legislature does not make the law, it only discovers and formulates it [*Die gesetzgebende Gewalt macht das Gesetz nicht, sie entdeckt und formulirt es nur*]." (*MEGA2* 1.2: 62/*MECW* 3: 58/*EW* 120).

47. "Critique of Hegel's Doctrine of the State" is in fact untitled. It has often been referred to as "Critique of Hegel's Philosophy of Right." "Critique of Hegel's Doctrine of the State" is more precise as to the contents of the manuscript, since it is a critique of the parts of Hegel's *Elements of the Philosophy of Right* that deal with "the idea of the state." Perhaps a better title would be "Critique of Hegel's Political Theory [*Staatsrecht*]," suggested by Hal Draper in DRAP 2: 35, #206, but the suggestion has not been taken up. The *MEGA2* title is "Zur Kritik der Hegelschen Rechtsphilosophie."

48. Cf. *The Communist Manifesto* (1848), where Marx and Engels speak glowingly of a bourgeoisie that "has subjected the country to the rule of the town . . . created enormous cities, vastly inflated the urban population as opposed to the rural, and so rescued a significant part of the population from *the idiocy of living on the land*" (*MEW* 4: 466/*MECW* 6: 488/*LPW* 5/*MER* 477 [my italics]). No country boys, these fishers in the afternoon.

49. See chapter III, section 4, "The Sociological Problem of the 'Intelligentsia,'" in Karl Mannheim, *Ideology and Utopia: With an Introduction to the Sociology of Knowledge*, trans. Louis Wirth and Edward Shils, with a preface by Louis Wirth (New York: Harcourt, Brace, 1949), 136–46.

50. A further complication is introduced by the sentence, quoted earlier in the text, that follows the sentence just quoted: "The state pervades the whole of nature with spiritual nerves . . . what is dominant is not matter, but form, not nature without the state, but the nature of the state, not the *unfree object*, but the *free human being* (*MEGA2* 1.1: 285/*MECW* 1: 306). The last phrase already anticipates a (Feuerbachian) reduction of the state to "man," a move that was shortly to become prominent in Marx's thinking about the human sphere.

51. On Ruge, good points of entry are provided by Mah, *The End of Philosophy*, Part III, "Arnold Ruge and the Crisis in Political Theory," 87–144, and by Breckman, *Marx, the Young Hegelians, and the Origins of Radical Social Theory*, chapter 6, "Arnold Ruge: Radical Democracy and the Politics of Personhood, 1838–1843," 221–57. Both Marx and Ruge had been the victims of censorship, an obvious point of connection and sympathy between them. Under Prussian pressure, the government of Saxony had suppressed Ruge's journal, the *Deutsche Jahrbücher*, in January 1843, shortly before the closing down of the *Rheinische Zeitung*.

52. There is a vast literature on the modern republican tradition, much of it stimulated by J. G. A. Pocock, *The Machiavellian Moment: Florentine Political Thought and the Atlantic Republican Tradition* (Princeton: Princeton University Press, 1975).

53. In a letter written in 1890, Engels asserted that Marx had told him that Ruge had prepared the letters for publication, and that in doing so "had inserted all kinds of nonsense" (Engels to Wilhelm Liebknecht, December 18, 1890, *MEW* 37: 527/*MECW* 49; see also DRAP 1: 261, #49; 2: 55, #471). Engels opposed a plan that was afoot to republish the letters. Unfortunately, the letters often appear in collections of Marx's writings without any editorial warning attached to them: see *MECW* 3: 133–45, 591 n. 18, *EW* 200–206, and *MER* 12–15. In *MEW* the letters appear at 1: 337–46, and although at *MEW* 1: 609 n. 144 there is a cross–reference to Engels's December 18, 1890, letter, Engels's objections to Ruge's editorial work are understated. The fact that Ruge did a very heavy editorial job on the letters is finally emphasized in *MEGA2* 1.2: 939–41.

Engels is not the only source on this matter. We now know that Ruge himself wrote to the progressive publisher Julius Fröbel, in a letter of December 19, 1843, that "Ich schreibe noch einige Briefe nach Originalen von Bacun, Feuerb, Marx und mir [I am still writing a few letters, following originals by Bakunin, Feuerbach, Marx and myself]" (*MEGA2* 1.2: 939, quoting Ruge's letter in the Fröbel Nachlaß, Zentralbibliothek Zürich). Observe that Ruge says that he is *writing* the letters—not that he is *editing* them. Accordingly, the published letters ought to be regarded as free variations, by Ruge, on the now lost originals that his colleagues had written to him. (Later, in his "Critical Notes on 'The King of Prussia and Social Reform'" [published August 1844], attacking an article by Ruge, Marx skewers claims in Ruge's "The King of Prussia . . ." as to the "unpolitical" nature of the Germans that are also present, although more briefly stated, in the "May 1843" letter that is putatively by Marx. One suspects that, in part, Marx was getting back at Ruge for putting words into his mouth. See *MEGA2* 1.2: 475–77, 449–52 [the letter is also printed in *MEGA2* 3.1: 48–53]/*MECW* 3: 134–38, 191–94/*EW* 201–2, 405–7).

54. For example, in 1840 Ruge declared that the plight of the impoverished masses [*Pöbel*] "will only be overcome through democracy, the courageous realization of the state *as the public essence*"; in 1842 he declared that "outside political life there are no free people, only resigned Christians"; and in 1845 he stated his wish for "politicization of all hu-

manity" and equally for the "humanization of the state." Quotations are from, respectively, Ruge, "Erinnerungen aus dem äusseren Leben, von Ernst Moritz Arndt" (1840), in *Die Hegelsche Linke: Dokumente zu Philosophie und Politik im deutschen Vormärz*, ed. Heinz and Ingrid Pepperle (Frankfurt: Röderberg, 1986), 186; Ruge, "Der christliche Staat: Gegen den Wirtemberger über das Preussenthum" (1842), in Ruge, *Gesammelte Schriften* (10 vols.; Mannheim, 1846), 3: 475; and Ruge, "Unsre letzten zehn Jahren" (1845), in Ruge, *Gesammelte Schriften*, 6: 62. I rely in part on Breckman, *Marx, the Young Hegelians, and the Origins of Radical Social Theory*, 245, 252, 240, which has an extensive discussion, 246ff., of what Breckman calls the "humanist republicanism" of Ruge.

55. The references to democracy in "Critique of Hegel's Doctrine of the State" and in "On the Jewish Question" are to be found at *MEGA2* 1.2: 30–33, 125–26/*MECW* 3: 29–32, 115–16/*EW* 86–90, 185–86 and at *MEGA2* 1.2: 152/*MECW* 3: 157/*EW* 223, respectively.

56. For one discussion, see Shlomo Avineri, *The Social and Political Thought of Karl Marx* (Cambridge: Cambridge University Press, 1968), 35–39; also 202–4, 208–12, and passim.

57. Ludwig Feuerbach, *The Essence of Christianity*, trans. George Eliot (Buffalo, N.Y.: Prometheus Books, 1989), appendix, §10; see also chapter XI, "The Significance of the Creation in Judaism," and chapter XXVI, "The Contradiction of Faith and Love," both passim.

58. Marx first articulated at length the notion of a radical opposition between state and civil society in "On the Jewish Question" (*MEGA2* 1. 2: 156–63/*MECW* 3: 160–68/*EW* 227–34); he first stated it, although very succinctly, in "Critique of Hegel's Doctrine of the State" (*MEGA2* 1.2: 78–79, 86, 89/*MECW* 3: 73, 77, 79–80/*EW* 137, 143, 146; and passim). Avineri offers a useful brief survey of Marx's thinking on the lessons and significance of the French Revolution; see Avineri, *Social and Political Thought of Karl Marx*, chapter 7, "The French Revolution and the Terror: The Achievements and Limits of Political Revolution," 185–201.

59. Similarly, in the third programmatic letter to Ruge, dated September 1843, it is stated that with the full development of political representation, the representative system of government is raised "from its political form to a general one" (*MEGA2* 1.2: 488/*MECW* 3: 144/*EW* 208). As noted already, the text of the letter is in principle problematic, and the possibility that Ruge made changes in the passage I have quoted is not excluded. But the same argument is prominent in "On the Jewish Question," which Marx quite possibly began writing as early as the following month (*MEGA2* 1.2: 155, 162–63/*MECW* 3: 159–60, 167–68/*EW* 225–26, 234; DRAP 1: 15).

60. G. W. F. Hegel, *Lectures on the Philosophy of World History: Introduction: Reason in History*, trans. H. B. Nisbet from the German edition of Johannes Hoffmeister, with an introduction by Duncan Forbes (Cambridge: Cambridge University Press, 1975), 24, 28, 29.

61. Some of Marx's acquaintances were aware of his plans. Arnold Ruge referred to the project in letters of May 20 and July 9, 1844, to a friend, Karl Moritz Fleischer. Ruge claims in the July 9 letter that Marx "wanted . . . to write the history of the Convention and to that end has read enormously" (Ruge, *Briefwechsel und Tagebuchblätter aus den Jahren 1825–1880*, ed. Paul Nerrlich [2 vols.; Berlin: Weidmannsche Buchhandlung, 1886]: 1: 354, 362).

62. The reasons for this difference are complex, but have much to do with the long existence in Germany of the so-called cameralist tradition, which aimed at systematizing and thus rendering teachable the practical knowledge that would be needed by German civil

servants. The authoritative study is David F. Lindenfeld, *The Practical Imagination: The German Sciences of State in the Nineteenth Century* (Chicago: University of Chicago Press, 1997).

63. See "Critique of Hegel's Doctrine of the State," *MEGA2* 1.2: 33, 89, 91/*MECW* 3: 32, 79–80, 81/*EW* 90, 146, 148; and passim. For more on the state/civil society split and on the need for its overcoming, see "On the Jewish Question," part 1, but especially *MEGA2* 1.2: 150–52, 162–63/*MECW* 3: 155–57, 168/*EW* 221–23, 234.

64. Besides referring to the French Revolution in "Critique of Hegel's Doctrine of the State" and in "On the Jewish Question," the Marx of 1843–early 1844 also referred to it in "Critique of Hegel's Philosophy of Right: Introduction," published, like "On the Jewish Question," in the *Deutsch-Französische Jahrbücher* in February 1844. (The Revolution is also referred to in two of the three programmatic letters to Arnold Ruge, those dated March and May 1843, that also appeared in the *Deutsch-Französische Jahrbücher*; these references may well have been Marx's own rather than insertions by Ruge, although we cannot quite know.) Selections from these texts, and from a large number of other texts ranging from 1842 to 1881 in which Marx alludes to the French Revolution can be found conveniently assembled in *Marx and the French Revolution*, trans. Deborah Kan Furet, ed. François Furet, selections by Karl Marx edited and introduced by Lucien Calvié (Chicago: University of Chicago Press, 1988).

65. The *MEGA2* editors note that "although Marx assembled and worked through an extensive literature . . . he could not realize his plan of writing a history of the Convention. The reason for this is not known. However it is presumably connected with the fact that at this time Marx's interest in problems of political economy greatly increased." (*MEGA2* 4.2: 725) But of course this begs the question—which is, *why* did he shift from political history to political economy?

66. Ruge to Ludwig Feuerbach, May 15, 1844, in Ruge, *Briefwechsel und Tagebuchblätter aus den Jahren 1825–1880*, ed. Paul Nerrlich (2 vols.; Berlin: Weidmannsche Buchhandlung, 1886), 1: 345. See also Ruge to Karl Moritz Fleischer, May 20, 1844, in *Briefwechsel* 1: 354.

67. Ruge to Karl Moritz Fleischer, July 9, 1844, in *Briefwechsel* 1: 362. At the time of Marx's banishment from France in early 1845, the *Trier'sche Zeitung* remarked on his plans to write on the history of the French Convention (so reports *MECW* 3: 606 n. 117), although its personnel does not seem to have had a direct connection to Marx and there is reason to think that by that time its information was out of date. In a short note to the paper, written and published in January 1846, Marx objected to the apparent presence of his name on its masthead, noted that he had not written "a single line" for it, and remarked upon the paper's "bourgeois-philanthropic and in no way communistic tendencies" (*MEW* 2: 625/*MECW* 6: 34).

68. Cf. *MECW*, whose editors note that Marx "worked on [the history of the French Convention] during several months of 1844, reading a lot of material, including the press of the time, memoirs of contemporaries, etc" (*MECW* 3: 606 n. 117). However, little of this material appears in *MECW*.

69. The *MEGA2* editors write, of the Levasseur notes, that they are "evidently the only surviving material from the broad preparatory work that Marx carried out in Paris at the end of 1843 and beginning of 1844 for the writing of a history of the Convention. He had already become particularly interested in this central episode of the French Revolution in summer 1843 in Kreuznach [Germany]" (*MEGA2* 4.2: 725). For a modern edition of Lev-

asseur, see René Levasseur (de la Sarthe), *Mémoires*, preface by Michel Vovelle, presented and annotated by Christine Peyrard (Paris: Messidor, 1989).

70. Furet, "Marx and the French Enigma (1851–1871)," in *Marx and the French Revolution*, 66–96; quotations at 66. The only published product of Marx's researches into the history of the French Revolution is to be found in Marx and Engels, *The Holy Family: or Critique of Critical Criticism*, chapter VI (c), where Marx criticizes Bruno Bauer's interpretation of the Revolution (*MEW* 2: 125–31/*MECW* 4: 118–24). *The Holy Family* was written in September–November 1844 and published in February 1845.

71. In addition, one finds in Marx's immediate intellectual vicinity two other instances, besides the *Lectures on the History of Philosophy*, of the kind of deductive, necessary history that the *LHP* offers.

One model is Bruno Bauer's attempt to "develop the 'idea of revelation' as a specific stage in religious development" (Toews, *Hegelianism*, 299) in his 1838 work, *The Religion of the Old Testament in the Historical Development of Its Principles*. See Bruno Bauer, *Die Religion des Alten Testamentes in der geschichtlichen Entwickelung ihrer Principien dargestellt* (2 vols.; Berlin: Dümmler, 1838; rpt. under the title *Kritik der Geschichte der Offenbarung*, 1 [einziger] Teil in 2 Bänden [Aalen: Scientia, 1983]).

The other model is Eduard Gans's attempt to work out "the immanent development of the concept of law" (Breckman, *Marx, the Young Hegelians, and the Origins of Radical Social Theory*, 261) as manifested in Gans's *The Right of Inheritance in World-Historical Development* (1824–35). Breckman has noted the affinity between Gans's work and Marx's discussion, in his November 1837 letter to his father, of his abortive attempt to work out a philosophy of law: "Marx expresses his determination to link the empirical history of law with the conceptual development of the idea of self-determining human subjectivity, the very approach that informed both Gans's four-volume *magnum opus* on the history of inheritance law and his long polemic against Savigny and the Historical School of Law" (Breckman, "Eduard Gans and the Crisis of Hegelianism: Associationism, Civil Society, and the Social Question," *Journal of the History of Ideas* 62 [2001]: 543–64; Marx's description of his abortive philosophy of law is to be found in *MEGA2* 3.1: 10–15/*MECW* 1: 11–17). Although never a student of Hegel's, Gans was his close proselyte and protegé; on the Gans–Hegel relation, see Michael H. Hoffheimer, *Eduard Gans and the Hegelian Philosophy of Law* (Dordrecht: Kluwer, 1995), 9–18.

Finally, it should be noted that in the third of his *Polemical Writings* (1837) the theologian David Friedrich Strauss raised the question, "whether and to what degree the gospel history is given *as* history by the idea of the unity of divine and human nature." Strauss identified three answers—all of the gospel history is deducible from the idea, some of it is, and none of it is—corresponding to what he called the "right," "center," and "left" Hegelian schools. Significantly, Strauss identified Bauer as a "right" Hegelian, who holds that the entirety of the Gospel history is deducible from the Idea (only subsequently did Bauer come to be identified as a "left" Hegelian). See David Friedrich Strauss, *Streitschriften zur Verteidigung meiner Schrift über das Leben Jesu und zur Charakteristik der gegenwärtigen Theologie*, 3 Hefte in 1 Band (rpt. Hildesheim: Olms, 1980), drittes Heft: *Die evangelische Kirchenzeitung* . . . (Tübingen: Osiander, 1837), III. Teil, "Verschiedene Richtungen innerhalb der Hegel'schen Schule in Betreff der Christologie," 95, 101–20.

While it is clear that Hegel's *History of Philosophy* was his one truly dialectical history, the idea of deducing history from "the idea" was clearly part of a broader Hegelian mindset, as the instance of Gans, who was not a student of Hegel's and who could have read the *LHP* only after their publication in the 1830s, especially shows. Of the works that I here mention, however, Hegel's *History of Philosophy* was closest to Marx, for he had very little interest in theology and he abandoned law for philosophy by 1838.

72. Note Hegel's German, as rendered in the first edition of his *Lectures on the History of Philosophy: "Die Zufälligkeit muß man mit dem Eintritt in die Philosophie aufgeben."* This could be more literally translated as "When one enters into philosophy, one must give up contingency." One might say that the difference between Hegel and Marx is that, whereas Hegel is attentive to the interpretive condition that leads one to render the world as rational (namely, that one is doing the job of a philosopher, and the job requires one to go for necessity and turn aside from contingency), Marx is much more inclined to think that the rationality ought actually to be there in the world, and to be *made to be there* if it is not. Quotation from Hegel, *Vorlesungen über die Geschichte der Philosophie*, in Hegel, *Werke* (18 vols., Berlin, 1832–45), 1st ed. of vols. 13–15 (Berlin, 1833–36), 13: 50.

73. Consider a passage from a fragment from Hegel's Jena period (1800–1806), "Continuation of the 'System of Morality,'" that would have resonated with Marx if he had known it. Here "men" come in as central to the story, and are curiously both impotent and powerful: "every single man is but a blind link in the chain of absolute necessity by which the world builds itself forth. The single man can devote himself to dominance [*Herrschaft*] over an appreciable length of this chain only if he knows the direction in which the great necessity wants to move, and if he learns from this knowledge to pronounce the magic words [*die Zauberworte*] that will evoke its form [*Gestalt*]." (G. W. F. Hegel, "Fortzsetzung des 'System der Sittlichkeit,'" in *Dokumente zu Hegels Entwicklung*, ed. Johannes Hoffmeister [Stuttgart-Bad Cannstatt: Frommann-Holzboog, 1974 (reprint of 1936 ed.)], 314–25, at 324–25.)

74. Zvi Rosen, *Bruno Bauer and Karl Marx: The Influence of Bruno Bauer on Marx's Thought* (The Hague: Nijhoff, 1977), 127–32 is illuminating on the relations between Marx and Bauer.

75. Bruno Bauer, *The Jewish Problem*, trans. Helen Lederer (Cincinnati: Hebrew Union College-Jewish Institute of Religion, 1958), 64. Bauer writes: "'But that is extreme! Too extreme!' one will say perhaps. . . . Well, let us investigate the wisdom of the *juste milieu*!" (The Lederer translation is not readily available. Some excerpts from Bauer's book are to be found in *The Young Hegelians*, ed. Stepelevich, 187–97.)

76. Bauer, *The Jewish Problem*, 71.

77. It should be noted that Marx opposed *on pragmatic grounds* the attack on the *juste milieu* that Bauer and his Berlin friends launched. In the *Rheinische Zeitung* in June and August 1842, Edgar Bauer published a five-part article, "Das Juste Milieu," attacking the moderation of Germany's liberals. In a letter to Dagobert Oppenheim dating from late August 1842, Marx suggested that he would be interested in criticizing Edgar Bauer's article. But Marx's reservations had less to do with Bauer's anti-*juste milieu* attitude than with the likelihood that such extremism would harm the *Rheinische Zeitung* in particular and the German opposition movement in general. Marx writes: "The subject must be discussed dispassionately . . . quite general theoretical arguments about the state political system are more suitable for purely scientific organs than for newspapers. The correct theory must be made clear and developed within the concrete conditions and on the basis of the existing state of things" (*MEGA2* 3.1: 31/*MECW* 1: 392). My translation: on the theoretical level Edgar Bauer is probably right, but he should not have discussed the matter publicly.

78. Terrell Carver, "Editor's Introduction," in Karl Marx, *Later Political Writings*, ed. and trans. Terrell Carver (Cambridge: Cambridge University Press, 1996), ix.

79. My claim that Marx was fundamentally not committed to democracy is a *historical* claim. It is not a claim that the political theorist's project of articulating a democratic version of Marxism is unjustified. What is unjustified is the attempt to attribute a democratic version of Marxism to Marx himself. "*Magnifique*," one might say, "*mais pas vrai*."

80. Brian Snyder, "Freedom for/from Politics in Marx," unpublished paper in my possession, 2001, 1–2.

81. Marx refers to "the democratic state" in "On the Jewish Question" (*MEGA2* 1.2: 152/*MECW* 3: 157/*EW* 223), and he discusses democracy in "Critique of Hegel's Doctrine of the State" (*MEGA2* 1.2: 30–33, 125–26/*MECW* 3: 29–32, 115–16/*EW* 86–90, 185–86). There is also a reference to "the democratic state" in the textually questionable letter of May 1843 to Ruge (*MEGA2* 1.2: 475–76/*MECW* 3: 134/*EW* 201).

82. This claim is borne out first by Marx's utter failure to elaborate on the notion of a democratic state. Second, it is interesting that a passage from the "Critique of Hegel's Doctrine of the State" quoted earlier, in which Marx asserts that "the legislature does not make the law, it only discovers and formulates it," is followed by a passage that Marx crossed out: " . . . so that in democracy, accordingly, the legislature does not decide the organization of the whole. . . ." (*MEGA2* 1.2: 62, 599/*MECW* 3: 58/*EW* 120). It is hard to interpret this passage, or its exclusion. But it does at least *suggest* (perhaps too transparently?) an identification of the *democratic* state with the *rational* state, which is the theme of the passage within which this sentence appears.

83. Norman D. Livergood, *Activity in Marx's Philosophy* (The Hague: Martinus Nijhoff, 1967). Livergood's book includes the earliest complete published translation into English of Marx's doctoral dissertation.

84. Persons wishing to get a feel for the character and magnitude of Marx's and Engels's reflections on politics might well begin their researches by consulting the volumes that Hal Draper wrote in an attempt to arrive at "a full and definitive treatment of Marx's political theory, policies, and practice": Draper, *Karl Marx's Theory of Revolution* (5 vols.; New York: Monthly Review Press, 1977–90), 1: 11.

One might also examine selected volumes of their works—say, *MECW*, vols. 8 and 9, covering the revolutionary and counter-revolutionary years 1848–49. There are also various collections of Marx's and Engels's journalism on specific subjects, including Marx, *The Eastern Question: A Reprint of Letters Written 1853–1856 Dealing with the Events of the Crimean War*, ed. Eleanor Marx Aveling and Edward Aveling (New York: Augustus M. Kelley, 1969 [reprint of 1897 edition]); Karl Marx and Friedrich Engels, *The First Indian War of Independence, 1857–1859* (Moscow: Foreign Languages Publishing House, 1960); and Karl Marx, *On Colonialism and Modernization: His Despatches and Other Writings on China, India, Mexico, the Middle East, and North Africa*, ed. Shlomo Avineri (Garden City, N.Y.: Doubleday Anchor, 1968). (It should be noted that most collections of Marx's and Engels's journalism are editorially defective: *inter alia*, they often attribute to Marx writings that were actually by Engels. But at least they give a quick sense as to what Marx and Engels wrote on specific topics.)

MEGA2 needs to be consulted for definitive editorial information and for authoritative presentations of Marx's and Engels's political texts. In addition, Hal Draper's *The Marx-Engels Cyclopedia* (3 vols.; New York: Schocken, 1985), vol. 2: *The Marx-Engels Register: A Complete Bibliography of Marx and Engels' Individual Writings* is extremely helpful, particularly in its checklists, 160–79, of Marx's and Engels's journalism for various newspapers.

85. Note that it was Engels who concerned himself with the politics of earlier times: see especially Engels's essays on the peasant wars in Germany, conveniently available in Friedrich Engels, *The German Revolutions: "The Peasant War in Germany" and "Germany: Revolution and Counter-Revolution,"* ed. and with an introduction by Leonard Krieger (Chicago: University of Chicago Press, 1967). After the failure of his projected history of the French Revolution Marx's inclination was to focus on contemporary history only.

The literature on Marx's and Engels's historiography is large. Two of Leonard Krieger's essays still provide a useful starting point: "Marx and Engels As Historians," *Journal of the History of Ideas* 14 (1953): 381–403, and "Uses of Marx for History," *Political Science Quarterly* 75 (1960): 355–78; rpt. in Krieger, *Ideas and Events: Professing History*, ed. M. L. Brick, with an introduction by Michael Ermarth (Chicago: University of Chicago Press, 1992), 296–320 and 273–95. Krieger's book also contains an essay focusing on Engels, "Detaching Engels from Marx," 321–51, reprinted from Krieger's edition of Engels, *The German Revolutions*.

Richard Hamilton demolishes Marx's and Engels's attempts to write modern political history, in Hamilton, *The Bourgeois Epoch: Marx and Engels on Britain, France, and Germany* (Chapel Hill: University of North Carolina Press, 1991). Although one could take issue with Hamilton on several grounds, he is resoundingly successful in showing how disconnected the predictions of Marx's and Engels's general theory were from the actual political situations prevailing in nineteenth-century Britain, France, and Germany.

86. Consider, *inter alia*, Jeffrey Mehlman, *Revolution and Repetition: Marx/Hugo/Balzac* (Berkeley and Los Angeles: University of California Press, 1977).

CHAPTER 3

A German version of part of the argument of chapter 3 appears as "Über die Grenzen einer gewissen Art von Sozialtheorie: Marx, der Rationalismus und der Markt," trans. Klaus-Michael Kodalle, in *Republik und Weltbürgerrecht. Kantische Anregungen zur Theorie politischer Ordnung nach dem Ende des Ost-West-Konflikts*, ed. Klaus Dicke and Klaus-Michael Kodalle (Köln: Böhlau, 1998), 363–98.

1. Because the matter becomes relevant in this chapter, I must here note that in this context I am using the terms *socialism* and *communism* to mean essentially the same thing—that is, I am using them to refer to the future society, devoted to human freedom and liberated from both the political state and from the market, that Marx and Engels envisaged as the outcome of history. Marx and Engels themselves waffled somewhat in their usage (which partly accounts for my waffling here), although their tendency was to prefer the term *communism* (see Tom Bottomore, "Communism," in *A Dictionary of Marxist Thought*, ed. Tom Bottomore, 2d ed. [Oxford: Blackwell, 1991], 102–5, at 103). (In the next section I note a distinction between "socialism" and "communism" that some commentators have drawn from Marx's "Critique of the Gotha Programme" [1875].)

2. A paradigmatic case is G. A. Cohen, *Karl Marx's Theory of History: A Defense* (Princeton: Princeton University Press, 1978), one of the founding works of analytical Marxism (on which I touch in chapter 4). Cohen seeks to clean up and in general improve Marx's historical materialism. He does so in a highly intelligent manner. Missing from Cohen's book (and from analytical Marxism more generally) are the historical grounds for

Marx's arguing as he did. Only if we investigate these grounds can we engage in a genuine confrontation with his work.

3. In what follows, whenever I refer to Marx's rejection of the market I also mean his rejection of private property. "Rejection of the market" *means* rejection of buying and selling and of everything that goes along with buying and selling—including, most important, private property and money. It would be irritating and redundant for me to refer in every case to Marx's rejection of "the market and private property and money and buying and selling. . . ." Conversely, when I refer to Marx's rejection of private property, I also mean his rejection of the market. Marx *himself* held that private property entails a market, as we shall see below, in the section "Marx's Unitarism and the Private Property—Market Relation."

4. To be sure, the ten-point program that appears toward the end of *The Communist Manifesto* envisages the abolition only of landed property, not of private property generally (it also calls for a heavy progressive income tax and abolition of the right of inheritance [*MEW* 4: 481–82/*MECW* 6: 505/*MER* 490/*LPW* 19–20]). But the omission of non-landed property was purely tactical: Marx and Engels held that the coming revolution in Germany would be a bourgeois revolution, not a socialist one, so that the best option for the proletariat would be to enter into a united front with the progressive members of the bourgeoisie. If one wants to enter into a united front with the bourgeoisie, one can hardly advocate the general abolition of private property. Of course, Marx and Engels also claimed (and in 1848 likely really believed) that the abolition of private property would nonetheless soon come, for "the bourgeois revolution in Germany can be merely the immediate prelude to a proletarian revolution" (*MEW* 4: 493/*MECW* 6: 519/*MER* 500/*LPW* 30). The revolutions that broke out in western and central Europe shortly after the publication of the *Manifesto* (and entirely independently of it) bore little resemblance to the revolutions that Marx envisaged. The discongruity led him in the 1850s to revise his approach to economics and politics.

5. Why does such a (relatively) specific account of production under communism never appear in any work written or co-written by Marx? I suspect that Marx himself was all too aware of unresolved problems raised by Engels's account. Engels was possibly also aware that there were problems, but Engels's tendency was always to thrust problems aside in the interests of clear exposition. Note, among other things, that Engels appears to assume that human needs are unchanging. But this was certainly not Marx's position: Marx held that needs develop over time (in 1974 I needed a Smith-Corona typewriter with a print ball, in 1985 an Osborne "portable," and now I need a notebook, unknown in 1974 or 1985). Clearly, if needs develop, the task of determining accurately what those needs are going to be next year or the year after is made more difficult. Even if needs do not develop, distribution was clearly going to be a headache. Marx certainly did not want to get into the task of trying to resolve such problems: he found it difficult enough to understand the complexities of capitalism. In any case, ultimately history will solve all problems, in Marx's view.

6. David Ramsay Steele, *From Marx to Mises: Post-Capitalist Society and the Challenge of Economic Calculation* (La Salle, Ill.: Open Court, 1992), chapter 2, "The Abolition of the Market," 25–47 (quote at 25). *From Marx to Mises* is one of the best books on the economic aspects of Marx's theory to have been written in the last twenty-five years. It deserves to be far better known than it is. It confirms by other means a conclusion that I initially reached by a much narrower, almost deductive, reading of Marx. With regard to the question of Marx and the market, my main contribution beyond Steele is to lay out in

a deeper way the intellectual foundations—the system of justification—that Marx thought he had for rejecting the market.

7. V. I. Lenin, *The Lenin Anthology*, ed. Robert C. Tucker (New York: Norton, 1975), 311–98, at 375–84 (chapter V, "The Economic Basis of the Withering Away of the State," sects. 3–4). Steele discusses Lenin's innovation, *From Marx to Mises*, 44–45. For the Marx text on which Lenin relied, see *MEGA2* 1.25: 13–15/*MECW* 24: 87–88/*LPW* 213–15.

8. Consider the following subtle attempt to update Marx. It is to be found in Terrell Carver's thought-provoking translation of *The Communist Manifesto*, which is the first truly new translation of the work since the familiar Samuel Moore translation of 1888 (which Engels edited and approved). Carver's translation was first published in Karl Marx, *Later Political Writings*, trans. and ed. Terrell Carver (Cambridge: Cambridge University Press, 1996), and is reprinted in *"The Communist Manifesto": New Interpretations*, ed. Mark Cowling (New York: New York University Press, 1998), 14–37.

Carver has published an illuminating essay about his translation, "Re-translating the *Manifesto*: New Histories, New Ideas," in *"The Communist Manifesto": New Interpretations,* 51–62. Carver makes it clear that in retranslating the *Manifesto* he wanted to do two things. First, he wanted to get back to the original, "pamphlet-style" work that was published in February 1848, and to offer a translation "which emphasises [the work's] role as a political intervention at the time it was written" (55). Second, Carver wanted to be attentive to the relation of Marx's texts to the present:

> if I did not think that these texts have something to communicate to present-day readers about the present, I would not be reading them. That something is a personal construction about politics which is deliberately associated with Marx, though this has disadvantages. Having satisfied canons of scholarly and commonsensical honesty, I often wonder if Marx is a useful sign under which to write politically? On balance I think he is, but persuading others of this requires a newly contextualised Marx as well as freshly reread texts, and considerable thought about translation. . . .
>
> Readers who—as translators—actually control the text, find themselves in the happy position of ventriloquist, making a dummy person say what they want "the author" to say. (53–54)

In his reflections on his *Manifesto* translation, Carver brilliantly highlights the dilemmatic situation of every translator and historian, for translators and historians are under an obligation both to be accurate in transcribing or describing *and* to make the translation or description connect in a meaningful way with the world of the present-day reader. On the whole, Carver's translation decisions seem to me to be defensible. Often they are far more than defensible. But consider Carver's translation of the following crucial sentence in the *Manifesto*, which (not accidentally) concerns private property:

> In diesem Sinn können die Kommunisten ihre Theorie in dem einen Ausdruck: Aufhebung des Privateigentums, zusammenfassen. (*MEW* 4: 475)

In Moore's translation, the sentence is rendered as follows:

> In this sense, the theory of the Communists may be summed up in the single sentence: Abolition of private property. (*MECW* 6: 498/*MER* 484)

Carver renders the sentence in the following way:

> In that sense communists can sum up their theory in a single phrase: the transformation of private property. (*LPW* 13)

Strikingly, Carver eliminates from the text the claim that communists look forward to the abolition of private property—for something that is to be *transformed* is surely not to be abolished.

In my opinion, at this point Carver goes astray. As noted in chapter 2, *Aufhebung* is a tricky word. It simultaneously means abolition, transcendence, and preservation. Which meaning or meanings did Marx intend here? I believe that to translate *Aufhebung des Privateigentums* as "the transformation of private property" is to underrate Marx's and Engels's radicalism. Note that the later Engels himself approved Moore's use of the term *abolition*. *Abolition* is a rather one-sided rendering of *Aufhebung*, at least if one cares to preserve something of the ambiguity of the original. Accordingly, I have translated the crucial phrase as "the transcending of private property." This is a compromise, of course. Both "transcending" and "transformation" are inferior to "abolition" if we are thinking of the *Manifesto* primarily as a *revolutionary* document. No revolutionary call to arms in English would contain the word "transcending," which is far too highfalutin for a revolutionary pamphlet, while "transformation" reeks of moderation. If, on the contrary, the translator's concern is to render accurately Marx's *theoretical* position, "transcending" is superior to both "abolition" and "transformation."

Why does Carver go astray here? Perhaps he was *too* concerned with making Marx suitable for present consumption. A Marx who wants to abolish private property is not very acceptable these days—and with good reason, I contend. "Abolition" of private property raises the gruesome specter of Communist economic failure in the years between 1917 and 1991, while "transformation" of private property does not. Rather than shade Marx so that he is more acceptable to current opinion and potentially more usable as a social and political thinker, I prefer to go in search of a Marx who really was—albeit a Marx highlighted in ways that accentuate the distinctive features of his work. Such a project requires coming to grips with Marx's reasons for holding the positions that he held. Softening Marx for present consumption leaves his justifying arguments in darkness.

9. Two general analyses of the system that prevailed in Russia and Eastern Europe under Communism can be recommended. The first, published while the system was still in operation, is Ferenc Fehér, Agnes Heller, and György Márkus, *Dictatorship over Needs* (Oxford: Basil Blackwell, 1983), which offers a good account of the ethical, political, and social consequences of living in such a social order. The second, published shortly after the collapse of the Communist system, is by the economist János Kornai: *The Socialist System: The Political Economy of Communism* (Princeton: Princeton University Press, 1992). Both books offer theoretical overviews: they do not enter into the complexities of each country's society and history. For a more variegated picture one would have to go to the work of historians, and other researchers and writers, sensitive to the ethical and political subtexts of these regimes.

It should be pointed out that those Marxists who argue, in defense of Marx's vision of a future socialism, that the Communist regimes did not live up to Marx's vision of socialism and that in consequence "socialism hasn't really been tried yet," are in a certain sense correct. What matters, however, is that the Communist regimes were *attempts* to implement Marx's vision of socialism. It seems to me that many of the pathologies that these regimes manifested—most egregiously, but not only, under Stalin and Mao—emerged out of their attempt to implement a social system that was impossible of implementation. The reaction, then, was to *force* the system on a "irrational" reality that resisted it.

10. See Warren Breckman, *Marx, the Young Hegelians, and the Origins of Radical Social Theory: Dethroning the Self* (New York: Cambridge University Press, 1999), 171–74; I also rely on Breckman, "Eduard Gans and the Crisis of Hegelianism: Associationism, Civil Society, and the Social Question," *Journal of the History of Ideas* 62 (2001), 543–64.

11. A notable exception to this generalization is Moses Hess, author of *The Holy History of Mankind* (1837), which was "Germany's first 'socialist' book," as Breckman has put it. Breckman also notes that "Hess's negation of . . . property contradicted not only the Saint-Simonians but virtually all of his German contemporaries as well"—including his fellow visionary and radical Hegelian, August Cieszkowski, who declared that "it is not a question of abolishing property but of renewing and universalizing it." (Breckman, *Marx, the Young Hegelians, and the Origins of Radical Social Theory*, 195)

12. For entry to Marx's life, see the vivid and lively account offered by Francis Wheen, *Karl Marx* (London: Fourth Estate, 1999). David McLellan, *Karl Marx: His Life and Thought* (New York: Harper & Row, 1973) juxtaposes an outline of Marx's life with summaries of his writings. Jerrold E. Seigel, *Marx's Fate: The Shape of a Life* (University Park: Pennsylvania State University Press, 1993), offers a dense, rather academic account of Marx's life and thought.

13. Marriages often bring children, and this one was no exception: on May 1, 1844, the first child of the Marx marriage, named Jenny after her mother, was born. Marx's productivity in the middle months of 1844 was undoubtedly helped by the fact that in June, Frau Marx took the baby back to Germany to show her to the grandmothers and to get some much needed tips from her mother on the care and feeding of babies. The baby was a challenge in the first few months, and as a result mother and baby returned to Paris only in September (see DRAP 1: 17–18; also Wheen, *Karl Marx*, 63). During this period Marx read political economy with great intensity and composed the "Economic and Philosophical Manuscripts." Also during this period Marx and Engels first got to know each other well. From August 23 to early September Engels stopped over in Paris on the way home from Manchester, where he had been working since spring 1843 in the office of the Ermen & Engels cotton business. During his Paris stay he spent almost all his time engaged in intense discussion and socializing with Marx (Wheen, 75–76). By the time he left for his home town of Barmen, he and Marx had forged an intellectual and personal connection far more momentous than the partnership between the Engelses and Ermens. One wonders how different the history of the twentieth century would have been had Marx's beloved wife and squalling, fussy baby stayed in Paris during the summer of 1844.

14. To be sure, limits are customarily placed on the right of private property. There are few places in the world where one can do absolutely anything one wants with, for example, a piece of land that one owns. But the limits that are placed on private property are acknowledged *as* limits, and do not impair the conceptual claim. To own a piece of property is not to own a physical object but is rather to own certain rights in regard to that object. Covenants, laws, and administrative and governmental regulations that limit the use that can be made of a piece of property at the same time limit the range of rights that can be legally bought or sold, but they do not abrogate the market in those rights that *can* legally be bought and sold.

15. After World War II, an uncle of mine "sold," for a dollar an acre, a piece of farmland in western Canada to the young man who had been farming it on a rental basis for the previous few years and who now wanted to start a family. This was not a market transaction but a gift masquerading as a market transaction. Paradoxically, if such morally ele-

vated behavior were to become widespread within capitalism it would risk damaging economic production, by impairing the capacity of markets to give good signals as to the likely cost and price of inputs and products. However, the risk of such an outcome seems small. It should also be noted that there is a capitalist form of philanthropy—namely, the transfer of property rights to charitable foundations—that seems entirely consistent with the maintenance of private property and the market.

16. See, for example, the following aphorism of the early Hegel: "The morning reading of the newspaper is a kind of realistic morning prayer. One takes one's orientation toward the world either from God or from what the world is [*Das Zeitungslesen des Morgens ist eine Art von realistischem Morgensegen. Man orientiert seine Haltung gegen die Welt an Gott oder an dem, was die Welt ist*]." (G. W. F. Hegel, "Aphorismen aus der Jenenser Zeit," no. 31, in Hegel, *Dokumente zu Hegels Entwicklung* [Stuttgart-Bad Cannstatt: Frommann, 1974 (reprint of 1936 ed.)], 360) Hegel very evidently favored the worldly, realistic orientation over the divine, transcendental one in his attempts to come to grips with the world.

17. I assert that Marx had to reject social democratic political intervention into the market (for that is what is at issue here) "at this moment in his thinking" because it is not entirely clear that this is the *only* moment in his thinking about the market, private property, governmental intervention, and related matters. First of all, I must again emphasize that Marx (and Engels) *do*, with apparent unequivocality, declare that the market, private property, and the political state ought to be, and eventually will be, things of the past. These rejections are an undeniable part of the Marx-Engels corpus of writings. Marx's wholehearted rejection of private property and the market is well documented by David Ramsay Steele. Remember, further, that abolition of private property (at least, abolition of private property in factors of production) was dogma—profoundly disastrous in its consequences—among those who ruled the Communist states of the twentieth century. Marx's followers were not exactly *wrong* to read Marx as they did.

But on the other hand, particularly in the thicket of his later economic writings, some of which are only now being published, there is much that tells against the anti-interventionist, antimarket view. I rely for this claim on the researches of Professor Michael Krätke, Vakgroep Politicologie, Faculteit der Politieke en Sociaal-Culturele Wetenschappen, University of Amsterdam. In a letter to me dated May 8, 2000, Prof. Krätke writes:

> I am not totally convinced that Marx did exclude the market as such or all kinds of markets from his view of a socialist society . . . in his later writings, in the manuscripts of the 1860s, when pointing at creations of modern capitalism that are already on the verge of turning into something more or less "socialist" . . . he is always talking about highly sophisticated forms of market relations. . . . Some markets would have to disappear in the course of the transition to socialism, like the slave trade and the venality of offices had to disappear in the long run in the course of the transition to capitalism, but not necessarily all of them.

It is obvious that further research into Marx's later economic views, and their relation to his project generally, are required. At this preliminary point, I see a sharp tension between Marx in his rationalist mode and Marx in a more empirical mode. I also see a sharp tension between Marx's vision of a utopian socialist future and his analysis of capitalism. In his rationalist/utopian mode, Marx *did* reject private property, the market, and politics. But when he turned to analyze the complexities of existing capitalism, the picture is different. For example, Prof. Krätke informs me that from the early 1860s until his death,

Marx kept studying the impact of British factory legislation, a classic instance of political intervention into the economy, and one that Marx approved of.

Krätke concludes that "Marx's real strength and merit is as an analyst, if not the leading analyst, of capitalism, and not as the author of an alleged theory of revolution or of socialism." I believe that this claim is correct. One of the aims of the present book is to highlight Marx's rationality-criteria, in order to facilitate their loosening. Then we would finally be in a position to discern what in Marx's work still lives for us, now. I have long been persuaded, but on general rather than on technical grounds, that Marx's account of the dynamic capitalist order—already present in Marx's and Engels's *The Communist Manifesto*—is the best thing about his work. I shall return to this matter in my conclusion.

See Michael R. Krätke, "How Political Is Marx's Political Economy? Political Theory in Marx's Economic Writings 1857/58 to 1867" (paper delivered at the Third European Social Science History Conference, Amsterdam, April 15, 2000); see also Krätke's numerous articles in *Historisch-Kritisches Wörterbuch des Marxismus*, ed. W. F. Haug, Bde. 1–3 (Hamburg: Argument, 1995–97), which focus on Marx's concern with the detailed functioning of capitalism and with the role of governmental intervention in particular (especially highlighted in the article "Banknote," 2: 21–28).

18. Fehér et al., *Dictatorship over Needs* (note 9). Of course, the economies of eastern Europe and the Soviet Union were hardly instantiations of the planned economy that Marx and Engels envisaged. Fehér, Heller, and Márkus make the point that planning in these societies "[bore] almost no relation to the Marxian idea of it, except for the common negative element present in both: negation of the regulative role of market mechanisms" (77). For this reason the authors refer to the economies in question not as planned, but as *command* economies. But the important point from our perspective is that Fehér, Heller, and Márkus provide ample reason for thinking that there were systematic grounds why a planned economy in the Marxian sense *was simply not possible*. For the bureaucrats who constructed the plans that were intended to regulate and guide these economies "[had] no systemic information about the real situation, needs, etc., in all those fields of social life which [were] not under their direct control" (80).

19. The idea that "Marxism" is rent by fissures is not at all new. For one approach to the notion of an internally incoherent Marx, see Alvin W. Gouldner, *The Two Marxisms* (New York: Oxford University Press, 1980)—a work that, if anything, underestimates the extent of the fissures within the system.

20. Or: *Alles was ich weiß, ist, ich kein Marxist bin*. As reported by Engels in letters to Eduard Bernstein of November 2–3, 1882, and of August 27, 1890, to Paul Lafargue (*MEW* 35: 388/*MECW* 46: 356; *MEW* 37: 450/*MECW* 49). This and related references come from Seigel, *Marx's Fate*, 281, 429 n. 62, and from Michael Krätke, "Marxismus als Sozialwissenschaft," in *Materialien zum Historisch-Kritischen Wörterbuch des Marxismus*, ed. W. F. Haug and Michael R. Krätke (Hamburg: Argument, 1996), 69–122, at 69.

21. See Allan Megill, "Recounting the Past: 'Description,' Explanation, and Narrative in Historiography," *American Historical Review* 94 (1989): 627–53, at 627, 647.

22. Lest there be some misunderstanding, note that I do not equate "cause" with "explanation by laws"; see Megill, "Recounting the Past," 632–34, 638, and passim.

23. Note that I am dealing here with the question of how Marx, in the period from late 1843 through late 1844, came to reject the market. I am not dealing here with Marx *generally*, or with his rejection of capitalism *generally*. I have these wider matters constantly in mind; it is just that they are not the focus of attention in the present book. If I were to

write a book focused on Marx's unfinished *Capital* and on the manuscript material surrounding that work, I would want to show how Marx holds in *Capital* that there are *three* justifications for rejecting capitalism: because it is *estranging*; because it is *irrational*; and because it is *exploitative*. My present focus of attention leads me to scant Marx's theory of exploitation, which he only began to develop in its final form in the 1850s, in the guise of his theory of surplus value.

24. Something *like* a disdain for "business" more generally comes out earlier, in an article by Marx, "Debates on Freedom of the Press," that was published in the *Rheinische Zeitung* in May 1842. Here Marx argues that freedom of the press is something higher than freedom of trade [*Gewerbe*] and that the writer [*Schriftsteller*] engages in a work that is an end in itself [*Selbstzwecke*], in contrast to such persons as printers and booksellers, for whom the press is a mere "material means" (see *MEGA2* 1.1: 121–69, at 162–63/*MECW* 1: 132–81, at 174–75). Here Marx seems to be appealing to the traditional distinction, rooted in Plato and in Christian theology, between the upward-striving realm of the spirit and the material body that holds us down. But it is hard to know how seriously to take Marx's argument here. Quite likely he appeals to this version of the spirit/matter distinction only because it supports the cause that he seeks to defend in this essay, namely, freedom of the press. Thus his *use* of the distinction does not necessarily mean that he was *committed* to it.

25. Bruno Bauer, *Die Judenfrage* (Brunswick, 1843); Bruno Bauer, "Die Fähigkeit der heutigen Juden und Christen, frei zu werden," in *Einundzwanzig Bogen aus der Schweiz*, ed. Georg Herwegh (rpt. Vaduz, Liechtenstein: Topos, 1977 [orig. Zurich, July 1843]), 56–71. A mimeographed translation of Bauer's *Die Judenfrage* into English is available in a few libraries: Bruno Bauer, *The Jewish Problem*, trans. Helen Lederer (Cincinnati: Hebrew Union College-Jewish Institute of Religion, 1958). Selections from Lederer's translation are more readily available in *The Young Hegelians: An Anthology*, ed. Lawrence S. Stepelevich (Cambridge: Cambridge University Press, 1983), 187–97.

26. C. B. Macpherson, *The Political Theory of Possessive Individualism: Hobbes to Locke* (Oxford: Oxford University Press, 1962), 3.

27. "Captain Hamilton informs us that the pious and politically free inhabitant of New England is a kind of Laocoön who does not make even the slightest effort to free himself from the snakes that are choking him. *Mammon* is his idol and he prays to him not only with his lips but with all the power of his body and his soul. For him the world is nothing but a Stock Exchange. . . . He is possessed by the spirit of bargaining [*Schacher*] and the only way he can relax is by exchanging objects. When he travels it is as if he carried his shop and office on his back and spoke of nothing but interest and profit . . . in North America . . . the very *proclamation of the Gospel*, Christian teaching, has become a commercial object and the bankrupt businessman is just as likely to go into evangelizing as the successful evangelist into business." (*MEGA2* 1.2: 165/*MECW* 3: 170–71/*EW* 237–38)

28. For one important instance, see Ludwig Feuerbach's widely noticed *The Essence of Christianity* (1841): in chapter XI, "The Significance of the Creation in Judaism," Feuerbach contends that Judentum is characterized by "Egoismus" and "Utilismus," rather than by love. In his discussion of "Judaism" Marx seems to have been more or less directly inspired by Feuerbach. But these general ideas floated around; Marx did not need Feuerbach to find them. See Feuerbach, *The Essence of Christianity*, trans. George Eliot (Buffalo, N.Y.: Prometheus, 1989), 205–17.

29. To my knowledge, the argument that Marx came to hate the market out of "Jewish self-hatred" has not been made in any precise way, but the general argument that Marx was

a self-hating Jew certainly has: see Arnold Künzli, *Karl Marx: Eine Psychographie* (Vienna: Europa Verlag, 1966), especially the section "Der jüdische Selbsthaß," 195–226, and Murray Wolfson, *Marx: Economist, Philosopher, Jew, Steps in the Development of a Doctrine* (New York: St. Martin's Press, 1982), throughout. Wolfson contends that in "On the Jewish Question" Marx identifies self-interest with "Jew" and "Judaism," and consequently is led to reject self-interest as evil (p. 90). But Wolfson gets things backwards here, for, as I have argued in my text, Marx takes "Jew" and "Judaism" as metaphors for self-interestedness; he does *not* see self-interestedness as specifically Jewish. On the other hand, Feuerbach (see note above) really was engaged in an attack on Judaism in the proper sense, although he was not self-hating, not being Jewish. See also the account of Marx in Sander L. Gilman, *Jewish Self-Hatred: Anti-Semitism and the Hidden Language of the Jews* (Baltimore: Johns Hopkins University Press, 1986), 188–208. Gilman shoehorns Marx into the larger language of anti-Semitism, significantly distorting, in the process, "On the Jewish Question."

30. Seigel reports some of Marx's anti-Semitic epithets concerning Lassalle, *Marx's Fate*, 113; on Marx's Jewish question generally, see Seigel, 112–19.

31. See Gerhard Scheit, who in his *Verborgener Staat, lebendiges Geld: Zur Dramaturgie des Antisemitismus* (Freiburg: Ça ira, 1999), puts Jesus's expulsion of the merchants from the temple at the center of his analysis of the dramatic representation, from the twelfth century onward, of anti-Semitism in the German literary tradition.

32. The words *Schacher* (noun, masc.), *Schacherer* (noun, masc.), and *schachern* (verb) have a problematic status in Germany and Austria today. One does not nowadays encounter these words in official, public German, since their currently unacceptable anti-Semitic connotations are well known. *Schacher* has often appeared in conjunction with *Wucher*, which has the meaning of "usury" and "profiteering," activities that, along with haggling, were seen as Jewish (as if Christians did not also try to buy low, sell high, and get what return on their money they could). The anti-Semitic animus of *Schacher* (and of *Schacher und Wucher* [or *Wucher und Schacher*]) was perfectly obvious to nineteenth-century writers and speakers of German. The term appeared in Jakob Friedrich Fries's scurrilously anti-Semitic pamphlet of 1816, *Über die Gefährdung des Wohlstandes und Characters der Deutschen durch die Juden* (Heidelberg: Mohr & Winter, 1816), 12, and no doubt in other anti-Semitic contexts as well.

Note the definition of *schachern* from an 1824 dictionary of economic and technical terms:

> *Schachern* . . . normally used only in a vulgar context [nur im gemeinen Leben üblich], where it means to trade, to engage in buying or trading; however, it is used only of profiteering [*gewinnsüchtig*] retail trade. According to Adelung [the authoritative German dictionary of the time], this word is borrowed from the Jews, who constantly utter it in their business activities; accordingly, it is also used only of a Jewish, profiteering mode of business [*nur von einer jüdischen, gewinnsuchtigen Art zu handeln gebraucht wird*]. (Johann George Krünitz, *Ökonomisch-technologische Encyklopädie, oder allegmeines System der Staats-, Stadt-, Haus-, und Landwirtschaft, und der Kunstgeschichte in alphabetischer Ordnung* [Berlin 1824], 368, cited by Michael Schmidt, "Schacher und Wucher: Ein antisemitisches Stereotyp im Spiegel christlicher und jüdischer Autobiographien der Goethezeit," *Menora: Jahrbuch für deutsch-jüdische Geschichte* 1 [1990], 235–77, and 247.)

See also the entries for *Schacher, schachern*, and related terms (e.g., *Schacherjude, Schacherjudenpack*) in Jacob and Wilhelm Grimm, *Deutsches Wörterbuch* (33 Bde.; München, 1984 [reprint of 1854–1971 edition]), 8: 1959–62 (vol. 8 was originally published in 1893). In the *Deutsches Wörterbuch* of Moriz Hayne (3 Bde.; Leipzig: Hirzel, 1890), 3: 238, *schachern* is illustrated by a quotation taken from the historian Heinrich von Treitschke: "die masse der deutschen israeliten . . . steckte noch tief im schacher und wucher." Friedrich Kluge, *Etymologisches Wörterbuch der deutschen Sprache*, 21, unveränderte Aufl. (Berlin: de Gruyter, 1975 [1. Aufl., 1883]) picks up on the use of the term *schachern* to apply to traveling salesmen, hence the meaning "als Händler herumziehen." Kluge also claims that the development of the word was affected by confusion with *Schächer*, robber, although, given the traditional hostility of farmers toward merchants and of Christians toward Jews, such a confusion is hardly needed to account for *Schacher*'s pejorative connotations. Finally, a www.google.com search for the terms *Schacher* and *Wucher* in conjunction (July 2001) brought up much relevant and somewhat disturbing material.

33. The common English translation of *Schacher* as "haggling" is worth thinking about. See Karl Marx, "On the Jewish Question," in *EW* 236, 237, and 241, where *Schacher* is translated four times as "haggling," once as "the spirit of bargaining," and once as "the market"; *verschachert* (239) is rendered as "put on the market." *Schacher* suggests the sort of activity that goes on at automobile dealerships and such, when there is no fixed and publicly known price for the commodity in question and where different persons will consequently end up paying different prices for the same or a similar commodity. Obviously, one can only get away with charging different people different prices if those who pay a higher price do not know that others are getting the same or similar commodity for a lower price. Veils and mirrors are thus required. (One suspects that the names of the French retail chains Monoprix and Prisunic, both founded in the early 1930s [www.monoprix.fr, accessed January 8, 2001], evoked negative memories of such haggling, and were intended as a statement that "we don't do that here, and hence are worthy of your trust.")

34. In this regard, the most relevant reference is G. W. F. Hegel, *Elements of the Philosophy of Right*, ed. Allen W. Wood, trans. H. B. Nisbet (Cambridge: Cambridge University Press, 1991), paragraphs 287–97 ("The Executive Power"), 328–97.

35. On Heinrich Marx's detachment from Judaism, Eugene Kamenka, "The Baptism of Karl Marx," *The Hibbert Journal* 61 (1958): 340–51 remains suggestive, although a bit too speculative. Heinrich's brother, Samuel, was the rabbi of Trier until his death in 1829.

36. David McLellan, *Karl Marx: His Life and Thought* (New York: Harper & Row, 1973), 4–7 gives a useful account of the views and standing of Marx's father.

37. Hans Rosenberg, *Bureaucracy, Aristocracy, and Autocracy: The Prussian Experience, 1660–1815* (Cambridge: Harvard University Press, 1958), 175; see also James J. Sheehan, *German History, 1770–1866* (Oxford: Oxford University Press, 1989), 427–29.

38. See Marx, "Debates on Freedom of the Press," May 12, 1842: "Laws are in no way repressive measures against freedom. . . . Laws are rather the positive, clear, universal norms in which freedom has acquired an impersonal, theoretical existence independent of the arbitrariness of the individual [*von der Willkühr des Einzelnen*]. A statute-book is a people's bible of freedom. . . . Law . . . is *true* law only when in it the unconscious natural law of freedom has become conscious state law." The claim here is that in a law-ordered universe we become free by becoming aware of what the laws are, and by turning those laws into "the inner laws of life of . . . action itself." Marx also asserts that "*there are no actual preventive laws*. Law prevents only as a *command*." He is asserting here the fundamental distinction between law as a correlation arising from the nature of things, and law as command, and adhering to the former, scientific conception. (*MEGA2* 1.1: 150/*MECW* 1: 162) See also Marx's August 1842 *RZ* article, "The Philosophical Manifesto of the Historical School of Law," where Marx attacks Gustav Hugo for articulating an "animal" conception

of law, one that is irrational and hostile to freedom (*MEGA2* 1. 1: 191–99, especially 194–95, 197–98/*MECW* 1: 203–10, especially 206–7, 209).

39. The section title is not Marx's but was added by the *MEGA2* editors: however, it accurately reflects the contents. Earlier editions used the section title "Estranged Labor," and it is this briefer title that is used in most (if not all) translations of the "Economic and Philosophical Manuscripts" into English.

40. For two useful studies, see István Mészáros, *Marx's Theory of Alienation* (New York: Harper & Row, 1970), and Bertell Ollman, *Marx's Conception of Man in Capitalist Society*, 2d ed. (Cambridge: Cambridge University Press, 1976 [1st ed., 1971]).

41. Perhaps the first time that Marx tried to apply such a procedure to a social or political question was in a fragment of an article that he never finished, "The Question of Centralization in Itself and with Regard to the Supplement to No. 137 of the *Rheinische Zeitung*, Tuesday, May 17, 1842," written in May 1842, where he declares that:

> The fate which a question of the time has in common with every question justified by its content, and therefore rational, is that the *question* and not the *answer* constitutes the main difficulty. True criticism, therefore, analyzes the questions and not the answers. Just as the solution of an algebraic equation is given once the problem has been put in its simplest and sharpest form, so every question is answered as soon as it has become a *real* question. World history itself has no other method than that of answering and disposing of old questions by posing new ones. (*MEGA2* 1.1: 170–71/*MECW* 1: 182–83)

Cf. Marx's assertion in "On the Jewish Question" that "to formulate a question is to answer it," and his assertion in the "Estranged Labor and Private Property" section of the EPM that one goes "a long way towards solving" the problem of the relationship between alienated labor and the course of human development by changing the question, for the "new way of formulating the problem already contains its solution" (*MEGA2* 1.2: 143, 374/*MECW* 3: 147, 281/*EW* 213, 333). What we have here is a method of definition and conceptual analysis. It was absolutely crucial to his work through to the end of his career. It is an intolerant method, for it banishes the thought that some matters of social and political concern admit of alternative answers and hence are infinitely discussable. However, when the questions are well posed, this way of proceeding can be powerfully illuminating.

42. When, in the first of the two passages that I quote in the text, Marx asserts that private property is "the *means* through which labor alienates itself," he appears to be suggesting that private property is a condition-by-which, rather than an active cause of alienation (that is, private property does not cause alienation—it only *makes it possible*). It should also be noted that in two statements closely related to the quoted passages, Marx writes in such a way as to suggest that he treats *estrangement* and *alienation* as synonyms, although strictly speaking they have slightly different meanings, with *estrangement* (*Entfremdung*) emphasizing the idea of something being or becoming "foreign" to the worker, and *alienation* (*Entäusserung*) emphasizing its becoming "external" to the worker. In the statements in question, Marx refers to "the concept of *estranged*, *alienated labor*" and to "the *estrangement of labor*, its *alienation*" (*MEGA2* 1.2: 374/*MECW* 3: 281/*EW* 333).

43. See Johann Gottlieb Fichte, *Science of Knowledge (Wissenschaftslehre)*, with First and Second Introductions, trans. and ed. Peter Heath and John Lachs (New York: Appleton-Century-Crofts, 1970), especially 154 and 233–34 (I: 165, 265 in the standard *Gesamtausgabe* pagination).

44. I cite Faust's meditations in his study, in Johann Wolfgang von Goethe, *Faust, First Part*, trans. Peter Salm (New York: Bantam, 1962), 76–77.

45. Moses Hess, "The Philosophy of the Act," in *Socialist Thought: A Documentary History*, rev. ed., ed. Albert Fried and Ronald Sanders (New York: Columbia University Press, 1992), 245–75. Hess's essay was first published in *Einundzwanzig Bogen aus der Schweiz* (note 25), 309–31.

46. "*Private property* is therefore the product, result, and necessary consequence of *alienated labor*, of the external relation of the worker to nature and to himself" (*MEGA2* 1.2: 372–73/*MECW* 3: 279/*EW* 331–32).

47. The ambiguity is between *logical derivation* and *causal assertion*. Marx's procedure in the EPM is heavily analytical. See, for example, the following quite typical passage: "it is clear from an analysis of this concept [i.e., the concept of alienated labor] that . . . private property . . . is in fact its [i.e., alienated labor's] consequence. . . ." (*MEGA2* 1.2: 372–73/*MECW* 3: 279/*EW* 332). It sounds as though Marx is here offering the results of a conceptual analysis. Yet in this part of the EPM Marx also seems to be offering causal assertions.

48. Engels deploys two modes of critique in his "Outlines of a Critique of Political Economy": an immanent, or internal, critique, in which he is intent on pointing out the contradictions of the political economists, and an external, moralizing critique (e.g., "This political economy or science of enrichment, born of the merchants' mutual envy and greed, bears on its brow the mark of the most detestable selfishness," etc. [*MEGA2* 1.3: 467/*MECW* 3: 418]). Marx's critique of political economy is more complex: it includes an immanent critique; a far lesser degree of external, moralizing critique than in Engels; and a "transformative" critique, inspired by Feuerbach's notion that one can arrive at a true humanism by finding how, in a given situation, man has been reduced to the status of a mere object, whose subjecthood now needs to be rescued. "Transformative" criticism might be regarded as a kind of synthesis of internal and external critique—less narrowly logical than the former, less moralizing than the latter. In essence, transformative criticism measures the existing world by the standard of whether it promotes or hinders human freedom. (The designation of Feuerbach's method as "transformative" is Shlomo Avineri's: *The Social and Political Thought of Karl Marx* [Cambridge: Cambridge University Press, 1968], 12.)

49. Louis Dupré gives a succinct account of Marx's misrepresentation of Hegel, in Dupré, "Recent Literature on Marx and Marxism," *Journal of the History of Ideas* 35 (1974): 703–14, at 709. In brief, Marx erroneously claimed that Hegel considered *all* objectification (making of objects) to be estranging. Koenraad Boey lays out Hegel's actual position in erudite detail: Boey, *L'aliénation dans la "Phénomenologie de l'Esprit" de G. W. F. Hegel* (Paris: Desclée de Brouwer, 1970). Nonetheless, Hegel's terminology is confusing and not entirely consistent, as Dupré notes.

50. In Marx, what *was* ontology is transported completely into the realm of experienced human life: "ontology" becomes something like "the fundamental features of human social life." Thus in the "Money" section of EPM Marx writes: "Only through developed industry, i.e. through the mediation of private property, does the ontological essence of human passion come into being . . . the science of man is therefore itself a product of the self-formation of man through practical activity" (*MEGA2* 1.2: 434/*MECW* 3: 322/*EW* 375). Note also an important implication, which is confirmed by, and consistent with, much else in Marx. This is that ontology (and science generally) *disappear* as independent activities. Ultimately, in Marx's view, there will be no separate science of man and no separate ontology of human existence, for these will be nothing other than the way that people understand themselves in the ordinary course of their social lives.

51. One could ask a similar question with regard to exploitation: Why not, by legislation and taxation, attempt to counter exploitation within the existing system? But since Marx did not have a worked-out theory of exploitation in the EPM, I leave this question aside here.

52. Marx perhaps comes closest to giving a starring role to the property/money/market complex in his "Excerpts from James Mill's *Elements of Political Economy*." Here he analogizes money to Christ, and the money economy generally to the Christian religion as interpreted by Feuerbach. In this interpretation, Christ/money equates to "*man* alienated." (See *MEGA2* 4.2: 448/*MECW* 3: 212–13/*EW* 260–61.) But note that Marx never attributed a causal role to Christianity—for Marx saw Christianity primarily as a *response to* the troubles of the material/social world, not as the *cause of* those troubles. Analogously, in 1844, even before his working out of the materialist conception of history—which is really a *productivist* conception of history—Marx seems to take the activity of production as the root of everything human.

53. Althusser advances this claim in his collection *For Marx*, trans. Ben Brewster (New York: Random House Vintage Books, 1969). See especially the essays "'On the Young Marx': Theoretical Questions" (December 1960), 49–86, and "Marxism and Humanism" (October 1963), 219–41.

54. See, for example, EPM, 2d MS: here Marx actually envisages the writing of *The German Ideology*, part 1, when he alludes to "the real course of development (*to be inserted here* [my italics] [*hier einzufügen*])" that leads to "the necessary victory of *capitalist* . . . private property" (*MEGA2* 1.2: 381/*MECW* 3: 288/*EW* 340). Marx makes a similar promise in the "Critique of Hegel's Dialectic" section: "History is the true natural history of man. (We shall return to this later [*Darauf zurückzukommen*].)" (*MEGA2* 1.2: 409/*MECW* 3: 337/*EW* 391). Further, especially in the "Private Property and Communism" section, Marx directly evokes the focus on the material transformation of nature that was to be a major theme in *The German Ideology*; see, for example, *MEGA2* 1.2: 395–98/*MECW* 3: 302–6/*EW* 354–57.

55. Bertell Ollman, *Alienation* (note 40). In his second (1976) edition, which I cite, Ollman responds to critics of the first (1971) edition: see vii–viii for an account of the changes or additions to the new edition, and appendix II, 263–76, for a "response to my critics." For a subtle exploration of the tension between holism and individualism in Marx, see Tim Shiell, "On Marx's Holism," *History of Philosophy Quarterly* 4 (1987): 235–46. As Shiell points out, some commentators have seen Marx as an ontological holist (holding, that is, that wholes or totalities have qualities that are not merely the sum of the qualities of the parts and relations making up those totalities). Other commentators have insisted, on the contrary, that Marx was an ontological individualist, who did not attribute "simple qualities" to wholes. Shiell concludes, on the basis of a terse but careful analysis of key texts, that "insofar as any ontology is attributable to Marx, it must be individualistic" (235). He also argues that *methodologically* Marx was (in part) a holist, for he held that the laws under which a particular aspect of social reality (e.g., population) falls vary according to the type of society; accordingly, the best lawful explanation of that social reality must take account not only of individual data points, but also of at least some properties of the social structure as a whole (240–42). Shiell also offers an explanation for Marx's methodological holism: Marx was committed to "radical change of the whole" of the extant social order, and this drove him, Shiell suggests, to a methodology consistent with his rejection of mere piecemeal improvement (244–45). I would add only that the methodological holism that

Shiell describes is also consistent with Marx's rationality-criteria: his commitment to universality and necessity involves constructing (or rather, attempting to construct) the object of one's attention (which necessarily will be a type rather than a particular) as a fabric of propositions so tightly interwoven that it will appear to possess a general character pervading all of its various parts.

56. Consider the relative weights of the terms *market* and *market price* (*Markt, Marktpreiß*), as compared with the term *exchange* (*Austausch*) in the "Economic and Philosophical Manuscripts." (I have located and counted these terms using "The Marx-Engels Internet Archive," which I discuss briefly in the bibliography of this book.) In the first of the three manuscripts making up the EPM the term *market* or *market price* appears twenty-five times. All of these uses appear in the first two-thirds of the First Manuscript, which is where Marx engages almost entirely in quoting or paraphrasing previous political economists (*MEGA2* 1.2: 327–59/*MECW*3: 235–66/*EW* 282–317). In the last third of the First Manuscript, Marx turns in another direction: first he polemicizes against a "romanticism" that sheds sentimental tears for feudalism and for landed property generally, and then, in the "Estranged Labor and Private Property" section, he offers his brilliantly original discussion of the estrangement of labor (*MEGA2* 1.2: 358–63, 363–75/*MECW* 3: 265–70, 270–82/*EW* 317–22, 322–34). As soon as Marx goes beyond the mode of paraphrase and quotation and instead speaks in his own voice, *Markt* and *Marktpreiß* drop out and only *Austausch*, appearing eleven times in the First Manuscript, is used. Neither set of terms is used in the Second Manuscript, of which only a few pages are extant. Finally, in the economic discussion in the Third Manuscript, where Marx is truly flying, the term *Markt* occurs three times, while *Austausch* occurs forty-one times (thirteen times in quotations, the rest of the time in Marx's own voice) (*MEGA2* 1.2: 383–99, 418–38/*MECW* 3: 290–326/*EW* 341–79). Marx's overwhelming concern with activity seems to be clearly, if perhaps unconsciously, indicated by this terminological preference on his part. (The specific passages in question are best located through The Marx-Engels Internet Archive; to offer three lists of page references here would be tedious and not very useful in any case, since single words are best searched for line by line.)

57. Toward the end of the "Need, Production, and Division of Labor" section of the EPM, Marx makes the following (Feuerbachian) argument, after several pages in which he has worked his way through discussions of the division of labor by various political economists:

> The *division of labor* and *exchange* . . . are the *perceptibly alienated* expressions of human *activity* and *essential powers* as *species*-activity and *species*-powers. . . .
>
> It is precisely in the fact that the *division of labor* and *exchange* are configurations [*Gestaltungen*] of private property that we find the proof, both that *human* life needed *private property* for its realization and that it now needs the supersession [*Aufhebung*] of private property. (*MEGA2* 1.2: 433/*MECW* 3: 321/*EW* 374)

In the *German Ideology* passage, quoted in the text, the divided activity of labor is *equated* with private property. In the EPM passage quoted here the divided activity of labor, and the activity of exchange, are apparently seen as forms of something more basic, private property. In the earlier EPM passage we see a Marx who is still within the orbit of the political economists whom he is attacking. Marx's apparent portrayal, in this passage, of private property as somehow more basic than the division of labor and exchange is inconsistent with Marx's own general tendency to see activity as basic.

58. *Qua* economist, Marx follows Adam Smith, who in his *Wealth of Nations* (1776) famously argued that the intensity of the division of labor is "limited by" the extent of the market: the larger the market, the more specialized the production that can be carried out. See: Adam Smith, *An Inquiry into the Nature and Causes of the Wealth of Nations*, ed. Edwin Cannan, with an introduction by Max Lerner (New York: Modern Library, 1937), Bk. I, chapter III, 17–21. Marx cites Smith's argument at *MEGA2* 1.2: 430/*MECW* 3: 320/*EW* 371. However, *methodologically* Marx is very far from Smith, who does not have Marx's analytic tightness and deep concern for searching out relations of mutual dependence.

59. The idea of the "circle of philosophy" is most famously expressed in Hegel's *Encyclopedia*, where he states that philosophy is a whole that presents itself "as a circle of circles in which each circle is a necessary moment." See G. W. F. Hegel, *Encyclopaedia of the Philosophical Sciences in Outline* (1817 ed.), trans. Steven A. Taubeneck, in Hegel, "*Encyclopaedia of the Philosophical Sciences in Outline*" and "*Critical Writings*," ed. Ernst Behler (New York: Continuum, 1990), introduction, §6, 51.

60. Hegel, *Encyclopedia*, introduction, §10, 53–54.

61. Pierre Laplace, *Théorie analytique des probabilités*, 3ième éd., rev. et augm. (Paris, 1820), ii–iii.

62. James Mill, *Elements of Political Economy*, 3rd ed., rev. and corrected (London: Henry G. Bohn, 1844), 4.

63. In the translation of Engels's "Outlines" that appears in *MECW*, *Schacher* is rendered as "huckstering." But this translation is inferior to "haggling." Engels refers to "simple, unscientific *Schacher*." But how can huckstering be unscientific? Huckstering can be greedy and pushy—that is, it can be immoral and impolite. But it surely cannot be unscientific. On the other hand, haggling certainly can be considered unscientific, for it is irregular and unpredictable, neither following nor establishing any universal and necessary benchmark of value.

Note also that science, in a quite general sense, was important to Arnold Ruge's conception of the *Deutsch-Französische Jahrbücher*. On the first page of his editor's introduction he writes that, in the journal, "the heavenly politics of the middle kingdom [*Mittelreich*; =Germany] will be abolished [*aufgehoben*] and the real [*wirkliche*] science of human things will be installed in its place" (Ruge, "Plan der Deutsch-Französische Jahrbücher," in *Deutsch-Französische Jahrbücher*, ed. Arnold Ruge and Karl Marx [Paris, 1844; rpt. Darmstadt: Wissenschaftliche Buchgesellschaft, 1967], 3).

64. See especially *Marxismusstudien*, ed. Iring Fetscher (5 vols.; Tübingen: Mohr, 1954–68). An early, widely noticed, and not entirely satisfactory publication in English was Erich Fromm, *Marx's Concept of Man*, with a translation from Marx's *Economic and Philosophical Manuscripts* by T. B. Bottomore (New York: Frederick Ungar, 1961). For an illuminating collection of essays that focuses on the problem of the relationship between "early" and "late" Marx that the "Economic and Philosophical Manuscripts" brought to the fore, see *Marx's Socialism*, ed. Shlomo Avineri (New York: Lieber-Atherton, 1972).

65. Who, one might ask, made the following statement? "Empirical observation [*Empirische Beobachtung*] must in each separate instance bring out empirically, and without any mystification and speculation, the connection of the social and political structure with production." It was Marx and Engels, in *The German Ideology* (*MEW* 3: 25/*MECW* 5: 35/*MER* 154). It is a commitment that, applied more generally, Marx seriously attempted to follow in the years after 1850, as he analyzed the workings of economic modernity. But

he kept his over-universalizing theories in place, in spite of his awareness of a host of considerations that contradicted them.

66. Karl Marx and Friedrich Engels, *Karl Marx Friedrich Engels Gesamtausgabe (MEGA)* (12 vols.; Frankfurt, Berlin, Moscow: Marx-Engels-Verlag and others, 1927–35), 1. Abt., 3. Bd.: *Die Heilige Familie und Schriften von Marx von Anfang 1844 bis Anfang 1845*, 2. Teil: "Aus den Exzerptheften: Paris, Anfang 1844–Anfang 1845," 493–550.

67. One exception: Sidney Hook, who made extensive use of *MEGA* in Hook, *From Hegel to Marx: Studies in the Intellectual Development of Karl Marx*, with a new foreword by Christopher Phelps (New York: Columbia University Press, 1994; 1st ed. 1936).

68. *MEGA2* 4.2: *Karl Marx Friedrich Engels Exzerpte und Notizen 1843 bis Januar 1845* (Berlin: Dietz, 1981); *MEGA2* 1.2: *Karl Marx: Werke, Artikel, Entwürfe, März 1843 bis August 1844* (Berlin: Dietz, 1982).

69. Bad handwriting is a minor leitmotif in Marx's career. When in fall 1862, during one of the Marx family's recurrent periods of extreme financial distress, Marx applied for work in a railway office, he was rejected on account of his poor handwriting (so Marx wrote to Kugelmann, letter of December 28, 1862 [*MEW* 30: 309/*MECW* 41: 436). Already in August 1835, two of his teachers commented as follows on the Latin essay that he wrote as part of his final exams: "the composition reveals a profound knowledge of history and of Latin. But what atrocious handwriting! [*Verum quam turpis litera!!!*]" (*MEGA1* 1.1 (2. Halbbd.): 170/*MECW* 1: 758). The aged Engels was supposedly obliged to give lessons in Marxian paleography to the German Social Democrats who were to inherit Marx's papers (Wheen, 84–85, not referenced). In the year 2000, retired archivists in Moscow were still being paid (in American dollars provided by the Volkswagen Foundation) to decipher Marx's handwriting.

70. In his *Republicanism and the French Revolution: An Intellectual History of Jean-Baptiste Say's Political Economy* (Oxford: Oxford University Press, 2000), Richard Whatmore persuasively argues that Say was not a political economist in the classical mold of Ricardo, but a modern republican who placed political economy within the larger context of fostering the modes of social behavior (manners, *moeurs*) required if republicanism were to thrive under modern conditions. Need we be surprised that (as Whatmore notes: 6, 218) Marx completely missed this aspect of Say's project?

71. On the dating of the Ricardo and Mill excerpts, see *MEGA2* 4.2: 758. The editors of *MEGA2* 4.2 (excerpts and notes, 1843–January 1845) suggest that Marx compiled the excerpts in summer/fall 1844. They also suggest (759) that he used these excerpts in the composition of the "Economic and Philosophical Manuscripts," which he broke off from writing in August 1844—which is prior to fall 1844. But there is reason for doubting that the Ricardo and Mill excerpts preceded the EPM. *MEGA2* 4.2 was published in 1981, edited by a Russian editorial team led by Nelly Rumjanzewa. The "Economic and Philosophical Manuscripts" appeared in *MEGA2* 1.2 ("works, articles, drafts, March 1843–August 1844"), published in 1982 and edited by a German editorial team led by Inge Taubert. The editors of the "Economic and Philosophical Manuscripts" offer a detailed account of Marx's manuscripts of this period (*MEGA2* 1.2: 685–709). They conclude that Marx's excerpts from Ricardo and Mill "with high probability originated only . . . after the "Economic and Philosophical Manuscripts" (696–97). Previously, it was generally assumed that the Ricardo and Mill excerpts preceded the EPM: for example, in the Pelican Marx Library *Early Writings* (*EW*), which is surely the most widely used edition of Marx's early writings in the English-speaking world, an excerpt from Marx's Mill excerpts

appears in the volume *before* the "Economic and Philosophical Manuscripts" (*EW* 259–78).

The timing is of some importance. If the "Economic and Philosophical Manuscripts" were written after the Ricardo and Mill excerpts, this tends to suggest to the historian that the Ricardo and Mill excerpts were a preparation for the EPM, and thus that the notion of the estrangement of labor, the most striking idea in the EPM, was the culmination of Marx's researches of 1844. If the Ricardo and Mill excerpts came after the EPM, as I believe they did (although the matter is not absolutely certain), this suggests that Marx articulated an important idea in the EPM and then arrived at another important idea in the excerpts. To be sure, elements of Marx's "irrationality of the market" argument are present in the EPM. Most notably, Marx insists that the current economic system is subject to chance and that it lacks a necessary foundation (I document this in my text). But in the EPM Marx does not actually *make* the argument.

72. Word counts done using "The Marx-Engels Internet Archive."

73. For a useful brief account, see G. Vaggi, "Natural Price," in *The New Palgrave: A Dictionary of Economics*, ed. John Eatwell, Murray Milgate, and Peter Newman (4 vols.; London: Macmillan, 1987), 3: 605–8.

74. David Ricardo, *Des Principes de l'économie politique et de l'impôt*, traduit par F.-S. Constancio, avec des notes explicatives et critiques par M. Jean-Baptiste Say, 3. éd., revue, corr. et augm. d'une notice. . . . (Paris, 1835).

75. Ricardo and Say are mentioned together at three places in the EPM. In the first reference, Ricardo and James Mill are said to be indifferent or even hostile to the existence of human beings, putting all their emphasis on interest and on increasing capital, whereas Smith and Say are said to be not so horrid. In the second reference, Marx places Ricardo and Say in a historical sequence—from Smith through Say to Ricardo and Mill—in which political economy allegedly becomes increasingly cynical. In the final reference, Marx places Ricardo and Say together, seeing them both as advocating thrift and execrating luxury, contra Lauderdale and Malthus, who are said to do the reverse. But there is no reference to their engagement over value. See *MEGA2* 1.2: 377–78, 384–85, 421–22/*MECW* 3: 284–85, 291–92, 309–10/*EW* 336, 343, 361.

76. Marx's characterization of Ricardo's position here is accurate so far as it goes, but it leaves out various qualifications. For Ricardo's views directly rendered, see David Ricardo, *On the Principles of Political Economy and Taxation*, chapter I, "On Value," in Ricardo, *Works and Correspondence* (9 vols.; Cambridge: Cambridge University Press, 1951–1973), 1: 11–51.

77. Marx here interprets David Ricardo, *Principles of Political Economy and Taxation*, chapter IV, "On Natural and Market Price," 88–92, at 92: "In speaking then of the exchangeable value of commodities, or the power of purchasing possessed by any one commodity, I mean always that power which it would possess, if not disturbed by any temporary or accidental cause, and which is its natural price."

78. On this point, see Whatmore, *Republicanism*, 205–6.

79. As Marx does in *The Communist Manifesto* (1848), where he refers to "free buying and selling [*den freien Kauf und Verkauf*]." But in this same passage—quoted toward the beginning of this chapter as one among a number of passages where Marx rejects private property and the market—Marx also uses the term *Schacher* four times. (*MEW* 4: 475–76/*MECW* 6: 498–500/*MER* 486/*LPW* 13, 15)

80. Of course, in an abstract sense we can explain the rise and fall of market price, since we know that if demand rises, prices will rise, and that if supply rises, prices will fall, *ceteris paribus*. But this knowledge was not good enough for Marx, since it could not be cashed out predictively. Marx wanted something not subject to unpredictable fluctuation. So he had to find a deeper level of social reality from which such unpredictability would be excluded. This deeper level is the level of production. The door is thus opened to Marx's historical materialism, which amounts to a history of production (see chapter 4), and to his analysis of capitalism, culminating in *Capital*, volume 1 and in the other *economica* of the later Marx. The later Marx's "labor theory of value" was, among other things, an attempt to provide the rational foundation that *Schacher* could not provide.

81. The symbol "\" indicates that in the manuscript Marx wrote the following word over the preceding word. I take the translation, although I make some alterations, from the translation of the culminating part of the "Excerpts" published in *EW* 259–78, at 259–60.

The passage that I quote, and the paragraph following it (which I do not quote), encapsulate Marx's two arguments against the market, namely, that it is irrational and that it is estranging (that is, dehumanizing). Although for many years I regularly assigned to students, and explicated, the truncated *EW* "Excerpts from James Mill," I managed to see the irrationality argument only when I read the passage in the wider context provided by the *complete* "Excerpts" and by the David Ricardo excerpts, as published in *MEGA2*. One is primed to see the estrangement argument in the James Mill excerpts but not the irrationality argument, in part because the irrationality argument is more difficult to see and in part because the James Mill excerpts do contain, toward their end, a brilliant discussion of the estranging character of production under capitalism and of what nonestranging production would feel like. See *MEGA2* 4.2: 464–66/*EW* 277–78.

82. This is a stricter, more rigid conception of lawfulness than can be found in Hegelian history as exemplified in the *History of Philosophy*. It was this Hegelian conception that the earlier Marx seems to have wanted to find exemplified in politics. Now he discovers that—at an *abstract* level, at any rate—political economy articulates a view that promises not just to see the world as rational *after the fact*, but to articulate laws that are predictive. This was a promise made within the context, and relying on the authority, of the Newtonian scientific paradigm; it was a promise that went beyond anything in Hegel, who promises, at most, a retrospective rationality: the owl of Minerva. . . . Marx found this retrospectivity unsatisfactory (recall God's showing of his posterior to Moses, evoked in chapter 1). Of course, the rub is that the complexities of economic reality *as they actually manifest themselves in the market* end up escaping the more rigorous grasp of the Newtonian model of lawfulness.

83. The nature of the movement of market prices has, of course, been a topic of concern to economists since Marx's time. See the very useful anthology, *The Random Character of Stock Market Prices*, ed. Paul H. Cootner (Cambridge, Mass.: MIT Press, 1964), which includes papers on the subject from 1900 through 1964. Cootner barely missed including Paul Samuelson, "Proof that Properly Anticipated Prices Fluctuate Randomly," *Industrial Management Review* 6 (1965): 41–49. The so-called random walk view has been challenged by Andrew W. Lo and A. Craig MacKinlay, *A Non-Random Walk Down Wall Street* (Princeton: Princeton University Press, 1999), who strive to identify sources of predictability in stock market prices; they of course do not argue that stock market prices are *overall* predictable.

84. Hegel, *Elements of the Philosophy of Right* (note 34), preface, 20 ("Was vernünftig ist, das ist wirklich; und was wirklich ist, das ist vernünftig" [Hegel, *Grundlinien der Philosophie des Rechts* (1821 ed.), Vorrede, in G. W. F. Hegel, *Werke*, Bd. 7 (Frankfurt am Main: Suhrkamp, 1970), 24]). But what, then, if some aspect of the world refuses to allow itself to "look rational"? From Marx's Left Hegelian perspective, the conclusion is obvious: one needs to change that aspect of the world, or abolish it. Hegel, that slacker at heart, was more tolerant. Thus he looked for the quintessence of rationality in the state, and saw civil society as too pervaded by particularity and arbitrariness [*Willkür*] to manifest full rationality (*Elements*, §182). But Hegel did not want to abolish civil society—nor politics either.

85. See Engels's discussion of this point, albeit from much later: Friedrich Engels, *Ludwig Feuerbach and the Outcome of Classical German Philosophy* (1888), in *MEW* 21: 261–307, at 266–68/*MECW* 26: 353–98, 358–61.

86. Cf. Notebook I ("The Chapter on Money") (October 1857) of the *Grundrisse*: "the problem [of the periodic depreciation of money] would have reduced itself to: how to overcome the rise and fall of prices. The way to do this: abolish prices." (*MEGA2* 2.1.1: 70/*MECW* 28: 72/*GRUND* 134)

87. Pierre-Josèphe Proudhon, *Système des contradictions économiques, ou Philosophie de la misère*, 2d ed. (2 vols.; Paris, 1850).

88. See Proudhon, *Philosophie de la misère*, chap 2, "De la Valeur" (1: 65–112). The first section (65–80) is titled "Opposition de la valeur d'*utilité* et de la valeur d'*échange*."

89. Proudhon, *Philosophie de la misère*, 1: 72–73.

90. Proudhon, *Philosophie de la misère*, I: 70. Note the appropriateness of the French term *mercuriale*—which evokes the element that once astounded people by its changeability, mercury (once known as *quicksilver*)—for designating "the price index." Also, mercury was used in the instruments that measured temperature and air pressure, both notoriously unstable. As I write this, the Dow Jones Industrial Average bounces up and down. Business reporters offer explanations of the day's action after it occurs, but tomorrow's action remains a mystery until it too has become a thing of the past.

91. I can do no more than note here Marx's lack of serious attention to the dynamics of the gendered-feminine activity of consumption (shopping): for an account of representations of female consumption in the nineteenth century, see Rita Felski, *The Gender of Modernity* (Cambridge: Harvard University Press, 1995), 61–90 and passim. Marx's productivist bias has massive consequences: it means an omission of fashion and whim. It seems clear that the worker's desire for potatoes for himself and his family (which will allow the production and continued reproduction of labor-inputs) has a different and much more predictable character than the desire for lace-equivalents and for the lace-like aspects of commodities like—say—potatoes, automobiles, watches, or personal computers that at first glance (but only at first glance) might seem to be perfectly well understandable only in terms of what they do, with no attention given to what they *signify*. These desires massively affect the economic system.

On the production side of the fence, it is notable that in Marx's time a very high proportion of factory workers were women, but Marx had a hard time integrating this fact into his general theory. For an interesting discussion, suggesting that Marx was "caught within a restricted and determinate net of contradictory ideas and principles" on this matter, see Mike Gane, "The Communist Manifesto's Transgendered Proletarians," in *"The Communist Manifesto": New Interpretations* (note 8), 132–41; quotation at 139.

92. Proudhon, *Philosophie de la misère*, chap. II, sect. III, "Application de la loi de proportionnalité des valeurs," 94–112, especially 110.

93. Proudhon, *Philosophie de la misère*, 1: 99.

94. Marx had already grasped, in his 1844 Excerpts from James Mill's *Elements of Political Economy*, that on occasion commodity producers will misanticipate demand, for James Mill himself made this point in a passage that Marx excerpted from Mill: "It may very well happen . . . that some one commodity or commodities may have been produced in a quantity either above or below the demand for those particular commodities." However, in line with the "invisible hand" assumption prevalent at the time, Mill held that *in the market as a whole* one finds "equality in the general sum of demands and supplies." (*MEGA2* 4.2: 461/*MECW* 3: 224/*EW* 273) Marx goes on to comment that in "a state of savage barbarism," where "man" produces only for himself, he produces "*no more* than his immediate needs. . . . Hence supply and demand coincide exactly" (*MEGA2* 4.2: 462/*MECW* 3: 224/*EW* 274). However, so far as I know it was only in 1847 that Marx went on to explore the implications of what he clearly saw as the noncoincidence of supply and demand in modern society. In the paragraphs that follow the 1844 passage just quoted, Marx actually goes on to discuss, quite brilliantly, the estranging, dehumanizing effects of the uncoupling of production from need, turning aside from an analysis of the market's alleged irrationality (*MEGA2* 4.2: 462–66/*MECW* 3: 225–28/*EW* 274–78). For James Mill's discussion of the "co-extensive" character of demand and supply, see his *Elements of Political Economy* (note 62), chapter IV, section III, especially 228–34.

95. Consider *The Holy Family* (written September–November 1844), where Marx criticizes political economy for "accepting the relationships of private property as human and rational" (*MEW* 2: 33/*MECW* 4: 32). By this time Marx had concluded that these relationships were both inhuman and irrational. He knew perfectly well that he was here deploying two sets of criteria for judging the existing order; what remained confused were their roles and relative standing. Further, in this passage Marx explicitly links political economy's violation of rationality to its acceptance of the notion that "value is determined quite accidentally [*der Wert eine rein zufällige Bestimmung ist*]." As for the criterion of humanness, it is clearly the contrary of estrangement.

96. See Malachi Haim Hacohen, *Karl Popper, The Formative Years, 1902–1945: Politis and Philosophy in Interwar Vienna* (New York: Cambridge University Press, 2000), 87–90.

97. Consider, in this regard, a well-known passage in *Capital* (vol. 1, chap. XIV, sect. 4), where Marx distinguishes between "the planned and regulated *a priori* system" by which, under capitalism, the division of labor is implemented in an individual workshop or factory, and the situation prevailing within the society as a whole, where the division of labor is "an *a posteriori* necessity imposed by nature, controlling the lawless caprice [*regellose Willkuhr*] of the producers, and perceptible in the fluctuations of the barometer [*Barometerwechsel*] of market prices" (*MEGA2* 2.5: 290/*MECW* 35: 361/*CAP* 1: 476). The *a posteriori* mode as Marx portrays it in this passage links up with two bad things: with the dehumanization implied in man's subjection to external forces, and, more relevant to our concerns here, with the irrationality of whatever is capricious, hence unpredictable, hence uncontrollable.

98. For a useful brief account, see Stephen H. Kellert, *In the Wake of Chaos: Unpredictable Order in Dynamical Systems* (Chicago: University of Chicago Press, 1993).

CHAPTER 4

1. The text of Engels's actual speech at Marx's graveside, which was delivered in English, presumably without notes, does not exist. I here quote a translation back into English of a text in German written by Engels, published on March 22, 1883, in the newspaper *Sozialdemokrat* (see DRAP 2: 108, #230, and 113, #317, and *MEGA2* 1.25: 1116).

2. Marx himself never used either the phrase *materialist conception of history* or the phrase *historical materialism*. Both were invented by Engels, who first used "materialist conception of history" in his review, published in August 1859, of Marx's *A Contribution to the Critique of Political Economy* (*MEW* 13: 469/*MECW* 16: 469). Engels went on to employ *materialist conception of history* in a variety of other writings. The most notable and widely read of these was his pamphlet, *Socialism: Utopian and Scientific*, published in 1880 (cobbled together out of parts of his *Anti-Dühring* [published 1877–78]); quotation at *MEGA2* 1.27: 608/*MECW* 24: 306/*MER* 700). Engels also used the phrase in the preface to the 2d edition (1870) of *The Peasant Wars in Germany*, as well as in: "The Housing Question" (1873); "Karl Marx's Funeral" (1883); preface to the 1st edition of *The Origin of the Family, Private Property and the State* (1884); and preface (1888) to *Ludwig Feuerbach and the Outcome of Classical German Philosophy*. Engels first used the term *historical materialism* in the preface to the English edition (1892) of *Socialism: Utopian and Scientific*. I rely on Zbigniew A. Jordan, *The Evolution of Dialectical Materialism: A Philosophical and Sociological Analysis* (New York: St. Martin's Press, 1967), 404 n. 67 for some references. I found additional references by searching "The Marx-Engels Internet Archive" (see bibliography) in July 1999. It would be overkill to provide specific page references here.

I treat *materialist conception of history* and *historical materialism* as identical in meaning. But their connotations, and risks, are slightly different. "Historical materialism" runs the risk of creating the mistaken impression that the view being designated was an ontological view in the traditional sense, concerned with the ultimate structure of the universe, for the word *materialism* has frequently been used in this sense. Except for its greater length, the term *materialist conception of history* is marginally to be preferred, since it highlights the fact that we are dealing with a conception of *history*. But even here there is a risk, for the materialist conception of history is as much a conception of society *now* as it is a conception of history.

3. As readers of chapter 1 will know, Engels misrepresents Darwin's theory, which involved no "law of development of organic nature" at all, but only postulated a mechanism by which the transmutation of species could take place.

4. Paul Q. Hirst, *Marxism and Historical Writing* (London: Routledge & Kegan Paul, 1985), vii.

5. The leap is not as long as it might seem at first glance. In his *Lectures on the History of Philosophy*, Hegel himself speaks of the "labor [*Arbeit*]" of spirit. For example, in an interesting passage near the end of the *Lectures* Hegel refers to the "inner working forward [*innerliches Fortarbeiten*]" of spirit, concerning which he says (following Hamlet's words to his father's ghost [=*Geist*, spirit]) "well labored, bold mole [of spirit] [*brav gearbeitet, wackerer Maulwurf*]." In his dissertation materials, Marx alludes to precisely this passage in Hegel (at *MEGA2* 4.1: 137/*MECW* 1: 506: see chapter 1, above). G. W. F. Hegel, *Lectures on the History of Philosophy*, trans. E. S. Haldane and Frances H. Simson (3 vols.;

London: Routledge and Kegan Paul, 1955 (1892]), 3: 546–47. In German: Hegel, *Vorlesungen über die Geschichte der Philosophie*, published in 1833–36 as vols. 13–15 of Hegel's Werke (18 vols., Berlin, 1832–45), 15: 685.

6. No work can be *purely* exegetical: all authors have some sort of active agenda. Still, the following works do seem to be mainly exegetical: Helmut Fleischer, *Marxism and History*, trans. Eric Mosbacher (New York: Harper & Row, 1973 [original German edition, 1969]); John McMurtry, *The Structure of Marx's World-View* (Princeton: Princeton University Press, 1978); William H. Shaw, *Marx's Theory of History* (Stanford: Stanford University Press, 1978); and the first half of Walter L. Adamson, *Marx and the Disillusionment of Marxism* (Berkeley and Los Angeles: University of California Press, 1985). All four authors bring to their study of Marx a large dose of the historian's concern with giving a correct account of what past authors said and meant. Their study of the texts is not a pretext for putting forward their own views, as is sometimes the case with writers having a more theoretical, and less historical, concern. For this they deserve our infinite respect and gratitude.

7. Letters in which Marx or Engels discuss the materialist conception of history in general (as distinguished from discussing particular historical situations to which it might be applied) include: (1) Marx to P. V. Annenkov, a Russian writer and landowner, dated December 28, 1846, in which Marx responds to Annenkov's request for Marx's views on Proudhon's recently published *Philosophy of Poverty*, offering an account of historical materialism in the process (*MEGA2* 3.2: 70–80/*MECW* 38: 95–106/*MER* 136–42). (2) Engels to Joseph Bloch, a mathematics student at the University of Berlin, dated September 21–22, 1890, in which Engels characterizes production as "the *ultimately* determining element in history" (*MEW* 37: 462–65/*MECW* 49). (3) Engels to Walther Borgius, a law student at Breslau, dated January 25, 1894, on the relation between necessity and accident in history (*MEW* 39: 205–7/*MECW* 50). These letters, and an additional letter to Franz Mehring dated July 14, 1893, are excerpted in *MER* 136–42 and 760–68 (note that *MER* misidentifies the January 25, 1894, letter as being to Starkenburg [DRAP 3: 27]). Another relevant letter is (4) Engels to Conrad Schmidt, an economics writer and Social Democratic activist, dated October 27, 1890, where Engels emphasizes that there is a "reacting back [*Rückwirkung*]" of commerce, the money market, state, politics, and law on "the economic development" (*MEW* 37: 488–95, at 490–91/*MECW* 49; an English version is also to be found in the *first* edition of *MER* [1972] 642–47, at 643–45, but was excluded from the second edition).

Since much of what Marx and Engels wrote on the materialist conception of history emanated from Engels, the question of the status of Engels's writings—as compared to Marx's—arises with particular insistence in this context. Engels's writings can be divided into four categories: (1) Those that Engels co-authored with Marx (e.g., *The German Ideology*, *The Communist Manifesto*). Marx seems to have agreed with and approved the joint text in all these cases, and for this reason I take these writings as providing evidence of Marx's views. (2) Those that Engels wrote by himself, but which we can reasonably assume give a Marxian account of the subject matter being addressed. I put the third part of *Socialism: Utopian and Scientific* in this category. (3) Those that Engels wrote by himself, but which extend a position adhered to by Marx to matters that Marx himself did not have occasion to investigate and write up on his own. An example of such a work is Engels's *The Peasant War in Germany*, which deals with the German peasant rebellion of 1525

(*MEW* 7: 327–413/*MECW* 10: 397–482. (4) Works in which Engels goes off on his own tangent. To this category I assign the second part of *Socialism: Utopian and Scientific*, where Engels puts forward an ontological materialism, a dialectic of the universe in general (*MEGA2* 1.27: 559–65/*MECW* 24: 298–305/*MER* 694–700); Engels developed this view at great length in his unfinished *Dialectic of Nature* (1873–82) (*MEGA2* 1.26: 1–558/*MECW* 25: 313–588).

8. The issue of the compatibility of the various accounts of historical materialism is one on which Fleischer, in *Marxism and History* (1969), and Adamson, in *Marx and the Disillusionment of Marxism* (1985), particularly focus. They represent an advanced stage in Marx scholarship, in which previously invisible distinctions are discovered. Many other commentators avoid the compatibility issue. One such author is McMurtry, whose *The Structure of Marx's World-View* is cast as an exegesis of the 1859 preface, with material from other Marx texts drawn upon in order to cast light on what Marx says in the preface. Another is G. A. Cohen, who in *Karl Marx's Theory of History: A Defence* (Princeton: Princeton University Press, 1978) is driven by a philosopher's concern with rationally reconstructing Marx's view and is not much interested in historical reconstruction. (I wish to acknowledge my debt, these past twenty-two years, to McMurtry's clear and interesting account of the 1859 preface.)

9. I exclude Engels's "dialectical materialism"—his ontological materialism—from this claim of compatibility. Dialectical materialism, classically articulated by Engels in the second part of *Socialism: Utopian and Scientific*, billed itself as a theory of *reality in general*. Dialectical materialism holds that reality is dialectical through and through, so that even the melting of ice needs to be seen in dialectical terms, an instance of the dialectical "law" of the transformation of quantity into quality. In contrast, historical materialism is a theory *of humankind*. Although such later commentators as V. I. Lenin and J. Stalin claimed that dialectical materialism was the joint view of Marx and Engels, Marx himself never wrote anything along this line. Instead, demonstrating his characteristic talent for avoiding irrelevancies, he stuck to history and society. The standard scholarly study is Jordan, *The Evolution of Dialectical Materialism* (note 2). Stalin's essay, "Dialectical and Historical Materialism" (1938), which characterizes "historical materialism" as "the extension of the principles of dialectical materialism to the study of social life," is the standard Soviet Marxist account: it can be found in, among many other places, *The Essential Stalin*, ed. Bruce Franklin (Garden City, N.Y.: Doubleday, 1972), 300–33; quotation at 300.

10. Persons interested in reading the whole of the 1859 preface and not just the fifteen sentences quoted in the epigraph can find it in *MEW* 13: 7–11 and, in English, in *MECW* 29: 261–65, *EW* 424–28, and *LPW* 158–62, among many other places.

11. The distinction between social statics and social dynamics was first articulated by the French positivist philosopher, and inventor of "sociology," Auguste Comte (1798–1857), in his *Course in Positive Philosophy* (1830–42). See passages excerpted in Auguste Comte, *Auguste Comte and Positivism: The Essential Writings*, 2d ed., ed. Gertrud Lenzer (New Brunswick, N.J.: Transaction, 1998), 263–97. I deploy the distinction here only because it is relevant; Marx was not influenced by Comte's theory, and regarded Comte as an apologist of capitalism, Bonapartism, and hierarchy.

12 . *The German Ideology* and *Socialism: Utopian and Scientific* offer very slightly different versions of the materialist conception of history. Interested readers are free to explore these other works on their own. *The German Ideology*, part 1, is to be found in *MEW* 3: 9–77; *MECW* 5: 19–93; and *MER* 146–200. (There are some differences, noted by

DRAP 2: 9–10, between the older *MEW* and the newer *MECW* version of *The German Ideology*.) *Socialism: Utopian and Scientific* is to be found in, among other places, *MEGA2* 1.27: 547–80, *MECW* 24: 281–325, and *MER* 683–717.

13. Readers interested in verifying the ambiguity that I note here might start by reading carefully the epigraph of this chapter. In sentences 1 and 2, Marx characterizes the relations of production, in their totality, as constituting the "real base" of society. In sentence 3 he alludes to "the mode of production" in a way that follows, with apparent seamlessness, sentence 2, thus appearing to suggest that "the mode of production" just is "the sum total of these relations of production." Yet in sentence 5 he begins to discuss "the material productive forces of society," and he does so in a way that seems to suggest that the productive forces are the spearhead of change within the social order. One would thus be inclined to assume that the productive forces *do* make up the "real base" of the social order and do constitute part of the "mode of production."

The tension between taking relations of production as the base and taking forces of production as, in the final analysis, the base emerges very clearly in G. A. Cohen's *Karl Marx's Theory of History: A Defence*. Cohen needs to be read at length to be appreciated, but I can point out several passages that get to the heart of the ambiguity. In *Karl Marx's Theory of History*, Cohen notes that the metaphor of "the economic base" is "explicitly defined by Marx: the base is the sum total of production relations" (87). Similarly, Cohen characterizes "mode of production" as "the way men work with their productive forces" (79). If I may gloss this, Cohen is here asserting that in Marx's account the mode of production does not include the productive forces themselves, which for Cohen fall into the category of "technology" rather than into the category of "economics." On the other hand, in his chapter VI, "The Primacy of the Productive Forces" (134–74), Cohen claims that Marx held that productive forces have primacy over productive relations (and over everything else within the social order). By this he means that the productive relations are to be *explained* by the productive forces (I shall return to this point below).

Why is Cohen so insistent on excluding productive forces from the economic base? I suspect that he is led to this position by an overinsistence on sharply separating the "material" and the "social" in Marx (thus he sees Marx as having established a "systematic opposition" between the two [30, 88–114]). Why this overinsistence? Cohen is perhaps overinfluenced, in his view of Marx, by traditional philosophical materialism (it should be noted, again, that it was Engels, not Marx, who used the terms "materialist conception of history" and "historical materialism"). But my claim is that in Marx's view productive forces are made up as much by socially developed *ideas* as they are by material entities (I would also claim that, besides being Marx's view, this is also true of reality). "The truth of thinking must be proved in practice" (Marx, "Theses on Feuerbach," #2). Because the practice in question involves an engagement with the material world, against which ideas are tested, materiality is intimately connected with ideas. Material things get created that embody ideas. These material things can acquire a life of their own, especially under capitalism. But this is no denial of the interrelatedness of idea and matter. Indeed, it is precisely the domination of material things over human activity that Marx wishes to see overcome.

14. The fact is, Marx simply *assumes* that all production worthy of the name is the production of material goods. He never justifies the assumption. Nor does he ever betray the thought or even the suspicion that the assumption might somehow require support. I cannot pursue the matter here. But note a telling statement appearing in an unpublished (but highly polished) chapter of *Capital*, excluded from *Capital*, volume 1, at what seems to

have been a late stage, titled "Results of the Immediate Process of Production" (probably written between June 1863 and December 1866 [DRAP 2: 76]). Here Marx observes that:

> On the whole, types of work that are consumed as services and not in products separable from the worker and hence not capable of existing as commodities independently of him, but which are yet capable of being directly exploited in *capitalist* terms, are of microscopic significance when compared with the mass of capitalist production. (Karl Marx, "Resultate des unmittelbaren Produktionsprozesses," in *Arkhiv K. Marksa i F. Engel'sa*, vol. 2 [1933 (rpt. Nendeln/Liechtenstein: Kraus, 1970)], 138/*CAP* 1: 1044).

Clearly, Marx had never heard of franchising, health-maintenance organizations, H & R Block, and a host of other, similar realities to be found in economic modernity, nor does it seem to have occurred to him that personal services (education, medical services, housecleaning, child care, and the like), although not produced in factories by means of mechanized mass production, might actually continue to be quite important as elements making up economic modernity.

15. The clearest survey of Marx's notion of productive relations is McMurtry's: *The Structure of Marx's World-View*, 12–13, 72–99, and passim. Also helpful is Cohen, *Karl Marx's Theory of History*, 63–70 and passim, although his characterization of productive relations as "relations of effective power over persons and productive forces" (63), with its emphasis on *control over* the productive forces, strikes me as underestimating that aspect of productive relations that Marx seems to want to see as *arising from* productive forces. Here, it seems to me, Cohen is to some extent imposing his own clarity and love of well-defined conceptual boundaries on Marx.

16. The analytic roots of the materialist conception of history are perhaps most clearly visible in a passage to be found near the end of the "Estranged Labor and Private Property" section of the "Economic and Philosophical Manuscripts" (1st MS). Here Marx claims to have "transform[ed] the question of the *origin of private property* into the question of the relationship of *alienated labor* to the course of human development. . . . This new way of formulating the problem already contains its solution" (*MEGA2* 1.2: 374/*MECW* 3: 281/*EW* 333). The theme, recurrent in Marx, of a problem already containing its solution is of course analytic—one *deduces* the result or solution by an *analysis* of the starting point, as in the solution of a mathematical equation or the derivation of a geometrical proof. As for the "course of human development" to which Marx alludes in this passage, this is the same "real course of development" that in the fragmentary second Manuscript Marx says is "to be inserted here," and that in the third MS he says he "shall return to . . . later" (*MEGA2* 1.2: 381, 409/*MECW* 3: 288, 337/*EW* 333, 391). In these passages of 1844 Marx is already pointing forward to his and Engels's articulation of the materialist conception of history in *The German Ideology*.

17. See Jon Elster, *Making Sense of Marx* (Cambridge: Cambridge University Press, 1985), especially 109–15 and 269–72.

18. Elster cites the following passage: "By forcing the great mass of society to carry out . . . work that goes beyond its immediate needs, the coercive power of capital creates culture: it fulfills a historical and social function" (quoted from Marx's MS, "*Zur Kritik der politischen Ökonomie [Manuskript 1861–63]*, *MEGA2* 2.3.1: 173, in *Making Sense of Marx*, 114–15). Elster also cites (at Elster, 115) a passage where Marx claims that "the interests of the species . . . always assert themselves at the cost of the interest of individuals" (from Marx's MS *Theories of Surplus Value* [1861–63]: see *MEW* 26.2: 111/*MECW* 31: 348 [chap. IX, sect. 2]). This second passage, however, seems of a different sort from

the first, for it evokes a general faith in the good ordering of the world but does not appear to make a functionally explanatory claim.

19. In *The Poverty of Philosophy* (chapter II, §1, 6th observation) Marx himself explicitly rejected functionalist explanation in a paragraph in which he tears into the providentialist conception of history that he finds in Proudhon. Marx attacks Proudhon's teleologism by way of the following example: The development of English industry led to a new market for wool. To take advantage of the market, Scottish landowners had to drive smallholders from the land, so that arable land could be transformed into pasture. Thus, landed property in Scotland "resulted in men being driven out by sheep. Now say that the providential aim of the institution of landed property in Scotland was to have men driven out by sheep, and you will have made providential history" (*MEW* 4: 138/*MECW* 6: 173). In short: Marx argues against converting the statement, "X caused Y," into the statement "X had the function of causing Y," if the situation is one wherein there is no intention or causal mechanism, aimed at the achieving of Y, that brings X about. To be sure, one could argue against the sin of functionalist explanation while still indulging in the sin. But Marx indulges in the sin very rarely, so far as I can see. I return to the topic of functional explanation below.

20. August von Cieszkowski, *Prolegomena zur Historiosophie*, with an introduction by Rüdiger Bubner and an appendix by Jan Garewicz (Hamburg: Felix Meiner, 1981 [first ed., 1838]). For a selection in English of Cieszkowski's writings, see August Cieszkowski, *Selected Writings*, ed. and trans. André Liebich (Cambridge: Cambridge University Press, 1979). An excellent study is Liebich's *Between Ideology and Utopia: The Politics and Philosophy of August Cieszkowski* (Dordrecht, Holland: Reidel, 1979). Cieszkowski is briefly discussed in Shlomo Avineri, *The Social and Political Thought of Karl Marx* (Cambridge: Cambridge University Press, 1968), 124–30.

21. See, crucially, *Prolegomena*, 128–33; quotation at 129 (an English translation is to be found in Cieszkowski, *Selected Writings*, 77–78). The term praxis is basically a synonym for action or activity, one that emphasizes a contrast with theory.

22. Moses Hess, "The Philosophy of the Act," in *Socialist Thought: A Documentary History*, rev. ed., ed. Albert Fried and Ronald Sanders (New York: Columbia University Press, 1992), 245–75. Hess's essay was first published in a widely noticed collection edited by the left-wing poet and journalist Georg Herwegh, *Einundzwanzig Bogen aus der Schweiz* (rpt.: Vaduz, Liechtenstein: Topos, 1977 [originally Zurich, 1843]), 309–31. Marx cites Hess's essay at *MEGA2* 1.2: 326, 393/*MECW* 3: 232, 300/*EW* 281, 352; note my discussion earlier, in chapter 3.

23. Arnold Ruge, "Erinnerungen aus dem äußeren Leben, von Ernst Moritz Arndt," in *Die Hegelsche Linke: Dokumente zu Philosophie und Politik im deutschen Vormärz*, ed. Heinz Pepperle and Ingrid Pepperle (Frankfurt: Röderberg, 1986), 172–88. Subsequent references are given parenthetically in the text. Ernst Moritz Arndt's *Erinnerungen aus dem äußeren Leben* is to be found in Arndt, *Werke: Auswahl in zwölf Teilen*, ed. August Leffson and Wilhelm Steffens (12 parts [4 vols.]; Berlin: Deutsches Verlagshaus Bong, 1912), 2: 1–282). For a discussion of Arndt's views, see John G. Gagliardo, *From Pariah to Patriot: The Changing Image of the German Peasant, 1770–1840* (Lexington: University Press of Kentucky, 1969), 199–210, 232, and passim.

24. Hegel, *Elements of the Philosophy of Right*, preface, 23.

25. Arndt saw the peasantry as "a forest . . . from which the mast and beams of power must be hewn"; thus it is worthy of special protection from the state (Arndt, *Erinnerungen*, "Über die Bauren," 199–233, quote at 199).

26. The 1840s saw much discussion of "the social question," of which Ruge's review of Arndt is only one instance. See, *inter alia*, Werner Conze, "Vom 'Pöbel' zum 'Proletariat': Sozialgeschichtliche Voraussetzungen für den Sozialismus in Deutschland," in *Moderne deutsche Sozialgeschichte*, ed. Hans-Ulrich Wehler (Köln: Kiepenheuer & Witsch, 1966), 111–36, 481–84.

It is interesting that the twenty-year-old Friedrich Engels also reviewed Arndt's *Erinnerungen*, in January 1841. Engels argued that Arndt's proposal that, in order to encourage social stability, it should be made easier to "entail" land (restricting its salability and divisibility) was retrogressive: "even if landed property were to fly from hand to hand I would rather have the surging ocean with its grand freedom than the narrow inland lake with its quiet surface. . . ." See *MEGA2* 1.3: 210–22/*MECW* 2: 146–49.

27. *Ludwig Feuerbach*, which the editors of *MECW* characterize as "one of the fundamental works of Marxism," was an important popularization of Marx's views (*MECW* 26: 659 n. 233). Here Engels writes that for Marx and for himself "the dialectic of concepts . . . became merely the conscious reflection of the dialectical motion of the real world and thus the Hegelian dialectic was placed upon its head; or rather, turned off its head, on which it was standing, and placed upon its feet" (*MEW* 21: 293/*MECW* 26: 383).

28. Elster, *Making Sense of Marx*, 109.

29. This passage is actually in a two-page section written by Engels, sandwiched between sections written by Marx. Given the co-authorship of *The Holy Family* and the congruence of the claim made here with views that Marx stated elsewhere (but not so early or so clearly), I take it as an Engelsian articulation of a view also held by Marx.

30. The first of these views is what dialectical materialism—with its insistence that movement-inducing laws (such as the law of the transformation of quantity into quality) are embedded within matter—is essentially about.

31. This connection is never admitted or acknowledged by Marx: of course, he would *not* admit or acknowledge it, for he wants to present himself as a great innovator, breaking from previous tradition. Still, one wonders whether, on the first page of the Feuerbach section of *The German Ideology*, Marx subliminally betrays the connection. I have been suggesting that Marx constructs the materialist conception of history as a rewriting of the history of philosophy and thus as an analogue of that history. Here at the beginning of *The German Ideology* one is intrigued to find Marx and Engels analogizing philosophy to industry, for they refer to philosophers as "industrialists of philosophy," concerned with selling their goods on a competitive market [*Die philosophischen Industriellen, die bisher von der Exploitation des absoluten Geistes gelebt hatten, warfen sich jetzt auf die neuen Verbindungen. . . .*] (*MEW* 3: 17/*MECW* 5: 27–28/*MER* 147).

32. I would identify at least four different balancings of the rationalist/empiricist opposition in Marx: those of 1839–44, 1845–56, 1857–58, and 1867. (I follow, here, some lines of thought suggested to me by a reading of Philip J. Kain, *Marx' Method, Epistemology, and Humanism: A Study in the Development of His Thought* (Dordrecht: Reidel, 1986) and of Adamson, *Marx and the Disillusionment of Marxism* [note 6], among other writings on Marx's method.)

33. On notions of progress in the nineteenth century, see Maurice Mandelbaum, *History, Man, and Reason: A Study in Nineteenth-Century Thought* (Baltimore: Johns Hopkins University Press, 1971), 51–61 and passim.

34. This idea is already present in the "Private Property and Communism" section of the "Economic and Philosophical Manuscripts," where Marx suggests that "communism, as accomplished [*vollendete*] naturalism = humanism, and as accomplished humanism =

naturalism: it is the genuine [*wahrhafte*] resolution of the conflict between man and nature" (*MEGA2* 1.2: 389/*MECW* 3: 296/*EW* 348). It is likewise to be found in *The Poverty of Philosophy*, chapter II, §3: "all history [*die ganze Geschichte*] is only a continuous transformation of human nature" (*MEW* 4: 160/*MECW* 6: 192).

35. It is a question here of "what Marx believed"—a tricky matter, as noted before. My suggestion that Marx was consciously making a wager in favor of progress is an inference from three facts. First, there is his obvious failure to provide adequate evidence. (The reader is invited to examine carefully sentence 12 of the epigraph of this chapter, where Marx's claim that "mankind always sets itself only such tasks as it can solve" remains almost comically undersupported: the support that Marx offers amounts to a tautological restatement.) Second, there is the fact that Marx was extremely intelligent, and surely would not have missed the lack of support for his claim. Third, there is the fact that Marx was perfectly willing to misrepresent states of affairs when doing so redounded, or seemed to redound, to the benefit of his revolutionary hopes. The idea here is that to assert that progress reigns in human history will itself encourage progress. This is a Kantian idea: see Kant, "Idea for a Universal History with a Cosmopolitan Purpose" (1784), 9th proposition, in Kant, *Political Writings*, ed. and with an introduction by Hans Reiss, trans. H. B. Nisbet, 2d, enl. ed. (Cambridge: Cambridge University Press, 1991), 41–53, at 51–53. While I suggest no deep influence here of Kant on Marx, I do suggest an affinity. My suggestion is that Marx did not hold to the materialist conception of history thinking that it had adequate justification. He held to it, rather, as a view that at certain moments was useful to hold. It also had the advantage of being consistent with his deepest philosophical commitments. I shall say more about this later.

36. Marx does not characterize forms of social consciousness and says surprisingly little about ideology. *The German Ideology* is mainly concerned with attacking a *specific* ideology—namely, that of the self-proclaimed radical wing of German philosophy, with a side glance at a number of self-proclaimed German socialist writers. It deals only glancingly with the notion of ideology itself. See *MEW* 3: 9–530/*MECW* 5: 19–539/*MER* 146–200 (pt. 1 only). Marx offers us no detailed account of ideology as such, and none at all of forms of social consciousness, for an obvious reason: he wanted to focus on "the material transformation of the economic conditions of production, which can be established with the accuracy of natural science"—to cite his statement in the 1859 preface (sentence 9 of the epigraph). John McMurtry, *The Structure of Marx's World-View*, does an excellent job of compensating for Marx's deficiencies: he explicates ideology and forms of social consciousness at 13–14, 123–44, and 145–56. Aside from McMurtry, so far as I know there is no literature on Marx's notion of social consciousness. There is, however, a substantial literature on Marx's concept of ideology. On this latter topic, perhaps the best place to start (after a reading of the relevant pages in McMurtry) is the reliable and unpretentious study by Martin Seliger, *The Marxian Conception of Ideology: A Critical Essay* (Cambridge: Cambridge University Press, 1977).

37. See, nonetheless, an important passage in *The German Ideology* that casts light on Marx's conception of the temporal relations among the different categories. The passage, about a page in length, also illuminates the 1859 preface passage. I quote only a part of it, the part most relevant to the question of different temporalities:

> This evolution [of history] . . . takes place only very slowly; the various stages and interests are never completely overcome, but only subordinated to the prevailing interest *and trail along beside the latter for centuries afterwards*. It follows . . . that an *earlier* interest, the peculiar form

> of intercourse of which has already been ousted by that belonging to a later interest, remains for a long time afterwards in possession of a traditional power in the illusory community (State, law). . . . This explains why . . . consciousness can sometimes *appear* further advanced than the contemporary empirical relationships, so that in the struggles of a *later* epoch one can refer to earlier theoreticians as authorities. (The entire passage is to be found at *MEW* 3: 72–73/*MECW* 5: 82–83/*MER* 194–95; my italics throughout.)

Here the suggestion seems to be that the legal and political superstructure and ideology may be significantly retarded, but that forms of social consciousness may be well ahead of them, close to being up to the measure of the current productive forces. If one wished to correlate this account with figure 4.1, I believe that one would do so by revising figure 4.1 slightly, moving forward the category "forms of social consciousness." Productive relations and productive forces would remain the vanguard of social development; the legal and political superstructure and ideology would be retarded, as they are in the diagram as given; but "social consciousness," at least in its guise as theory, would be *almost* up to the level of the forces and relations of production—and thus would be in advance of current legal and political arrangements and ideology. The revision cunningly allows a space for the critical theorist to operate, while in no way denying the primacy of productive forces and relations.

38. Cohen defends "Functional Explanation: In General" in his chapter IX, and discusses "Functional Explanation: In Marxism" in chapter X, in Cohen, in *Karl Marx's Theory of History: A Defence*, 249–77, 278–96. (Incidentally, persons wishing to explore issues in and around analytical Marxism ought to consult the expanded edition of *Karl Marx's Theory of History*, published by the Oxford and Princeton university presses in 2000. It contains a new introduction, "Reflections on Analytical Marxism," and four new chapters.)

39. But see Jon Elster, "Cohen on Marx's Theory of History," *Political Studies* 28 (1980): 121–28, at 125–28.

40. See Cohen, *Karl Marx's Theory of History*, 278–85. I quote, however, from the abbreviated (and clearer) account that Cohen gives in his "Functional Explanation: Reply to Elster," *Political Studies* 28 (1980): 129–35, at 129.

41. Here and below, I have found important guidance in Timothy Shiell, "On Marx's Holism," *History of Philosophy Quarterly* 4 (1987): 235–46. Shiell's piece came to me early in the game, since it was originally written years ago in a class that I taught, or rather, in which students taught me. See also the discussion of "MI" [methodological individualism] in Terrell Carver and Paul Thomas, "Introduction," in *Rational Choice Marxism*, ed. Carver and Thomas (University Park: Pennsylvania State University Press, 1995), 1–10, and Mark E. Warren's searching study, "Marx and Methodological Individualism," analyzing Elster on MI, in the same collection, 231–57.

42. There are interesting discussions of the appearance/essence distinction in Marx in Seigel, *Marx's Fate: The Shape of a Life* (University Park: Pennsylvania State University Press, 1993), 316–18 and in Adamson, *Marx and the Disillusionment of Marxism*, 60–61. It seems clear that Marx's emphasis on a sharp distinction between appearance and essence correlates with pessimism on his part concerning the likelihood of revolution in the immediate future. Thus the distinction tends to drop out of the optimistic Marx of the period 1845–48, and returns to his thinking after 1851, by which time it was clear that the revolutions of 1848 had failed to produce the kind of change he wished for. I see his emphasis

on the appearance/essence distinction in the 1850s and after as a stratagem on his part for preserving an underlying hope at a time when the world of appearances had disappointed that hope.

43. G. W. F. Hegel, *Phenomenology of Spirit*, trans. A. V. Miller with a foreword by J. N. Findlay (Oxford: Oxford University Press, 1977), preface, §20, 11.

44. Martin Jay, *Marxism and Totality* (Berkeley and Los Angeles: University of California Press, 1984), 65; cited in Shiell, "On Marx's Holism," 235.

45. The next question, of course, is: why was Marx hostile to the existing order? I cannot pursue this question in detail. I can only note that there are two types of answer to the question, namely, "logical" and "psychological." Among "logical" answers, three suggest themselves, namely, that Marx hated the existing order (a) because it is estranging, (b) because it is exploitative, and (c) because it is irrational.

Let us imagine a reformed capitalism, in which estrangement had been reduced to a minimum and in which exploitation had been either eliminated or compensated for. In my opinion, at the end of the day Marx would still have rejected capitalism, on grounds of its irrationality. (As Marx says in *Capital*, volume 2, "in capitalist society . . . any kind of social rationality [*der gesellschaftliche Verstand*] asserts itself only *post festum* [too late to have any effect]" [*MEW* 24: 317/*MECW* 36: 314/*CAP* 2: 390 (chapter 16)]. For Marx, this just wasn't good enough.)

As for "psychological" answers to the question, these amount to claims that Marx was emotionally predisposed toward rejecting the existing order—perhaps on Oedipal grounds, perhaps because he was innately a "negating genius." I do not claim to be able to assess this latter type of answer—which in any case I find less interesting than the first type.

46. I want to reiterate that he may well offer good explanations in his investigation of specific issues *within* capitalism—for example, with regard to issues of currency and banking. This, however, is a matter for further research. Given limitations of time, space, energy, and inclination, I cannot pursue this line of investigation in the present book. Cf. chapter 3, note 17.

47. Significantly, the first hint of the materialist conception of history in Marx's writings, which appears just before the end of the first of the "Economic and Philosophical Manuscripts," arises within the context of what Marx presents as an analytic line of argument (involving analysis of concepts). In brief, Marx characterizes what we can now recognize as historical materialism as involving an attempt to answer the question "How . . . does *man* come *to alienate his labor*, to estrange it?" Marx attempts to "solv[e] this problem by *transforming* the question of the *origin* of *private property* into the question of the relationship of *alienated labor* to the course of human development." And he concludes, in a characteristically analytic way, with the observation that "This new way of formulating the problem already contains its solution [*Diese neue Stellung der Frage ist inclusive schon ihre Lösung*]." (*MEGA2* 1.2: 374/*MECW* 3: 281/*EW* 333)

48. See Allan Megill, "Recounting the Past: 'Description,' Explanation, and Narrative in Historiography," *American Historical Review* 94 (1989): 627–53, at 647–50.

49. Cf. the early, apparently rationalist Wittgenstein, who writes in the *Tractatus Logico-Philosophicus* (1921) that "if a question can be framed at all, it is also *possible* to solve it" (Ludwig Wittgenstein, *Tractatus Logico-Philosophicus*, trans. D. F. Pears and B. F. McGuinness with the introduction by Bertrand Russell [London: Routledge & Kegan Paul, 1974], §6.5).

50. Arthur M. Prinz, "Background and Ulterior Motive of Marx's 'Preface' of 1859," *Journal of the History of Ideas* 30 (1969): 437–50; quote at 437; see also 449–50. As Prinz notes, article 20 of the Prussian constitution "proclaimed freedom of science and its teaching" (439), and Marx's emphatic insistence in the 1859 preface on the scientific character of his views does sound, in part, like an appeal to the censor to permit the work of a man who in March 1843 had been branded a dangerous radical, and who had been rebranded as such in 1848–49, to be published and to circulate legally. The peroration of the preface, with its quoting of Dante, sounds awfully like an attempt to bend the will, flatter the erudition, and curry the favor of censor:

> my views . . . are the results of conscientious investigation lasting many years . . . at the entrance to science, as at the entrance to hell, the demand must be posted:
> Here all mistrust must be abandoned
> And here must perish every craven thought.
> (*MEW* 13: 11/*MECW* 29: 265/*MER* 6)

Conversely, paragraph 100 of the Prussian penal code stipulated a prison term of up to two years to "anyone who incited one class of the population to hatred and contempt of other classes." Notably, the "actors" in the 1859 preface are productive forces, not classes, and the proletariat is not mentioned. See Prinz, 437–38.

51. I remember, as a child in Saskatchewan, hearing the British Guyanian political leader Cheddi Jagan being interviewed on the Canadian Broadcasting Corporation radio station in Regina. Jagan extolled the merits of "scientific socialism," a phrase that must have mystified most of his listeners, as it did me. "Scientific socialism" took its justification from historical materialism, and could not have existed without it. (In an e-mail message of December 12, 2000, Nadira Jagan-Brancier informed me that Cheddi Jagan visited Canada in October 1961.)

52. In addition to his "retrograde" model of ideology, Marx had a second, "inversion" model: as Marx and Engels suggest in *The German Ideology*, in ideology "men and their relations appear upside down, as in a camera obscura" (*MEW* 3: 26/*MECW* 5: 36/*MER* 154). How the "inversion" model hooks onto the "retrograde" model is not entirely clear. However, one can say in broad terms that the "retrograde" model is Hegelian and that the "inversion" model is Feuerbachian. One needs to take both models into account if one is to grasp Marx's conception of ideology. Usually the retrograde model is overlooked—as it is by Adamson, in a passage in which he points out, rightly, that the inversion model does not make sense of modern Americans' attachment to the "rugged individualism" of "the robber baron, the independent entrepreneur, the cowboy, the pioneer," but in which he does not note Marx's other model; see Adamson, *Marx and the Disillusionment of Marxism*, 66.

53. Marx and Engels make the same point in *The Communist Manifesto* (1848), where they deny that "the history of ideas" can have any independent history: "What else does the history of ideas prove, than that intellectual production changes its character in proportion as material production is changed? The ruling ideas of each age . . . ," and so on (*MEW* 3: 26/*MECW* 6: 503/*MER* 489/*LPW* 18). Again, it must be emphasized that Marx and Engels are here talking about *ideological* ideas—ideas detached from an immediate dialectical relationship to practice—not about scientific ideas.

54. See the following passage from *The Holy Family* (late 1844): "One must be acquainted with the studiousness, the craving for knowledge, the moral energy and the unceasing urge for development of the French and English workers, to be able to form an

idea of the human nobility of that movement" (*MEW* 2: 89/*MECW* 4: 84 [chapter VI.1.a]). Here the workers seem well fitted to be the philosophers of the future, the legitimate heirs of philosophy's mantle.

55. In his "Appendix I: Karl Marx and the Withering Away of Social Science," in *Karl Marx's Theory of History*, 326–44, G. A. Cohen develops these points, linking them to, among other things, the metaphoric of unveiling that is so important for Marx (see, for example, *MEGA2* 2.6: 110/*MECW* 35: 90–91/*CAP* 1: 173 [chapter 1, section 4]). I would not quite say, though, that "by unifying social theory and social practice, socialism [in Marx's view] suppresses social science" (Cohen, 338). I would say, rather, that social science *becomes* social practice. Science disappears as a separate enterprise because all practice becomes scientific—which is to say that science does not really disappear. And the rationality-criteria remain in place.

56. Walter Benjamin, "Theses on the Philosophy of History," in Benjamin, *Illuminations*, ed. Hannah Arendt, trans. Harry Zohn (New York: Schocken, 1969), 253–64, at 253.

57. Cf. Wittgenstein, *Tractatus Logico-Philosophicus*, 6.54: "My propositions serve as elucidations in the following way: anyone who understands me eventually recognizes them as nonsensical, when he has used them—as steps—to climb up beyond them. (He must, so to speak, throw away the ladder after he has climbed up it.)"

58. Helmut Fleischer, *Marxism and History* (note 6), 8–9.

59. See Bryan S. Turner, "Asiatic Society," in *A Dictionary of Marxist Thought*, ed. Tom Bottomore, 2d., rev. ed. (Cambridge: Harvard University Press, 1991), 36–39, which neatly summarizes 125 years of discussion of this topic.

60. See Karl Marx, *Ethnological Notebooks (Studies of Morgan, Phear, Maine, Lubbock)*, ed. Lawrence Krader (Assen: van Gorcum, 1972).

61. Although the letter to Zasulich is only about three hundred words long, Marx devoted a great deal of time and attention to Zasulich's question. There exist four drafts of the letter, three of them substantially longer than the letter Marx actually sent: see *MEGA2* 1.25: 219–40 (the material is all in Marx's impeccable written French). The letter to Zasulich, Marx's drafts for the letter, and other interesting material related to the later Marx's views on Russia, all in English translation, are included in *Late Marx and the Russian Road: Marx and "the Peripheries of Capitalism,"* ed. Teodor Shanin (New York: Monthly Review Press, 1983). Interestingly, the Russian Marxists long suppressed Marx's letter—indeed, twenty years later Zasulich, Plekhanov, and Axelrod, luminaries of Russian Marxism at the time, denied that any such letter had ever been received. The problem was that, *plus catholiques que le pape*, they were unable to assimilate Marx's views to the standard historical materialist account of a sequence from feudalism through capitalism to socialism. Already, as early as 1883, they put their orthodox historical materialism into practice by throwing in their lot with the Russian proletariat, even though it was almost nonexistent. They thus turned aside from what they now saw as the benighted, superstitious, utterly backward peasantry (which unfortunately made up the vast majority of Russia's population). On this move, which surely ought to be seen as a fateful error, see Esther Kingston-Mann, *In Search of the True West: Culture, Economics, and Problems of Russian Development* (Princeton: Princeton University Press, 1999), 141.

Engels preceded Marx in suggesting an alternative path to socialism, in a response he wrote to queries from a Russian Populist: see "On Social Relations in Russia" (1874), where he asserts that the peasant commune might be raised "to this higher form [of socialism] without it being necessary for the Russian peasants to go through the intermediate stage of bourgeois small holdings" (*MEW* 18: 565/*MECW* 24: 48/*MER*, 665–75, at 673). In all likelihood, this was a matter that Marx and Engels discussed off and on between themselves over a period of years.

62. Richard W. Miller, *Analyzing Marx: Morality, Power and History* (Princeton: Princeton University Press, 1984), 11.

63. In *Marx and the Disillusionment of Marxism*, 24–39, Walter Adamson argues that Marx had *four* conceptions of history—the anthropological, pragmatological, and nomological conceptions identified by Fleischer, plus a fourth, "counter-evolutionary" conception, which Adamson finds in the discussion, in the *Grundrisse*, of method and of the place of Greek art in history (See *MEGA2* 2.1: 35–45/*MECW* 28: 37–48/*GRUND* 100–11/*MER* 236–46). Adamson contends that Marx here diverges from the claim that there is only one necessary world-historical pattern into which everything must fit. But I do not see that Marx developed this insight beyond his very unclear articulation of it in this 1857 text.

CONCLUSION

1. One should bear in mind the primary meaning of *autopsy*, visible in the original Greek: a self-seeing (*aut-opsia*).

2. Readers who wish to pursue the question of Marx's method in detail might consult the following commentaries, among others: Philip J. Kain, *Marx' Method, Epistemology, and Humanism: A Study in the Development of His Thought* (Dordrecht: Reidel, 1986); Derek Sayer, *Marx's Method: Ideology, Science and Critique in "Capital"* (Hassocks, Sussex: Harvester, 1979); Hiroshi Uchida, *Marx's "Grundrisse" and Hegel's "Logic,"* ed. Terrell Carver (London: Routledge, 1988); and Jindřich Zelený, *The Logic of Marx*, trans. and ed. Terrell Carver (Oxford: Blackwell, 1980). A number of important Marxian texts relevant to method are assembled in Karl Marx, *Texts on Method*, trans. and ed. Terrell Carver (Oxford: Blackwell, 1975). A study that explores the *Grundrisse* generally is Roman Rosdolsky, *The Making of Marx's 'Capital,'* trans. Peter Burgess (London: Pluto Press, 1977). An important methodological influence on the later Marx was Hegel's *Science of Logic*, which he took up and read in late 1857. Marx excitedly noted his rediscovery of Hegel in a letter to Engels of January 16, 1858 (*MEW* 29: 260/*MECW* 40: 249).

3. For a useful account, see Maurice Mandelbaum, *History, Man, and Reason: A Study in Nineteenth-Century Thought* (Baltimore: Johns Hopkins University Press, 1971), 10–20, especially 10–11.

4. Eugen von Böhm-Bawerk, "Karl Marx and the Close of His System," in "*Karl Marx and the Close of His System," by Eugen von Böhm-Bawerk and "Böhm-Bawerk's Criticism of Marx," by Rudolf Hilferding*, ed. Paul M. Sweezy (New York: Augustus M. Kelley, 1949), 1–101, at 101.

5. The claim came to be known as Say's Law, and was based on the premise that "the production of a given output necessarily generates incomes sufficient to purchase that output" (as Thomas Sowell summarizes matters, *Say's Law: An Historical Analysis* [Princeton: Princeton University Press, 1972], 36). Sowell discusses "the Marxian challenge" to Say's Law at 168–90.

6. See Ludwig von Mises, "Economic Calculation in the Socialist Commonwealth," in *Collectivist Economic Planning*, ed. F. A. von Hayek (London: George Routledge, 1938),

87–128 (originally published in the important social-science journal *Archiv für Sozialwissenschaften* in 1920). In brief, von Mises argued that the claim made by socialists that "a socialist system of production" will have "greater rationality" than production based on private ownership of the means of production cannot be sustained. Their claim cannot be sustained because, in the absence of "exchange relations," one has no adequate way of determining the value of production-goods. Technical considerations alone cannot serve to guide production in a rational way, since there are many different ways of producing the same product. How is one supposed to choose among them? Only when a functioning market exists, with the result that one can discern the prices of the various inputs, can one overcome "the difficulty arising from the complexity of the relations between the mighty system of present-day production on the one hand and the efficiency of enterprises and economic units on the other" (von Mises, 128–30).

Perhaps it is worth pointing out that von Mises's style of thinking is remarkably close to Marx's: like Marx, von Mises demonstrates a commitment to deductive reasoning, to an ultimate consistency, and to "rationality." It is not surprising that, with this orientation, von Mises is able to perceive something that not every reader of Marx sees, namely, *Marx*'s commitment to rationality. The difference between the two thinkers is that, whereas Marx argues that social rationality cannot be achieved *with* the market, von Mises argues that it cannot be achieved *without* the market. Von Mises's well-known antistatist tendencies can also be seen as having a parallel in similar tendencies in Marx, but this is not a matter that I can pursue here.

7. I rely here on Owen W. Linzmayer, *Apple Confidential: The Real Story of Apple Computer, Inc.* (San Francisco: No Starch Press, 1999), 1–12.

8. It needs to be emphasized that a precondition for participation in the process of choice that is here alluded to is a certain degree of economic sufficiency and personal independence. Dependent poor people have little in the way of market choice. The market as such cannot guarantee that they will. This is one of the reasons why there needs to be a state—preferably a democratic state—that is willing and able to correct the market at those points where its outcomes impair personal independence and fail to conduce to the general good. Nor is the state the only institution that should be doing this, although the state's coercive power does enable it to handle problems that charitable foundations, churches, cooperatives, self-help societies, and the like will unfortunately not be able to adequately address.

9. See two of Friedrich von Hayek's classic papers, "Economics and Knowledge" (1937) and "The Use of Knowledge in Society" (1945), reprinted in Hayek, *Individualism and Economic Order* (London: Routledge & Kegan Paul, 1949), 33–56 and 77–91. In many works, Israel Kirzner has developed and popularized the notion of the market as a discovery mechanism. See, for example, Israel M. Kirzner, *Discovery and the Capitalist Process* (Chicago: University of Chicago Press, 1985), and Kirzner, *The Meaning of Market Process: Essays in the Development of Modern Austrian Economics* (London: Routledge & Kegan Paul, 1992), especially chapter 9, "Economic Planning and the Knowledge Problem," 152–62. Usefully concentrated is Kirzner's pamphlet, *How Markets Work: Disequilibrium, Entrepreneurship and Discovery* (Saint Leonards, Australia: Centre for Independent Studies, 1998 [Occasional Paper 64]), especially section IV, "The Theory of Entrepreneurial Discovery," 20–39. Hayek's emphasis was on the market as a mechanism for bringing together knowledge that otherwise exists only as "dispersed bits of incomplete and frequently contradictory knowledge" (Hayek, 77). Kirzner's emphasis is on the market as a mechanism that actually *creates* knowledge—knowledge that would not have existed

without it. This would include, for example, the knowledge of a certain four-year-old that she wants a robot dog (which was designed by a group of people in Japan and manufactured somewhere in China in order to be sold in the United States), and the knowledge that I want and need the notebook computer on which I am right now typing this sentence.

10. See *Encyclopaedia Britannica*, 14th ed., vol. 11 (London: Encyclopaedia Britannica Company, 1929), s. v. "Hitler, Adolf," 598.

11. Karl R. Popper, *Conjectures and Refutations: The Growth of Scientific Knowledge*, 2d ed. (New York: Basic Books, 1962). As Popper suggests in his preface, the thesis of his book is that "*we can learn from our mistakes*" (vii). Among other things, the market is a device for the continuous testing out of new ideas. In the medium and long term, failure on the market allows "us," collectively, to learn from mistakes while also benefiting from lucky guesses. One problem is that, in the short term, we do have to put up with the mistakes. It also needs to be emphasized that self-interest (greed) alone is not enough for an adequately functioning market system; one also needs civic order, a reliable legal system, relative honesty (leading to a corresponding level of trust), individual freedom, general access to basic goods and resources, and surveillance and regulation. The absence of any of these conditions risks disaster.

12. Although *glasnost* did not manage to save the system, it was at least an improvement on Communism's earlier institution for gathering information, the secret police. This institution, which reached its acme with the GDR's information-mad *Stasi*, was an entirely understandable (even rational) response to the system's overwhelmingly recalcitrant information problem (a problem that arose not just out of the absence of markets but also—and perhaps more importantly—out of the absence of properly functioning political institutions).

13. Maurice Dobb, *An Essay on Economic Growth and Planning* (London: Routledge and Kegan Paul, 1960).

14. Adam Smith's phrase, in Smith, *An Inquiry into the Nature and Causes of the Wealth of Nations*, ed. Edwin Cannan, with an introduction by Max Lerner (New York: Modern Library, 1937), Bk. IV, chap, II, 423.

15. Robert Skidelsky, *Keynes* (Oxford: Oxford University Press, 1995), 1.

16. I evoke a complex set of issues, including such diverse matters as social justice, gender relations, racial and ethnic relations, affirmative action, child welfare, the organization of health care, the functioning of the legal system, and (perhaps of central importance) the role and function of government. I can do no more than note the existence of a substantial literature in ethical and political philosophy that attempts to deal with the philosophical bases of such issues. A fundamental work is John Rawls's *A Theory of Justice* (Cambridge: Harvard University Press, 1971), which initiated a discussion to which a large number of theorists, including (among many others) Robert Nozick, Michael Walzer, Michael Sandel, and Ronald Dworkin, have contributed. The specialized literature continues onward with few signs of abating. But we do not need to worry about it very much, for the central point that I want to make here is easy to understand, and (I believe) incontrovertible.

17. One comes closest to finding an ethically oriented Marx in the writings of his Feuerbachian phase. See especially the introduction to his projected "Critique of Hegel's Philosophy of Right" (late 1843, published February 1844), where he declares that:

> To be radical is to grasp things by the root. But for man the root is man himself. . . . The criticism of religion ends with the doctrine that *for man the supreme being is man*, and thus with the *categorical imperative to overthrow all conditions* in which man is a debased, enslaved, neglected and contemptible being." (*MEGA2* 1.2: 177/*MECW* 3: 182/*EW* 251)

Clearly, this has to be a different sort of ethical imperative than the transcendent law envisaged by Kant, but it does seem to be an ethical imperative. After February 1844, however, the question of Marx's relation to ethics becomes more complicated.

Although I disagree with what I see as its "moderating" view of Marx, Philip J. Kain's *Marx and Ethics* (Oxford: Oxford University Press, 1988) is perhaps the best overall introduction to the issues in question, in part because it so scrupulously surveys other, competing attempts to deal with Marx's relation to ethics. Kain summarizes his conception of the evolution of Marx's views on ethics at 11–12, and deals interestingly with questions of justice and ethics under communism at 176–203. Kain believes that Marx thought that conceptions of justice and ethics would still apply under communism. He disagrees with such commentators as Allen Wood, George Brenkert, George Schedler, and Allen Buchanan, who dispute this view.

I think that the other commentators are right. I also think that Kain is right in pointing out that problems would arise under communism that would inevitably require the deployment of principles of justice and morality. I just do not think that this fact is compatible with Marx's underlying theory. I think that Kain improves Marx. I think that he is justified in doing so. But I think that we also need the unimproved Marx, if we are to understand how, under the Leninist-Stalinist variant of Marxism, human beings by the thousands and millions could be smashed to make the tasty omelet of communism.

18. For a contemporary version, see Robert Nozick, *Anarchy, State, and Utopia* (New York: Basic Books, 1971).

19. For a contemporary version, see John Rawls, *A Theory of Justice*.

20. Hannah Arendt, *The Human Condition*, 2d ed., with an introduction by Margaret Canovan (Chicago: University of Chicago Press, 1998 [1958]). Much of Arendt's discussion of politics is to be found in chapter V, "Action," 175–247. See the useful index, s.v. "Marx, Karl," for Arendt's various scattered Marx references.

21. See Jürgen Habermas, "Labor and Interaction: Remarks on Hegel's Jena *Philosophy of Mind*," in Habermas, *Theory and Practice*, trans. John Viertel (Boston: Beacon, 1973), 142–69.

22. Arendt, *The Human Condition*, 51.

23. Hannah Arendt, *Love and Saint Augustine* [originally published in German in 1929, translated and revised late 1950s(?)–early 1960s], ed. and with an interpretive essay by Joanna Vecchiarelli Scott and Judith Chelius Stark (Chicago: University of Chicago Press, 1996); Hannah Arendt, *Rahel Varnhagen: The Life of a Jewess* [written 1930s and later, first published 1958], ed. Liliane Weissberg, trans. Richard and Clara Winston (Baltimore: Johns Hopkins University Press, 1997).

24. Marx's expressions of love for his wife are many. Here is an example from a quite amazing letter of June 21, 1856, to Jenny, who was away visiting in Trier at the time: "But the love, not for Feuerbachian man, nor for Moleschott's metabolism, nor for the proletariat, but the love for the sweetheart, that is, for you, makes the man a man again" (*MEGA2* 3.8: 30–32, at 31/*MECW* 40: 54–57, at 56). The whole letter is in a similar vein, and is worth reading by people who foolishly think that they know Marx already. To be sure, sweet words do not pay the rent, and living with Marx was not easy for Jenny, given Marx's devotion to his work and his carelessness about money.

Karl and Jenny had seven children who were born alive, of whom four died in infancy or childhood. It should also be noted that in all likelihood Marx was the father of the child of the family maid, Helene Demuth, a boy born in June 1851. The child would have been conceived in the single sleeping room of the Marx family apartment while Frau Marx was away in the Netherlands fruitlessly seeking to borrow money from Marx's mother's sister's husband Lion Philips (whose son went on to found what became the multinational Philips corporation that we know today). The birth, and rumors surrounding it, seem to have caused Frau Marx much grief. (Francis Wheen surveys the evidence on this matter in *Karl Marx* [London: Fourth Estate, 1999], 170–76.)

25. "The immediate, natural, necessary relation of human being to human being is the *relationship* of *man* to *woman*. . . . It is possible to judge from this relationship the entire level of development of humankind." (*MEGA2* 1.2: 388/*MECW* 1: 295–96/*EW* 347)

"If you love unrequitedly, i.e., if your love as love does not call forth love in return, if through the *vital expression* of yourself as a loving person you fail to become a *loved person*, then your love is impotent, it is a misfortune" (*MEGA2* 1.2: 438/*MECW* 3: 326/*EW* 379).

26. Marx, *On Suicide*, ed. Eric A. Plaut and Kevin Anderson, trans. Plaut, Gabrielle Edgcomb, and Anderson (Evanston, Ill.: Northwestern University Press, 1999). Although the text appears in *MECW* 3: 597–612, it is not adequately annotated, nor was it adequately annotated in its appearance in *MEGA1* I.3: 391–407. Hence the Anderson-Plaut edition, which includes the German original, is indispensable. The text was excluded from *MEW* and has not yet appeared in *MEGA2*.

27. Karl Marx, *Ethnological Notebooks (Studies of Morgan, Phear, Maine, Lubbock)*, transcribed and edited, with an introduction by, Lawrence Krader (Assen, Netherlands: van Gorcum, 1972). Eventually Marx's ethnological excerpts and notes will appear in a new edition in *MEGA2*, 4. Abt., Bd. 27 (excerpts and notes of 1879–81).

28. Of Lizzy Burns, Engels wrote as follows, in a letter of 1892: "My wife was of real Irish proletarian stock, and her passionate feeling for her class, which was inborn, was worth infinitely more to me and had stood by me in all critical moments more strongly than all the aesthetic nicey-niceness and wiseacreism [*Schöngeisterei und Klugtuerei*] of the 'eddicated' and 'senty-mental' [*'jebildeten' und 'jefühlvollen'*] daughters of the bourgeoisie could have done" (Engels to Julie Bebel, March 8, 1892, in *MEW* 38: 298/*MECW* 49). As for Frau Marx, besides keeping the family on an even keel (even, on occasion, begging for money), she acted as Marx's secretary—"writing letters, producing fair copies of his articles for newspapers (his handwriting being illegible) and keeping careful records of the dispatch of his journalism" (David McLellan, *Karl Marx: His Life and Thought* [New York: Harper & Row, 1973], 270). Obviously, both men were very lucky with regard to the main women in their lives.

29. I cite the much expanded 4th edition (1891; English trans., 1902). A convenient cheap version of the 4th edition is Friedrich Engels, *The Origin of the Family, Private Property and the State*, with an introduction by Michèle Barrett (Harmondsworth: Penguin, 1985); chapter II, "The Family," 58–115; quotes at 92, 93, 113, 114.

30. Hannah Arendt, "What Is Freedom?" in Arendt, *Between Past and Future: Eight Exercises in Political Thought* (New York: Viking Press, 1961), 149.

31. From the song "Denn wovon lebt der Mensch?," in Bertolt Brecht, *Die Dreigroschen Oper*, in Bertolt Brecht, *Die Stücke in einem Band* (Frankfurt am Main: Suhrkamp, 1978), 191.

32. In this regard, André Malraux, more than Brecht, represents Marx's view: as in Katov's gift of the cyanide, in Malraux, *Man's Fate*, trans. Haakon M. Chevalier (New York: Vintage Books, 1990; orig. French ed., 1933), "Six O'Clock in the Evening," 311–26.

Bibliography

This bibliography lists only writings by Marx and Engels and not items from the vast secondary literature. I have listed several Marx-Engels items that I did not end up citing but that I nonetheless consulted and found useful. Full publication data for all works cited in this book, except for those that I cite by way of abbreviations, are given at the first citation within a given chapter. The key to abbreviations, which appears after the contents and before the preface, decodes the abbreviated reference forms that I have used for frequently cited items, and also gives the publication data for those items.

A word should be said about the several comprehensive Marx-Engels editions listed here. By far the best edition is the *Karl Marx Friedrich Engels Gesamtausgabe (MEGA)* (abbreviation: *MEGA2*) that began appearing in East Germany in 1972 and that, since 1990, has been continuing under the auspices of the Internationale Marx-Engels-Stiftung.[1] It is a truly heroic effort of scholarship. It is also the only edition that conforms to the rigorous standards of modern textual editing. In its presentation of Marx's manuscripts it stands as a first-rate example of how textual editors can make accessible to scholars an original text that is itself quite inaccessible. Although under the East German regime there was a tension between, on the one hand, the ideological demands of the party, and, on the other, the commitment of the actual editors to producing a truly critical edition, ideological tendentiousness was pretty much confined to the volume introductions and to some of the tertiary apparatus (annotations, indexes). Accordingly, the scientific level of *MEGA2* is extremely high, and this includes almost everything that was done under the Communist regime. The editorial introductions to specific texts are often a model of informativeness, while the detailed apparatus gives the reader the sense that he or she is reading—but in legible form—Marx's own manuscripts, with their multitude of additions, erasures, underlinings, and the like.

Indeed, one can find editorial indications as to the lines and other markings that Marx made in the margins or his manuscripts, markings that are clues as to what, on reflection, he thought was worthy of special notice.

One also finds a physical description of each manuscript: the type of paper, whether the pages were bound together, the color of the ink, whether there were also markings in colored crayon or in pencil, whether Marx supplied page numbers, whether the manuscript shows signs of later use, and so on. One would be inclined to say that this edition is the next best thing to reading the original manuscripts, except that, given the extreme illegibility of Marx's handwriting, it is *better* than being there. Without *MEGA2* I would certainly not have written this, or any, book on Marx. Historians feel uneasy about working without original sources; failing that, an edition that can stand in for the original sources is required. Previous editions were simply not up to an editorial standard that would allow proper historical work to be done. Second, there are things that I was able to see via *MEGA2* that I had not been able to see before turning to it: most important, only in using *MEGA2* 4.2 ("Karl Marx Friedrich Engels Exzerpte und Notizen 1843 bis Januar 1845") did I discern the role that Marx's conviction that the market is irrational plays in his thinking.

A "redimensioning" of *MEGA2* occurred in 1992, somewhat reducing the originally envisaged size of the project. The best current information on *MEGA2* will be found on the Website of the Berlin-Brandenburg Academy of Sciences (BBAW), which in late 2000 took over responsibility for the project. Particularly useful is a document on the BBAW Website titled "Marx-Engels Gesamtausgabe Redimensionierung des Projektes: Der revidierte Plan der Marx-Engels-Gesamtausgabe," www.bbaw.de/vh/mega/revplan.html (17 August 2001). But see also, in print, Jacques Grandjonc and Jürgen Rojahn, "Der revidierte Plan der Marx-Engels-Gesamtausgabe," *MEGA-Studien* 2 (1995): 62–89. An important resource is the journal *MEGA-Studien*, which began publication in 1994, continuing the earlier *Marx-Engels Jahrbuch*. As I write this, a list of its contents to date appears on the Website of the International Institute of Social History (IISG) in Amsterdam (www.iisg.nl).

MEGA2 is distinct from, and supersedes, the original *Marx-Engels Gesamtausgabe*, or "Old *MEGA*" (abbreviation: *MEGA*), which was published in 1927–35 and was brought to a premature halt by Stalin's purges. The Old *MEGA* has been expensively reprinted, in Germany and Japan; the later reprintings should not be confused with the "New *MEGA*." *MEGA2* will also supersede the Marx-Engels *Werke* (*MEW*), which began publication in East Germany in 1956: *MEW* simply does not have the richness of editorial work to be found in *MEGA2*, and the desire to proselytize—to present Marx and Engels in what was deemed to be the most pedagogically appropriate light—influenced the organization of the material, so that one cannot have faith in its honesty. I defy readers to find the "Economic and Philosophical Manuscripts" in *MEW* without getting special assistance. Still, until *MEGA2* is complete, *MEW* will remain an essential resource. The English-language *Collected Works* (*MECW*) appears to be more or less based on *MEW*, with some improvements; it does not systematically integrate (or integrate at all?) material from *MEGA2*, even though its publication began in 1975, after *MEGA2* had begun to appear. Neither its textual base nor its organization is fully conducive to serious scholarly work, although it does have the tremendous merit of making most of the Marx-Engels material available, in a single edition, in English.

A word also should be said about the best single aid to Marx research, the indispensable three-volume *Marx-Engels Cyclopedia*, by the late Hal Draper. Draper's dedication to Marx scholarship and his meticulous care are marvels to behold. The *Cyclopedia* presents a large amount of information about Marx's and Engels's lives and writings in a systematic and compact manner. It includes a *Marx-Engels Chronicle*, which gives a month-by-month, and even day-by-day, account of Marx's and Engels's doings, a *Marx-Engels Register* that lists and briefly discusses all their writings, and a *Marx-Engels Glossary* that lists, briefly identifies the persons, periodicals, parties or other organizations, and the like mentioned in the *Chronicle* and in the *Register*. Published in 1985 by Schocken Books, *The Marx-Engels Cyclopedia* is now out of print. Anyone who tries to do research on Marx without unearthing a copy of the Draper *Cyclopedia* is making a big mistake.

Finally, there is a Marx-Engels Website, The Marx-Engels Internet Archive, that contains a variety of searchable texts by Marx and Engels. In the absence of a computer-searchable version of *MEGA2* it remains a convenient, although imperfect, tool. It exists on different sites, some less well maintained than others. To find the sites, search the phrase "Marx/Engels Internet Archive" using any major search engine. It may be best to use a search engine that also accesses material that has disappeared from the Web, such as www.google.com. It is then up to the user to determine by experiment which site allows one to do what needs to be done. The most useful feature that these sites offer is the ability to locate specific words and phrases in the Marx and Engels works that have been put on the Web (which, to be sure, amount to only a very small part of their total output).

WRITINGS BY MARX AND ENGELS

Marx-Engels Collected Writings

Marx, Karl, and Friedrich Engels. *Gesamtausgabe (MEGA)*. 12 vols. Frankfurt, Berlin, Moscow: Marx-Engels-Verlag and others, 1927–35.

Marx, Karl, and Friedrich Engels. *Werke*. 43 vols. Berlin: Dietz, 1956–83. (Cited in text as *MEW*.)

Marx, Karl, and Friedrich Engels. *Karl Marx Friedrich Engels Gesamtausgabe (MEGA)*. Eventually 114 conceptual vols. (bound as approximately twice as many physical vols.). Berlin: Dietz, 1972. (Cited in text as *MEGA2*.)

Marx, Karl, and Friedrich Engels. *Collected Works*. 50 vols. New York: International Publishers, 1975–2003[?]. (Cited in text as *MECW*.) As of September 2001, only volumes 48–50 have not yet been published.

MARX-ENGELS EDITIONS ADDITIONAL TO THE COLLECTED WRITINGS

Engels, Friedrich. *The German Revolutions: "The Peasant War in Germany" and "Germany: Revolution and Counter-Revolution."* Ed. Leonard Krieger. Introduction by Leonard Krieger. Chicago: University of Chicago Press, 1967.

Marx, Karl. *Economic and Philosophic Manuscripts of 1844*. Trans. Martin Milligan. Ed. Dirk J. Struik. Introduction by Dirk J. Struik. New York: International Publishers, 1964.

Marx, Karl. *Ethnological Notebooks (Studies of Morgan, Phear, Maine, Lubbock)*. Ed. Lawrence Krader. Assen: van Gorcum, 1972.

Marx, Karl. *Mathematische Manuskripte*. Ed. Wolfgang Endemann. Kronberg Taunus: Scriptor, 1974.

Marx, Karl. *Mathematical Manuscripts*. Trans. C. Aronson and M. Meo. London: New Park, 1983.

Marx, Karl. *Texte aus der Rheinischen Zeitung von 1842/43, mit Friedrich Engels' Artikeln im Anhang*. Ed. Hans Pelger, with the assistance of Elisabeth Krieger-Neu. Trier: Karl-Marx-Haus, 1984.

Marx, Karl. *Texts on Method*. Trans. and ed. Terrell Carver. Oxford: Basil Blackwell, 1975.

MARX-ENGELS: POPULARLY PRICED EDITIONS

The Pelican Marx Library

Marx, Karl. *Capital: A Critique of Political Economy*. Trans. Ben Fowkes. Introduction by Ernest Mandel. 3 vols. Pelican Marx Library. Harmondsworth: Penguin, 1975.

Marx, Karl. *Early Writings*. Trans. Rodney Livingstone and Gregor Benton. Introduction by Lucio Colletti. Pelican Marx Library. Harmondsworth: Penguin, 1975.

Marx, Karl. *Grundrisse: Foundations of the Critique of Political Economy*. Trans. Martin Nicolaus. Foreword by Martin Nicolaus. Pelican Marx Library. Harmondsworth: Penguin, 1973.

Marx, Karl. *Surveys from Exile* (Political Writings, vol. 2). Ed. David Fernbach. Pelican Marx Library. Harmondsworth: Penguin, 1973.

Other Editions

Engels, Friedrich. *The Origin of the Family, Private Property and the State*. Introduction by Michèle Barrett. Harmondsworth: Penguin, 1985.

Marx, Karl. *Later Political Writings*. Trans. and ed. Terrell Carver. Cambridge: Cambridge University Press, 1996.

Marx, Karl. *The Portable Karl Marx*. Selected, trans. in part, and with an introduction by Eugene Kamenka. Harmondsworth: Penguin, 1983.

Marx, Karl, and Friedrich Engels. *The Marx-Engels Reader*. 2d ed. Ed. Robert C. Tucker. New York: Norton, 1978.

Marx, Karl, and Friedrich Engels. *Basic Writings on Politics and Philosophy*. Ed. Lewis S. Feuer. Garden City, N.Y.: Doubleday, 1959.

NOTES

1. For an informative discussion of *MEGA2* and its background, see Kevin Anderson, "Uncovering Marx's Yet Unpublished Writings"; Rolf Hecker, "The MEGA Project: An Edition between a Scientific Claim and the Dogmas of Marxism-Leninism"; and Jürgen Rojahn, "Publishing Marx and Engels after 1989: The Fate of the MEGA"; all in *Critique: A Journal of Socialist Theory* 25 (1998): 179–87, 188–95, and 196–207.

Index

About the Author

Allan Megill was educated at the universities of Saskatchewan and Toronto and at Columbia University. He is a historian of ideas with a particular interest in modern European thought and in the philosophy of history. He currently teaches at the University of Virginia. He is the author of *Prophets of Extremity: Nietzsche, Heidegger, Foucault, Derrida*; co-editor (with John S. Nelson and Donald N. McCloskey) of *The Rhetoric of the Human Sciences: Language and Argument in Scholarship and Public Affairs*, and editor of *Rethinking Objectivity*.